45

THE CHURCH, THE AFTERLIFE AND THE FATE OF THE SOUL

THE CHURCH, THE AFTERLIFE AND THE FATE OF THE SOUL

PAPERS READ AT
THE 2007 SUMMER MEETING AND
THE 2008 WINTER MEETING OF
THE ECCLESIASTICAL HISTORY SOCIETY

EDITED BY

PETER CLARKE

AND

TONY CLAYDON

PUBLISHED FOR
THE ECCLESIASTICAL HISTORY SOCIETY
BY
THE BOYDELL PRESS
2009

First published 2009

A publication of the Ecclesiastical History Society
in association with The Boydell Press
an imprint of Boydell & Brewer Ltd
PO Box 9, Woodbridge, Suffolk IP12 3DF, UK
and of Boydell & Brewer Inc.
668 Mt Hope Avenue, Rochester, NY 14620, USA
website: www.boydellandbrewer.com

ISBN 978-0-95468-095-4

ISSN 0424-2084

A CiP catalogue record for this book is available
from the British Library

Details of previous volumes are available from Boydell & Brewer Ltd

This book is printed on acid-free paper

Typeset by Pru Harrison, Hacheston, Suffolk
Printed in Great Britain by
CPI Antony Rowe, Chippenham and Eastbourne

CONTENTS

Preface   ix

List of Contributors   xi

List of Abbreviations   xiv

Introduction   xvii

Naked or Clothed? Eschatology and the Doctrine of Creation   1
FRANCES YOUNG

What Happened to the Last Judgement in the Early Church?   20
JOSEPHINE LAFFIN

Timor Mortis: The Fear of Death in Augustine's Sermons on   31
the Martyrs
ELENA MARTIN

Philosophy, Hagiology and the Early Byzantine Origins of   41
Purgatory
MATTHEW J. DAL SANTO

Saints and Soteriology in Sophronius Sophista's *Miracles of Cyrus*   52
and John
PHIL BOOTH

Death and the Afterlife in Jonas of Bobbio's *Vita Columbani*   64
ALEXANDER O'HARA

Individual and Collective Salvation in Late Visigothic Spain   74
JAMIE WOOD

Anglo-Saxon 'Purgatory'   87
SARAH FOOT

Byzantine Visions of the End   97
LESLIE BRUBAKER

CONTENTS

The Afterlife of Bishop Adhémar of Le Puy   120
CONOR KOSTICK

Michael Glykas and the Afterlife in Twelfth-Century Byzantium   130
YANNIS PAPADOGIANNAKIS

Ghosts and Ghostbusters in the Middle Ages   143
R. N. SWANSON

Agreements to Return from the Afterlife in Late Medieval *Exempla*   174
CATHERINE RIDER

Fixing the Eschatological Scales: Judgement of the Soul in Late   184
Medieval and Early Modern Irish Tradition
SALVADOR RYAN

'An Afterlife in Memory': Commemoration and its Effects in a Late   196
Medieval Parish
CLIVE BURGESS

Performing the Passion: Strategies for Salvation in the Life of   218
Stefana Quinzani (d. 1530)
CORDELIA WARR

Christ's Descent into Hell in Reformation Controversy   228
DAVID BAGCHI

Revelation and Reckoning: Angels and the Apocalypse in   248
Reformation England, c. 1559–1625
LAURA SANGHA

Heaven and Heavenly Piety in Colonial American Elegies   258
ADRIAN CHASTAIN WEIMER

'But where shall my soul repose?': Nonconformity, Science and   268
the Geography of the Afterlife, c. 1660–1720
ANDREW CAMBERS

The Chinese Rites Controversy: Confucian and Christian Views   280
on the Afterlife
PAUL RULE

CONTENTS

Strategies for the Afterlife in Eighteenth-Century Malta   301
FRANS CIAPPARA

Apparitions and Anglicanism in 1750s Warwickshire   311
SASHA HANDLEY

Rescuing the Perishing Heathen: The British Empire versus   323
the Empire of Satan in Anglican theology, 1701–1721
ROWAN STRONG

'In their madness they chase the wind': The Catholic Church   336
and the Afterlife in Late Chosŏn Korea
ANDREW FINCH

The 'Restitution of All Things' in Evangelical Premillennialism   349
MARTIN SPENCE

'Angels Seen Today': The Theology of Modern Spiritualism   360
and its Impact on Church of England Clergy, 1852–1939
GEORGINA BYRNE

Civilians, Soldiers and Perceptions of the Afterlife in Britain   371
during the First World War
MICHAEL SNAPE

Life Beyond the Grave: New Churches in York and the   404
Afterlife, c. 1982–2007
DAVID GOODHEW

African Christianity and the Eclipse of the Afterlife   413
PAUL GIFFORD

PREFACE

'The Church and the Afterlife' was one of four themes suggested by Professor Robert N. Swanson for his Presidency of the Ecclesiastical History Society in 2007–8; this theme was enthusiastically endorsed by the Society's Committee. It proved to be a rich and fertile theme as the papers in this volume illustrate. They comprise the eight plenary papers delivered at the Summer Meeting in 2007 and the Winter Meeting in 2008, and a selection of the communications offered at the Summer Meeting.

We are grateful to the members of the Society who afforded their time and expertise in compiling peer review reports on the communications submitted for this volume, and to the authors for their efficiency and efforts in producing timely revisions and answering numerous editorial queries.

The Society wishes to thank the University of Leicester for hosting the Summer Meeting, and especially the staff of New Hall for their co-operation at this event, and is particularly indebted to John Doran, Dr Stella Fletcher and Dr Nigel Aston for organizing the excursions. Thanks are also due to Dr Williams's Library, London, and its Director Dr David Wykes for accommodating the Winter Meeting.

As the incoming Editors, we would like to thank the previous Editors, Dr Jeremy Gregory and Dr Kate Cooper, and Professor Swanson as Chair of the Society's Publications Committee for their support and guidance. We are also grateful to Dr Tim Grass, the Assistant Editor, who has been a model of efficiency, diligence and patience in copy-editing this volume and seeing it through the press. We are further indebted to the Society for funding Tim's post, which has considerably eased our editorial task.

As Editors we introduced an innovation into the Summer Meeting programme in 2007, a Round Table discussion. The Editors, the President and the previous year's President, Professor David Bebbington, were the main participants. The idea was to assess how the President's theme had developed in the light of the papers delivered and to review the historical problems and issues that had arisen in the process. The event was an interesting experiment and will be repeated. We are grateful to the Society for permitting us this indulgence.

Peter Clarke
University of Southampton
Tony Claydon
Bangor University

CONTRIBUTORS

R. N. SWANSON (*President*)
> Professor of Medieval History, University of Birmingham

David BAGCHI
> Lecturer in the History of Christian Thought, University of Hull

Phil BOOTH
> Research Student, Trinity Hall, University of Cambridge

Leslie BRUBAKER
> Professor of Byzantine Art History; Director, Centre for Byzantine, Ottoman and Modern Greek Studies; University of Birmingham

Clive BURGESS
> Senior Lecturer in History, Royal Holloway, University of London

Georgina BYRNE
> Vicar in the Halas Team with responsibility for Romsley, Worcestershire

Andrew CAMBERS
> Lecturer in History, Lancaster University

Frans CIAPPARA
> Senior Lecturer in History, University of Malta

Matthew J. DAL SANTO
> Junior Research Fellow, Trinity College, University of Cambridge

Andrew J. FINCH
> Ambleside, Cumbria

CONTRIBUTORS

Sarah FOOT
   Regius Professor of Ecclesiastical History, University of Oxford

Paul GIFFORD
   Professor of African Christianity, School of Oriental and African
   Studies, University of London

David GOODHEW
   Vicar of St Oswald's, Fulford, York

Sasha HANDLEY
   Simon Fellow, University of Manchester

Conor KOSTICK
   Post-Doctoral Fellow of the Irish Research Council for the
   Humanities and Social Sciences, Trinity College, Dublin

Josephine LAFFIN
   Lecturer in Church History, Adelaide College of Divinity and
   Flinders University of South Australia

Elena MARTIN (*EHS postgraduate bursary*)
   Doctoral Fellow, Durham University

Alexander O'HARA
   Research Student and Carnegie Scholar, University of St
   Andrews

Yannis PAPADOGIANNAKIS
   A. G. Leventis Lecturer in Patristics, University of Oxford

Catherine RIDER
   Lecturer in History, University of Exeter

Paul RULE
   Honorary Associate, History, La Trobe University, Melbourne,
   Australia; EDS/Stewart Distinguished Fellow, Ricci Institute for
   Chinese-Western Cultural History, University of San Francisco;
   Member, Macau Ricci Institute

Salvador RYAN
> Academic Co-ordinator and Lecturer in Church History, St Patrick's College, Thurles, Co. Tipperary, Ireland

Laura SANGHA (*EHS postgraduate bursary*)
> Research Student, University of Warwick

Michael SNAPE
> Senior Lecturer in Modern History, University of Birmingham

Martin SPENCE (*EHS postgraduate bursary*)
> Research Student, Corpus Christi College, University of Oxford

Rowan STRONG
> Associate Professor of Church History, Theology Program, Murdoch University, Perth, Australia

Cordelia WARR
> Lecturer in Art History and Visual Studies, University of Manchester

Adrian Chastain WEIMER (*Michael J. Kennedy Postgraduate Prize*)
> Research Student, Harvard University

Jamie WOOD
> Research Student, University of Manchester

Frances YOUNG
> Emeritus Professor of Theology, University of Birmingham

ABBREVIATIONS

ActaSS	*Acta sanctorum*, eds J. Bolland and G. Henschen (Antwerp, etc., 1643–)
AHR	*American Historical Review* (New York, 1895–)
ANF	Ante-Nicene Fathers, eds A. Roberts and J. Donaldson, 10 vols (Buffalo, NY, 1885–96 and subsequent edns)
ARG	*Archiv für Reformationsgeschichte* (1903–)
BJRL	*Bulletin of the John Rylands Library* (Manchester, 1903–)
CChr	Corpus Christianorum (Turnhout, 1953–)
CChr.CM	Corpus Christianorum, continuatio medievalis (1966–)
CChr.SG	Corpus Christianorum, series Graeca (1974–)
CChr.SL	Corpus Christianorum, series Latina (1953–)
CathHR	*Catholic Historical Review* (Washington, DC, 1915–)
CYS	Canterbury and York Society (London, etc., 1907–)
DOP	*Dumbarton Oaks Papers* (Washington, DC, 1941–)
DNB	*Dictionary of National Biography* (London, 1885–)
EETS	Early English Text Society (London/Oxford, 1864–)
EHR	*English Historical Review* (London, 1886–)
es	extra series (of EETS)
ET	English Translation
HistJ	*Historical Journal* (Cambridge, 1958–)
HThR	*Harvard Theological Review* (New York/Cambridge, MA, 1908–)
IWM	Imperial War Museum
JECS	*Journal of Early Christian Studies* (1993–)
JEH	*Journal of Ecclesiastical History* (Cambridge, 1950–)
JMedH	*Journal of Medieval History* (Amsterdam, 1975–)
JThS	*Journal of Theological Studies* (London, 1899–)
LW	*Luther's Works*, eds J. Pelikan & H. Lehmann, 55 vols (St Louis, MO/Philadelphia, PA, 1955–75)
MGH	Monumenta Germaniae Historica inde ab a. c. 500 usque ad a. 1500, eds G. H. Pertz et al. (Hanover, Berlin, etc., 1826–)
n. d.	no date
n. pl.	no place

ABBREVIATIONS

NPNF I	A Select Library of Nicene and Post-Nicene Fathers of the Christian Church, ed. P. Schaff, 14 vols (New York, 1887–92 and subsequent edns)
NPNF II	A Select Library of Nicene and Post-Nicene Fathers of the Christian Church: A New Series, eds P. Schaff et al., 14 vols (New York/Oxford, 1890–1900 and subsequent edns)
NRSV	New Revised Standard Version
ns	new series
ODCC	*Oxford Dictionary of the Christian Church*, ed. F. L. Cross (Oxford, 1957; 2nd edn 1974; 3rd edn 1997; 3rd edn revised 2005); 2nd edn onwards with E. A. Livingstone
ODNB	*Oxford Dictionary of National Biography,* eds H. C. G. Matthew and Brian Harrison (Oxford, 2004)
os	old series
P&P	*Past and Present: A Journal of Scientific History* (London/Oxford, 1952–)
PG	Patrologia Graeca, ed. J. P. Migne, 161 vols (Paris, 1857–66)
PL	Patrologia Latina, ed. J. P. Migne, 217 vols + 4 index vols (Paris, 1841–61)
PS	Parker Society (Cambridge, 1841–55)
RS	*Rerum Brittanicarum medii aevi scriptores*, 99 vols (London, 1858–1911) = Rolls Series
SC	Sources Chrétiennes (Paris, 1941–)
SCH	Studies in Church History (London/Oxford/Woodbridge, 1964–)
ScHR	*Scottish Historical Review* (Edinburgh/Glasgow, 1904–)
SCH.S	Studies in Church History: Subsidia (Oxford/Woodbridge, 1978–)
Speculum	*Speculum: A Journal of Medieval Studies* (Cambridge, MA, 1925–)
UNHCR	United Nations High Commission for Refugees
WA	*D. Martin Luthers Werke: Kritische Gesamtausgabe*, eds J. K. F. Knaake, G. Kawerau et al. (Weimar, 1883–)

INTRODUCTION

Whatever the advances in medical science, the current ultimate death rate among humans remains what it always has been, 100 per cent. What happens after death, if indeed there is anything after death, is one of the great conundrums of human existence. For Christians, and for the Church in all its branches, belief in the afterlife and an eventual Last Judgement is a basic component of the faith, a belief restated with every recitation of the traditional creeds. That there will be a Last Judgement, at some unknown and unpredictable future point, requires that there be some kind of 'life' beyond death. What actually happens in the period between death and the end of time is a matter of speculation, and faith; yet the presumed existence of that interval between bodily death and the final definitive judgement on the fate of the soul, the expectation of an afterlife, raises questions which cannot be avoided or evaded. What happens at death? Where do the dead go? What happens to them there? Even more importantly for the living, can anything be done in this life to prepare for the next? How (if it is even possible) can the living influence their fates to ensure a successful transit through the afterlife and a favourable judgement at the Day of Doom?

Arguably such questions, matters of specific relevance to Christians as individuals and the Church as an institution, originate with the foundation of the faith. Christianity was, in a sense, born in the afterlife. In the aftermath of his own death Christ harrowed hell, liberating the patriarchs from their limbo to make them the first of the saved (although at the same time posing a theological problem – as David Bagchi points out in his essay in this volume – with his promise on the cross to be on that same day with the Good Thief in paradise). Since then the Church and its members have had to wrestle with the problems raised by the afterlife, institutionally, doctrinally, and individually. The need for Christians to negotiate the afterlife, and to prepare for the Last Judgement, has stimulated a range of responses, both practical and intellectual. As the Church has evolved in time and space, and as the world has changed around it, so the questions and uncertainties – and, of course, the certainties – provoked by the presumption that there is an afterlife have themselves been transformed. Chronologically, speculations and analyses range across the centuries, their continuation both as theological concerns and as responses to current anxieties being exemplified in the recent debate within the Roman Church regarding the existence of the *limbus infantium* (limbo of infants) and the afterlife of unbaptized children. In between, there are major evolutionary milestones, such as the development and consolidation of purgatory, its later rejection (at least by Protestants) at the Reformation, and in the nineteenth and early twentieth centuries the issues raised by spiritualism. Initially, the geographical focus lies on the Church's traditional European and east Mediterranean heartlands, but expands with the Church itself to require examination of the significance of the Christian approach(es) to the afterlife in missionary contexts, as the Church institutionally, and Christianity ideologically, has had to sell its image of the afterlife in processes of conversion, and responded to the threat or challenge of rival understandings.

Over time the afterlife has acquired its own unstable geography, with the fundamental split between heaven and hell, and beyond that most notably the Catholic interpolation of purgatory. Faced with the possibility of the eternal torments of hell, and the transient but still terrifying prospect of purgatory, the afterlife has been both a threat and a promise; small wonder therefore that Christians have regularly sought to develop strategies for eternity, seeking to ameliorate divine wrath through prayer and charitable deeds, or throwing themselves wholly on divine mercy by adopting a theology of justification through faith (alone or not). Visionaries have had glimpses of the hereafter; ghosts, and saints, have returned from the lands of the dead to warn and exhort. Even in the twenty-first century the shape and significance of the afterlife, indeed its existence, continue to offer challenges and create uncertainties, with the Church now seeming to be increasingly uncertain about how to deal with its less attractive features.

* * *

The impact of belief in the afterlife on the Church's history and evolution, and the manifold ways in which it has impacted on and been reflected in the lives, expectations, and aspirations of Christians across the centuries, is the central theme of this volume. Yet, while providing the central theme, it does not impose a monolithic shape on the volume: as the essays demonstrate, the responses to the demand to believe in the afterlife have varied over time, creating their own dynamics in the Church's history. For the contributors, as ecclesiastical historians, the afterlife, like the past, may be 'another country'; but here their task is to merge those two countries into one, with the essays as part of an ongoing process of exploration and mapping. The overall richness of the theme necessarily impacts on the structure and content of this introduction, which is intentionally limited in its scope. Within a brief space it can neither offer a full survey of the contents of the essays, nor mention all of them individually. While many readers may confine their attention only to articles which immediately appear to have direct personal relevance, much wider reading is certainly to be encouraged: this is one essay collection where the whole is indeed greater than the sum of its parts, as subsidiary themes resonate across time and space.

* * *

The Christian afterlife has emerged and developed as a complex phenomenon. On one level its creation has been as a theological construct, an aspect of the resolution of some of the questions and uncertainties which lie at the heart of the faith, niggled at and formalized by generations of thinkers with arguments of varying degrees of assurance and internal consistency. As Frances Young demonstrates with reference to the Church's earliest centuries, the theologians' afterlife has had to make sense as an integral part of a totalized and holistic cosmology. However, it has also had to be approached and understood through a prism of contingency and uncertainty. As Josephine Laffin shows in her complementary consideration of the pastoral and artistic approaches to the afterlife in the same centuries, the theology also had perhaps to be watered down and simplified to make it acceptable and accessible to the faithful. At that less abstruse level, and looking more widely, developments in understanding of the afterlife raise the issue of how far the laity might contribute to the development of doctrine. This is particularly of concern with purgatory's emergence as a doctrinal concept which in some senses represents a response to preceding 'popular' recognition and assertion of the possibility that souls could in fact be saved by prayer even after death. Such understanding logically, and so theologically, required the existence of a place of punishment – or purgation – which was not actually hell. This is an evolution primarily associated with Catholicism of the central and late Middle Ages. However, there was a complex prehistory, aspects of which are considered by Matthew dal Santo (Byzantium) and Sarah Foot (Anglo-Saxon England). To establish a settled theology of the afterlife was no easy matter, and could become contentious in certain contexts. David

Bagchi's paper shows how the issue of Christ's own experience of the afterlife, in the 'Harrowing of Hell', complicated the doctrinal debates of the sixteenth century. The entrenched confessional differences of succeeding centuries only added to the complexities.

The theology, the intellectualizing, of the afterlife is only one facet of the overall theme. For individual Christians it is the practicality of the afterlife, as something which would actually be a sensory experience at and after death, which has been the main area of concern. What actually happens after death? Is the afterlife something which can be prepared for in this life, requiring 'strategies for eternity' to negotiate safe passage through to an eternity of bliss and avoid an eternity of suffering? How much is the afterlife an other life, a parallel existence with the possibility of communication across the divide? Most importantly, if there is an afterlife, how much is it a place of judgement, pain, and punishment? Almost unavoidably – although this was a factor which was deliberately not emphasized in the call for papers for the conference from which these essays derive – discussion of the afterlife easily slides into consideration of the fate of the soul, and in due course to eschatology. That transition, which becomes symbiosis, is admirably traced and exemplified for one Christian tradition in Leslie Brubaker's survey and analysis of Byzantine imagery and artistic conventions.

The concern with the soul's fate can be 'positive', as several of the papers in the volume indicate; but there is also a 'negative' element. The modern world finds the afterlife – or more precisely a judgemental afterlife in which not everyone will be a winner – something of a problem, one perhaps to be pushed to the back of the mind. While this is not necessarily an exclusively modern phenomenon, nevertheless it does seem to be more characteristic of the modern world than of earlier centuries. The deeply disturbing picture of some types of African Christianity presented by Paul Gifford is complemented in the somewhat coyer sidelining of the afterlife reported in David Goodhew's contribution on the independent churches which have flourished in York in recent decades. For a world which finds it hard to cope with death (except as an audio-visual experience), hell and judgement are far too daunting and disturbing to contemplate and worry about.

The inability, or refusal, of many modern Christians to engage with the afterlife can perhaps be explained as an aspect of modern and maybe primarily westernized cultures' inability to engage with death. In earlier centuries widespread (but not automatically universal) acceptance of the fact of an afterlife, and of the reality of the afterlife as a process and extended experience which determined the ultimate fate of the soul, made it a much more central feature of Christian existence. 'In the midst of life we are in death' might almost be glossed as 'In the midst of this life we have to prepare for and connect with the afterlife.' If the afterlife was a place of judgement, it had to be planned for, either to seek to avoid its pains (the purpose of most of the Church's pastoral activity), or through strategic management of affairs in this life to reduce the intensity of any punishment or purgation which might fall due after death. Clive Burgess's paper on late medieval Bristol recreates such strategic approaches in pre-Reformation England; the later continuation of such attitudes in Catholic Europe is clearly demonstrated in Frans Ciappara's examination of the situation in eighteenth-century Malta. For Protestants, their rejection of the concept of purgatory and of the possibility of any further purification of the soul between death and the Last Judgement meant that strategies for eternity could only be this-worldly, with a good life as the only acceptable form of pre-emption. As Adrian Chastain Weimer argues in her discussion of elegies in colonial America, Protestant strategies for the afterlife were based on the firm establishment of models of holy living which provided templates for the living and an assurance of salvation. The Protestant afterlife, with its rigid duality of heaven and hell, might seem theologically more straightforward than one which integrated the concept of purgatory; yet it still had to address the question of the gap between death and judgement and the problem of the fate of the soul. Protestants might be vehemently self-assured of what that intervening experience would not be like – no purgatory – yet the form it would actually have was still a matter of speculation and uncertainty. Such speculation was necessarily affected by theology, and by the need to correlate theology with changing understandings of the physical cosmos. How souls might fare in an afterlife potentially constrained by the physical structure and limitations of an increasingly known Copernican universe clearly taxed some theologians of the late seventeenth century, as Andrew Cambers demonstrates. Yet even in the early twentieth century, an afterlife was needed to make sense of this life, and of death itself, perhaps especially in the context of the industrialization of war. Understanding of that afterlife may often have been theologically naïve and simplistic among British soldiers in the First World War but, as Michael Snape shows, an afterlife was expected, and the churches had to respond to those expectations and address the needs and hopes of the living. His paper provokes something akin to a sense of déjà vu as clerics offered theological validation of a popular call for a process of salvation in the afterlife aided by the prayers of the living which seems to replicate – perhaps only superficially – the emergence of purgatory several centuries before.

'Strategies for eternity' dissolve the duality of this life and the afterlife which is imposed by making death a rigid point of division. Clearly, death does divide, but it need not separate. One perennial human concern has been to test the fixity of the division, as a challenge faced on two fronts. As a missionary faith, Christianity has had to confront other afterlives, to seek either equilibrium with them or their replacement with an exclusively Christian (even if denominational) understanding. Historically, that challenge extends from the Roman catacombs and the amphitheatres of martyrdom right through to the present day, in processes of conflict, toleration, syncretism or displacement. In its totality, this may be a strand insufficiently represented in this volume, but its importance is acknowledged in the inclusion of Paul Rule's discussion of the Chinese Rites controversy of the seventeenth and eighteenth centuries (neatly complemented by Andrew J. Finch's analysis of the clash between Catholicism and the pre-existing religions in eighteenth- and nineteenth-century Korea), and alluded to by Paul Gifford in his discussion of modern African Christianity. A slightly different perspective – based on missionary aspiration rather than experience – is provided by Rowan Strong's commentary on early eighteenth-century Anglican approaches to mission to unconverted heathens, as expressed for home consumption.

In a rather different context, conflict over the nature and immediacy of the afterlife is expressed in debates over the permeability of the barrier between this world and the next. Accidental encounters with the dead as visitors or exiles from the other side, and deliberate attempts to establish contact with the souls of the deceased, enmeshed Christians in a world – very much this world – inhabited by ghosts and spirits. Interpretation of such phenomena (debates on the reality of their existence, and the reactions of ecclesiastical authorities to their alleged appearances) has provided a further strand in the history of Christian engagement with the afterlife and concern for the fate of the soul, feeding an additional tension between ecclesiastical teaching and believers' practices. Again, this may be a tension inherent in the faith from its early days. While there seems to be no sign that anyone actually advanced it as a formal argument (or, if anyone did, that it was treated as a significant argument), one response to those who considered ghosts incompatible with Christian faith might be that Christianity itself is partly founded on a ghost story. No matter how physically Christ appeared in the locked Upper Room, how did he get there? What happened on the road to Emmaus?

If the dead can speak, they are potentially the best guides to the afterlife; but the theological acceptability of ghosts, and of processes for making contact with the dead, has always been questionable in orthodox belief. The widespread human desire for contact with the world of the dead, especially to gain reassurance about the fate of individual souls, conflicts with theological understandings which challenge the reliability of such contacts and see them as demonic manifestations. Such tension clearly existed in the Middle Ages (as the papers by Robert Swanson and Catherine Rider demonstrate); its later problematic persistence is shown in the integration of apparitions in the negotiation of pastoral and parochial relations in eighteenth-century Warwick-shire, examined by Sasha Handley, and in the ambivalent attitudes of Victorian and early twentieth-century British churchmen to the practices and beliefs of spiritualism, discussed by Georgina Byrne.

* * *

In the nature of things, the papers in this volume can only offer an incomplete survey of a theme of immense potential richness. These essays are dots – often scattered clusters rather than singletons – in a pointillist picture whose full shape is not yet apparent. Nevertheless, they throw down a challenge by directing attention to the remaining gaps, and to the questions which remain unconsidered. As usual in a volume of *Studies in Church History*, established scholars join with post-graduate students in a collective attempt to deal with a major theme in Christian and ecclesiastical history. In doing so, they seek to develop both an understanding of the Church's past and an appreciation of its contribution to the formation of the present world.

Robert Swanson
University of Birmingham

NAKED OR CLOTHED? ESCHATOLOGY AND THE DOCTRINE OF CREATION

by FRANCES YOUNG

A PAPER on life after death in the early church should probably begin with the underworld: Sheol in the Hebrew Bible, Hades in Greek mythology, with parallels in ancient Mesopotamia, Egypt and Persia. It should reflect on the universally connected theme of judgment and its importance for theodicy, and address the wide variety of beliefs discernible in the New Testament and its background, especially in the apocalyptic literature. It should consider the so-called intermediate state, and the supposed distinction between the Greek concept of the immortality of the soul and the Hebrew idea of resurrection: which takes us full circle, since the latter notion assumes the picture of shades in the underworld brought back to full-bodied living – as indeed the traditional *Anastasis* icon of the Eastern Orthodox tradition makes dramatically clear, Christ springing up from the grave and hauling Adam up with one hand and, often though not invariably, Eve with the other.

But two considerations have led in another direction: (i) all this is well-trodden ground and hardly needs another survey; and (ii) in detail one could hardly cover in a single essay the sheer variety of ideas and the complexity of their relationships, assumed as they are in a whole range of potentially relevant texts, described in apocalyptic tours of the cosmos or adumbrated in accounts of mystical union with the divine. So all that is presumed, especially the remarkable and perennial production (from the third century BC to the Middle Ages) of apocalypses unveiling the fate of the dead, which Bauckham[1] has comprehensively studied. Instead the focus here will be on the one aspect of the afterlife which has in any sense been formally defined by its presence in the creeds, namely, the resurrection of the body; and the significant connection between resurrection and creation will be pursued.

The first part of this paper will advance the thesis that the doctrine of *creatio ex nihilo* so deepened the sense that the union of body and soul

---

[1] Richard Bauckham, *The Fate of the Dead: Studies on the Jewish and Christian Apocalypses*, Supplements to Novum Testamentum 93 (Leiden, 1998).

is essential to human nature as a creature made and redeemed by God for eternal life, that Platonizing Fathers of the fourth century, who might have been expected to focus on the immortality of the soul and to have a negative view of the body, in fact defended the resurrection of the body as the hallmark of Christian hope. The second part will turn back to the second century to explore the Christian antecedents of this, and suggest that belief in resurrection may even have contributed to the emergence of the idea that God created out of nothing. It seems clear that it was not until the fourth century, beginning with the Arian controversy, that the corollaries of *creatio ex nihilo* for Christology and anthropology were realized.[2] For completeness, third century ambiguities about the resurrection of the flesh should be considered,[3] along with the way they paralleled ambiguities about *creatio ex nihilo*. However, the main aim is to show how significant for the notion of bodily resurrection was the argument from *creatio ex nihilo*; so the final part of the paper returns to the fourth century to confirm this point from development in the thought of Augustine.

Gregory of Nyssa

Much of the fourth century was dominated by the argument with Arians, who suggested that the pre-existent Logos was a creature – maybe the first and greatest of the creatures, but still a creature. One of the outcomes of this was to clarify the distinction between God, who is uncreated, and everything else that has come into being from nothing, a point that is highlighted by Gregory of Nyssa in his work *De opificio hominis* (*On the Making of Humankind*).[4] This means that God is immutable, but created nature cannot exist without change – for its very passage from non-existence to existence is a kind of motion and change.

2 This paper is a sequel to the one entitled 'Creation and Human Being: the forging of a distinct Christian discourse', forthcoming in *Studia Patristica*. There I traced the impact of the doctrine of *creatio ex nihilo* on the anthropology of those key fourth-century Fathers who are generally regarded as somewhat Platonist, concentrating particularly on Augustine, and referring across to the Cappadocians. In that paper I also set out reasons for the now commonly accepted view that the notion of *creatio ex nihilo* emerged in the second century in debate with Platonism and Gnosticism.
3 I refer to Origen, misunderstandings of Origen and reactions against views taken to be Origenist; see further Brian E. Daley, *The Hope of the Early Church: A Handbook of Patristic Eschatology* (Cambridge, 1991), esp. ch. 5.
4 Gregory of Nyssa, *De opificio hominis* 16.10, 12 [hereafter: *Op. hom.*]; Greek text in PG 44: 123–256. Paragraph numbers are from the ET in NPNF II, 5: 387–427.

But this mutability is not to be understood as negative:[5] if God's power is sufficient to bring things into existence from nothing, then the transformation of that creation is also within divine power. To press this point Gregory challenges first those who suggest matter is co-eternal with God, then those who deny the resurrection. It is well known that Gregory's spirituality expressed itself in terms of eternal *epektasis* (continual reaching out in the desire for fuller knowledge of God) and progress. He had indeed taken mutability positively in a way that is arguably unprecedented. Scholarship has tended to relate this to his positive evaluation of God's infinity;[6] this work suggests that 'creation out of nothing' was an equally important driver.[7]

So what does Gregory say here specifically about resurrection? He begins his discussion[8] from the inherent mutability of creatures – the great thing about this is that it means human beings will not stay settled even in evil. Since motion is constant, eventually, when the limit of evil is reached, there will be a turn around, and once more human nature will be on course towards good. So paradise will be restored, along with the grace of God's image. Our hope, he says, is for something beyond anything we can envisage. He then turns to those who wonder why this heavy and corporeal existence has to wait for the consummation of all things before the life of human beings is set free for blessedness and *apatheia* (impassibility).[9] Before proceeding with Gregory's argument, we should note that these points – the natural reversion towards good and the weight of the body, like so much else in Gregory's work, bespeak a quasi-scientific or philosophical mode of thought. So will his reply to this question about the delay in consummation, turning as it does on the notion of the pre-existent Form of humankind behind Adam. But this philosophical mode of thought is made to serve another perspective. Gregory attributes the delay to the time it takes for the full number of humankind to be produced by animal generation rather than the method proper to unfallen human nature. When the full complement of human nature has reached its predetermined measure, then the trumpet of the resurrection will sound, awaken the dead and

[5] Gregory of Nyssa, *Op. hom.* 23.5; 25ff.
[6] E.g. E. Mühlenberg, *Die Unendlichkeit Gottes bei Gregor von Nyssa* (Göttingen, 1966); R. E. Heine, *Perfection in the Virtuous Life* (Philadelphia, PA, 1975).
[7] The above paragraph is borrowed, with abbreviations, from 'Creation and Human Being'.
[8] Gregory of Nyssa, *Op. hom.* 21.
[9] Ibid. 22.

transform to incorruptibility those still alive, in the same way as those who have been raised – so that the weight of the flesh is no longer heavy, and its burden no longer holds them down to earth, but they rise up through the air to be with the Lord (here Gregory exploits 1 Corinthians 15: 51–52 and 1 Thessalonians 4: 17).[10] Scripture enjoins hope and confidence in the future.

Gregory associates resurrection with world re-formation (*anastoicheiōsis*), and the next objection he addresses is that it is inconceivable that the processes and the time intervals that are going on now could come to an end.[11] Here we begin to see how Christian insistence on the beginning and end of the world transforms his otherwise somewhat Platonist conceptions. Anyone who takes the view that the universe is eternal cannot also believe that in the beginning the heaven and earth were made by God; and if there was a beginning of motion, so there must be an end – we should therefore believe Scripture on both these matters. It is at this point that he challenges those who suggest that matter is co-eternal with God, and then those who deny the resurrection. Gregory rehearses the standard arguments in his own way: the immaterial God cannot have made matter out of the divine self, nor could the one God have something other than the divine self exist alongside it from eternity; therefore, he asserts, just as we suppose the power of the divine will to be a sufficient cause for the things that exist to have come into being out of nothing, so we are not trusting in something improbable when we refer world re-formation to the same power. Creation out of nothing and resurrection are acts of a kind, and they mutually support each other in challenging certain fundamental philosophical assumptions, namely, that nothing comes from nothing, and that the soul's liberation is to be released from the body.

Gregory turns to the evidence of resurrection in Scripture, and pursues this at some length;[12] but still there are those who doubt that such a thing is possible even for God, pressing such awkward questions as: what about those who have been consumed in fire or eaten by wild beasts? what about ship-wrecked sailors devoured by fish?[13] Gregory dismisses all this questioning as unworthy of God's power and authority. Of course death means dissolution, he acknowledges; the

---

[10] Ibid. 22.6.
[11] Ibid. 23–24.
[12] Ibid. 25.
[13] Ibid. 26.

elements return to the elements, earth to earth, moisture to water. But
what is possible for God must not be judged by the limits of human
capacity or imagination. What once belonged to the person will be
restored. The most notable thing about ourselves, he says, is the first
beginning of our existence;[14] and here he embarks on a disquisition
about the various views of the soul and its relationship with the body.
He eventually affirms that as a human being is one, consisting of soul
and body, so the beginning of existence is one, common to both parts,
neither soul nor body antecedent to the other.[15] The profound interde-
pendence of soul and body is then outlined, drawing on contemporary
medical philosophy, and producing a picture of the soul which makes it
very like what we would call the central nervous system.[16] For Gregory
a human being is a psychosomatic whole. It is this wholeness that is to
be restored in the resurrection. The work ends by quoting Paul – we are
to put off the old humanity, and put on the one that is renewed after
the image of the Creator (Colossians 3: 9–10) – and then praying for us
all to return to that divine grace in which humanity was first created
when God said, 'Let us make humankind in our image and likeness'
(Genesis 1: 26).

This work on *The Making of Humankind* purports to be a continuation of Basil's *Hexaemeron* (*On the Six Days of Creation*). The really
striking thing about the *Hexaemeron* is its general tone of sheer wonder
at creation, its affirmation that nothing is superfluous or wrong or out
of place; indeed, everything contributes to the rich tapestry of the
created order and its beauty.[17] Basil draws upon the then current
scientific understanding of the cosmos and the natural world to foster
this wonder at creation. Yet the development of this 'creation spirituality' is grounded in the assertion that God is the sole source: a dualism
with matter is absolutely ruled out.[18] Creation out of nothing means
that this wonderful reality is finite; its beginning implies its end,[19] but
none of it was conceived by chance or without reason[20] – it must be
looked at *sub specie aeternitatis*, Basil implies. The problem with philos-

14 Ibid. 27.9.
15 Ibid. 29.
16 Ibid. 30.
17 e.g. Basil, *Hexaemeron* 1.11; 3.10; 7; 8; 9.
18 Ibid. 2.
19 Ibid. 1.3.
20 Ibid. 1.6.

ophy is precisely its inherent atheism – its failure to rise to knowledge of God through its much ado about explaining nature.[21]

In exploring human nature, its formation and re-formation, Gregory follows a similar agenda. His picture of how the dissolved particles of the body are imprinted with an identity and are reconstituted by the soul's knowledge of them might seem quasi-scientific – indeed a parallel with modern notions of the persistence of DNA has been drawn.[22] Yet the fundamental drive is to affirm God's creativity. Gregory explicitly makes an analogy between two miracles, resurrection being no more extraordinary than reproduction:

> The growth of the body with its many parts out of a sperm, which is substance that is both shapeless and formless, is nothing short of miraculous. If God can bring this about, there is no doubt He can restore life and shape to matter … .[23]

> The features of parents and forefathers appear in their children and grandchildren. We do not understand the 'how' of those extraordinary things. But seeing that God gives those features of rotten and ruined bodies to others, it would be foolish if we would not admit that He can give back to the soul its own elements.[24]

The fact that many changes occur to the human body over time without its losing its identity implies the continuity of change after death. Analogies with sleep or animal hibernation make resurrection plausible. It must be very easy for God who creates out of nothing.

The same sense of someone entering into the inherited parameters of the intellectual debates of antiquity, but with a distinctive countercultural position, can be picked up from Gregory's dialogue *De anima et resurrectione*.[25] Here he adopts a genre which invites comparison with Plato's *Phaedo*: his sister Macrina, rather than Socrates, discusses the nature of the soul on her deathbed. She roundly rejects the immortality of the soul as pagan nonsense. A definition is given which picks up the

[21] Ibid. 1.2. This paragraph is drawn from 'Creation and Human Being'.
[22] Vasiliki Limberis, 'Resurrected Body and Immortal Flesh in Gregory of Nyssa', in E. D. Moutsoulas, ed., *Jesus Christ in St. Gregory of Nyssa's Theology: Minutes of the Ninth International Conference on St. Gregory of Nyssa, Athens 7–12 September 2000* (Athens, 2005), 515–28. I am indebted to this article for the quotations from *In sanctum pascha* which appear in this paragraph.
[23] Gregory of Nyssa, *Op. hom.* 27.9.
[24] Idem, *In sanctum pascha*.
[25] Greek text in PG 46: 11–160; ET in NPNF II, 5: 430–68.

detailed presentation of a complex, psychosomatic whole already found in the *Making of Humankind*: 'The soul is an essence created, and living, and intellectual, transmitting from itself to an organised and sentient body the power of living and grasping objects of sense, as long as the natural constitution capable of this holds together.'[26] But to treat death simply as the dissolution of this complex being has already been dismissed: you can only think that if you remove from consideration the Deity who upholds the world. Creation proclaims the Creator. This premise prepares the ground for arguing that reconstitution is less problematic than the initial creation from nothing. Gregory explores at greater depth here the questions about the re-assembly of the dissolved particles, as well as introducing discussion of the emotions, dismissing Plato's famous charioteer analogy, and identifying the emotions as growths, somewhat like warts, on the soul's thinking part, rather than being essential to the soul. Focussing on the biblical idea of humanity being created in God's image, Gregory suggests that in the re-formation of human nature which is the resurrection, all this will be stripped away so that there will be nothing to impede contemplation of the Beautiful, nothing to prevent participation in the Good, both identified with God. To the one purified of its emotions and negative habits, love alone will remain – that is, an inherent affection for the Beautiful, grounded in its simplicity and godlikeness. This Platonic-sounding dream is then confirmed by reference to Paul's hymn to love in 1 Corinthians 13.

Like other Platonists Gregory assumes that the 'body weighs us down', but the important point for this discussion is that even the body, which weighs us down, although woven from the very same particles of matter, will be transformed, its threads worked up into something more subtle and ethereal, restored to us with a brighter and more entrancing beauty. For the soul still wrapped in earthly passions there will be agonized struggle when God is drawing it to the divine self and scraping the foreign matter off by force – the analogy with metal dross being purified in fire creates the impression of a Platonic interpretation of the apocalyptic image of hell. Speculating about the 'how' of creation, or indeed of reconstitution, is to engage in meddlesome prying: the problems of conceiving how a child or old man will be when resurrected are dismissed with other objections. But nature and

---

[26] NPNF II, 5: 433 (PG 46: 29B). The following paragraphs summarize Gregory's lengthy reasoning and there is no attempt to provide detailed references to a text which does not have convenient standard subdivisions.

Scripture alike point to the hope that in the resurrection we are born again in our original splendour.

So Gregory of Nyssa surely supports our first thesis: that *creatio ex nihilo* so deepened the sense that the union of body and soul is essential to human nature as a creature made and redeemed by God for life eternal, that bodily resurrection became its inevitable corollary, despite tendencies to a Platonist outlook. Turning to our second thesis, that belief in resurrection generated insistence on the goodness of the material creation and may even have contributed to the very emergence of the idea that God created out of nothing, will allow us to explore the specifically Christian background to Gregory's challenges to Platonism.

Creation and Resurrection in Second-Century Debates

The connection between creation and resurrection goes back beyond the articulation of a specific doctrine of *creatio ex nihilo*. It is already found in 2 Maccabees 7: 28, where the mother pleads with her seventh son to suffer martyrdom:

> I beg you, my child, to look at the heaven and the earth and see everything that is in them, and recognize that God made them not out of things that existed. And in the same way the human race came into being. Do not fear this butcher ... Accept death, so that in God's mercy I may get you back again along with your brothers.[27]

This text is often taken to be a reference to creation out of nothing, on the assumption that the idea was already accepted in Jewish circles. Certainly it would have been read that way later; but here it is not advanced as a theoretical argument concerning the presence or absence of a material substrate; rather, implying no more than that the world came into existence when it previously was not there, it is entirely compatible with human creation 'out of clay' found in Genesis 2. The context in 2 Maccabees is God's power to bring life out of death; birth is called in as a parallel mystery: 'The Creator of the world, who shaped the beginning of humankind and devised the origin of all things, will in his mercy give life and breath back to you again' (2 Maccabees 7: 23). Thus it is simply a paraenetical observation that fear can be dismissed

---

[27] All biblical quotations in this paper are taken from the NRSV.

because God brought you into existence when you did not exist *as you* before, and can therefore restore that existence if you put your hope and trust in God.[28]

In Romans 4 a similar connection between creation and resurrection is made. The thrust of Paul's argument concerning Abraham's faith is that he believed that God could bring life out of death, for:

> he did not weaken in faith when he considered his own body, which was already as good as dead ..., or when he considered the barrenness [i.e. *nekrōsis* or deadness] of Sarah's womb ....
> Now the words, 'it was reckoned to him [as righteousness]', were written not for his sake alone, but for ours also. It will be reckoned to us who believe in him who raised Jesus our Lord from the dead ... (Romans 4: 19, 23–24)

Earlier in the discussion Paul speaks of 'those who share the faith of Abraham' in the God 'who gives life to the dead and calls into existence the things that do not exist' (Romans 4: 17). Again it is unlikely that Paul was making a point about the something or nothing out of which God brought things into existence.

One of the many reasons for contesting the presence of an unambiguous doctrine of creation out of nothing at this early stage is the fact that some second-century writers, such as Justin Martyr and Athenagoras, assume that God as Creator imposed form on a material substrate.[29] The case of Athenagoras is particularly pertinent to our investigation since, assuming he was the author,[30] he provides us with the first treatise on the subject of resurrection. He is clearly facing opponents who disbelieve, and he challenges them about the connection between creation and resurrection: either they must deny to the creation of human beings any cause, or, if they do ascribe creation to God, they must examine what that presupposes and show why they regard resurrection as an untrustworthy doctrine – in other words, they need to demonstrate that God, despite being Creator, either cannot or

---

[28] This paragraph repeats points made in 'Creation and Human Being'.
[29] For Athenagoras, see *Legatio* 15.2; cf. 4.1–2, which is more ambiguous.
[30] W. R. Schoedel takes it to be an anti-Origenist work of the third century in his introduction to the text and translation quoted here: *Athenagoras: Legatio and De Resurrectione* (Oxford, 1972) [hereafter: *De res.*], following R. M. Grant, 'Athenagoras or Pseudo-Athenagoras?', *HThR* 47 (1954) 121–29. The case against authenticity has been subjected to vigorous critiques by L. W. Barnard, *Athenagoras: A Study in Second Century Christian Apologetic* (Paris, 1972), and others. See further Daley, *Hope of the Early Church*, 230 n. 4.

will not restore dead bodies so as to reconstitute the human beings they were before.[31] As to God's power to do this, the original creation of our bodies is enough to show that it suffices for their resurrection; if God first gave them form when they did not exist before, he can just as easily raise them up after their dissolution.[32]

So, where 2 Maccabees and Paul used creation as encouragement to faith in God, even in the face of death, this author turns that tradition into a philosophical defence of the notion of resurrection. Whatever the objections raised, such as what happens to those eaten by wild animals or turned into food for fish after drowning, Athenagoras will find a reasoned way through and trump it with the power and wisdom of the Creator.

> Moreover one cannot say that it is a work unworthy of God to raise up and reconstitute a decomposed body; for if the lesser work – the making of a corruptible and passible body – is not unworthy of God, how much more is the greater work – the making of an incorruptible and impassible body – not unworthy of God.[33]

Of course, some at this time did indeed think it was unworthy of God to get mixed up with the creation of physical things. The apparent crudities of collecting all the bits of matter that had belonged to each body is finessed by the notion of a body which transcends what we know in our present existence: Paul's idea of a spiritual body (1 Corinthians 15: 35–57), together with his sense that the soul needs to be clothed rather than naked (2 Corinthians 5: 1–6),[34] undoubtedly contributes to the picture. Without the composition of soul and body you would not have a human being; so even a transformed human being must be such a composite. This necessitates the resurrection.[35]

The connection between creation and resurrection is further developed by the observation that the reason for creating human beings was not God's own need – rather it was for humanity's sake and out of God's wisdom and goodness; and so God 'decreed an unending existence to those who bear his image in themselves, are gifted with intelli-

31 Athenagoras, *De res.* 2. 2–3.
32 Ibid. 3.1.
33 Ibid. 10.6. Note the form of argument, often referred to as *Qal wahomer*, or 'from light to heavy', and regarded as a particularly Jewish form of reasoning.
34 The title of this paper was taken from this passage.
35 Cf. Athenagoras, *De res.* 15.2, 5.

gence and share the faculty for rational discernment'. That being the
case, the two parts, soul and body, are receptive to the appropriate
changes, 'including, along with the other changes affecting age, appearance or size, also the resurrection'.[36] Resurrection from the dead is
taken to be 'transformation for the better', or 'survival in a incorruptible form', and Christians expect this because of their confidence in the
will of the Creator, who

> made man that he might participate in rational life and, after
> contemplating God's majesty and universal wisdom, perdure and
> make them the object of his eternal contemplation, in accordance
> with the divine will and nature allotted to him. The reason then for
> man's creation guarantees his eternal survival, and his survival
> guarantees his resurrection, without which he could not survive *as
> man*. From what we have said it is clear that the resurrection is
> demonstrated by the reason for man's creation and the will of the
> Creator.[37]

Against others the author insists that the resurrection does not take
place primarily for judgement but because of the will of the Creator
and the nature of those created.[38] Interestingly enough, the author of
this treatise eventually notes for himself that all the arguments brought
forward to confirm the resurrection are of the same kind and spring
from the same basic idea, namely the origin of human beings in the act
of creation.[39]

Clearly this treatise anticipates a great deal that we found in Gregory
– in fact it maps the *topoi* of discussion that keep recurring in the
patristic period.[40] It affirms the goodness of materiality; it insists that
the union of body and soul constitutes a created human person; it
emphasizes the connection between creation and resurrection; yet so far
creation out of nothing is not explicitly articulated.

Justin Martyr had also accepted that God created out of pre-existent
matter. His pupil Tatian, however, was already moving on in the argu-

---

[36] Ibid. 12.5–7.
[37] Ibid. 13.2.
[38] Ibid. 14.6.
[39] Ibid. 18.1.
[40] For example, Tertullian's (fl. 200) treatise *On the Resurrection of the Flesh* (*De resurrectione carnis*) and the fourteenth *Catechetical Lecture* of Cyril of Jerusalem (d. 386) cover much the same ground.

ment. God was definitely alone, he asserts;[41] matter is not, like God, without beginning; it was brought into existence by the Creator who begat our world, having first created the necessary matter. Tatian goes on to say that it is 'on this account' that 'we believe that there will be a resurrection of bodies'. Tatian confesses that he did not know who or what he was before he was born; but being born, after a former state of nothingness, he obtained a certainty of his existence. In just the same way, having come to be and through death existing no longer, he would exist again. Even if all trace of his physical existence were to be obliterated by fire, dispersed through waters or torn in pieces by wild beasts, there is nothing to stop the creative power of God restoring him to his original pristine condition.

Behind this argument is the utter rejection of the immortality of the soul, which Tatian spells out later.[42] He has recognized that the notion of the soul's immortality is incompatible with the doctrine of creation. The soul is mortal; and yet it is possible for it not to die. If it does not know the truth, it dies, dissolved with the body; but united with Spirit, it ascends. In other words the creative activity of God is at the root of any afterlife. 'Tatian's rejection of natural immortality is fundamentally theocentric', wrote Jaroslav Pelikan:

> Neither for his original birth out of the nothingness of non-being nor for his ultimate rebirth out of the nothingness of death can man take the credit, but it belongs to God's sovereignty and discretion to create a human being in the first place and re-create him after he has been annihilated by death . . . .
> Whatever immortality a man may obtain is thus by participation in the immortality and incorruptibility of God.

Pelikan speaks of 'a necessary corollary from the confession . . . that God is the Maker of heaven and earth'.[43]

And this involves another corollary – that the material aspect of human existence is given due recognition. Tatian is particularly conscious of the complexity of human nature and the inability of the soul to be by itself without the body – both reach dissolution in death, and neither can rise without the other. He is clear, then, that body and

---

41 Tatian, *Oration to the Greeks* 5, 6 [hereafter: *Orat.*]; *Tatian, Oratio ad Graecos and fragments*, ed. and trans. Molly Whittaker, OECT (Oxford, 1982).

42 Tatian, *Orat.* 13.

43 Jaroslav Pelikan, *The Shape of Death* (London, 1962), 17–18.

soul belong together and after death may be reconstituted by the Creator God who created them together in the first place.

So Tatian espoused the notion of *creatio ex nihilo* and asserted its bearing on resurrection,[44] in conscious opposition to philosophy in general and Platonism in particular. But second-century discussion of cosmology and eschatology was also affected by views later to be designated by the term 'Gnostic'. Indeed, it is in an evidently Gnostic work that the consequences of losing the connection between creation and resurrection can be observed, namely, the *Epistle to Rheginos* (or *Treatise on the Resurrection*)[45] found in the Nag Hammadi library, and probably dating from the late second century – in other words, in all likelihood, approximately contemporary with Athenagoras's treatise.

This short work responds to a question about death and the afterlife, but generally seems to treat 'death' and 'resurrection' as having metaphorical connotations only: for while the Lord 'existed in flesh', he lived 'where you remain', a place which 'I call "Death"!' It goes on to assert that he was Son of God so that he might vanquish death, and Son of Man so that 'restoration to the Pleroma' might occur. He was 'originally from above', 'a seed of the Truth'; he 'transformed [himself] into an imperishable Aeon and raised himself up, having swallowed the visible by the invisible, and he gave us the way of our immortality'. The Apostle is quoted (rather roughly, it has to be said): 'we suffered with him, and we arose with him, and we went to heaven with him'. So the elect were revealed: 'We are manifest in this world wearing him', and then 'drawn to heaven by him', unrestrained by anything. 'This is the spiritual resurrection which swallows up the psychic in the same way as the fleshly.' After exploring the need for faith, the question is posed again, 'What is the resurrection?' The answer is: 'It is always the disclosure of those who have arisen.' The appearance of Moses and Elijah in the Transfiguration narrative is alluded to and used as proof that the resurrection is no illusion; rather, the world is an illusion. The resurrection is the 'revelation of what is, and the transformation of things, and a transition into newness'. The recipient of the letter is urged to 'flee from the division and the fetters, and already you have the resurrec-

[44] The second-century writer Theophilus of Antioch made similar moves: see *Ad Autolycum* 2.4, where he argues that creation out of pre-existent matter makes God no better than a human craftsman; cf. ibid. 1.4, 7 for the connection between creation and resurrection.
[45] Trans. Malcolm L. Peel, in *The Nag Hammadi Library in English*, ed. James Robinson (Leiden, 1977), 50–53.

tion'. This is to 'enter into the wisdom of those who have known the Truth'.

It is hardly surprising, then, that this work has been characterized as 'permeated with Valentinian symbols and imagery', and as spelling out the views of those criticized in 2 Timothy 2: 18 for asserting that 'the resurrection has already taken place'.[46] In the genre of epistle, in its language and its allusions, it could almost pass as Christian, yet it clearly assumes that redemption is escape from matter and evil, and if it apparently speaks of being clothed in the Lord, or even of receiving flesh 'when you ascend into the Aeon', it turns out to be something 'better than flesh', and resurrection is actually rising up to the Pleroma or the All. If nothing else, then, this treatise proves that it is not so straightforward as has been assumed to distinguish resurrection and immortality – both terms could refer to the same thing, though with very different connotations in different contexts.

But its main importance for our argument here lies in the fact that creation is never mentioned – the connection has been lost. It shows how the argument with Gnosticism about the goodness of the material creation would inevitably involve the defence of bodily resurrection, as well as the true enfleshment of Jesus Christ in the incarnation. Creation, incarnation and resurrection all hung together. A brief look at Tertullian's treatise on the *Resurrection of the Flesh*[47] shows how clearly he saw the connections. From both heathen and heretic alike comes invective against the flesh, he asserts,[48] and he proceeds to offer a different view – of the glory of the flesh, created by God out of nothing, redeemed in Christ and to be resurrected. The opening chapters of the treatise suggest that he sees the resurrection as the basis of the whole Christian position; and his cross-references to other treatises, *Against Marcion* and *On the Flesh of Christ*, indicate his awareness of how all these doctrines cohere. 'First they crash in respect of the resurrection of the flesh,' he says, 'and afterwards they crash in respect of the unity of the deity.' He continues: 'Just as the foundations [of the unity of the deity] are shaken by denial of the resurrection of the flesh, so by the vindication of [the resurrection], [the unity of the deity] is established.'[49]

---

[46] Peel's introduction: ibid. 50.

[47] *Tertullian's Treatise on the Resurrection*, ed. and trans. Ernest Evans (London, 1960).

[48] Tertullian, *On the Resurrection* 4.

[49] Ibid. 2; here I have used and corrected Evans's translation and inserted explanations from the context.

It is this point which underlies my claim that resurrection had something to do with the emergence of the doctrine of creation out of nothing. It would be impossible to demonstrate a linear connection: Athenagoras apparently affirms one without the other, and the doctrine's basis undoubtedly lay in the arguments against alternative cosmogonies. On the one hand, God did not create out of the divine self (as Gnostic myths of the fragmentation of the divine might suggest) or everything would be divine; on the other hand, God did not create out of an eternal material substrate (as Platonists argued) or God's *monarchia* (his sovereignty as the single first principle) would be threatened – there would be two first principles. Tertullian was the first to set out these alternatives, rejecting both in favour of *creatio ex nihilo*.[50] Yet it was also Tertullian who saw how the incarnation and resurrection of Christ hang together with God's act of creation out of nothing, and that must surely be significant. His treatise *On the Resurrection of the Flesh* could have been written as an answer to the *Epistle to Rheginos*, it so precisely sets out to deny the positions taken up there. Metaphorical and spiritual interpretations of resurrection were alike heretical in Tertullian's view. The rejection of anti-materialist positions and the assertion of creation out of nothing surely derived a good deal of their punch from faith in the physical resurrection of Christ and the promised general resurrection.[51]

Such, then, is the case for my second thesis: that we can trace such a long-standing connection between creation and resurrection, both alike attesting God's power, that it can plausibly be argued that belief in resurrection, founded on the resurrection of Jesus Christ, not only reinforced insistence on the goodness of the material creation, but also contributed to the emergence of the idea that God created out of nothing.

Augustine of Hippo

To conclude, it is worth returning to the fourth century and Augustine of Hippo. The final book (22) of the *City of God* is his most extended treatment of the resurrection, though earlier books (such as 10, 13, 20 and 21) anticipate some of the material discussed at the climax. Here we

---

[50] Tertullian, *Against Hermogenes*.
[51] A similar argument could be adduced from the works of Irenaeus, who was also, of course, opposing Gnostic heresies.

see how his thinking, like that of Gregory of Nyssa, was indebted to the traditions we have been exploring,[52] though developed in his own inimitable way, with much reference to Scripture, as well as asides targeted at the Platonists, whose views, Augustine keeps arguing, should logically lead to Christian truth if they were not misguided about certain crucial matters: for example, despite saying that 'in the celestial sphere there are immortal bodies of beings whose blessedness is immortal', they assert that 'escape from any kind of body is an essential condition for our happiness', whereas Christians affirm that 'the resurrected body will be eternal', 'incorruptible and immortal and will present no obstacle to that contemplation by which the soul is fixed on God'.[53]

The following points provide a summary of Augustine's views:

1. The promises of God are to be relied upon because God is the originator of the creation, with all its marvels and surprises.[54] Belief in the physical resurrection of Christ, the coming resurrection to the new age of humankind and the immortality of the body is now generally accepted, Augustine affirms, because of the persuasive power of prophecy, the fearless proclamation of the martyrs and demonstrations of divine power, including contemporary miracles,[55] though created existence is itself the most powerful testimony.[56] The goodness of creation is rooted in God.[57]

2. There is a resurrection of the soul, from the death of irreligion and wickedness to righteousness and faith; this first resurrection is here and now, and is a resurrection of mercy. The second resurrection is of judgement, and anyone who does not want to be condemned then must rise up in the first. The resurrection to come is of bodies, and through fire their corruptible elements will perish, and 'our substance itself will acquire the qualities … suited, by a miraculous transformation, to our immortal bodies … renewed for the better even in their flesh'.[58]

3. The objections to the idea that bodies and material flesh could belong to heaven are met by appeal to the same Creator God – should it

---

[52] Latin text in CChr.SL 47–48 (Turnhout, 1955); ET in *Concerning the City of God,* trans. Henry Bettenson, intro. David Knowles, Penguin Classics (Harmondsworth, 1972).
[53] Augustine, *City of God* 10.29.
[54] Ibid. 22.1–3.
[55] Ibid. 22.5, 7–9.
[56] e.g. ibid. 22.4, 24.
[57] Ibid. 11.24.
[58] Ibid. 20. 6, 16.

not be regarded as more amazing that immaterial souls are bound within earthly bodies? For 'the interweaving of material with immaterial substances', the one being 'heavenly' and the other 'terrestrial', 'is surely a greater miracle of divine power than the conjunction of the material with the material'.[59] Platonist appeals to the weight of bodies cannot set limits to the power of Almighty God, as if God were not able to make our bodies capable of dwelling in the heavens.[60]

4. The classic problems of people being consumed by wild beasts or fire, drowned, or born with defects receive the classic answer: nothing is beyond the resources of the Creator. It is unthinkable that the Creator should lack the power to revive them all and restore them to life. Loss of nail-parings and hair-cuttings are not inimical to the general point that nothing will 'perish' from the person at the resurrection. The original substance of the person will be reused rather as an artist reuses or remixes material to produce a work without defects. The Almighty Artist can correct all disharmony and distortion, yet will retain the marks of the glorious wounds of the martyrs. At the resurrection to eternal life the body will most likely have the size and dimensions which it was to attain at maturity, according to the design implanted in the body of each person, with any necessary rearrangements to produce the harmony and beauty of the whole. The same flesh will arise, but re-formed as a spiritual body, the grace of which Augustine cannot describe because he has had no experience of it.[61]

5. Other questions designed to derail the idea – like, 'What about abortions or miscarriages?' or 'What will be the height and size of the resurrection body?' – are met by appeal to the apostolic statement that we shall all attain to the stature of the full maturity of Christ.[62] To reach that stature and be shaped in his likeness, refers not so much to literal size as to the inner person and the condition of immortality.[63] The point is that no weakness will persist, though sexual differentiation will, being regarded as natural, not a defect; but there will be no lust or childbirth, so the female organs will be part of a new beauty arousing praises of God 'for his wisdom and compassion, in that he not only created out of nothing but freed from corruption that which he

---

59 Ibid. 22.4.
60 Ibid. 22.11.
61 Ibid. 22.12–14, 19–20.
62 Ibid. 22.12.
63 Ibid. 22.15.

created'.[64] The Body of Christ is what is meant by perfect humanity – so the gradual building up of the Church is what will find fulfilment at the resurrection.[65] When Augustine attempts a description,[66] it is of a society in heaven, which is genuinely a body politic, at peace and bound in the closest possible harmony, where God is the goal of all longings, and 'we shall see him for ever, love him without satiety and praise him without weariness'.

To appreciate the significance of all this, it is important to scroll back through Augustine's earlier writings. His first instinct was to place sensible and material reality well below the intellectual in the hierarchy of existence, treating it as a drag downwards, while arguing in Platonic fashion for 'the indestructibility of the soul as a philosophically evident truth',[67] a position he never entirely abandoned, though he would also root the soul's immortality in its creation in the image of God and natural kinship to the transcendent world of Truth and Beauty. As for the body, in the 390s he could suggest that being 'raised a spiritual body', as Paul suggested in 1 Corinthians 15, implied a lack of material flesh and blood, taking seriously the words 'flesh and blood cannot inherit the Kingdom of God' (1 Corinthians 15: 50); whereas later he would speak of spiritual flesh.[68] In the *Confessions* Augustine focused on the vision of God promised to the purified soul, for which he yearns; he also offers praise to his Creator, taking creatureliness very seriously;[69] but he hardly touches on expectations for eternity or what the resurrection might mean. Over the years he had, of course, alluded to resurrection in sermons and other ecclesiastical writings, and in his completed work on *The Literal Meaning of Genesis* he considers the bodily state in the resurrection, but it is not until the *City of God* that he fully sets out his appreciation of the Christian critique of Platonism and explores at length the integration of soul and body as the ultimate human reality to be realized at the resurrection.[70] Here he even integrates this with his

64 Ibid. 22.17.

65 Ibid. 22.18.

66 Ibid. 22.30.

67 Daley, *Hope of the Early Church*, 142. See also Brian E. Daley, 'Resurrection', in Allan D. Fitzgerald, ed., *Augustine through the Ages: An Encyclopedia* (Grand Rapids, MI, 1999); other entries on 'Soul', 'Body' and 'Anthropology' helpfully trace Augustine's developing views.

68 Augustine, *City of God* 22.21.

69 In 'Creation and Human Being', I argued that this was the key to the *Confessions* and the much-debated question of its unity.

70 I am indebted to the work of a graduate student, Rowena Pailing, for demonstrating the exceptional character of the *City of God* in this respect.

more Platonic desire to contemplate God by discussing at length what it means 'to see God in the body',[71] – whether one would see God through the eyes of the body. He adopts the view that in the resurrected state those physical eyes must have some function, even though the incorporeal God cannot be seen in a physical way; he suggests that seeing the physical bodies of the new heaven and new earth will involve seeing God in utter clarity, present everywhere and governing the whole transformed material creation. Hence the power of God the Creator so to transform the whole person that the goal of the original creation is realized, beyond time in eternity, fully informs Augustine's vision. Now, too, despite all the oddities and speculations that discussion of bodily resurrection kept raising, it is possible to appreciate the thrust of that ancient creedal affirmation and its deep connection with the doctrine of creation.

Finally, as a postscript, it may be observed that the argument advanced here suggests that the heuristic model for studies of this kind should shift from the evolutionary notion of doctrinal development – surely a child of modernity – to that of discourse formation through argument and deduction. A deep-seated connection between resurrection and creation contributed to *arguments* that resulted in the idea of creation out of nothing; the implications of that doctrine, which took time to work out, then had a major impact on the formation not only of Christological discourse but also the Christian conception of the nature of the human creature and its eternal destiny. This study points up the importance for that *discourse formation* of dawning recognition of the coinherence of one doctrine with another.

University of Birmingham

---

[71] Augustine, *City of God* 22.29.

WHAT HAPPENED TO THE LAST JUDGEMENT IN THE EARLY CHURCH?

by JOSEPHINE LAFFIN

T HE Last Judgement was one of the most important themes in Christian art from the twelfth to the sixteenth centuries. It can be found in glittering mosaics on the west wall of the cathedral on the island of Torcello in the Venetian lagoon, on the sculptured centre portal of the west façade of Notre Dame in Paris, in Luca Signorelli's haunting frescos in the Chapel of the Madonna of San Brizio in Orvieto, and in Michelangelo's masterpiece in the Sistine Chapel. Numerous other churches had their own 'dooms'. A dramatic but not untypical example from the twelfth century can be found above the entrance to the Church of Sainte-Foy at Conques. Christ is enthroned as an austere judge, dividing the saved from the damned. The procession to heaven is neat and orderly while hell is chaotic, being depicted as a hideous mouth devouring the damned, a common representation in medieval art. In ominous foreboding, this Romanesque Last Judgement rivals the thirteenth-century hymn, the *Dies Irae*, as a reminder of the coming 'day of wrath and doom impending'.[1]

To step down into the ancient Roman catacombs is to enter a very different world from the Romanesque and Gothic churches of the Middle Ages. Depictions of the Last Judgement are almost completely absent from the wall and ceiling paintings which survive from the third to fifth centuries, and from relief sculpture on sarcophagi. It was not a popular theme in early Christian iconography. Why not? The expectation that there would be a final judgement was grounded in the New Testament, affirmed in creeds, and acknowledged by the great majority of early Christian writers, so why was this apparently core belief seldom reflected in the art of the period?

One explanation – the once common assumption that the early

---

[1] For the Last Judgement in medieval art, see S. G. F. Brandon, *The Judgment of the Dead* (New York, 1967), 118–31; Uwe Geese, 'Romanesque Sculpture', in Rolf Toman, ed., *Romanesque: Architecture, Sculpture, Painting* (Cologne, 1997), 328–33; idem, 'Gothic Sculpture', in Rolf Toman, ed., *Gothic: Architecture, Sculpture, Painting* (Cologne, 1998), 310–12; Veronica Sekules, *Medieval Art*, Oxford History of Art (Oxford, 2001), 85.

church was so concerned about idolatry that it was hostile to art – has been convincingly refuted by Mary Charles Murray.[2] Scholars have turned their attention to investigating why artists depicted some aspects of Christian teaching but not others. Much of the focus to date has been on the scarcity of crucifixion and resurrection scenes.[3] The paucity of images of the Last Judgement is only noted in passing, if at all, and most of the theories advanced to explain the late development of crucifixion and resurrection iconography do not apply to it.[4] This paper will first explore possible reasons why early Christians avoided depicting judgement and damnation. It will then look more closely at the literary sources and suggest that the disjunction between the visual and the textual evidence may not, in fact, be as great as one might expect from the prominence of the judgement theme in creedal statements and later Christian tradition.

The Visual Evidence: Early Christian Art

Given the fact that the earliest surviving Christian art comes predominantly from the Roman catacombs, the simplest explanation for the lack of representations of the Last Judgement is that they were not needed. As Jerome observed, just going down into the grim darkness of

---

[2] Mary Charles Murray, 'Art and the Early Church', *JThS* 28 (1977), 303–45. There is now considerable literature on early Christian art. A recent major work is Jeffrey Spier et al., *Picturing the Bible: The Earliest Christian Art* (New Haven, CT, and London, 2007). See also Jas Elsner, *Imperial Rome and Christian Triumph: The Art of the Roman Empire AD 100–450* (Oxford and New York, 1998); Paul Corby Finney, *The Invisible God: The Earliest Christians on Art* (New York and Oxford, 1994); Robin Margaret Jensen, *Understanding Early Christian Art* (London and New York, 2000); John Lowden, *Early Christian and Byzantine Art* (London, 1997). For the Roman catacombs, see Vincenzo Fiocchi Nicolai, Fabrizio Bisconti and Danilo Mazzoleni, *The Christian Catacombs of Rome: History, Decoration, Inscriptions* (Regensburg, 2002); L. V. Rutgers, *Subterranean Rome* (Leuven, 2000); Graydon Snyder, *Ante Pacem: Archaeological Evidence of Church Life Before Constantine* (Mercer, GA, 1985).

[3] Felicity Harley's forthcoming monograph, *Crucifixion Iconography: Beginnings and Development, ca. 200–600*, will be a seminal work. I am grateful to Dr Harley for reading a draft of this paper and providing helpful comments. For the development of resurrection iconography, see Anna Kartsonis, *Anastasis: The Making of an Image* (Princeton, NJ, 1986).

[4] Felicity Harley provides a survey of the theories in 'Images of the Crucifixion in Late Antiquity: The Testimony of Engraved Gems' (unpublished Ph. D. thesis, University of Adelaide, 2001), 16–33. That early Christians might have been deterred from pictorializing the crucifixion because of the stigma associated with that form of execution does not apply to the Last Judgement. Neither do the Christological concerns identified by Kartsonis, as they pertain to how Christ's death could be understood in terms of his human and divine natures (*Anastasis*, 33–39).

the catacombs could remind one of a descent into hell.[5] It is hardly surprising that grieving relatives commissioned scenes which illustrated God's saving actions in the Old and New Testaments, images which could bring comfort and hope. Hence the most common images in the catacombs from the third and early fourth centuries include Noah receiving the dove, Jonah regurgitated by the sea creature, and Shadrach, Meshach and Abednego surviving the fire in the furnace. The earliest representations of Jesus usually depict him as a beardless young man. In narrative scenes he appears as a miracle worker, healing the woman with the haemorrhage and raising Lazarus from the dead. He also seems to be symbolized as a philosopher teaching his disciples, and as a loving shepherd caring for his flock.[6]

Not all images in the catacombs are so benign, however. Deliverance from danger is accompanied by the destruction of opponents in fourth- and fifth-century representations of Samson smiting the Philistines and the Israelites crossing the Red Sea. There is a consensus among art historians that the artists who worked in the catacombs drew on and adapted well-known pagan images, and there was no shortage of battle scenes in late antique art. The funerary context was not necessarily a deterrent.[7] Thus, for example, the porphyry sarcophagus which contained the body of Constantine's mother Helena is decorated with Roman soldiers triumphing over barbarians. There was also a precedent for judgement scenes: they sometimes adorned the sarcophagi of Roman magistrates. André Grabar suggests that imperial judicial imagery could have influenced depictions of Susanna appearing before Daniel and, from the fourth century, the trials of martyrs and Jesus appearing before Pilate.[8] It may even have evolved into a representation of the Last Judgement, in the form of Christ presiding over a council of the apostles.[9]

The earliest known depiction of the Last Judgement, a Roman

---

[5] Jerome, *Commentary on Ezekiel* 60, quoted by James Stevenson, *The Catacombs: Life and Death in Early Christianity* (London, 1978), 24.

[6] The conventional interpretation that the Good Shepherd and philosopher images should be identified as representations of Jesus has not gone unchallenged. For a discussion on the possible meanings of this iconography, see Jensen, *Understanding Early Christian Art*, 37–46.

[7] See the chapter 'Art and Death', in Elsner, *Imperial Rome and Christian Triumph*, 145–65.

[8] André Grabar, *Christian Iconography: A Study of Its Origins* (London, 1969), 49.

[9] As evidence Grabar cites 'an isolated work', the (undated) Barbarini terracotta plaque in the Dumbarton Oaks collection (ibid. 44).

sarcophagus relief dated to the late third or early fourth century, is an illustration of the parable of the separation of the sheep from the goats (Matthew 25: 31–46). It features Jesus in the gentle guise of a philosopher-shepherd.[10] According to Paulinus of Nola (355–431), a similar image adorned the apse of his church in Fundi.[11] As Felicity Harley argues with regard to crucifixion iconography, such evidence reveals that it was possible to depict the Last Judgement pictorially. The fact that it is so rare does not necessarily imply that the subject was consciously avoided; it could simply have been insufficiently popular.[12]

It is worth remembering that the artists who produced the earliest Christian art may not themselves have been Christian, and they may well have worked for both Christian and pagan patrons. Contrary to what is sometimes assumed, not all catacombs would have been under ecclesiastical control or for the exclusive use of Christians. The Via Latina catacomb, rediscovered in the mid-twentieth century, indicates that in the fourth century affluent Roman families could bury both their pagan and their Christian dead in family tombs.[13] The Last Judgement would doubtless have been too disturbing and confrontational a theme for that context.

Yet Christianity was in the ascendant in the fourth century, and in the wake of the Emperor Constantine's patronage the greater self-confidence of the Christian community was reflected in art. In particular, in the catacombs there was a trend away from the youthful shepherd image to more regal depictions of Christ, now shown as an older man with halo and beard. Some of these 'portrait' images have been interpreted as representations of Christ the judge.[14] Whether on his own, or with Peter, Paul and other saints, Christ may be seated in judgement, but as James Stevenson notes, the image seems to be a benign one. There is no hint of possible condemnation.[15]

[10] Margaret English Frazer, 'Sarcophagus Lid with Last Judgment', in Kurt Weitzmann, ed., *Age of Spirituality: Late Antique and Early Christian Art. Catalogue of the Exhibition at the Metropolitan Museum of Art, 1977* (New York, 1979), 558.

[11] Jensen, *Understanding Early Christian Art*, 160.

[12] Harley, 'Images of the Crucifixion', 33.

[13] Antonio Ferrua, *The Unknown Catacomb: A Unique Discovery of Early Christian Art* (Florence, 1990), 156. See also Mark Johnson, 'Pagan-Christian Burial Practices of the Fourth Century: Shared Tombs?', *JECS* 5 (1997), 37–59. Johnson argues (at 58–59) that Christians and pagans were indeed buried in the same tombs, and that there was no ecclesiastical control over tomb decoration in burial places not owned by the Church.

[14] Fabrizio Bisconti, 'Art in the Paleochristian Period', in Marco Bussagli, ed., *Rome: Art & Architecture* (Cologne, 1999), 178–211, at 203; Stevenson, *Catacombs*, 108.

[15] Stevenson, *Catacombs*, 108.

This is equally true of the magnificent apse mosaics in the basilicas of Santa Pudenziana (c. 400) and Santi Cosma e Damiano (c. 526–30) in Rome. Here we have the risen Christ in apocalyptic majesty. For Fabrizio Bisconti, this reveals 'a new stress on judgement and the next world'.[16] Robin Jensen likewise remarks: 'the Santa Pudenziana iconography of Christ emphasizes his role as mature lord and judge; the Son who, according to the church's creed, has now ascended to heaven, where he sits on the right hand of the Father to judge the living and the dead'.[17] On the other hand, although Thomas Matthews acknowledges that one of the 'chameleon guises' of Christ is that of 'future judge of all',[18] he argues that Christ is primarily identified in the apse mosaics as a philosopher/teacher: 'Implicit in such images is the bold claim of Christians to have bested their pagan adversaries in the intellectual realm.'[19] The mosaics affirm the supreme teaching authority of Christ, mediated through the Church, and most directly through the clergy – who would sit or stand immediately below the apse. It is possible to accept that this interpretation has some merit without fully embracing Matthews's controversial denial of any influence on early Christian art of imperial iconography. A similar blurring of the eschatological dimension with an emphasis on the power and authority of the Church can be found in the scenes where the risen Christ is depicted handing the scroll of the law to the apostles, most notably St Peter, as in the fourth-century mausoleum of Constantine's daughter Constanza in Rome.

A slightly more negative depiction of judgement from the sixth century can be found in the basilica of Sant' Apollinare Nuovo in Ravenna. However, Jesus is once again a youthful shepherd, and although one of the angels has a rather sour expression on its face, the goats do not appear to be unduly perturbed at being separated from the sheep. We are still a long way from the gruesome depictions of damnation of the second half of the Middle Ages. It seems reasonable to conclude, on the basis of these works of art, that early Christians 'did not speculate about the resurrection and the end of the world and were unafraid of judgement'.[20] What then of the textual evidence?

16 Bisconti, 'The City of the First Christians', 210.

17 Robin Margaret Jensen, *Face to Face: Portraits of the Divine in Early Christianity* (Minneapolis, MN, 2005), 157.

18 Thomas F. Matthews, *The Clash of Gods: A Reinterpretation of Early Christian Art*, rev. edn (Princeton, NJ, 1999), 150.

19 Ibid. 111.

20 Mary Charles Murray, *Rebirth and Afterlife: A Study of the Transmutation of Some Pagan*

The Textual Evidence: The Eschatology of the Early Church Fathers

Most patristic writers made some reference to the final destiny of humankind, but their reflections on eschatological themes usually have to be gleaned from documents devoted primarily to other topics.[21] For example, in the mid-second century Bishop Polycarp of Smyrna turned a stern reminder of the coming judgement into an ethical exhortation, with particular emphasis on the need to show love and forgiveness and not judge others.[22] One would expect that Polycarp's contemporary, Bishop Ignatius of Antioch, would have been concerned about the so-called 'last things' as he fervently awaited his martyrdom. In fact, Ignatius was far more interested in ecclesiology than eschatology.[23] He did not mind those who disobeyed their bishop and corrupted the faith being consigned to an 'unquenchable fire', but he recommended that Christians treat their pagan neighbours as brothers, no matter how much opposition they faced.[24] Rather than await the Day of Judgement with fear, Ignatius preferred loving acceptance of God's gracious gift of salvation in Christ,[25] and he seems to have expected immediate access to God after his death.[26]

The North African writer Tertullian (c. 160–c. 225) certainly looked forward to the Last Judgement, and he proclaimed that one of the joys which the saved would experience would be watching the torments of the wicked in hell.[27] Thankfully for those who do not find this prospect

Imagery in Early Christian Funerary Art, British Archaeological Reports International Series 100 (Oxford, 1981), 111, with particular reference to images of Noah.

[21] For a survey of early Christian writings, see Brian Daley, *The Hope of the Early Church: A Handbook of Patristic Eschatology* (Cambridge, 1991); Joanne McWilliam Dewart, *Death and Resurrection,* Messages of the Fathers of the Church 22 (Wilmington, DA, 1986). For an introduction to eschatology, see William J. La Due, *The Trinity Guide to Eschatology* (New York and London, 2004); Zachary Hayes, *Visions of a Future: A Study of Christian Eschatology* (Wilmington, DA, 1987).

[22] Polycarp, *Letter to the Philippians* 2.1–3; 6.1–2.

[23] 'Ignatius was aware of the key elements in traditional Christian eschatology ... But such matters were peripheral rather than central for him': Christine Trevett, *A Study of Ignatius of Antioch in Syria and Asia,* Studies in the Bible and Early Christianity 29 (Lewiston, NY, 1992), 152–53. See also William Schoedel, *Ignatius of Antioch: A Commentary* (Philadelphia, PA, 1985), 21, 27–29.

[24] Ignatius, *Letter to the Ephesians* 16.2; 10.3.

[25] Ibid. 11.1.

[26] Idem, *Letter to the Romans* 6.1–2.

[27] Tertullian, *The Shows* 30. Tertullian's attitude has been charitably described as 'melancholy optimism' in response to pagan persecution of Christians: Eric Osborn, *Tertullian: First Theologian of the West* (Cambridge, 1997), 219.

appealing, other late second- and early third-century theologians were more restrained. Bishop Irenaeus of Lyons (c. 130–c. 200) did not dwell on the fate of the damned. In his writings, God is not vindictive, and hell not so much a place of torture and punishment as the state of self-imposed misery that results when people choose to turn away from God.[28]

What is most striking about Irenaeus's eschatology is his literal interpretation of prophetic and apocalyptic biblical passages, and his insistence, against his Gnostic opponents, that salvation must involve the material world. He expected a brief reign of the Antichrist on earth, followed by the return of Christ as judge. With the Antichrist and his followers cast into 'the lake of fire', the just would rise from their graves to live in a renewed physical world of incredible vitality and fruitfulness. After a thousand years (by which Irenaeus 'may have simply meant a very long time'[29]), Christ would surrender this kingdom to the Father, who would then be all in all. A new heaven and a new earth would be created. Those deemed worthy would enter heaven, which would contain wonders beyond comprehension, while those who were left behind would either be cast into the eternal fire or remain in the earthly paradise, growing in knowledge and love of God. The latter option is consistent with Irenaeus's understanding of salvation as an organic process rather than a single, transformative event. Irenaeus's literal understanding of an earthly kingdom of Christ was rejected by most later theologians, but his point that salvation must also involve the body remained strongly embedded in the Christian tradition.[30]

Irenaeus offered little reflection on the state of souls between the death and resurrection of their bodies: they would 'go away to the invisible place allotted to them by God'.[31] Writing during a time of persecution and plague in the mid-third century, Bishop Cyprian of Carthage (d. 258) cheerfully envisaged family reunions on the other side of the grave and described relatives in heaven eagerly waiting to

[28] 'But on as many as, according to their own choice, depart from God, He inflicts that separation from Himself which they have chosen of their own accord': Irenaeus, *Against Heresies* 5.27 (ANF, 1: 556). See also Denis Minns, *Irenaeus*, Outstanding Christian Thinkers Series (London, 1994), 127–28.

[29] Minns, *Irenaeus*, 126.

[30] For more on early Christian thinking about the resurrection of the body, see, in this volume, Frances Young, 'Naked or Clothed? Eschatology and the Doctrine of Creation', 1–19.

[31] Irenaeus, *Against Heresies* 5.31.2 (ANF, 1: 560).

greet and embrace their loved ones. Cyprian accepted that some humans would be eternally damned, but he was confident that Christians who faithfully followed their Lord would be granted immediate access to Christ's kingdom when they died.[32]

Clement of Alexandria (c. 150–c. 215) expected that all souls would have to undergo some kind of remedial and educational punishment in their progression towards fulfilment in God. He also raised the possibility of universal salvation, as it is the divine will that ultimately all people will be saved.[33] This suggestion is most famously associated with the controversial theologian Origen (c. 185–c. 254), as it was included in the condemnation of supposed aspects of his teaching at the Fifth Ecumenical Council in Constantinople in 553. It is difficult to summarize Clement's and Origen's eschatological beliefs because their scattered references to this topic lack consistency.[34] Henri Crouzel writes of Origen's questioning of the eternity of damnation: 'Origen hesitates, not seeing how to reconcile all the statements in Scripture: sometimes he makes no pronouncement, sometimes he ventures an opinion in one direction, sometimes in the other'. Yet Origen was convinced of the ultimate goodness of God, and 'he seems to preserve the hope that the Word of God will attain such force of persuasion that, without violation of free will, it will in the end overcome all resistance'.[35]

Significantly, although the creed issued at the Council of Nicea in 325 affirmed that Christ will come to judge the living and the resurrected dead, it did not actually state that one of the outcomes of that judgement could be eternal damnation. That reticence allowed a range of different opinions to be expressed in the fourth and early fifth centuries, on the occasions when the Fathers ventured beyond the Trinitarian and Christological issues which were the primary focus of debate. Thus Basil the Great (d. 379) believed in eternal damnation, but his brother, Gregory of Nyssa (d. c. 395), was much more optimistic. Gregory continued Origen's emphasis on the purgative nature of punishment, and he articulated more clearly the hope of universal

---

[32] Cyprian, *On Mortality* 26 (ANF, 5: 475), quoted in Daley, *Hope of the Early Church*, 41–43. Christian tomb inscriptions convey a similar belief in a peaceful existence in heaven, and the hope that family ties had not been completely broken: Danilo Mazzoleni, 'Inscriptions in the Roman Catacombs', in Nicolai et al., *Christian Catacombs of Rome*, 173–74.

[33] See, for example, Clement, *Stromata* 7.2, quoted in Daley, *Hope of the Early Church*, 47.

[34] For discussion of Clement's and Origen's eschatological beliefs, see Daley, *Hope of the Early Church*, 44–60; Dewart, *Death and Resurrection*, 114–36.

[35] Henri Crouzel, *Origen* (Edinburgh, 1989), 264–65.

salvation. This was based in part on the Platonic assumption that evil has no existence in its own right and will ultimately disappear with the triumph of goodness.[36]

Bishop Ambrose of Milan (c. 339–97) often exhorted his congregation not to fear death, and several times advised against too literal an understanding of a courtroom image of judgement. The salvation of the Good Thief demonstrated that 'no one can be excluded' from God's forgiveness.[37] Jerome (c. 345–420) also placed his hope in a judge who would be merciful as well as fair, at least to Christian sinners. In various writings he reiterated that blessedness or punishment would be experienced immediately after death, but he was agnostic about how this would come about, and whether the latter would be for eternity:

> We should leave this to the knowledge of God alone, who holds in his scales not only mercy but punishments, and who knows whom he should judge, and in what way, and for how long. Let us only say, as befits our human fragility, 'Lord, do not reproach me in your anger; do not destroy me in your rage ...'[38]

In the heat of the controversy over sin, grace and predestination, Augustine of Hippo (354–430) was driven to affirm the reality of eternal damnation for a great proportion of the human race. Nevertheless, he was a pastor as well as a theologian, and he stressed that God should be approached as a loving father rather than fearsome judge. 'Augustine tries to avoid preying on people's terror of the Last Judgment', comments Bonnie Kent.[39] Although he maintained that the punishment of hell would be everlasting, he did accept that the ancient practice of praying for the dead could move God to forgive sinful Christians, which implies that some punishment after death could be remedial and temporary.[40]

---

[36] See, for example, Gregory of Nyssa, *On the Soul and Resurrection* (NPNF II, 5: 444); idem, *The Great Catechism* 26 (NPNF II, 5: 496). See also Daley, *Hope of the Early Church*, 87; Anthony Meredith, *The Cappadocians* (London, 1995), 92–93.

[37] Ambrose, *On the Psalms* 39.17, quoted by Daley, *Hope of the Early Church*, 99.

[38] Jerome, *Commentary on Isaiah* 18.66.24, quoted by Daley, *Hope of the Early Church*, 104.

[39] Bonnie Kent, 'Augustine's Ethics', in Elenore Stump and Norman Kretzmann, eds, *The Cambridge Companion to Augustine* (Cambridge, 2001), 205–33, at 219–20. See also, in this volume, Elena Martin, '*Timor Mortis*: The Fear of Death in Augustine's Sermons on the Martyrs', 31–40.

[40] 'Not all men who endure temporal pains after death come into these eternal punishments which are to come after the judgement. Some, in fact, will receive forgiveness in the world to come for what is not forgiven in this': Augustine, *City of God* 21.13 (*Concerning the*

Conclusion

From these early Christian roots the notion of purgatory as a separate interim state would grow, mystics would see visions of the trials ahead, and devotional practices aimed at securing a speedy passage to heaven would come to dominate late medieval piety.[41] It is surely no coincidence that depictions of the Last Judgement became common at the same time. However, both the visual and the textual evidence from the first Christian centuries suggest that early Christians may not have been as concerned as their medieval successors by the prospect of a final judgement. Bishops like Polycarp, Ignatius, Irenaeus and Cyprian had more pressing pastoral concerns, as they faced persecution and divisions within the Christian community. After the era of persecutions ended, a series of doctrinal controversies focused the attention of fourth- and fifth-century theologians on Trinitarian and Christological issues rather than eschatology. 'Ordinary' Christians faced the challenge of living in a society where different religious cults could attract the allegiance of family members, creating pressures which must have been at their most acute during times of death and distress. They were, therefore, unlikely to commission representations of the Last Judgement, there being simpler symbols which artists could use to communicate Christian hope for salvation.

Despite the many inconsistencies and differences of opinion, there was in patristic eschatology an overriding emphasis on hope: the hope that death would not bring an end to life; that the body would be resurrected one day; and that ultimately one would be held to account by a God who was loving and merciful. That hope found expression in the simple soteriological images of the catacombs (Jonah, the Good Shepherd, Jesus healing and raising the dead) and in the glorious mosaics of the risen Christ in early Christian basilicas. The inscrutable Last Judgement was not denied, but neither was it emphasized as in the medieval 'dooms'. Why it became so popular in the Middle Ages deserves much fuller treatment elsewhere. What can be concluded here is that the

---

City of God, trans. Henry Bettenson, intro. David Knowles, Penguin Classics (Harmondsworth, 1972), 990–91). See also Daley, *Hope of the Early Church,* 138–39.

[41] R. N. Swanson, *Religion and Devotion in Europe, c. 1215–c. 1515* (Cambridge, 1995), 191–224, esp. 191: 'Devotional practice in the years between 1215 and 1515 offers a kaleidoscope of responses to the demands of faith, yet the whole period seems to be overshadowed by four words … *Timor mortis conturbat me* – the fear of death sets me in turmoil'.

scarcity of images of judgement and damnation in early Christian art offers a profound insight into early Christian eschatological beliefs. As Robin Jensen contends in her defence of the importance of integrating art and text history:

> Most religious communities are diverse enough to allow a rather broad scope and range of interpretation, but yet narrow enough to cohere as a group, guiding researchers back to certain core beliefs. Unless it is about to go into schism, fundamental continuity among these different modes of expression should be presumed about any group. Thus both verbal and visual eventually come down to the same thing and reinforce one another.[42]

That seems to have been true of the Last Judgement in the early church.

Flinders University

---

[42] Jensen, *Understanding Early Christian Art*, 182.

TIMOR MORTIS:
THE FEAR OF DEATH IN AUGUSTINE'S
SERMONS ON THE MARTYRS*

by ELENA MARTIN

IN the late fourth and early fifth centuries Augustine of Hippo preached a number of sermons at the annual celebrations of martyr festivals. These festivals commemorated the martyr's 'birthday': the day of the martyr's death on earth and entrance into the eternal life of heaven. They were popular occasions, drawing in larger and more diverse crowds than ordinary services, and attracting a certain air of festivity and merriment in North Africa.[1] Martyr festivals provided the ideal location for the discussion of the afterlife: eschatological hopes had long given meaning to martyrdom, exposing the order permeating chaos, pointing towards beauty amid human suffering, and revealing death as the gateway to true life.[2]

In his sermons delivered at martyr festivals Augustine frequently responds to the persistent anxieties and existential fears of his listening audience. While some work has been done on Augustine's attitudes towards the fear of death (*timor mortis*),[3] this contribution focuses on

---

* I would like to thank the Arts and Humanities Research Council and the Ecclesiastical History Society for the financial support that has enabled me to undertake this research. I am also very grateful to Dr Carol Harrison for her advice and comments on this paper. Any remaining errors are my own.

[1] For background, see Jan Den Boeft, ' "Martyres sunt sed homines fuerunt": Augustine on Martyrdom', in A. A. R. Bastiaensen, A. Hilhorst and C. H. Kneepkens, eds, *Fructus centesimus: Mélanges offerts à Gerard J. M. Bartelink à l'occasion de son soixante-cinquième anniversaire*, Instrumenta Patristica 19 (Dordrecht, 1989), 115–24; W. H. C. Frend, 'The North African Cult of Martyrs: From Apocalyptic to Hero-Worship', in E. Dassmann, ed., *Jenseitsvorstellungen in Antike und Christentum: Gedenkschrift für Alfred Stuiber*, Jahrbuch für Antike und Christentum, Ergänzungsband 9 (Münster, 1982), 154–67; Tarcisius J. Van Bavel, 'The Cult of the Martyrs in St. Augustine: Theology Versus Popular Religion?', in M. Lamberigts and P. van Deun, eds, *Martyrium in Multidisciplinary Perspective: Memorial Louis Reekmans*, Bibliotheca Ephemeridum Theologicarum Lovaniensium 117 (Leuven, 1995), 351–61.

[2] Carole Straw, 'Settling Scores: Eschatology in the Church of the Martyrs', in Caroline Walker Bynum and Paul Freedman, eds, *Last Things: Death and the Apocalypse in the Middle Ages*, The Middle Ages Series (Philadelphia, PA, 2000), 21–40.

[3] Robert Dodaro, ' "Christus Iustus" and Fear of Death in Augustine's Dispute with Pelagius', in Cornelius Mayer and Adolar Zumkeller, eds, *Signum pietatis: Festgabe für Cornelius*

how Augustine uses the figures of the martyrs to transform his listeners' concerns about their own mortality into an eager expectation of eternal life in heaven. In this pastoral context Augustine's reflections on the afterlife are rather more optimistic than those found in his written works.

As J. Kevin Coyle observes, Augustine's reflections on the afterlife vary according to context: his sermons do not always reveal the same picture as his writings.[4] While Augustine's preaching was by no means divorced from his theology, his sermons delivered at martyr festivals required a different approach to subjects such as death and the afterlife. Martyr festivals were celebrations of the victory of life over death, Christ over the devil, the Church over her pagan oppressors. This sense of triumph was expressed in a variety of ways: prayer, celebration of the Eucharist, singing, dancing, and offering food and wine at the martyrs' graves.[5] Augustine harnessed the heightened emotions associated with the martyr festivals as he used the atmosphere of celebration and the prospect of heavenly rewards to dispel the fear of death and to instruct, inspire and incite his listeners towards spiritual progress.

Recent scholarship on late antique sermons draws attention to the importance of the sermon as a tool that reveals information about both the preacher and the preacher's audience.[6] While the rhetorical nature of sermons warns us against a hasty acceptance of Augustine's words, we are invited to see glimpses of the afterlife through the eyes of some of his listeners. Augustine affirms that death is the one thing that we can be certain of in this life, but, even then, we cannot be certain of when the day of our death will arrive.[7] As this day moves closer, people take great pains to delay it: they are preoccupied with obtaining the

Petrus Mayer OSA zum 60 (Würzburg, 1989), 341–61; Éric Rebillard, *In hora mortis: Évolution de la pastorale chrétienne de la mort aux IVe et Ve siècles dans l'occident latin* (Rome, 1994), esp. 51–92.

[4] J. Kevin Coyle, 'Adapted Discourse: Heaven in Augustine's *City of God* and in His Contemporary Preaching', *Augustinian Studies* 30 (1999), 205–19.

[5] Peter Brown, 'Enjoying the Saints in Late Antiquity', *Early Medieval Europe* 9 (2000), 1–24; Johannes Quasten, ' "Vetus superstitio et nova religio": The Problem of Refrigerium in the Ancient Church of North Africa', *HThR* 33 (1940), 253–66.

[6] See, for example, Pauline Allen and Wendy Mayer, 'Computer and Homily: Accessing the Everyday Life of Early Christians', *Vigiliae Christianae* 47 (1993), 260–80.

[7] *Sermo* 306D.4; *Enarratio in Psalmum* 38.19. All references to Augustine's *Sermones* are to John E. Rotelle, ed., Edmund Hill, trans., *The Works of Saint Augustine: A Translation for the Twenty-First Century*, part III, vols 1–11 (New York, 1990–97) [hereafter: *S.* and *WSA* III respectively]. References to the *Enarrationes in Psalmos* [hereafter: *En. Ps.*] are to the same series, trans. Maria Boulding, vols 15–20 (New York, 2000–04).

necessary food, retaining their health, and acquiring medicine for illnesses.[8] Faced with the prospect of imminent death, people tremble with fear, they beg for their lives to be extended by even just one day, and they turn to superstitious cures and remedies to heal illnesses and postpone death.[9] The fear of death is common to those people who believe in an afterlife and those who do not. People who totally deny any form of life after death still desperately cling to this life of suffering and pain.[10] Some people are afraid of death, even though they are unsure of whether there is an afterlife: whether death is followed by judgement or is simply the end of existence.[11] Even when people do believe in an afterlife, they struggle to delay death and hold on to the present life.[12] Augustine describes this fear as a universal feeling experienced by all living creatures, originating from Adam's sin, and arising from our natural longing to stay alive.[13] But among human beings fear of death also has its origin in the incorrect understanding of divine revelation and Christian teaching on the afterlife. This misunderstanding has far-reaching consequences because faith in the resurrection is central to Christianity and, if this faith is absent, then the most fundamental tenets of Christian teaching perish: creation and order; the Fall and sin; Christ's incarnation and resurrection; God's mercy and grace; redemption and salvation.[14]

Furthermore, the fear of death leads to inordinate obsession with the preservation of the body and the excessive desire for temporal goods and false pleasures. This *cupiditas* – the improper love of the world and the self – enchains people to the transient world and leads to spiritual paralysis, as fear and despair turn the individual inwards and away from God, who created mankind from nothing and who is the source of all life.[15] Augustine asserts that the soul is immortal in that it shares in God's immortality, but it can indeed be deprived of life when it is separated from God: 'The death of the body is everlasting punishment;

---

[8] S. 280.3, 305A.8, 306D.4.

[9] S. 280.3, 302.4, 335D.3, 345.2. Cf. *Tractates on the Gospel of John*, 43.12(1–2). All references to the *Tractates* are to the translation by John W. Rettig, Fathers of the Church 78–79, 88, 90, 92 (Washington, DC, 1988–95) [hereafter: *Io. Ev. Tr.*].

[10] S. 280.3.

[11] S. 301.3.

[12] S. 280.3.

[13] S. 297.3–4, 299.8, 335B.1.

[14] See further S. 361.2.

[15] S. 335E.3.

the death of the soul is the absence of God'.[16] The result of the fear of death is, therefore, eternal death: by putting their own lives before God, people might delay the death of the body, but they hasten the death of the soul.[17] For those who have turned away from God, what is done in this life is fixed and eternal: prayers for the departed give no relief to the wicked.[18] At the Final Judgement these people will be damned to 'the second death', the unending torture of body and soul in the inextinguishable fires of hell.[19] With this in mind, Augustine qualifies the fear of bodily death with the fear of eternal death: 'Be afraid of the second death', he says, 'where the soul is not wrenched from the flesh, but the soul is tormented with the flesh. Don't be afraid of the transitory death, be afraid of the permanent one; there is no worse death than where death does not die ...'.[20] Here Augustine does not intend to arouse fear, but to explain the right order of what should be feared and avoided, and what should be loved and anticipated. He asks his audience: 'What am I to say? What sharp, well-aimed threats, what burning exhortations can I apply to hard and sluggish hearts, frozen in the ice of earthly numbness and dullness, to make them shake off the lethargy of the world, and catch fire at the prospect of eternity?'[21] But Augustine does not terrify his audience with threats of infernal fire. Instead he tries to inflame their hearts with the love of eternal life.

Acutely aware of the limits of language, Augustine speaks of heaven as something which transcends our own reality and experience: it is that which 'neither eye has seen nor ear has heard'.[22] He does not speak of the bountiful gardens of paradise or the resplendent palaces of light that are encountered in other North African sources from late antiquity.[23] This is especially the case in his sermons, where he spends less

---

[16] *S.* 65.8 (*WSA* III/3: 196). Cf. *The City of God Against the Pagans*, trans. R. W. Dyson, Cambridge Texts in the History of Political Thought (Cambridge, 1998), 13.2 [hereafter: *Civ.*].

[17] *S.* 273.1.

[18] *Civ.* 21.24.

[19] *S.* 306.5, 306E.9. Cf. *Civ.* 13.2.

[20] *S.* 335B.5 (*WSA*, III/9: 219).

[21] *S.* 302.2 (*WSA*, III/8: 301).

[22] *S.* 299D.1, 301.8, 302.7, 305A.9, 328.6, 331.3.

[23] Jan N. Bremmer, 'Contextualising Heaven in Third-Century North Africa', in Ra'anan S. Boustan and Annette Yoshiko Reed, eds, *Heavenly Realms and Earthly Realities in Late Antique Religions* (Cambridge and New York, 2004), 159–73; A. P. Orbán, 'The Afterlife in the Visions of the *Passio SS. Perpetuae et Felicitatis*', in Bastiaensen et al., *Fructus Centesimus*, 269–77.

time deliberating on the details of the afterlife than he does in his treatises.[24] Augustine's sermons depict a more abstract image of heaven
which is presented as a transformed, regenerated and perfect version of
this present life. Everything that we love and hope for in this life will be
found in heaven: everything that causes pain or suffering will be absent.
While this present life is marred with insecurity, uncertainty, change,
suffering, grief and death, the passing nature of this life encourages us
to have faith in the real life that begins after death.[25] Against the
eudemonistic traditions of the philosophers, Augustine affirms that the
ultimate happiness of mankind cannot be found in this present fallen
existence but can only be attained in the life after death.[26] The future
life is the true life; it is the realization of everlasting happiness and
eternal blessedness. It is an existence of inexpressible tranquillity, calm,
and peace; a place of rest and refreshment in the true embrace of the
presence of God; where the saints enjoy the direct vision of God;[27]
where individual identity is not lost, but existence is as a community of
saints, equal with the angels;[28] a place where, Augustine says, 'we shall
see, we shall praise, we shall remain'.[29]

Central to Augustine's vision of the afterlife is the resurrection of the
dead, as he rejects devaluations of the body found in Manichaeism and
Platonism by appealing to the authority of Scripture, and particularly
Paul, to describe heaven as a paradise for the whole person, body and
soul.[30] The same bodies that are inhabited on earth will rise again and
be changed from mortality to immortality, placed under the control of
the will, and renewed in conformity with Christ.[31] All bodies will be
transformed to their perfect potential, but the wounds of the martyrs
will remain visible: Augustine explains, 'the glorious martyrs will be

[24] Coyle, 'Adapted Discourse', 219: 'In the homiletic discourses, Augustine does not
discuss matters such as the [resurrected] body's weight, height, or hair … . The one truly
graphic description of risen bodies is in the *City of God*.' See further *Civ.* 21 for Augustine's
explanation of how the bodies of the damned will endure unending punishment, and for a
description of the resurrected bodies of the saints in the eternal City of God.

[25] *S.* 306.6–7.

[26] Ibid.; *Civ.* 19.

[27] *S.* 277.13–19. Cf. *Civ.* 22.29.

[28] *S.* 303.2.

[29] *S.* 305A.8 (*WSA*, III/8: 331). Cf. *Civ.* 22.30.

[30] See further M. Alfeche, 'The Use of Some Verses in 1 Cor. 15 in Augustine's Theology
of Resurrection', *Augustiniana* 37 (1987), 122–86.

[31] *En. Ps.* 140.16. See also, in this volume, Frances Young, 'Naked or Clothed? Eschatology and the Doctrine of Creation', 1–19.

resplendent with the special light that distinguishes them, and the bodies in which they suffered unseemly torments, will be turned for them into seemly robes of honour ...'.[32] With this description of heaven Augustine shows that death is not loss but gain; it is not the end of life but the entry into a truer and fuller life.[33] He preaches a message of consolation: 'when you die, you will not be dead ...'.[34]

This message is supported with references to the victories of the martyrs, whose suffering and death forms a second baptism which allows them to enter heaven immediately at the moment of their deaths.[35] This is why the martyrs were not mourned but were held in great honour,[36] and why Christians did not pray *for* the martyrs but rather prayed *to* the martyrs for intercession.[37] Augustine uses the belief in the martyrs' privileged state of life after death to preach against the fear of death. He interprets martyrdom as a revelation of eternal life and presents the martyrs as witnesses who bear testimony to the truth of the resurrection of the dead.[38] Martyrdom is described as a magnificent spectacle that can be seen and interpreted in various ways according to the different intentions and dispositions of the spectators.[39] Those who do not believe in an afterlife look on with the eyes of the flesh and they think that the martyr has been defeated and has suffered a bad death.[40] But those people who do believe in an afterlife look on with the eyes of faith, and, with the illumination of the light of faith, they perceive hidden sights and concealed truths that others are not permitted to see: the martyrs lay down their bodies but their souls do not die; and they do not attain temporal salvation in this life but do receive eternal salvation in heaven.[41] These hidden truths are apparent to the faithful in the description of the martyrs' suffering: as they endure horrific torture the martyrs receive heavenly visions in advance of their imminent participation in the vision of God;[42] their calm and

---

32   *S.* 280.5 (*WSA*, III/8: 75). Cf. *Civ.* 22.19.
33   *S.* 299E.1–2.
34   *En. Ps.* 36(3)15 (*WSA*, III/16: 141).
35   *S.* 280.4, 302.7.
36   *S.* 273.2, 309.1.
37   *S.* 284.5, 285.5, 297.3, 306E.1.
38   *S.* 328.2, 335A.1.
39   *S.* 274.1, 277.1, 280.1–2, 300.1, 313A.3.
40   *S.* 299E.1–2, 313D.4, 335E.2.
41   *En.Ps.* 40.2, 137.3, 14; *S.* 286.6, 301.2, 306D.1–2.
42   *S.* 280.4, 314.1, 316.2.

collected words reveal the inner working of the Holy Spirit;[43] their blood proclaims the eternal life;[44] their relics contain miraculous power which bears witness to the truth of immortality.[45] Even the martyrs' names declare the eternal life: Perpetua and Felicity point towards the perpetual felicity of heaven;[46] Perpetua and Victoria reveal the everlasting victory of life over death;[47] Vincent demonstrates the victory over the Devil.[48]

Interpreting martyrdom as a revelation of eternal life, Augustine affirms the truth of resurrection and immortality and urges his listeners to perceive that truth for themselves. He says: 'Look at them [the martyrs] very carefully, dearly beloved; you can't do it with your eyes, but think about them with mind and heart, and see that precious in the sight of the Lord is the death of his holy ones ...'.[49] Augustine appeals to the theological virtues of faith, hope and love to encourage his audience to perceive their own deaths in the same manner, looking beyond the surface of desolation and loss, and hoping for the things that can be seen only with the eyes of faith. He advises them: 'Believe what you can't yet see, so that you may earn the right to see what you believe.'[50]

Yet, while here Augustine appeals to the rewards of heaven to console his listeners, elsewhere his doctrines of original sin, election and predestination led him to advocate a strikingly negative position on human destiny. The philosophy of the Platonists, and the competing theologies of the Origenists, Manichees, Donatists and Pelagians, pushed Augustine towards definitions of the Fall, redemption, and salvation, which formed the framework for his theology. Within this framework we find some of Augustine's more extreme ideas on the afterlife: the damnation of infants; the impossibility of posthumous salvation for non-Christians; the small number of the predestined elect; and the eternity of hell.[51] In an aspect of his theology which has been described as 'horrifying' and 'terrifying', Augustine maintains that God, in his mercy, chooses to save a number of people from justly deserved

---

[43] S. 275.1, 276.2.
[44] S. 299F.1.
[45] Civ. 21.9, 10; S. 275.3, 317.1.
[46] S. 159A.11, 280.1, 281.3, 282.1, 3.
[47] S. 335A.1–2.
[48] S. 274, 275.2–3, 276.1, 4.
[49] S. 329.2 (WSA, III/9: 183).
[50] S. 301.9 (WSA, III/8: 287–88).
[51] For example Civ. 21.13, 17, 23.

damnation, but God does not bestow his grace upon all: the vast majority of humankind is damned to eternal punishment.[52] It is not difficult to imagine how this view could have struck the fear of death into the hearts of even the most pious Christians.

Here, then, there is a tension between Augustine's theology and his preaching. His sermons convey a relatively optimistic outlook on salvation, presenting a far more positive image of heaven than the exclusive abode of the select few suggested by his views on election and predestination. In one sermon he goes so far as to say, 'Whoever wishes to enjoy bliss should be hurrying along to the kingdom of heaven. It is not closed to anyone, except those who have excluded themselves from it.'[53] With these words Augustine presents heaven as being within reach of all who desire it, and closed only to those who choose to exclude themselves from it by turning away from God. The emphasis here is not so much on God's election, but rather on the moral responsibility and willed decision of the individual.

In a similar vein Augustine describes the present life as a pilgrimage along the path to eternal life which was first laid down by Christ.[54] This is not the hard and narrow path of Matthew 7: 14, along which only a few can travel, but it is a path that has been made smooth and wide by the martyrs: Augustine asks, 'How can the way still be rough, when it has been smoothed by the feet of so many walking along it?'[55] The martyrs are guides who go ahead and lead the way to eternal life.[56] They were just like us: they were human; they were born like us; they shared the mortal condition; and they were afraid of suffering and death.[57] But they conquered fear because they understood the right order of love: they swapped cupidity for charity, temporal goods for eternal happiness, and this life for the next life.[58] Augustine says, 'The holy martyrs, witnesses of God, preferred to live by dying, in order not to die by living; in order not to deny life by fearing death, they despised life by loving life.'[59] This qualification of life and love enabled the

[52] Gerald Bonner, *Freedom and Necessity: St. Augustine's Teaching on Divine Power and Human Freedom* (Washington, DC, 2007), 14, 20.
[53] *S.* 326.1 (*WSA*, III/9: 170).
[54] *S.* 304.3, 306.2, 345.6.
[55] *S.* 306.10 (*WSA*, III/9: 24).
[56] *S.* 302.7, 325.1.
[57] *S.* 159A.3, 273.9, 277.2, 284.3, 297.1–3, 299.8, 299F.4, 305A.2, 330.4, 335B.3, 335C.1, 335H.2.
[58] *S.* 169.15, 281.3, 284.4, 306A, 335B.2, 4.
[59] *S.* 299D.1 (*WSA*, III/8: 256).

martyrs to be brave by fixing their hopes on heaven, to endure temporary torture and receive eternal rewards, and to give up their bodies and save their souls.[60] But the martyrs did not achieve this by themselves; they could only conquer the fear of death with Christ as their helper and protector.[61] Acknowledging their own weakness, the martyrs prayed for God's guidance and received the interior working of grace to strengthen them in their battles.[62] Augustine provides the martyrs' actions as a moral lesson for his listeners, encouraging them to imitate the martyrs so that they too will arrive at the same destination.[63] Here he suggests that heaven is extremely close and that grace is openly available. By imitating the martyrs, praying to the martyrs for intercession,[64] and drinking from the fountain of grace,[65] they too can receive the desire for eternal life,[66] the strength to endure the trials of this life,[67] and the reward of an eternal crown in heaven.[68] Thus, everyone who follows the martyrs will receive eternal life: Augustine says that God 'does not grant health to everyone through the martyrs; but to all who imitate the martyrs, he does promise immortality'.[69]

In conclusion, Augustine's reflections on the afterlife in his sermons on the martyrs focus on the accessibility of heaven for all the faithful and the moral responsibility of human beings in their progress towards eternal life. These emphases might sit uncomfortably with the doctrine of predestination, but it must be remembered that Augustine was preaching within a pastoral context, responding to the anxieties of his audience with perceptive concern and the sensitive desire to console.

---

[60] *S.* 277A.2, 299F.2–3, 304.4, 313C.1, 314.1, 335B.2, 4.

[61] *S.* 280.4, 306A, 331.1. For the anti-Pelagian undertones of this assertion, see Dodaro, 'Christus Iustus', 349.

[62] *En. Ps.* 140.22; *S.* 274, 276.1–2, 277A.2, 280.1, 281.1, 283.4, 284.1–3, 285.1, 299C.4, 302.8, 305A.2, 5, 313A.5, 328.3, 329.2, 330.1, 332.3, 335B.4, 335F.2, 335J.1. For Augustine this point distinguishes the true martyrs of the Catholic Church (*martyres veri*) from the false martyrs of the Donatist Church (*martyres falsi*). While the Donatist martyrs appear to have conquered the fear of death by welcoming martyrdom, Augustine repeatedly asserts that it is the cause, not the punishment, which makes a martyr (*S.* 325.2, 327.1–2, 328.4, 7, 335.2, 335C.5, 335G.2, 359B.16–20). The true martyr's motivation is pure and chaste love; this love is shed abroad in the heart by the Holy Spirit, which is received only by those who are in the unity of the Catholic Church (*Io. Ev. Tr.* 93.1).

[63] *S.* 159A.1, 302.9, 306.10, 315.8, 317.3, 325.1, 335C.12, 335D.3, 335H.1.

[64] *S.* 332.3, 335H.2.

[65] *S.* 299F.4, 315.8, 317.4, 345.6.

[66] *S.* 297.8, 299A.2, 301.3, 7–8, 313A.2.

[67] *S.* 305A.10, 306C.3, 5.

[68] *S.* 331.5.

[69] *S.* 286.5 (*WSA*, III/8: 103).

He understood the problem of the fear of death to be a serious and urgent matter: fear leads to spiritual paralysis, paralysis to moral passivity, and passivity to eternal death. It is because of this that Augustine allows himself to emphasize the more positive aspects of the afterlife in order to stimulate his listeners, shake them out of the lethargy of fear, and touch the hearts of the indifferent and the complacent by inciting a hope for heavenly rewards. Knowing that the prospect of hell could send his already fearful audience further into the depths of despair, Augustine prefers to reflect on the inexpressible wonders of heaven and the glorious revelations of eternal life disclosed through martyrdom. Linking mortality with morality, Augustine encourages his audience to adopt an eschatological outlook, to redirect their attention beyond death and towards eternal life, and to persevere and make progress in this life, not in spite of, but precisely because of, the inevitability of death.

University of Durham

PHILOSOPHY, HAGIOLOGY AND THE EARLY
BYZANTINE ORIGINS OF PURGATORY

by MATTHEW J. DAL SANTO

O N 8 June 1438, the Council of Ferrara-Florence began proceedings aimed at the reunion of the Eastern and Western Churches. One of the first issues discussed was the Latin doctrine of purgatory.[1] This article examines a particular moment in the divergence of eschatological doctrine between the Latin, Greek and Syriac Churches – indeed, representatives of the West Syrian 'Jacobites' and East Syrian 'Nestorians' were at Ferrara too.[2] It argues that a debate concerning the *post mortem* activity of the saints proved crucial for the formation of various Christian eschatological orthodoxies. The catalyst for this debate was the sixth-century revival of Aristotelian philosophy, especially Aristotelian psychology which emphasized the soul's dependence on the body. This threatened the cult of the saints and the Church's sacramental 'care of the dead'. Defenders of the hagiological and cultic status quo rejected Aristotle's claims and asserted the full *post mortem* activity of the soul after separation from the body by developing a novel doctrine of immediate *post mortem* judgement. This led to the formulation of eschatological opinions which, if not normative in their day, came to be considered so by later generations. One of these ideas was *post mortem* purgation.

* * *

In his *Dialogues* (c. 593), Pope Gregory the Great (590–604) asserted the necessity of believing in a 'cleansing fire after death'.[3] Gregory's

---

[1] For Greek-Latin debates leading up to Florence-Ferrara, see G. Dagron, 'La perception d'une différence: les débuts de la "Querelle du purgatoire" ', in *15e Congrès international des études byzantines: Actes* 4 (Athens, 1976), 84–89, repr. in G. Dagron, *La romanité chrétienne en Orient* (London, 1984), ch. 13.

[2] On the 'Nestorians', see S. Brock, 'The "Nestorian" Church: A Lamentable Misnomer', *BJRL* 78 (1996), 23–35. Syriac refers to the liturgical language which was common to both the West Syrian church, whose Christology tended to emphasize Christ's single divine-human nature (and has been labelled Miaphysite, Monophysite or anti-Chalcedonian), and the East Syrian ('Nestorian') church, whose Antiochene Christology emphasized the distinct properties of Christ's separate divine and human natures.

[3] *Grégoire le Grand: Dialogues*, ed. A. de Vogüé, trans. P. Antin, 3 vols, SC 251, 260, 265

endorsement became a primary authority for later formulators of
Catholic purgatory during the thirteenth century. Although Augustine
of Hippo (354–430) considered the *post mortem* purgation of the souls of
imperfect Christians possible, Gregory was the first Latin to make it an
article of faith, explicitly linking *post mortem* purgatorial expiation with
the Church's intercession for the dead.[4] What prompted Gregory
towards such a momentous shift? Gregory developed his thoughts on
the afterlife in the context of a broader debate concerning the saints,
especially the miracles which they performed *post mortem*.[5] This debate
implied a thoroughgoing reassessment of patristic anthropology
generally, especially as this was viewed from the perspective of the 'last
things'.[6] Around 582 Eustratius of Constantinople's *On the State of Souls*
defended the saints' *post mortem* miracles against unnamed 'philosophers' who contended that human souls were inactive after death
because the soul depended upon the body for mobility and perception.[7]
The philosophers' arguments recall Aristotle's definition of the soul
as the form that endowed the body with growth, perception and reason,
with only a controversial claim to separate existence. Eustratius,
however, reaffirmed the activity of the disembodied soul, including its
retention of the body's faculties, which enabled the souls of the
saints to intercede for believers and to perform miracles for supplicants.[8]

There are close links between the ideas Eustratius rebutted and the
opinions attributed to Stephen Gobar, a Miaphysite disciple of the great
Christian Aristotelian, John Philoponus.[9] Gobar was active in Constantinople during the 570s and his writings reflect a strong sense of

---

(Paris, 1978–80). On the eschatological questions of the fourth dialogue, see M. van
Uytfanghe, 'Scepticisme doctrinal au seuil du moyen âge? Les objections du diacre Pierre
dans les *Dialogues* de Grégoire le Grand', in J. Fontaine et al., eds, *Grégoire le Grand: Actes du
colloque de Chantilly, 15–19 septembre, 1982* (Paris, 1986), 315–26.

4 J. Le Goff, *La naissance du purgatoire* (Paris, 1982), 124–28.

5 See also M. Dal Santo, 'Gregory the Great and Eustratius of Constantinople: The
Dialogues on the Miracles of the Italian Fathers as an Apology for the Late Sixth-Century Cult of
Saints', *JECS* (forthcoming).

6 On the latter, see N. Constas, ' "To Sleep, Perchance to Dream": The Middle State of
Souls in Patristic and Byzantine Literature', *DOP* 55 (2001), 91–124.

7 *Eustratii Presbyteri Constantinopolitani: De statu animarum post mortem*, ed. P. van Deun,
CChr.SG 60 (Leuven, 2006) [hereafter: *De stat.*].

8 N. Constas, 'An Apology for the Cult of Saints in Late Antiquity: Eustratius Presbyter
of Constantinople, *On the State of Souls after Death*', *JECS* 10 (2002), 267–85.

9 Ibid. 281.

sixth-century Christian Aristotelianism.[10] Gobar contested the prayers and masses offered for the dead; and Eustratius concluded his vindication of the saints' miracles with a defence of these cultic practices. The two issues – the reality of the saints' *post mortem* miracles and the Church's sacramental care of the dead – were intimately related.[11] If human souls were inactive after separation from the body, little could be gained by the prayers of the faithful.[12]

Straightforward from a high medieval perspective, the *post mortem* activity of souls was problematic for sixth-century audiences, forcing defenders of the saints into lengthy apologies. Did not St Paul say that he longed to die and be with Christ,[13] as Gregory the Great noted? Gregory affirmed: 'We firmly believe that Christ is in heaven. Should we, then, not believe that the soul of Paul is there too?'[14] Moreover, in 2 Corinthians the Apostle described death as a shedding of the 'tent' of the body and an apparently immediate entry into a 'heavenly dwelling, not made with hands'.[15] The 'high' view of the saints held by Eustratius and Gregory also entailed an immediate *post mortem* judgement *in addition to* the Final Judgement that would follow the resurrection. Certainly, this was the implication that flowed from their teaching that just as the souls of the saints entered into heaven directly upon separation from their bodies, so the souls of sinners descended immediately into hell.[16] Even in hell the disembodied souls of the damned remained active, 'not in the same way as the souls of the saints, but in the sense that they are alive and move about and experience remorse'.[17]

[10] Gobar's teachings are referred to in Photius (815–97), *Bibliotheca*, cods. 230–41, in *Photius: Bibliothèque*, ed. R. Henry, 5 (Paris, 1967): 67–79; A. von Harnack, 'The "Sic et Non" of Stephen Gobarus', *HThR* 16 (1923), 205–34; G. Bardy, 'Le florilège d'Étienne Gobar', *Revue des études byzantines* 5 (1947), 5–30; 7 (1949), 51–52.

[11] G. Dagron, 'L'ombre d'un doute: L'hagiographie en question, VIe–XIe siècle', *DOP* 46 (1992), 59–68, at 63, col. 1; J. Ntedika, *L'évocation de l'au-delà dans la prière pour les morts: Étude de patristique et de liturgie latines (IVe–VIIIe s.)* (Louvain, 1971).

[12] The same combination of themes appears in Gregory's *Dialogues* which end with a demonstration of the *post mortem* power of the mass: *Dial.* 4.57–60 (SC 265: 184–200). See Dal Santo, 'Gregory the Great'.

[13] Phil. 1: 23.

[14] *Dial.* 4.26.2 (SC 265: 84).

[15] 2 Cor. 5: 1. Eustratius employed the same biblical authorities to defend the same proposition: *De stat.* (CChr.SG 60: 719–28, 733–38). See Dal Santo, 'Gregory the Great'.

[16] Gregory, *Dial.* 4.29 (SC 265: 98–100); Eustratius, *De stat.* (CChr.SG 60: 2209–23). On Gregory's eschatology, see C. Carozzi, *Le voyage de l'âme dans l'au-delà d'après la littérature latine: Ve–XIIIe siècle* (Rome, 1994), 61.

[17] Eustratius, *De stat.* (CChr.SG 60: 2161–64).

Two later Christian thinkers, Anastasius of Sinai (d. c. 700) and the Pseudo-Athanasius (d. before 750) highlight the innovatory nature of such eschatological opinions.[18] 'Question and Answer' writers, both considered it absurd to imagine the *post mortem* existence of the soul apart from the body. According to Anastasius, between the death of the body and its resurrection the disembodied soul dwelt either in Paradise or Hades, temporary waiting rooms where it received a premonition of its destiny without experiencing its consequences, which was impossible without the body. The eschatological realities of heaven or hell were only realized after the resurrection, not before as Gregory and Eustratius argued.[19] Anastasius also denied the *post mortem* activity of the souls of the saints owing to the soul's dependence upon the body.[20] Indeed, what seems to have tipped Eustratius and Gregory towards a doctrine of immediate *post mortem* judgement in contrast to Anastasius was their equally opposed concern to shore up the cult of the saints.

Anastasius and Pseudo-Athanasius were faithful to the ancient eschatology of St Irenaeus of Lyons (d. c. 200). Irenaeus condemned the belief that souls went directly to heaven or hell before reunification with the body at the resurrection.[21] Yet, this was the very doctrine which sixth-century defenders of the saints asserted was orthodox.[22] The cult of the saints provoked a definitive break with the past at the end of the sixth century as the Church realized the ramifications of the cult of the saints and prayer for the dead for its eschatology and anthropology. The old eschatology of the *post mortem* inactivity of souls before

---

[18] *Anastasii Sinaitae: Quaestiones et responsiones*, eds M. Richard and J. A. Munitiz, CChr.SG 59 (Leuven, 2006) [hereafter: *Qu. et Resp.*]; Pseudo-Athanasius, *Quaestiones ad Antiochum ducem* (PG 28: 554–710). For Anastasius's biography, see J. Haldon, 'The Works of Anastasius of Sinai: A key Source for the History of Seventh-Century East Mediterranean Society and Belief', in A. Cameron and L. Conrad, eds, *The Byzantine and Early Islamic Near East*, 1 (Princeton, NJ, 1992): 107–47. On dating Pseudo-Athanasius, see G. Thümmel, *Die Frühgeschichte der ostkirchlichen Bilderlehre: Texte und Untersuchungen zur Zeit vor dem Bilderstreit*, Texte und Untersuchungen zur Geschichte der altchristlichen Literatur 139 (Berlin, 1992), 246–52.

[19] *Qu. et Resp.* 21 (CChr.SG 59: 38).

[20] Dagron, 'L'ombre'. Compare D. Krausmüller, 'God or Angels as Impersonators of Saints: A Belief in its Context in the *Refutation* of Eustratius of Constantinople and the Writings of Anastasius of Sinai', *Gouden Hoorn* 6/2 (Winter 1998–99) [online journal], <http://www. isidore-of-seville.com/goudenhoorn>, accessed 31 March 2008.

[21] C. E. Hill, *Regnum Caelorum: Patterns of Future Hope in Early Christianity* (Oxford, 1992), 9–17.

[22] Ntedika, *Évolution*, 159. In the ninth century, Photius asserted that fathers like Irenaeus unintentionally erred in stressing the resurrection: *Photius*, ed. Henry, 5: 67–79.

the resurrection was incompatible with the *post mortem* activity of the soul these practices assumed.[23] The 'Question and Answer' writers display Christian communities grappling with these questions under Muslim rule in Egypt at the beginning of the eighth century. At the western end of the Mediterranean the same is true for Julian of Toledo's (d. 690) *Prognosticon*.[24]

Where does Gregory's belief in *post mortem* purgation fit into this? *Post mortem* purgation was attractive because it offered a solution to a secondary problem raised by immediate *post mortem* judgment, namely the fate of Christians who were not saints but not unrepentant sinners either.[25] According to Irenaeus's resurrection-orientated eschatology, an individual's ultimate *post mortem* fate was deferred until the Last Day. A system of immediate *post mortem* judgement, however, orientated towards the afterlife of the soul made the *post mortem* status of ordinary souls a matter of urgency.[26] Moreover, given the necessity of upholding the cult of the saints and prayer for the dead, the traditional solution – soul sleep or temporary repose in Paradise or Hades until the resurrection – was no longer satisfactory. Fiery purgation offered a handy solution by maintaining the complete activity of all souls *post mortem* and presupposed that the soul possessed sensory abilities apart from the body. Simultaneously, the *post mortem* purgation of the imperfect preserved the distinctness of the saints' glory in heaven and enhanced the imperative for the living to offer sacrifices for the dead.

After the 'Triumph of Orthodoxy' (843), Byzantine Christianity popularly assumed the *post mortem* activity of intermediate souls, especially in hagiography, even if their precise condition prior to the resurrection remained uncertain.[27] Yet, later uncertainty was not for want of earlier speculation. In the seventh century a Cypriot abbot had proposed the existence of an eternal third condition, somewhere

---

[23] M. van Uytfanghe, 'L'essor du culte des saints et la question de l'eschatologie', in *Les fonctions des saints dans le monde occidental: Actes du colloque organisé par l'École française de Rome avec le concours de l'Université de Rome 'La Sapienza', Rome, 27–29 octobre 1988* (Rome, 1991), 91–107, esp. 92, 107.

[24] *Sancti Iuliani Toletanae Sedis Episcopi: Opera*, 1, CChr.SL 115 (Turnhout, 1976): 9–126. See also, in this volume, Jamie Wood, 'Individual and Collective Salvation in Late Visigothic Spain', 74–86.

[25] See *Dial.* 4.26.

[26] P. Brown, 'The Decline of the Empire of God: Amnesty, Penance, and the Afterlife from Late Antiquity to the Middle Ages', in Caroline Bynum and Paul Freedman, eds, *The Last Things: Death and the Apocalypse in the Middle Ages* (Philadelphia, PA, 2000), 41–59, at 42–43.

[27] Constas, ' "To Sleep, Perchance to Dream" '; Dagron, 'Perception', 84.

between heaven and hell.[28] Even Anastasius of Sinai could imagine the slow ascent of the soul through the tollgates of heaven, tested by demons, uncertainly dependent upon the intercession of angels or saints.[29] In the West the doctrine of purgatory proclaimed at the Second Council of Lyons (1274) solved this problem. Like the Byzantine position, the medieval Latin one was reached after six centuries of intermittent, at times inconsistent, speculation. The two communities did not realize their divergence until their confrontation at Ferrara in 1438. Between the sixth century and the Second Council of Lyons in 1274, however, Greek and Latin representations of the fate of intermediate souls beyond the grave were closer than later polemics portray.[30] The reality of the miracles performed by the saints beyond the grave and the efficacy of the Church's care for the dead encouraged Greeks and Latins alike during the early Middle Ages to assert the *post mortem* activity of all human souls, imperfect or otherwise. The differing eschatological orthodoxy of Greeks and Latins can be seen as a response to the complex anthropological questions which the doctrine of *post mortem* activity raised.

The cult of the saints also had an impact upon East Syrian ('Nestorian') eschatology and this is illustrated by the ideas of the early sixth-century theologian Narsai of Nisibis (d. after 503). Unlike Gregory or Eustratius, Narsai conceded that human souls could not be active after separation from the body.[31] For Narsai the soul was totally dependent upon the body. Before the resurrection the soul 'slept', unable to resume its activity until the body too had reawakened.[32]

[28] C. P. Kyris, 'The Admission of the Souls of Immoral but Human People into the *limbus puerorum* according to the Cypriot Abbot Kaïoumos (Seventh Century AD) compared to the Quran's Al-Araf (Suras 7.44–6, 57.13)', *Revue des études sud-est européennes* 9 (1971), 461–77.

[29] F. Nau, 'Les récits inédits du moine Anastase: contribution à l'histoire du Sinaï au commencement du VIIe siècle', *Revue de l'Institut catholique de Paris* 1–2 (1902), 1–70, at 48; commentary in B. Flusin, 'Démons et sarrasins: l'auteur et le propos des *Diègmata stériktika* d'Anastase le Sinaïte', *Travaux et mémoires* 1 (1991), 381–409. This became the most common Byzantine view of the afterlife: C. Mango, *Byzantium: The Empire of New Rome* (London, 1980), 157.

[30] For example, Bede's (d. 735) 'Byzantine' description of the *post mortem* fate of the imperfect: *Historia ecclesiastica* 3.19, ed. and trans. Bertram Colgrave and R. A. B. Mynors, *Bede's Ecclesiastical History of the English People* (Oxford, 1969), 272–74. See also, in this volume, Sarah Foot, 'Anglo-Saxon "Purgatory" ', 87–96.

[31] Narsai of Nisibis, *De la valeur de l'âme et comment elle dirige le corps, sa demeure*. For a French translation, see P. Krüger, 'Le sommeil des âmes dans l'œuvre de Narsai', *Orient Syrien* 4 (1959), 193–210.

[32] Ibid. 202.

Narsai also eschewed a 'high' view of the saints' *post mortem* activity, which allowed him to avoid both immediate *post mortem* judgement and the problem of the *post mortem* activity of the souls of the imperfect.[33] Strengthened by Aristotelian psychology, the Church of the East rejected the eschatological views of Pope Gregory and Eustratius and later Latin and Byzantine traditions, views that strongly contributed to the Latin doctrine of purgatory.

* * *

What brought these psychological issues to the fore during the sixth century for Christian writers in Greek, Latin and Syriac? An explanation can be found in the uneasy confrontation between Christian doctrine and practice (including the cult of the saints and prayer for the dead) and a resurgent interest in Aristotle across the Mediterranean throughout the sixth century.[34] Aristotelianism promoted empirical enquiry capable of undermining the claims of theologians and hagiographers alike, not least because Aristotle was an essential foundation for Galenic medicine.[35] Above all, Aristotle confronted Christians with a distinctive teaching on the soul as the body's 'life principle' or 'form'. For Aristotle, even if soul were a separate substance, the soul primarily provided the body's physical matter with its various nutritive, sensory and rational functions.[36] Through the soul's 'indissoluble admixture with the body', it could only be imagined with difficulty as existing

[33] See P. Krüger, 'Traduction et commentaire de l'homélie de Narsai sur les martyrs', *Orient Syrien* 3 (1958), 299–316.

[34] C. Wildberg, 'Philosophy in the Age of Justinian', in *The Cambridge Companion to the Age of Justinian*, ed. M. Maas (Cambridge, 2005), 316–40. On the positive reception of Aristotle in Syriac, see S. Brock, 'From Antagonism to Assimilation: Syriac Attitudes to Greek Learning', in N. Garsoïan, T. Mathews and R. W. Thomson, eds, *East of Byzantium: Syria and Armenia in the Formative Period* (Washington, DC, 1982), 17–34, repr. in S. Brock, *Syriac Perspectives on Late Antiquity* (London, 1984), ch. 5; E. C. D. Hunter, 'The Transmission of Greek Philosophy via the "School of Edessa"', in C. Holmes and J. Waring, eds, *Literacy, Education and Manuscript Transmission in Byzantium and Beyond* (Leiden, 2002), 225–39.

[35] G. Dagron, 'Le saint, le savant, l'astrologue: étude de thèmes hagiographiques à travers quelques recueils de questions et réponses des Ve–VIIe siècles', *Hagiographie, cultures et sociétés, IVe–XIIe siècles: actes du colloque organisé à Nanterre et à Paris (2–5 mai 1979), Centre de recherches sur l'antiquité tardive et le haut moyen âge, Université de Paris X* (Paris, 1981), 143–56, repr. in idem, *La romanité chrétienne en Orient: héritages et mutations* (London, 1984), ch. 4.

[36] *Aristotle: De anima (On the Soul)*, trans. H. Tancred-Lawson (London, 1986), 71–73; cf. S. Everson, 'Psychology', in J. Barnes, ed., *The Cambridge Companion to Aristotle* (Cambridge, 1995), 170, 181; R. Sorabji, 'Body and Soul in Aristotle', in J. Barnes, M. Schofield and R. Sorabji, eds, *Articles on Aristotle, 4: Psychology and Ethics* (London, 1974), 42–64.

apart from the body's physical matter.[37] Early Byzantine interest in Aristotle peaked in Greek around 550 with John Philoponus (c. 490–570s).[38] It was reflected in Latin by Boethius (c. 480–524), and in Syriac by Sergius of Reš'aina (d. 535) and Paul the Persian, who provided the Arab world with the foundation of its knowledge of Aristotle in the eighth century.[39]

Of these Christian traditions, the 'Nestorian' Church of the East could clearly accommodate Aristotle the least problematically. Despite the use St Maximus the Confessor (c. 580–662) and Boethius made of Aristotle elsewhere, the Greek- and Latin-speaking Churches rejected outright Aristotle's claims regarding the soul and the afterlife. Leading Latin and Greek writers consistently attributed bodily functions to the disembodied soul. Severus of Antioch (d. 538) affirmed the ability of disembodied souls to see and recognize each other in the next life, a proposition later confirmed by Gregory the Great.[40] Taking inspiration from the relationship between the saints' souls and bodily relics, Maximus adumbrated the non-Aristotelian psychology of early Byzantine Christianity, Latin and Greek:

> For the soul after the death of the body is not simply called soul …. *Even after it has departed the body, the whole human being is predicated of it as part of its species according to its condition.* In the same way, although the body is by nature mortal, because of how it came to be, it is not an independent entity. … For like the soul, *it has the whole human being predicated of it* as part of its species according to its condition.[41]

[37] See Aristotle, *De anima*, 1.4.407b (trans. H. Tancred-Lawson, 142).
[38] R. Sorabji, 'John Philoponus', in idem, ed., *Philoponus and the Rejection of Aristotelian Science* (London, 1987), 1–40.
[39] On Boethius, see J. Marenbon, *Boethius* (Oxford, 2003); H. Chadwick, *Boethius: The Consolations of Music, Logic, Philosophy and Theology* (Oxford, 1981). On Sergius and Paul, see H. Hugonnard-Roche, 'Note sur Sergius de Reš'aina, traducteur du grec en syriaque et commentateur d'Aristote', in G. Endress and R. Kruk, eds, *The Ancient Tradition in Christian and Islamic Hellenism* (Leiden, 1997), 121–43; D. Gutas, 'Paul the Persian on the Classification of the Parts of Aristotle's Philosophy: A Milestone between Alexandria and Baghdad', *Der Islam* 60 (1983), 231–67.
[40] Severus, a Miaphysite, was later claimed as father of the West Syrian or 'Jacobite' tradition: *Ep.* 117, in *A Collection of Letters of Severus of Antioch (From Numerous Syriac Manuscripts)*, 2, ed. and trans. E. W. Brooks, Patrologia Orientalis 14 (Paris, 1920): 284–90. For Gregory, see *Dial.* 4.34 (SC 265: 112–16).
[41] Maximus the Confessor, *Ambiguum* 7 (*St Maximus the Confessor, On the Cosmic Mystery of Jesus Christ*, trans. P. M. Blowers and R. L. Wilken (New York, 2003), 73); the italics are mine.

For Maximus the *post mortem* activity of the souls of the saints visible in the miracles performed by their relics suggested a *communicatio idiomatum* between the soul and the body, which not only allowed human souls to possess the attributes of the body *post mortem* but also the body to possess those of the deified soul.[42] Like Gregory and Eustratius, Maximus was a Neo-Chalcedonian,[43] for whom the exchange of properties between the divine and human natures within the one Person of Christ was an important dogma.

The Syriac-speaking Church of the East responded differently to this revival of Aristotle, canonizing a view of the afterlife antithetical to the teachings of most Greek and Latin writers.[44] A synod of the East Syrian Church at Baghdad in 790 anathematized 'all those who say that souls feel, know, act, praise [God] or have use [of intercessions] after their departure from the body. For, no such thing comes to them until they put on their bodies [once again]'.[45] Catholicos Timothy I expounded that prayers and masses only obtained benefits for the deceased at the moment of the soul's reunion with the body at the resurrection: only the whole human being could experience eschato-logical reward or punishment and enjoy the good works done on its behalf by others.[46] Indeed, when Timothy wrote that '[t]he activity of the soul is the life of the body', he had Aristotle's psychology in mind.[47] Although Aristotelian psychology was an important influence, East Syrian anthropology was also affected by 'Nestorian' Christology.[48] Just as the Byzantine and Latin concept of a related body and soul seems

---

[42] This also reflects his Christology, although psychology was another model for this: Maximus, *Ambiguum* 42 (*Maximus*, trans. Blowers and Wilken, 83).

[43] The Neo-Chalcedonians supported the Cyrilline interpretation of the Council of Chalcedon as proclaimed at the Second Council of Constantinople (553), which emphasized the unity of Christ's Person.

[44] See G. Khouri-Sarkis's thoughts on the Syrian Catholic Missal in Krüger, 'Sommeil', 195–96.

[45] For the Syriac text with German translation, see O. Braun, 'Zwei Synoden des Katholikos Timothy I', *Oriens Christianus* 2 (1902), 283–311; A. Guillaumont, 'Sources de la doctrine de Joseph Hazzâyâ', *Orient Syrien* 3 (1958) 3–24.

[46] For the Syriac text with Latin translation, see *Timothei Patriarchae I: Epistulae*, vol. 1, ed. O. Braun (Rome and Paris, 1915), Corpus Scriptorum Christianorum Orientalium, Series Secunda 67.

[47] Ibid. 24–25.

[48] See further D. Krausmüller, 'Conflicting Anthropologies in the Christological Discourse at the End of Late Antiquity: The Case of Leontius of Jerusalem's Nestorian Adversary', *JThS* 56 (2005), 415–49. On psychology and Christology more generally, see H. Chadwick, 'Eucharist and Christology in the Nestorian Controversy', *JThS* 2 (1951), 145–64, esp. 160–62.

modelled on the Neo-Chalcedonian doctrine of the interpenetration of the natures of Christ in the hypostatic union, so the East Syrians' commitment to the distinctness of soul and body seems to reflect their insistence upon Christ's separate divine and human natures.

* * *

The different Greek, Latin and Syriac responses to Aristotelian thought contributed to the divergent doctrinal paths of the Chalcedonian and East Syrian Churches concerning the cult of the saints and the care for the dead. The strong Semitic tradition and positive reception of Aristotle among East Syrians ensured that their views of man (living and dead) would be defined in terms different from those espoused further west.[49] They provide an alternative to the more familiar Latin and Greek traditions from which to judge the mutual claims of both these traditions to normativity. Both Latins and Greeks affirmed throughout the medieval period that the integrity of the human individual went essentially unchanged by death, so that the *post mortem* activity of the soul and its separability from the body remained constant features of representations of the afterlife in both of these traditions. Jacques Le Goff mistakenly believed that the problem of the soul's corporeality did not influence the development of purgatory.[50] On the contrary, attributing the properties of the body to the disembodied soul was controversial and contributed a vital impetus to the elaboration of ideas on the *post mortem* fate of the imperfect, notably the Latin doctrine of purgatory.

A particular view of the human person was being fought over during the philosophical and hagiological debates of the sixth and seventh centuries, at the centre of which stood the mutual relation of the soul and the body, the integrity of human personality *post mortem*. Gregory the Great's firm conviction of the latter throughout the *Dialogues* often shocks the modern reader; but his view of the indestructibility of personal existence by death is arguably far closer to modern Western representations of the afterlife than those considered orthodox by the early medieval Church of the East.[51] Certainly, it is closer to the anthro-

---

[49] F. Gavin, 'The Sleep of the Soul in the Early Syriac Church', *Journal of the American Oriental Society* 40 (1920), 103–20.

[50] Le Goff, *Naissance*, 16.

[51] See the interesting remarks concerning out-of-body experiences and the ethics of (particularly brain) transplants in modern popular cinema and television in C. Bynum, 'Why all the Fuss about the Body? A Medievalist's Perspective', *Critical Inquiry* 22 (1995), 1–33; eadem, *The Resurrection of the Body in Western Christianity, 200–1336* (New York, 1995).

pology on which the Latin Middle Ages were founded, whose formal doctrine of purgatory and popular representations, literary and otherwise, of the dead intervening in the affairs of the living would not have been possible if the Syriac-speaking Narsai and Timothy had written the psychological and eschatological theology of the Latin Church.

Trinity College, Cambridge

SAINTS AND SOTERIOLOGY IN SOPHRONIUS SOPHISTA'S *MIRACLES OF CYRUS AND JOHN*

by PHIL BOOTH

TENSIONS between public and private forms of religiosity have been endemic to Christianity since its institutionalization during the first four centuries AD. That process was in part characterized by the clerical curtailment of alternative routes of divine access which bypassed the structures of the Church and the controls which it operated: most notably, Scripture and sacrament. Acts had imagined the last Christian days as a spiritual age of prophecy, visions and dreams,[1] but the rapid association of such phenomena with rigorist, schismatic or heretical groups – particularly the Gnostics, Montanists and Manichaeans – rendered them suspect if scripturally unassailable.[2] Dreaming – 'the paradigm of the open frontier',[3] 'epiphany's most open level'[4] – became strictly delineated by episcopally defined typologies which restricted access to the divine and necessitated arbitration, thus protecting the centrality and authority of the Church.[5] Those typologies not only emphasized the relative rarity of divinely inspired dreams (as opposed to the physiological or demonic), they also stressed the special status of the recipient. They thus partook of a late antique professionalization of the holy by which an emergent spiritual elite attempted to exercise an unprecedented monopoly on the supernatural.[6]

If control of dream access was implicated in the establishment of

---

[1] Acts 2: 17; cf. Joel 2: 28.
[2] See I. Moreira, *Dreams, Visions and Spiritual Authority in Merovingian Gaul* (Ithaca, NY, 2000), 22–29.
[3] P. Brown, *The Making of Late Antiquity* (Cambridge, MA, 1978), 65.
[4] R. Lane Fox, *Pagans and Christians* (Harmondsworth, 1986), 149.
[5] The starting point for dreams in late antiquity remains the classic account of E. R. Dodds, *Pagan and Christian in an Age of Anxiety* (Cambridge, 1965). More specifically, see P. Cox Miller, *Dreams in Late Antiquity: Studies in the Imagination of a Culture* (Princeton, NJ, 1994). On dreaming and Christianity in East and West see, respectively, G. Dagron, 'Rêver de Dieu et parler de soi: la rêve et son interprétation d'après les sources byzantines', in T. Gregori, ed., *I sogni nel medioevo* (Rome, 1985), 37–55; J. Le Goff, 'Le christianisme et les rêves (IIe–VIIe siècle)', in idem, *L'imaginaire médiéval* (Paris, 1985), 265–316.
[6] See Brown, *The Making*.

episcopal paradigms of authority, then it was similarly implied in their subsequent dissolution. In the late sixth century clerical and imperial attempts to monopolize the holy were increasingly destabilized. As contemporary crisis undermined the perceived efficacy of the ecclesial and imperial institutions, a population burdened by increased taxation and the ravages of periodic warfare turned from more formal modes of authority to those alternatives which offered more dependable or more immediate edification – the saints and their icons.[7] As a corollary to that process, the dream realm was once more reopened. The quintessential manifestation of the 'open frontier', the incubatory shrine,[8] was again extensively represented in the literary record, an expression of both burgeoning popularity and the new cultural relevance of the discourses which such shrines inherently epitomized. Thus the composition of the various *Miracles of Cosmas and Damian* in late sixth-century Constantinople soon inspired contemporary imitations both in the imperial city itself (the *Miracles of Artemius*; the *Miracles of Therapon*) and elsewhere (the *Miracles of Demetrius*; the *Miracles of Cyrus and John*).[9]

The basic constituents of such miracles were all fundamentally similar: a diseased individual, perhaps disappointed by secular physicians, comes to the saint(s) and requests a remedy; after a compulsory test of the patient's faith, he or she is visited by the saint(s) in a dream and consequently cured, either directly or upon the achievement of some saintly prescription. This basic narrative pattern of illness-intervention-healing is simultaneously soteriological, for the virtues required for recovery are precisely those required for resurrection. In approaching the saints, therefore, the sick anticipate an appearance before Christ upon the Last Day. As analogies for redemption, these miracle narratives intersected with debates upon the afterlife in two

---

[7] J. F. Haldon, 'Ideology and Social Change in the Seventh Century: Military Discontent as a Barometer', *Klio* 68 (1986), 139–90.

[8] Incubation is the ancient practice whereby a sick individual visits a healing shrine, experiences a dream of the relevant deity or saint, and is consequently healed.

[9] For the Miracles of Cyrus and John, see N. F. Marcos, *Los Thaumata de Sofronio: Contribucion al estudio de la incubatio Cristiana* (Madrid, 1975); J. Gascou, trans., *Sophrone de Jérusalem: Miracles des Saints Cyr et Jean* (Paris, 2006). Here I have used Marcos's critical edition with the textual emendations suggested by Gascou and by J. Duffy, 'Observations on Sophronius's Miracles of Cyrus and John', *JThS* 35 (1984), 71–90; idem, 'The Miracles of Cyrus and John: New Old Readings from the Manuscript', *Illinois Classical Studies* 12 (1987), 169–77. For the prologue I have used Pauline Bringel's critical text, *Sophrone de Jérusalem, Préface et Panégyrique* [online text] (15 June 2005), at <http://halshs.ccsd.cnrs.fr/halshs-00003975>, accessed June 2006. All translations are my own.

salient ways: first, they asked who could experience divine favour, and thus also what could be done upon earth to ensure salvation; but second, they asked how it was possible for the saint(s) to intervene, in what posthumous state their souls now existed, and how such a state had been achieved. Sixth- and seventh-century miracle collections responded to these issues in various, idiosyncratic ways, but this paper will concentrate upon the most sophisticated of such responses: the Alexandrian *Miracles of Cyrus and John* by Sophronius Sophista, monk and future patriarch of Jerusalem (634–39).[10]

At its most basic, Christian incubation involved the direct revelation of a divine protector. In presenting narratives structured around visionary experiences, however, the authors of these cults were acutely aware of the centrifugal pull which unrestricted, unmediated supernatural access might exert.[11] In Bishop John of Thessalonica's *Miracles of Demetrius* that potential pull is counteracted by an emphasis on high civic status as pre-requisite to the incubatory experience.[12] The cult is consequently fully integrated into the bureaucratic and clerical structures of the city. In the *Miracles of Artemius*, by contrast, the visitation of the saint can often only occur once the supplicant has completed the obligatory rituals;[13] the dream experience is thus contextualized within,

---

[10] On Sophronius himself, see the fundamental account of C. von Schönborn, *Sophrone de Jérusalem: Vie monastique et confession dogmatique* (Paris, 1972). On the *Miracles*, see esp. Marcos, *Los Thaumata*, 1–239; P. Maraval, 'Fonction pédagogique de la littérature hagiographique d'un lieu de pèlerinage: l'exemple des Miracles de Cyr et Jean', in E. Patlagean and P. Riché, eds, *Hagiographie, cultures et sociétés: IVᵉ–XIIᵉ siècles* (Paris, 1981), 383–97; D. Montserrat, 'Pilgrimage to the Shrine of SS Cyrus and John at Menouthis in Late Antiquity', in D. Frankfurter, ed., *Pilgrimage and Holy Space in Late Antique Egypt* (Leiden, 1997) 257–79; idem, ' "Carrying on the Work of the Earlier Firm": Doctors, Medicine and Christianity in the *Thaumata* of Sophronius of Jerusalem', in H. King, ed., *Health in Antiquity* (London, 2005), 230–42; V. Déroche, 'Tensions et contradictions dans les recueils de miracles de la première époque byzantine', in D. Aigle, ed., *Miracle et karama: Hagiographies médiévales comparées* (Turnhout, 2000), 145–66.

[11] On the tension between open and restricted models of dream access in early and late antique Christianity, see Le Goff, 'Le christianisme et les rêves'; Moreira, *Dreams, Visions*, 13–38.

[12] See J. C. Skedros, *Saint Demetrios of Thessaloniki: Civic Patron and Divine Protector 4ᵗʰ–7ᵗʰ Centuries CE* (Harrisburg, PA, 1999), 115–20. For the *Miracles of Demetrius* (with accompanying French epitomes), see P. Lemerle, *Les plus anciens recueils des Miracles de Saint Démétrius et la pénétration des slaves dans les Balkans*, 2 vols (Paris, 1979), vol. 1.

[13] The majority of miracles recall the performance of the 'customary rites', and frequently involve the Saturday nocturnal vigil performed by devotees of the saint. See, for example, *Miracle* 33, the context of which is entirely ritualized. For the text with accompanying English translation, see V. S. Crisafulli and J. W. Nesbitt, eds, *The Miracles of St. Artemios: A Collection of Miracle Stories by an Anonymous Author of Seventh-Century Byzantium* (Leiden, 1997).

and dependent upon, the liturgical rhythms of the shrine. In the *Miracles of Cyrus and John*, however, the civic and ecclesial contexts of cultic practice are consistently marginalized, and the visitation of the saints is predicated instead upon the adoption of ascetic virtue. These divergent schemes not only disseminated divergent models of proper cultic practice; they offered, by virtue of the soteriological analogy inherent to them, divergent strategies for salvation. Conflicting systems for saintly appeasement thus represented genuine differences over how redemption could best be ensured.

In the Artemius collection, the necessity of ritual as pre-requisite to healing serves not only to protect the centrality of the ecclesial context, but also to comment on the perceived necessity of liturgy to spiritual advancement both within and beyond the earthly life. In Sophronius's scheme, however, the soteriological role of liturgy is far more ambiguous. The attainment of health, and thus also of salvation, is predicated rather upon a process of ascetical self-transformation to which ritual performance as mediated by the clerical hierarchy is largely immaterial. Liturgical acts are subordinated to the achievement of ascetic virtue, and it is the saints themselves who provide the anthropological paradigm for that process. In their unwavering and Christ-like obedience to God, the saints have ascended towards a synergy of divine and human activities, and consequently they exist posthumously as *Christomimētoi*, 'imitators of Christ'. This theological anthropology is consonant not only with Sophronius's later Christology, but also with the position espoused in Eustratius Presbyter's late sixth-century psychological treatise, *On the State of Souls After Death*. Sophronius's *Miracles* thus reveal the contours of a broader contemporary debate upon the afterlife in which convictions concerning soteriology, sainthood and Christology all broadly intersected.

Narratives of Redemption

To understand the soteriological analogy which Sophronius constructs around his narratives of saintly healing, it is expedient first to elucidate his conception of disease. The crucial passage concerns an illness of the testicles:

> But [the patient] was perhaps ashamed at such an illness, and wanted to keep his infirmity hidden; but we have been commanded to feel shame not at the diseases of the body, but

55

PHIL BOOTH

rather those of the soul ... And the Lord said that those sent into
eternal shame were not those weighed down by bodily diseases (for
he himself has borne our infirmities and our illness), but rather
those who are sick in the soul and the doers of evil. For some
illnesses are involuntary, those of the body and known in relation
to the body. Others are voluntary and products of our will, those
which damage the beauty of the autonomous and intelligent soul.[14]

Bodily disease should not be a source of shame for the infirm, for it is
an intrinsic product of the Fall: '[The patient's] affliction was terrible,
and beyond both reason and description. For it was not natural like
those many diseases which are caused by an abundance of humours or
generated by other occurrences, and which the body by necessity is
allotted to serve after the transgression in paradise.'[15]

Bodily diseases are thus emblematic of mankind's blameless corruption in the Fall. In the movement from illness through saintly intervention to restoration, therefore, Sophronius's patients replicate the
movement of the human person from corruption through judgement
to redemption. That equivalence is deeply entrenched throughout the
Miracles, where Sophronius repeatedly represents the progression from
sickness to health as one from corruption to salvation.[16]

In alleviating disease, Cyrus and John re-enact both the historical
and the cosmological role of Christ. Hence they are 'imitators of Christ'
(*Christomimetoi*),[17] 'bearers of Christ' (*Christophoroi*);[18] their involvement
on earth is a *sunkatabasis*, 'condescension'.[19] Imitation extends beyond
action to their metaphysical union, described in terminology highly
reminiscent of the lexicon of contemporary Christology. Thus the
posthumous pairing of the saints, so that they invariably appear and
operate together, imitates the union of divine and human natures in the
incarnation:

How could we not be amazed at the junction of this indissoluble
pair? How could we not glorify the union of their strange combi-

[14] *Miracles* 16.1–2 (Marcos, *Los Thaumata*, 274–75).
[15] Ibid. 21.1 (Marcos, *Los Thaumata*, 282).
[16] The analogy is further reinforced by the consistent ambiguity of recurrent words in
Greek, e.g. *pathos*, disease/passion; *charis*, favour/grace; *soteria*, bodily health/salvation; and
lutrosis, release/redemption.
[17] *Miracles* 38.9 (Marcos, *Los Thaumata*, 334).
[18] Ibid. 30.8 (Marcos, *Los Thaumata*, 304).
[19] Ibid. 9.3; 23.2; 62.1 (Marcos, *Los Thaumata*, 257, 285, 379).

56

nation? For we see the unmixable mixed, the irreconcilable reconciled, the uncontrolled controlled, the unembraceable embraced, the warlike pacified, contraries made allies, and from this communion the creation of oneness in things which resist that creation.[20]

In imitating the incarnate Christ, the saints also prefigure his eventual judgement:

> I remember saying in the preceding that I would write two or three tales through which the zeal and severity of the saints would be made known, for the help of those who are rather indifferent, and for the benefit of those who are more steadfast, so that each might learn that [the saints] know not only how to reward the best but also to punish the worst. And in this they mimic Christ their own Master, who spreads out his kingdom to all, but does not concede it entirely to all, but rather to those who heed it in his message, and maintain faith both in what they do and in his commands. But to those who do not do this, he gives the sleepless worm, eternal hell and external darkness.[21]

In supplicating the saints, the sick anticipate their appearance at the Last Judgement. Psychological diseases, as willingly adopted and hence reprehensible, are thus an impediment not only to saintly intervention but also to redemption. Those seeking cures must be free from the passions, 'for the saints pay great attention to the *apatheia* of souls than the curing of bodies'.[22]

The adoption of ascetic virtue is therefore prerequisite to the dispensation of healing just as it is to salvation.[23] Both remedy and redemption are dependent on the reciprocal interaction of personal endeavour and divine grace, so that the ascetic virtues of self-control, perseverance and obedience are the primary preconditions for the saints' bestowal of both health and 'the things lacking in men for the attainment of perfection'.[24] The narrative of the suffering body is, then,

---

[20] Ibid., Prologue, 11.1–9 (Bringel, *Sophrone*, 26). Cf. Schönborn, *Sophrone*, 225–28, who applies the same analysis to Sophronius's sermon *On Peter and Paul*.
[21] *Miracles* 29.1 (Marcos, *Los Thaumata*, 298).
[22] Ibid. 1.6 (Marcos, *Los Thaumata*, 244).
[23] Frequently a patient must undergo an extraordinary test of faith before being cured. See, for example, ibid. 69, in which a Roman patient awaits the saints in the open air for eight years. Cf. ibid. 13, where a patient is overcome by the demon of *accidie* and abandons his supplications at the shrine; rebuked by the saints, he is subsequently healed.
[24] Ibid. 64.6 (Marcos, *Los Thaumata*, 383).

not simply a metaphor for the movement towards redemption, but also for the spiritual progression of the monk. Illness is analogous to asceticism; saintly intervention to divine grace; health to spiritual perfection.[25] The *Miracles* thus contain a complex, tripartite analogy:

(somatic/psychological) illness > intervention > healing
(involuntary/voluntary) sin > judgement > redemption
(body/soul) corruption > grace > perfection

The process by which a patient attains health, redemption and perfection is an ascetic self-transformation which culminates in a quasi-mystical experience of the saints – the dream. As analogies both for the eschatological and the spiritual movements of the Christian life, however, Sophronius's narratives are remarkably unencumbered by clerical mediation.[26] External rituals equivalent to those recommended by the author(s) of the Artemius collection are almost entirely absent.

Indeed, a remarkable feature of the healing-saint genre in general is the marginalization specifically of the eucharist as a vehicle to propitiate or experience the relevant saint(s).[27] In Sophronius's scheme the sacraments serve as an initial moment of glorious enlightenment contingent upon conversion to Chalcedonian orthodoxy:

> And when the divine martyrs saw [the heretic patient Stephen] sincerely promising and hurrying with all his might to honour his agreement with the martyrs concerning the faith, again they appeared to him in a dream, standing at the altar of Christ and offering bloodless sacrifice, which they brought and offered to him. And as he again partook of the sacrament they showed him the Church, Bride of the Saviour, flashing in bright clothes, divinely ornamented and with an incomparable beauty which it is not possible to describe in human words. And coming forward to the august altar, again she [the Church] took the sacraments of Christ which lay there and offered them to Stephen. And when the

[25] On the concept of illness as asceticism in the patristic tradition, see J.-C. Larchet, *The Theology of Illness* (New York, 2002), 64–68.
[26] It should also be noted that enigmatic dreams are exceptional, and only once does one glimpse a possible ecclesiastical arbitration of divine power through dream interpretation; see *Miracles* 11.8.
[27] On the place of the eucharist in the genre, see I. Csepgregi, 'Mysteries for the Uninitiated: The Role and Symbolism of the Eucharist in Miraculous Dream Healing', in I. Perczel, R. Forrai and G. Geréby, eds, *The Eucharist in Theology and Philosophy: Issues of Doctrinal History in East and West from the Patristic Age to the Reformation* (Leuven, 2006), 97–130.

saints asked her if what was given sufficed for perfection, she replied with these words: 'I want him to abound in divine gifts, and with this to acquire more than what is given. For now I have received him as one who is enlightened, and from now on he shall be called my son.'[28]

While indubitably dramatic, such scenes are limited to instances of heresy or paganism.[29] The efficacy of the sacrament is thus restricted to conversion, and its continued relevance to spiritual progression within the Christian life is wholly ambiguous. As a strategy for the afterlife, participation in the eucharist, in comparison to asceticism, seems remarkably ineffective.[30]

Christology, Sainthood and the Afterlife

The ascetical scheme which Sophronius presents summons his audience to self-transformation as a route to salvation. But the ultimate paradigm for humankind's redemption remains the obedience and sinlessness of Christ: 'It was the Lord who first revealed to us the path of justice, and first uncovered the way to the complete abandonment of the soul's passions, saying to all in his mercy, "Learn from me".'[31]

The saints are those who have approximated to Christ in their obedience to divine will and in consequence earned the *post mortem* epithet of *Christomimētoi*. The precise nature of that posthumous existence, and with it the ability of saints to interfere in terrestrial affairs, did not, however, go unquestioned in contemporary theology. In the late sixth century the Constantinopolitan presbyter Eustratius composed an apology for the cult of the saints in response to a radical challenge by sceptical theologians who argued that saintly apparitions represented the movement of the saints' forms not by their souls but rather by divine angels.[32] In *Miracle* 51 that position is explicitly refuted:

---

[28]   *Miracles* 38.10–11 (Marcos, *Los Thaumata*, 335).

[29]   Thus the eucharist is only mentioned at *Miracles* 12, 31, 32, 36, 37, 38 and 39, all of which involve conversion to Christianity or to Chalcedonian orthodoxy. In all such instances the rituals are performed entirely by the saints, and clerics themselves are absent. See also the memorable quasi-baptism performed by the saints in the shrine's bath complex: ibid. 52.3–4.

[30]   Compare Sophronius's defence of eucharistic efficacy (ibid. 36.16), which demonstrates an awareness of the problematic relationship between sacrament and asceticism in his scheme.

[31]   Ibid. 16.4 (Marcos, *Los Thaumata*, 275). See also Schönborn, *Sophrone*, 144–47, 179–89.

[32]   For the critical edition of Eustratius's text, see now *Eustratii Presbyteri Constantino-*

There was a plague, and those who were sick before it was diag-
nosed died. [The presbyter] George fell ill, and with the hours of
his life fulfilled, he departed from the present life. And he saw
angels taking him up and leading him, and the martyrs Cyrus and
John meeting them, and interceding so that their presbyter might
be returned to them, which the angels, enslaved by their being to
the divine command, said they could not do. But they [the angels]
told them [the saints] that they were awaiting their supplication
made to God, and the reception of his second command. And so
the martyrs took this response and turned to prayer, bending their
knees to God and begging that their servant be given to them. And
as they did this, a voice descended from heaven ordering [the
angels] to give the presbyter to the martyrs, and determining
twenty more years [for George] in the flesh.[33]

The rather forced differentiation of divine and saintly wills in *Miracle* 51
serves most obviously to preserve the saints' ability to intervene on
behalf of their supplicants. Appreciated, however, from the perspective
of dyenergist Christology, of which Sophronius as patriarch was later
principal proponent, that differentiation can be seen to avoid a
monenergizing position which would subordinate the saintly activity to
that of the divine.[34] Indeed, when Eustratius refuted the 'saints as angels'
arguments of his theological adversaries, it was precisely to the
Christological language of energies that he resorted. According to that
argument, the souls of the saints remained posthumously active in an
unconfused and co-operative union of divine and human energies
enabled by divine synergy.[35] That is precisely the same theological

politani *De statu animarum post mortem (CPG 7522)*, ed. Peter Van Deun, CChr.SG 60
(Turnhout and Louvain, 2006). For discussion, see esp. D. Krausmüller, 'Gods or Angels as
Impersonators of Saints: A Belief and its Contexts in the "Refutation" of Eustratius of
Constantinople and in the Writings of Anastasius of Sinai', *Golden Horn* 6/2 (1998–9) [online
journal], <http://isidore-of-seville.com/goudenhoorn/62dirk.html>, accessed September
2005; N. Constas, 'An Apology for the Cult of the Saints in Late Antiquity: Eustratius Presbyter of Constantinople, *On the State of Souls after Death* (CPG 7522)', *JECS* 10 (2002), 267–85.

[33] *Miracles* 51.10–11 (Marcos, *Los Thaumata*, 364). A similar discrimination between
angel and saint is made in the *Miracles of Artemius* 34.

[34] Monenergist Christology acknowledged the two natures of Christ but proposed a
single operation, the disputed 'theandric activity' of Pseudo-Dionysius the Areopagite.
Conversely, dyenergist Christology conceived both divine and human energies operating
simultaneously in synergy, and argued that Pseudo-Dionysius had actually proposed a 'new
theandric activity'. On both, see now S. Hovorun, *Will, Action and Freedom: Christological
Controversies in the Seventh Century* (Leiden, 2008).

[35] Constas, 'An Apology', 275.

anthropology which Sophronius would later apply to the wills and energies of Christ.[36] The Christological preservation of the natural human energy was fundamental to Sophronius's soteriology, since the presence of human nature in its fullness within the incarnation provided the mediating model for humankind's resurrection.[37] Through voluntarily aspiring to Christlike obedience, therefore, the individual ascends towards the same synergy of human and divine energies, that is, towards the posthumous existence enjoyed by the saints.[38] For Sophronius, then, the divine suppression of the human energy implied in monenergism not only compromised a Christocentric soteriology, it also undermined the full ontology of synergized saintly activity after death.

That concern for the posthumous preservation of the saints' agency is accompanied by an emphasis on the sustained integrity of their individuality. That individuality is most obviously manifested in descriptions of the saints' appearance:

> Your narrator was asleep, and saw himself coming into one of the oratories of those in his own monastery. When he came to its doorway, he met the apostle and martyr Thomas coming out from the group inside. And he recognised the saint from his clothes, from his form and from all the characteristics of that form ...[39]

The precise mechanism by which the souls of the saints were imprinted with their physical, bodily characteristics was a contemporary subject of considerable contention,[40] and it intersected with emerging debates on the veneration of icons. For the authors of incubatory cults, the terrestrial iconography of the saints was a genuine representation of their celestial existence,[41] and all such authors include tales which celebrate

[36] While the dispute over monotheletism crystallized in the period immediately following Sophronius's death, the differentiation of divine and human wills in the incarnation is nevertheless fundamental to his theology. For that theology, see Schönborn, *Sophrone*, 157–238.

[37] Ibid. 179–99.

[38] Ibid. 228–38.

[39] *Miracles* 70.18 (Marcos, *Los Thaumata*, 398). For similar references see ibid. 8.11; 52.3; 70.12 (Marcos, *Los Thaumata*, 256, 365, 397).

[40] See D. Krausmüller, 'The Real and the Individual: Byzantine Concepts of the Resurrection, Part 1', *Golden Horn* 5/1 (Summer 1997) [online journal], <http://isidore-of-seville.com/goudenhoorn/51dirk.html>, accessed 1 September 2005; idem, 'Timothy of Antioch: Byzantine Concepts of the Resurrection, Part 2', *Golden Horn* 5/2 (Winter 1997–98) [online journal], <http://isidore-of-seville.com/goudenhoorn/52dirk.html>, accessed 1 September 2005.

[41] See esp. *Miracles of Artemius* 34; *Miracles of Cosmas and Damian* 13. For the text of the

the efficacy of the saints' icons.[42] Sophronius offers no explicit theological exposition on that connection, but it is at least apparent that soteriology, Christology, anthropology, sainthood and iconography were all systemically connected in his thought.[43]

Conclusion

Iconographic representation and incubation were complementary phenomena: dreams stimulated the production of icons; icons conditioned the dream experience.[44] The burgeoning popularity of both in the sixth and seventh centuries was furthermore predicated upon the same 'ideological reorientation'. The post-Justinianic crisis of empire precipitated a broad cultural shift in religious sensibilities and a subsequent devolution in established paradigms of spiritual authority which refocused attention from terrestrial to celestial authority, and from the mediation of public ritual and hierarchy to the direct revelation of heavenly intercessors and their iconography.[45] Like icons, incubation offered an opportunity for the unmediated experience of divinity, but the authors of incubatory cults attempted to condition that experience through the imposition of certain prerequisites. Those prerequisites were determined not simply by convictions of what constituted proper cultic practice, but also of effective soteriological strategy. The remarkable absence of liturgical rituals from Sophronius's scheme is a comment not on the absence of such rituals from the shrine itself, nor on the lack of competing exhortations to participate in liturgy, but

latter, see L. Deubner, *Kosmas und Damian: Text und Einleitung* (Leipzig, 1907); trans. A.-J. Festugière, *Sainte Thècle, Saints Côme et Damien, Saints Cyr et Jean (extraits), Saint George* (Paris, 1971), 83–213.

[42] In Sophronius's text, see *Miracle* 36. It is possible that such instances are later iconophile interpolations, although references within the *Miracles of Cyrus and John* are few, tangential and certainly not inconsistent with the broader theological scheme. On the issue of interpolation, see L. Brubaker, 'Icons before Iconoclasm?', in G. Cavallo et al., eds, *Morfologie sociali e culturali in Europa fra tarda antichità e alto medioevo: XLV Settimana internazionale di studio* (Spoleto, 1998), 1215–54.

[43] For the intersection of sainthood and Christology in late antiquity, see R. Williams, 'Troubled Breasts: The Holy Body in Hagiography', in J. W. D. Drijvers and J. W. Watt, eds, *Portraits of Spiritual Authority: Religious Power in Early Christianity, Byzantium and the Christian Orient*, Religions in the Graeco-Roman World 137 (Leiden, 1999), 63–78; and, in this volume, Matthew J. dal Santo, 'Philosophy, Hagiology and the Early Byzantine Origins of Purgatory', 41–51.

[44] See Dagron, 'Rêver de Dieu', 42–43.

[45] See Haldon, 'Ideology and Social Change'.

rather on the author's own ambiguous attitude towards such acts as a successful preparation for the world beyond. Indeed, the monastic tradition in which Sophronius had been trained had long proved ambivalent towards the hierarchy and rituals of the Church, and the post-Justinianic decentralization of spiritual authority served not to contradict but rather to complement a monastic spirituality inspired largely by Evagrius and Pseudo-Macarius and thus lacking a developed sacramental, liturgical or ecclesiological understanding.[46] It is this spirituality which primarily informs Sophronius's perspective.

The *Miracles of Cyrus and John* thus partake of a contemporary debate upon Christian practice which simultaneously reveals concomitant anxieties concerning soteriology, Christology and eschatology. The transition from illness to health presented in these narratives serves as an analogy for the movement both from sin to redemption, and from ascetic struggle to mystical enlightenment. Sophronius's scheme, however, circumvents the sacramental context of the saints' shrine and presents ascetic self-transformation as the principal route to both remedy and redemption. Ascetic endeavour in imitation of Christ allows the individual to attain to the sanctity of the saints, and thus also to the posthumous synergy of divine and human activities. That status, in turn, guarantees a level of *post mortem* continuity in which personal agency and individuality are preserved. The *Miracles* are, then, not simply beneficial tales designed for the spiritual edification of the reader, but a complex theological system in which the place of humankind, the incarnation and the afterlife are all inextricably intertwined.

Trinity Hall, University of Cambridge

---

[46] On the sacramental minimalism of early Byzantine ascetic theory, and the attempted reconciliation of ascetic and sacramental theologies in the wake of the Persian and Arab invasions (not least by Sophronius himself), see P. Booth, 'John Moschus, Sophronius Sophista and Maximus Confessor between East and West' (unpublished Ph. D. thesis, University of Cambridge, 2008).

DEATH AND THE AFTERLIFE IN JONAS OF BOBBIO'S
*VITA COLUMBANI**

by ALEXANDER O'HARA

I
N the seventh century Christians in the Latin West turned with a
novel concern to the issues of death and the afterlife. This is a
period that has been characterized as marking the 'rise of the other
world', a development that was rooted in a belief in the imminence of
Doomsday and an increasing preoccupation with sinfulness.[1] This shift
to a more metaphysical mentality can be noticed in a number of areas
ranging from changes in burial and liturgical practices to literary works
and the rise in power of the monasteries as intercessory places of prayer.

In this paper, however, I wish to consider one area in which we can
see 'the awareness of the other world that seems to increase in the age
we are describing'.[2] Hagiography is one area where we can detect a
heightened interest in the fate of the soul after death. My focus will be
on the composite saint's Life, the *Vita Columbani abbatis et discipulorum-
que eius*, written by Jonas of Bobbio between 639 and 643,[3] and how, in
particular, the accounts of miraculous deaths and visions of the afterlife
characteristic of Book II reflect the institutional concerns of the
monastic communities for whom Jonas was writing. This near-
contemporary account, widely regarded as one of the most important
hagiographical works of the seventh century, narrates in two books the

* I am grateful to Professor Sarah Foot for her helpful comments at the conference and in
the subsequent revising of the article for publication.

    1   Peter Brown, *The Rise of Western Christendom: Triumph and Diversity A.D. 200–1000*, 2nd
edn (Oxford, 2003), 260–62; idem, '*Gloriosus obitus*: The End of the Ancient Other World', in
William E. Klingshirn and Mark Vessey, eds, *The Limits of Ancient Christianity: Essays on Late
Antique Thought and Culture in Honor of R. A. Markus* (Ann Arbor, MI, 1999), 289–314.
    2   J. N. Hillgarth, 'Eschatological and Political Concepts in the Seventh Century', in J.
Fontaine and J. N. Hillgarth, eds, *The Seventh Century: Change and Continuity* (London, 1992),
212–31, at 212.
    3   Jonas of Bobbio, *Vita Columbani abbatis et discipulorumque eius*, in *Ionae Vitae Sanctorum*,
ed. B. Krusch, MGH, Scriptores rerum Germanicarum in usum scholarum (Hanover and
Leipzig, 1905), 144–294. On the *Vita*, see now Albrecht Diem, 'Monks, Kings and the Trans-
formation of Sanctity: Jonas of Bobbio and the End of the Holy Man', *Speculum* 82 (2007),
521–59; Clare Stancliffe, 'Jonas's *Life of Columbanus and his Disciples*', in John Carey et al., eds,
Studies in Irish Hagiography: Saints and Sinners (Dublin, 2001), 189–220; and Adalbert de
Vogüé's introduction to his French trans., *Vie de Saint Colomban et de ses disciples*
(Bellefontaine, 1988).

saintly deeds (and misdeeds) of the Irish abbot and monastic founder, Columbanus, and his followers in the years following the saint's death. While Book I deals with the maverick figure of Columbanus and his monastic foundations in Burgundy (Annegray, Luxeuil and Fontaine) and Lombard Italy (Bobbio), Book II concerns Columbanus's abbatial successors and the miraculous deaths of a number of nuns at Eboriac (Faremoutiers), a community to the south east of Paris founded after Columbanus's death by a noble family closely associated with the saint.

Monastic dissent, miraculous deaths, and visions of the afterlife are all prominent features of Book II, and Jonas's treatment of death and the afterlife may be considered as part of what has been termed a 'transformation of sanctity', a process whereby the emphasis on the individual's sanctity shifted to that of the community.[4] This transformation arguably stemmed from the new attitude to death and the afterlife. This was one of the driving forces behind the construction of scores of new monasteries in the seventh century whose purpose, beyond that of the salvation of the members of the community, was to pray for the souls of the founders and for the wellbeing of the kingdom.[5]

The revolution in the perception of the afterlife witnessed during the early Middle Ages arguably took place because the ecclesiastical elites of the time were so adamant that the end of the world was upon them. This was obvious to Gregory the Great, Pope from 590 to 604, who could see from the ruins of Rome and the looming menace of the Lombards clear signs of the end of time.[6] Hell, for example, could now be glimpsed off the coasts of Sicily. As he told his friend, Peter, there were, on the islands around Sicily:

> more open pits burning with fires from hell than in any other region. And these are becoming larger every day, as well-informed people tell us, for, with the end of the world approaching, it seems that the openings to hell are enlarged in order to receive the great number of lost souls who will be gathered there to be cast into eternal punishment.[7]

---

[4] Diem, 'Monks, Kings and the Transformation of Sanctity', 521–27, 556–59.

[5] On this process see, for example, Mayke de Jong, 'Carolingian Monasticism: The Power of Prayer', in Rosamond McKitterick, ed., *The New Cambridge Medieval History, 2: c. 700–c. 900* (Cambridge, 1995), 622–53.

[6] On Gregory's apocalypticism and its influence on his thought, see R. A. Markus, *Gregory the Great and His World* (Cambridge, 1997), 51–67.

[7] Gregory the Great, *Dialogues*, 4.36.12, trans. Odo J. Zimmermann (Washington, DC, 1959), 236.

This was ample evidence for those who did not believe in the existence of hell. Some years later the Irish abbot Columbanus was musing on life in Northern Italy shortly before his death at Bobbio in 615.[8] Life, he told his monks in one of his sermons, was 'nothing ... except a way, a mirage, fleeting and void, or a cloud, uncertain and feeble, and a shadow, like a dream'. They should, accordingly, 'hurry like pilgrims to their true homeland'.[9] Heaven, the *vera patria*, was thus the singular goal of existence; and life, merely a wearisome interlude to better things. Like his twentieth-century compatriot, the playwright Samuel Beckett, who similarly chose a life of voluntary exile in France, Columbanus had an equally grim outlook on life. But in contrast to Beckett's nihilism which stemmed from an atheistic perspective on life, Columbanus's bleak vision of human existence arose from his utter conviction of the existence of the other world. The transitory nature of life, with its fleeting pleasures and hardships, confirmed the ascendancy of the afterlife.

The inanity of human life is a pervasive feature in Columbanus's writings and underpinned the Irish monk's decision to depart his native country as a *peregrinus* for the rest of his life. His undertaking of ascetical exile (*peregrinatio pro Christo*) in c. 590 was the very literal response to the notion of the Christian life as a journey towards Heaven. His ascetical odyssey brought him to Merovingian Gaul and eventually to Lombard Italy in 612. In both of these societies his charisma as a holy man and the ascetic rigour of his monasticism won him and his monastic communities renown. His monasticism, evident from his surviving monastic Rules and Penitential, was a punitive and elite form confidently described by Columbanus as 'the training of all trainings'.[10] A system of unwavering ascetical severity, it was, nevertheless, initially appealing. Columbanus received the patronage of Merovingian kings and aristocrats, while his last monastic foundation, at Bobbio in the Apennines, was on land donated by the Lombard king.

---

8 On Columbanus, see the saint's own writings in *Sancti Columbani Opera*, ed. and trans. G. S. M. Walker, Scriptores Latini Hiberniae 2 (Dublin, 1960), with introduction; Donald Bullough, 'The career of Columbanus', in M. Lapidge, ed., *Columbanus: Studies on the Latin Writings* (Woodbridge, 1997), 1–28. On the impact of Columbanian monasticism, see the articles in H. B. Clarke and M. Brennan, eds, *Columbanus and Merovingian Monasticism* (Oxford, 1981); and F. Prinz, *Frühes Mönchtum im Frankenreich: Kultur und Gesellschaft in Gallien, den Rheinlanden und Bayern am Beispiel der monastischen Entwicklung (4. bis 8. Jahrhundert)* (Munich and Vienna, 1965), 121–51.

9 Columbanus, *Instructio* 6.1 (*Sancti Columbani Opera*, 87).

10 Ibid. 4.1 (*Sancti Columbani Opera*, 79).

Although Columbanus is one of the most significant and enigmatic figures of early medieval Europe, he was also a controversial figure whose orthodoxy had been in question during his lifetime and was still in doubt even after his death. The Gallic bishops had viewed him with suspicion over his adherence to the Irish method of calculating the date of Easter and over his determination that his monasteries should be independent from their jurisdiction.[11] Just over a decade after his death in 626/7 a disaffected Columbanian monk named Agrestius had, at the Council of Mâcon in Burgundy, attacked Columbanus and his monastic practices as heretical.[12] Although the then abbot of Luxeuil, Eustasius, successfully defended Columbanian monastic practices, the affair had clearly caused a rift within the communities.[13] The production of the *Vita Columbani* can arguably be seen as a reaction against accusations of Columbanus's heterodoxy and the undermining of his monastic observances exemplified by the Agrestius affair. It was produced by a community (Bobbio) which was peripheral to these events, but one, nonetheless, that may have been more zealous in defending Columbanian practices and the saint's reputation.

A considerable part of Book II (twelve out of twenty-five chapters) describes the deathbed dramas of the female religious community of Eboriac. In these chapters Jonas not only wrote about those nuns who experienced beatific deaths and visions of the afterlife; he was equally concerned to relate the wretched and demonic deaths of those nuns who had attempted to flee from the community or caused internal dissent through their disobedience and religious pride. This is apparent from his statement that while 'we have not omitted to relate to posterity the great gifts which were given for good merit and religious devotion we likewise consider it appropriate to tell about a thing that we know for certain to be useful to terrify those women who are hard and ignoble of mind'.[14]

---

[11] See now Clare Stancliffe, 'Columbanus and the Gallic Bishops', in G. Constable and M. Rouche, eds, *Auctoritas: Mélanges offerts au Professeur Olivier Guillot* (Paris, 2006), 205–15.

[12] See Jonas, *Vita Columbani* 2.9 (*Ionae Vitae Sanctorum*, ed. Krusch, 246–51).

[13] It would appear that not long after the Council, perhaps within the year, the Columbanian observances or Rule were modified by the introduction of elements of the Rule of St Benedict. This perhaps meant an easing of some of the more draconian practices which included beatings and incarceration for the disobedient. The Rule 'for beginners' was certainly more appealing to those aristocratic monks and nuns who now largely constituted the Columbanian communities: see Stancliffe, 'Jonas's *Life of Columbanus*', 211.

[14] Jonas, *Vita Columbani* 2.22 (*Ionae Vitae Sanctorum*, ed. Krusch, 277–78).

Jonas describes, for example, how some young nuns, who had been tempted by the devil, tried to flee the monastery and notes the divine punishments inflicted on them when they refused to repent. Their moment of death was attended by demons in the guise of a 'crowd of advancing Ethiopians'.[15] The other nuns became terrified as a noise sounded from the roof of the little cell and the door was suddenly flung open as dark shadows loomed in the doorway. The demons beckoned the dying nuns by name, who screamed out 'Wait, wait, stop a little, stop' before dying.[16] Some time afterwards, when they had been buried at the edge of the monastic cemetery, balls of fire could be seen burning above their graves, while voices could be heard reverberating within. When, after six months, the abbess opened the graves she found that only glowing embers remained. The bodies had been completely burnt by fire. Jonas concludes:

> The severity of the inflicted sentence lasted for three years so that the terror of the damned might be the cause of fear to the remaining companions and the punishment of the dead would be a reproof to the living. … those who were destroyed increased the salvation of the living as a result of religious devotion and a vigorous zeal.[17]

The salutary lesson of these accounts was clear: only those nuns who persevered in the monastic observances could be assured of a blessed afterlife.

The prominent feature of internal dissension in Book II is one closely linked to the themes of death and the afterlife that are especially characteristic of the second part of the *Vita*. This becomes apparent when we consider Jonas's treatment of death and the afterlife in the first book dealing with Columbanus. While Book II abounds in descriptions of miraculous deaths, divine and demonic beings, and visions of the afterlife, such features are almost wholly absent from Book I. Most notably, Jonas was remarkably silent about the death of Columbanus himself. He simply noted that the saint died after he had spent a year in the monastery at Bobbio.[18] In the second part of the

---

15 Ibid. 2.19 (273–74).
16 Ibid. (274).
17 Ibid. (275).
18 Ibid. 1.30 (223–24). Besides this, there is only one account in the whole of the first book which deals with a miraculous death, but this is not so much concerned with the dying monk as with providing yet another example of Columbanus's spiritual power. The power

work, however, Jonas contrasted instances of beatific deaths (with attendant angels, bright lights and pleasant smells) with the ignominious and demonic deaths of those who attempted to undermine the monastic observances or who sought to leave their communities. For the members of the Columbanian communities, attainment of a blessed afterlife depended on how they behaved in the monastery. What was particularly emphasized in these accounts was the importance of obedience to the abbot or abbess,[19] the formal acknowledgement of wrongdoing (or repentance) in confession for those who transgressed the Rule,[20] the pitfalls of religious pride,[21] and the need for a total commitment to mortification.[22] The dying nun Ercantrudis, for example, realised that one of the nuns had not dedicated herself completely to the monastic life. The culprit, Jonas noted, 'was being empty to the world and yet desiring the secular life outside, and did not at all show devotion of mortification, but was completely alive to the world'.[23] In contrast, Ercantrudis had given herself fully to the mortifications of the monastic life and so merited to see a miraculous bright light and to hear angels singing at her death.[24]

Let us take another example. Almost twenty years after Columbanus's death, Gibitrudis, a nun of Eboriac, had an odd experience of the afterlife.[25] Jonas was at the monastery around the time that

of the saint's prayer is so great that it prevents one of his Irish monks (somewhat confusingly also named Columbanus) from dying a natural death until the monk, annoyed at being detained on earth, tells his abbot to allow him to die in peace. Jonas does not then even describe the death of the Irish monk or mention anything about his soul's journey to heaven: ibid. 1.17 (183–85).

[19] See, for example, the case of Leudeberta who was warned of her impending death while she was asleep. She was instructed that in no way should she deviate from the teachings of her abbess as she was about to die: ibid. 2.18 (271).

[20] Seen in the cases of the Luxeuil monks who left the monastery without the consent of their abbot: ibid. 2.1 (231–32); and the supporters of Agrestius: ibid. 2.10 (254).

[21] See the case of Domma: ibid. 2.16 (266–68).

[22] Ibid. 2.22 (277–79).

[23] Ibid. 2.13 (263).

[24] Ibid. (264).

[25] Ibid. 2.12 (260–62). Eboriac appears to have been a double monastic foundation having both a male and a female community. On female religious communities in Merovingian Gaul: Jo Ann McNamara, 'A Legacy of Miracles: Hagiography and Nunneries in Merovingian Gaul', in J. Kirshner and S. F. Wemple, eds, *Women of the Medieval World* (Oxford, 1985), 36–52; Suzanne F. Wemple, *Women in Frankish Society: Marriage and the Cloister 500 to 900* (Philadelphia, PA, 1981); and now Lindsay Rudge, *Texts and Contexts: Women's Dedicated Life from Caesarius to Benedict* (unpublished Ph. D. thesis, University of St Andrews, 2007).

the nun died and noted how the scent of balsam could miraculously be smelt in the little cell where her body lay. He was there a month later when he celebrated mass for Gibitrudis's soul. This time the smell of perfume that filled the church was so strong that it was as if Jonas could smell a plethora of oils and spices. It was evident to the community by these divine smells that their recently departed companion was among the blessed in the afterlife. But Jonas had, in fact, witnessed the nun's second death. For six months previously she had successfully pleaded to God that she should die in place of her relative, the community's abbess Burgundofara, who was then on the point of death. Gibitrudis's petition had been answered while she was praying in church; a voice had proclaimed to her that the abbess would be spared while she would be 'freed earlier from the chains of the flesh'.[26] She died shortly afterwards and her soul, escorted by angels 'above the sky' to heaven, was placed before 'the tribunal of the eternal Judge'. While she was looking about her at the crowds of the blessed dressed in white, she heard a voice boom from the throne of judgement: 'Go back, because you have not fully left worldliness.'[27] She was duly whisked back to her body and commanded to amend herself because she had harboured ill feelings towards three nuns whom she had not fully forgiven for an offence they had caused her. Back on earth she told her startled companions what had happened and summoned the three nuns to seek their forgiveness. From this miracle account, therefore, Jonas drew a moral lesson concerning the dangers of communal discord.

Jonas amply illustrates the dangers of discord in the chapters dealing with Abbot Eustasius of Luxeuil (d. 629). Following the account of how Agrestius's charges of heterodoxy against Columbanian monastic practices were successfully rebutted by the abbot at the Council of Mâcon, Jonas turns to consider the fate of the rebel monks. A string of calamities befell those who had rebelled against the Columbanian practices. One dissenter became possessed by demons and hanged himself.[28] Rabid wolves broke into the monastic confines of Remiremont, a Columbanian monastery that had supported Agrestius, tearing two members of the community to pieces.[29] Divine punishment again struck the community when a bolt of lightning ripped through the

---

[26] Jonas, *Vita Columbani*, 2.12 (*Ionae Vitae Sanctorum*, ed. Krusch, 261).
[27] Ibid.
[28] Ibid. 2.10 (253–54).
[29] Ibid. (253).

monastery, killing more than fifty.[30] Agrestius was spared this disaster because, as Jonas says, God wished to give him the chance of repentance. But as Agrestius did not take this opportunity, he was struck down by his own slave; murdered, it was said, because of his illicit relations with the man's wife.[31] These cases of divine punishment can be contrasted with Eustasius's death some years later.[32] When it came to describing the moment of the abbot's death, Jonas simply noted that Eustasius, after a period of thirty days of penitential suffering, 'by the force of the victories achieved, entered the celestial kingdoms with Christ as his guide'.[33]

Although Jonas mentions a number of occasions when dying monks and nuns had visions of heaven, he does not go into any great detail about these visions. In the case of the nun Gibitrudis heaven for her was a place of judgement and God a judge of her sins.[34] When Abbot Athala of Bobbio was dying, he instructed some of his monks to take him outside his cell where there was a standing cross.[35] He prayed for a long time there for his sins to be forgiven, and then he saw a vision of heaven which lasted for many hours. Jonas does not describe what Athala saw; the vision itself indicated that his sins had been forgiven.[36] This is likewise the case where the appearance of angels or the scents of sweet perfumes are sufficient indicators that the soul of the departed would ascend to heaven. The important thing about these events was that they would serve as 'acts of encouragement' (*hortamina*) for living members of the communities.[37]

Jonas's accounts should be seen in the context of a literary trend that was developing during the seventh century as hagiographical works came to focus more acutely on the afterlife. It was a period when Latin Christianity, according to Peter Brown, became 'for the first time, an "otherworldly" religion in the true sense. Religious imagination and religious practice came to concentrate more intently on death and the fate of the dead.'[38] A fundamental text in this regard was Gregory the

---

[30] Ibid. (254).
[31] Ibid.
[32] Ibid. (256–57).
[33] Ibid. (257).
[34] Ibid. 2.12 (261).
[35] Ibid. 2.6 (238–40).
[36] Ibid. (239–40).
[37] See, for example, ibid. 2.11 (257).
[38] Brown, *Rise of Western Christendom*, 261.

Great's *Dialogues*, completed in 594.[39] The *Dialogues*, a collection of Italian miracle stories arranged in four parts or books, take the form of a series of conversations between Gregory and the deacon Peter. The final part of the work, Book IV, deals with miracles concerning the afterlife, miracles that demonstrated the imminence of Doomsday. These are much more vivid and precise evocations of heaven and hell than any found in Jonas's *Vita*. These miracles were indeed signs that the world was coming to an end, as Peter sensed: 'It seems that the spiritual world is moving closer to us manifesting itself through visions and revelations.' 'That is right', Gregory replied, 'for, as the present world approaches its end, the world of eternity looms nearer, manifesting itself by ever clearer signs. ... the end of the world merges with the beginnings of eternal life.'[40] The function of these miracles in Book IV was, therefore, eschatological. They were intended to convince their audience of the imminence of the otherworld so that all their energies would be directed towards the fate of their souls in the afterlife.

The *Dialogues* were widely disseminated during the course of the seventh century and had a considerable impact on subsequent hagiographical writing. The work may even have influenced Jonas in his treatment of death and the afterlife, where some phrases and scenes recall those of the *Dialogues*.[41] However, there is an important difference between the Gregorian accounts and those in the *Vita Columbani*. Jonas's accounts of miraculous deaths and otherworldly visions did not herald the ascendance of the afterlife as they did in the *Dialogues*; they tried to convince a specific group to follow a certain monastic regime, a regime that had been seriously undermined. They were not eschatological, as were Gregory's; they were institutional. In Book II of Jonas's *Vita*, it was the monastery and community that offered the surest route to a blessed afterlife. But achieving heavenly bliss depended on following a severe ascetical programme within a certain monastic system. As we have noted, however, the period following Columbanus's death was

[39] The authenticity of the *Dialogues* has been queried but not disproved. It is still considered a genuine Gregorian work by most scholars. On doubts as to its authenticity, see, however, Francis Clark, *The Pseudo-Gregorian Dialogues*, 2 vols (Leiden, 1987); Marilyn Dunn, 'Gregory the Great, the Vision of Fursey, and the Origins of Purgatory', *Peritia* 14 (2000), 238–54.
[40] *Dialogues* 4.43.1–2 (trans. Zimmerman, 251).
[41] Adalbert de Vogüé, 'La mort dans les monastères: Jonas de Bobbio et les Dialogues de Grégoire le Grand', in *Mémorial Dom Jean Gribomont (1920–1986)*, Studia Ephemeridis 'Augustinianum' 27 (Rome, 1988), 593–619.

characterized by a reaction against his mode of monasticism. In Book II Jonas addressed these issues by looking at the big questions: death and the afterlife. His aims were to edify and to terrify. He was not a mystic in the same sense that Gregory the Great was: he was not interested in giving a topographical evocation of the afterlife. Rather, he was reaffirming Columbanian monastic practices by clearly contrasting the fates of past members of the Columbanian communities.

Although the severity and punitive nature of Columbanian monasticism was destined from the outset not to last, St Columbanus was, like St Benedict, a catalyst of monasticism in the West. His monasteries, particularly Luxeuil and Bobbio, had a profound impact on Frankish and Lombard societies. In Merovingian Gaul Luxeuil became the source of a dynamic monastic movement that would transform the role of the monastery in society. During the course of the seventh century monastic foundations mushroomed, especially in the northern part of the country, as monasteries became ever more expressions of royal and aristocratic dynastic power. But perhaps Columbanus's greatest legacy lay in his influence as a moral teacher, a teacher who taught with particular fervour the necessity of a penitential way of life. As we have seen from some of the instances of death and the afterlife in Jonas's *Vita Columbani*, it was only those who faithfully adhered to such a penitential philosophy within the monastery who could be assured of a blessed afterlife.

University of St Andrews

INDIVIDUAL AND COLLECTIVE SALVATION IN LATE VISIGOTHIC SPAIN

by JAMIE WOOD

BISHOP Julian of Toledo is remembered primarily as a key actor in the processes of king-making and -unmaking that went on in the Visigothic kingdom of the 670s.[1] In the early part of the decade Julian's *Historia Wambae Regis* legitimated King Wamba's hold on the throne in opposition to a rebellion. The text also provides us with the first reference to unction in the early medieval West, while Julian's actions in putting the same king through penance when he appeared to be on the brink of death in 680 and then insisting that the king could not resume his royal duties when he recovered have long attracted the attention of scholars of penance and conspiracy theorists alike. As the Bishop of Toledo, capital of the Visigothic kingdom, Julian was the main ecclesiastic in Visigothic Spain, presiding over four councils of Toledo (from the twelfth in 681 to the fifteenth in 687).[2] Perhaps as a result of his historical significance in a poorly documented era, Julian's plentiful writings about the end of time have been largely ignored; after all, they seem not to deal with 'historical' events. This is a shame, since Julian's *Liber prognosticum futuri saeculi* was the most widely disseminated work of late seventh-century Spain: hundreds of manuscripts survive and there are well over one hundred references to the work in medieval library catalogues.[3] The great success of the *Prognosticum* can be attributed to the contents of its three books, which deal with the origins of human death, the fate of the soul after death, and the fate of the body at the resurrection, and thus address a series of theoretical and practical issues connected to death and its aftermath. The text was so popular because it was very easy to use, briefly

---

[1] For the most recent bibliography on Julian, see Alberto Ferreiro, *The Visigoths in Gaul and Iberia. A Supplemental Bibliography, 1984–2003* (Leiden, 2006), 238–42.

[2] Joaquín Martínez Pizarro, *The Story of Wamba. Julian of Toledo's Historia Wambae Regis* (Washington, DC, 2005).

[3] J. N. Hillgarth, ed., *Sancti Iuliani Toletanae Sedis Episcopi Opera. Pars I*, CChr.SL 115 (Turnhout, 1976), xxv–xxxvii; idem, 'St. Julian of Toledo in the Middle Ages', *Journal of the Warburg and Courtauld Institutes* 21 (1958), 7–26, at 20.

summarizing a wide range of patristic opinions on death, the second coming of Christ and its aftermath.

However, it is not only from the reception of the *Prognosticum* that we should judge it historically significant; by examining the context of its production and the way in which Julian constructed his work valuable historical data can be obtained. The historical texts of late antiquity and the early Middle Ages have long been recognized as contingent constructions that are as much about influencing what contemporaries think about the past and the present as they are about accurately representing that past.[4] This paper argues that in the *Prognosticum* Julian was engaging in a similar process; he was seeking to influence contemporary identities and practices – mainly ideas about what it was to be orthodox – by controlling the future (or at least what people thought about it). Additionally, it will be argued that in writing the *Prognosticum* Julian was trying to fill a gap in the 'marketplace'; no previous Visigothic author had written about the end in such detail, nor had they given it such bodily and communal emphasis.

What follows is divided into three parts. The first section examines evidence for reading and writing about eschatology in Visigothic Spain (sixth and seventh centuries). The second part explores Julian's eschatological writings, particularly his *Prognosticum*. Finally, some brief suggestions are made about the possible social significance of these writings. The focus of the paper is less on the content of Julian's eschatology and more on its context, as this best allows us to demonstrate that the *Prognosticum* was not simply an exercise in antiquarianism but stood within a long-established tradition in Visigothic Spain of writing about the end of time.

* * *

Historically there have been two schools of thought on the influence of eschatology in the Visigothic kingdom. One side sees the ecclesiastics of the kingdom, including the father of the Spanish church Isidore of Seville, as largely unbothered by such issues, while the other sees the kingdom as riddled with concern about the end of time. Recently,

---

[4] See, for example, Walter Goffart, *The Narrators of Barbarian History (A. D. 550–800): Jordanes, Gregory of Tours, Bede, and Paul the Deacon* (Princeton, NJ, 1988); Walter Pohl, 'History in Fragments: Montecassino's Politics of Memory', *Early Medieval Europe* 10 (2001), 343–74; Rosamond McKitterick, *History and Memory in the Carolingian World* (Cambridge, 2004).

García Moreno has suggested that the anti-Jewish measures enacted by King Sisebut in the 610s were underpinned by a belief that the world was about to end and that the Jews had to be converted before that event could occur. Whilst it is unlikely that Sisebut was wholly inspired by a belief in an imminent apocalypse (his actions can be understood better as part of an effort to promote an image of an orthodox Visigothic monarchy), there is considerable evidence that the elite of Visigothic Spain were interested in eschatology and were predisposed to interpret and describe events in such terms.[5] This interest is evidenced throughout the history of the kingdom and found expression in a wide range of writings. These texts were not hysterical outpourings but reflected concerns of a pastoral and practical nature.

In the mid-sixth century the Iberian bishop Apringius of Beja wrote a *Tractatus in Apocalypsin*. Apringius's was an original piece because, unusually for a commentary on the *Apocalypse*, it did not draw on the work of Tyconius, whose typological, historical and anti-eschatological reading of the text 'determined the Western church's exegesis for the next eight hundred years'.[6] The text is based mainly on the writings of Irenaeus, Hippolytus, Tertullian, Prudentius and Jerome, and it 'shows an optimistic and Christ-centred vision of history' common in Iberian writers such as Orosius.[7] Interestingly, given the later anti-Jewish flavour of much Visigothic writing, Apringius also tried to refute Jewish messianic and apocalyptic ideas. Perhaps owing to this polemical objective, the text lacks the emphasis on the body that Julian was to add to Visigothic eschatology over a century later. Although Apringius's work was not very influential in subsequent centuries, there was some interest in it in seventh-century Spain, as Isidore of Seville makes clear in his *De viris illustribus*: 'Apringius ... explained the *Apocalypse* of the Apostle John, with a literal sense and a brilliant discussion, nearly as

[5] J. N. Hillgarth, 'Eschatological and Political Concepts in the Seventh Century', in J. Fontaine and J. N. Hillgarth, eds, *Le septième siècle: Changements et continuités / The Seventh Century: Change and Continuity* (London, 1992), 212–31, at 225; L.A. García Moreno, 'Expectatives milenaristas y escatolólogicas en la España tardoantigua (ss. V–VIII)', in *Spania. Estudis d'antiguitat tardana oferts en homenatge al professor Pere de Palol i Salellas* (Barcelona, 1996), 103–09.

[6] Paula Fredriksen, 'Apocalypse and Redemption in Early Christianity. From John of Patmos to Augustine of Hippo', *Vigiliae Christianae* 45 (1991), 151–83, at 157.

[7] A. M. Jorge, 'Church and Culture in Lusitania in the V–VIII Centuries: A Late Roman Province at the Crossroads', in Alberto Ferreiro, ed., *The Visigoths: Studies in Culture and Society* (Leiden, 1999), 99–122, at 115.

well as the old ecclesiastics are considered to have put forth.'[8] An independent Spanish apocalyptic tradition was clearly already developing in the sixth century. This tradition brought together patristic opinions for very practical purposes, in this case to refute Jewish opinions about the end of time.[9]

Isidore of Seville himself demonstrated a repeated concern to ensure orthodox eschatological beliefs remained in the ascendancy. Most notably this found expression in the acts of the Fourth Council of Toledo (633), over which Isidore, as chief ecclesiastic in the kingdom, presided. These acts reveal that there was some debate within the kingdom as to the canonicity of the Apocalypse:

> The authority of many councils and the synodical decree of the bishops of the Romans order and decide that the book of the Apocalypse of John the apostle be accepted among the sacred books. And because there are many who do not accept his authority and hold preaching in the church of God in contempt, if anyone hereafter either does not accept it or does not preach [it] in the church from Easter to the time of the masses of Pentecost, he shall receive the sentence of excommunication.[10]

The desire to encourage and enforce orthodoxy of belief about the end of time, together with the anti-Jewish character of much other Visigothic writing about the end, suggests that the bishops thought that this had some social importance whether as a boundary marker for their community, as a method of ensuring that correct practice was observed, or both. For example, a chapter of Isidore's *De fide Catholica contra Iudaeos* is entitled: 'the Jews will believe in Christ at the end of the world'.[11] Additionally, all three versions of Isidore's *Chronicle* evidence hostility to those who might attempt to find out the date of the end of the world, each ending with the stark injunction: 'The remaining time of the world is not ascertainable by human investigation.'[12] As we shall

8 Isidore, *De viris illustribus*, 17, in C. Codoñer Merino, ed., *El 'De viris illustribus' de Isidoro de Sevilla* (Salamanca, 1964), 143.
9 R. Gryson, ed., *Commentaria minora in Apocalypsin Johannis*, CChr.SL 107 (Turnhout, 2003), 11–97.
10 Fourth Council of Toledo, canon 17, in G. Martínez Díez and F. Rodríguez, eds, *La colección canónica hispana*, 6 vols (Madrid and Barcelona, 1966–2002), 5: 205–06 (the translation is mine).
11 Isidore of Seville, *De fide Catholica contra Iudaeos*, 2.5 (PL 83: 508–10).
12 Isidore, *Chronica maiora*, 418, in J. C. Martín, ed., *Isidori Hispalensis Chronica*, CChr.SL

see, later in the same century, Julian was similarly hostile to those trying to find out the time of the end.

Other extant writings from the mid- to late seventh century contain a significant number of references to the end of time. In the 640s Braulio of Zaragoza wrote to Abbot Aemilian in Toledo asking him to obtain a copy of Apringius's commentary.[13] When writing to Braulio in 650 or 651 Fructuosus of Braga refers to the proximity of the end of time.[14] Ildefonsus of Toledo discusses the end of the world in a letter to Quiricius of Barcelona, which was probably written in the 650s or 660s.[15] Again in the mid-seventh century, Taio of Zaragoza used imagery taken from the Apocalypse to describe a recent revolt when writing to Quiricius.[16]

Important though these references are for demonstrating an interest in the end of time on the part of the Visigothic ecclesiastical elite, there does not seem to have been a systematic attempt to explain what was to happen when the end arrived. Likewise, although several of the 'reference' works produced in Visigothic Spain, notably Isidore's *Sententiae* and *Etymologies*, refer to death and the resurrection, there is no great detail on these issues, nor is there an attempt to deal with matters connected to the fate of the body after death. Nor is there any effort to define orthodox or unorthodox practice.[17] Similarly, in the Visigothic law codes reference to the management of the bodies of the deceased (for example, the protection of graves) is dealt with only cursorily. Perhaps, as so often in Visigothic-era writing, the answer lies with Isidore. His *Chronicle* concludes with the following statement:

112 (Turnhout, 2003), 206–09; Richard Landes, 'Lest the Millennium be fulfilled: Apocalyptic Expectations and the Pattern of Western Chronography 100–800 CE', in W. Verbeke, D. Verhelst and A. Welkenhuysen, eds, *The Use and Abuse of Eschatology in the Middle Ages* (Leuven, 1988), 137–211.

13 Braulio, *Epistolae* 25–26, in L. Riesco Terrero, ed., *Epistolario de San Braulio: Introducción, edición crítica y traducción* (Seville, 1975), 122; Roger Collins, 'Literacy and the Laity in Early Mediaeval Spain', in Rosamond McKitterick, ed., *The Uses of Literacy in Early Mediaeval Europe* (Cambridge, 1990), 109–33, at 115, repr. in Roger Collins, *Law, Culture and Regionalism in Early Medieval Spain* (London, 1992), ch. 15.

14 Braulio, *Epistolae* 43 (Riesco Terrero, ed., *Epistolario*, 164): 'mundi iam termino propinquante'.

15 *Hildefonsi responsio* (PL 96: 196).

16 *Taionis Caesaraugustani episcope sententiarum libri quinque, praefatio* (PL 80: 727–30); cf. Recceswinth, *De omnium heresum erroribus abdicatis*, in K. Zeumer, ed., *Leges Visigothorum*, 12.2.2, MGH Leges nationum Germanicarum 1 (Hannover, 1902), 412–13.

17 For example, Isidore, *Etymologies* 11.2.31–37, in W. M. Lindsay, ed., *Isidori Hispalensis episcopi Etymologiarum sive originum libri XX* (Oxford, 1911); Isidore, *Sententiae* 1.27–31; 3.66, in P. Cazier, ed., *Isidorus Hispalensis Sententiae*, CChr.SL 111 (Turnhout, 1998), 81–90, 328–30.

Therefore everyone should think about his passing over, as it says in Holy Scripture: 'in all your works be mindful of your most recent and in eternity you will do no wrong'. For when each person departs from the world, then that is the end of the world for him.[18]

Sentiments such as this would have encouraged members of the Christian community to focus upon the afterlife in a very personal way. However, as we have seen, the writings of Isidore and his followers did not provide much detail to reassure someone considering their passing over. This was to be addressed by Julian, who focused not only upon the fate of the body of the individual but also upon how that individual related to the larger community in the afterlife. Julian therefore answered questions that arose naturally from Isidore's unsystematic approach to death and the end of time.

* * *

The previous analysis has revealed that in Spain from the sixth to the mid-seventh century there were various specific references to the end of time and some extended commentaries on the matter. The majority of these writings can be related to concrete social contexts or interactions. In some cases they were the result of the Christian elite's attempts to impose orthodox belief and practice; in others they derived from specific communications between members of the ecclesiastical hierarchy; while sometimes it was controversy between Jews and Christians – whether of a real or imagined nature will be examined presently – that produced them. In none of these instances can it be shown that concern for the end of days was related to a dusty antiquarianism that had little to do with contemporary religious and social relations and practices.

It is in this context that we can best understand Julian of Toledo's writings about the end. As was noted in the introduction, Julian's significance as a writer on eschatology has been largely ignored by scholars, who have preferred to focus on his role as a historian and a historical actor. However, Felix of Toledo, Julian's biographer, notes that his subject wrote four works (out of sixteen) that made significant reference to the end of days: the *Librum prognosticorum futuri saeculi*; the *De comprobatione sextae aetatis*; collected excerpts from the books of Augustine against the heretic Julian (presumably the fifth-century

---

18   Isidore, *Chronica* 418 (Martín, ed., *Isidori Hispalensis Chronica*, 206–09).

Bishop of Eclanum, who argued with Augustine); and a *libellum* 'on divine judgements, collected from the holy volumes'.[19]

It is worth discussing briefly the *De comprobatione* since it shares some common features with earlier Visigothic-era texts. It was written in 686 and was, according to the author, intended to combat Jews who were misusing the doctrine of the six ages of the world. They apparently argued that the fifth age had not yet been completed and therefore that the Messiah could not yet have arrived.[20] However, commentators are largely agreed that this was little more than a rhetorical trope – the real audience for Julian's arguments was the Catholic population of Spain.[21] Indeed, it has recently been argued that there were actually very few Jews in Spain in the seventh century and that the main influx occurred in the aftermath of the Islamic invasions of the early eighth century.[22] It therefore seems more likely that the anti-Jewish content of the *De comprobatione* was part of an appeal to established literary tradition within the writings of the Hispano-Visigothic *literati*, complementing efforts by the Spanish episcopacy and monarchy to demonstrate their orthodoxy through emphasizing opposition to the Jews. This is made more likely by the dedication of the work to King Ervig.[23] Finally, we should also interpret this attempt to encourage orthodoxy in the wider context of persistent attempts by the bishops to inculcate correct Catholic beliefs within the population of the Iberian Peninsula.[24] Against this background, it is of additional interest that Julian's six ages were structured exactly as Isidore ordered and divided the ages in the third redaction of his *Chronicle*. Julian also repeated Isidore's injunction not to try to calculate the time remaining until the end of the world as its date was known only to God.[25]

---

[19] Felix of Toledo, *Vita Iuliani* 7–10 (PL 96: 445–52).

[20] Julian of Toledo, *De comprobatione sextae aetatis libri tres* 3.10.35 (Hillgarth, ed., *Sancti Iuliani*, 212). For the wider context of production, see J. Campos, 'El "De comprobatione sextae aetatis libri tres" de San Julián de Toledo', *XXVII Semana española de teología (La patrología Toledano-Visigoda)* (Madrid, 1969), 245–59, esp. 245–50. For the *Prognosticon futuri saeculi*, see T. Stancati, 'Alle origini dell'Escatologia cristiana sistematica: Il Prognosticon futuri saeculi di San Giuliano di Toledo (sec. VII)', *Angelicum* 73 (1996), 401–33.

[21] Campos, 'El "De comprobatione"', 254–57; Hillgarth, ed., *Sancti Iuliani*, lxv–lxvi.

[22] M. Toch, 'The Jews in Europe 500–1050', in P. Fouracre, ed., *The New Cambridge Medieval History*, 1: *c. 500–c. 700* (Cambridge, 2005), 547–70.

[23] Julian, *De comprobatione*, praefatio, 1.2.3 (Hillgarth, ed., *Sancti Iuliani*, 145).

[24] Pierre Cazier, *Isidore de Séville et la naissance de l'Espagne catholique* (Paris, 1994), 295–308.

[25] Julian, *De comprobatione* 3.10.34 (Hillgarth, ed., *Sancti Iuliani*, 211); cf. Campos, 'El "De comprobatione"', 254–57.

Julian's *Prognosticum* can be understood as a natural extension of earlier trends, seeking to address questions that previous writings raised but did not answer. There are continuities with earlier Visigothic texts in the context of production, on certain specific issues, and in the way the work was composed. All of this places the text firmly within established patterns of eschatological discourse among the ecclesiastical elite of the Visigothic kingdom. The remainder of this paper is therefore dedicated to examining Julian's *Prognosticum*.

It is firstly necessary to note that the seed for the work was sown during a conversation between Julian and Bishop Idalius of Barcelona in Toledo on Good Friday 688. As previously noted, an interest in afterlife and eschatology was manifested through, and presumably developed out of, discussion between members of the ecclesiastical elite. The three books of the work dealt with the individual and communal aspects of the seventh and final age in a systematic manner, explaining the opinions of a very wide range of earlier writers on the issue of the seventh age to a Christian audience.[26] Indeed, the presence of such a broad range of texts dealing with the end is itself evidence for concerted interest in the matter in early medieval Spain.

Julian was highly creative in his approach to his sources, as Hillgarth, the editor of the *Prognosticon*, noted: 'The exegesis of Jerome, the etymologies of Isidore, the curious analyses of the problems of the resurrection of the body, may not appeal to us today but they were well calculated to appeal to a world intensely concerned with the Last Things.'[27]

While Isidore, for example, was interested in eschatology and knew many of the texts on which Julian drew – especially the writings of Augustine and Gregory – he did not see fit to produce detailed texts summarizing them. Julian, on the other hand:

---

[26] The identifiable sources of Julian's *Prognosticum* (Hillgarth, ed., *Sancti Iuliani*, 11–126) are: Ambrose, *Expositio evangelii Lucae*; Augustine, *De civitate dei*, *De cura pro mortuis gerenda*, *De diversis quaestionibus ad Simplicianum*, *De doctrina christiana*, *De Genesi ad litteram*, *De Trinitate*, *Enchiridion*, *Enarratio in Psalmos*, *Epistolae*, *In Ioannis evangelium tractatus*, *Retractationum libri II*, *Sermones*; Cassian, *Conlationes*; Cyprian, *Ad Fortunatum de exhortatione martyrii*, *De mortalitate*; Eugenius of Toledo, *Fragmentum ex aliquo opere suo deperdito*; Gregory the Great, *Dialogi*, *Homilia in evangelia*, *Moralia in Job*, *Homiliarum in Ezechielem prophetam libri duo*; Ildefonsus of Toledo, *De cognitione baptismi*; Isidore, *De ecclesiasticis officiis*, *Differentiarum libri II*, *Etymologiae*, *Sententiae*; Iulianus Pomerius, *De natura animae vel qualitate eius*, *De animae natura dialogus*; Jerome, *Epistolae*, *Commentariarum in epistulas ad Ephesios*, *Commentariorum in Ioelem liber unus*, *Contra Iovinianum*; John Chrysostom, *Homilia prima de cruce et latrone*; Origen, *Homilia VII in Leviticum*; Taio of Zaragoza, *Sententiarum*.

[27] Hillgarth, ed., *Sancti Iuliani*, xviii.

---

treated themes of central importance to Christian thought, but which in several cases had not previously received full and coherent coverage. ... Julian produced a single treatise that dealt, in three easily comprehended parts, with the questions of the origins of death, the fate of souls after death, and the final resurrection of the body.[28]

The first book, *On the origin of human death*, not only deals with theological, theoretical or etymological issues, such as how sin first entered the world (chapter 1), from where sin was named (chapter 4) and the three kinds of bodily death (chapter 5), but it also refers to a number of highly practical issues concerning death. For example, a group of chapters cover the different kinds of fear of bodily death and how people might be consoled or saved from the desperation it engendered (chapters 11–15, 17). The end of this book covers issues which must have been of even more practical concern. Chapters 20 and 21 are clear that it is to the benefit of the dead if they are buried in or near churches, where they might be kept safe and sustained by the protection of the martyrs, while chapters 18 and 22 consider the administration of burials, funerals, and donations offered for the dead.

While the subject matter of the second book is of an even more abstract nature (the fate of the soul after death), Julian still shows an acute concern for matters that would have been of importance to a more general audience. For example, the relationship between the body and the soul receives significant coverage (chapters 15–17), while the related issue of the connection between the living and the dead is examined towards the end of the book (chapters 26–27, 29–31). Chapter 29 discusses whether the dead could know about the activities of the living, while chapter 30 explores whether the dead could make themselves visible to the living. The book closes by opposing those who say that the soul does not live on after death (chapter 33), the final chapter (37) emphasizing that 'souls of the saints reign in the heavens with Christ'.[29]

The third and longest book explores what happens to the body at the resurrection. There is a huge amount of detail about what to expect at the Final Judgement and its aftermath, such as the separation of the just from the unjust, who will sit with the Lord at the Judgement, what

---

[28] Roger Collins, *Early Medieval Spain. Unity in Diversity, 400–1000* (Basingstoke, 1983), 78.
[29] Hillgarth, ed., *Sancti Iuliani*, 41–76.

happens to the impious after judgement, that a new heaven and a new earth will begin after the Judgement, and, in the final chapter, the endless praise for God which will occur at the 'end without end' (chapter 62).[30] However, like the other sections, this book also has a more 'practical' emphasis upon the body. Chapters 19 to 31 deal with a wide range of issues concerning the bodies of the resurrected, mainly concerning whether the bodies of those who rise again will be in the same state as when they died. These range from fairly basic information, such as whether they will still be 'old' or 'young', 'male' or 'female', and whether they will need to consume food and drink, to more obscure matters, such as whether those who have been eaten by beasts or mutilated in their former lives will maintain their bodily integrity. The third book is characterized by continuities on some specific points of content with previous Visigothic-era literature. For instance, in chapter 1, like Isidore before him, Julian states that no one knows the time and day of judgement. On other occasions, notably chapter 39, the Apocalypse is appealed to as a direct source of authority.[31]

Like earlier Visigothic texts, Julian's *Prognosticum* was not simply a scholarly exercise in theological speculation or an antiquarian compilation with little contemporary relevance, but instead it sought to answer questions that would have been of fundamental practical interest to every member of the Christian community. However, unlike previous Visigothic-era writings, Julian's text offered something new in terms of content: an emphasis upon the fate of the individual's body after death. In producing such a systematic work, Julian aligned himself with an established tradition that sought to compile and summarize the works of previous centuries to encourage orthodox practice and belief. That these specific issues had never before been dealt with in one place (until Julian), that the text stood in continuity with a series of earlier Spanish texts but added something new, and that Julian was concerned with very real issues connected to the body, all suggest that Julian was attempting to create a work that was of social and practical relevance.[32]

---

30 Ibid. 77–126.

31 Chapters 3 and 43 show further opposition to attempts to determine how long the Final Judgement will last and what will happen during it.

32 Peter Brown, *The Body and Society: Men, Women and Sexual Renunciation in Early Christianity* (New York, 1988); S. A. Stofferahn, 'The Power, The Body, The Holy: A Journey through Late Antiquity with Peter Brown', *Comitatus* 29 (1998), 21–46.

There are other clues which suggest that Julian intended to produce something of practical utility. One of these is the emphasis which he placed on the brevity (*brevitas*) of the *Prognosticum*.[33] Julian refers to the brevity of his work on four occasions in the preface. On two occasions he talks of collecting information with *brevitas*; he then talks of constructing a brief book (*brevis volumen*); finally he states that his *brevitas* sated the thirst of many readers.[34] The emphasis on brevity seems to have been closely linked to Julian's desire to make the work as practically useful as possible. A letter to Julian from Bishop Idalius of Barcelona, to whom the *Prognosticum* was dedicated, reinforces this point neatly:

> doubts have been driven away and secret things have been brought forward into the light, when both the opinions of the ancient fathers and proofs have been drawn out towards the public by the fruitful toil of your skill of new brevity. Truth springs forth from their opinions, but new and most true brevity [springs forth] from your toil.[35]

Brevity therefore facilitated access to the truth in the most efficient manner possible. In focusing on the brevity of his treatment Julian was adhering to a long-established tradition. Again this had been filtered through Isidore. For Isidore brevity was the best way to ensure that his message remained in the mind of the reader. He made this explicit in his *Sententiae*:

> Often extended narrative causes the memory of reading to be forgotten for the reason of length. Because, if it is concise, it is read without effort, when the book has been removed the meaning is drawn back into the soul, and those things which have been read, being recalled, will be extracted with very little effort.[36]

That Julian's brief and useful extracts were intended for a practical application can be inferred from the acts of the Fourth Council of

---

[33] Hillgarth, 'St. Julian of Toledo in the Middle Ages', 15–17.
[34] Julian, *Prognosticorum futuri saeculi libri tres, praefatio,* 1.45, 55, 61, 65 (Hillgarth, ed., *Sancti Iuliani,* 12–13).
[35] Idalius of Barcelona, *Epistola Idalii ad Iulianum* 1.68–73 (Hillgarth, ed., *Sancti Iuliani,* 5); in his *Epistola Idalii ad Sunfredum* 1.7 (Hillgarth, ed., *Sancti Iuliani,* 7), Idalius states that the work was written with 'remarkable and new brevity'.
[36] Isidore, *Sententiae* 3.14.8, in P. Cazier, ed., *Isidorus Hispalensis Sententiae,* CChr.SL 111 (Turnhout, 1998), 240 (the translation is mine).

Toledo held in 633. It legislated for bishops distributing instructional manuals to priests under their care, who, in turn, were supposed to use these resources to tend to their flocks more effectively: 'When priests are appointed in parishes, they should accept a *libellum* from their official bishop so that the learned succeed to the churches assigned to them, lest … through ignorance they do despite to the divine sacraments'.[37]

* * *

While there was clearly a considerable amount of interest in matters eschatological in the Visigothic kingdom in the sixth and seventh centuries, we should not just read the eschatological texts of Julian as a one-dimensional reflection of such beliefs, but as congruent with other contemporary trends. Just as the anti-Jewish writings were not necessarily about, or addressed to, actual Jews, the eschatological writings did not simply reflect fears or beliefs concerning the end of the world. Julian's works on eschatology filled a gap left by Isidore and other Visigothic writers: we have seen that, for example, they dealt with the fate of the body and the soul after death in a more systematic manner than had previously been done. But, like the didactic writings of Isidore, which also summarized the opinions of a large number of earlier thinkers for pastoral purposes, those of Julian were intended to emphasize the orthodoxy of the Hispano-Visigothic episcopal and secular hierarchy. It is therefore no coincidence that his work on divine judgement and the *De comprobatione* were both dedicated to King Ervig. The rhetorical and didactic or scholarly features of these writings should not be seen as opposed. The encouragement of orthodox beliefs served to strengthen the hierarchy and thus the position of the bishops and monarchy with regard to those lower down the scale.

It is also likely that Julian was seeking to influence contemporary beliefs about the end. Otherwise why would he have devoted such attention to altering the emphases of his sources, underlining his opposition to certain beliefs and practices and creating a rhetorical opposition to those who did not hold the same beliefs as his orthodox community? The practical, didactic underpinning of the work is strongly suggested by the emphasis which Julian and his correspondent placed on brevity. Just as scholars such as Walter Goffart and Walter

---

[37] Fourth Council of Toledo, canon 26, in Martínez Díez and Rodríguez, eds, *La colección canónica hispana*, 5: 216 (the translation is mine).

Pohl have shown that rewriting the past of a community was a common way through which early medieval writers sought to influence the identity of that community, so this paper has tried to show that Julian of Toledo sought to do the same when writing about the future.[38] His writings about the end of the world and its aftermath were intended to establish what an orthodox Spanish Christian ought to think about their ultimate fate as individuals and their place within the community. In this sense Julian's writings acted to integrate individual and community by creating a consensus about the afterlife and ultimately about the end of time.

University of Manchester

---

[38] Goffart, *The Narrators of Barbarian History*, 432–37; Pohl, 'History in Fragments'.

ANGLO-SAXON 'PURGATORY'

by SARAH FOOT

Since a countless multitude of misshapen spirits, far and wide, was being tortured in this alternation of misery as far as I could see and without any interval of respite, I began to think that this might be Hell, of whose intolerable torments I had often heard tell. But my guide who went before me answered my thoughts, 'Do not believe it,' he said, 'this is not Hell as you think.' ... As he led me on in open light ... [we came to] a very broad and pleasant plain ... [where] there were innumerable bands of men in white robes, and many companies of happy people sat around; as he led me through the midst of the troops of joyful inhabitants, I began to think that this might perhaps be the kingdom of Heaven of which I had often heard tell. But he answered my thoughts: 'No,' he said, 'this is not the kingdom of Heaven as you imagine.'[1]

VISIONS played a prominent role in Bede's narrative in his *Ecclesiastical History* of the growth of the English Church. Some divine revelations offered consolation to their recipients, but a cluster of visions in the final book, where the one just quoted occurs, is quite different. Far from providing their recipients with the reassurance of a promised share in the heavenly kingdom, this vision of a layman called Dryhthelm, and the other revelations of life after death that Bede recounted immediately after it, offer profoundly unsettling accounts of the tribulations suffered by the wicked and, perhaps yet more alarmingly, the pains inflicted on the venial sinner. These visions reflect an increasing emphasis on the judgement of individuals which is one of the characteristics of the final book of Bede's *History*.[2]

Dryhthelm's vision has attracted considerable attention. It is the longest of the vision-narratives included in Bede's *History* and also

[1] Bede, *Historia ecclesiastica* 5.12, ed. and trans. Bertram Colgrave and R. A. B. Mynors, *Bede's Ecclesiastical History of the English People* (Oxford, 1969), 490–93 [hereafter: *HE*].

[2] Ralph Walterspacher, 'Book V of Bede's *Historia ecclesiastica gentis Anglorum*: Perspectives on Salvation History and Eschatology', *Archa Verbi: Yearbook for the Study of Medieval Theology* 1 (2004), 11–24, at 11–15.

stylistically the most sophisticated and carefully crafted. In the early Middle Ages it circulated as an independent text, separately from the *Ecclesiastical History*, either alone or together with other visions.[3] According to Bede, this man was married and living a devout life with his household until he fell seriously ill and died one night. When at dawn he came back to life and suddenly sat up, he terrified all those gathered round his body in mourning. His vision inspired the layman to adopt an entirely new lifestyle; dividing all his possessions between his wife, his sons and the poor, he joined the minster at Melrose, where he lived a life of particular penitence in a secret retreat. Only at the end of the story, just before his death, did Bede reveal the visionary's name. For the whole of the extended narrative Dryhthelm remained anonymous; Bede thus made him an archetypal sinner telling a remarkable story of the consequences of sin through which universal message he demonstrated the road to salvation.[4] Dryhthelm's example served to make Bede's readers so fear judgement and eternal punishment that they would repent and reform their lives.[5] The tale reveals something of the Anglo-Saxon theology of the afterlife, especially a view of the geography of the other world where lay places of waiting and purgation: 'Do not believe it', he said, 'This is not Hell as you think. ... this is not Heaven as you imagine it.' If neither in heaven nor in hell, where was Dryhthelm, and why was that neither-heaven-nor-hell place not one location but – quite explicitly – two discrete environments?

Several recent articles have explored aspects of the development of a theology of purgatory in the early medieval West, all challenging Le Goff's assertion that purgatory was 'born' in the twelfth century.[6] This essay explores the early Anglo-Saxon idea of *post mortem* purgation to see what it reveals of contemporary belief about the afterlife. Where did the dead go who were not consigned immediately to heaven or

[3] M. L. W. Laistner and H. H. King, *A Hand-List of Bede Manuscripts* (Ithaca, NY, 1943), 107–08.

[4] Bede, *HE* 5.12 (trans. Colgrave and Mynors, 498–99).

[5] Claude Carozzi, *Le voyage de l'âme dans l'au-delà d'après la littérature latine Ve–XIIIe siècle*, Collection de l'Ecole française de Rome 189 (Rome, 1994), 231; Walterspacher, 'Book V', 17.

[6] Graham Robert Edwards, 'Purgatory: "Birth" or "Evolution" ', *JEH* 36 (1985), 634–46; Peter Brown, 'The Decline of the Empire of God: Amnesty, Penance and the Afterlife from Late Antiquity to the Middle Ages', in Caroline Bynum and Paul Freedman, eds, *Last Things: Death and the Apocalypse in the Middle Ages* (Philadelphia, PA, 2000), 41–59; Marilyn Dunn, 'Gregory the Great, the Vision of Fursey, and the Origins of Purgatory', *Peritia* 14 (2000), 238–54; Marina Smyth, 'The Origins of Purgatory through the Lens of Seventh-Century Irish Eschatology', *Traditio* 58 (2003), 91–132.

hell? What kind of space was this? How long might purgation last? What was it for? And did it work? It concentrates on vision literature from the eighth century, but although emphasizing the textual, not the visual, it does not forget that early Anglo-Saxon churches were highly decorated with images. At Wearmouth scenes from St John's vision of the Apocalypse were drawn on the north wall, representing both the heavenly paradise but also, surely, the bottomless pit into which Satan was dragged for his thousand-year reign.[7] Heaven and hell were part as much of the visual as of the auditory and literary repertoire of Anglo-Saxons; but what about purgatory?

Central to Jacques Le Goff's argument that purgatory (a developed theology creating a third place in the other world with a defined function) was not born until the twelfth century are the notions of time and space. His argument that there was no noun *purgatorium* before the 1150s (even though there was the adjective *purgatorius* found in phrases such as *ignis purgatorius*) is critical to his case, for Le Goff was unequivocal in his view that without a word to describe it, one cannot have the concept of purgatory.[8] Some reviewers struggled with the starkness of this linguistically-turned understanding, yet it is an important one. Le Goff's demonstration that early medieval theologians failed to agree on a geography of the afterlife renders his argument particularly powerful; only when the other world became demarcated into three exclusive areas – heaven, hell and a space in between – can we talk confidently of a notion of purgatory. Plentiful as were early medieval visionary accounts of otherworldly experience (all dependent on the same limited range of literary models), they display remarkably little consistency about the shape of the other world and the nature of the afterlife to be anticipated by such souls not self-evidently destined for either heavenly bliss or infernal torment. That there was some period after death when recompense might be made for earthly sins was agreed,[9] but the lack of any word to define a place for purification reflects the absence of an agreed and thought-through theology of purgatory. The texts we shall

---

[7] Bede, *Historia abbatum*, ch. 6, ed. Charles Plummer, *Bedae Opera Historica*, 2 vols (Oxford, 1896), 1: 369.

[8] Jacques Le Goff, *La naissance du purgatoire* (Paris, 1981); trans. Arthur Goldhammer, *The Birth of Purgatory* (Chicago, IL, 1983); for a sceptical reading, see R. W. Southern, 'Between Heaven and Hell', *Times Literary Supplement*, 18 June 1982, 651–52, and A. Ja. Gurevich, 'Popular and Scholarly Medieval Cultural Traditions: Notes in the Margin of Jacques Le Goff's book', *JMedH* 9 (1983), 71–90.

[9] As emphasized by Southern, 'Between Heaven and Hell', and Edwards, 'Purgatory'.

examine reflect instead various, often contradictory phases in the process of articulating such a theology. It is not that the afterlife was not spatially defined, but that there were conflicting ideas as to its geographical shape, models that depended on the vantage point from which the visionary viewed the other world's regions. Three seventh- and eighth-century vision-narratives illustrate this well.

Bede's *Ecclesiastical History* supplies a condensed version of one episode in the vision of the Irish monk Fursa, an independently- circulating text of Frankish origin.[10] There angels took the saint's spirit out of his body; when he looked back at the world he saw a dark valley and four fires burning separately that threatened to consume the world. His angelic guides explained to which sins the fires related – falsehood, covetousness, discord and injustice – and guided him safely through the conflagration before he could be burnt. An evil spirit threw a suffering soul straight at the saint, hitting him and scorching his shoulder and jaw; Fursa here understood that he shared in the punishment of a soul who had not repented of his sins before death.[11] The full version of the vision makes the point more explicitly; there the angel accompanying Fursa and the evil spirit debate whether there is a place of punishment for those sins not purged on earth. When the demon laments that there is no such place, the angel corrects him saying, 'You do not know the mysteries of God, there may be such a place'.[12] Fursa did not visit the infernal regions themselves; the fire in which he was marked lay neither in heaven nor hell, although it was clearly a purging fire, occupied only by sinners. But how this place related to either the heavenly or infernal regions is hard to tell, not least because Fursa's other-worldly geog- raphy is most imprecisely drawn. A clear message of the whole narra- tive is that the question of the *post mortem* punishment of sins is shrouded in mystery and unknowable to any of the living. A different, more geographically-precise account occurs in the vision of Dryhthelm quoted at the beginning, where the afterlife is delineated on a hori- zontal plane.

So concrete a geographical relationship is established between the four different spaces that Dryhthelm was taken to visit, it is as if the layman walked through earthly countryside.[13] At the outset, he and his

---

[10] Bede, *HE* 3.18 (trans. Colgrave and Mynors, 270–77); Carozzi, *Le voyage*, 100–12.
[11] Bede, *HE* 3.18 (trans. Colgrave and Mynors, 274–75).
[12] *Visio Fursei*, ch. 9, lines 20–22 (ed. Carozzi, *Le voyage*, 684; discussed ibid. 110).
[13] Carozzi, *Le voyage*, 236–37. For a similarly vivid evocation of an imagined space,

guide went towards the direction in which the sun rises at the time of the summer solstice, namely towards the north-east. On their left appeared a 'deep and broad valley of infinite length', with a raging fire on one side and hail, ice and snow on the other. 'Both sides were full of the souls of men, tossed from one side to the other as if by the fury of the tempest.' From this unnamed place they proceeded until, directly in front of them, fell away a great pit from which masses of noisome flame spurted up. Into this burning pit Dryhthelm watched a crowd of laughing and jeering demons drag five human souls. Although the spirits threatened Dryhthelm with their fiery tongs, they dared not touch him. Like a light in the darkness, the rising of the winter sun led him and his guide to the right towards the south-east. In the open, the two confronted an amazingly high wall with no obvious entry, on top of which they soon miraculously found themselves. Here lay the flowery plain with the white-robed bands of joyful men. Finally, by walking straight on through the blessed spirits they found before them a more beautiful light and sweet singing but, just as Dryhthelm had hesitated on the edge of the infernal region, so he could not cross the threshold into the heavenly kingdom.

This vision provides a clear fourfold description of the other world, where heaven lies in the east (straight ahead after the pair had turned right from their north-easterly trajectory to walk south-east) and hell lies in the north. In between the two extremes lie two unnamed places of waiting: a provisional hell and a provisional heaven. As the angel explained, the valley with alternating fire and cold chastens souls who failed to make recompense for their sins before death, yet because they did confess on their deathbeds they can hope, with the prayers of the living and celebration of masses, to be freed even before the Day of Judgement. Similarly in the flowery place await the souls of those who died practising good works 'but who are not in such a state of perfection that they deserve to be received immediately into the kingdom of Heaven'.[14] It is tempting to see the influence of Augustine on this recommendation of the benefit of prayers, alms and masses for the suffering dead, although the scheme described here – where the redeemably bad suffer in the dark valley – does not exactly match

---

compare Bede's detailed account of the shape of the earth, conceived as a ball divided into five circular zones of different temperatures: *De temporum ratione*, ch. 34, trans. Faith Wallis, *Bede: the Reckoning of Time* (Liverpool, 1999), 96–99 [hereafter: *DTR*].

[14] Bede, *HE* 5.12 (trans. Colgrave and Mynors, 494–95).

Augustine's statement in his *Enchiridion* that prayer for the *non valde mali* (not very bad) could be propitiatory.[15] Dryhthelm's vision shows us an other world laid out essentially on one horizontal plane, divided into four areas: two permanent sites of blessedness or torment and two places of waiting, one markedly more agreeable than the other. Yet the two waiting areas are more than antechambers to heaven and hell, for in the more hellish of the two one does not necessarily have to antici-pate an infinitely infernal future; purged souls may in due course escape to ultimate bliss.

In our final vision, seen by a monk from Wenlock and retold by Boniface in a letter, the coordinates of the other world are yet more confusing.[16] This shows some familiarity with both Fursa's and Dryhthelm's visions while incorporating a number of original features.[17] Taken out of his body while ill, our visionary first looked down on the earth (surrounded like a ball with the flames of an enor-mous fire) and watched dying souls enter the other-worldly regions, where angels and demons disputed over their spirits. His own past sins came to accuse him, while his few virtues also spoke up in his defence. In the bowels of the earth, fiery pits spewed terrible flames; on their margins clung the souls of wretched men resembling black birds who enjoyed a brief respite before being cast back into the pits. This, the guiding angel explained, was in anticipation of the relief God would grant to such souls at the Day of Judgement, when they would finally come to rest eternal. Beneath these fires in the lowest depths, the monk heard unspeakable groaning and weeping of souls in distress; to these souls the loving kindness of God would never come, as they were destined to be tortured in the undying flame forever. Without explaining how the spheres related one to another, the vision reports further the monk's sight of a place of wondrous beauty where a multi-tude of handsome men enjoyed extraordinary happiness in a fragrant atmosphere. Beyond this place (God's paradise), lay a pitch-black fiery river, boiling and glowing, dreadful and hideous to regard, over which

[15] Augustine, *Enchiridion*, 110, ed. J. Rivière, Bibliothèque Augustinienne 9 (Paris, 1947), 304; Edwards, 'Purgatory', 645 n. 82.

[16] Boniface, *Epistola* 10, ed. Michael Tangl, *Die Briefe des Heiligen Bonifatius und Lullus* (Berlin, 1916), 7–15; also Patrick Sims-Williams, 'A recension of Boniface's letter to Eadburg about the monk of Wenlock's vision', in Katherine O'Brien O'Keeffe and Andy Orchard, eds, *Latin Learning and English Lore*, I: *Studies in Anglo-Saxon Literature for Michael Lapidge* (Toronto, 2005), 194–214, at 203–07.

[17] Carozzi, *Le voyage*, 199–200.

rested a log as a bridge.[18] Happy souls left the paradisal fields 'anxious to cross to the other side', but while some crossed swiftly in safety, others slipped and fell into the infernal stream. Yet, each of those who fell came up on the opposite bank 'far more brilliant and beautiful than when he fell into the foaming and pitchy river', the trial having purged their souls of trifling sins. On the far side of the river stood shining walls of great splendour, length and height: the heavenly Jerusalem.[19]

For all its lack of precision and geographical ambiguity, Boniface's report of the Wenlock monk's experience lets us draw a picture of the other world. In a vertical image we have at the base a permanent Gehenna, the pits of lower hell where the light and mercy of God never penetrated. But the upper hell above this region, where the souls of the suffering dead took the form of black birds, was just a 'provisional hell', where the sinful were punished only until the Last Judgement, when they would be released to eternal blessedness. This place of waiting and seemingly of purgation endured temporally between the times of death and judgement; like the equivalent place in Dryhthelm's other world, it was not simply hell's antechamber. There was, however, another place of purgation: the fiery river where souls were purged of venial sins before they entered the heavenly Jerusalem. Sims-Williams saw this as a quadripartite other world, seeing the provisional hell of the fiery pits with black birds as mirrored by the flowery plains where the venial sinners linger in joyful idleness before crossing into the heavenly Jerusalem, and comparing this with Dryhthelm's four-fold other world.[20]

More compelling to my mind is the lack of symmetry that the Wenlock vision displays. Three different sorts of sinner appear: the definitively wicked who burn in the eternal fires of hell; the moderately sinful, who committed more than venial sins but who were not beyond redemption and would suffer in the fiery pits with occasional remission until released at the Last Judgement; and thirdly those whose sins were small enough to be washed away in the river of fire, where they were immersed in direct proportion to the degree of their error. The Wenlock vision depicts not only two heavens and two hells, like Dryhthelm's, but also two spatial and temporal manifestations of the exaction of satisfaction for sin. One occurs in an infernal region, just

[18] Compare Gregory, *Dialogues* 4.37 (ed. A. de Vogüé, SC 265: 130–32).

[19] For the literary models employed here, see Patrick Sims-Williams, *Religion and Literature in Western England, 600–800* (Cambridge, 1990), 249–58.

[20] Sims-Williams, *Religion and Literature*, 259–60.

above the lower hell but clearly within its sight; here the sinful endure the unknowably lengthy torment of burning in fiery pits until the end of time. A second place of purgation lies elsewhere, tantalizing between the provisional paradise and heaven itself, and is experienced in quite a different temporal frame. As if in a celestial snakes and ladders, joyful souls hasten onto the log with the walls of the heavenly Jerusalem gleaming in front of them, only to find themselves immersed no less nastily, if much more briefly, in the burning river. Dryhthelm's other world similarly had two waiting areas, but it is only his two hells that really resemble those seen by the Wenlock monk. Dryhthelm's paradise led straight to heaven and was not separated by the second area of testing or punishment. Neither the time nor the space of the other world is satisfactorily explained in the Wenlock vision, reflecting its dream-like origins.[21]

Two clear conclusions emerge from this discussion of visions of the afterlife in seventh- and eighth-century Anglo-Saxon England. First, although the other world could be described in quasi-terrestrial terms, as if it were an extension of the world known to the living, there was then no clear notion of the shape or organization of its space. Both Dryhthelm and the Wenlock monk talk of climbing up to the heavenly Jerusalem, and Fursa and the monk from Wenlock see hell in the depths: it is interesting that the other world could effectively be depicted either in vertical terms or on a predominantly horizontal plane. Second, no single concept explained how time functioned after death. These examples all stress the benefit to be derived for the souls of the departed from the prayers, alms and celebration of masses by the living, and all indeed draw a direct relationship between the actions of the living and the fate of the dead. That message was central to all three narratives, which reflect a degree of rapprochement between the worlds of the living and of the dead. These accounts show further a translation into the afterlife of the notion of tariffed penance (a sliding scale determining the penance required for each sin according to its severity), by now well-established for the living.[22] That satisfaction for all sin was probably not possible on earth need not be a cause of despair for the dying or the bereaved if satisfaction could still be exacted from the soul after its death. But how long the sinful soul must suffer *post mortem*

21 Carozzi, *Le voyage*, 215.
22 Dunn, 'Gregory the Great'.

punishment, and the relationship between a judgement of his deeds on his death – the conflict between the virtues and vices that we saw most overtly in Fursa's vision – and the ultimate Last Judgement at the end of time, remain entirely unclear. Indeed the spatially most explicit narrative – Dryhthelm's – is temporally the vaguest.

Some of the ideas articulated in these vision-narratives, specifically the idea that prayer for the dead could be efficacious, occur in other Anglo-Saxon texts of similar date, such as references to masses for the dead in the penitential attributed to Archbishop Theodore,[23] or an Advent homily of Bede's which recommended prayer, alms, fasting and the saying of masses for those awaiting judgement.[24] Wills reflect lay perceptions of the spiritual benefits of generosity to the Church, almsgiving and particularly the manumission of slaves at the time of death.[25] One of the miserable souls whom the Wenlock monk encountered in the afterlife was worried because the slave-girl whom he had wanted to manumit on his deathbed had still not been freed.[26] Such examples and similar pronouncements in later pre-Conquest texts suggest that, although the English were interested in the fate of the soul between the death of the body and the Last Judgement, many anticipated a preliminary judgement immediately after death and had clear notions of *post mortem* purgation (a period of punishment in a place where fire predominated); even later Anglo-Saxon homilists expressed little interest in where that place lay or what the condition of purgation might be.[27] One could even argue that tenth- and eleventh-century

23 Theodore, *Penitential* 2.5, ed. Paul Willem Finsterwalder, *Die Canones Theodori Cantuariensis und ihre Überlieferungsformen* (Weimar, 1929), 318–19; quotation from 2.5.9.

24 Bede, *Homelia* 1.2, trans. Lawrence T. Martin and David Hurst, *Bede the Venerable, Homilies on the Gospels, Book I: Advent to Lent* (Kalamazoo, MI, 1991), 17. Cf. Council of *Clofesho* (AD 747), ch. 30, cf. chs. 26–7, eds Arthur West Haddan and William Stubbs, *Councils and Ecclesiastical Documents relating to Great Britain and Ireland*, 3 vols (Oxford, 1869–78), 3: 376, 372–3.

25 On Anglo-Saxon wills in general, see Julia Crick, 'Posthumous Obligation and Family Identity', in William O. Frazer and Andrew Tyrrell, eds, *Social Identity in Early Medieval Britain* (London, 2000), 193–208.

26 Boniface, *Epistola* 10 (ed. Tangl, *Briefe*, 13). See also Council of Chelsea (AD 816), ch. 10 (eds Haddan and Stubbs, *Councils*, 3: 583–84).

27 For the question of double judgement, see T. A. Shippey, *Poems of Wisdom and Learning in Old English* (Cambridge and Totowa, NJ, 1976), 30–31. Bede stressed the second judgement to be expected on Doomsday: *DTR*, ch. 70 (trans. Wallis, *Reckoning*, 243–46); *Explanatio Apocalypsis* 1.6.11, trans. E. Marshall, *The Explanation of the Apocalypse by the Venerable Beda* (Oxford 1878), 41–42. For later Anglo-Saxon views of judgement, see Milton McC. Gatch, 'Eschatology in the Anonymous Old English Homilies', in his *Eschatology and Christian*

texts, and importantly drawings, often seem to show a greater interest in hell than in heaven. Some contemporary images show hell as a kind of 'living-dead existence' in pits set underneath hills or mounds in the English landscape, much closer to the viewer than he might suspect.[28] In part this must reflect contemporary perceptions of the imminence of Judgement Day, in which frame of mind the fate of souls between death and their appearance before the judgement seat seemed of rather less pressing concern than were the flames of eternal punishment.

Neither in our analysis of the seventh-century vision narratives nor in these few references to later pre-Conquest texts and images have we encountered evidence that the Anglo-Saxons had an idea of purgatory in its later medieval sense. The geography of the other world appears far from settled throughout this period and its temporal framework remains equally vague. On the lips of our visionaries, the afterlife had various shapes, allowing for punishment for past sins to be exacted in multiple environments. Although heaven and hell generally lay at the outer edges of the other world, the nature and relationship of the places in between varied; they functioned as more than waiting rooms in which the unjudged might ponder their ultimate fate uneasily, or the insufficiently-shriven pay for sins unrepented at the time of death. Fursa's other world remained tripartite; Dryhthelm's had four major zones, yet the afterlife could, in the imagery of the monk from Wenlock, encompass five separate places, each with a slightly different function. One has to conclude, paraphrasing the words of Dryhthelm's angelic guide: 'this is not purgatory as you would imagine it'.

Christ Church, Oxford

Nurture. Themes in Anglo-Saxon and Medieval Religious Life (Aldershot, 2000), 117–65, at 161–65.
[28] Sarah Semple, 'Illustrations of Damnation in Late Anglo-Saxon Manuscripts', Anglo-Saxon England 32 (2003), 231–45, at 240.

BYZANTINE VISIONS OF THE END

by LESLIE BRUBAKER

AS is well known, western medieval apocalyptic literature owes a considerable debt to Byzantine apocalyptic literature, which itself built on Roman and Jewish sources. The classic studies are now Evelyne Patlagean's 'Byzance et son autre monde', published in 1981; Paul Alexander's *The Byzantine Apocalyptic Tradition*, published posthumously in 1985; and Jane Baun's edition and commentary of three Middle Byzantine apocalyptic texts that appeared in 2007. In addition, Paul Magdalino has recently published several articles on the theme.[1] On top of this, numerous studies connect specific Byzantine apocalypse traditions to particular political events, most notably the Islamic conquests of the seventh and eighth centuries.[2] Byzantine eschatology has been even more thoroughly studied, and, with the subtitle 'Views on death and the last things', was the subject of a recent (1999) Dumbarton Oaks symposium.

But though Byzantine apocalyptic and prophetic literature flourished, Byzantine eschatology was firmly entrenched in Greek theological writings, and Byzantine images of the transition to the other world – that is, deathbed and funerary scenes – were relatively commonplace, visualization of the afterlife itself was largely limited to representations

---

[1] E. Patlagean, 'Byzance et son autre monde: observations sur quelques récits', in *Faire croire: Modalités de la diffusion et de la reception des messages religieux du XIIᵉ au XVᵉ siècle*, Collection de l'École française de Rome 51 (1981), 201–21; P. Alexander, *The Byzantine Apocalyptic Tradition* (Berkeley, CA, 1985); P. Magdalino, ' "What we Heard in the Lives of the Saints we have Seen with our own Eyes": The Holy Man as Literary Text in Tenth-Century Constantinople', in J. Howard-Johnston and P. Hayward, eds, *The Cult of Saints in Late Antiquity and the Middle Ages: Essays on the Contribution of Peter Brown* (Oxford, 1999), 88–112; idem, 'Une prophétie inédite des environs de l'an 965 attribuée à Léon le Philosophe (Ms Karakallou 14, fol. 253r–254r)', *Travaux et mémoires* 14 (2002), 391–402; idem, 'The Year 1000 in Byzantium', in idem, ed., *Byzantium in the Year 1000* (Leiden, 2003), 233–70; J. Baun, *Tales from Another Byzantium: Celestial Journey and Local Community in the Medieval Greek Apocrypha* (Cambridge, 2007). For a recent overview, see A. Timotin, 'Byzantine Visionary Accounts of the Other World: A Reconsideration', in J. Burke et al., eds, *Byzantine Narrative. Papers in Honour of Roger Scott* (Melbourne, 2006), 404–20.

[2] See the articles collected in A. Cameron and L. Conrad, eds, *The Byzantine and Early Islamic Near East* I: *Problems in the Literary Source Material*, Studies in Late Antiquity and Early Islam 1 (Princeton, NJ, 1992). Byzantine prophetic literature also flourished: see, for example, C. Mango, 'The Legend of Leo the Wise', *Zbornik Radova Vizantološkog Instituta* 6 (1960), 59–93; repr. in idem, *Byzantium and its image* (London 1984), essay 16.

of the Anastasis or of the Last Judgement from the later Byzantine period. The publication of the papers delivered at the symposium on 'Views on Death' in *Dumbarton Oaks Papers* 55 (2001), for example, contains not a single article on Byzantine visual imagery – an almost unheard-of state of affairs for that journal.

Though there are excellent articles on early symbolic visual references to heaven, one synthetic study on the theme of Christ's descent into Hades, and some notable publications of specific monuments,[3] there is no comprehensive overview of Byzantine visualizations of the end. For this reason, I will start with a brief survey of what material we have, and then turn to the questions that these works pose: first, why Byzantine representations of the other world were so limited; and, second, how and why Byzantine images of heaven and hell changed over time. I will conclude with a consideration of shifting social responses – as visualized in Byzantine painting – to the afterlife.

As noted, images of the transition to the afterlife are far more common in Byzantium than images of the afterlife itself. Four basic formulae have been identified: the lament of mourners around the deathbed; the funeral procession; the entombment; and the funeral ceremony itself.[4] The deathbed scene showed family or companions clustered round the bed of the dying person, and remained consistently familiar in the Byzantine world, as is clear from two miniatures painted nearly 400 years apart. The first is from a ninth-century manuscript made in Constantinople (figure 1); the second is a late thirteenth-century manuscript made in Trebizond (figure 2). In the earlier image, we see Gorgonia, the sister of Gregory of Nazianzus, as she whispers her dying words ('I will lie down in peace', from Psalm 4: 8) to Gregory of Nyssa, while her family stands at the foot of the bed, her mother covering her face in grief.[5] The image tells us that, in death, Gorgonia's

---

[3] See, for example, B. Brenk, 'Die Anfänge der byzantinischen Weltgerichtsdarstellung', *Byzantinische Zeitschrift* 57 (1964), 106–26 and, despite its title, idem, 'The Imperial Heritage of Early Christian Art', in K. Weitzmann, ed., *Age of Spirituality: A Symposium* (New York, 1980), 39–52; A. Kartsonis, *Anastasis, The Making of an Image* (Princeton, NJ, 1986); S. Der Nersessian, 'Program and Iconography of the Frescoes of the Parecclesion', in P. Underwood, ed., *The Kariye Djami* 4 (Princeton, NJ, 1975), 303–49.

[4] See C. Walter, 'Biographical Scenes of the Three Hierarchs', *Revue des études byzantines* 36 (1978), 233-60; and idem, *Art and Ritual of the Byzantine Church* (London, 1982), 137–44, using slightly different terminology.

[5] Paris, Bibliothèque nationale de France, MS gr.510, fol. 43v, discussed and reproduced in L. Brubaker, *Vision and Meaning in Ninth-Century Byzantium: Image as Exegesis in the Homilies of Gregory of Nazianzus*, Cambridge Studies in Palaeography and Codicology 6 (Cambridge, 1999), 119–21.

Fig. 1 Paris, Bibliothèque nationale de France, MS gr.510, fol. 43v: Gregory and his family; funeral of Kaisarios; death of Gorgonia (courtesy of the Bibliothèque nationale de France).

Fig. 2 Venice, Hellenic Institute, MS 5, fol. 192r: Alexander the Great on his
deathbed (courtesy of the Hellenic Institute, Venice).

sanctity is assured: she has been given a holy confessor (Gregory of Nyssa), not recorded in the accompanying funeral oration, and her transition from life to death is accompanied by an appropriately liminal psalm verse.[6] In figure 2, we see Alexander the Great on his deathbed, surrounded by mourners, including his horse Bucephalus who, the text tells us, drenched his bed with tears.[7] We cannot expect Alexander to pray or have a Christian confessor, but his importance is nonetheless signalled by the extraordinary response of a mute beast to his death. Though these two examples date from the ninth and thirteenth centuries, deathbed scenes such as these appeared by the sixth century in Byzantium and were basically adaptations of pre-Christian Roman conventions.[8] In the tenth and twelfth centuries respectively they became associated with the Virgin Mary and Christ. Scenes of the 'going-to-sleep' of the Virgin – *dormitio* in Latin, *koimesis* in Greek – which draw on this tradition, first appear in the tenth century;[9] while ritualized scenes of the lament over Christ's body (the *threnos*) appear in the twelfth, after which they went on to have a pronounced impact on western art.[10]

Funeral processions also appeared early in Byzantine imagery, and, again, they were adapted from Roman depictions. The ninth-century example in figure 1 – the funeral procession of the brother of Gregory of Nazianzus – is one of the latest preserved Byzantine depictions of the event,[11] which by the tenth century was largely replaced by images of the entombment and, especially, of the funeral ceremony itself. Representations of the entombment had, however, surfaced already by the

6   On the rare use of quotations in the inscriptions of this manuscript, and their significance, see L. Brubaker, 'When Pictures Speak: The Incorporation of Dialogue in the Miniatures of Paris.gr.510', *Word & Image* 12 (1996), 94–109.

7   Venice, Hellenic Institute, MS 5, fol. 192r, reproduced in N. Trahoulias, *The Greek Alexander Romance, Venice Hellenic Institute Codex gr. 5* (Athens 1997), 433.

8   See Walter, *Art and Ritual*, 139–40.

9   A. P. Kazhdan et al., *The Oxford Dictionary of Byzantium*, 3 vols (Oxford, 1991), 1: 651–53, with additional bibliography, to which should be added S. Mimouni, *Dormition et assomption de Marie, Histoire des traditions anciennes*, Théologie historique 98 (Paris, 1995) and B. Daley, ' "At the Hour of our Death": Mary's Dormition and Christian Dying in Late Patristic and Early Byzantine Literature', *DOP* 55 (2001), 71–89.

10   K. Weitzmann, 'The Origin of the Threnos', in M. Meiss, ed., *De Artibus Opuscula XL. Essays in Honor of Erwin Panofsky* (New York, 1961), 476–90, remains the classic study. Giotto's much-vaunted Lamentation at the Arena Chapel is a straight crib from Byzantine images of the *threnos*.

11   See Walter, *Art and Ritual*, 137–38. For another example from the same manuscript (Paris, MS gr.510, fol. 104r), see Brubaker, *Vision and Meaning*, 137–41.

sixth century, and in the oldest representations Old Testament figures are entombed in caves or chapels.[12] In the ninth century, for the first time, Christ was shown entombed (figure 3): in the Khludov Psalter (843–47), for example, Joseph of Arimathaea and Nicodemus convey his body into a roughly hewn tomb carved into the hillside.[13] This new emphasis on Christ's death stressed his human nature, which was important in ninth-century Byzantium in the aftermath of Iconoclasm, the debate about the validity of religious portraiture that occupied the empire from roughly 720 until 843.[14] The pro-image faction, which won, argued that it was Christ's human nature that allowed the Godhead to be seen and thus depicted, and so representations of Christ that stressed his humanity were favoured ever after in Byzantium.[15]

After the ninth century, however, representations of the entombment in cave-tombs are rarely found except for scenes of Christ's burial (very sacred representations are nearly always exceptionally conservative in their iconography in Byzantium); instead, figures are shown being laid out in large coffins or sarcophagi. Figure 4 shows the laying out of Gregory of Nazianzus, and actually conflates elements of the laying out with elements of the funeral service: the youth on our left lowers Gregory's feet into the sarcophagus; the middle aged man on our right lowers the saint's head (held firmly by the halo); while the grey-bearded man in the centre censes the body. To have the three ages of man so carefully delineated here is extremely unusual, but presumably this should be understood as an attempt to link the life cycle with its conclusion, death.[16] Conflations of the deathbed scene or the

---

[12] See, for example, the sixth-century Vienna Genesis (Vienna, Österreichische Nationalbibliothek, MS theol.gr.31), reproduced in the facsimile volume of H. Gerstinger, *Die Wiener Genesis* (Vienna, 1931).

[13] Moscow, Gosudarstvennyi istoricheskii muzei (State Historical Museum), cod. 129, fol. 87r, reproduced in the facsimile volume M. Ščepkina, *Miniaturi Khludovskoi Psalt'iri* (Moscow, 1977). For another, slightly later, example, see Paris, MS gr.510, fol. 30v, discussed and reproduced in Brubaker, *Vision and Meaning*, 297–99.

[14] The bibliography on Iconoclasm is immense. The most recent overviews are, from a theological perspective, C. Barber, *Figure and Likeness: On the Limits of Representation in Byzantine Iconoclasm* (Princeton, NJ, 2002), and, from a cultural and historical perspective, L. Brubaker and J. Haldon, *Byzantium in the Era of Iconoclasm* (Cambridge, 2009).

[15] The patriarch Germanos (715–30) was an early exponent of this point, the implications of which were first explored by J. Martin, 'The Dead Christ on the Cross in Byzantine Art', in K. Weitzmann, ed., *Late Classical and Mediaeval Studies in Honor of Albert Mathias Friend Jr* (Princeton, NJ, 1955), 189–96.

[16] Paris, MS gr.510, fol. 452r, discussed and reproduced in Brubaker, *Vision and Meaning*, 136–37. See also E. Sears, *The Ages of Man: Medieval Interpretations of the Life Cycle* (Princeton, NJ, 1986), 90–94.

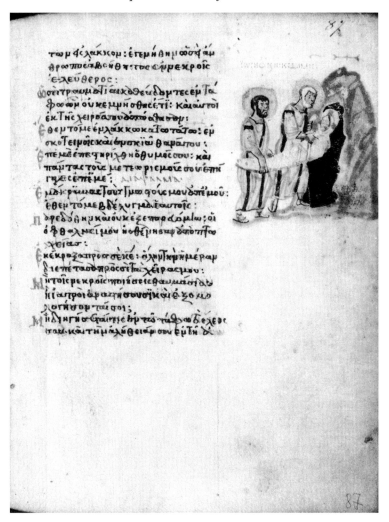

Fig. 3 Moscow (Gosudarstvennyi istoricheskii muzei (State Historical
Museum), gr. 129, fol. 87r: entombment of Christ (courtesy of the State
Historical Museum, Moscow).

Fig. 4 Paris, Bibliothèque nationale de France, MS gr.510, fol. 452r (detail):
funeral of Gregory of Nazianzus
(courtesy of the Bibliothèque nationale de France).

Fig. 5 Constantinople, Chora Monastery, Koimesis of the Virgin
(Copyright Dumbarton Oaks, Washington, DC).

entombment with the funerary service occur with increasing frequency
in later Byzantine imagery: for example, the *koimesis* of the Virgin at the
Chora monastery in Constantinople (1316–21) joins elements of the
deathbed scene with accoutrements of the funeral service such as the
figures swinging a censer and presenting the funerary liturgy (figure 5).
    Images of the afterlife are more restricted: there are a scant handful
of images of the second coming; even fewer of parables set in heaven
such as the story of Lazarus and the rich man; and a sprinkling of other
scenes, most notably a sequence connecting the Virgin with the fate of
dead souls. Three themes account for the vast majority of images,
however: prophetic visions; the Anastasis (which became known in the
west as Christ in limbo); and the Last Judgement. We will skim through

the 'occasional' scenes – which are of course particularly interesting precisely because they are so unusual – and then turn to prophetic visions, the Anastasis and the Judgement.

The depiction of Christ's second coming (*Parousia* in Greek) is derived from Matthew 25: 31–34: 'When the Son of Man comes in his glory and the angels with him, he will sit in state on his throne, with all the nations gathered before him .... Then the king will say to those on his right hand, "You have my father's blessings; come, enter and possess the kingdom that has been ready for you since the world was made."' The earliest image appears in a copy of the *Christian Topography* (figure 6), a sixth-century text that was copied and illustrated in Constantinople in the second half of the ninth century.[17] It shows Christ (the Son of Man), in glory, with angels below, and, in two tiers beneath them, the blessed (or 'the resurrected dead' as they are called in the accompanying text).[18]

This is an extremely unusual image, and it only appears in Byzantium (and its appendages) in other copies of, or excerpts from, the *Christian Topography* text, where the author argues that the world was shaped like the Ark of the Covenant – hence the arched form here – and pays particular attention to the second coming, which introduces what he calls the 'second condition'. The passage that introduces this miniature reads:

> Except in the second condition, neither the angels nor men enter heaven. Only the Lord Christ, raised from the dead, has entered it as a precursor for us, as long as the present condition still lasts, giving to you the assurance that, just as he entered heaven, so too all of you will take your place in the ascending hierarchy under his rule. May you judge us worthy, O friend of men, us who are under your rule and believe in you.[19]

Later Byzantines, who knew perfectly well that the world was round, and not shaped like the Ark of the Covenant, ridiculed this text but

[17] Vatican City, Biblioteca Apostolica Vaticana, MS Vat.gr. 699, fol. 89r. On this image, see H. Kessler, 'Gazing into the Future: The *Parousia* Miniature in Vatican gr. 699', in C. Moss and K. Kiefer, eds, *Byzantine East, Latin West: Art Historical Studies in Honor of Kurt Weitzmann* (Princeton, NJ, 1995) 365–75.

[18] Book 7.94: W. Wolska-Conus, ed. and trans., *Cosmas Indicopleustès, Topographie chrétienne* III, SC 197 (Paris, 1973), 162–63.

[19] Book 5.247: W. Wolska-Conus, ed. and trans., *Cosmas Indicopleustès, Topographie chrétienne* II, SC 159 (Paris, 1970), 358–59. See Kessler, 'Gazing into the Future', esp. 366, whence the English translation.

Fig. 6 Vatican City, Biblioteca Apostolica Vaticana, MS Vat.gr.699, fol. 89r:
second coming of Christ (courtesy of the Biblioteca Apostolica Vaticana).

nonetheless copied it, often in luxurious formats. There are a number
of reasons for this,[20] but the point of importance to us here is that this is
an unusual image, made to further the ideas of a strange text. It is nonetheless interesting for a number of reasons, most notably, for our
purposes, because it shows graphically just how hierarchical Byzantine
eschatological systems were.

The parable of Lazarus and the rich man (Luke 16: 19–31) appears as

---

[20] On which, see L. Brubaker, 'The Christian Topography (Vat.gr.699) Revisited: Image,
Text, and Conflict in Ninth-Century Byzantium', in E. Jeffreys, ed., *Byzantine Style, Religion
and Civilisation: In Honour of Sir Steven Runciman* (Cambridge, 2006), 3–24.

Fig. 7 Paris, Bibliothèque nationale de France, MS gr.510, fol. 149r (detail):
parable of Lazarus and the rich man
(courtesy of the Bibliothèque nationale de France).

a narrative sequence in one Byzantine manuscript, a ninth-century
copy of the *Homilies* of Gregory of Nazianzus (figure 7), where it illustrates the sermon 'On the Love of the Poor'.[21] According to Luke, the
rich man 'fared sumptuously every day' and Lazarus lay outside his
gates 'desiring to be fed with the crumbs which fell from the rich man's
table'. Here, the rich man, identified by an inscription, is shown
wearing purple, as Luke describes him, but on horseback rather than at
table – this is not unusual in this manuscript, where men are constantly
shown riding horses in scenes where they have no real business to,
probably because the recipient of the book was a noted rider.[22] In any

[21] Paris, MS gr.510, fol. 149r (Brubaker, *Vision and Meaning*, 131–32); PG 35: 857–909 (the
parable appears at 904 B14–C3).
[22] Ibid.

event, the rich man rides toward Lazarus, who reclines on the grass, while – as Luke says – a dog licks his sores. Lazarus then dies, as represented by a mummy laid out on the hillside; and Luke tells us that he 'was carried by the angels into Abraham's bosom', as we see below.[23] The rich man also dies, and we see him, in the upper left, laid out on a bier attended by two mourners. Below this, the rich man sits in hell,[24] lifts his eyes 'and seeth Abraham afar off, and Lazarus in his bosom'. He points to his parched mouth, requesting water. Abraham refuses, saying 'Son, remember that thou in thy lifetime receivedst thy good things, and likewise Lazarus evil things: but now he is comforted, and thou art tormented. And beside all this, between us and you there is a great gulf fixed: so that they which would pass from hence to you cannot; neither can they pass to us that would come from thence'. The divide between the elect and the damned is carefully emphasized in this image, with the painter grouping the scenes from Lazarus's life, death and afterlife on the right, in contrast with the rich man's life, death and afterlife on the left.

This careful composition finds only faint echoes elsewhere in Byzantium,[25] and all other pictorial examples of the episode (of which there are not many) are restricted to a depiction of the rich man gesturing for water as he looks at Lazarus reclining in the bosom of Abraham.[26] The expansive ninth-century miniature forms part of a manuscript to which we have referred consistently, a copy of Gregory's *Homilies* commissioned by the patriarch Photius, perhaps the greatest scholar Byzantium ever produced, for the emperor Basil I (867–86).[27] It is full of unprecedented images, and so, as with the image of the second coming – in another ninth-century manuscript, but one that was almost certainly produced in the same circle as this one[28] – we once again have an unusual image, or in this case sequence of images, composed for an unusual manuscript.

The same is true of our final anomalous sequence, which appears in

[23] The scene is inscribed 'Lazarus on the bosom of Abraham'.
[24] As we are told by the inscription: Ο ΠΛΟΥCΙΟC ΕΝ ΤΗ ΚΑΜΙΝΩ.
[25] See J. M. Plotzek, 'Lazarus, Armer', in E. Kirschbaum, ed., *Lexikon der christlichen Ikonographie* III (Rome, 1971), 31-33.
[26] See, for example, Florence, Biblioteca Mediceo-Laurenziana, MS Laur. plut. 6.23, fol. 144r, reproduced in T. Velmans, *Le Tétraévangile de la Laurentienne*, Bibliothèque des cahiers archéologiques 6 (Paris, 1971), fig. 243.
[27] Brubaker, *Vision and Meaning*, 201–38.
[28] Ibid. 113.

two manuscripts of sermons about the Virgin Mary written in the twelfth century by the monk James of the Kokkinobaphos monastery.[29] The second sermon, 'On the Nativity of the Virgin', traces the story of humanity's fall and redemption through the Virgin's willingness to bear Christ. James weaves together the biblical story of Adam and Eve and an account of Mary's birth and childhood, arguing that humanity was condemned until Mary arrived, and that the righteous gained salvation through her son. There is a whole narrative sequence of the fall of Adam and Eve, and then James writes, 'For death ruled from Adam to Moses, even over the sinless ones', and he describes them in Hades asking each newcomer whether there is any news of their future saviour.[30] Figure 8 shows the bright realm of the angels contrasted with the dark kingdom of Hades, which is divided into three sections. Adam and Eve occupy the top storey (though in fact James very unusually blames Adam for the fall and does not even mention Eve in this section of the text); the 'sinless ones' – an all male, and clothed, group – appear against a slightly lighter background; and the sinners, sexless and unclad, are prodded into their black space by two more angels. New members join each group: the sinless soul, represented (as is common in middle and late Byzantine imagery) as a child, is carried forth in an angel's arms; the new sinners, undifferentiated from the habitués, are hurried forward by two additional angels. However, though Byzantine texts about death and the afterlife insist that all people are alike when they go to meet their maker, the sinless and the sinners are clearly differentiated here.

The next stage in the narrative is Mary's procession to the temple, led by a convoy of candle-bearing prophets and patriarchs and followed by her parents.[31] Below, angels announce the event to the souls in Hades, who rise up from their sarcophagi and rejoice, because they

[29] Vatican City, MS Vat.gr.1162, and Paris, MS gr.1208, reproduced in I. Hutter and P. Canart, *Das Marienhomiliar des Mönches Jakobos von Kokkinobaphos, codex Vaticanus graecus 1162*, Codices e Vaticanis selecti 79 (Vatican City, 1991); C. Stornajolo, *Miniature della Omilie di Giacomo Monaco (cod.Vatic.gr.1162) e dell'Evangeliario greco Urbinate (cod.Vatic.Urbin.gr.2)*, Codices e Vaticanis selecti, series minor 1 (Rome, 1910); H. Omont, 'Miniatures des homélies sur la Vierge du moine Jacques (MS grec 1208 de Paris)', *Bulletin de la Société française de reproductions de manuscrits à peintures* 11 (1927), 1–24. The most recent study is K. Linardou's as yet unpublished Ph. D. dissertation, 'Reading two Byzantine Illustrated Books: the Kokkinobaphos Manuscripts (Vaticanus graecus 1162 and Parisinus graecus 1208) and their Illustration' (University of Birmingham, 2004).

[30] Linardou, 'Reading two Byzantine Illustrated Books', 43–46.

[31] Vatican City, MS Vat.gr.1162, fol. 62v; Paris, MS gr.1208, fol. 80r: Linardou, 'Reading two Byzantine Illustrated Books', 80–82.

Fig. 8 Paris, Bibliothèque nationale de France, MS gr.1208, fol. 41r: realm of the angels and Hades (courtesy of the Bibliothèque nationale de France).

Fig. 9 Paris, Bibliothèque nationale de France, MS gr.1208, fol. 66v:
Christ enters Hades; Christ leaves Hades; the Virgin Mary, Adam, Eve
(courtesy of the Bibliothèque nationale de France).

know that Mary's coming will lead to their salvation. Many are recognizable and are identified: Adam and Eve are now among the sinless, or at least among those who anticipate resurrection.

As James comes to the end of his sermon, he has Adam speak for all the patriarchs in Hades and praise Mary: 'O daughter, what an offshoot has shot up from our pains of childbirth!'[32] Through her, James explains, death has been defeated and paradise has been re-opened for the righteous. The miniature plays this out in a visual narrative (figure 9). Once again, heaven/paradise is bright and on the right hand of God (our left), in contrast to the darkness of Hades. In the top register Christ enters Hades, breaking down the door and trampling Hades; naked and sexless souls raise their arms in supplication but are held back by an angel. In the middle zone Christ leaves Hades, taking the righteous with him, amongst them Adam, Eve and John the Baptist, who holds a scroll inscribed 'Behold the Lamb of God' (John 1: 29); more souls appear in the lowest tier. From this miniature it would appear that – at least in these manuscripts – the sinless are identifiable and clothed, while sinners are anonymous, sexless, and naked. Finally, in the lower left, we see Mary enthroned, with Eve (in red) prostrate at her feet; Adam stands behind her, gesturing in speech: his words – 'O daughter, what an offshoot has shot up from our pains of childbirth!' – follow immediately below the miniature.

The final scene shows Mary, labelled the 'container of the uncontainable', a popular epithet for the Virgin in the later Byzantine period, enthroned, and flanked by glorifying angels, in the garden of paradise, with the Old Testament prophets who have been saved by Christ's advent below.[33] As with the previous scene, this composition finds vague earlier parallels,[34] but its role as a visual conclusion to a sermon worked out in words and in images is unprecedented. The sequence is also an excellent introduction to representations of heaven and hell, and of the sinless and the sinful, in Byzantium.

Unlike the Parousia in the *Christian Topography*, the parable of Lazarus and the rich man in the *Homilies* of Gregory of Nazianzus, and the *majestas Mariae* in the Kokkinobaphos manuscripts, prophetic

---

[32] Vatican City, MS Vat.gr.1162, fol. 48v; Paris, MS gr.1208, fol. 66v: Linardou, 'Reading two Byzantine Illustrated Books', 63–65.

[33] Vatican City, MS Vat.gr.1162, fol. 50v; Paris, MS gr.1208, fol. 69v: Linardou, 'Reading two Byzantine Illustrated Books', 66–68.

[34] In this case from the eleventh century: see Linardou, 'Reading two Byzantine Illustrated Books', 67 n. 3.

Fig. 10 Paris, Bibliothèque nationale de France, MS gr.1208, fol. 162r: Vision
of Isaiah (courtesy of the Bibliothèque nationale de France).

visions, the Anastasis and the Last Judgement were frequently depicted in Byzantium. The most common prophetic visions were those of Isaiah 6 and Ezekiel 1, but there are a few representations of Daniel's vision of the four empires (Daniel 7), and numerous generic images that combine aspects of Isaiah's and Ezekiel's visions to present a *majestas domini*.[35] These generic visions were especially common in the early Byzantine period (fifth to seventh century); specific visions, with identifiable protagonists, come to the fore in the ninth century and last until the end of the Byzantine empire in 1453.[36] Figure 10 shows Isaiah, at God's command, being fed a burning lump of coal by angels, to purify his lips (Isaiah 6: 6–7). God, represented as the Ancient of Days in our twelfth-century image, is enthroned and surrounded or flanked by the angelic host. We are meant to understand that the vision is of heaven, but few details are provided. This is true of all depictions of prophetic visions I know, and so they are not very useful for our purposes. The Anastasis is more profitably explored.

The Anastasis (Greek for resurrection) is the emblematic scene of hell in Byzantium (figure 11). Based (probably) on the apocryphal *Gospel of Nicodemus*, its first preserved appearance is in the mid-ninth century, and it is virtually ubiquitous thereafter.[37] It pictures Christ's descent into Hades during the three-day period between his death and his resurrection, to save the sinless souls awaiting his coming. In its basic format, it shows Christ, who has broken down the gates of Hades, rescuing Adam and Eve (always dressed in red[38]) by pulling Adam out of his sarcophagus. Often, other righteous dead are represented by the Old Testament kings David and Solomon; hell is a pit, with a gate.

This basic format became increasingly elaborated. At Nea Moni (the New Monastery) on the island of Chios, built at the order of Constantine IX Monomachos between 1042 and 1055, the pit of hell is flanked by mountains, and an anonymous throng of the righteous

35 C. Ihm, *Die Programme der christlichen Apsismalerei vom vierten Jahrhundert bis zur Mitte des achten Jahrhunderts*, Forschungen zur Kunstgeschichte und christlichen Archäologie 4 (Wiesbaden, 1960); D. Pallas, 'Eine Differenzierung unter den himmlischen Ordnungen (ikonographische Analyse)', *Byzantinische Zeitschrift* 64 (1971), 55-60; C. Belting-Ihm, 'Theophanic Images of Divine Majesty in Early Medieval Church Decoration', in W Tronzo, ed., *Italian Church Decoration of the Middle Ages and Early Renaissance: Functions, Forms and Regional Traditions*, Villa Spelman colloquia 1 (Baltimore, MD, 1989), 43–59.

36 See, for example, Brubaker, *Vision and Meaning*, 281–90, with bibliography.

37 Kartsonis, *Anastasis*.

38 See L. James, *Light and Colour in Byzantine Art* (Oxford, 1996), 103.

Fig. 11 Constantinople, Chora monastery, Anastasis
(Copyright Dumbarton Oaks, Washington, DC)

crowd behind Adam, Eve, David and Solomon.[39] Less than half a
century later, in the church at Daphni (just outside Athens), Adam and
Eve have moved to the favoured side with David and Solomon, and
John the Baptist, leading other prophets, has joined the righteous
souls.[40] Most interestingly, we have the new appearance of Hades
himself to the scene. His feet are fettered and he is half-clad – either
because our mosaicist is following the ancient pictorial convention of
depicting personifications partially clad, or because our artisan is
adapting the convention of showing sinners sexless and naked to a
sinful figure known (by the Byzantines) to be male. The most elaborate
Anastasis of all, an early fourteenth-century fresco in the Chora monastery at Constantinople (figure 11), contains all these elements, plus
additional figures (Abel is probably the youth leading the crowd on our
right), but Christ grasps both Adam and Eve, though they are now
divided, with Adam on Christ's favoured right side. We see an increasingly complex depiction of the righteous in hell, with only Satan as a

[39] D. Mouriki, *Nea Moni on Chios: The Mosaics* (Athens, 1986), pl. 48.
[40] E. Diez and O. Demus, *Byzantine Mosaics in Greece: Hosios Lucas and Daphni*
(Cambridge, 1931), fig. 100.

representative of the darker side of Hades. Images of the Last Judgement make up for this apparent lack.

I am not going to trace the visual history of Last Judgement scenes here, other than to say that the narrative does not really take off until the eleventh century.[41] Nor am I going to discuss the admittedly fascinating variations of urban Last Judgement imagery that appear in small village churches, especially in Greece, where the sinners are punished for rural crimes (such as moving boundary stones) that tell us a lot about rural life in the later Byzantine period: these have been the subject of several articles and are about to be the subject of a major book by Sharon Gerstel.[42] Instead, I am going to focus on one late, urban example: the Last Judgement sequence that is spread across the walls and ceiling of the side chapel of the Chora monastery in Constantinople, built and decorated between 1316 and 1321 by Theodore Metochites (figure 11).[43] The room was probably intended as his funerary chapel, so the iconography is particularly appropriate. The Last Judgement, appropriately enough, was painted on the chapel's ceiling.

In the centre of the ceiling, an angel unfurls the scroll of heaven; Christ sits in judgement with his heavenly court, while souls are evaluated by angels below. The righteous, fully clothed and clearly male, kneel to (our) left (Christ's right); the sinners, nude and sexless, are pushed into the river of fire by angels. Christ, backed by the angelic host, is flanked by the Virgin (on his favoured right side) and John the Baptist, who intercede with him on behalf of humanity. Lazarus, represented as a child, reposes in the bosom of Abraham, overlooking the torments of the damned. The saved are allowed through the gates of paradise, guarded by the fiery cherubim, and welcomed by the Good Thief, to whom Christ had promised admittance to paradise at the crucifixion.

Though more elaborate than many, this is nonetheless a fairly standard Last Judgement sequence, and corroborates several details speculated about above. The righteous wear clothes, and they are gendered (they are also, aside from Eve, all male, but that is a narrative for a different article); sinners are sexless and naked. Good souls in transition,

[41] For a brief overview, see Kazhdan et al., *Oxford Dictionary of Byzantium*, 2: 1181–82.

[42] See S. Gerstel, 'The Byzantine Village Church: Observations on its Location and on Agricultural Aspects of its Program', in J. Lefort, C. Morrisson and J.-P. Sodini, eds, *Les villages dans l'empire byzantin (IVᵉ–XVᵉ siècle)*, Réalités Byzantines 11 (Paris, 2005), 165–78.

[43] Underwood, ed., *Kariye Djami*; the Last Judgement sequence is closely studied in Der Nersessian, 'Frescoes of the Parecclesion'.

as we saw in the Kokkinobaphos manuscripts (and in images of the Koimesis of the Virgin), are represented as children, as is Lazarus in the bosom of Abraham. Heaven is a garden; hell is a black pit, punctuated by rivers of fire. Late Byzantine representations of the Last Judgement such as this one display a set of conventions associated with images of the afterlife, most of which do not appear in earlier Byzantine images. What can we conclude?

In the late antique / early Byzantine period, there are numerous texts about death and the afterlife, but very few representations. Admittedly, there is not much imagery preserved from the fourth to the seventh centuries, but, as Beat Brenk demonstrated,[44] there are a number of symbolic representations of the afterlife (mostly on sarcophagi) and there are a handful of images of funeral processions or scenes of entombment.

It is in the ninth century that we start to find more representations, and also indications that responses to death and the afterlife are shifting. Except for representations of Christ's burial, entombment in caves is replaced by burial in sarcophagi: so far as I am aware, this is not because burial practices changed dramatically, but rather because rituals of death – like all other Byzantine rituals – became increasingly regulated during the ninth and tenth centuries. Funeral processions continue to be depicted, but drop out of visual fashion by the tenth century; again, this is not because funeral processions ceased in Byzantium but instead corresponds to a shift from representing the funerary rites of 'ordinary' people (like Gregory of Nazianzus's brother and sister) to concentrating on the Virgin, Christ, and special saints (for example, St Nicholas, who comes to the fore in the ninth century, and whose laying out in a sarcophagus is represented on most of the many middle and late Byzantine icons that show scenes from his life).[45]

Prophetic visions, the Anastasis, and the Last Judgement were, as noted earlier, the most commonly represented visualizations of the afterlife in Byzantium. Early representations of prophetic visions were, however, normally (though not always) generic; they only ubiquitously turn historic in the ninth century.[46] And there were no early Byzantine

[44] Brenk, 'Die Anfänge der byzantinischen Weltgerichtsdarstellung'; idem, 'Imperial Heritage'.
[45] On Nicholas, see N. Patterson Ševčenko, *The Life of Saint Nicholas in Byzantine Art* (Turin, 1983); eadem, 'Canon and Calendar: The Role of a Ninth-Century Hymnographer in Shaping the Celebration of Saints', in L. Brubaker, ed., *Byzantium in the Ninth Century: Dead or Alive?* (Aldershot, 1998), 101–14.
[46] See the references in notes 35–36 above.

representations of the Anastasis: while it is just possible that the iconography was developed in the late seventh or eighth century, our earliest preserved examples date to the ninth, and the classic formulation is a tenth- or eleventh-century invention.[47] Last Judgement imagery, like prophetic visions, appears in the early Byzantine period, but usually in symbolic form;[48] the narrative is latent until the eleventh century. So we are really looking at a relatively late development, albeit one that – at least in the case of the Anastasis, which became a major church feast in the tenth century[49] – became immensely popular.

In terms of funerary scenes, we see a tightening of the genre, and perhaps the increased impact of liturgical practice, across the ninth century. In terms of envisioning the afterlife, we see more or less the exact opposite, with a shift from generic and symbolic to particular and narrative, beginning in the ninth century but only really taking off in the eleventh and twelfth. The difference is that funerals are of this world; the afterlife, obviously, is not. But it was increasingly made recognizable – in part by incorporating it in elaborate visual and literary stories (and it is worth remembering that the Kokkinobaphos visual narratives about the Virgin are also, of course, written narratives, and they are matched by a variety of unillustrated texts about the afterlife: the various apocalyptic texts that appeared in such number across the tenth and eleventh centuries, and proto-novels like the twelfth-century *Timarion*[50]). The afterlife was also made recognizable by establishing a set of visual conventions, as has been outlined above: the dressed male is righteous and saved, the naked sexless being is a sinner. In one way or another, what we see from the ninth/tenth century on, and especially from the eleventh/twelfth, is the ordinary being made 'strange', and the strange being made familiar. To us, the afterlife is a distant country; to the Byzantines, it looked increasingly like home – an admittedly dysfunctional, not to mention patriarchal, home, but recognizable nonetheless.

University of Birmingham

---

[47] Kartsonis, *Anastasis*, 40–67, 165–203.

[48] Brenk, 'Die Anfänge der byzantinischen Weltgerichtsdarstellung'.

[49] Kartsonis, *Anastasis*, 177–85.

[50] Baun, *Tales from Another Byzantium*; R. Romano, ed., *Pseudo-Luciano, Timarione* (Naples, 1974); ET in B. Baldwin, *Timarion* (Detroit, MI, 1984).

THE AFTERLIFE OF BISHOP ADHÉMAR OF LE PUY

by CONOR KOSTICK

My brothers should not grieve that my life has come to an end, because never was I so useful to them in the past as I will be in the future, providing they are willing to keep the commandments of God. As a matter of fact I, and all my brothers whose life has ended as mine has, will stay with them, and I will appear and give them much better advice than hitherto.[1]

BISHOP Adhémar of Le Puy was the papal legate appointed to journey on the First Crusade (1096–99) by Pope Urban II.[2] Adhémar led a sizeable contingent of troops and non-combatants from Provence in the company of the elderly crusader Count Raymond IV of Toulouse. The bishop distinguished himself at one of the critical battles of the First Crusade, that near Dorylaeum (1 July 1097). Adhémar played what was perhaps an even more critical role in helping prevent the disintegration of the crusade during its lowest moment. Although the Christian army captured Antioch at night on 3 June 1098, within five days they had themselves become the besieged, with the arrival of an enormous Muslim army under the command of Kerbogha, *atabeg* (governor) of Mosul. Many prominent knights abandoned the crusade, letting themselves down over the walls of the city at night on

---

[1] Raymond of Aguilers, *Historia Francorum qui ceperunt Iherusalem*, ed. John France (unpublished Ph. D. thesis, University of Nottingham, 1967), 139 (PL 155: 620B): 'Et ne doleant, fratres mei, si ego vitam finivi, quoniam nunquam eis profui tantum quantum prodero, si praecepta Dei servare voluerint. Etenim cum illis habitabo, et omnes fratres mei qui vitam, ut ego, finierunt; et eis apparebo, et multo melius quam hactenus consiliabor eos.' I am grateful to Professor France for permission to quote from his thesis, which I consider a superior edition to those of the *Recueil des historiens des croisades: Historiens occidentaux*, 5 vols (Paris, 1844–95), 3: 235–309; *Le 'Liber' de Raymond d'Aguilers*, eds J. H. Hill and L. L. Hill (Paris, 1969); and that in PL 155: 591–668A, to which, nevertheless, references are also given here, as they are more accessible than the thesis.

[2] For the role of Bishop Adhémar of Le Puy and his authority on the First Crusade, see J. H. Hill and L. L. Hill, 'Contemporary Accounts and the Later Representation of Adhémar, Bishop of Le Puy', *Medievalia et Humanistica* 8 (1955), 30–38; J. A. Brundage, 'Adhémar of Puy: the Bishop and his Critics', *Speculum* 34 (1959), 201–12; H. E. Mayer, 'Zur Beurteilung Adhémars von Le Puy', *Deutsches Archiv für Erforschung des Mittelalters* 16 (1960), 547–52; I. S. Robinson, *The Papacy 1073–1198* (Cambridge, 1990), 350–52.

ropes. The papal legate was a key figure in addressing this panic, rallying the princes to make them swear an oath that they would not abandon the expedition. The victory of the Christian forces on 28 June 1098 should have secured Adhémar's position as the most authoritative figure on the crusade, but a plague that subsequently broke out in the city took his life on 1 August.

Surprisingly, however, this was not the end of Adhémar's involvement in the leadership of the First Crusade, at least in the sense that he was popularly believed by the crusaders to have returned to them to offer advice and to intercede for them with God. A contemporary account of Adhémar's experience of the afterlife comes from the hand of a crusading priest, Raymond of Aguiliers. Raymond was a member of the chaplaincy of Count Raymond of Toulouse, raised to the priesthood during the expedition. Crucially, he shared a tent with the key intermediary between this world and the next, a lowly visionary, Peter Bartholomew.

Peter Bartholomew was a servant who had risen to extraordinary prominence during the crusade, by declaring that the saints Andrew and Peter had visited him. He claimed that they had shown him the location of the Lance that had pierced Christ's side. Although sceptical, not least because, as Colin Morris has shown,[3] Adhémar would have known that the Byzantines claimed to have the same relic at Constantinople, the legate nevertheless utilized popular enthusiasm for the relic in order to bring about a successful mobilization of the army against the *atabeg* of Mosul on 28 June 1098. The crusade as a whole included many who were sceptical about the visions of Peter Bartholomew. But he had strong support amongst the poor and, in the aftermath of a victory against Kerbogha that seemed miraculous, even the senior princes legitimized the visionary. A letter they wrote to Pope Urban II emphasized the part played by the Holy Lance in the success of the Christian army.[4]

On 3 August 1098, the night after the burial of Adhémar, Peter Bartholomew claimed that the legate had visited him in the chapel of

[3] C. Morris, 'Policy and Visions: The Case of the Holy Lance at Antioch', in J. Gillingham and J. C. Holt, eds, *War and Government in the Middle Ages: Essays in Honour of J. O. Prestwich* (Woodbridge, 1984), 33–45.

[4] Letter of Bohemond and the other princes to Pope Urban II, in H. Hagenmeyer, ed., *Epistulae et chartae ad historiam primi belli sacri spectantes quae supersunt aevo aequales ac genuinae: Die Kreuzzugsbriefe aus den Jahren 1088–1100* (Innsbruck, 1901), 163.

Count Raymond of Toulouse. In the vision, Adhémar explained that he had been in hell for the period between his death and his burial due to his lack of belief in the Holy Lance. While burning in the flames of hell, the bishop was relieved by the Lord himself, who presented Adhémar with a robe that protected him from the fire. The robe was that which the legate had given away to a poor person on the occasion of his ordination as bishop of Le Puy.

Adhémar explained that a candle, offered in prayer by the bishop's friends, and three denarii that the legate himself had given as alms in the name of the Holy Lance were the most effective items in restoring him as he departed hell. The legate had a message for Bohemond I, prince of Taranto and one of the crusade's senior princes: he was not required to fulfil a vow to take the body of the bishop to Jerusalem. Adhémar then committed his *familia* (his following) to Count Raymond of Toulouse, whose services to them would be rewarded by God. Adhémar explained that none should grieve at his death, because he would stay with them, offering better advice than previously. Those who doubted should open the bishop's tomb where they would see that his face had been entirely burned. The vision of the legate concluded with a warning to all to fear the punishments of hell and a number of practical commands, including one that the Count of Toulouse, together with those of his choosing, appoint a new bishop of Le Puy.[5]

What can we learn of the contemporary concept of the afterlife from this report? Most notably, we see that there was no neutral space in which the dead bishop resided, no place of purgatory, although there was a purging process.[6] Until he returned to earth to be with and to guide the crusade, Adhémar was in hell. The main reason for this was the fact that he had expressed reservations about the authenticity of the Lance and was therefore punished. Nevertheless, Adhémar's experience in hell was mediated by both his own past actions and those of the living in a manner that prefigures the development of indulgences. It was the prayers of those who paid for a candle for him and his own contribution for the sake of the Lance that restored Adhémar. It was an act of charity to the poor, the giving away of a robe, which led to Christ himself returning the robe and preventing all harm but for burns to the

---

[5] Raymond of Aguilers, *Historia Francorum*, ed. France, 138–40 (PL 155: 0619D). The see of Le Puy was not filled until 1102, when Pons de Tournon was appointed.

[6] For the wider context to this issue, see n. 22 below.

face that, according to Adhémar's confession, had rightfully been earned through his scepticism regarding the Lance.

Some nine months later, in April 1099, Count Raymond of Toulouse held up the crusade with a deeply unpopular effort to besiege the city of 'Arqa. By this time the visionary, Peter Bartholomew, was expressing near-uncritical support for the goals of Count Raymond, and this cost him his life. Arnulf, chaplain to Robert I, Count of Normandy, challenged the authenticity of the Lance and the visions of Peter Bartholomew,[7] leading to a dramatic trial by fire and the eventual death of Peter. In his extensive reporting of this episode, three more references to the afterlife of Bishop Adhémar were detailed by the historian Raymond of Aguilers.

Raymond wrote that in the debate about the authenticity of the Lance the legate visited another Provençal priest, Peter Desiderius,[8] who recalled:

> I saw the bishop of Le Puy after his death and the blessed Nicholas with him, and after saying many things the bishop said this to me: 'I am in a choir with the blessed Nicholas, but because I doubted the Lance of the Lord, I, who in particular ought to have believed, was led to Hell. And there the hair on the right of my head and half my beard was burned. And although I am not suffering punishment, nevertheless, I cannot see God clearly until my hairs and beard grow back as they were.'[9]

This time Adhémar was portrayed as visiting the crusaders, rather than being invisible amongst them. His true celestial home was given as being among a chorus with St Nicholas. The association of Nicholas,

[7] For Arnulf, chaplain to Robert I, Duke of Normandy, before becoming Patriarch of Jerusalem in 1099 and again from 1112 to 1115, see R. Foreville, 'Un chef de la première croisade: Arnulf Malecouronne', *Bulletin philologique et historique du comité des travaux historiques et scientifiques, 1953–1954* (1955), 377–90. See also B. Hamilton, *The Latin Church in the Crusader States* (London, 1980), 12–13.

[8] For references to Peter Desiderius, see J. Riley-Smith, *The First Crusaders* (Cambridge, 1997), 216.

[9] Raymond of Aguilers, *Historia Francorum*, ed. France, 230–31 (PL 155: 639A–B): 'Ego vidi post obitum eius episcopum Podiensem et beatum Nicolaum cum eo, et post multa alia, dixit mihi episcopus haec "Ego sum in uno choro cum beato Nicolao, sed quia de lancea Domini dubitavi, qui maxime credere debuissem, deductus sum in infernum, ibique capilli mei ex hac parte capitis dextera, et medietas barbae combusta est, et licet in poena non sim, tamen clare Deum videre non potero, donec capilli et barba sicut ante fuerant, mihi succreverint." '

the fourth-century bishop of Myra (south-west Turkey), with the crusade is probably connected to the translation of the saint's relics to the southern Italian port of Bari in 1087. A new church to house the relics was being built at the time of the crusade, and Pope Urban II held a council there in 1098. Interestingly, some of the sculptures of the church at Bari match exactly those of a frieze at the abbey of Saint-Gilles, Gard.[10] Count Raymond of Toulouse was also count of Saint-Gilles, suggesting that the appearance of Nicholas in this vision might be due to something more than the growing popularity of the fourth-century saint. It seems as though there might have been a specific Provençal interest in the presence of Nicholas's relics at Bari.

Likewise, the Normans of southern Italy held St Nicholas in such great veneration that after the victory of the First Crusade over Kerbogha, *atabeg* of Mosul (28 June 1098), Bohemond I of Taranto, the leader of the Italian Normans, sent a pious donation to the church of St Nicholas at Bari, namely Kerbogha's tent.[11] Across a broad spectrum of crusaders, then, it would have seemed appropriate that Adhémar was now keeping the company of St Nicholas.

The vision of Peter Desiderius again portrayed Adhémar as having suffered burns in hell for having doubted the authenticity of the Lance and added the further punishment that the legate was not to be allowed to see God until his beard and hair had regrown. As with the vision of Peter Bartholomew, there was no special place where the consequences of sin could be remitted, no purgatory, but there was a sense that the afterlife had rewards or punishments that were not absolute judgements: one's condition could be altered.

There is a paradox here between the idea of eternal life and having a corporeal nature, that is, a body that grows older. But this paradox would have been more evident to the Scholastic theologians of the next generation than to the clergy on the First Crusade. Raymond of Aguilers, addressing the popular element among the crusaders, was no dialectician. For him, to judge by the fact that the celestial Adhémar expected his hair and beard to grow in the same manner as if he were still alive, the passage of time in the afterlife directly matched human experience.

---

[10] A. Kingsley, 'Bari, Modena and St.-Gilles', *The Burlington Magazine for Connoisseurs* 43: 245 (August 1923), 58–67.

[11] 'Historia belli sacri', in *Recueil des historiens des croisades: Historiens occidentaux*, 5 vols (Paris, 1844–95), 3: 206.

The second reference to the afterlife of Adhémar that emerged in the debate about the authenticity of the Holy Lance and the visions of Peter Bartholomew was a report by Raymond of Aguilers that, while sick in Antioch in the summer of 1098, a priest and member of the following of Adhémar, the otherwise unknown Bertrand of Le Puy, saw the legate. Accompanying the Bishop of Le Puy was Heraclius,[12] his standard-bearer, who had been struck in the face by an arrow at the battle against Kerbogha. Adhémar told Bertrand that he was sick because he did not believe in the Lance of the Lord. Although Bertrand protested that he believed in it as much as he did in the Passion of the Lord, the legate replied that this was not enough.[13]

Again, the main theme of the vision was its insistence on the importance of the Holy Lance. It also reveals, as with the vision of Peter Bartholomew, that it was popularly believed that fallen crusaders gathered together again in the afterlife, with the Bishop here being depicted as being reunited with his standard bearer.

The third reference to Adhémar to be recorded as a result of the controversy over the Holy Lance was a rather poignant moment as Peter Bartholomew lay dying in the tent of the chaplaincy of Count Raymond of Toulouse. Peter challenged Raymond of Aguilers, asking him why, in his secret thoughts, he had joined with those who wanted Peter to undergo the trial by fire. Raymond would not admit the truth of this accusation until Peter explained that his knowledge was certain, for there was a night when the blessed Virgin Mary and the Bishop of Le Puy revealed to Peter what Raymond was denying.[14] What we learn concerning the afterlife of the legate here is that Adhémar kept company with the Virgin Mary and could see into the thoughts of the living.

Thus far we have Peter Bartholomew, Bernard of Le Puy and Peter Desiderius claiming to have met with Adhémar after his death. A fourth visionary, the Provençal priest Stephen of Valence,[15] also saw him around 18 April 1099, during the siege of 'Arqa, in a major vision once more recorded by Raymond of Aguilers.

Adhémar appeared to Stephen of Valence and struck him with a rod to get his attention as he was returning home during the night.

---

12 For Heraclius I of Polignac, see Riley-Smith, *First Crusaders*, 211.
13 Raymond of Aguilers, *Historia Francorum*, ed. France, 239–42 (PL 155: 640C–D).
14 Ibid. 256 (PL 155: 643A).
15 For Stephen of Valence, see Riley-Smith, *First Crusaders*, 223.

Adhémar reprimanded Stephen for twice neglecting instructions regarding the cross that the bishop used to carry in front of the army. The legate desired that Stephen obtain the cross that had been left in Latakia, without which, according to the blessed Mary, the Christians would lack wisdom. When Stephen heard the name Mary, he asked to see her, and she was revealed, in wonderful form and attire. With her were St Agatha and an unnamed virgin with two candles.

Stephen then asked Adhémar whether he could have a candle in order to bring it to Count Raymond of Toulouse, as a physical item of evidence that would prove the truth of the vision to those sceptics who continued to deny that the legate's beard and hair were burnt in hell, among other things. Adhémar in turn made this request to Mary, who sent him back to Stephen with a refusal, but with the instruction that a small ring owned by Stephen was useless to him, but it would be valuable to Count Raymond if in the future he solicited the Lady who sent it to him in times of need.

Finally, Stephen asked Adhémar whether he had any instruction for his brother, William Hugh of Monteil. The legate answered that William should ask the bishop-elect of Le Puy to say three masses for the souls of their parents. Adhémar added that in future the Holy Lance should not be displayed, except by a priest clad in sacred vestments, and that instead the cross should be carried in front of the army. The legate then demonstrated this, holding the cross on a spear, with a man in priestly robes following behind with the Lance in his hands. Next, Adhémar began the contemporary popular Easter antiphon 'Rejoice, Virgin Mary: you alone in the entire world have destroyed all heresies',[16] whereupon hundreds and thousands of men joined in and the holy group departed.[17]

The main content of this vision concerned a reorganization of the political centre of the crusade. The vision was designed to appeal above all to those southern French followers of Adhémar who had joined the *familia* of the count after the death of their lord. The subordination of the Holy Lance to the cross of the dead legate was, in fact, a powerful symbol that the bishop's following should no longer defer to their Provençal comrades. The vision took place during a siege that many outside the immediate following of Count Raymond of Toulouse saw as a diversion from the true goal of the expedition.

---

[16] 'Gaude Maria virgo: cunctas haereses sola interemisti in universo mundo.'
[17] Raymond of Aguilers, *Historia Francorum*, ed. France, 325–26 (PL 155: 654D–655B).

The policy of Count Raymond at this time was to step up the siege of 'Arqa and to await assistance from the Byzantine Emperor, Alexius I Comnenus. Raymond of Aguilers noted that the majority of people rejected this policy, but the crusade remained at an impasse due to the large entourage of Count Raymond.[18] Prayers, fasting and alms for the people were proclaimed in the hope of resolving the situation, and this sense of crisis formed the background to the vision of Stephen of Valence.

Although the implicit message, therefore, of Stephen's vision was a political one concerning the leadership of the expedition, it does provide further evidence for how contemporaries understood the after-life of Bishop Adhémar. In reporting the vision, Stephen of Valence confirmed the story that the bishop had been scarred in hell. He placed the bishop in the company of the Virgin Mary and strengthened their association by having the bishop lead a celestial host in the antiphon 'Rejoice, Virgin Mary'.

The final two appearances of Adhémar in the work of Raymond of Aguilers confirm that he remained a popular figure among the crusaders. Both took place around the time of the capture of Jerusalem. The first was a reappearance of the legate before Peter Desiderius with an instruction to deal with the sense of discouragement that existed among Christian forces thwarted in their initial attacks on the city. Adhémar told Peter Desiderius to speak to the princes and all the people, telling them to be sanctified from their unclean acts, after which they should go around Jerusalem in bare feet. Should they do this and attack the city with vigour, they would capture the city in nine days.[19] After this vision was discussed in the chancery of Count Raymond of Toulouse, it was decided to ask the Christian army to follow this course of action, but not to announce the source of the instruction, through fear that it would be disbelieved.

The bare-footed walk of the crusaders around Jerusalem is a famous incident, and it is interesting that the clergy advocating this course of action felt that there might be some resistance to the idea by the crusaders. This is the second reference to scepticism regarding the validity of the visions, the first being the concern of Stephen of Valance to obtain proof of his vision.

The many stories that subsequently arose, which placed Adhémar to

---

[18] Ibid. 266 (PL 155: 645A).
[19] Ibid. 325–26 (PL 155: 654D–655B).

the fore in the decisive attack on the city, show that whatever scepticism existed concerning the visions, it was not so strong as to preclude a popular belief that the legate was with the Christian army at the culmination of the expedition. As Raymond of Aguilers recorded in his final report on the afterlife of the legate: 'On this day lord Adhémar, the bishop of Le Puy, was seen by many in the city. Indeed, many of them bore witness that he was the first to go climbing the walls; he was urging his companions and the people that they should climb.'[20]

The seven visions of Bishop Adhémar of Le Puy on the First Crusade had complex meanings for contemporaries. They intertwined commentary on the particular political situation with more deeply rooted notions of the afterlife.[21] Between them the visions allow the afterlife of the bishop to be reconstructed with a certain amount of vivacity. Adhémar spent two days in hell, during which time his suffering was alleviated by the Lord himself, presenting the bishop with a protective cowl that the bishop had once given away as a charitable act. Importantly for theological developments concerning the afterlife, the visions also show that, for contemporaries, the prayers of the living had a beneficial effect on the condition of the departed. Once freed from hell, Adhémar returned to the crusade, at times marching with it invisibly, at other times appearing with celestial company, including St Nicholas and the Virgin Mary, and the other martyrs of the expedition. He assisted the crusade in the capture of Jerusalem; at which point his interventions in the affairs of living humans came to an end.

Jacques Le Goff has made a strong case for believing that the clergy did not have a developed notion of purgatory until the late twelfth century. A. Ja. Gurevich in reply has pointed out that it was nevertheless popularly believed that a person could earn heaven after a period of punishment for their sins, assisted by the prayers of the living.[22] What the history of Raymond of Aguilers reveals is that while he had no notion of a place of purgatory, he did have a concept of the afterlife that allowed a person to move from hell to the company of God and the

[20] Ibid. 348 (PL 155: 660A): 'In hac die dominus Ademarus, Podiensis episcopus, a multis in civitate visus est. Etiam multi de eo testantur, quod ipse primus murum ascendens, ad ascendendum socios atque populum invitabat.'

[21] For further analysis of the political content of the visions, see C. Kostick, *The Social Structure of the First Crusade* (Leiden, 2008), 120–49.

[22] See Jacques Le Goff, *The Birth of Purgatory* (Chicago, IL, 1984), and the critique by A. Ja. Gurevich, 'Popular and Scholarly Medieval Traditions: Notes in the Margins of Jacques Le Goff's Book', *JMedH* 9 (1983), 71–90.

saints. Protected by Christ's intervention and the prayers of his friends, Adhémar nevertheless suffered whipping and burning before being purged himself of his sins, in particular that of doubting the authenticity of the Holy Lance. Once his body was buried, Adhémar's soul came out of hell and took its place alongside the saints.

Perhaps the strongest impression created by the reports concerning Adhémar is that of continuity between the worlds of the living and the deceased. For the visionaries and historians such as Raymond of Aguilers, there was perceived to be a direct continuity between the activities of the legate while alive and those after his death, even to the belief that his burnt hair and beard were in the process of growing back. Their afterlife had a heaven (from which at various times St Nicholas, Mary and the Lord descended) and hell (to which Adhémar was temporarily condemned), but it also co-existed with the timeframe and immediate experiences of the living. For those experiencing and believing the visions of the First Crusade, the afterlife was not something transcendental and abstract, but a state of being in which the dead could walk alongside and assist the living.

Trinity College, Dublin

MICHAEL GLYKAS AND THE AFTERLIFE IN TWELFTH-CENTURY BYZANTIUM*

by YANNIS PAPADOGIANNAKIS

FROM the range of sources on Byzantine religious life, and Byzantine views on the afterlife in particular, the correspondence of Michael Glykas stands out as precious but neglected evidence. Glykas's correspondence with people from all walks of life and his engagement with their preoccupations and with other controversial issues of the day reflect a dense network of communication and links with monks, laymen, members of the imperial family and imperial bureaucrats, situating him at the heart of the moral universe of twelfth-century Byzantine culture. Glykas's correspondence and, in particular, his collection of 'Questions and Answers' (*Kephalaia*) shed light on the kinds of religious issues that were being raised in twelfth-century Byzantium, and they also highlight the multifarious issues and pastoral challenges which Christian theologians had to be prepared to deal with in their pastoral, pedagogical work.

In the process of responding to these enquiries, which clearly resonated with central contemporary concerns,[1] Glykas offers an extensive overview of the most significant Byzantine ideas on the afterlife, rendering his correspondence a rich and informative source. Thus in his answers Glykas offered 'a plain man's guide to the theology of salvation'[2] which is supported by, and reflected in, the rich manuscript tradition of this work. In the absence of more detailed history of Glykas's reception, it is difficult to assess fully how influential his views became. However, one of the oldest, carefully copied manuscripts of Glykas's *Kephalaia* was used for the catechesis of the monks of the monastery of *Megiste Laura* on Mount Athos, an unmistakable sign of the authority that accrued to this work.

---

* I would like to thank Dr Joseph Munitiz for his helpful comments on this paper. The paper is a development of my wider current research on late antique and Byzantine collections of questions and answers, including Glykas and his *Kephalaia*.

[1] For Middle Byzantine eschatological concerns, see Jane Baun, *Tales from Another Byzantium* (Cambridge, 2007).

[2] Paul Magdalino, *The Empire of Manuel I Komnenos, 1143–1180* (Cambridge, 1993), 371 n. 181.

Our knowledge about Glykas's life leans heavily on the identification of Glykas with the figure of Michael Sikidites, who as an imperial
secretary dabbled in magic and because he was involved in a plot
against the emperor was imprisoned and partly blinded.[3] After his
imprisonment Glykas became a monk in 1164.

Apart from his correspondence, Glykas also wrote a *Chronicle*, in
which he demonstrated his scientific knowledge in his account of the
creation of the world, and the *Verses from Prison*, in which he allegedly
recounted in verse his experience of imprisonment and appealed to the
Emperor Manuel for his release.[4] While his views on a number of issues
have been regarded by modern scholars as 'the voice of traditional
common sense ... representing the Orthodoxy that was common to the
educated and the uneducated, the powerful and the poor',[5] his opinion
on the corruptibility of the eucharist stirred up controversy and was
rejected or vehemently opposed by his orthodox contemporaries.[6]

The Kephalaia *or* erotapokriseis

This paper will focus on Glykas's *Theological Chapters [Kephalaia] on the
Problems [Apora] of the Holy Scripture,* hereafter *Kephalaia*.[7] The *Kephalaia*
subscribe loosely to a literary format (*erotapokriseis*) that had a classical
pedigree and had been adapted by Christian authors to suit their needs
for debate and instruction.[8] In Byzantine literature, collections of questions and answers were very popular throughout the centuries.[9]

3 On Glykas, see Magdalino, *Empire*, 370–82, 404–06; idem, *L'orthodoxie des astrologues*
(Paris, 2006), 122–30. For the identification, see O. Kresten, 'Zur Sturz des Theodoros
Styppeiotes', *Jahrbuch der österreichen Byzantinistik* 27 (1978), 49–103, at 90–92. This identification has been accepted by most scholars but is now challenged by Emmanuel
Bourbouhakis, ' "Political" Personae: The Poem from Prison of Michael Glykas: Byzantine
Literature Between Fact and Fiction', *Byzantine Modern Greek Studies* 31 (2007), 53–75, at
56–58.
4 Reappraisal in Bourbouhakis, ' "Political" Personae'.
5 Magdalino, *Empire*, 371.
6 On his eucharistic views, see Michael Angold, *Church and Society in Byzantium under the
Comneni 1081–1261* (Cambridge and New York, 1995), 128–29; Mahlon H. Smith III, *And
taking bread . . .: Cerularius and the Azyme Controversy of 1054* (Paris, 1978), 119–35.
7 Ed. Sophronios Eustratiades, 2 vols (Athens, 1906; Alexandria, 1912). All references
below are to this edition; translations are my own.
8 Averil Cameron, 'Texts as Weapons: Polemic in the Byzantine Dark Ages', in A. K.
Bowman and G. Woolf, eds, *Literacy and Power in the Ancient World* (Cambridge, 1994),
198–215; Yannis Papadoyannakis [*sic*], 'Instruction by Question and Answer in Late Antiquity: the Case of Late Antique and Byzantine Erotapokriseis', in Scott Johnson, ed., *Greek
Literature in Late Antiquity: Dynamism, Didacticism, Classicism* (Aldershot, 2006), 91–105.
9 On the literary form of *kephalaia* and its widespread use by the Byzantines, see Endre

What the title *Kephalaia* does not convey is that this collection of ninety-six letters which was put together by Glykas[10] preserves enquiries from named people – laymen and monks – on a variety of issues.[11] As characterized by Paul Magdalino, 'They were questions that arose ... from the consciences of devout believers genuinely troubled by uncertainties and discrepancies in the church's teaching, and concerned to make full sense of what the scriptures and the fathers had to say about human life, death, sin and salvation.'[12] Thus this collection affords a priceless glimpse into the nature of the concerns of Byzantine society, a glimpse into a universe that is not well served by the historical record.

Enquiries vary widely: 'Can demons predict the future?', 'What are the properties of magnets?', 'Is the shape of heaven spherical or flat?', 'Does the monastic habit absolve one of sin?', 'How strictly should one fast on Wednesdays and Fridays?' Disputed issues such as the *Filioque* and the unleavened bread controversy are also reflected. The answers to these enquiries often read like exercises in tackling difficult (and not always easy to solve) problems, a feature they share with earlier collections of questions and answers. This accounts for a certain openendedness in some answers, which are rather tentative (and read more as *ad hoc* interventions) and perhaps only intended to be suggestive. One particular hallmark of Glykas's collection, when compared with earlier *erotapokriseis*, is that Glykas deliberately formulated his answers in dialogue with patristic authors and ideas. As a result there is a dense clustering of authorities and proof-texts going as far back as the earliest Christian centuries. Given the current state of the edition, which is based on only seven out of the forty-nine extant manuscripts, and characterized by interpolations and later supplementation with additional authorities in support of Glykas's claims, it is hard to be sure and to document with any certainty and in any detail the full extent of his borrowings. It will not be possible here to do full justice to the complex

von Ivánka, 'Κεφάλαια – eine byzantinische Literaturform und ihre antiken Wurzeln', *Byzantinische Zeitschrift* 47 (1954), 285–91. On the literary form of *erotapokriseis*, see Annelie Volgers and Claudio Zamagni, eds, *Erotapokriseis: Early Christian Question-and-Answer Literature in Context* (Louvain, 2004), with bibliography.

[10] Thus *Kephalaia*, ed. Eustratiades, 1: 95–96. See also E. Kurtz, in his review of Eustratiades's edition in *Byzantinische Zeitschrift* 17 (1908), 166–72, at 168.

[11] For identity and prosopography, see Magdalino, *Empire*, 372–76. According to the introduction by the editor (*Kephalaia*, ed. Eustratiades, 1: 53–55), while not all questions can safely be attributed to the person from whom they are supposed to have originated, the fact that they were genuine enquiries does not seem to be in doubt.

[12] Magdalino, *Empire*, 372.

and multi-layered nature of Glykas's responses, but by discussing the cluster of enquiries that deal with death and its aftermath, I hope to show the significance of this text for understanding Byzantine attitudes to the afterlife.

The Afterlife

Nicholas Constas has remarked that:

> The Byzantines had no 'system' around the last things. Eschatology remained for them an open horizon within theology, an openness perhaps intended to draw experience and thought toward that which lies beyond the bounds of the world of space and time.[13]

While Byzantine eschatology originated in the Bible, the biblical notion of the afterlife and the inherited early Christian notions that built on it were ambiguous and subject to a diversity of interpretations, which in turn led to the creation of a variety of imaginative structures.[14] Nowhere does this process become more apparent than in Glykas's responses to questions on the afterlife.

An enquiry by the monk Kyr Domestikos Isaiah on where the souls of the departed go once they are separated from the body after death, leads Glykas to an exploration of the issue.[15] Glykas begins with Pindar, who claimed that the souls of the pious dwell in heaven. But since Pindar may not be known to all, Glykas says, he turns to Anastasius of Sinai who located the abode of the righteous on the inner side of the firmament. He then provides more proof-texts from one of his favourite sources, the pseudo-Athanasian *Quaestiones ad ducem Antiochum*,[16] which are indebted to Anastasius of Sinai's seventh-century collection of questions and answers.[17] In this influential and oft-quoted proof-text it is

---

[13] Nicholas Constas, '"To Sleep, Perchance to Dream": The Middle State of Souls in Patristic and Byzantine Literature', *DOP* 55 (2001), 91–124, at 124.

[14] Ibid. 120. For a review of attitudes on the afterlife, see Baun, *Tales*, 120–29, and for visual expression of this variety, see, in this volume, Leslie Brubaker, 'Byzantine Visions of the End', 97–119.

[15] *Kephalaia*, ed. Eustratiades, 1: 240–46 (Q. 20).

[16] PG 28: 597–700.

[17] For the reliance of pseudo-Athanasius on Anastasius's collection, see *Anastasii Sinaitae Quaestiones et responsiones*, eds Marcel Richard and Joseph A. Munitiz (Turnhout, 2006), lii–lv. Glykas seems to have had access to both collections: see J. A. Munitiz, 'In the Steps of Anastasius of Sinai: Later Traces of His Erotapokriseis', in B. Janssens, B. Roosen and P. Van Deun, eds, *Philomathestatos: Studies in Greek Patristic and Byzantine Texts Presented to Jacques Noret for His Sixty-fifth Birthday* (Leuven and New York, 2005), 435–54, at 448.

argued that 'the souls of the righteous dwell in heaven along with the Good Thief for whom Christ opened paradise. Christ did not open paradise for him alone, however, but for the souls of all the saints as well.'[18] Glykas also cites Gregory the Great, Anthony, Theodoret, Basil, Gregory of Nazianzus and Paul. As for the wicked, after their death their souls end up in Hades, where they contemplate the evils that they have committed during their lives. In support of this claim Glykas cites the sixth-century monastic author Dorotheos of Gaza.[19]

At this point Glykas blends in a concept that by his time had worked its way deep into the imagination and the structure of eschatological expectations of the Byzantines, namely that of the tollgates (custom houses).[20] According to this view,

> otherworld beings, whether angels or demons, attended the actual hour of death, assisting with the parting of soul from body. If the departed's moral or penitential status were ambiguous, angels and demons might argue over whose the soul should be. The soul then underwent its own particular judgement, often passing through a multi-stage ordeal or examination. Its sins and good deeds were reviewed, sometimes read out of books, sometimes weighed, sometimes tested by fire.[21]

In that same response Glykas refers to the location of Hades, which according to the testimony of pseudo-Athanasius was below the earth.[22] Glykas also cites the liturgical hymns of Andrew of Crete (c. 660–740). Concluding his response, Glykas refers to the parable of the rich man and Lazarus (Luke 16: 19–31) as the text par excellence for Byzantine eschatology.[23]

Another issue that looms large among the enquiries on the afterlife

---

18 *Kephalaia*, ed. Eustratiades, 1: 241 (Q. 20).

19 'Fear of the Punishment to Come', *Discourse* 12, ed. L. Regnault, SC 92 (Paris, 1962), 384–88. Further details in Constas, ' "To Sleep, Perchance to Dream" ', 100.

20 George Every, 'Toll Gates on the Air Way', *Eastern Churches Review* 8 (1976), 139–50.

21 Jane Baun, 'Last Things', in T. F. X. Noble and J. M. H. Smith, eds, *The Cambridge History of Christianity, 3: Early Medieval Christianity, c. 600–c. 1100* (Cambridge, 2008), 606–24, at 607; see also Baun, *Tales*, 125–26.

22 *Kephalaia*, ed. Eustratiades, 1: 245 (Q. 20).

23 See Outi Lehtipuu, *The Afterlife Imagery in Luke's Story of the Rich Man and Lazarus* (Leiden, 2006); also Monique Alexandre, 'L'interprétation de *Luc* 16.19–31, chez Grégoire de Nysse', in J. Fontaine and C. Kannengiesser, eds, *Epektasis: mélanges patristiques offerts au cardinal Jean Daniélou* (Paris, 1972), 425–41; Constas, ' "To Sleep, Perchance to Dream" ', 99; Baun, *Tales*, 315.

is that of Paradise and the resurrection of the body. Like any question that goes straight to the heart of the faith, it had been asked by many in the past and would continue to be asked (and debated) by subsequent generations. More specifically, in Question 7 the monk Kyr Ioannes Aspiotes asks about the nature of the resurrected body and whether the blessed will eat solid food (*brosin aistheten*) in paradise. This enquiry provides Glykas with the opportunity to expound his view on the resurrected body which will be identical with that of Adam before the Fall. Glykas refers to a sort of *apokatastasis*, understood as a restoration to an original, proper condition. This means, in Glykas's view, that the resurrected bodies will not be prone to decay; they will be incorruptible (*aphtharta*), and will not need food, drink or clothes. In the resurrected state there is to be no age differentiation or diversity in external appearance.[24] To support his claim he employs the Pauline image of the seed (1 Corinthians 15: 35–42).[25] Just as seeds can differ in size and weight but all nevertheless become flowering sheaves that look alike, so will the bodies in their resurrected state. For human beings, Glykas argues, were prone to thirst, hunger and other passions as a consequence of the Fall. Their restoration to their original condition will reverse these. To this end Glykas cites John of Damascus and Gregory of Nyssa, the former to underpin the view that it is impossible for human beings to be incorruptible in their resurrected state if they can eat and drink, and the latter to support the view that human beings in their resurrected state will be like angels in heaven, in no need of food and drink.[26]

The most compelling proof of this for Glykas, however, is the nature of Christ's risen body, which did not need burial clothes, sleep, food or drink. For this interpretation he appeals to John of Damascus. The ultimate goal of the resurrected human being is to stand in the presence of Christ and to contemplate God's glory. Glykas also refers to the episode in Luke 24: 41–43 when the risen Christ is seen to eat, arguing that his body was not subject to the laws of nature and that this was a concession by Christ intended to convince his disciples. Glykas continues by arguing that the body will be pure and resplendent and there will be no

---

[24] For an overview of the patristic debate regarding the age and shape of resurrected bodies, see Christian Gnilka, 'Neues Alter, neues Leben: Eine antike Weisheit und ihre christliche Nutzung', in idem, *Sieben Kapitel über Natur und Menschenleben* (Basel, 2005), 105–48, at 129–48.

[25] For analysis of resurrection imagery, see Caroline Walker Bynum, *The Resurrection of the Body in Western Christianity, 200–1336* (New York, 1995).

[26] *Kephalaia*, ed. Eustratiades, 1: 73–74 (Q. 7).

need for divisions such as day or night. This is what lies in store for the righteous too. But what about the resurrected state of the body of sinners? In Glykas's view their body too will be incorruptible (*aptharton*), for Christ died for the sake of all humanity. Their body will also be subtle (*lepton*), light and spiritual (*pneumatikon*, meaning, according to Glykas, vivified by the Holy Spirit).[27] But their body will differ from that of the righteous just as the seed of grain differs from the seed of barley.[28]

The same persistent enquirer, monk Kyr Ioannes Aspiotes, wants to know whether there will be sexual differentiation in the resurrected state (Question 8)[29] and (Question 9) whether one must give credence to those who say that those who will be resurrected will not recognize each other then (*tote*). And if they do recognize each other, sinners will recognize the righteous but the righteous will not recognize the sinners.[30]

Relying rather heavily on Gregory of Nyssa – among other patristic authorities – Glykas posits two phases in the creation of human beings, the first and most pristine being that there was a single human being that was not prone to sexual differentiation.[31] Hence when human beings will be restored to their original condition in Paradise they will not bear the marks of their gender.[32]

When it comes to answering Question 9, on whether resurrected human beings will be able to recognize each other, Glykas adduces the parable of the rich man and Lazarus in order to show that just as the rich man was able to recognize Lazarus, so will we be able to recognize each other. For Glykas the parable foreshadows what will take place in the future; he cites with approval a similar interpretation of the parable by John of Damascus.[33] Not only that, but resurrected human beings

---

27 Ibid. 2: 273–74 (Q. 78).
28 Ibid. 1: 88 (Q. 7).
29 Ibid. 1: 89 (Q. 8).
30 Ibid. 1: 116 (Q. 9).
31 Johannes Zachhuber, *Human Nature in Gregory of Nyssa: Philosophical and Background Theological Significance* (Boston, MA, 1999), 154–59; Morwenna Ludlow, *Universal Salvation: Eschatology in the Thought of Gregory of Nyssa and Karl Rahner* (Oxford, 2000), 46–50.
32 See Bernard Flusin, 'Avant la différenciation sexuelle: Remarques sur la huitième "difficulté" de Michel Glykas', in P. Legendre, ed., *'Ils seront deux en une seule chair': scénographie du couple humain dans le texte occidental* (Bruxelles, 2004), 217–33; J. Warren Smith, 'The Body of Paradise and the Body of the Resurrection: Gender and the Angelic Life in Gregory of Nyssa's *De hominis opificio*', HThR 92 (2006), 207–28.
33 *Kephalaia*, ed. Eustratiades, 1: 117 (Q. 9).

will be able to recognize those who lived before their times by some special dispensation that will endow the 'eye of their soul' with intuitive power (or spiritual insight).[34] This same spiritual insight will enable the resurrected human beings to recognize each other, since any other mark of identification will be absent from the resurrected bodies. This will happen after the Last Judgement (Glykas cites here Maximus the Confessor) during which the books recording the content of one's conscience will be wide open and everybody will be judged on the basis of these contents.[35]

Now, after the Last Judgement, according to Glykas, the righteous will be able to see the wicked being tormented in hell but will not be able to help them (even their relatives or friends) or feel sympathy for them. They will miss this capacity (or it will have been suspended) so that they can continue to enjoy their state of blessedness. The sinners, however, will not be able to see each other in the outer place to which they will have been expelled. This view is supported with some passages from John Chrysostom and the parable of the rich man and Lazarus, in which Abraham, despite being charitable and hospitable and despite the fact that the rich man was beseeching him, beheld the rich man in torment but could not help him.[36] On this issue of 'kindred recognition',[37] Glykas cites as authorities Theodore the Studite, the Gospels and John Chrysostom.[38]

Other enquiries, such as Question 10 from a monk named Isaiah, deal with such issues as whether, after their restoration (*apokatastasis*), the righteous are going to progress in virtue and in glory or not.[39] This enquiry prompts Glykas to argue, echoing Gregory of Nyssa and citing Gregory of Nazianzus, that when the righteous stand in the presence of God and behold his glory, each will be illuminated and partake of it according to the degree of their purity, just as the sinners will feel the darkness in their minds that derives from their alienation from God. This will be part of a process of progressing in virtue, knowledge and glory. And there will be no end, no measure and no satiety to this

---

[34] Nicholas Constas, 'Death and Dying in Byzantium', in Derek Krueger, ed., *Byzantine Christianity* (Minneapolis, MN, 2006), 124–45, at 144.
[35] *Kephalaia*, ed. Eustratiades, 1: 120 (Q. 9).
[36] Ibid. 1: 125–26 (Q. 9).
[37] See also Constas, 'Death', 144.
[38] *Kephalaia*, ed. Eustratiades, 1: 123–28 (Q. 9).
[39] Ibid. 1: 129 (Q. 10).

participation in God's glory, for God is infinite.[40] As mentioned earlier, this idea recalls Gregory of Nyssa's doctrine of perpetual progress. Glykas, then, is injecting his response with the dynamism that characterizes Gregory's doctrine of perpetual progress.[41] Despite his reliance on Gregory's doctrine, however, Glykas stops well short of adopting here or elsewhere in his responses Gregory's idea of universal salvation.

But how is one to influence the fate of the departed? The answer is given in the process of answering Questions 21 and 51 that pertain to the cult of the saints and their involvement in human affairs. The title of Question 21 reads: '(to the same) whether one should give credence to those who say that the departed souls of the saints rest in some place and do not pray on our behalf before Christ'. This enquiry is part of a wider, earlier but still continuing debate on the intercessory role of the saints after death. The debate harks back to a sixth-century controversy about the role of the saints and their intercessory power.[42] Eustratius, a leading presbyter of Constantinople, in his apology for the cult of the saints, refuted the views of anonymous opponents who denied the ability of dead souls to involve themselves in, or be affected by, the affairs of the living.[43] Moreover Eustratius's opponents argued that the widespread saintly apparitions were in fact produced by a divine power simulating the forms of dead martyrs and saints. These views, which posed a threat to the cult of the saints and the Church's care for the souls of the dead,[44] were still resonating in the eleventh and twelfth centuries.[45] In parts of his response Glykas seems to be following loosely the argumentation of Eustratius. Like Eustratius's response to these assertions, Glykas's response draws on and carefully weaves together an impressive array of scriptural verses, patristic texts and saints' lives.[46]

---

[40] Ibid. 1: 132–33 (Q. 10).

[41] Ludlow, *Universal Salvation*, 63–64.

[42] On the controversy, see Nicholas Constas, 'An Apology for the Cult of Saints in Late Antiquity: Eustratius Presbyter of Constantinople, *On the State of Souls After Death* (CPG 7522)', *JECS* 10 (2002), 267–85; see also, in this volume, Phil Booth, 'Saints and Soteriology in Sophronius Sophista's *Miracles of Cyrus and John*', 52–63, and Matthew J. dal Santo, 'Philosophy, Hagiology and the Early Byzantine Origins of Purgatory', 41–51.

[43] *Eustratii Presbyteri Constantinopolitani De statu animarum post mortem (CPG 7522)*, ed. Peter van Deun, CChr.SG 60 (Turnhout and Louvain, 2006).

[44] Further details in Constas, 'An Apology', 278–79; idem, ' "To Sleep, Perchance to Dream" ', 110–12.

[45] Gilbert Dagron, 'L'ombre d'un doute: L'hagiographie en question, VIe–XIe siècle', *DOP* 46 (1992), 59–68, at 67; Constas, ' "To Sleep, Perchance to Dream" ', 111–12.

[46] Constas, 'An Apology', 273–74.

Glykas goes on to argue that since the saints were given as a gift the ability to stand with *parrhesia* (courage and frankness of speech, but also implying liberty of approach) before God and pray for us and bring down to us all kinds of spiritual gifts, and since the soul of the saints is alive and active after death, it can be sent by God to our assistance. Glykas then cites Basil of Caesarea to support this claim and states emphatically that 'when we pray for their help and their succour, sometimes they [the saints] themselves appear to us on their own, at other times divine angels are sent instead of them, and sometimes it is the grace of the Holy Spirit'.[47] For Glykas, the saints' souls are not confined to one place but instead stand before the glory of God. This he supports with a citation from the Gospels (John 17: 24). If saints stand before Christ and see his glory, Glykas continues, what stops them from interceding on our behalf?[48] There follow more proof-texts from the Bible, Theodore the Studite and Gregory of Nazianzus (the parable of the rich man and Lazarus), among others. The ultimate exemplar for the ascent to heaven remained Christ, who after his resurrection paved the way to heaven for the righteous.[49]

Having supported the intercessory role of the saints, Glykas moves on to grapple with the issue of whether benefactions can completely remove the sins of the departed.[50] Glykas endorses what had been standard practice in Byzantium (and in Eastern Christianity to date), *mnemosyna*, a series of memorial services – accompanied by memorial meals at the house of the deceased – which were conducted on the third, ninth and fortieth days after death and again on the first anniversary.[51] Glykas presents this custom as having been enjoined by the apostles.[52] His endorsement, though, is not unqualified. Citing Dionysius

[47] *Kephalaia*, ed. Eustratiades, 1: 248 (Q. 21).
[48] Ibid. 1: 251 (Q. 21).
[49] Ibid. 1: 251–52 (Q. 21).
[50] Ibid. 2: 55–61 (Q. 50), to the same (Neilos the monk). Following the editor Eustratiades, Constas notes that Glykas is here drawing partly on the section on the feast of *Protopsychosabbaton* (Saturday of All Souls, the first Saturday of Great Lent in the Orthodox calendar) in the liturgical calendar (*synaxarion*) dedicated to the prayers and memorial offerings for the dead: Constas, ' "To Sleep, Perchance to Dream" ', 102.
[51] Constas, 'Death and Dying', 137; Gilbert Dagron, 'Troisième, neuvième et quarantième jour dans la tradition byzantine: temps chrétien et anthropologie', in *Le temps chrétien de la fin de l'antiquité au moyen age, IIIᵉ–XIIIᵉ siècle* (Paris, 1984), 419–30.
[52] Perhaps he had in mind the *Apostolic Constitutions* 8.42.1, ed. M. Metzger, SC 336 (Paris, 1987), 258. The Byzantine practice of *mnemosyna*, however, was interpreted by some as an imitation of Christ's resurrection on the third day and his ascension into heaven on the fortieth: Constas, ' "To Sleep, Perchance to Dream" ', 103.

the Areopagite, Glykas claims that some sins cannot be forgiven but others can. As an example of the first case Glykas mentions those who not only oppressed those in need but took away everything from them: these cannot hope to be forgiven. Examples of the second are those who were of pure and good conscience but whose premature death did not allow them to make amends for any minor sins committed. Citing Chrysostom, Glykas argues that they will benefit the most not only from *mnemosyna* but also from almsgiving. The righteous can benefit too from almsgiving in that their reward will be increased.[53]

Elsewhere, when discussing a related enquiry (Question 69) concerning the nature of the Kingdom of Heaven and the Final Judgement, the origin of the eschatological fire, the sleepless worm and the outer darkness,[54] Glykas criticizes the naive literal interpretation of such images. Instead, he allegorizes their meaning. The Kingdom of Heaven is to stand before God, to behold his glory and to partake of the fervent spiritual joy (*agalliasis*), whereas Gehenna, the purifying fire, the outer darkness, the sleepless worm and the gnashing of teeth stand for exclusion or falling from blessedness.[55] The fire stands for the light that will shine upon the righteous but will also be fire that will burn the sinners. Citing the apostle Paul's saying, 'the fire will test what sort of work each has done' (1 Corinthians 3: 13), Glykas turns to the language of refining gold, asserting that if the light shines upon gold (i.e. the righteous), the gold will become more resplendent. By contrast, if it shines upon wood or hay (i.e. the sins of the wicked), it will set it on fire. But then Glykas hastens to add: 'what kind of fire this will be and how it will burn the wicked in the day of the Last Judgement only God knows'.[56]

What is certain for Glykas, though, is that this will not happen immediately after death. He emphasizes this in his response to a different enquiry regarding whether the soul is surrendered to the purifying fire that burns the body right after death.[57] This teaching Glykas attributes to Gregory the Great's responses, rejecting it and adding that there is no scriptural basis for it. Instead he cites one of his favourite authorities, pseudo-Athanasius's *Quaestiones ad ducem Antiochum*, where it is clearly stated that both the righteous and the wicked are in a state

---

53 *Kephalaia*, ed. Eustratiades, 2: 59 (Q. 50).
54 Ibid. 2: 215–29 (Q. 69).
55 Ibid. 2: 228 (Q. 69).
56 Ibid. 2: 221 (Q. 69); see also discussion in Baun, *Tales*, 138–44, 300–12.
57 *Kephalaia*, ed. Eustratiades, 2: 380 (Q. 85).

in which they only have a foretaste of their rewards and their punishments.[58]

Conclusion

Glykas's answers regarding the Last Things drew on a repertoire of patristic opinion as well as otherworld images and ideas which enjoyed great currency in his time. If he consulted a number of authorities in his answers, this does not mean that he was a mere compiler of arguments and ideas, for Glykas did not lack independence and the intellectual courage to disagree with some of the authorities that he was citing. Instead he drew on, and engaged with, various sources to clarify and develop his views on the issues upon which he was asked to pronounce. The tensions that are reflected in his correspondence are a reminder that views on the afterlife were fraught with ambiguity. They had to be debated and at times defended against alternative opinions. Such enquiries reflect a current of feeling among many Christians in twelfth-century Byzantium that the end of time was nearing, even if Glykas thought that it was still some way off.[59] What is not in doubt, however, is an increased preoccupation with the afterlife, as the extensive literature that sprang up describing the afterlife, Paradise, and the relationship between the soul and body in Paradise attests. The hitherto unedited, neglected and largely inaccessible *Dioptra* of Philip the Monk, from the late eleventh century, is a case in point as it became extremely popular at the time of its composition and afterwards.[60] For all his attempt to provide an imaginative solution to a perennial intractable problem, the strain of fitting heterogeneous materials together is at times obvious in the various solutions that were current in varying degrees in his writings.

What makes Glykas's collection significant, not least for Byzantine notions of the afterlife, is that it illuminates how this process of structuring religious belief and practice was necessitated by contemporary concerns and anxieties, exposing the mechanisms and strategies that shaped what came to be shared Byzantine views on the afterlife. It is only by examining this type of less commonly used source, alongside

---

[58] Ibid. Constas (' "To Sleep, Perchance to Dream" ', 113 n. 77) sees in this an allusion to the debate on purgatory that was to erupt few years after Glykas's death.

[59] Magdalino, *Empire*, 406.

[60] Constas, ' "To Sleep, Perchance to Dream" ', 100–01.

others, that we can illustrate and understand such processes in any detail.

Finally, throughout Glykas's responses on the issues related to the afterlife, the awareness that he is approaching a great mystery, concerning which the last and most definitive word belongs to God, is never allowed to slip from view. Glykas's apophatic inclination translates into a persistent reticence to overdetermine how things will unfold in the *eschaton* (age to come), lending to his approach a certain (perhaps calculated) open-endedness and inconclusiveness imbued with the awareness of the profound mystery that surrounds the Last Things.

Wolfson College, Oxford

GHOSTS AND GHOSTBUSTERS IN THE MIDDLE AGES

by R. N. SWANSON

THE dead are the silent majority in the Church's history – as they are, indeed, in humanity's. The life after death is a matter of faith and conjecture more than tried and tested certainty, predicated on a soul which survives the death of the body. That raises issues about the nature and structure of the afterlife, its pains and delights. For the late medieval Church, the afterlife raised particular concerns and anxieties, its complex division into heaven, hell, and purgatory promising a future which had to be planned for. Strategies for eternity were a major force in religious practice, with death as the threshold to something unknown until experienced.

The dead did not always sleep peacefully; they had a nasty habit of turning up unexpectedly and might even be recalled. The continued presence of the dead, or of some of them, is a surprisingly regular feature of medieval religion, in assorted manifestations and formulations, providing the stuff of narratives across the centuries. In the complex range of relationships between the living and the dead, between this world and the afterlife, ghosts' visits to the world of the living to recount the benefits or pains they experience in the afterlife reciprocate the journeys by living humans into the afterlife, to see the delights of heaven and the horrors of hell and purgatory.[1] This paper examines that continued presence, that propensity to return, and what those returnees revealed of the afterlife.

* * *

Ghosts make good stories. They have their own history, as part of the history of the afterlife, real or imagined.[2] They are also socially constructed, to reflect their times. Here the main concern is with the years from 1100 to the Reformation. After 1100 sources become more

---

[1] A. Guiance, *Los discursos sobre la muerte en la Castilla medieval (siglos VI–XV)* (Valladolid, 1998), 381.

[2] R. C. Finucane, *Appearances of the Dead: A Cultural History of Ghosts* (London, 1982); J.-C. Schmitt, *Ghosts in the Middle Ages: The Living and the Dead in Medieval Society* (Chicago, IL, and London, 1998). Abbreviated translations of several tales are in A. Joynes, ed., *Medieval Ghost Stories: an Anthology of Miracles, Marvels, and Prodigies* (Woodbridge, 2001).

abundant, and the subsequent consolidation of ideas about purgatory makes the afterlife more prominent. After 1100, relations between the living and the dead supposedly also became more firmly defined (at least for clerics), with a growing sense of separation and alienation summarized in the phrase: 'we [the living] do not communicate with the dead'.[3] This 'growing desire to reinforce the boundaries between the living and the dead' is partly explained – or hypothesized – from contemporary changes in the role of ghosts ('in élite literature at least'), and the appearance of 'the angry ghost ... endowed with power to harm the living'.[4] The argument is not entirely convincing, but it serves to limit coverage here.

At the other chronological extreme, the Protestant reformers' rejection of preceding ghost-lore, discarding the idea of returning souls alongside purgatory and the cult of saints, brought a definitive caesura between the worlds of the living and the dead. Arguably, the Reformation's theological rejection of ghosts is part of the construction of the 'Middle Ages'; after all – to quote Jean-Claude Schmitt – 'What is more "medieval", if not "Middle-Agesish" [moyenâgeux] than the tales of ghosts [revenants]?'[5]

* * *

What exactly are these 'ghosts', and how do we know about them? The definition, and the range of sources which deal with ghosts, clearly affect how they can be discussed.

In common modern understanding ghosts are usually incorporeal, ungraspable, yet often visible. Medieval ideas extend the range to other forms of spirit manifestation. Ghosts, while seemingly a specific category, only rarely attract specific attention in medieval sources. They were not the only visitors from the other world, one inhabited by many races whose differing manifestations established contact with the living. Medieval ghosts often appear not simply as wraiths of dead humans, but as inhabitants of a world of spirits which may be good or bad, but they are not necessarily – or even presumptively – human. They fit into a wider category of apparitions, which includes other spectral manifes-

---

[3] M. McLaughlin, 'On Communion with the Dead', *JMedH* 17 (1991), 23–34.

[4] Ibid. 32, 31.

[5] J.-C. Schmitt, 'Préface', in Jean Gobi, *Dialogue avec un fantôme*, ed. M.-A. Polo de Beaulieu (Paris, 1994) [hereafter: 'Gobi'], ix.

tations such as the Wild Hunt, or diabolical night-flying female spirits.[6] Issues surrounding ghosts and their appearance and reliability as informants merge into a wider debate about the discernment of spirits which are often invasive forces impacting on the living.[7] Visits by angels and demons also crowd in, but are categorically different, since they are rightful inhabitants of that same other world. The ghosts' preceding human lives, as legal immigrants into the afterlife who now return, mark them out, yet they often appear alongside those other inhabitants of the other world or may be mistaken for them. A ghost at Beaucaire in 1211 was initially accompanied by a demon; later an angel seems to act as his advisor when dealing with questions from his human interrogators.[8]

Ghosts are, generally, visions; but not all visions are of ghosts.[9] Manifestations were both to humans and through humans. While ghostly appearances might appear random or accidental, some among the living had regular contact with the dead, being in effect mediums. The best documented case occurred in southern France in the early 1300s. This person was not possessed by the spirits but had frequent communication with them.[10] A more 'traditional' medium is reported in fifteenth-century Berne, with adherents among the townsfolk; but he was eventually hanged as a thief.[11] The dead spoke through him, seeking aid to cut their time in purgatory. This case was perhaps theologically challenging, as the possessing spirits should have been considered demonic rather than human;[12] yet the believers clearly had no qualms on the matter. Some 'mediums' may have been involuntary: it was seemingly accepted that the dead sometimes invaded the bodies of

---

[6] On the hunt in general, see C. Lecouteux, *Chasses fantastiques et cohortes de la nuit au moyen âge* (Paris, 1999).

[7] N. Caciola, *Discerning Spirits: Demons and Demonic Possession in the Middle Ages* (Ithaca, NY, and London, 2003).

[8] S. E. Banks and J. W. Binns, eds, *Gervase of Tilbury, Otia imperialia: Recreation for an Emperor* (Oxford, 2002) [hereafter 'Gervase'], 762–65 (later discussion clarifies the status of these guardian angels: ibid. 776–81).

[9] Cf. G. W. Adams, *Visions in Late Medieval England: Lay Spirituality and Sacred Glimpses of the Hidden Worlds of Faith*, Studies in the History of Christian Traditions 130 (Leiden and Boston, MA, 2007), which treats ghosts in ch. 1.

[10] Below, 164.

[11] N. Caciola, 'Spirits seeking Bodies: Death, Possession and Communal Memory in the Middle Ages', in B. Gordon and P. Marshall, eds, *The Place of the Dead: Death and Remembrance in Late Medieval and Early Modern Europe* (Cambridge, 2000), 66–86, at 69, with discussion to 73; Johannes Nider, *Formicarium*, ed. G. Colvenerius (Douai, 1602), 181–82.

[12] Caciola, 'Spirits seeking Bodies', 69–70.

the living.[13] Ghosts were choosy about who they spoke to, and through whom they spoke. The girl who conversed with the Beaucaire ghost in 1211 was initially the only channel for communication – but others did ask questions later.[14] A fifteenth-century writer advised that a ghost be asked whom it would accept as its questioner.[15]

While medieval ghosts manifested in varied ways, some visitations are ignored here. The dead seen in dreams are discounted, despite their fairly frequent occurrence.[16] Poltergeists and similar visitors, or inhuman manifestations, are also omitted, except for shape-shifters which became humanoid when conversing with the living. Such shape-shifting creates its own definitional problems, as the manifestation may not be visually recognizable. One ghost in an English record of around 1400 appeared first as a raven and a dog, later as a she-goat, before taking a human form probably nothing like his earthly appearance.[17] This is significant. Ghosts which make a point of conversing with humans, which have a reason for their presence, might be expected to be recognizable, to be visible manifestations. Often, though, they are merely auditory phenomena, or if visible are not immediately recognized. If invisible, or occupying another body, they must identify themselves by sound.[18] Even when visible, they may appear in unrecognizable form – and not necessarily as human. They must again identify themselves orally and prove their identity from shared memories. Possibly the most striking instance of this is the priest Walchelin in the twelfth century, who takes some persuading that he is actually talking to his own brother's ghost.[19]

[13] Ibid. 78–81. James of Clusa denied that a good spirit, already certain of its ultimate fate – 'certus de sua predestinatione' – would ever invade another body: Jacobus de Clusa, *Tractatus optimus de animabus exeuntis a corporibus* (Leipzig, 1497) [hereafter 'Clusa'], sig. Biv^v.

[14] Gervase, 759–85. The ghost said she could only serve as a conduit while she remained a virgin: ibid. 768–69.

[15] Clusa, sig. Biv^v.

[16] Schmitt does include them in his analysis. One of the most vivid is the lengthy conversational encounter reported in M. P. Harley, *A Revelation of Purgatory by an Unknown Fifteenth-Century Woman Visionary: Introduction, Critical Text, and Translation* (Lewiston, NY, and Queenston, Ont., 1985), 60–65, 78–84 (trans. at 113–19, 132–38).

[17] His human form is described as looking 'like one of the dead kings in pictures' ('ad instar vnius regis mortui depicti'), possibly looking like an image from the series of the Three Living and the Three Dead: M. R. James, 'Twelve medieval Ghost-Stories', *EHR* 37 (1922), 413–22, at 417; for the earlier forms, see ibid. 415, 417. These tales are translated, with further commentary, in A. J. Grant, 'Twelve Medieval Ghost Stories', *Yorkshire Archaeological Journal* 27 (1924), 363–79; also incompletely in Joynes, *Medieval Ghost Stories*, 120–25.

[18] Gobi, 52–53, 58, 72, 74–75, 103–04 (cf. ibid. 40–42).

[19] M. Chibnall, ed., *The Ecclesiastical History of Orderic Vitalis, Volume IV, Books VII and*

* * *

The stories of these ghostly manifestations are indeed stories; but they are also sources. Most late medieval tales largely conform to clerical expectations and agendas.[20] Their frequent stereotyping, shaped to serve clerical purposes and reinforce Catholic doctrine and practices, tempers their utility. Some are more fictionalized than others: tales with lengthy dialogue are clearly constructs, which may evolve further as they switch cultural contexts. The stories recorded by chroniclers and others can also be challenged. Those included in Walter Map's *De nugis curialium* seem to provide evidence for belief in ghosts in twelfth-century England and Wales;[21] but they have also been interpreted as fictions, 'composed in order to entertain' – with a claim that 'some of his ghosts were ... originally intended to be jokes'.[22]

The tales' purpose and function are also problematic. Some simply exist, with no immediately obvious point or purpose. Some are lengthy statements which circulated widely as tracts, even going into print.[23] Many occur in collections of sermon *exempla*, as illustrative anecdotes to grab attention and convey a message, or in the sermons themselves.[24] Clerical dominance of both the experiences and the dissemination and use of the tales superficially confirms an 'association between the clerical thought-world and the functions and forms of spirits of the dead'. Clerics, as the Church's agents, 'expressed and shaped popular attitudes towards ghosts in general',[25] as the medieval Church 'instructed the living by making use of the dead'.[26] This takes things rather close to an imposed distinction between elite and popular culture and religion

---

VIII, Oxford Medieval Texts (Oxford, 1973), 236–49, esp. 246–49.

[20] Finucane, *Appearances*, 84.

[21] M. R. James, ed. (rev. C. N. L. Brooke and R. A. B. Mynors), *Walter Map: De nugis curialium; Courtiers' Trifles* (Oxford, 1983), 161, 202–07, 345.

[22] M. Philpott, 'Haunting the Middle Ages', in C. Sullivan and B. White, eds, *Writing and Fantasy* (London and New York, 1999), 48–61, at 50, 55.

[23] Gobi, 166; W. Seelmann, 'Arnt Buschmans Mirakel', *Jahrbuch des Vereins für niederdeutsche Sprachforschung* 6 (1880), 32–67, at 35–37.

[24] See, for example, the *exempla* extracted from Jean Gobi's *Scala coeli* in Gobi, 123–49. Sermons for All Souls often give a string of such tales: Jacobus de Voragine, *The Golden Legend: Readings on the Saints*, trans. W. G. Ryan, 2 vols (Princeton, NJ, 1993), 2: 280–90; T. Erbe, ed., *Mirk's Festial: a Collection of Homilies by Johannes Mirkus (John Mirk)*, EETS es 96 (1905), 269–71.

[25] Finucane, *Appearances*, 86.

[26] C. Lecouteux, *Fantômes et revenants au moyen âge* (Paris, 1986), 222: 'instruit les vivants en se servant des morts'.

which is highly questionable.[27] It is certainly true that the ghosts in many of the tales (especially the *exempla*) become 'somewhat stereotypical figures whose exploits and utterances conformed to orthodox templates about the importance of confession, the sanctity of vows, the value of intercessory prayers'.[28]

How far the tales really reflect the extent of Church control over the afterlife, and popular acceptance of it, is elusive. Their use as *exempla* may show a Church seeking to ensure control, so that everyone participating in the economy of salvation and exploiting strategies for eternity was using the same templates. Alternatively – as has been suggested for Castile – the absence of ghost stories in a context of elaborate funeral rituals may reflect a close connection between the living and dead, making it unnecessary for ghosts to appear to remind people of their needs.[29]

For these tales had audiences, and while the messages might be controlled, they had to fit easily into a thought-world which was not exclusively clerical – one which had often provided the clerics' initial formation. The tales' integration into a broader medieval cosmology is nevertheless open to discussion. Jean-Claude Schmitt stresses the difference between *miracula* and *mirabilia*, between 'a suspension of the natural order ... through the will of the Creator' and events which 'even if they did not contradict the natural order, amazed the beholder, who did not understand what caused them'. He places ghost stories (those of the twelfth and thirteenth centuries at least) in the latter category.[30] Often, however, the issue of causation is irrelevant: in sermon *exempla* the key issue is not the ghostly presence, but the moral lesson. The *exemplum* aims to make a succinct point without saying much about the protagonists.[31] In this respect, the earlier chronological limit applied here cuts arbitrarily through the longer tradition of ghost stories. Many tales were indeed new to the late Middle Ages, but others were old. The awareness and anticipation of visitors from the afterlife derived from old traditions as well as new occurrences, which in turn were passed on and integrated into the accepted pattern. Gregory the

---

[27] See comments in N. Caciola, 'Wraiths, Revenants and Ritual in Medieval Culture', *P&P* no. 152 (August 1996), 3–45, at 5–6.

[28] P. Marshall, *Beliefs and the Dead in Reformation England* (Oxford, 2002), 16.

[29] Guiance, *Discorsos*, 412–13.

[30] Schmitt, *Ghosts*, 79–81; quotations at 79.

[31] Above, 147.

Great's *Dialogues* repeatedly provided later templates. *Exempla* were regularly adapted and translated over time and space. The cumulative and repetitive impetus operating here was important yet is easily forgotten. As Aaron Gurevich has commented, 'Eye-witness evidence … becomes part of tradition, and its part in tradition confirms its authenticity.'[32] Each addition to the tradition confirms the existing corpus, but is in turn confirmed and validated by such precedents, which form the mindset into which further novelties can be integrated.

The traditions within which the ghost stories must be accommodated were neither static, nor uniform. There are discernible differences over time and space, both in the rate of occurrence and the nature of the tales. The stories from Iceland and Scandinavia differ from those of the sermon *exempla*, possibly reflecting pre-Christian beliefs – certainly beliefs which appear unaware of purgatory and which accordingly accommodate ghosts while unconcerned with the fate of souls.[33]

A final point here: ghosts, and belief in ghosts, are only rarely mentioned in bureaucratic records. Few have been found in inquisition material;[34] appropriate evidence is almost undetectable in English official records.[35] This is worrying: there is no real control against which to assess the clerically-generated tales.

* * *

Despite the narratives, few theological writers seem to discuss these ghosts – possibly because they were of only peripheral interest. Alcher of Clairvaux, a twelfth-century author whose *Liber de spiritu et anima* was wrongly ascribed to St Augustine and thereby achieved considerable subsequent circulation, says very little about souls which return from the dead. His meticulous dissection of the components and qualities of the soul and the spirit devotes only one brief chapter explicitly to ghosts, accepting that they appeared but unsure how they should be explained.[36] Aquinas is similarly unforthcoming. His *Summa* includes a

---

[32] A. Gurevich, *Historical Anthropology of the Middle Ages* (Oxford, 1992), 216 n. 15.

[33] Lecouteux, *Fantômes*, deals almost exclusively with Scandinavian and Icelandic material, with no solid analysis of how ghosts were integrated into post-conversion mentalities. (I could not consult the 2nd edn, published in 1996.)

[34] Others may not yet have been highlighted or noticed.

[35] One of the few instances is in A. T. Bannister, 'Visitation Returns of the Diocese of Hereford in 1397', *EHR* 44 (1929), 446.

[36] PL 40: 779–832, at 799–800.

discussion of 'separated souls', in which the existence of ghosts is accepted, but not analysed.[37]

Later writers seem equally reticent. *Dives and Pauper*, an early fifteenth-century English tract, hints at a strand of popular instruction which possibly communicated 'official' doctrine to parishioners. Dives asks Pauper, 'Is there any danger to man or woman in charging a friend when dying to come again and give information about how he fares?' Pauper condemns such activity, for several reasons. Any such apparition may be diabolical rather than genuine, an appearance to misinform and undermine faith. If genuine, it would still be counter-productive, replacing faith in the soul's survival after death by experiential knowledge, which merited less reward. A genuine appearance could only occur by divine permission, since souls are incorporeal and lack inherent power to appear in visible form to humans; such engagements therefore tempt God. Sure knowledge of a soul's fate after death is also contrary to God's intention, reducing commitment to charitable acts for that soul. Other souls would then also suffer, while the survivor would lose the merit of his or her charity.[38] When Dives responds that some clerics endorsed such engagements as reflecting a natural and legitimate desire to increase knowledge, Pauper agrees that it is lawful to desire knowledge, 'but it is not lawful to desire to know ... by that means, or by any unlawful means, not by teaching of the fiend or by teaching of those who are dead'.[39] Dives immediately then asks how the spirits of the dead can actually walk about. Pauper initially replies that such spirits are devilish misrepresentations of the dead or else had assumed their bodies to do harm. However, he admits that God sometimes permits spirits to return, either to seek help, or to show that souls do live on after death and so strengthen those of weak belief. These spirits are harmless, except to those who refuse to believe that they are suffering and will not help them in their need.[40]

Two late fifteenth-century printed works show that ghosts did stimulate some specific academic analysis; both appeared in several editions, indicating wide interest.

---

[37] Thomas Aquinas, *Summa Theologiae*, XII: 1a, 84–89 (London and New York, n. d.), 160–61, 164–65.

[38] Priscilla Heath Barnum, ed., *Dives and Pauper*, 2 vols in 3, EETS os 275, 280, 323 (1976–2004), 1/i: 169–70. See also, in this volume, Catherine Rider, 'Agreements to Return from the Afterlife in Late Medieval *Exempla*', 174–83.

[39] Barnum, ed., *Dives and Pauper*, 1/i: 160–61.

[40] Ibid. 1/i: 171–72.

James of Clusa (d. 1465) produced the *Tractatus peroptimus de animabus exutis a corporibus.*[41] He cites various academic authorities to substantiate his points,[42] with the sources for his ghostly examples including Gregory the Great and Peter Damian.[43] One section of the tract considers how to communicate with and question spirits when they appear; the afterlife as such is less important.[44] A driving concern is to differentiate between good and bad spirits, but Clusa accepts that the Christian dead may manifest. Indeed, a key distinction is that ghosts, being Christian souls, can only appear to Christians: apparitions to infidels, Saracens, Jews and others can only be demonic.[45] If the spirit is actually a Christian soul, Clusa assumes that it wants help to get through purgatory: its needs should be investigated, and the reasons for its being in purgatory; but it must not be asked about matters superfluous, curious or superstitious, unless it desires voluntarily to reveal them.[46] Clusa accepts the sinlessless of a desire for ghostly visitations, if motivated by a wish to know a soul's fate and offer appropriate assistance; but it is sinful to desire such visitations out of levity or vanity. After all, if the dead can appear spontaneously to request aid, why should prayers by the living motivated by a desire to give aid be improper? This is not tempting God, because it aims to benefit the souls, and any visitation – as Clusa repeatedly stresses – requires divine permission. Nor is the desire motivated by superstition or for purposes of divination, but solely to discover truth.[47]

The purgatory from which these souls return receives some attention. The existence of general and individual purgatories is accepted, the latter being terrestrial and lasting until the Day of Judgement.[48] Purgatorial punishments are imposed by divine justice, possibly with demons as rejoicing spectators, but neither they nor angels are actively tormentors.[49]

[41] Clusa. See also L. Thorndike, *A History of Magic and Experimental Science*, 8 vols (New York, 1923–58), 4: 288–91 (for his tract on demons, see ibid. 283–88).

[42] E.g. Clusa, sigs Bi^r–Bii^r.

[43] Ibid. sigs Av^v–Avi^r.

[44] Ibid. sigs Biii^v–Cii^r.

[45] Ibid. sig. Aii^r.

[46] Ibid. sig. Biv^r.

[47] Ibid. sig. Bii^r. God's control over when and where ghosts are released from purgatory is repeatedly affirmed at sigs Bi^v–Bii^v. Clusa stipulates that the preliminaries to an interrogation should include prayers to God to cause the spirit to appear and explain itself: ibid. sig. Biv^r.

[48] Ibid. sig. Av^r.

[49] Ibid. sigs Avi^r–Bi^r.

Ghosts are also considered in a section of the *Speculum peregrinarum questionum* of Bartholomaeus Sibylla (d. 1493).[50] He allows diverse denizens of the other world to cross into this one, giving a complex list of contexts in which that might happen. The only inhabitants of the afterlife barred from appearing to the living are the children in limbo, who can gain no benefit from such manifestations.[51] Of the other dead, the souls of saints can appear to help humans under siege,[52] while the damned may appear by divine permission prior to judgement, to teach and instil fear in the living.[53] For Sibylla, the basic difference between saints and the damned was that saints have grace to appear whenever they wish, while the damned need divine permission.[54] Souls in purgatory can emerge to implore suffrages.[55] Spectral manifestations are not, however, solely of dead humans. Good and bad angels also appear in assumed bodies, the latter sometimes at the instigation of witches.[56] It is therefore necessary to determine whether a spirit is good or bad. Following established tradition, Sibylla treats this as a matter of sensation and perception: once the encounter's initial shock (invariably a sense of terror) has abated, a good feeling indicates the presence of a good spirit, while a continuing bad feeling indicates a bad spirit.[57]

Sibylla also acknowledges that the dead might actually or putatively manifest in other, non-ghostly, ways. Dream visions are a different issue,[58] and dreams of the dead are not necessarily visitations by the dead. Yet the dead may appear in dreams to give advice, to warn, and to ask for prayers.[59] Sibylla denies that people possessed by spirits should be believed if they claim to be overtaken by the soul or spirit of someone dead. That is false: the possession is demonic.[60]

* * *

Most of the learned analysis seems to be late, reflecting a fully mature doctrinal approach, and a general trend which condemned all spirits as

---

[50] Lyons, 1534 [hereafter, 'Sibylla']. The relevant section is fols 61r–63r.
[51] Ibid. fol. 61v.
[52] Ibid. fol. 61r.
[53] Ibid. fol. 61r–v.
[54] Ibid. fol. 61v.
[55] Ibid.
[56] Ibid. fol. 61r.
[57] Ibid. fol. 61v. Cf. W. A. Christian, Jr, *Apparitions in Late Medieval and Renaissance Spain* (Princeton, NJ, 1981), 193.
[58] Sibylla, fol. 61v, also fols 75r–76v.
[59] Ibid. fol. 75v.
[60] Ibid. fol. 127v.

demonic. There is an inherent inconsistency in the assumption that ghosts were necessarily diabolical projections, just as there is in the assumption that all spirit possessions of the living – including possession by identifiable souls – were necessarily diabolical.[61] By the 1400s ghosts were perhaps being denied the opportunity to prove they were ghosts.[62] This may explain cases where spirits treated as demons act like purgatorial ghosts seeking liberation from the effects of sin by demanding prayers, masses and other good deeds supposedly to liberate the souls of the people they purported themselves to be.[63]

Care was certainly needed when dealing with ghosts which might be deceits. Evil spirits claimed to be the Christian dead, so all had to be tested, and could be found wanting. In 1458 one seemingly benign ghost was unable to recite a prayer when tested, thereby revealing itself as a diabolic spirit.[64] In the thirteenth century Jacques de Vitry reported a more dangerous case, of a young Catholic woman tempted into Catharism by what looked like the ghost of her dead mother in glory, ascribing her state to her adherence to Cathar belief. The apparition was a demonic fraud: when the woman sought advice from Catholic priests, their masses and prayers compelled the devil to bring back the real mother, bewailing her fate and urging her daughter to remain a true Catholic.[65]

Evidence of how ghosts actually fitted into the contemporary belief system generally derives from less academic tales and *exempla*. Until purgatory congealed as a major factor in religious belief and practice in the thirteenth century, ghosts arguably had little place in formal theology. They did, though, have a place in popular beliefs: part of the impetus for purgatory's formalization undoubtedly lay in tales of returning souls seeking aid to alleviate, if not eliminate, their sufferings

---

[61] P. A. Sigal, 'La possession demoniaque dans la région de Florence au XVe siècle d'après les miracles de saint Jean Gualbert', in *Histoire et société: Mélanges offerts à Georges Duby, III: Le moine, le clerc et le prince* (Aix-en-Provence, 1992), 101–12, at 105–06.

[62] Suggested in Caciola, *Discerning Spirits*, 254.

[63] See for example *ActaSS* Jul. 2, 421, and Bernardino of Siena's comment that a spirit 'Aliquando est diabolus loquens in persona hominis mortui et petit ut dicantur missae pro anima sua', cited in G. Zarra, 'Purgatorio "particolare" e ritorno dei morti tra Riforma e Controriforma: l'area italiana', *Quaderni storici* 50 (August 1982), 475. Such appeals might be deceptions: see 162–63 below.

[64] Petrus Madonis, *Flagellum maleficorum* ([?Lyons, 1491]), sig. b.2r.

[65] C. Muessig, 'Heaven, Earth and the Angels: Preaching Paradise in the Sermons of Jacques de Vitry', in C. Muessig and A. Putter, eds, *Envisaging Heaven in the Middle Ages* (London and New York, 2007), 57–72, at 63.

in the afterlife. One such was the vision of the priest Walchelin, recorded by Orderic Vitalis. While clearly linked to traditions of the Wild Hunt, at its core was a personal encounter between the priest and his brother, as the latter sought relief from his tortures.[66]

How should ghosts be accommodated within Christian belief? What did they represent? If ghostly visitations occurred to seek aid for deceased souls, those souls clearly had to be capable of being aided, to be potentially able to achieve salvation. Logically, souls in hell should not return to earth, because no-one could help them. The only reason why the damned might legitimately return would be to offer warnings for amendment.[67]

While many early ghost tales almost presuppose purgatory, they often do so from hindsight. Possibly, if purgatory had not existed, such stories may have forced its invention; but its invention did not eradicate the complexities of the afterlife which the tales created. Equally, while ghost stories after 1250 (an arbitrary cut-off date) reflect ideas of the afterlife which include purgatory, the tales' purposes remain complex. The tripartite afterlife of heaven, hell and purgatory, and the tripartite salvational construct to which they are usually tied, was not universally accepted. An elusive strand within medieval Christianity argued for the possibility of universal salvation even of 'the damned' – and asserted that the final purpose of Creation could not be fulfilled until every soul had returned to its Creator, as the ultimate universal destiny.[68] Such an understanding should reject ghosts and purgatory, yet one of its prime recorded exponents communicated with ghosts and understood the afterlife to include some form of purification.[69] More radically, some people rejected the very idea of an afterlife: in 1491 Thomas Tailour at Newbury said that death was really the end, the soul being snuffed out like a candle.[70]

Acceptance that ghosts were – chiefly – souls returned from purga-

---

[66] Jacques Le Goff, *The Birth of Purgatory* (London, 1984), 177–81; Chibnall, *Orderic*, 236–49; Lecouteux, *Chasses fantastiques*, 91–101.

[67] Lecouteux, *Fantômes*, 120.

[68] P. Dronke, 'The Completeness of Heaven', in Muessig and Putter, eds, *Envisaging Heaven*, 44–56; N. Watson, 'Visions of Inclusion: Universal Salvation and Vernacular Theology in Pre-Reformation England', *Journal of Medieval and Early Modern Studies* 27 (1997), 145–87.

[69] See here 152, 164–66 (esp. 166).

[70] D. P. Wright, ed., *The Register of Thomas Langton, Bishop of Salisbury, 1485–93*, CYS 74 (1985), 70; see also J. H. Arnold, *Belief and Unbelief in Medieval Europe* (London, 2005), 2, 225–26.

tory solved part of the problem of their existence, but not all of it. Why did they appear where they did? One explanation was that souls might mingle together in a general or common purgatory, or might have an individual purgatory, a specific terrestrial site associated with their major sins, to which they returned as ghosts. How this worked doctrinally is unclear; nor is it known how widespread such an understanding was, as most references to purgatory make no such distinction.[71]

Ghosts' integration into the tripartite afterlife of late medieval Catholicism helped to resolve the problem of their existence, but did not eliminate the earlier beliefs in the wandering dead. Here a distinction may be needed between 'revenants', the returning bodies of the dead, and 'ghosts' as returning souls. Old – maybe continuing – beliefs accepted that the dead wandered. A key issue was the state in which they wandered. Corpses could be mere shells, available for demonic possession to terrify the living. As such they clearly fell within the learned discourse.[72] The dead even had to be protected against such invasion, through the prayers recited when dedicating a cemetery.[73] The argument that revenants were possessed gave a learned refinement to reality; but not all revivified corpses were demonically possessed. Some simply revived, returning to terrorize their neighbours, sometimes as killers themselves or harbingers of death.[74] How these should be interpreted within the Christian cosmology is unclear: while revivified, and sometimes fitted into the system by acknowledging that God had permitted their return, they were probably not reanimated (repossessed of a soul). Some – notably in Icelandic sagas – may not actually be part of a recognizably Christian thought-world at all. Their contagious murderousness arguably had little to do with the Christian afterlife.[75] Yet some of the revivified dead must have been reanimated. Walter Map mentions living men who abducted women from groups of the dead dancing at night, and by whom they later had children. These dead were not being troublesome, just enjoying themselves; the living were the intruders. These abducted women cannot have been unsouled shells if they returned to the Christian world.[76]

[71] This distinction is a theme of Zarra, 'Purgatorio', 466–97. A threefold purgatory appears in Harley, *Revelation of Purgatory*, 79–83, 133–37.
[72] See Caciola, 'Wraiths', 11–14.
[73] Ibid. 13.
[74] Ibid. 15–24.
[75] See, for example, ibid. 15–16.
[76] James, *Walter Map*, 160, 348–50; Caciola, 'Wraiths', 38.

The physicality of revenants is often striking: these were not spirits, but walking corpses, which could terrify and terrorize, and even become vampires.[77] As physical beings, they provoked physical responses: for them the 'afterlife' was firmly earthbound. Among lay reactions, one was to destroy the corpse by burning – a purifying process of elimination akin to the treatment of heretics and witches.[78] Where a corpse merely had to be quietened, all it needed was a proper burial.[79]

The search for quiet, for a decent burial to pacify and placate a soul, shifts attention from the corporeality of the revenant to the incorporeality of the ghost – although some late medieval ghosts retained their materiality, being grasped and held fast.[80] This shift from revived body to returned soul contributes to the process which made the ghost a visitor from purgatory seeking aid in a clericalized understanding of the afterlife. The transition – and with transition the tension – between possibly conflicting lay and clerical responses to the dead appears in a twelfth-century tale reported by William of Newburgh. Here lay people wished to burn a wandering corpse to end the nuisance it caused; but the local bishop insisted on first placing a letter of absolution in the man's tomb, which provided the desired pacification.[81] Just how this absolution worked is unclear, as no theological validation is given. Some later cases also mention absolution, with the ghost first making a confession.[82] Other 'absolutions' may not be sacramental acts to remove the guilt of sin, but judicial absolutions from excommunication. Spirits in such cases might indeed be from purgatory, seeking to reduce the penalties they faced there.[83]

* * *

Against the *exempla*, a few detailed accounts offer more than isolated fragments of evidence. Between 1200 and 1460, three lengthy inter-

[77] R. Howlett, ed., *Chronicles of the Reigns of Stephen, Henry II, and Richard I*, 4 vols, RS (London, 1884–9), 2: 474–82 (for the vampire, see 481–82), trans. Joynes, *Medieval Ghost Stories*, 100–02.

[78] Caciola, 'Wraiths', 21.

[79] James, *Walter Map*, 204.

[80] James, 'Ghost-Stories', 418.

[81] Howlett, ed., *Chronicles*, 2: 474–75; trans. Joynes, *Medieval Ghost Stories*, 97–98.

[82] E.g. James, 'Ghost-Stories', 418. The priest made the ghost's captors swear not to reveal any of the confessed sins.

[83] James, 'Ghost-Stories', 419–20; Erbe, *Mirk's Festial*, 281. See also comment in C. S. Watkins, 'Sin, Penance and Purgatory in the Anglo-Norman Realm: The Evidence of Visions and Ghost Stories', *P&P* 175 (May 2002), 3–33, at 23–24, 27 (esp. n. 80).

views with specific ghosts say something about the afterlife, and about how contemporaries dealt with ghosts.[84] There is also the record of a heresy investigation in early fourteenth-century France. None of this material is new, yet it merits reconsideration precisely as evidence of the afterlife.

The first case is reported by Gervase of Tilbury. It occurred in Beaucaire in July 1211, following a young man's accidental but violent death.[85] He later appeared to a young female cousin and communicated with a priest, in a series of apparitions lasting some weeks. Gervase was apparently among those who questioned the ghost via the priest.[86] He reports events in an almost blasé manner. Describing the ghost's first visit, he refers blandly to the 'instinct, implanted by nature in the hearts of mortals, to shrink from the dead and respond to their visits in a confused state of mind', the ghost calming his cousin's fears 'in the usual way of those who come back by divine consent'.[87]

This ghost is invisible throughout, and usually inaudible except to its chosen interlocutor. This caused some confusion: a visiting prior was asked to move, because he was almost standing on the ghost's foot. The visitation was clearly considered an opportunity worth exploiting, with several people eventually asking questions. Gervase frequently cites Gregory the Great's *Dialogues,* noting occasional differences between the papal and spectral understandings of the afterlife.[88] Despite Gregory's authority, Gervase prefers to believe the ghost because 'he has more first-hand knowledge'.[89]

This ghost's presence seems to lack specific purpose but has been explained psychologically.[90] His return is divinely sanctioned, yet he seeks no personal *post mortem* commemorations. While violent, his death was spiritually complete: he had time to repent, to make confession and to receive the last rites. There was, apparently, nothing to keep him on earth. He initially ascribes his return to affection for his cousin,

---

[84] Had they not occurred in dreams, the conversations reported in Harley, *Revelation of Purgatory,* could also be included: see above, n. 16.

[85] The case appears in Gervase, 759–85; see also Schmitt, *Ghosts,* 87–97. It and the Alès manifestation (below, 159–60) are considered in M.-A. Polo de Beaulieu, 'De Beaucaire (1211) à Alès (1323): les revenants et leurs révélations sur l'au-delà', in *La mort et l'au-delà en France méridionale (XIIᵉ–XVᵉ siècle)*, Cahiers de Fanjeaux 33 (Toulouse, 1998), 319–41.

[86] Gervase, 770–71.

[87] Ibid. 760–61.

[88] Ibid. 762–65, 768–75.

[89] Ibid. 774–75: 'magis experto magis consentio'.

[90] Schmitt, *Ghosts,* 92.

but later it appears that she had made him swear when dying to return from the dead 'to make his condition known to her'. Her repeated extraction of promises to return explain his repeated visits, but he adds that 'The real reason for my return is the hope that by my words the faithlessness of unbelievers may be turned to faith, and the faith of believers may burn more brightly.'[91] Those unbelievers included the Albigensians (Beaucaire lay in Cathar territory), whose 'death and extermination' were declared 'pleasing to God';[92] but they are mentioned almost in passing. The reported dialogues (which Gervase acknowledges to be incomplete) include comments on the afterlife, especially purgatory.

The ghost says that he dwells in the air among spirits, experiencing purifying fires.[93] His state is directly affected by events on earth: his clothing changes to resemble his earthly garments when they are distributed to the poor; and he must wear a girdle of fire until a borrowed belt is returned to its rightful owner.[94] All souls which will be saved enter purgatory, other than saints, who go to heaven.[95] Purgatory is a place of days and nights,[96] where souls are cleansed in agony tinged with joy. The souls there receive some respite at weekends, and when masses are celebrated or other deeds done on their behalf.[97] Each soul has a guardian angel – all called 'Michael' to name the office rather than an individual – and the souls join in commemoration of St Michael's Day by praising their personal angels.[98] The sufferings of the damned are visible from purgatory, but they are not yet in hell. That subterranean pit will remain empty until after the Day of Judgement – until then the damned suffer aerial torments while anticipating the fullness of their damnation.[99] The just are meanwhile in the bosom of Abraham, pending admission to heaven.[100] Some of the ghost's pronouncements clearly relate to contemporary debates. Announcing that the saints have

[91] Gervase, 760–63, 770–71.
[92] Ibid. 778–79.
[93] Ibid. 762–65.
[94] Ibid. 764–67. A similar belief about the quality of the clothing worn by the dead is suggested by J. Duvernoy, ed., *Le registre d'inquisition de Jacques Fournier, évêque de Pamiers (1318–1325)*, 3 vols (Toulouse, 1965), 1: 541.
[95] Gervase, 772–73.
[96] Ibid. 776–77.
[97] Ibid. 774–77.
[98] Ibid. 778–81.
[99] Ibid. 768–69, 772–73.
[100] Ibid. 768–69.

varying degrees of glory, St Bernard's is declared imperfect because he opposed the Feast of the Immaculate Conception.[101] Debates about the beatific vision are addressed when the ghost says that he had already seen the Virgin, but not yet God. God would be seen indistinctly when the ghost was released from purgatory, and fully after the Day of Judgement.[102]

The second manifestation, of the ghost of Guy of Corvo, occurred in Alès, in southern France, in 1323 or 1324. The story was subsequently widely diffused across Europe, its differing versions reflecting differing imperatives and manipulations, as yet incompletely analysed.[103] This was a high-profile case, its protagonists including one of the leading contemporary Dominicans, Jean Gobi, with a report being presented to Pope John XXII. From an initially short statement, the tale grew into a lengthy dialogue with detailed comments on various aspects of contemporary spiritual activity. It has a strongly didactic aspect throughout, using the ghost to reinforce a range of points. The ghost is always invisible but is heard moving and has a voice. There are at least two meetings, the lengthy preliminaries to the first recalling the preparations enjoined by James of Clusa.[104] Duly conjured, the ghost promised to answer questions 'as allowed by my nature and what is permitted to me'.[105] The subsequent discussions range over many issues, although the ghost is sometimes reticent: 'it is not the divine will that I should answer all your questions'.[106] This is an exhausting process; the ghost is almost silenced at one point by the weight of his sufferings but is speedily reinvigorated by a burst of devotional activity.[107] Not every issue relates to the afterlife: the dialogue also provides pastoral instruction for its future readers. One section is almost an *ars moriendi*;[108] another comment digs at the secular clergy, as less effective in divine service than the regulars.[109]

Guy is suffering in purgatory for his sins committed on earth,

---

[101] Ibid. 774–75.

[102] Ibid. 766–67.

[103] The fullest survey of the evidence currently available is in Gobi, with a French translation of the short version of events at 51–61, and of the fuller tract at 71–107. For date, see 22–23.

[104] Gobi, 72–74.

[105] Ibid. 75.

[106] Ibid. 103.

[107] Ibid. 93–94.

[108] Ibid. 82–86.

[109] Ibid. 98.

awaiting release from punishment when he has suffered enough – although the soul seems rather annoyed that it suffers for the misdeeds of a body to which it is no longer joined.[110] He has returned to seek prayers to reduce the sufferings, and to warn his wife so that she might avoid similar punishments.[111] He avers the separation of heaven and hell, and as he is neither damned nor yet fully saved cannot say who is in either. The punishments of purgatory and hell occur in firmly separated places.[112] Here purgatory is double: Guy suffers at night in the personal purgatory of his former home, but by day mingles with other souls in the general purgatory, at the centre of the earth.[113] Although he is suffering, he is supported by a guardian angel.[114] There is detailed – perhaps pedantic – analysis of how masses work for the dead, individually or collectively, and of other ways to aid the deceased.[115] At the first encounter Guy asserts the effectiveness of *post mortem* commemorations: those from which he has benefited mean that he will quit purgatory at Easter. He invites Gobi to return then, 'and if you do not hear me, know that I will be in heaven'.[116]

As evidence of and from the afterlife, Guy's most important information concerns the immediate judgement after death, in the brief interval before the separation of body and soul when it is decided whether the soul will go to hell or to purgatory. That judgement made, the journey is immediate. However, prayers for the soul before it leaves the body may delay the arrival in purgatory if they force a recalculation of the time due to be spent there.[117] Purgatory itself is not really described, other than as a place of fire and freezing.[118] Also noteworthy is what is almost Gobi's parting shot: a transfer to the ghost of the benefits of the indulgences Gobi had gained over the preceding year, and from which it immediately receives comfort.[119] Sermon *exempla* and other tales of ghostly encounters also affirm the effectiveness of indulgences in purgatory, often in similar contexts of transfer.[120]

---

[110] Ibid. 77.
[111] Ibid. 77, 98, 104.
[112] Ibid. 78–80.
[113] Ibid. 81–82.
[114] Ibid. 90.
[115] Ibid. 86–93.
[116] Ibid. 90; see also 108.
[117] Ibid. 99–100.
[118] Ibid. 101.
[119] Ibid. 104.
[120] e.g. J. T. Welter, ed., *Le speculum laicorum: Édition d'une collection d'exempla composée en*

The third ghost story comes from fifteenth-century Germany. The lengthy tale of the encounter between Arnt Buschman and his grandfather's ghost, dated to 1437 (but written at least a year later) survives in several vernacular manuscripts, in a Latin translation, and in print. While regionally fairly popular, it never achieved continental distribution.[121] The reported conversations are at times disjointed and occasionally appear self-contradictory.[122]

Immediately notable is the alleged delay between the death of the grandfather Henry Buschmann and his apparition: some forty years. Moreover, this ghost appears initially not as a human, but as a dog. It is some time before Arnt realises that it is a ghost rather than an evil spirit, and only after taking clerical advice does he formally conjure the ghost to declare itself, allowing the conversations and apparitions to begin. They last for about six months, ending when the ghost secures release from purgatory. Apart from the initial clerical involvement in advising Arnt on how to proceed, this is very much a lay experience, and strongly domestic.

The text's purpose is heavily didactic: this ghost story certainly aims to reinforce faith among the laity. It might almost be placed among the *pastoralia* produced in the pre-Reformation centuries as part of the so-called pastoral revolution arising from the Fourth Lateran Council of 1215.[123]

Like Guy of Corvo, Henry Buschman is also weakened by the interviews, but is reinvigorated by prayer.[124] He has a guardian angel.[125] The idea of double purgatory is implicit, but perhaps differently formulated, as some souls suffer a localized terrestrial purgation prior to the

---

Angleterre à la fin du XIII siècle (Paris, 1914), nos 326–27 (cf. no. 86, for a transfer of merits from good deeds); M. Sensi, *Il perdono di Assisi* (Assisi, 2002), 211–12, 214, 219, 300, 326–27. Intriguingly, indulgences are not transferred in the Middle English version of the Alès apparition, *The Gast of Gy*, in C. Horstmann, ed., *Yorkshire Writers: Richard Rolle of Hampole and his Followers*, 2 vols (London, 1895–6), 2: 292–333. See also Gobi, 148–49.

[121] For the German text, see Seelmann, 'Arnt Buschmans Mirakel', 40–67, listing manuscripts and incunabula editions, with brief textual consideration at 35–40. A modern French translation (based on a printed text not noted by Seelmann) is in C. Lecouteux, *Dialogue avec un revenant, XVᵉ siècle* (Paris, 1999).

[122] The text primarily relates the meetings between Arnt and his grandfather, but two other ghosts are also briefly mentioned: Lecouteux, *Dialogue*, 51.

[123] Succinctly surveyed by L. E. Boyle, 'The Fourth Lateran Council and Manuals of Popular Theology', in T. J. Heffernan, ed., *The Popular Literature of Medieval England*, Tennessee Studies in Literature 28 (Knoxville, TN, 1985), 30–43.

[124] For weakness, see Lecouteux, *Dialogue*, 55, 58, 62; for reinvigoration, see ibid. 59–60.

[125] Ibid. 74.

general purgatory.[126] Here the devil is an active tormentor in purgatory.[127] Henry is obliged to appear where he does on earth, but for reasons known only to God.[128] He can only say what God allows, and not what he does not authorize.[129] Like other ghosts, Henry seeks and stipulates actions to liberate him from purgatory.[130] Fragments of his tale construct a narrative to explain his delayed appearance to seek relief – but they do not quite add up. Thus, Henry's soul had originally been scheduled for purgatory, but intercession by the Virgin and St James had allowed him to be punished on earth, being tortured by an evil spirit until his sins were purged.[131] Yet he had experienced a poor death, having made an incomplete confession, and so was suffering more than he might have.[132] His sufferings were extended because his children had neglected him after death, and he had not been allowed to return to reveal his sufferings. This neglect was not wholly deliberate. His children had asked a pious relative[133] to summon his soul to reveal its state. This is a rare acknowledgement of the possibility of actual necromancy in the ghost stories. However, it conforms to the learned discourse since the relative was deceived by evil spirits: when she recalled Henry, the devil appeared in his guise and requested pilgrimages, masses and charity.[134] These were done, but did not benefit Henry's soul because they were commissioned at diabolical instigation rather than as required by the Church.[135] The devil returned at the

---

[126] Ibid. 71.

[127] Ibid. 79.

[128] Ibid. 54.

[129] Ibid. 59.

[130] For the required commemorations, see ibid. 48–49.

[131] Ibid. 79.

[132] Ibid. 64–65.

[133] Lecouteux's translation first calls her an aunt, then a kinswoman (*cousine*), and finally a niece (ibid. 66–68). The German text calls her a niece throughout (Seelmann, 'Arnt Buschmans Mirakel', 53–54).

[134] Although she was also now suffering, her salvation was assured. She had engaged in magic unwittingly, and the local priest had actually authorized her to contact spirits (Lecouteux, *Dialogue*, 67–68). In precise contemporary terminology, necromancers 'claim that, by means of superstitious rites, they are able to raise the dead from the earth in order to speak on occult matters': M. D. Bailey, *Battling Demons: Witchcraft, Heresy, and Reform in the Late Middle Ages* (University Park, PA, 2003), 40; see also Lecouteux, *Fantômes*, 76–79. Most late medieval 'necromancy' had a different focus, and as a learned and clerical art it adopted the formal clerical attitude to ghosts: they could not be summoned. Learned necromancers intentionally and knowingly summoned only demons; but like the false Henry Buschman, these could appear as simulacra of the dead: R. Kieckhefer, *Magic in the Middle Ages* (Cambridge, 1989), ch. 7, esp. 152–53.

[135] Is this a let-out clause for other cases where possessing spirits request similar com-

year's end and reported that the offices had worked, so Henry's children ended the commemorations. This left his soul stranded, but he still gained a share in the general prayers and offices for the dead.[136]

Henry now appeared to Arnt because his father (Henry's son) had been loyal to him but had died before he could complete the disbursements intended to benefit Henry's soul.[137] The encounter with Arnt procures Henry's final release: the commemorative acts have the desired effect, as does a transfer of 'indulgences' (*aflates*), but these are slightly problematic. Henry takes as many as he needs yet will remain in purgatory for two more days until all the masses commissioned for his soul are said.[138] Even so, before leaving he is already changed: in one apparition he shines like the sun, having already seen the face of Christ.[139] He already knows his future: on leaving purgatory he will go to the place where Christ took the souls of those released at the Harrowing of Hell. He will stay there ten days and then join the third choir of angels in heaven.[140]

Apart from these 'autobiographical' remarks, little more is revealed of the afterlife; yet some of the points are striking. Henry is not reticent about commenting on the fates of others. Arnt's father is reported as suffering, because he had not fulfilled the distributions for Henry's soul, but this would cease – having already lasted twenty-five years – when a defaulting debtor dies, who will have to assume the penalties in his stead.[141] Henry also explains the fates of other souls, like the widow now placed in the eighth choir of angels.[142]

Henry's purgatory has some strange features. Some souls suffer a terrestrial purgatory after death, but not all of them then go to God. One person reportedly suffered for three years on earth, and was then sent to hell.[143] The most bizarre tale concerns a father whose spirit was suffering on earth at his son's home. There he behaved as an instrument of divine retribution, killing his son's children after their baptisms

memorative works for dead souls? See 153 above. The ghost offers a warning against false spirits: Lecouteux, *Dialogue*, 54.
   [136] Ibid. 66–67.
   [137] Ibid. 54.
   [138] Ibid. 62–63; Seelmann, 'Arnt Buschmans Mirakel', 51.
   [139] Lecouteux, *Dialogue*, 74–75.
   [140] Ibid. 82. For a Spanish woman who claimed to see her dead son as an angel when visited by the Virgin, see Christian, *Apparitions*, 177.
   [141] Lecouteux, *Dialogue*, 54–55.
   [142] Ibid. 83.
   [143] Ibid. 70–71.

(seven thus far) to punish him for his own and his relatives' sins – and he would continue to do so until the son's wife drove him to confession and penance.[144]

These three tales have a certain generic overlap; the fourth statement is very different. It appears in testimony offered to the inquisition in southern France in 1319 by and about Arnaud Gélis, a sacristan at Pamiers who was on the fringes of the clerical world.[145]

Gélis acted as a messenger for souls, his contacts with the dead giving him a particular role within his community (he had a kins-woman with similar powers).[146] Despite their subsequent denials, he apparently had several adherents.[147] His quasi-clerical functions affected his view of the afterlife, imposing a Christian perspective; but one not firmly Catholic. His other world is firmly earth-bound, with two parallel dimensions occupying the same terrestrial space. The earth was crowded with the invisible dead, who had to be accommodated, and considered. Even energetic walking might harm them: 'People who move their arms and hands from their sides when they walk about ... knock many souls of the dead to the ground.'[148] This is also a somewhat uncharitable afterlife: if the dead fall over, they cannot rise of their own accord but must wait for help from other souls who knew them while alive. Those who did not know them simply walk over them.[149]

The dead with whom Gélis mingled were mostly Christians and sought Christian salvation, by serving out their own *post mortem* purifi-cation and asking Gélis to contact their relatives to have them commis-sion masses and other charitable acts for their souls (although some make no requests for aid).[150] He had also seen Jewish ghosts, whose ex-perience was different, and who remained separate from the Christians. Nevertheless, they would still be saved by Mary's intercession.[151] The

144 Ibid. 71. The son later improves, partly thanks to Arnt's intervention: ibid. 72.
145 Duvernoy, *Registre*, 1: 129–43, 533–52; extracts translated in J. Duvernoy, *Inquisition à Pamiers: cathares, juifs, lépreux ... devant leur juges* (Paris, 1966), 34–39. See also E. Le Roy Ladurie, *Montaillou* (Harmondsworth, 1980), 345–51.
146 Duvernoy, *Registre*, 1: 136.
147 For one accusation that he was lying, see ibid. 1: 551.
148 Ibid. 1: 544–55.
149 Ibid. 1: 135, 534, 543. The souls kept together in groups who had known each other while alive: ibid. 1: 541.
150 Contrasting with other cases, these requests are fairly minor, e.g. three masses, or food for three paupers for one day (ibid. 1: 129, 131). See also ibid. 1: 135. If Gélis did not pass on the messages, he was beaten: ibid. 1: 136.
151 Ibid. 1: 135–56, 535, 543–44.

dead kept their earthly physical shapes but were more beautiful.[152] Dead clerics were recognizable by their clothing (a former bishop of Pamiers still had his mitre), but others simply wore albs.[153] Most of the Christian souls were undergoing terrestrial purification, prior to admission to heaven – but this was not the purgatory of contemporary Catholicism.[154] The 'good ladies' of tradition, Gélis said, were the great and rich who were being dragged in carts by devils over mountains and valleys, and across plains.[155]

A striking feature of Gélis's testimony is his emphasis on the connection between the dead and churches. The adult dead were constantly on pilgrimage, moving from church to church to purify their souls and secure salvation (the greater their need for penance, the faster they moved). They had a real affinity with their own parish churches, and with the churchyards where they were buried. They spent the night in churches. Any who had not made a pilgrimage to Compostela whilst alive did so after death.[156] However, they rested from Saturday evening to Monday morning, could return to their family homes on Saturdays, and enjoyed wine and a good warm fire, but were fastidious about entering unclean houses.[157] (The Saturday relief recalls ideas that the torments of souls in purgatory are reduced – or even fully abated – at weekends.)[158] The dead preferred offerings of oil in lamps to altar candles, because the latter got blown out when walking.[159] Dead women liked to return to check on young grandchildren; others returned to help people to sleep more soundly.[160] Some of the dead suffered for specific causes, and passed on messages of warning, or requesting appropriate action.[161] Dead children, if baptized, went immediately to the place of rest or to glory; but the unbaptized went to limbo, pending their salvation.[162]

---

[152]   Ibid. 1: 136–37, 543.

[153]   Ibid. 1: 130, 134.

[154]   Only one ghost reports a journey through purgatorial fire, possibly as an alternative method of purification: ibid. 1: 130, 135, 542; Ladurie, *Montaillou*, 1: 348–49.

[155]   Duvernoy, *Registre*, 1: 544. On these women, see Lecouteux, *Chasses fantastiques*.

[156]   Duvernoy, *Registre*, 1: 134–35, 137, 537.

[157]   Ibid. 1: 132, 137, 533, 535, 537, 551.

[158]   M.-A. Polo de Beaulieu, 'Recueils d'exempla méridionaux et culte des âmes du purgatoire', in *La papauté d'Avignon et le Languedoc (1316–1342)*, Cahiers de Fanjeaux 26 (1991), 257–78, at 271–73.

[159]   Duvernoy, *Registre*, 1: 544.

[160]   Ibid. 1: 135, 545.

[161]   Ibid. 1: 131–32, 540, 548.

[162]   Ibid. 1: 134, 538, 541–42.

The promise of salvation for unbaptized infants links to the most idiosyncratic feature of Gélis's testimony, his belief in universal salvation, based on information supplied by the ghosts.[163] These ghosts were undergoing penance, but none were suffering real punishment or in an eternal hell. Their penance would end; they would then move to a place of rest, the terrestrial paradise, to await the Last Judgement, when ultimately all would be saved.[164] Those at rest felt nothing bad, but they did not see the face of God, and would not until the Day of Judgement.[165] Occasional qualifications demanded belief in Christ, or baptism, but how these refined the overall idea is unclear.[166] Moreover, Gélis still accepted the existence of hell, but said that no soul would enter it until the Day of Judgement.[167]

How the ecclesiastical authorities reacted to this case is unknown: many of Gélis's beliefs were judged erroneous (but not heretical), and he duly abjured. He was later sentenced, but his punishment is not recorded.[168]

* * *

This material gives considerable – but at times conflicting – information on the afterlife and the permeability of the barriers between this world and the next, which impacted on the relationship between the living and the dead. One important consideration would be where the 'other world' physically was.

The crowded terrestrial afterlife in Arnaud Gélis's testimony is highly idiosyncratic;[169] but the idea that the afterlife had a terrestrial element was perhaps widely shared. Ghosts were seen dancing in churchyards, claiming territorial space where the living could be in danger, but might also be protected. Some of the oddest episodes concern the dead who rise from their graves to attack someone at prayer,[170] or turn against a human who interrupts their own special

---

[163] E.g. ibid. 1: 129–30, 133.

[164] Ibid. 1: 133 (but the truly saintly will reach heaven earlier), 135, 541, 544, 551. Angels are messengers in the prelude to the move to the place of rest: ibid. 1: 543. See also 154 above.

[165] Duvernoy, *Registre*, 1: 551.

[166] Ibid. 1: 131–32.

[167] Ibid. 1: 133, 136. Jews, Saracens and heretics who implore divine mercy will also be saved, as will apostate Christians who return to do penance after death among Christians (ibid. 1: 136, 544; cf. 535). The souls of heretics who contemned God will be utterly annihilated (ibid. 1: 542, see also 139).

[168] Ibid. 1: 138–43.

[169] Above, 164.

[170] Lecouteux, *Fantômes*, 74; see also 214.

midnight masses – masses celebrated by a priest from among the dead for a congregation of the dead.[171] The churchyard was also a place of intimacy, where the living were particularly expected to pray for the dead – and might gain indulgences for doing so. The dead might acknowledge such prayers with their own 'amen'.[172] More actively, a fairly common *exemplum* has the dead rise from their graves to defend someone who habitually prayed for their souls while walking through a churchyard, who was being mugged in the cemetery.[173]

There were so many dead, so many potential returnees, that the living possibly had to protect themselves from being pestered. Some customary practices of medieval Catholicism may reflect acceptance of the possibility – even probability – that ghosts could and would return, unless dissuaded. The regularity of ghostly appearances on the seventh or thirtieth days after their death, or on its anniversary, replicates the timetable of *post mortem* commemorations frequently encountered in pre-Reformation Catholicism.[174] While these commemorations did aim to ease the soul through purgatory, were they also meant to keep it there, and to prevent it from coming back? Something similar might be suggested for the practice of providing a written statement of absolution to accompany a corpse into the afterlife, as mandated by the Use of Salisbury.[175]

Further evidence of a concern with the invisible dead, and awareness of their presence, occurs in a Yorkshire tale of c. 1400. The ghost explains his visibility to his seer: 'You should know, therefore, that because today you have not heard mass nor the Gospel of John, nor have seen the consecration of the Lord's body and blood, I have now confronted you; otherwise I would not fully have the power to appear to you.'[176] This explanation draws attention to several late medieval popular devotional practices. Here, however, they have a specific functional value in warding off ghosts. Even if such attributes were only a regional belief,

---

171   Ibid. 74–75; Lecouteux, *Chasses fantastiques*, 37–39.
172   Schmitt, *Ghosts*, 138.
173   Jacobus de Voragine, *Golden Legend*, 2: 285; Schmitt, *Ghosts*, 138 (and n. 41).
174   Finucane, *Appearances*, 65–66.
175   A. J. Collins, ed., *Manuale ad usum percelebris ecclesie Sarisburiensis*, Henry Bradshaw Society 91 (1960), 157. The York Manual omits this point, but has a special form of absolution for those holding appropriate papal indulgences for plenary remission: W. G. Henderson, ed., *Manuale et processionale ad usum insignis ecclesiæ Eboracensis*, Surtees Society 63 (1874), 48–49, 99. See also 156 above.
176   James, 'Ghost-Stories', 416.

they suggest wide awareness of the possibility of ghostly encounters, and of how they might be avoided.

The same tale records other protective measures. At the place agreed for a subsequent meeting between ghost and seer, the latter prepared for the encounter by drawing a great circle on the ground, and had with him the four gospels with 'other holy words' – presumably charms. He stood in the middle of the circle, placing four small reliquaries (*monilia*) in the shape of a cross at the edges. The reliquaries bore *verba salutifera*, referred to as *Ihesus Nazarenus etc.*, again perhaps used as charms.[177] The seer became in some ways a necromancer, maybe still fearful that the ghost was a demon.[178]

Expectations that returning souls would be from purgatory, and seeking assistance, doubtless affected expectations about who would and could return. Suicides, with their most unnatural of deaths, might be expected to appear regularly among medieval ghosts, but they are rarely mentioned.[179] The obvious theological reason for their absence is that they were damned: their return would be pointless, because they could not be helped.[180] Yet the processes for their disposal – being extracted from the house without using the threshold, being placed in barrels and sent floating down river, and various forms of profane or extra-social burial – have affinities with practices used for other corpses to prevent ghostly returns, or at least they have been so interpreted.[181]

That the dead might be unseen did not mean that they were in turn unseeing: far from it. According to the ghost of Beaucaire, the dead maintain constant watch over the living. They should remember this: 'a spirit has all things under his glance, and no obstacle can block his vision: shameful deeds should therefore be avoided at all costs, because they are seen by numberless spirits, while modesty is fostered by so many witnesses'.[182]

---

[177] Ibid. 417.

[178] On necromancy, see above, 162.

[179] A. Murray, *Suicide in the Middle Ages,* II: *The Curse on Self-Murder* (Oxford, 2000), 472–80.

[180] Above, 154.

[181] However, these readings may be misinterpretations, misreadings of practices which were merely customary, or which may not actually have existed in the Middle Ages: Murray, *Suicide,* II: 23–28, 34, 36–53; see esp. 38, 51–52 (but cf. 479–80).

[182] Gervase, 766–67.

* * *

So far, the focus has been on 'normal' ghosts: the dead who returned from purgatory either to seek help for their souls, or to offer warnings. This restrictive categorization reflects one implicitly adopted by medieval commentators. For them, whether evil or not, ghosts are always sinners. Saints' posthumous appearances are not treated in the same way as ghostly manifestations (a distinction also found in modern analyses). How this affected the Church's attitude to the afterlife is not clear. Yet, by putting the posthumous appearances of saints into a separate category, even if the reality of saintly apparitions could still be debated,[183] the Church possibly sought to control the terms of the debate about the afterlife, and to reinforce boundaries between the living and the (ordinary) dead.

If saints are, in Peter Brown's words, the 'very special dead',[184] their *post mortem* apparitions also make them 'very special ghosts'. By definition, they would not be evil-minded visitors, but they could be rather tetchy, sometimes punishing people who treated them lightly. Equally, they would not be restless souls, but divine agents.

The cultic contexts of many medieval saints' apparitions mean that they are not treated in the same way as the unsaintly dead; few visitations (or alleged visitations) are recorded in non-cultic sources.[185] The saints' ghostly status is sometimes suggested, as in a couple of Castillian tales (dream visions, not full apparitions) where they appear among a cohort of the dead.[186] Reports sometimes treat a saint's appearance as almost incidental. Gervase of Tilbury records that St Simeon (which St Simeon is not specified) appeared fortuitously to a knight caught in a storm whilst hunting in a forest, and gave him a hunting-horn to protect himself against thunder and lightning. The saint simply appeared, identified himself, gave the horn, and then went off in

---

183   See below.
184   The title of ch. 4 in P. R. L. Brown, *The Cult of the Saints: Its Rise and Function in Latin Christianity* (Chicago, IL, 1981).
185   Notable exceptions are the cases discussed in Christian, *Apparitions.*
186   Guiance, *Discorsos*, 398–404. (In both cases the company includes demons, the visions being concerned with the fate of recently deceased souls which they claim.) For a spirit (a ghost?) with poltergeistic tendencies as emissary for an encounter with a saint (with resemblances to a dream vision), see H. E. D. Blakiston, 'Two more Medieval Ghost Stories', *EHR* 38 (1923), 85–87, at 86–87. It is often difficult to tell whether the saints appear as waking visions, or as dreams.

pursuit of the tale's more marvellous element, a giant fire-breathing dog also seen by the terrified knight.[187]

Saintly apparitions could be contested, especially if they challenged official stances. Chiara Signorini appeared before the Milanese inquisition in 1519, charged with witchcraft. In her defence, she invoked the Virgin, saying that she had often appeared to her in visions and was the source of her powers. The inquisitors accepted the fact of the apparitions but challenged their use to claim divine approval of and participation in Signorini's activities. The apparitions transform in the questioning, from signs of divine approval to proofs of diabolical attachment. Chiara Signorini ends up as a convicted devil-worshipper, party to a pact which explained her seemingly magical powers and ability to cast spells on others. Circumstantial details change, but the core relationship is static: the basic pattern of conversations and agreements originating with Mary's apparition is replicated in the final confession of the dealings with the devil. Here a saintly apparition, even of the Mother of God, was reduced to the status of any other ghost in the learned construction of the afterlife.[188] A woman in Spain who claimed visions of the Virgin in 1523 was also condemned after investigation for 'trickery and falsehood', and punished by whipping.[189]

As ghosts, saints may mimic – or share – characteristics of 'normal' ghosts and demons. The Wild Hunt has a parallel of sorts in the appearance of a force of heavenly knights led by identifiable saints to aid the crusaders at Antioch in 1098.[190] Similarly, saints could be choosy about how and to whom they appeared. While it was a necessary element in the fiction of the Virgin's apparition to Chiara Signorini, Mary, like many ghosts, was supposedly invisible to everyone except Signorini.[191]

---

[187] Gervase, 692–95. The dog entered the priest's house through closed doors, set fire to it and killed the priest's illegitimate offspring. Lecouteux interprets this as St Simeon following his own hound, and punishing sin: *Chasses fantastiques*, 68–69.

[188] C. Ginzburg, *Clues, Myths, and the Historical Method* (Baltimore, MD, and London, 1986), 6–16.

[189] Christian, *Apparitions*, 159–79 (sentence at 179).

[190] R. Hill, ed., *The Deeds of the Franks and the Other Pilgrims to Jerusalem* (Oxford, 1962), 69; see also J. V. Tolan, *Saracens: Islam in the Medieval European Imagination* (New York, 2002), 114 and refs. For allegedly similar manifestations in anti-Moorish battles in Spain, see J. F. O'Callaghan, *Reconquest and Crusade in Medieval Spain* (Philadelphia, PA, 2003), 194–99; cf., in this volume, Conor Kostick, 'The Afterlife of Bishop Adhémar of Le Puy', 120–29.

[191] Ginzburg, *Clues*, 8.

* * *

Ghosts were everywhere, but they were not necessarily menacing. They appeared chiefly to seek help, not to terrify. They returned because they sought salvation and needed ghostbusters.

The medieval Church, however, lacked such specialists. While exorcism could deal with the demonic, there was no specific clerical order to assuage wandering and repentant Christian souls. This absence follows almost by definition from the Church's official late medieval stance: if ghosts were not actually souls, but demonic illusions, they had to be treated accordingly. They needed not pastoral care, but exorcism. The exorcist may be the closest approximation to an 'official ghostbuster'; but it is a poor approximation. The exorcist's role was to identify diabolical spirits, but there was seemingly no provision for dealing with a non-diabolical ghost. The first priority in any interview with a spirit was to establish its status as good or bad, and then whether it had to be formally exorcized. But ghosts, as Christian souls, should not have been exorcized, or affected by exorcisms.[192] A notable feature of the major narratives is that the ghosts largely determine the timetable for their eventual disappearance.

Paradoxically, the outcome is not that medieval ghostbusting was rare, but that it could be universal. Within the economy of salvation, every Christian could assume the role, because what most ghosts sought was *post mortem* commemorations to ease their journey to salvation. That, indeed, is explicit in most visitations, confirmed not just by the initial appeals, but by later assurance that they worked. Two of Gervase of Tilbury's tales provide suitable *exempla*. A monk appeared to one of his brethren to request prayers, masses, and charitable works for a year from him and the rest of the community. If this proved insufficient, the ghost would reappear at the year's end to make further arrangements. The second meeting did happen, but the soul had already been freed by the commemorative acts.[193] In Gervase's second tale a bishop of Pozzuoli conjured a soul from the purgatorial fires of a nearby volcano. It requested a daily mass for a year to secure its release. The bishop

---

[192] While the failure of exorcisms and other ceremonies is sometimes noted, why this happens is rarely considered. H. P. Broedel suggests that for James of Clusa exorcism could not affect Christian souls (*The Malleus maleficarum and the Construction of Witchcraft: Theology and Popular Belief* (Manchester and New York, 2003), 48), but I do not find it explicit in his text: from Broedel's reference at 63 n. 40 this may be an over-reading of Thorndike's summary of the tract (see n. 41).

[193] Gervase, 112–15.

asked how he would know whether this had been successful; the ghost asked him to return in a year's time, and if he (the ghost) did not answer the bishop's call, he would have been released 'through God's mercy and your prayers.' Predictably, when the bishop returned the soul did not respond, 'So the man of God presumed ... that it really was free.' Gervase adds a gloss, explaining that while souls are allowed to appear to 'make known the wretchedness and exigency of their condition', when their purgation is completed and they transfer to higher delights, 'they do not present themselves to our sight any more'.[194]

Gervase speaks of action by monks and priests, but opportunities to aid souls grew greatly over later centuries as the process of *post mortem* commemoration became an essential element of late medieval religion – establishing, in the now somewhat hackneyed phrase, 'a cult of the living in support of the dead'.[195] The Church and its members might almost be seen as engaged in a process of constant pre-emptive ghost-busting: certificates of deathbed absolution, indulgences and the gamut of commemorative practices all sought to ensure that the dead got through purgatory, and maybe obviated any need for them to return as ghosts to seek help. Indeed, if some aspects of contemporary religious behaviour were also understood to make it harder for ghosts to make contact, thereby preventing such encounters,[196] this ghostbusting assumes another dimension.

* * *

Ghosts, like saints, were victims of the Reformation, as a contested element in that great upheaval. Among Catholics, ghosts were still accepted – indeed, almost flaunted – as proof of purgatory and the soul's continued existence after death; but officially Protestants rejected them. Ghosts had no role in their revised Christianity: with purgatory abolished, and salvation dependent on accepting Christ during life, miserable sinners could not return after death seeking help to end their misery. For Protestant divines ghosts inhabited demonic realms, as signs of Satan's power.[197] Ghosts were no longer people, a view matching the

[194] Ibid. 588–91.
[195] The phrase derives from A. Galpern, 'The Legacy of Late Medieval Religion in Sixteenth-Century Champagne', in C. Trinkaus and H. A. Oberman, eds, *The Pursuit of Holiness in Late Medieval and Renaissance Religion: Papers from the University of Michigan Conference*, Studies in Medieval and Renaissance Thought 10 (Leiden, 1974), 141–76, at 149.
[196] Above, 167–68.
[197] Finucane, *Appearances*, ch. 4; P. Marshall, 'Deceptive Appearances: Ghosts and

changed attitude to the corpse manifested in the revised English burial service of 1552.[198] Whatever the afterlife was, formally the dead were now to be confined within it (although subsequent history showed that the boundary with the afterlife remained permeable).[199]

The evidence is at present too fragmentary, too insubstantial, to construct a full history of the integration of the returning dead into appreciations of the afterlife in pre-Reformation Europe. Important regional differences may be obscured; no clear chronological evolution can be delineated; potentially important aspects need further attention. It is, though, clear that the returning dead were important informants on the medieval afterlife. They had an active role in constructing awareness both of what happened after death, and of the need for individuals to establish strategies for eternity before crossing a frontier maybe not so final after all.

University of Birmingham

Reformers in Elizabethan and Jacobean England', in H. Parish and W. G. Naphy, eds, *Religion and Superstition in Reformation Europe* (Manchester and New York, 2002), 188–208; Zarri, 'Purgatorio', 488–89.

[198] E. Duffy, *The Stripping of the Altars: Traditional Religion in England, 1400–1580* (New Haven, CT, and London, 1992), 474–75.

[199] For continuing Anglican interest in ghosts and apparitions, see, in this volume, Sasha Handley, 'Apparitions and Anglicanism in 1750s Warwickshire', 311–22; Georgina Byrne, '"Angels Seen Today": The Theology of Modern Spiritualism and its Impact on Church of England Clergy, 1852–1939', 360–70.

AGREEMENTS TO RETURN FROM THE AFTERLIFE IN LATE MEDIEVAL *EXEMPLA**

by CATHERINE RIDER

ONE of the ways in which medieval Christians thought about the links between this life and the afterlife was by telling ghost stories – a topic which has attracted the attention of several historians.[1] In these stories, a dead person often appears to a living relative or friend and asks them to give alms or to perform other good works on their behalf, in order to speed up their passage to heaven. The dead person usually appears spontaneously, although sometimes this occurs after relatives have said prayers for them. This paper, however, will examine a group of stories about less spontaneous apparitions. These are stories in which two people agree that whichever of them dies first will come back and tell the other about the afterlife. They have sometimes been mentioned in studies of medieval ghost stories,[2] but they have not been examined in their own right.

Stories about agreements to return from the afterlife were circulating from at least the early twelfth century, when the Benedictine abbot Guibert of Nogent claimed that his mother had made such an agreement with another woman, and William of Malmesbury included a similar tale in his *Deeds of the English Kings*.[3] They continue to occur until at least the sixteenth century, when the Swiss horse-wrangler Chonrad Stoeckhlin claimed that he had made an agreement with his friend, and further claimed that his friend had indeed come back.[4] The

* I am grateful to Julia Crick for commenting on a draft of this paper and to Sophie Page for sharing unpublished work.

[1] Claude Lecouteux, *Fantômes et revenants au moyen age* (Paris, 1986); Jacques Le Goff, *The Birth of Purgatory*, trans. Arthur Goldhammer (Aldershot, 1984); Jean-Claude Schmitt, *Ghosts in the Middle Ages*, trans. Teresa Lavender Fagan (Chicago, IL, 1998); C. S. Watkins, 'Sin, Penance and Purgatory in the Anglo-Norman Realm: The Evidence of Visions and Ghost Stories', *P&P* 175 (May 2002), 3–33. See also, in this volume, R. N. Swanson, 'Ghosts and Ghostbusters in the Middle Ages', 143–73.

[2] Schmitt, *Ghosts*, 87, 113–14, 137.

[3] *A Monk's Confession: The Memoirs of Guibert of Nogent*, trans. Paul J. Archambault (University Park, PA, 1996), 68; William of Malmesbury, *De gestis regum Anglorum*, ed. William Stubbs, RS 90, 2 vols (London, 1889), 2: 295–96.

[4] Wolfgang Behringer, *Shaman of Oberstdorf: Chonrad Stoeckhlin and the Phantoms of the Night*, trans. Erik Midelfort (Charlottesville, VA, 1998), 10–12.

same story is told in the *Decameron* of Boccaccio and occurs in European folklore.[5] One place in which the story is often found is in *exempla*, short moral stories which were collected from the early thirteenth century onwards for use in preaching. Many *exempla* were collected by friars, but collections made by monks and secular priests also survive.[6]

These stories shed light on two aspects of the relationship between the living and the afterlife which have not been much discussed by the recent historiography. Firstly, they stress the friendship between the living person and the dead one, showing us an afterlife in which personal, emotional relationships, often with non-family members, remain important after death. Secondly, although some medieval writers presented asking a dead friend to return as legitimate, others argued that it was dangerous, unorthodox or even magic. These stories thus allow us to explore which forms of interaction with the afterlife were deemed acceptable, and why. Moreover, the emphasis on the emotional bond between the living and the dead was one factor that helped most, although not all, writers to conclude that this way of finding out about the afterlife was licit.

Stories about agreements to return occur in many *exemplum*-collections,[7] but this paper will focus on four in particular, from different regions and compiled by writers in different monastic orders. All four collections include numerous tales of ghosts and apparitions, and many stories that their authors claim are based on contemporary events:

1. Caesarius of Heisterbach, *Dialogue of Miracles*: Caesarius was master of novices at the Cistercian monastery of Heisterbach. His *Dialogue* was written in around 1219–22, primarily as an educational tool for use in the monastery. Caesarius includes four *exempla* about agreements to return from the dead.[8]

2. Thomas of Cantimpré, *Bonum universale de apibus*: Thomas was a member of the community of Augustinian canons at Cantimpré, near Cambrai, but later became a Dominican friar. He compiled the *Bonum*

---

5 Ibid. 14–16; Schmitt, *Ghosts*, 215.

6 See Claude Bremond, Jacques Le Goff and Jean-Claude Schmitt, *L'Exemplum*, Typologie des sources du moyen âge occidental 40 (Turnhout, 1982).

7 Frederic Tubach, *Index Exemplorum: A Handbook of Medieval Religious Tales* (Helsinki, 1969), nos 1464 (where they are not distinguished from other apparitions), 2214, 3976.

8 Caesarius of Heisterbach, *Dialogue on Miracles*, trans. H. von E. Scott and C. C. Swinton Bland, 2 vols (London, 1929), 1: 42–43; 2: 320–21, 330, 332–33. On Caesarius, see Bremond et al., *L'Exemplum*, 59.

universale, which includes one *exemplum* about an agreement to return from the afterlife, between 1256 and 1263.[9]

3. Stephen of Bourbon, *The Seven Gifts of the Holy Spirit*: Stephen was another Dominican friar, based in Lyons. He left his treatise unfinished at his death in 1262. He included at least two *exempla* about agreements to return, although the modern edition of his text is still incomplete, so there may be others.[10]

4. *Liber exemplorum ad usum praedicantium*: an anonymous collection compiled in around 1275 by an English Franciscan friar. This includes two *exempla* about agreements to return.[11]

The stories follow a fairly consistent pattern. This example comes from Stephen of Bourbon:

> I heard from Brother Humbert [of Romans], master-general of the Friars Preachers [1254–63] that two young scholars, companions from the same *natio* [national grouping at a university], entered the religious life and conducted themselves in that religious life well and devoutly before both God and men. When one of them was dying and the other wept for him, saying that he was desolate to remain in a strange land [i.e. alive], the sick man replied that if God allowed and it was possible, he would console him even after death, by telling him of his condition [in the afterlife].

The dying scholar was true to his word and after death appeared to his friend 'very sad and distressed': he was suffering the pains of purgatory (*penam purgatorii*) because he had kept his old shoes when given new ones, against the rules of the order. He asked his friend to return the spare shoes to the prior and seek absolution for him in the chapter, which his friend did. Then the dead man returned, 'very happy and bright', and showed his living friend a vision of all the souls ascending to heaven.[12]

---

[9] Thomas of Cantimpré, *Bonum universale de apibus* 1.20, c. 4 (Douai, 1605), 74–75. On Thomas, see Henri Platelle, *Les exemples du livre des abeilles* (Turnhout, 1997), 13–18.

[10] Stephanus de Borbone, *Tractatus de diversis materiis predicabilibus,* Part 1, eds Jacques Berlioz and Jean-Luc Eichenlaub, CChr.CM 124 (Turnhout, 2002), 188–89; Part 3, ed. Jacques Berlioz, C.Chr.CM 124B (Turnhout, 2006), 95. See also A. Lecoy de la Marche, *Anecdotes historiques, légendes et apologues tirés du recueil inédit d'Etienne de Bourbon* (Paris, 1877). On Stephen, see Jean-Claude Schmitt, *The Holy Greyhound: Guinefort, Healer of Children since the Thirteenth Century,* trans. Martin Thom (Cambridge, 1983), 11–12.

[11] *Liber exemplorum ad usum praedicantium*, ed. A. G. Little (Aberdeen, 1908), 91, 95–96.

[12] Stephen of Bourbon, *Tractatus*, 1: 188–89; the translation is mine.

The vision of souls ascending to heaven is unusual in stories about agreements to return,[13] but in other respects this story is typical: the dead friend comes back, explains how he is being punished for some sin committed during life, and asks the living friend to help. Variants exist, however, in which the dead person is either damned or saved outright. In these cases they simply inform their living friend about their status, and if they have gone to hell, they sometimes tell their friend to change his or her life in order to avoid the same fate.[14] These stories thus make moral points similar to those made by many other apparition stories: they demonstrate the dangers of sin and the power of good works and prayers to help the dead in the afterlife.[15] They also serve to reinforce the doctrine of purgatory, which Jacques Le Goff has argued was formalized in the twelfth century, even if the concept of a middle place between heaven and hell was much older.[16]

Friendship

In other respects, however, these *exempla* differ from stories of spontaneous apparitions. For example, in many of them the agreement to return is made between friends, although there are exceptions (in one of Caesarius of Heisterbach's stories, a father agrees to appear to his daughter[17]). Who the friends are varies: they can be monks, scholars, cathedral canons, nuns or laymen. This is in contrast to the stories of spontaneous apparitions, in which ghosts appear to a wider range of people: friends, family members, spouses, or fellow monks or friars.[18] Moreover, the closeness of the friends is often emphasized. In Stephen of Bourbon's first *exemplum*, the two scholars are 'companions' who enter religion together. In Caesarius of Heisterbach an abbot agrees to come back to 'a monk whom he loved more closely than the rest' and the nun Acselina to a 'spiritual sister in the convent singularly beloved

---

[13] Although similar visions appear in other contexts: Patrick Sims-Williams, *Religion and Literature in Western England 600–800* (Cambridge, 1990), 255.

[14] Caesarius, *Dialogue*, 2: 330, 332.

[15] Schmitt, *Ghosts*, 128, 134–35.

[16] Le Goff, *Birth of Purgatory*, 132; A. Ja. Gurevich, 'Popular and Scholarly Medieval Cultural Traditions: Notes in the Margin of Jacques Le Goff's Book', *JMedH* 9 (1983), 71–90, at 79. See also, in this volume, Sarah Foot, 'Anglo-Saxon "Purgatory"', 87–96.

[17] Caesarius, *Dialogue*, 2: 330.

[18] Le Goff, *Birth of Purgatory*, 293–94.

by her'.[19] In Thomas of Cantimpré, a canon of St Victor in Paris agrees to appear to 'a certain companion of his, who loved him greatly',[20] while in the Franciscan *exempla* two monks 'friendly between themselves' make the agreement, as do two rich men 'bound together by mutual love'.[21] There are exceptions, such as in Stephen of Bourbon's other *exemplum*, in which a nun appears to her abbess without the personal bond being stressed,[22] but often these stories present an afterlife in which friendship relations are important.

The kind of friendship which they describe does not look like the formal friendship (*amicitia*) which Julian Haseldine has identified in some twelfth-century sources. *Amicitia* could exist between acquaintances or strangers, and it did not necessarily involve an emotional attachment.[23] Rather, these *exempla* depict an emotional bond between two people who live in close proximity to each other, and they sometimes emphasize that it is stronger than other similar relationships: in the story by Caesarius quoted above, Acselina's friend was 'singularly' loved by her. In emphasizing personal bonds, often within monastic settings, these stories depict relationships which look more like the twelfth-century monastic friendships studied by Jean Leclercq and Brian Patrick McGuire. McGuire argues that Caesarius of Heisterbach presents friendship as an accepted part of monastic life, and that the Dominicans picked up this Cistercian interest in personal friendships.[24] Nevertheless, the *exemplum*-collectors recognized that monasteries were not the only settings in which close friendships could form, since they sometimes tell the same story of scholars or laymen. In this, they were probably reflecting the world around them: as Ruth Mazo Karras has argued, close bonds could form between young men in many settings, both religious and secular.[25]

The agreement-to-return stories thus present a slightly different

---

[19] Caesarius, *Dialogue*, 2: 320, 332.

[20] Thomas of Cantimpré, *Bonum Universale*, 75: 'socius quidam eius, qui eum multum dilexerat'.

[21] *Liber exemplorum*, 91, 95: 'sibi invicem familiares', 'amore mutuo confederati'.

[22] *Tractatus*, 3: 95.

[23] Julian Haseldine, 'Introduction', in idem, ed., *Friendship in Medieval Europe* (Stroud, 1999), xvii–xxiii, at xix.

[24] Jean Leclercq, *The Love of Learning and the Desire for God*, 2nd edn (New York, 1974), 226–28; Brian Patrick McGuire, *Friendship and Community: The Monastic Experience 350–1250* (Kalamazoo, MI, 1988), 404–06.

[25] Ruth Mazo Karras, *From Boys to Men: Formations of Masculinity in Late Medieval Europe* (Philadelphia, PA, 2003), 29, 96–97, 128.

picture of the afterlife from that which is usually emphasized by historians. Studies of the relationship between the living and the dead in the Middle Ages often focus on commemoration, either by monasteries or within the parish, giving a picture of an afterlife defined by the duty of the living to pray for the dead.[26] This is undoubtedly an important form of interaction between the living and the dead, but *exempla* about agreements to return suggest that other factors could also be present. In particular, they present an afterlife in which emotional bonds are important for their own sake. The dead person does not necessarily ask for anything, sometimes simply informing their friend about their condition in the afterlife. There is not always unfinished business which would make it necessary for them to appear, which is perhaps why a prearranged agreement is needed.

Magic

It is likely that some people really made agreements like this with their friends: Chonrad Stoeckhlin certainly claimed to have done. Either the *exempla* themselves, or the fact that people might imitate them, raised questions in the minds of some writers about whether it was legitimate to ask someone to come back from the afterlife in this way. The issue was discussed in another kind of source aimed at educating the clergy: confession manuals which summarized theology and canon law.[27] Under the heading of magic (*sortilegium*), John of Freiburg, a Dominican friar who wrote an influential *Summa for Confessors* in around 1295, asked 'Whether it is licit to ask a dying person to reveal his state after death?' John argued, quoting Thomas Aquinas, that this was indeed licit, as long as the person doing the asking accepted that the outcome of their request was subject to God's will. If God's permission was acknowledged, 'there seems to be no reason why this should be said to be a sin, unless perhaps he asks in a spirit of testing, because he doubts

---

[26] Clive Burgess, '"Longing to be Prayed For": Death and Commemoration in an English Parish in the Later Middle Ages', in Bruce Gordon and Peter Marshall, eds, *The Place of the Dead* (Cambridge, 2000), 44–65; Patrick Geary, 'Exchange and Interaction between the Living and the Dead in Early Medieval Society', in idem, *Living with the Dead in the Middle Ages* (Ithaca, NY, 1994), 77–92; Le Goff, *Birth of Purgatory*, 293–94; Otto Gerhard Oexle, 'Die Gegenwart der Toten', in Herman Braet and Werner Verbeke, eds, *Death in the Middle Ages* (Leuven, 1983), 19–77.

[27] On these, see Pierre Michaud-Quantin, *Sommes de casuistique et manuels de confession au moyen âge* (Louvain, 1962).

in his faith in the future state'.[28] The version of the story told earlier by
William of Malmesbury suggests what John might have meant by 'testing': a dying cleric agreed that if he came back from the afterlife,

> he would have been taught that, as the Platonists say, death does
> not extinguish the spirit, but rather lets it loose, as if from a prison,
> to God, its beginning. If he did not [come back], it should be
> conceded to the Epicurean sect, who think that when the soul is
> separated from the body it vanishes into the air, passing away into
> the wind.[29]

Perhaps unsurprisingly, the cleric later revealed that he was in hell for
unspecified 'crimes' (*criminibus*).

• Other writers disagreed with John of Freiburg, however, and argued
that it was always wrong to ask a dying friend to return. One English
exemplum-collection, the *Speculum laicorum*, included a version of the
story in which the dead man revealed that he was in purgatory precisely
because he had promised to return from the afterlife.[30] The early
fifteenth-century English devotional text *Dives and Pauper* offered more
details. It took up John of Freiburg's point that asking a dying friend to
return might reflect doubts about the afterlife, saying that if the dead
friend did indeed return, then this would render the living friend's faith
in the afterlife less commendable, since he or she would have learned
by experience that there was life after death. *Dives and Pauper* also
warned that demons might appear in the dead person's place, a fear
which can also be found in some other ghost stories, which depict
ghosts and devils as looking very similar to each other, so that the living
sometimes mistake one for the other.[31] The concerns found in these

[28] John of Freiburg, *Summa Confessorum* (Lyons, 1518), fol. 32v (bk. 1, title 11, qu. 23):
'Utrum liceat ab aliquo moriente requirere quod revelet statum suum post mortem? ...
subiiciendo tamen hoc divino iudicio ... nulla ratio videtur quare debeat dici hoc esse
peccatum nisi forte ex dubitatione fidei de futuro statu quasi tentando inquirat.' On John,
see Leonard Boyle, 'The *Summa Confessorum* of John of Freiburg and the Popularisation of
the Moral Teaching of St Thomas and some of his Contemporaries', repr. in idem, *Pastoral
Care, Clerical Education and Canon Law 1200–1400* (London, 1981), 245–68.

[29] William of Malmesbury, *De gestis*, 2: 295: 'Si fiat, edocturus quod, secundum
Platonicos, mors spiritum non extinguat, sed ad principium sui Deum tanquam e carcere
emittat; sin minus, Epicureorum sectae concedendum, qui opinantur animam corpore
solutam in aerem evanescere, in auras effluere.'

[30] J. A. Herbert, *Catalogue of Romances in the Department of Manuscripts in the British
Museum*, 3 vols (London, 1883–1910), 3: 391.

[31] Priscilla Heath Barnum, ed., *Dives and Pauper*, 2 vols in 3, EETS os 275, 280, 323
(London, 1976–2004), 1/i: 169–70; Watkins, 'Sin', 23–24.

texts may have further been compounded by the fact that some magical texts included rituals to conjure up the dead in order to gain information from them, and some people claimed to be able to do this: a later example is that of Anna Megerler, who claimed in 1564 that she had the spirits of two executed criminals trapped in crystal, who informed her about distant events.[32]

In these *exempla*, then, we find a belief which inhabits a grey area between faith and doubt about the afterlife, and between legitimate concern for a friend and magic. Medieval writers hesitated as to how to classify these stories, but most came down on the side of John of Freiburg. One reason for this may be that the afterlife presented by these stories resembles that found in other apparition stories, whose orthodoxy does not seem to have been questioned. For example, as in some stories of spontaneous apparitions, the dead person often appears with their fate illustrated in their body. The saved dead appear, like the scholar in Stephen's story, 'with a great light' (*cum magna claritate*), while the damned are 'very ugly and horrible' (*deformis valde atque horribilis*). In one version of the story told by Caesarius of Heisterbach, a dead abbot has the fact that he is in purgatory shown graphically in this way: his upper body is bright, but his legs are 'ulcered and black as coals.'[33] These details would have reinforced expectations of the afterlife generated by other ghost stories, in which clothing and colours similarly signify the fate of the dead person's soul.[34]

John of Freiburg also suggested other reasons why it could be legitimate to ask someone to come back from the afterlife. One of these comes back to the theme of friendship. Citing Aristotle's *Metaphysics*, John argued that the desire to know things was natural: 'mankind naturally desires to know'.[35] This 'natural' desire for knowledge of a person's fate might be expected particularly to apply to friends and loved ones. Nevertheless, it had limits, as John recognized when he stated that people should acknowledge that any return was dependent

---

[32] Sophie Page, 'Magic and the Pursuit of Wisdom: The Familiar Spirit in the *Liber Theysolius*', forthcoming in *La Corónica*; Lyndal Roper, 'Stealing Manhood: Capitalism and Magic in Early Modern Germany', in eadem, *Oedipus and the Devil: Witchcraft, Sexuality and Religion in Early Modern Europe* (London, 1994), 130.

[33] *Liber exemplorum*, 91, 95; Caesarius, *Dialogue*, 1: 43, 2: 320; Stephen of Bourbon, *Tractatus*, 3: 95.

[34] Schmitt, *Ghosts*, 204.

[35] John of Freiburg, *Summa confessorum*, fol. 32v: 'Homo autem naturaliter scire desiderat: 1 Metaphysica.'

on God's will. The *exempla* which presented making agreements to return from the dead as legitimate did not usually go beyond these limits, and they likewise stressed the importance of seeking God's permission. In Thomas of Cantimpré's collection the friend agrees to return 'if God should permit', and the same is true of one pair of friends in the *Liber exemplorum*, and even of the scholar of necromancy (who might be expected to worry less about this) in the collection of Caesarius of Heisterbach.[36]

Another way in which asking a friend to return from the afterlife could be distinguished from magical ways of contacting the dead was with regard to the information which the living friend sought. Magical methods of contacting the dead tended to seek practical information (as Anna Megerler did), rather than simply finding out what had happened to them: the early medieval writer Isidore of Seville, whose definitions of magic influenced many later writers, defined 'necromancy' as [bringing] 'the dead back to life *to prophesy and answer questions* [my emphasis]'.[37] The *exempla* which present making agreements to return as legitimate, by contrast, only ask about their friend's condition in the afterlife, although the dead friend sometimes offers other information, such as the dead man's revelation in Thomas of Cantimpré's collection that he had been right to refuse a bishopric while alive because in that position, he would have risked damnation.[38] These *exempla* do not say explicitly that their protagonists asked their friends to return for the right reasons, but *exempla* and confession manuals were produced in the same settings, by friars and other churchmen engaged in pastoral care, so that the contents of one set of sources would probably have been known to the authors of the other.

Conclusion

Stories about agreements to return are only one medieval image of the afterlife among many. *Exemplum*-collections also contain many other stories of ghosts and apparitions, some of which deal with the same themes as the *exempla* discussed here. For example, the thirteenth-

---

[36] *Liber exemplorum*, 91; Caesarius, *Dialogue*, 1: 43; Thomas of Cantimpré, *Bonum universale*, 75: 'si deus permitteret'.

[37] William Klingshirn, 'Isidore of Seville's Taxonomy of Magicians and Diviners', *Traditio* 58 (2003), 59–90, at 85.

[38] Thomas of Cantimpré, *Bonum universale*, 75.

century Italian Franciscan Servasanto da Faenza told a ghost story that expressed the same doubts about the orthodoxy of trying to find out what has become of a dead friend in the afterlife. In this story, a Florentine painter became concerned about the fate of his master, who had been a heretic. The painter prayed to know what had become of his master, and eventually he had a vision of the dead man, 'very black and deformed, and he struck him with great fear. And after this he appeared to him every night, and distressed him very much.'[39] A local Franciscan friar explained that the only way to stop the apparitions was for the painter to stop praying for his master and to confess his sin in doing so.

Another theme that stories about agreements to return from the afterlife share with other ghost stories is the idea of purgatory: this is often where the dead friend has gone. It is possible that the doctrine of purgatory made stories about agreements to return particularly appealing, both to *exemplum*-collectors and to the laity they preached to, by heightening anxieties about what had happened to friends in the afterlife. Stories about the return of a dead friend from purgatory could reassure their living friends that the dead person had gone to purgatory rather than hell and so would eventually be saved. Moreover, if the dead were thought to be in a definite place of purgation, then it may have been easier to conceive of them as being able to come back on request.

Despite these similarities to other ghost stories, the agreement-to-return *exempla*, with their emphasis on an afterlife in which friendship, as well as formal commemoration, is crucial, and in which the dead can honour a prearranged agreement, offer a distinctive view of the afterlife. They thus highlight the variety of forms which relations with the afterlife could take in the late Middle Ages. Because of the questions which remained about the legitimacy of asking the dead to come back, they also show how the boundary between orthodox and unorthodox ways of interacting with the afterlife was not always clearly defined and was disputed by churchmen engaged in pastoral care.

University of Exeter

---

[39] Servasanto da Faenza, *Antidotarium anime sive liber aureus* (Louvain, 1485), fol. 145v (tractatus 9, ch. 6): 'niger nimium et deformis, ac magnum illi timorem incussit. Et post hec omni nocte illi apparebat et nimium eum affligebat.'

FIXING THE ESCHATOLOGICAL SCALES: JUDGEMENT OF THE SOUL IN LATE MEDIEVAL AND EARLY MODERN IRISH TRADITION

by SALVADOR RYAN

THE *Annals of Loch Cé*, a native Irish chronicle compiled in north Roscommon in the years 1588–9, contains the following entry for the year 1568:

> A cold, stormy year of scarcity was this year; and this is little wonder, for it was in it Mac Diarmada died, i.e. Ruaidhrí, the son of Tadhg, the son of Ruaidhrí Óg, i.e. king of Mag-Luirg and Airtech and Tir-Tuathail and chief lord over the whole territory of Clann-Maelruanaidh, and some more of the districts and fair territories of Connacht ...

The entry recording Mac Diarmada's death was commissioned by his son, Brian. It is interesting that the remainder of the account focuses not merely on his father's considerable status as a secular and ecclesiastical lord, as might have been expected, but more importantly on the qualities that ensured his safe passage to the next life:

> He left not the value of one groat of inheritance; but he earned the blessings of patrons and ecclesiastics, poets and doctors, the poor and widows, strangers and orphans, the infirm and pilgrims, martyrs and victims of heavy sickness, guests and exiles ...

> He obtained, moreover, prodigious bounty and gifts from the elect Trinity ... until he experienced pure penance and great penitence for his faults after spending nearly eighty years.[1]

Here was a man of considerable local stature who spurned riches, won the blessings of the most vulnerable in Gaelic Irish society, and died in old age after sincere penance. His chronicler could thus be confident in recording that 'his soul afterwards journeyed to the general Pasch without end or limit, in saecula saeculorum'.[2]

---

[1] W. M. Hennessy, ed., *The Annals of Loch Cé*, 2 vols (London, 1871, repr. Dublin, 1939), 2: 396–405: quotations at 397–99, 401, 403.

[2] Ibid. 403.

The late medieval period was not a time to be complacent about death or, more crucially, salvation. Philippe Ariès notes that a shift in how the end of time was portrayed can be discerned in Europe from the twelfth century onwards, involving the superimposition of the judgement scene of Matthew 25 onto the scene from the Book of Revelation, rendering the return of Christ a far more terrifying prospect for people in the later Middle Ages than had been the case for their predecessors.[3] With the second coming now linked to the Last Judgement, the appearance of Christ in the sky at the end of time heralded a process of reckoning in which the heavenly court would seek to impose strict justice and during which one's soul would literally hang in the balance of St Michael's scales. A tense preoccupation with such a terrifying scenario swept through the high Middle Ages and gave rise to an anxiety for the fate of humanity which wanly concluded that the majority of souls could expect to be lost. This was the age of the chilling *danse macabre* which portrayed the universal power of death, which imposed itself particularly starkly in the great plague which struck Europe in the fourteenth century. The vision of Christ's return in judgement was regularly depicted above rood lofts in churches as a haunting reminder of the necessity of living a good life. Christ would come at the end of time, his wounds all fresh and bleeding, to exact justice.[4] This study examines how the judgement of the soul was portrayed in late medieval and early modern Ireland, particularly in the devotional verse of Gaelic Irish poets, and it attempts to answer how, in an environment in which eternal damnation was feared by so many, individuals such as Brian Mac Diarmada managed to be confident of their loved ones' salvation.

Gaelic Irish bardic poets belonged to a professional order of versifiers (mostly lay men) who composed both secular and religious works between the thirteenth and seventeenth centuries. Poems commissioned by patrons, both secular and ecclesiastical, were destined to be recited in public or semi-public settings, in the large banqueting halls of the Irish aristocracy, but also in churches on occasions such as important feast days. While the language and metre of these compositions was stylized and complex, recent studies have drawn attention to the importance of the message conveyed and the absolute necessity of

---

3 Philippe Ariès, *The Hour of our Death*, trans. Helen Weaver (Oxford, 1991), 97.

4 Eamon Duffy, *The Stripping of the Altars: Traditional Religion in England, 1400–1580* (New Haven, CT, and London, 1992), 157, 309.

ensuring that the poem remained intelligible to what were often large audiences.[5] Some four hundred bardic religious compositions (out of a corpus of about two thousand poems) are extant and, while the style and language of the poetry remains unchanged throughout this period, its devotional content and intensity develops rapidly, in keeping with the evolution of various forms of piety in England and the Continent. However, there were also important continuities, particularly the retention of a great deal of the devotional language of the late medieval world right into the seventeenth century. For that reason, the late medieval and early modern Irish tradition is understood here as coterminous with the Irish bardic tradition.

Accused

Bardic poets routinely present a scene that was very familiar to European Christians. At the end of time, Christ was expected to appear in the sky lying upon a cross, his wounds bleeding afresh. The flowing blood of Christ accuses humanity in its sin and strikes terror into the unrepentant. Tadhg Óg Ó hUiginn (d. 1448) remarks that 'uncovered shall be thy cross at the Sessions: whenever his pardon is about to be given us, his wrath, though slow, must break forth as the red cross points me out to him'.[6] Ó hUiginn describes how Christ the Judge was expected to display his wounds as evidence against sinners and thereafter to exact retribution: 'The red blood drawn by the lance for you, O children of Eve, and his flesh all torn, shall be avenged on the Last Day.'[7] The sense of terror accompanying the moment of judgement, which was to take place on Mount Zion, is succinctly captured in the words: 'We shall see Him coming above us on the hill to judge; we are the flock of birds, He the hawk; dread the doom.'[8] Another poet pleads for the evidence against him to be put aside: 'Hide from us thy red cross, so that thy wrath be not seen; close thy gaping side.'[9] The sixteenth-century poet, Aonghus Fionn Ó Dálaigh, likewise adverts to

[5] See especially Salvador Ryan, 'A Slighted Source: Rehabilitating Irish Bardic Religious Poetry in Historical Discourse', *Cambrian Medieval Celtic Studies* 48 (2004), 75–101.
[6] Lambert McKenna, ed., *Dán Dé* (Dublin, 1922), poem 3, stanza 18.
[7] Ibid., poem 6, stanza 20.
[8] Ibid., stanza 19.
[9] Ibid., poem 16, stanza 17. See Salvador Ryan, 'Reign of Blood: Devotion to the Wounds of Christ in Late Medieval Gaelic Ireland', in Joost Augusteijn and Mary Ann Lyons, eds, *Irish History: A Research Yearbook* (Dublin, 2002), 137–49.

the indictment of humanity on the Last Day: 'Christ will bring up against his children his stigmata, the three nails, the painful point of the ruddy thorn, the throbbing anger of the sore foot.'[10] The instruments of Christ's Passion, which commanded a significant role in late medieval religious iconography and devotional literature, were also believed to function as witnesses to mankind's iniquity on the Day of Doom, exhibiting themselves as the murder weapons by which the Son of God was tortured and killed in an act of what the Gaelic Irish called *fingal* or kin-slaying.[11] The sights and sounds of Christ's Passion and Death were expected to be re-enacted on the Last Day, the instruments functioning as harbingers of condemnation. Ó Dálaigh remarks that 'dread shall sound the riveting of the blunt nails',[12] exclaiming in another poem: 'God's wounds pursue me! Save me from the guilt of his blood.'[13] The sixteenth-century poet, Domhnall, son of Dáire Mac Bruaideadha, states that 'we should fear too the flashing reddened spear, tempered in the Lord's blood, and the rope that dragged out his bright arms so that neither of them was left unwounded'.[14] Such a depiction of Judgement Day was standard fare, being found, for instance, in sermons such as for the First Sunday in Advent in John Mirk's *Festial*, compiled c. 1382–90, a favourite English preaching manual that was also used in Ireland.[15]

On the Day of Judgement outstanding debts would be settled. Irish poets refer frequently to the necessity of mankind paying the *éiric* or blood-price that was incurred by putting Christ to death illegally. While poets generally agree that the passion and death of Christ restored the peace between God and humanity broken by Adam and Eve's sin by the payment of a tribute (literally *síodh na cána*), the subsequent rejection of that peace by individuals who chose to persist in unrepentant sin would be severely dealt with at the end of time. The five wounds of Christ, which functioned as 'peace gifts' on Calvary,

---

[10] Lambert McKenna, ed., *Dánta do chum Aonghus Fionn Ó Dálaigh* (Dublin, 1919), poem 5, stanza 8.

[11] See Salvador Ryan, 'Weapons of Redemption: Piety, Poetry, and the Instruments of the Passion in Late Medieval Ireland', in Henning Laugerud and Laura Skinnebach, eds, *Instruments of Devotion: The Practices and Objects of Religious Piety from the Late Middle Ages to the 20th Century* (Aarhus, 2007), 111–25.

[12] McKenna, ed., *Aonghus Fionn*, poem 19, stanza 9.

[13] Ibid., poem 21, stanza 11.

[14] Lambert McKenna, ed., *Aithdioghluim Dána*, 2 vols (Dublin, 1939–40), 2, poem 58, stanza 21.

[15] Theodore Erbe, ed., *Mirk's Festial: A Collection of Homilies by Johannes Mirkus (John Mirk)* (London, 1905).

would then cry out for vengeance in the presence of persistent sinners who died unshriven. Late medieval *exempla* often recounted how Christ offered sinners salvation in the final moments before death if they would only trust in his blood (often flowing from his side); in cases where they refuse, Christ is depicted as casting his blood in their faces and allowing demons to snatch them off to hell.[16]

It was not only the wounds of Christ and the instruments of his Passion that would function as witnesses for the prosecution in the heavenly court. Detailed lists of an individual's transgressions were believed to be kept by the devil or his demons which would be read aloud on the Last Day. The thirteenth-century poet, Donnchadh Mór Ó Dálaigh, notes that 'when the soul of each of us is placed in our bodies, a demon comes to it, noting our sins; when good confession undoes the sin, the Devil cannot see it, for a hole appears in the book'.[17] The key to obviating embarrassing disclosures on Judgement Day, therefore, was the making of a sincere and honest confession, the importance of which was increasingly emphasized in the wake of the Fourth Lateran Council of 1215 which decreed annual confession for all adults. His contemporary, Giolla Brighde Mac Con Midhe, notes how after death 'a dark red troop' will come for him, accusing him of the eight deadly sins.[18] He continues with a salutary reminder: 'O man who escaped secretly to meet a woman with soft hair, your solitary trysting with a woman in the wood will be screamed aloud on the day that all are gathered together.'[19]

Weighed

The drama of the Day of Doom was heightened with the appearance of St Michael the Archangel with his scales in which the deeds of individuals were to be weighed. In his role as steward of justice, St Michael was simultaneously an object of fear and a sign of hope. Philip Bocht Ó hUiginn (d. 1487) depicts both the demons and St Michael as intent on his condemnation: 'My foes' tongues will harm me on Dispute Day, the

---

[16] Ryan, 'Reign of Blood', 146 n. 66.
[17] McKenna, ed., *Dán Dé*, poem 30, stanzas 4–5.
[18] N. J. Williams, ed., *The Poems of Giolla Brighde Mac Con Midhe* (Dublin, 1980), poem 21, stanza 19. The number eight follows the eight capital sins listed by the desert father, John Cassian (c. 360–435), which greatly influenced the early Irish penitentials.
[19] Ibid., stanza 23.

Scales Steward on the other side assailing me.'[20] His kinsman, Tadhg Óg Ó hUiginn, enlists the protection of St John against the threat of Michael's judgement: 'Stand warrant for me with thy Master, O John; great the danger from Michael's doom; 'tis no light task to be my warrant against the doom of the judgment scale.'[21] However, more often than not, Michael appears as a defender of souls and as a result his cult enjoyed widespread popularity in late medieval Ireland.[22] A fifteenth-century tomb panel from Jerpoint Abbey in County Kilkenny depicts St Michael as *Psychopompos* or 'guide of souls', conducting a soul-like figure to paradise in the folds of a napkin.[23] The native Irish annals routinely highlight when a notable figure dies close to the feast day of the saint at Michaelmas. The beginning of the judicial year was hailed as particularly promising as it was thought that Michael might feel an urge to tip the scales of justice in favour of the sinner around this time.

In the weighing of souls, St Michael was expected to do all he could to secure a favourable result, particularly for those who expressed devotion to him. Philip Bocht Ó hUiginn, in a more positive view of the angel, implores: 'Michael, ever-blooming tree, true master of the eternal home, is my battle-shield against the world; may he counter-weigh my debts (in the scales).'[24] Meanwhile, Aonghus Fionn Ó Dálaigh, appealing to the angel's vanity – Irish poets routinely regarded heavenly beings as having all-too-human weaknesses! – suggests to Michael that the power of his miracles will gain greater renown if 'thou hidest my sins on doomsday'.[25] In an unattributed poem, a poet beseeching Christ to hear the intercessory prayer of St Michael was not averse to exercising a little blackmail to ensure that his case would be heard. The argument he employs is so illustrative of the ingenuity of the Gaelic Irish approach to spiritual politics that it merits quoting at length. Addressing Michael at first and then, finally, Christ, the poet begins:

> The Lord's tribute-steward will stand by me on Testament Day; if, then, Jesus rejects me, will it not be to reject two?

---

20 Lambert McKenna, ed., *Philip Bocht Ó hUiginn* (Dublin, 1931), poem 6, stanza 12.
21 McKenna, ed., *Dán Dé*, poem 1, stanza 1.
22 See Helen M. Roe, 'The Cult of St Michael in Ireland', in Caoimhín Ó Danachair, ed., *Folk and Farm: Essays in Honour of A. T. Lucas* (Dublin, 1976), 251–64.
23 Ibid. 255, 262.
24 McKenna, ed., *Philip Bocht*, poem 11, stanza 32.
25 McKenna, ed., *Aonghus Fionn*, poem 32, stanza 8.

I talk not of my own rejection, but of God's rejection of Michael; to be slighted by Jesus is equal shame for him and me.

The pleader stands to represent me at my sin's trial; if I merit not Heaven, urge Thy rights on the archangel (not on me).[26]

Of course there were also other ways in which the result of the weighing of souls could be skewed in favour of the sinner. A host of intercessors were at hand to add the merits of their lives (and more often their deaths) to the scales, which resulted in a sinner's good deeds (those of the soul) outweighing the bad (those of the body). Philip Bocht Ó hUiginn requests that Catherine of Alexandria present the severed head of her martyrdom as surety for him.[27] The following verses illustrate what effect this was expected to have:

I fear the tilting up of the soul's end of the scale; its lowness brings victory; let me see, dear friends [Saints Michael and Catherine] the other end tilted up by you.

O famous Catherine, though the angel may find (in his scale) excessive weight at my foe's end, fail not to counter-weigh it.

In fear of the light measure I merit, be sure, Catherine, to put thy martyrdom at my end of the scales; help me, O child of God![28]

In a rather humorous admission of the use of sleight of hand at the heart of the celestial judiciary, Ó hUiginn admits: 'I suppose 'tis unjust – but even so, if the maid and the angel both help me, they can save my soul.'[29]

For those who repented of sin before judgement, the symbols of Christ's Passion and Death, observed earlier as accusers of humanity, could be called upon to weigh in on the side of the sinner. An unidentified Franciscan poet adverts to the use of the nails of crucifixion to save humanity: 'Mary's Son will balance against our heavy sin-burden the weight of the nails.'[30] A similar tale can be found in the *Liber Exemplorum*, a thirteenth-century collection of morality tales, in which a dying man's evil deeds are portrayed as outweighing his good deeds

---

[26] Lambert McKenna, ed. and trans., 'St Michael', *Irish Monthly* (1930), 514 (stanzas 7, 11, 35).

[27] McKenna, ed., *Philip Bocht*, poem 14, stanzas 34–35.

[28] Ibid., poem 18, stanzas 10, 11, 14.

[29] Ibid., stanza 15.

[30] McKenna, ed., *Aithdioghluim*, poem 89, stanza 8.

until a nail from the cross falls into the lighter scale.[31] Philip Bocht Ó hUiginn demonstrates how the wounds of Christ fulfilled a double function at the Last Judgement and could be called upon both to condemn and to save sinners. Addressing Christ, he requests: 'Urge not against me – or, rather, let me appeal to – thy pierced hand; if the pierced side be appealed to, we shall both be appealing to the same thing (I on my behalf, thou against me).'[32] The blood of Christ, which was expected to flow in condemnation of sinners and as consolation to the just on the Last Day, could also function as the most efficacious of counter-weights at the weighing of souls. Tadhg Óg Ó hUiginn pleads with God: 'avenge not on us thy Son's burial, but pour his wine-blood into the scale (against our sin).'[33] The story of a dying friar who sees devils and angels weighing his deeds in a balance and asks for a drop of Christ's blood to be added to the weight of his good actions was a staple of medieval *exempla* illustrating the vastness of God's mercy for those who chose to avail themselves of it.[34] While examples of the Virgin Mary placing her rosary beads in the scale to help increase the weight of a client's good deeds, which were common in English wall paintings, are not found as frequently in Ireland, the Virgin was nevertheless expected to interfere with the weighing when the opportunity arose.[35] A seventeenth-century Irish collection of medieval *exempla* includes the story of a boastful and unchaste cleric who nevertheless had a lively devotion to the Virgin Mary. One night he had a dream in which he appeared before the judgement seat of God and a troop of devils arrived carrying the many scrolls on which his sins were written. The Virgin Mary, in turn, arrives with one small roll detailing his good deeds. When placed in the scales the scale of his good deeds rises quickly on account of their lightness; however, when Mary places her blessing on the small roll, the weight suddenly increases and surpasses the cleric's sins, ensuring his salvation.[36]

---

31 Íde Ní Uallacháin, *Exempla Gaeilge: an cnuasach exempla Gaeilge sa ls. 20978–9 i Leabharlann Ríoga na Bruiséile* (Maynooth, 2004), 182.

32 McKenna, ed., *Philip Bocht*, poem 17, stanza 17. For the wider context see Ryan, 'Reign of Blood'; idem, 'Weapons of Redemption'.

33 McKenna, ed., *Dán Dé*, poem 9, stanza 28.

34 Ní Uallacháin, *Exempla Gaeilge*, 182.

35 See, for instance, a fourteenth-century example at Slapton, Northamptonshire, and a fifteenth-century example at South Leigh, Oxfordshire. For further examples, see 'Medieval Wall Painting in the English Parish Church: A Developing Catalogue' (last updated May 2006), <http://www.paintedchurch.org>, accessed 15 March 2008.

36 Ní Uallacháin, *Exempla Gaeilge*, 125.

Defended

The weighing of souls was not the final act in the eschatological drama. When souls were in most need of clemency, they could appeal to a variety of intercessors to overturn unfavourable judgements. Appeals could be made from those who exhibited a measure of devotion, however paltry, to the Virgin Mary and a wide variety of saints, but also to the blood of Christ, the cross and the various instruments of his Passion. The cross, which instilled terror in those who witnessed its appearance on the Last Day, is nevertheless called upon as intercessor by Tadhg Óg Ó hUiginn: 'O cross, whereon God shed his blood, undertake and achieve my defence; owing to my many sins, I flee to thee.'[37] Just as saints were expected to do on the Day of Judgement, the cross was invited to bring its merits before the heavenly court as a plea-bargain for the sinner; in this case, Ó hUiginn mentions that it had the back of Christ's hand affixed to its blood-stained wood, that Christ's foot poured its blood out on it and that his pierced body was stretched on it.[38] While the merits of the cross in this instance are clearly transferred directly from Christ's blood, in a poem by Donnchadh Mór Ó Dálaigh the cross is portrayed as having itself suffered wounds: 'Lay not on me the blame for thy wounds, O hacked cross of the Lord.'[39] The wounds of Christ impressed upon St Francis's body were likewise called upon by Philip Bocht Ó hUiginn to atone for the actual wounds that Christ suffered: 'Francis's wounds requite the nails piercing thee; the saint's breast-wound requites the deep-wounded breast.'[40] In a gesture reminiscent of Christ and the Virgin Mary in the iconography of the double intercession (Christ displaying his wounds to the Father and Mary her exposed breast), which was found across late medieval Europe, Francis is depicted as baring his breast in a gesture of supplication 'pleading for the forgiveness of all my conduct which wounds thy breast'.[41] This gesture is also attributed to the cross in Ó hUiginn's poetry, when he asks it to 'take hold of his grace, which will soften his wrath against me; that I may keep away my

[37] McKenna, ed., *Dán Dé*, poem 3, stanza 19.
[38] Ibid., stanza 20.
[39] Ibid., poem 28, stanza 31.
[40] McKenna, ed., *Philip Bocht*, poem 1, stanza 24.
[41] Ibid., stanza 5. See Salvador Ryan, 'The Persuasive Power of a Mother's Breast: The Most Desperate Act of the Virgin Mary's Advocacy', *Studia Hibernica* 32 (2002–3), 59–74.

sins, show him thy four woods'.[42] The wounds of Christ and the instruments of his Passion became important intercessors for those whose trust in them was sincere; their frequent appearance on late medieval Irish tomb sculpture attests to the patron's wish to record a personal devotion which would shepherd him through death and judgement to paradise.[43] The paradox of these symbols as both salvific and condemnatory is captured in Philip Bocht Ó hUiginn's reference to the 'marks of the cross accusing us; till, owing to it, we enjoy the next life'.[44] Intercession could also be expected from the twelve apostles with their individual merits; John the Baptist, St Dominic and St Catherine of Alexandria also feature prominently as intercessors in late medieval Irish sources. Although St Patrick was traditionally held to have been accorded the particular privilege of judging the Irish by Christ, the bardic poets did not normally capitalize on this boon, preferring to appeal to more universally venerated saints (such as the twelve apostles, Francis and Dominic). If all failed, however, the Virgin Mary was recognized as the advocate par excellence; according to an unidentified poet, 'she lays waste God's wrath'.[45] Ultimately, in the words of sixteenth-century poet Fearghal Ó Cionga, 'the Virgin – and this is the strongest possible claim to my salvation – will prevail over her Son'.[46]

Saved

The account left by Brian Mac Diarmada of his father Ruaidhrí Óg's death in 1568, in the *Annals of Loch Cé*, contains important information that led his audience to conclude, with him, that his soul was saved. In the aftermath of the Fourth Lateran Council, with its emphasis on sincere and complete confession, the key to a favourable judgement lay in true contrition and open admission of guilt. The thirteenth-century poet Giolla Brighde Mac Con Midhe concludes that 'the best recipe for seeking heaven is confession and repentance'.[47] As the revelation of one's sins was expected to shame those gathered at the Last Judgement, he recommends that the necessary embarrassment be faced before death in confession rather than afterwards: 'Confession with its grass

---

42 McKenna, ed., *Philip Bocht*, poem 5, stanza 52.
43 See Ryan, 'Weapons of Redemption', 111–25.
44 McKenna, ed., *Philip Bocht*, poem 7, stanza 4.
45 McKenna, ed., *Aithdioghluim*, poem 87, stanza 10.
46 Ibid., poem 59, stanza 36.
47 Williams, ed., *Giolla Brighde*, poem 22, stanza 14.

showing is a creation pleasing to the eye but fraught with filth; the craftsman of the elements is displeased with it when the earth-side is not uppermost'.[48] Those who carry unconfessed sin exact the vengeance of God in judgement, according to Tadhg Óg Ó hUiginn and are akin to 'a tree on fire'.[49] Ruaidhrí Óg, however, experienced 'pure penance'.[50] In his poem on the fifteen signs before judgement Donnchadh Mór Ó Dálaigh refers to the scene in Matthew 25 where Christ reveals how his followers will be judged ultimately on their charity. Christ reveals that

> I was the beggar in Thy doorway in thirst and hunger, not getting price of bit or sup, while you were in comfort.
> I was every poor man, the woman in rags, every beggar, naked and destitute ...[51]

Brian Mac Diarmada carefully noted that during life his late father won the praise of these very categories of people. Giolla Brighde Mac Con Midhe, in citing the tradition that few rich men go to heaven, remarks that 'the ocean's swift, terrifying, rough wave is not violent against the man with the worthless ship'.[52] The fact that Ruaidhrí Óg left not a groat of inheritance (presumably on account of his generosity to the poor) assured him of a smoother path to eternal life. Those who 'roofed their house'[53] (confessed) in advance of the storm could comfort themselves in the knowledge of Christ's blood covering their house 'as the ark'.[54] But not all managed to travel the road of penance when the 'weather was still fine', as described by one bardic poet. What happened when the evening came with its dark clouds and the unsuspecting sinner was caught unaware? On that occasion, inappropriately prepared to meet the Christ of judgement, believers needed to rely on the support of spiritual patronage and on the prospect of a 'fixing of the eschatological scales'.

[48] Ibid., stanza 20. The idea of good confession was that the penitent would reveal the earth-side of himself to the confessor rather than the more attractive and grass-covered upper-side. The sins that were not revealed in confession could not be absolved.
[49] McKenna, ed., *Dán Dé*, poem 4, stanza 3.
[50] Hennessy, ed., *Annals of Loch Cé*, 396–405.
[51] Lambert McKenna, ed., 'The Signs of the Judgement', *Irish Monthly* (1927), 262–63 (stanzas 26–27).
[52] Williams, ed., *Giolla Brighde*, poem 21, stanza 16.
[53] McKenna, ed., *Aithdioghluim*, poem 62, stanza 4.
[54] McKenna, ed., *Philip Bocht*, poem 11, stanza 31.

Conclusion

Preoccupation with the afterlife and, more particularly, with reaching the kind of afterlife that promised blissful union with God rather than eternal punishment, was a staple concern in late medieval and early modern Irish society. In this way, Irish Christians differed little from their European counterparts when it came to eternal questions. The surviving 'Book of Piety' commissioned by Máire Ní Mháille, a Donegal noblewoman in 1513, complete with her favourite devotional legends and religious instructions, treats of issues such as why God shortens the sinner's life, four things which prevent holiness, three things which lead to heaven, three things which lead to hell, and three reasons why one should despise the world.[55] Many people considered it infinitely more important to fix their gaze on the afterlife rather than become too attached to what was described in the *Salve Regina* as a 'vale of tears'. Preparation for individual judgment, therefore, was regarded as forming the most crucial element of one's life. The cultivation of devotion to the Virgin Mary and the saints as intercessors, the recitation of prescribed prayers promising salvation, and recourse to the merits of Christ's passion and death were the key instruments which might be employed to secure one's eternal future. While the religious works of Irish bardic poets attest to the currency of these familiar themes in the late medieval and early modern periods, the unique character of the argumentation employed by native Irish versifiers, who were more accustomed to eulogizing secular princes than heavenly ones, adds a dash of colour to a world which we are more used to viewing more dimly.

St Patrick's College, Thurles

---

55 Salvador Ryan, 'Windows on Late Medieval Devotional Practice: Máire Ní Mháille's "Book of Piety" (1513) and the world behind the texts', in Rachel Moss, Colmán Ó Clabaigh and Salvador Ryan, eds, *Art and Devotion in Late Medieval Ireland* (Dublin, 2006), 1–15, at 4.

'AN AFTERLIFE IN MEMORY': COMMEMORATION AND ITS EFFECTS IN A LATE MEDIEVAL PARISH*

by CLIVE BURGESS

INVESTIGATIONS of the more routine expressions of pre-Reformation spirituality inevitably tend to dwell on the conventions employed by individuals to ease the progress of the soul. The pious attestations and exhortations that some men and women recorded may merit the closest attention for the insight they afford into beliefs and aspiration; but hardly less instructive, and much more common, are the services and good works that individuals commissioned both to express repentance and expedite deliverance. Focusing in this way on individuals poses problems, however. While a few had the means to establish a 'freestanding' institution – such as an almshouse – the great majority channeled penitential activity into the arena, and to the benefit, of their parish. Individuals ordinarily acted as parishioners, contributing towards and depending upon the services of a well-defined, broader community, within which they did their best to enhance collective memory and experience to their own advantage by securing the benefit of others. If anything, ensuring the benefit of others was reckoned the essential, practical prerequisite for personal advantage. As a result, if we accept that the desire to be saved – and as expeditiously as possible – spurred on most contemporary Christians, the doctrinal emphases in the centuries before the Reformation predicated a series of distinctive consequences, two of which are of particular significance here. First, many parishioners assured themselves of long remembrance, amounting to an afterlife in the world and in the consciousness of those that came after. Such enterprise worked as a vital precondition assisting any soul striving towards the greater afterlife in

---

* This paper strays close to ground that I have covered elsewhere, particularly in my ' "Longing to be Prayed for": Death and Commemoration in an English Parish in the Later Middle Ages', in B. Gordon and P. Marshall, eds, *The Place of the Dead: Death and Remembrance in Late Medieval and Early Modern Europe* (Cambridge, 2000), 44–65. It is offered, however, as a convenient gathering of a number of ideas that afford a fruitful approach to understanding some, at least, of the purposes underpinning late medieval pious practice and achievement. Notes are kept to a minimum.

heaven. Second, the impact of commemoration, and of ensuring it, profoundly affected the standards and observances of parish life in many – possibly most – pre-Reformation English local communities. Communal commemoration, and the investment this entailed, greatly improved the spiritual efficacy of many a parish regime, cultivating a cult of memory to ensure on the one hand that the living served and helped to save the dead, and on the other that the dead served and sustained the living. Self-evidently, focusing on individuals misses much of the point of what was afoot.

In so far as the Reformation recast those processes deemed necessary for securing the afterlife and prompted hostility towards commemoration as an aid to salvation, the achievements of earlier parishioners were all too often either discarded or destroyed, and their cumulative impact has, until recently, been little considered. But the most striking survival from the pre-Reformation regime is, probably, the buildings, with many of our parish churches as they now exist dating wholly or in the main from the fourteenth and fifteenth centuries. Most of these have, of course, been changed – either 'purged' in the sixteenth and seventeenth centuries, or heavily restored in the nineteenth – and many historians may shy away from 'reading' buildings. Nevertheless, given that the late fourteenth and fifteenth centuries saw a relatively low population, the spate of rebuilding and ambitious enlarging begins to suggest something of the impact that penitential and commemorative practice, albeit operating in conjunction with other priorities, may have had on local religious observance. When exploring the impact of such practice on parish development, however, it proves crucial to bear the broader context in mind – and to this extent, considering parish buildings (edifices which epitomized the institutional achievements of the local community) helps to point us in the most profitable direction. For, by contrast with the situation after the Reformation, when parishes had become almost the sole constituents of the institutional Church (save for cathedrals in a number of the larger cities), earlier circumstances produced their own distinctive milieu. Parishes had previously taken a relatively lowly place in a far richer ecclesiastical environment, comprising monasteries and nunneries in the regular Church, and colleges, hospitals and almshouses, and even fraternities, in the secular sphere – with parishes, of course, fitting into the latter.[1] Moreover,

---

[1] For a rough, but instructive, impression of the institutional richness of the pre-Reformation Church, it is worthwhile contemplating the bulk of D. Knowles and R. N.

while we may tend to conceive of the Church primarily as discharging a pastoral function, many of the larger and influential foundations just mentioned would, first and foremost, have fulfilled a liturgical purpose. As a result of the constant celebration of high-grade worship, which was their prime duty, such institutions benefited not only their founders but also, and more importantly, Christian society – in practice, the realm – against mishap. For the unstinting and decorous praise that these establishments offered up called down the grace of God onto Christian society, and the general conception of the latter tended to equate with the political society – be it local or national, and usually both – with which one associated and identified. An important principle flows from this observation. Many of England's monasteries and colleges had been founded as the result of a penitential motive – guaranteeing founders long-term and prestigious commemoration – but this was not selfish; the benefit accruing did not solely profit the founder and his or her kin. Monks and canons also served the broader advantage of Christian society by the faithful and decorous celebration of the liturgy. Thus penance coalesced productively with, and helped to secure, the broader benefits for Christian society that were bound to result from the 'increase of divine service'.

Bearing this background in mind but turning, now, to reflect on the institution most closely embedded in the localities, parishes may have been founded between the tenth and the twelfth century primarily to satisfy a pastoral *raison d'être*, but with time – and especially in the fifteenth century – they adapted. Cumulatively, penitential activity by parishioners brought about change, enabling parishes to integrate within the broader Church. Although local churches naturally continued to discharge pastoral functions, like teaching the laity and administering the sacraments, the rites of lay penitence, which invariably prompted commemorative activity, wrought important liturgical and institutional effects. In short – and to emphasize the 'political sub-text' – if abbeys and hospitals and colleges and the like might benefit the realm by extending sophisticated liturgical service, so increasingly could many parishes.[2] Successive governments, depending upon the agency of bishops working in the localities to advance royal interests, encouraged

Hadcock, *Medieval Religious Houses: England and Wales*, 2nd edn (London, 1971).
  [2] I have argued this point in more detail elsewhere; see my 'An Institution for all Seasons: The Late Medieval English College', in C. Burgess and M. Heale, eds, *The Late Medieval English College and its Context* (Woodbridge, 2008), 3–27.

the 'increase of divine service' from as broad a constituency as possible – and the most numerous constituency in the Church was the parish, after all – to benefit both the locality and the realm.[3]

* * *

If differing somewhat from conventional assessments of the late medieval Church, such reasoning presents an intriguing prospect whose outline – as a result of the heavy losses subsequently inflicted on commemorative formulae and practice – ordinarily needs to be pieced together from decidedly exiguous data. But some parishes preserve far better evidence than the great majority of their counterparts, and this can reveal with welcome clarity the role that penitential activity played in enhancing local experience. One such – and among the best such, in pre-Reformation England – is the parish of All Saints', Bristol, on whose archive the following concentrates. To neglect such a parish on the grounds of atypicality, because it possesses an unusually ample archive, would of course be absurd, so, first, some brief comments may be offered by way of background both about the town and this parish in the later Middle Ages.

By the fifteenth century, Bristol was England's third largest town (after London and Norwich), but, since it had only become important as a settlement after the diocesan map of England had been drawn in the late seventh century, it remained a town rather than a city. Straddling two dioceses, the old town, to the north of the River Avon, lay in the diocese of Worcester, with the newer suburbs to the south of the river in the diocese of Bath and Wells. At the heart of the old town, All Saints' came under the jurisdiction of the diocese of Worcester, and its patron was the abbey of St Augustine, Bristol's largest conventual institution. All Saints' occupied a restricted space, bounded to the north by Corn Street and to the east by the High Street, and served a communicant population in the mid sixteenth century of just under two hundred souls. To gain some sense of context, it may be noted that the average population in the town's parishes was nearer four hundred, although some, like neighbouring St Nicholas, or St Mary Redcliffe to the south of the Avon, served far larger communicant populations of some eight

---

3 On the role of bishops, see A. K. McHardy, 'Liturgy and Propaganda in the Diocese of Lincoln during the Hundred Years War', in S. Mews, ed., *Religion and National Identity*, SCH 18 (Oxford, 1982), 215–27; eadem, 'Some Reflections on Edward III's Use of Propaganda', in J. S. Bothwell, ed., *The Age of Edward III* (Woodbridge, 2001), 171–92.

hundred souls apiece.[4] Far from being physically imposing, All Saints' was for the most part tucked away behind adjacent tenements, possessing only a restricted street frontage. But two factors must be noted. First, considering its communicant numbers, a somewhat disproportionate number of these appear wealthy – perhaps fittingly, in view of the parish's central location in the town – and a fair few of its parishioners played a part in Bristol's municipal government.[5] Second, it housed the Kalendars' Guild, a fraternity whose name reflects the fact that its main celebration fell at the beginning of every month.[6] While having earlier restricted its membership to the secular clergy, by the fifteenth century the laity might also join, and from this time it supported a prior and three additional priests. These occupied a house (rebuilt in the 1440s) above the north aisle of the church and to its west end; from the 1460s the prior presided over a newly stocked library, open to the public at regular intervals. The point perhaps to be pondered so far as the Kalendars were concerned, however, is that their existence inevitably made for a heavy clerical presence within All Saints'.

Small, possibly quite 'well-heeled', and supporting a heavy clerical presence – such factors helped to define this parish. Nevertheless, far and away All Saints' most remarkable characteristic presently lies in its preservation of an extraordinary range of archival material illustrative of later fifteenth- and early sixteenth-century lay aspiration and practice, and of the effects of these as they combined.[7] Items within the archive all have their equivalents elsewhere, with the possible exception of the benefaction list: similar lists, of which there were probably many, functioning as glorified bede rolls, proved plum targets for destruction, closely associated as they were with the doctrine of purgatory. As suggested, it is the range of surviving materials that is so extraordinary. In common with many another parish, a number of parishioners' wills

---

[4] The 'houselling populations' for Bristol's parishes are taken from the mid sixteenth-century Chantry Certificates – most easily accessible in J. Maclean, ed., 'Chantry Certificates, Gloucestershire', *Transactions of the Bristol and Gloucestershire Archaeological Society* [hereafter: *TBGAS*] 8 (1883–84), 229–308.

[5] I am indebted to Dr James Lee for advice on this point.

[6] N. Orme, 'The Guild of Kalendars, Bristol', *TBGAS* 96 (1978), 32–52, is essential reading on this fraternity and its fortunes in the fifteenth century.

[7] Full transcriptions of the great majority of the All Saints' archive are now available in three volumes of the Bristol Record Society: Clive Burgess, ed., *The Pre-Reformation Records of All Saints', Bristol: Parts 1, 2 and 3*, Bristol Record Society's Publications 46, 53, 56 (1995, 2000 and 2004) [hereafter: *ASB 1, ASB 2* and *ASB 3*].

can be gathered, from both the Bristol Corporation's Great Orphan Book, and from the Prerogative Court of Canterbury registers.[8] The total surviving, however, of about forty wills for the fifteenth and early sixteenth centuries serves as a salutary reminder of quite how much material illustrative of contemporary aspirations has evidently been lost, even for a parish generally well served with surviving evidence. The remainder of the archive, however, was produced 'in house' and apparently kept in the parish chest, for a time at least, for 'domestic' purposes. Perhaps the most striking compilation, generally of 'tidied' material deemed worthy for formal preservation either because it recorded declarations or possessions or because it lauded those who had worked hard for the parish, is the All Saints' Church Book.[9] In addition to 'constitutions' – that is, rules that had been passed to guide the conduct of parish affairs – it contained the benefaction list, already mentioned, in at least three redactions written down between about 1480 and 1510. It also logged two inventories, one from the late fourteenth century and the other from c. 1470, and, for the years from c. 1410 until c. 1470, it preserved a 'tidied' set of churchwardens' accounts and also listed epitomes descriptive of successive wardens' achievements on behalf of the parish. Other records in the parish archive include a reasonably complete series of audited churchwardens' accounts, beginning c. 1460 and extending well into the sixteenth century, which means that the earliest ten years or so of the audited accounts exist in parallel with the 'tidied' version in the Church Book.[10] The accounts and sundry other documentation for the Halleways' chantry represent a rarer survival, however. Joan Halleway oversaw the inception of this commemorative arrangement c. 1450, and detailed financial records, recording income from its endowment and expenditure on both ceremonial observances and the maintenance of its properties, survive in a reasonably complete series from the early 1460s almost until the chantry's dissolution in the 1540s. In common with many of Bristol's late medieval parishes, All Saints' also preserves a good series of contemporary deeds, disclosing property transactions, the names of the parish's managers and much about other administrative procedure.[11]

[8] These are all printed in the first section of *ASB 3*.
[9] Printed in *ASB 1*.
[10] Printed in *ASB 2*.
[11] The Halleway chantry materials and All Saints' deeds respectively constitute the second and third sections of *ASB 3*.

In all, we may derive a relatively good impression of parish management in All Saints', and it is worth noting how different categories of evidence reveal various aspects of commemorative activity. To schematize, wills and the benefaction list disclose something about movable gifts (such as vessels and vestments) made to priests and the parish; the benefaction list and deeds reveal more about the real property (providing endowments for services) entrusted to the church, often given *pre obit* and omitted from wills. Although it proves impossible in the following to say much about the continuous effort devoted to commemorative services, even a cursory glance at records surviving for the Halleways' chantry suggests something of the care lavished on one such endeavour for the best part of a century. Although much material has undoubtedly been lost, considerably more survives for All Saints' than for most parishes. But it is worth commenting, if briefly, on how little (about parish life, at least) the wills tend to tell us, which must give pause, since most regimes furnish us only with wills, if we are lucky – everything else produced by contemporaries having perished. Had we nothing else, All Saints' wills could impart a decidedly inadequate impression of parishioners' activity. The Halleways' chantry accounts, for instance, disclose in detail how one major commemorative benefaction was managed – discretely, as it turns out – and reveal that the annual budget for this one suffrage, certainly in the fifteenth century, usually exceeded that dealt with by the churchwardens in their separate, parish accounts. Thomas Halleway, a mayor of Bristol whose fortune underwrote the perpetual chantry founded in his name, omitted any mention of this undertaking in his will. In the absence of deeds and chantry accounts – which is now the situation in the great majority of parishes, even though such documentation was once commonly available – historians would have no way of assessing, or even guessing, the very considerable significance of his commemorative arrangements. Such lessons, and the measure of loss that has been visited on most parish archives, need to be noted.

* * *

A number of observations may now pave the way towards a more detailed discussion of the activities within All Saints'. First, in addition to the established duty of maintaining their priest by tithe, thirteenth-century synodal decrees assigned to the laity in every parish the duty of maintaining the fabric of nave and tower, and of providing the vessels and vestments necessary for the seemly celebration of the

liturgy.[12] Second, by the fifteenth century, the response to these obligations was far exceeding basic provision. As already noted, rather than
maintenance, building anew was ubiquitous; similarly, rather than
providing the necessities for seemly celebration, many parishes accrued
an ever-increasing abundance of sophisticated liturgical equipment,
and some supported a plurality of priests. Such bounty resulted from
the penitential teachings of the Church, resting chiefly on the doctrine
of purgatory that had been preached and honed, also from the
thirteenth century, by the friars as well as by other clergy.[13] Without
going into undue detail, the essentials of this doctrine emphasized *inter
alia* the importance of charity, and of good works, in particular
prompting the wealthy (the penitentially challenged) to give. This they
did in order to receive, and in particular to benefit from, the prayers of
the poor (whose prayers, as a result of implicit closeness to Christ, were
reckoned as powerful), as well as from succeeding generations of
co-parishioners, both clerical and lay. Thus, in addition to frequent and
generous gifts to the poor, the laity regularly gave money and items,
such as cups or books, to the clergy, and were also openhanded to their
respective parish communities. The rationale for the latter was that by
gifts of equipment or money – to help towards the rebuilding of the
nave roof, shall we say – the donor relieved succeeding generations of
the community from similar obligations. In so doing, moreover, he or
she enriched both the parish environment as well as the liturgy celebrated within, further benefiting parish and parishioners. The donor
could claim to be remembered as a benefactor. In sum, what emerges
very clearly from a parish like All Saints', Bristol, is how the dead, and
those about to die, laid claim to the prayers of the living, and of generations yet to come, by a calculating generosity – or, in effect, by a self-
interested altruism. The donation of money and/or of goods and equipment, the provision of furniture and fixtures, and the devise of property
or premises and dwellings ensured a response from the living, obliged

---

[12] F. M. Powicke and C. R. Cheney, eds, *Councils and Synods with other Documents relating to
the English Church II, AD 1205–1313* (Oxford, 1964), 1: 128, 367; 2: 1006, 1122–23. C. Drew,
Early Parochial Organisation in England. The Origins of the Office of Churchwarden, St Anthony's
Hall Publications 7 (York, 1954) provides useful discussion on the impact of such obligations.

[13] For convenient discussion of this doctrine and its impact, see E. Duffy, *The Stripping of
the Altars: Traditional Religion in England, 1400–1580*, 2nd edn (New Haven, CT, and London,
2005), ch. 10; also my 'A Fond Thing Vainly Invented', in S. J. Wright, ed., *Parish, Church and
People: Local Studies in Lay Religion, 1350–1750* (London, 1988), 56–84.

to remember benefactors in assiduous prayer; benefactors assured themselves of an afterlife. Such contracts with posterity worked with every appearance of efficiency: we can certainly see that those able to, gave; we may also discern characteristics of the commemorative response, which we shall shortly consider.

What must be emphasized in the interim, however, as the factor effectively underpinning any such contract, was the development of managerial expertise within the parish. As the church derived cash, equipment and property, it was obliged to depend upon a competent managerial structure able to safeguard gains and orchestrate and guarantee the required response. Those agents who worked to secure the desired result also laid claim on commemoration by the wider parish, which had certainly benefited from their labour – as the material relating to successive churchwardens' achievements in the All Saints' Church Book clearly reveals.[14] Managerial expertise, upon which everything else depended (as donors would never have been persuaded to give had they not been confident that largesse would have its desired effects), was undoubtedly a good work, and evidently these 'enablers' too were carefully remembered as benefactors. But one or two further observations on this topic also prove relevant. First, that some managers, having been appointed as churchwardens, clearly used this office as a first rung on the ladder to greater things – most obviously, a role in municipal government. In such circumstances, the understandable desire that such men felt to acquit themselves well, facilitating subsequent progress among the town's elite, obviously advanced parish interests too. Second, it is relevant to note that 'masters' of the parish, as directors of parish affairs, usually had a proven competence in parish, craft or town management, and, as successful men of affairs in a number of spheres, were evidently a force to be reckoned with.[15] As wealthy men, likely to be among the most generous benefactors in their generation to the parish, they had a keen – often very personal – interest that their local commemorative regime, in which they had invested time, energy and means, should work as well as possible. Such factors worked to the long-term and intrinsic advantage of parish

[14] Respectively, the series of epitomes of successive pairs of churchwardens and the tidied version of old accounts, to be found in *ASB 1*, 45–49 and 49–135.

[15] The Masters of the parish receive more attention in my 'Pre-Reformation Churchwardens' Accounts and Parish Government: Lessons from London and Bristol', *EHR* 117 (2002), 306–32.

administrations functioning as commemorative regimes: their management was both competent and committed – which might not, *prima facie*, have been assumed. But we should now turn to consider some more precise examples of contemporaries' planning and activity.

* * *

Numerous entries in the All Saints' Church Book's benefaction list have the merit of mentioning something, at least, of donors' motivation. Among those who gave sums of money, we are told that William Palmer, a goldsmith of London, who gave 40s., Robert Derkyn, a London mercer, who gave 20s., and Martin Symondson, a hardwareman 'of this parish', who also gave 20s., specifically did so 'to be prayed for'.[16] Thomas Abyndon, parishioner and inn-holder, 'at his decease gave unto this church in money 40s.' and is said to have done so 'as a good doer'.[17] Others gave items, usually with a liturgical purpose in mind. Richard Ake 'gave to the use of the vicar for the time being one antiphonal, price £10, in order to be prayed for among the benefactors of the church. God have mercy on his soul'.[18] Other donations exhorted prayer, sometimes blatantly. Alice Chestre gave 'a hearse cloth of black worsted with letters of gold of H & C & A & C and a scripture in gold, *Orate pro animabus Henricus Chestre et Alicie uxoris eius*'. She reportedly made this benefaction 'for the love and honour that she had unto Almighty God and to all Christian souls, and for the ease and succour of all this parish unto whom she owed her good will and love in her day'.[19] Some of the other comments elicited by her extensive benefactions are worth highlighting. She was generous on behalf of her late husband, Henry, and herself, 'to the worship of almighty God and his church, and to have both their souls prayed for specially amongst all other good doers'. In what amounts to an editorial note, made presumably by the scribe, Sir John Thomas (who became vicar of All Saints' in the late fifteenth century), we find the memorandum, 'We all that are now and they that are to come are bound to pray for her.'[20] She achieved her aim: clergy and parishioners evidently knew that they were obliged to remember both her and her husband.

16 *ASB 1*, 15.
17 Ibid. 21–22.
18 Ibid. 13.
19 Ibid. 17. As the subsequent exhortation makes clear, the initials are those of her late husband, Henry, and herself.
20 Ibid.

While many probably envisaged a response which was to some extent, at least, informal (Alice Chestre clearly hoped that any who saw her hearse cloth might react spontaneously to the prompt embroidered on it), All Saints', like every other parish, had also evolved formalized responses. It is plain that the parish had a bede roll, a list of names of 'good doers', to be read out every Sunday. Clement Wilteshire, in his will written in 1488, bequeathed to the vicar, 'Sir John Thomas, a gown of scarlet, which had formerly belonged to William Coder, to pray for my soul and the soul of my [late] wife, Margery, and the souls of our parents, brothers, sisters, kin and friends, on every Sunday among the other dead of the parish of All Hallows' according to the usage there'.[21] Thomas Baker *alias* Spicer, while depending on much the same provision in his will made in 1492, perhaps wanted something slightly more. He bequeathed Sir John Thomas 20s., 'in recompense to him for tithes and offerings forgotten by me or inadequately reckoned, and with the intention that every Sunday he may specially exhort the parishioners there to pray for my soul'.[22] Quite what the special exhortation would have comprised, or how long this would have been continued, is not clear; but it is plain that parishioners formally remembered benefactors, apparently during High Mass.

Weekly commemoration had also evidently long been practised – indeed, reference in an early fifteenth-century will, made by Robert Crosman in 1405, discloses something of its longevity. To the vicar of All Hallows', Crosman left '40d if he put the above names [those of his wife and of both his and her parents] on the table of memory and rehearse them every Sunday'.[23] While most testators admittedly fail to specify such a service – plausibly because it was so basic a commemorative device that executors could be expected to employ it as a matter of course – Crosman's request reveals that names might be engraved on a table of memory, presumably a plaque or board. Thus they could be permanently displayed and, in addition, formally recited once a week.[24] Whether 'tables of memory' and the bede roll were one and the same,

---

21 *ASB 3*, will 16, clause 5. Clement Wilteshire died suddenly while serving as mayor of Bristol in 1492, probably at Christmastide. The will that survives for him was evidently made, following common precautionary practice, some years before his decease; those granted the opportunity recast their wishes in the days or hours before death.
22 Ibid., will 18, clause 4.
23 Ibid., will 3, clause 11.
24 He may, unusually, have bothered to specify this since he was not a parishioner of All Saints' when he died, although it had clearly been his parents' parish and he would probably

or whether each supplemented the other – one, in practice, displaying names, and the other designed to be read out – is an imponderable.[25] Whether the benefaction list in the All Saints' Church Book was to be read out loud is similarly difficult to determine. As it stands, we have several different redactions, by turns 'shrinking' material devoted to benefactors whose activities were receding into the ever more distant past, thus allowing more room for recent additions. The conscious endeavour for brevity, or manageability, does perhaps suggest that the most recent redaction was for recital. Or perhaps it was the case that a table of names was rehearsed on Sundays, while the list preserved (in its different forms) in the church book may have been the 'data base' for a recitation that took place annually. For there was, indeed, another, annual celebration of benefactors, clearly meant to differ from Sunday formalities. Material in the Bristol archives suggests that each parish observed its General Mind, so called, on its own distinct day, but, as a result of the detail available in its archive, we know more about the rationale underpinning, and the activities comprising, this celebration in All Saints'.[26]

It is, first, virtually obligatory to reproduce the prologue to the benefaction list in the Church Book: it affords probably the clearest statement we are likely to encounter anywhere of quite why names of benefactors had been collected and what the annual recitation of them was meant to trigger.[27] Immediately preceding the benefaction list, on a fresh folio towards the beginning of the Church Book, the following is set down as a heading:

> The names of good doers and well willers by whom livelode, tenements and other goods have been given unto the church of All Hallows in Bristol, unto the honour and worship of Almighty God and [the] increasing of divine service, to be showed and declared unto the parishioners on the Sunday before Ash Wednesday and at high Mass and yearly to be continued as follows.

have grown up there. He obviously felt obliged to be precise as to the location of this observance.

[25] In the unbound churchwardens' accounts for 1478–79, for instance, there is a payment for bedes being hung up in the church, and later taken down and folded up (*ASB 2*, 93), which may possibly suggest some overlap between tables of memory and bede rolls.

[26] Parishes in Bristol each appear to have had different days for their General Mind, as mentioned in my 'Longing to be prayed for', 54.

[27] *ASB 1*, 4.

The recitation of names on the Sunday before Ash Wednesday is singled out as special and as more elaborate than was customary on other Sundays. The prologue proper is then given, emphasizing that the practice of reciting the names of benefactors was long established, and classifying the range of deeds that might count as benefactions, confirming that donors had always been conscious of the desirability of having their names rehearsed:

> Where it has been of a laudable custom of long continuance used, that on this day, that is to say the Sunday before Ash Wednesday, the names of good doers and well willers by whom livelode – tenements, buildings, jewels, books chalices, vestments and with other divers ornaments and goods, as follows – has been given unto the church unto the honour and worship of Almighty God and increasing of divine service, to be rehearsed and shown yearly unto you by name, both man and woman, and what benefits they did for themselves and for their friends and for others by their lifetimes, and what they left for them to be done after their days.

The reason for such activity is then explained, as the tone of the preface becomes decidedly exhortatory, urging others to do likewise:

> That they shall not be forgotten but had in remembrance and be prayed for of all this parish that be now and all of them that be to come, and also for an example to you all that be now living that you may likewise to do for yourself and for your friends while they be in this world, that after the transitory life you may be had in the number of good doers rehearsed by name and in the special prayers of Christian people in time coming that by the infinite mercy of Almighty God, by the intercession of our blessed lady and of all the blessed saints of heaven, in whose honour and worship this church is dedicated, you may come to the everlasting bliss and joy that our blessed lord has redeemed you unto. AMEN.

Contemporary belief as to the efficacy and point of intercession stands revealed. 'Rehearsal by name and in the special prayers of all Christian people in time coming' was manifestly held to be an effective means of prompting God's mercy and the intercession of the Blessed Virgin and of all the saints, and thus of securing redemption. The importance attached to benefaction and formal commemoration is explained, and the generosity of contemporaries, particularly those burdened by worldly success and its inevitable 'wages', wholly understandable.

And what generosity it was! In the course of the 1440s, an individual donor, Richard Haddon, rebuilt the north aisle of the church (along with the Kalendars' House above it) and also reglazed the windows of 'Our Lady's aisle', doing so particularly in memory of his parents.[28] At about the same time, other parishioners, both clerical and lay and mentioned in the benefaction list, 'clubbed together' to rebuild the south – or 'Cross' – aisle.[29] Thus, in the course of a decade or so in the mid-fifteenth century, what may very well have been orchestrated generosity saw the rebuilding and enhancement of both aisles of the church. Moreover, in addition to smaller acquisitions – such as vestments, altar cloths, candlesticks, images, and the like, all of which are listed 'under' their donors in the benefaction list – others were more generous still in replacing the major fittings within the church, continuing the refurbishment of its interior. Thus Alice Chestre, two years before she died in 1485, being in good prosperity and health of body, and considering that the rood loft in the church

> was but single and no thing of beauty, according to the parish intent [that is, with their permission], and taking to her counsel the worshipful of the parish with others having best understanding and insight in carving, to the honour and worship of God and His saints, and of her special devotion to this church, let make a new rood loft in carved work with twenty-two images at her own proper cost – of the which images, three are principal, a Trinity in the middle, a Christopher in the north and a Michael in the south . . .[30]

As well as being remembered as a particularly generous benefactress (although not entirely unrivalled in the community), it is worth noting how such a donor might affect the devotional tenor of the church. Quite simply, the generosity of the few had a significant effect on the spiritual lives of the many. As a result, if a wealthy parishioner could be persuaded to rebuild or beautify part of the church (in addition to, or rather than, simply enlarging their house, for instance), a little might go a long way in terms both of the general benefit and, thus, in procuring long-lasting commemoration.

---

[28] Ibid. 9; but my forthcoming monograph on All Saints' includes a much fuller discussion of Haddon's generosity and of the vicissitudes visited on his legacy.

[29] Sir Thomas Marshall, vicar of the church in the 1430s and 1440s, had paid for glazing two windows in the Cross aisle (ibid. 8), and Thomas Halleway had, at some unspecified date, given the sum of £20 to the Cross aisle (ibid. 14).

[30] Ibid. 16–17.

* * *

Moving on from donations, we profit by considering the services that parishioners established; these fell into two main categories – chantries and anniversaries. Taking chantries first, it is simply worth saying that, ordinarily, these provided for a priest to celebrate a daily mass at an existing altar within the church; in that the founder was usually obliged to guarantee the priest's stipend, foundation was not a responsibility to be taken lightly. Chantries themselves fell into two types: temporary chantries intended to last for a limited duration after the founder's death; and perpetual chantries, everlasting institutions to be served by an unbroken succession of priests. To deal with the first of these, temporary chantries, it is worth saying that they were, understandably, much the more numerous manifestation of the form, with the majority lasting for a year or two, although some were to last for ten or a dozen years. An heir or a widow usually 'found' these services, literally as a 'death duty', as the beneficiary of a property devise who might be expected to pay the priest's stipend for the stipulated duration. Some, indeed, continued for longer than required, presumably as the widow or heir concerned (it was usually the former) felt that they were also benefiting from the service. The priest certainly celebrated a daily mass for the donor and other named beneficiaries (such as his or her family, and invariably 'for all the faithful departed'); but this was only part of the commemoration. For the community received the services of an extra priest, who, although not able to celebrate more than once in any day, might help in the parish, swelling the ranks in the choir and assisting with liturgical duties – and all 'for free'. It is quite clear that the parish counted this as an important and generous benefaction. Indeed, in the benefaction list, it is striking how the temporary chantries that parishioners had provided regularly took pride of place, mentioned before any other benefaction that he or she had made, with a careful note of how much in total had been paid to the priest. Given that a priest's salary was ordinarily in the region of £6 per annum, the sum amassed over an extended duration (say £60 for a ten year stint) did indeed amount to a considerable sum, exceeding most other benefactions. Hence, in addition to benefiting from merit accruing from the masses celebrated, founders were also remembered as important benefactors as a result of underwriting a 'free' stipendiary for parish purposes, perhaps helping to teach the young, and adding to the ranks of liturgists at the parish mass and canonical hours. Moreover, founders of temporary chantries often provided their priests with vessels and vestments. These were, of course, intended to serve the priest for the duration of the chantry but would thereafter remain in the parish's possession; these too might amount to a generous bequest. To take one example, Katherine Laynell provided her and her husband's celebrant with a mass book worth 10 marks, a double gilt chalice, weighing 25 oz. and worth £7 13s. 4d., with cruets of silver, a fine corporas cloth, a pair of large latten candlesticks and vestments of blue velvet with flowers originally priced at £25. All this passed to the parish on completion of the chantry, originally intended to last for ten years, but which, as a result of Katherine's largesse, was extended by two years during her life and for a further three after her death.[31]

While, by definition, such windfalls would not have been envisaged where perpetual chantries were concerned – although their celebrants were entrusted with rich vessels and vestments, whose employment would have embellished proceedings within the church – the foundation of such services, establishing a 'free' priest forever, represented a rare and munificent gift. Only one perpetual chantry was successfully established in All Saints', founded by Thomas and Joan Halleway in the 1440s.[32] In time, their mass became amalgamated into the parish's liturgical round, 'doubling' as the morrow mass – the first early morning mass of the day – for the benefit of the parish as much as the Halleways' souls. Should this appear at all presumptuous on the part of the parish, encroaching on the Halleways' provision, it may be countered that, in one respect, the utility of the Hallways' provision was only magnified, which must have redounded to their spiritual credit. If men of business as well as labourers attended the morrow mass, because they could not easily attend the main parish mass later in the day, they would certainly have been reminded of the Halleways' largesse, as well as being exhorted to pray for their souls. But, in a more substantial respect, the rare survival of the Halleways' Chantry Accounts presents us with a fascinating balance sheet, which repays close consideration. To provide their service with an income in perpetuity, the Halleways set aside three blocks of property situated in various parts of Bristol that had to be managed by the parish. Thus, from one point of view, the parish not

---

[31] Ibid. 17–18.

[32] All the material relating to the Halleways' foundation (and including a general introduction) is printed in the second section of *ASB 3*. It should also be noted that Richard Haddon's attempt to establish a perpetual chantry in All Saints' (also in the 1440s and 1450s) foundered in the early 1470s.

only gained a 'free' priest, but also derived both property and influence in the broader purlieus of Bristol. But what, from another point of view, is unequivocally revealed by the accounts is that the managerial investment, the sheer hard work necessarily involved in maintaining and letting the many different tenements that constituted each of the three main endowments, was both unremitting and demanding. It took considerable time and effort year after year to maintain the service; a 'free' priest certainly came at a price. To enfold the Halleways' mass within the fabric of parish life was hardly to the founders' detriment, representing no more nor less an appropriation than the parish had earned.

Anniversaries also fell into two groups: those that were to last for a limited duration – for instance, for five, ten, or twenty years – which, like temporary chantries, were ordinarily 'found' by legatees; and those that were intended to be perpetual, which, correspondingly, were usually supported by a property endowment.[33] Insofar as anniversaries were customarily intended to support one major commemorative celebration annually, they represented much the cheaper option and were more numerous than chantries. Indeed, where perpetual anniversary foundation was concerned, there seems indeed to have been something of a spate in All Saints' in the later decades of the fifteenth century. But, before investigating this, a word of explanation is needed. An anniversary – also interchangeably known as a year's mind or an obit – essentially reran the funeral service for the benefit of a nominated individual or group, celebrating the funerary liturgy and associated observance, albeit in the absence of the corpse but on an appropriate date. This comprised the *exequies* on the eve, that is the psalms of *Placebo* and *Dirige*, and the mass of *Requiem* on the morrow, celebrated by the parish priest with the assistance of perhaps half-a-dozen auxiliary clergy. At these services the parish hearse would be set out, draped with a hearse cloth and accompanied by tapers burning at its head and foot – just as if the body were present. This would be accompanied by prolonged tolling of the bells in the parish belfry, and by the town crier or bede-man perambulating the town, ringing a hand bell and exhorting that prayers be offered for those commemorated. Invariably the most expensive element of the observance was the provision of doles for the

[33] I discuss the form and number of late medieval Bristol's anniversaries in 'A Service for the Dead: The Form and Function of the Anniversary in Late Medieval Bristol', *TBGAS* 105 (1987), 183–211.

parish poor and, often, the poor from farther afield; each pauper ordinarily received a loaf of bread at the church, presumably in return for having attended the *Requiem* and for his or her specific prayers. Where a chantry priest's stipend amounted to at least £6 annually, an elaborate anniversary could be provided for a sum in the region of 10s. or 13s. 4d., which certainly illustrates the relative economy of anniversary provision. It should be noted, however, that most anniversary provisions specified that perhaps as much as a half of any such sum should be given as penny doles or loaves, evidently anticipating the attendance of many paupers. For a reasonable sum, an anniversary founder could be assured of a barrage of well-directed prayer on a significant day, from clergy, from parishioners and from numerous poor, some of whom would probably have come from neighbouring parishes and even farther afield, summoned by bells.

Perpetual anniversaries invariably rested on property endowments, and, as noted, certainly in All Saints' – and elsewhere – their inception and thus the provision of endowments, usually granted to the custody of the parish, seems to have become more common in the later fifteenth century.[34] The most notable aspect of this development, however, is that, where the anniversary might account for approximately 10s. or 13s. 4d. per annum, the total rent deriving from the endowment was invariably worth considerably more – perhaps four or five times this sum – and the difference went into the parish coffers. Admittedly, the parish would be charged with maintaining the endowment and was obliged, were the property not to be forfeit, to remember a benefactor in perpetuity; but, where we might pay most heed to the anniversary, such a service was simply the commemorative return owed for a generous property devise. The latter had much the greater impact so far as the parish was concerned; and in All Saints', Bristol, in the later fifteenth and early sixteenth centuries, a number of parishioners embarked on such provision – Agnes Fylour, Henry and Alice Chestre, Thomas and Maud Baker and Joan Pernaunt among them. As a result, All Saints' found itself in possession of an increasing property portfolio of tenements dotted around Bristol (in addition to those supporting the Halleways' chantry, which were however accounted for separately), and an increasing annual income. Where income as recorded in the church-

---

[34] I scrutinize similar developments in London in my 'London, the Church and the Kingdom', in M. Davies and A. Prescott, eds, *London and the Kingdom: Essays in Honour of Caroline M. Barron* (Donington, 2008), 98–117.

wardens' parish accounts stood at approximately £13 10s. per annum in the 1480s, anniversary endowments had helped to boost this to something in the region of £17 10s. by 1500, and to approximately £20 per annum by the 1520s.[35] The extra could be devoted to various ends. It could certainly be used to employ more clergy – or musicians, perhaps – to enhance the liturgy on high days and holy days. In All Saints', more specifically, a healthy credit balance certainly seems to have given the parish the confidence, when the opportunity arose, to embark on buying back property that had once been part of a perpetual chantry endowment for the Haddon family, lost in acrimonious circumstances some fifty years previously.[36] This purchase-cum-acquisition further augmented parish income, of course, which stood at some £30 per annum by the end of the 1520s.

The foundation of perpetual anniversaries clearly signified more than the regular commemoration of a generous benefactor. It seems, at one and the same time, to have depended upon the existence of a capable parish management, maintaining and letting the properties that comprised the endowment, which in itself would further have honed parish expertise and influence. As a natural corollary, such foundation naturally also meant more property and income for the parish, which in turn enabled the parish, as a matter of routine, to mount a more sophisticated liturgy. Reflecting thus on the developing status of the parish leads me to reconnect with suggestions made earlier, for it is clear that, by the early sixteenth century, commemoration and the generosity supported, and furthered, by an efficient regime had significantly changed a parish like All Saints'. While it naturally still discharged its pastoral duties – and insofar as parishioners' responses were concerned, it seems to have done so with success – it might also discharge a much more ambitious liturgical role, if anything resembling that of a small college. In sum, the penitential and commemorative response ensured a number of significant liturgical effects. It provided for opulent equipment and fittings, as well as for a plurality of clergy at any one time, a burgeoning property portfolio and an increasing income. Penitential activity and the commemorative response worked, albeit in conjunc-

---

[35] The acquisition of properties devised ostensibly for anniversaries may be traced in detail in the All Saints' deeds, printed in the third part of *ASB 3*; the subsequent increase in parish income, which can be deduced from surveying the parish accounts, is discussed in more detail in *ASB 2*, 15–16.

[36] See above, n. 28; the reacquisition is discussed in more detail in my 'Pre-Reformation Churchwardens' Accounts', 326–28.

tion with other factors, to transform the parish into an institution better able to take its place among the larger institutions of the secular church, making some contribution, at least, towards the spiritual benefit of Bristol and that of the realm. Its competences were not only pastoral but also liturgical. It was the second of these that was effectively felled at the Reformation, particularly as a result of legislation in Edward's reign confiscating endowments devised for 'superstitious purposes', which occasioned a profound deterioration in parish capabilities and an equal change in its identity.

* * *

Two considerations need to be explored in conclusion. First, it is important to avoid creating too restrictive an impression of parish procedures. While the preceding discussion has dwelt on the movables and immovables either bequeathed or devised by parishioners for commemorative purposes, which, cumulatively, wrought a significant effect on the spiritual regime offered in All Saints', there were undoubtedly other means of acquisition that did not require such acknowledgment. They remain, by comparison, hazy, if only because there was no need to remember the contributors so assiduously, which means many fewer records; but the parish certainly supported clerks by rates that had to be assessed on and gathered from householders within the parish.[37] Such rating systems might also be employed to provide for funds to underwrite building campaigns or to provide for sumptuous equipment. Indeed, while the All Saints' archive affords no list of benefactors and the sums that each had given (according to their means) in procuring a particular item resembling those often found elsewhere,[38] there is a hint that the parish had made a really spectacular acquisition relying, in part at least, on such procedures. The epitome for wardens William Peyntour and Robert Walsche reveals that 'in their day [1454–55] was brought in on All Hallows eve the best suit, price £100'.[39] Careful scrutiny of various references scattered throughout the

---

[37] This much is plain from the rules set down 'for the clerk's finding' (*ASB 1*, 2), and from the 'top-up' payments to clerks that churchwardens commonly allowed for in the parish accounts.

[38] For instance, the Church Book of St Ewen's, Bristol, names those who gave 'to the making of a cross of silver and over gilt' in 1454: printed in B. R. Masters and E. Ralph, eds, *The Church Book of St Ewen's Bristol, 1454–1584*, Publications of the Bristol and Gloucestershire Archaeological Society, Records Section 6 (1967), 27–29, 33.

[39] *ASB 1*, 47.

All Saints' archive confirms that this sum was not (as I first assumed) given in error, even though there is no list of benefactors. But in the description of the Halleways' largesse to the parish (Thomas having died in 1454 and Joan in 1455), there is the telling detail that they gave £20 to the best suit of vestments, which sum the vicar at the time, Sir William Rodberd, also equalled.[40] One is left wondering whether this suit should be identified with the 'vestments of cloth of gold tissue' mentioned in the inventory compiled in 1469 by Richard Haddon and John Schoppe – vestments not otherwise assigned to any particular donor in the benefaction list.[41] The parish would appear to have paid for this by combining donations with (apparently still considerable) monies collected from rates. Indeed, we do well to remember both that the sums accruing from rates could be appreciable and that the regimes gathering them might evidently be proficient (though, as noted, we are much less well informed about the latter because they were less ostentatiously predicated on commemoration). But, even in parishes depending upon 'collection' regimes, memory would have played its part, for surely one of the most effective sanctions for refusal to participate would have been a concomitant exclusion from the body of the faithful. In life this may have meant compelling those who refused to participate to abstain from their housel; in death, those abstaining would have been omitted from the collective memory that celebrated 'all the faithful departed' in parish prayers and services. The prospect of such oblivion was literally dreadful, which sanction seems invariably to have been turned to productive effect in regimes either rich or poor, commemorative or collective – in practice, fusing both systems and encouraging all-important participation from those who could give no less than from those who might pray.

The second point to be considered, however, is the question of typicality: how normal was All Saints' and may any wider lessons be drawn from its archive? Or, to put it more bluntly, which was extraordinary – this parish or its archive? While small, in both area and communicant population, many of All Saints' parishioners were clearly reasonably wealthy; the parish also supported an unusually heavy presence of clergy, both parish and guild priests. This last factor is worth dwelling on as it highlights perhaps the most telling aspect to shed some light at

[40] Respectively, ibid. 14 and 8.
[41] Ibid. 41.

least on the basic question about All Saints'. An already heavy clerical presence did not deter parishioners: they wanted, and procured, more clergy, apparently to further embellish liturgical procedures. This must give pause. For while, as argued, there was a strong commemorative desire – according with the basic human urge to be remembered – that prompted largesse, such multiplication of priests was optional. Parish-ioners wanted more, however: unusual circumstances, that might have relieved parishioners of the need for generosity, proved to be no disin-centive at all. Parishioners were evidently caught up in an objective that transcended parish boundaries. It might therefore appear that it was not so much that All Saints' parishioners were acting in extraordinary ways, but what is extraordinary is that we know so much about them. If we knew as much about many other parishes, which we emphatically do not, I wonder whether the question would even arise. It may well be the case, however, that if we discount the response there as an aberration, we perhaps underestimate what was afoot elsewhere by the early decades of the sixteenth century, certainly in the urban context. The provinces, too, with their market towns and smaller communities, many of which were doing reasonably well at this time, certainly looked to larger towns both for the fashions worth following and guid-ance in how certain practices might be realized. As noted, many a parish regime embarked on ambitious rebuilding. The resulting churches, that are still so noteworthy an aspect of the English scene, were hardly likely to have remained understaffed and badly equipped or, for that matter, their parishioners uncommemorated.

Royal Holloway, University of London

PERFORMING THE PASSION: STRATEGIES FOR SALVATION IN THE LIFE OF STEFANA QUINZANI (d. 1530)

by CORDELIA WARR

IN Italy, the years around 1500 were fraught for a number of reasons. There were renewed fears about the second coming of Christ and the end of the world.[1] The expansion of the Ottoman Empire gave rise to a sense of instability and impending doom.[2] In this climate many people became increasingly concerned about their fate in the afterlife and the need to be prepared for death and judgement. Central to this was the doctrine of purgatory. Yet, in the first decades of the sixteenth century, ideas surrounding purgatory were highly contested as heretical ideas from northern Europe began to filter into northern Italy. This paper investigates Catholic beliefs about the alleviation of purgatorial suffering through a case study of one holy woman from the north of Italy, the Dominican tertiary, Stefana Quinzani, who, according to a letter of 4 March 1500 written by Duke Ercole d'Este, endured every Friday 'the whole of the Passion in her body, stage by stage, from the Flagellation to the Deposition from the Cross'.[3]

Stefana was born in 1457 in Orzinuovo and died in 1530.[4] She spent much of her life in nearby Crema and Soncino, both of which are situated between Brescia and Milan. Crema had passed from the jurisdiction of Milan to that of the Republic of Venice in 1449.[5] However, the Milanese did not lose Soncino to the Venetians until the end of the

* I would like to thank Gabriele Neher of the University of Nottingham for her generous help on aspects of Brescian history during this period.

1 Stephen D. Bowd, *Reform before the Reformation: Vicenzo Querini and the Religious Renaissance in Italy* (Leiden, 2002), 16.

2 Jonathon B. Riess, *The Renaissance Antichrist: Luca Signorelli's Orvieto Frescoes* (Princeton, NJ, 1995), 135–36. For the expansion of the Ottoman Empire, see Colin Imber, *The Ottoman Empire, 1300–1650: The Structure of Power* (Basingstoke, 2002), 27–66.

3 Edmund G. Gardner, *Dukes and Poets in Ferrara: A Study of the Poetry, Religion and Politics of the Fifteenth and Early Sixteenth Centuries* (London, 1904), 375.

4 For brief details of Stefana's life, see Maiju Lehmijoki-Gardner, *Worldly Saints: Social Interaction of Dominican Penitent Women in Italy, 1200–1500* (Helsinki, 1999), 49.

5 Nicolai Rubinstein, 'Italian Reactions to Terraferma Expansion in the Fifteenth Century', in J. R. Hale, ed., *Renaissance Venice* (London, 1973), 197–217, at 202–04.

fifteenth century. The French subsequently took over the small fortress town in 1509 and the Venetians did not regain complete control until 1525. Brescia too suffered as a city located at the interstices of Venetian and Milanese power. It was sold to Venice in 1426, and, although it remained nominally under Venetian power until seized and then sacked by the French in 1512, there was considerable tension during the Milanese siege of 1438 led by Niccolò Piccinino.[6] Thus Stefana lived during a period of major upheaval.

Adele Simonetti has recently undertaken a detailed study of the sources for Stefana's life,[7] the first to do so since Paolo Guerrini and Pietro De Michele published the results of their research in 1930 on the fourth centenary of Stefana's death.[8] Two *vitae* were written about Stefana by men who had known her: Bartolomeo da Mantova and Battista di Salò. Both were Dominican friars and both had at some time served as Stefana's confessor.[9] A Latin compilation put together by Domenico de Calvisano and based on the lost *vita* by Battista di Salò is still extant in the Dominican archives in Rome.[10] A sixteenth-century manuscript, also in the Dominican archives, contains a vernacular *leggenda*.[11] Simonetti identifies this manuscript as being written by Bartolomeo da Mantova. The *vita* published by Guerrini in 1930, from a manuscript in the Vatican library,[12] is, according to Simonetti, based closely on that of Bartolomeo da Mantova, with the major differences being that all the references to Bartolomeo in the first person have been replaced by references to him in the third person, and biographical and chronological references have been added.[13] Simonetti concluded that

[6] For a detailed study of this period in the history of Brescia, see Giovanni Treccani degli Alfieri, *Storia di Brescia*, 4 vols (Brescia, 1963), 2: 3–400.

[7] Adele Simonetti, 'Le vite e gli agiografi della beata Stefana Quinzani', *Hagiographica* 8 (2001), 191–231.

[8] P. De Micheli, 'Il quarto centenario della morte della beata Stefana Quinzani terziaria domenicana (1530–1930)', *Memorie domenicane* 47 (1930), 3–150; Paolo Guerrini, *La prima 'legenda volgare' de la beata Stefana Quinzani d'Orzinuovi secondo il codice Vaticano-Urbinate latino 1755* (Brescia, 1930). Quotations from Guerrini's Italian text have had the punctuation altered slightly; punctuation was lacking in the original manuscript.

[9] Simonetti, 'Le vite', 203, 209.

[10] Ibid. 197–98 (citing Rome, Santa Sabina, Archivium Generale Ordinis Praedicatorum, MS X 2857).

[11] Ibid. 199 (citing Rome, Santa Sabina, Archivium Generale Ordinis Praedicatorum, MS 2868b).

[12] Vatican City, Biblioteca Apostolica Vaticana, Urb.lat. MS 1755.

[13] Simonetti, 'Le vite', 199.

Bartolomeo originally wrote his *vita* while Stefana was still alive.[14] She dates the *vita* between 1506 and 1518, but probably before 1512 because the writer of the Vatican manuscript mentions that he died at least eighteen years before Stefana.[15] The Vatican manuscript, written after Stefana's death, was used by the Dominican biographer Serafino Razzi (1531–1611).[16] Razzi's compilation of the lives of Dominican holy men and women, the first edition of which was published in Florence in 1577, contains sections on a number of contemporary or near contemporary *beatae* including Stefana Quinzani and Lucia Brocadelli da Narni (1476–1544).[17] It is the Vatican manuscript, published by Guerrini, on which I shall base my discussion.[18]

Stefana's sufferings of the passion were significant for the afterlife, because her prayers during and after them were considered efficacious for departed souls.[19] Through them it was believed that she could help those already in purgatory and those who might otherwise have undergone purgatorial suffering. This is demonstrated by some of the episodes related in the *vita* published by Guerrini, by information in her correspondence, and by the records of her suffering the pains of Christ's passion. These passion ecstasies became public knowledge and some were attended by high ranking citizens who acted as witnesses. Two public episodes during which Stefana suffered the passion occurred in Crema on 17 February 1497[20] and in Mantua on 16 July 1500.[21] According to her *vita* Stefana also experienced the pains of the

---

14 Ibid. 199–200.

15 Ibid. 201–02; Guerrini, *La prima 'leggenda volgare'*, 101.

16 Guerrini, *La prima 'leggenda volgare'*, 73. For more details on Razzi's life, see Guglielmo di Agresti's brief biography in his introduction to Serafino Razzi, *Vita di Santa Caterina de' Ricci, con documenti inediti antecedenti l'edizione*, a cura di Guglielmo M. di Agresti OP (Florence, 1965), xviii–xxii.

17 Serafino Razzi, *Vite de i santi e beati, cosi huomini, come donne del sacro ordine de frati predicatori*, 2 parts (Florence, 1577), 2: 136–49, 151–54.

18 Guerrini, *La prima 'leggenda volgare'*. Throughout, all translations from Guerrini's edition of the Vatican manuscript are my own.

19 Gabriella Zarri, 'Living Saints: A Typology of Female Sanctity in the Early Sixteenth Century', in Daniel Bornstein and Roberto Rusconi, eds, *Women and Religion in Medieval and Renaissance Italy*, trans. Margery J. Schneider (Chicago, IL, and London, 1996), 219–304, at 221; Richard C. Trexler, *Public Life in Renaissance Florence* (Ithaca, NY, and London, 1991), 35.

20 Maiju Lehmijoki-Gardner, *Dominican Penitent Women* (New York, 2005), 192–97, provides a translation of the notarial document recording this ecstasy based on the text published in Giuseppe Brunati, *Vita o gesta di santi bresciani*, 2 vols (Brescia, 1855), 2: 55–62.

21 Lehmijoki-Gardner, *Dominican Penitent Women*, 294–95 n. 15. See also Brunati, *Vita o gesta*, 2: 62–64; Guerrini, *La prima 'leggenda volgare'*, 103.

passion at other times during her life,[22] and the notarial document recording her passion ecstasy in 1497 reported that these happened '[e]very Friday'.[23]

During her ecstasies, Stefana is recorded as having cried out 'souls, souls', reflecting her belief that her own suffering could be tendered against the sins of those in purgatory.[24] Through the torments that she endured, Stefana believed that she was able to prepare herself for the next life, as well as alleviating the pains of others who were about to die, or who were already in purgatory. Towards the end of the ecstasy of 1497, Stefana 'makes fervent prayers to Jesus Christ, and she prays for the souls of the people'.[25] This is a theme which is repeated throughout her *vita*. In chapter 21, which deals with love of one's neighbour, we are told that 'I have heard it said that in order to save a soul she would go even as far as the end of the world'.[26] Her hagiographer then goes on to claim that Stefana had suffered all the torments of the martyrs 'and all this for the souls of sinners'.[27] Later in this chapter a specific example is given:

> One can say of a certain prelate in particular, whose name I will not mention, that if she [Stefana] had not been there and if she had not undergone great suffering for him and if she had not made the greatest entreaties in her prayers, he would already have been dead for a number of years and according to what had been shown to her, he would have been damned.[28]

Her *vita* consistently indicates that Stefana saw her sufferings as having a direct effect on the afterlife of those around her. In chapter 39 of the *leggenda* this is demonstrated through the testimony of a priest who, with a companion, was watching over Stefana during the night because she was extremely ill. As Stefana was tossing and turning, the priest:

---

22 Guerrini, *La prima 'leggenda volgare'*, 101.
23 Lehmijoki-Gardner, *Dominican Penitent Women*, 194.
24 Ibid. 106.
25 Ibid. 196.
26 Guerrini, *La prima 'leggenda volgare'*, 115: 'Io ho oldito a dire: per salvare una anima andaria per fina al fine del mundo'.
27 Ibid. 115: 'se io dicesse che tutti li martirii che hanna portato li martiri ley ha sostenuti, non credo mentiria, e questo tutto per le anume di peccatori'.
28 Ibid. 117: 'Se potria dire de uno certo prelato in particulare, el nome del quale voglio tacere, che se ley non fusse stata et non havesse sostenuta grande passione per quello et fatte grandissime instantie nele sue oratione, sarebbe morto già più anni et secundo che gera dimonstrato saria damnato'.

… began to comfort her, exhorting her to suffer patiently for the souls of the sinners, and then she cried out loudly: 'Oh heavenly country, souls.' And immediately she became as though dead and remained thus for a considerable time, and at length, having returned to herself, he asked her: 'Where have you been, mother? Have you been in paradise?' She replied to him: 'My son, my lover appeared to me saying: "My daughter, you must suffer for sinners. Do you not see how much they have offended me?" '[29]

Stefana was also granted knowledge about the fate of her followers: 'When she wanted to see the state of her sons, it was shown to her. And so she said to me one day of the holy cross: "My son, this night I have seen the state of all my sons, alive and dead" '.[30]

This is presented as being closely linked to her suffering. For example, she told one of her followers:

'… From the beginning of Lent until now' – which was within the octave of Easter – 'all my bones have been extracted from me, and many times it seemed to me that they had been taken out of my body and then were placed inside' with so much pain that it sometimes seemed as though she had died and she fell to the ground through the great pain. But no one knew why this was. He [Stefana's follower] said: 'The reward which follows from such suffering makes you undergo it willingly.' She replied: 'It is true, son.' He said: 'On Good Friday did you not suffer for my brother? Did you not free him of the pains of purgatory?' She replied: 'He and many others were freed on that day.' This brother had died in the previous August and, according to what [Saint] Paul had said, he should have remained in purgatory for ten years, and so through the merits of this bride of Christ, he did not complete eight months.[31]

---

[29] Ibid. 138–39: 'Comenciò alhora luy a confortarla exortandola che patientemente, sustenisse per le anime de peccatori, e lei cridò alhora forte: "O Iesu, anime, anime". Facto un poco de intervallo disse: "O patria celeste, anime," et immediate rimase como morta e così per un gran spacio rimase, et tandem ritornata a se gran spacio rimase, et tandem ritornata a se luy la interrogò: "Dove siti stata Madre? Sèti stata in paradiso?" La ge rispose: "Figliol mio, l'amatore mi è apparso dicando: figliola, el t'è necessario patire per li peccatori. Non vedetu quante offese me fanno?" '

[30] Ibid. 128: 'Quando voleva vedere el stato de li sui filioli giera dimostrato, unde ley me disse un giorno de sancta croce, "Filiol mio, questa notte ho veduto el stato de tutti li miei filioli et vivi et morti" '.

[31] Ibid. 146: ' "… dal principio de la quadragesima per fina a questa hora" – chi era infra

In chapter 7 of the *leggenda*, which deals with bodily mortification, we are informed that she flagellated herself three times each night in emulation of Saint Dominic and that one of the strokes of the iron rod was made in order to help souls in purgatory.[32] Stefana underwent this suffering in the belief that she was able to influence the amount of time that souls suffered in purgatory, or even remove the suffering completely. In chapter 16 of her *leggenda* she exhorts one of her 'sons': '[E]ndure with a good soul and do not doubt that I have been assured that you are one of the elect, and I hope to be able to do such a thing for you that you will not suffer any of the pains of purgatory'.[33]

Later, in chapter 22, we are told of the sufferings which she endured in order to alleviate the purgatorial sufferings of a certain Baptista, a gentleman from Crema, who had defended her when allegations about her morality had circulated in the town.[34]

These accounts of Stefana's interventions in the afterlife are significant for three main reasons. First, they offer an insight into the beliefs of contemporary elites, since during her lifetime she was well known and well connected. She is one of several Dominican tertiaries from this period to have been actively engaged with local ruling families, particularly the d'Este.[35] Several of Stefana's letters are known.[36] They demonstrate the extent to which she was embedded in the religious life of the local nobility. She wrote, for example, to Lucrezia Gonzaga, wife of Count Nicolò Gambara di Verolanuova, who sought comfort before

la octava di pascha – "tutti li mei ossi mi sono stati estorciti, et spesse volte apparevami che fussero stati tolti fora dil corpo e poi fussero posti dentro" cum tanti dolori e pene che molte volte pareva cha mancasse e cadeva in terra per grande dolore. Ma niuno ha saputo dove procedesse. Dicando lui, "El fructo el quale seguita per tale passione vi fa voluntiera sustenire". Respose, "L'è vero, figliol" Dicando lui, "El giorno del venerdì sancto non patesti per mio fratello? L'haveti liberato dalle pene del purgatorio?" Respose, "Lui e molti altri furno liberati quel giorno". Questo suo fratello era morto a l'austo precedente e, secondo che paulo aveva ditto, doveva stare in purgatorio per dece anni, e così per meriti de questa sposa de cristo non ge stete otto mesi compiti.'

[32] Ibid. 97.
[33] Ibid. 109: 'tollerate de bon animo e non dubitati che io sono stata certificata che voi siete del numero de li eletti e spero far tal cosa per voi che non sentireti pena alcuna dil purgatorio'.
[34] Ibid. 118.
[35] Gardner, *Dukes and Poets*, 364–66.
[36] They have been published by Paolo Guerrini, 'Lettere inedite della B. Stefana Quinzani', *Memorie Domenicane* 54 (1937), 6–31. See also Vittorio Tolasi, *Stefana Quinzani. Donna, suora e beata (1457–1530). Inediti dell'epistolario Gonzaga e sintesi del processo di beatificazione* (Brescia, 1972), 20–61.

her death on 25 January 1505.[37] Letters also survive to Isabella d'Este.[38] Stefana is known to have visited Mantua in 1500. Francesco Gonzaga and Isabella d'Este wanted her to stay in order to found a Dominican convent.[39] Stefana thus forms part of an interconnected web of Dominican religious women and the ruling families of Ferrara and Mantua.[40] In Ferrara, Lucia Brocadelli da Narni was supported by Duke Ercole d'Este until his death in 1505,[41] whilst in Mantua Osanna Andreasi (1449–1505) had strong links with Ercole's daughter Isabella d'Este and her husband Francesco Gonzaga.[42] This Este nexus of sanctity and polity coincided with an 'exceptionally active' period for Dominican female penitents in the north of Italy which started at the end of the fifteenth century and continued until the 1530s.[43] This period has been connected with 'a revival of the cult of Catherine of Siena' (1347–1380).[44] Catherine had been canonized in 1461 by Pius II, thus engendering new interest in her life.[45]

Second, Stefana's public profile meant dissemination of her brand of spirituality beyond the cloister. It has been noted that in the late fifteenth and early sixteenth centuries 'religious women's public participation was tolerated, even encouraged'.[46] It is difficult to hear the 'real' voices of these holy women, to untangle them from those of their hagiographers and biographers,[47] even where, as in the case of Stefana

---

[37] Guerrini, La prima 'leggenda volgare', 83–84.

[38] Idem, 'Lettere inedite', 29–30, 31.

[39] Idem, La prima 'leggenda volgare', 80.

[40] For a discussion of holy women and court culture, see Zarri, 'A Typology of Female Sanctity'.

[41] On Ercole d'Este's support of Lucia Brocadelli, see Thomas Tuohy, Herculean Ferrara: Ercole d'Este (1471–1505) and the Invention of a Ducal Capital (Cambridge, 1996), 176–81; Gardner, Dukes and Poets, 366–81, 401–04.

[42] On Isabella d'Este and Osanna Andreasi, see Julia Cartwright, Isabella d'Este Marchioness of Mantua 1474–1539: A Study of the Renaissance, 2 vols (London, 1903), 1: 79, 255, 275; 2: 139, 312.

[43] Lehmijoki-Gardner, Worldly Saints, 139.

[44] Gardner, Dukes and Poets, 363; Tuohy, Herculean Ferrara, 176.

[45] For the history of the publication of editions of Catherine's life in the decades after her canonization, see Marie-Hyacinthe Laurent, 'Essais de bibliographie catherinienne: Les premières éditions italiennes', Archivum Fratrum Praedicatorum 30 (1950), 348–68. For a brief discussion of the impact of Catherine's canonization on the visual arts in Siena, see Diana Norman, Painting in Late Medieval and Renaissance Siena (New Haven, CT, and London 2003), 207, 267–71.

[46] Lehmijoki-Gardner, Worldly Saints, 16.

[47] For an introduction to the major issues involved in the study of hagiographic literature concerning women during this period, see John W. Coakley, 'Friars as Confidants of Holy Women in Medieval Dominican Hagiography', in Renate Blumenfeld-Kosinski and

Quinzani, those who wrote about them were their contemporaries and had known them personally. Stefana is described as almost begging God that she should not become 'known'.[48] Yet Lehmijoki-Gardner has observed that for many Dominican penitents, their 'religious experiences often took place in secular spaces' and were therefore subject to observation by others.[49] Stefana, who came from a relatively poor background, lived in the houses of a number of noble families before the foundation of her convent.[50] It was not until 1519, eleven years before her death, that she founded her religious community.[51] Even then, it appears that the convent, dedicated to Santa Caterina e San Paolo, was 'open'. Stefana remained a tertiary and did not take the vows of a second-order Dominican nun, which would have required strict enclosure.[52] Like her contemporaries Osanna Andreasi and Lucia Brocadelli, Stefana is presented in her *leggenda* as having made a conscious choice to follow an active, rather than purely contemplative, life. God told her: 'I want you to maintain and practice the *vita activa*, because there is greater perfection in the life which contains both *vita activa* and contemplation.'[53]

Finally, of course, Stefana's passion sufferings and her contemporaries' understanding of these must be seen in relation to the development of the late medieval doctrine of purgatory and its defence against Luther's attacks, in the years between the Council of Ferrara-Florence (1438–1445) and the Council of Trent (1545–1563). The former council had decreed that: '[If] truly penitent people die in the love of God before they have made satisfaction for acts and omissions by worthy fruits of repentance, their souls are cleansed after death by cleansing pains.' It went on to specify that: 'the suffrages of the living faithful avail them in giving relief from such pains, that is, sacrifices of masses, prayers, almsgiving, and other acts of devotion which have been

---

Timea Szell, eds, *Images of Sainthood in Medieval Europe* (Ithaca, NY, and London, 1991), 222–46; Kimberley Benedict, *Empowering Collaborations: Writing Partnerships between Religious Women and Scribes in the Middle Ages* (New York, 2004).

[48] Guerrini, *La prima 'leggenda volgare'*, 60.

[49] Lehmijoki-Gardner, *Worldly Saints*, 90.

[50] Ibid. 98; Guerrini, *La prima 'leggenda volgare'*, 98–100, 111.

[51] Guerrini, *La prima 'leggenda volgare'*, 80; Lehmijoki-Gardner, *Worldly Saints*, 63.

[52] On the enclosure of nuns, see James A. Brundage and Elizabeth M. Makowski, 'Enclosure of Nuns: The Decretal *Periculoso* and its Commentators', *JMedH* 20 (1994), 143–55.

[53] Guerrini, *La prima 'leggenda volgare'*, 154: 'io voglio mò che tu tenga et exerciti la vita activa perchè di magior perfectione è la vita la quale in se contiene e la vita activa e la contemplatione'.

customarily performed by some of the faithful for others of the faithful in accordance with the church's ordinances'.[54] Similarly, the Council of Trent declared that 'purgatory exists, and that the souls of the faithful detained there are helped by the prayers of the faithful.'[55]

Between the two councils, Luther's attacks on the Church's manipulation of the belief of the faithful in purgatory had been countered in Leo X's bull *Exsurge Domine* of 1520.[56] The text of the bull contains forty-one items which were condemned as heretical. Items 37 to 40 concern purgatory, with item 40 stating that: 'The souls freed from purgatory through the suffrages of the living are less happy than if they had made atonement for themselves.'[57]

Such heretical ideas had reached Brescia and the surrounding areas during Stefana's lifetime.[58] In response there was a marked increase in lay piety. Luther did not publicize his ninety-five theses until 1517, twenty years after Stefana's first recorded passion 'performance', but by the time that the *vitae* on which the *leggenda volgare* is based were written, Brescia had been forced to make official plans to deal with the infiltration of heretical ideas, so it is legitimate to interpret the source as a form of anti-Reformation polemic.[59]

Thus the repeated references to Stefana's self-inflicted and vision-induced suffering in the *leggenda volgare* published by Guerrini can be seen to reflect the religious situation of the years leading up to and immediately after Stefana's death. The stress on Stefana's ability to help those in purgatory through her own suffering demonstrated the heresy of the teaching condemned in item 40 of Leo X's *Exsurge Domine* in public practice. This emphasis reflected Stefana's beliefs; those of her elite patrons; those of her confessor, who wrote the account of her spiritual life on which the *leggenda* relied so heavily; and perhaps those of the wide audience to which both passion performance and later accounts were addressed. The language of the *leggenda* published by

[54] Norman Tanner, *Decrees of the Ecumenical Councils*, 2 vols (London, 1990), 1: 527 (session 6, 6 July 1439).

[55] Ibid. 2: 774 (session 25, 3–4 December 1563).

[56] The main sections of the bull are published in B. J. Kidd, ed., *Documents Illustrative of the Continental Reformation* (Oxford, 1967), 75–79.

[57] Ibid. 78: 'Animae ex purgatorio liberatae suffragiis viventium minus beantur quam si per se satisfecissent.'

[58] Treccani degli Alfieri, *Storia di Brescia*, 2: 447–50.

[59] Gabriele Neher, 'Moretto and Romanino: Religious Painting in Brescia 1510–1550. Identity in the Shadow of La Serenissima' (unpublished Ph. D. thesis, University of Warwick, 1999), 175.

Guerrini shows a familiarity with elements of Brescian and Cremonese dialect.[60] The two manuscripts known to Guerrini were both addressed to Dominican nuns from Soncino, where Stefana had lived for much of her life, and who may have been literate only in the vernacular.[61] Not only did the *vita* preserve Stefana's memory amongst her compatriots, it reinforced Catholic belief about suffrages for the dead in the face of the advance of Luther's ideas. This was particularly appropriate for nuns, who were expected to pray for the souls of others.

University of Manchester

---

[60] See Guerrini, *La prima 'leggenda volgare'*, 72–73, for a brief discussion of the linguistic make-up of the text.

[61] Ibid. 72–76, for details of the addressees of the manuscripts. There was a strong tradition of vernacular literacy – active and passive – in Italian convents in the fifteenth and sixteenth centuries. See K. J. P. Lowe, *Nuns' Chronicles and Convent Culture in Renaissance and Counter-Reformation Italy* (Cambridge, 2003), 11–34.

CHRIST'S DESCENT INTO HELL IN
REFORMATION CONTROVERSY

by DAVID BAGCHI

BY far the shortest of the *Thirty-nine Articles* of the Church of
England is the third, 'Of the going down of Christ into Hell'. In
its entirety it reads: 'As Christ died for us, and was buried, so also
is it to be believed, that he went down into Hell'.[1] One might be
forgiven for thinking that the brevity of the article, together with the
notable absence of polemic, indicates the doctrine's relative unimpor-
tance amid the other great debates of the day. In fact, the descent of
Christ into hell was one of the most controverted of all the creedal articles in the Reformation era.[2] Article III is so short, not because it was a
routine recital of the Apostles' Creed, but because no further elaboration or explanation of the doctrine could command consent in the
febrile climate of early Elizabethan England: disagreement over what
was meant by 'hell', what was meant by Christ's 'descent', and over the
doctrine's fundamental significance, was rife. This particular manifestation of the afterlife – be it only Christ's afterlife, and only a temporary
destination at that – is not the most obvious candidate as a theological
cause célèbre of the Reformation era. But the intensity and the

---

[1] For a brief account of the evolution of the article, see E. C. S. Gibson, *The Thirty-Nine Articles Explained with an Introduction* (London, 1906), 159.

[2] For treatments of the doctrine in this period, see especially E. Quilliet, 'Descente de Jésus aux Enfers', in A. Vacant and E. Mangenot, eds, *Dictionnaire de Théologie Catholique*, 4 (Paris, 1920), cols 565–619; Erich Vogelsang, 'Weltbild und Kreuzestheologie in den Höllenfahrtsstreitigkeiten der Reformationszeit', *ARG* 38 (1941), 90–132; Constance I. Smith, 'Descendit ad inferos – Again', *Journal of the History of Ideas* 28 (1967), 87–88; Dewey D. Wallace, Jr, 'Puritan and Anglican: The Interpretation of Christ's Descent into Hell in Eliza-bethan Theology', *ARG* 69 (1978), 248–87; Jerome Friedman, 'Christ's Descent into Hell and Redemption through Evil: A Radical Reformation Perspective', *ARG* 76 (1985), 217–30; Markwart Herzog, *'Descensus ad inferos': Eine religionsphilosophische Untersuchung der Motive und Interpretationen mit besonderer Berücksichtigung der monographistischen Literatur seit dem 16. Jahrhundert*, Frankfurter theologische Studien 53 (Frankfurt am Main, 1997); Peter Marshall, 'The Map of God's Word: Geographies of the Afterlife in Tudor and early Stuart England', in Bruce Gordon and Peter Marshall, eds, *The Place of the Dead: Death and Remembrance in Late Medieval and Early Modern Europe* (Cambridge, 2000), 110–30; idem, 'The Reformation of Hell? Protestant and Catholic Infernalisms in England, c. 1560-1640', *JEH* (forthcoming). I am grateful to Professor Marshall for letting me see his study in advance of publication.

longevity of the debates it fuelled make it at least an intriguing footnote to the study of the period.

The purpose of this essay is not to provide a blow by blow account of the various controversies: the last person to do that was Johann August Dietelmair in 1741, whose comprehensive effort had, according to one German historian, 'all the charm of a telephone directory'.[3] My intention is rather to try to elucidate what lay at the heart of the various descent controversies, and also to try to shed light on a peculiar feature about them: the doctrine of Christ's descent into hell was unusual, and perhaps unique, in its ability to undermine and cut across confessional allegiances. Although Catholics, Lutherans and Reformed all contributed to the debate, it was a topic on which party lines shifted. In an era which we are used to thinking of as marked by confessional certainty, it may be instructive to examine an area of Christian doctrine in which the confessional compasses spun out of control.[4] Indeed, the tendency of this doctrine towards what might be termed denominational disorientation has been a focus of recent writing on the subject.[5]

<hr/>

[3] Herzog, 'Descensus', 21. Dietelmair's monograph was *Historia dogmatis de descensu Christi ad inferos litteraria* (Nuremberg, 1741; 2nd edn Altdorf, 1762).

[4] See, for instance, Robert Kolb, 'Christ's Descent into Hell as Christological Locus in the Era of the Formula of Concord: Luther's "Torgau Sermon" Revisited', *Lutherjahrbuch* 69 (2002), 101–18, at 105 n. 14, where it is noted that: '[t]he issue of the soteriological significance of Christ's descent into hell cuts across the usual "party lines" of the period; Melanchthon, his Philippist disciples, as well as Gnesio-Lutheran students of his like Chemnitz, interpreted it as part of Christ's triumph; Johannes Brenz (1499–1570) and Andreae shared a position similar to that of their Calvinist opponents in viewing it as a part of his suffering.'

[5] The figure of our own time who is most closely associated with this doctrine – and who indeed based an entire theology upon it – is the Roman Catholic theologian Hans Urs von Balthasar. Balthasar's orthodoxy was such that he was nominated to the cardinalate shortly before his death in 1988; but in the book *Mysterium Paschale: The Mystery of Easter* (trans. Aidan Nichols; Edinburgh, 1990), in which he sets out his famous 'theology of Holy Saturday', his understanding of the descent shows many points of contact with that of Luther and Calvin, not to mention more recent Protestant theologians. Recent commentators have found these similarities striking, with some emphasizing the rich possibilities for ecumenical encounter, others his gross neglect of traditional Catholic teaching. An example of the first category is David Lauber, *Barth on the Descent into Hell: God, Atonement and the Christian Life* (Aldershot, 2004). The case for Balthasar's heterodoxy is made by Alyssa Lyra Pitstick, *Light in Darkness: Hans Urs von Balthasar and the Catholic Doctrine of Christ's Descent into Hell* (Grand Rapids, MI, 2007). The fact that Pitstick's splendid piece of conservative Catholic polemic was issued by a publishing house normally associated with the Reformed tradition adds to the sense of denominational disorientation typical of this doctrine.

* * *

A fundamental question in the Reformation debates was whether Christ descended into hell in order to conquer it (the traditional idea of the 'harrowing of hell'), or in order to suffer its torments as part of his work of redemption. To frame the same question in liturgical terms, should Holy Saturday be regarded as a foretaste of the Christ's victory on Easter Sunday, or as a continuation and intensification of his passion and death on Good Friday? The victory or harrowing motif has been associated with Catholicism and Lutheranism, while the suffering motif has been associated with Calvinism. The victory motif is associated with a literal descent that took place after Christ's death, as celebrated by the liturgies of the Easter vigil, and by the familiar literary, dramatic and artistic representations of the harrowing of hell. The suffering motif is generally associated with the idea of a spiritual descent, as Christ's mental anguish and fear of death both on the cross itself (as expressed by his great cry of dereliction, 'My God, my God, why hast thou forsaken me?', in Matthew 27: 46), and in the Garden of Gethsemane, with his prayer 'Let this cup pass from me' (Matthew 27: 39).

The story of how this dichotomy came about is itself an intriguing one. The doctrine first attained creedal status in the so-called fourth formula of the Synod of Sirmium in 359, and indeed the belief seems to have originated in the East, probably in Syria. But it achieved definitive status in a Western symbol, the Apostles' Creed, in the form *descendit ad inferos* ('to those below') or *ad inferna* ('to the lower regions').[6] *Inferi* and *inferna* both render the Greek word *Hades*, which in turn is how the Septuagint renders the Hebrew *sheol*. This is significant, because the New Testament uses two rather different words which are both normally translated as 'hell' in English: the first is *Hades*, indicating simply the place where people go when they die, and lead an existence which is recognizable as a rather dull version of life on earth, as shadows of their former selves; the second is *Gehenna*, which signifies the place of punishment. So it is likely that the *descensus* article was originally intended simply to reinforce the fact of Christ's death: he died; his body was buried in the ground; and his soul went to the place where the souls of the dead go. But fairly quickly the belief took on a richer meaning than that. The spread of this belief seems to be connected with the popularity of the second part of *The Gospel of*

[6] J. N. D. Kelly, *Early Christian Creeds*, 3rd edn (London, 1972), 378–83.

Nicodemus (also known as *The Acts of Pilate*), an apocryphon of the fifth or sixth century which dramatically portrays the harrowing of hell in a way typical of Gnostic redeemer-myths.[7] It was this stock of stories that went on to influence portrayals of the harrowing of hell in the Middle Ages. The harrowing according to *The Gospel of Nicodemus* had no place for Christ's preaching to the imprisoned spirits in 1 Peter 3–4, and, partly because of the influence of Augustine, scholastic theologians hardly ever interpreted that passage in connection with the descent into hell.[8] The verse of Scripture most often associated with it was Psalm 15 (16): 10, 'For you will not abandon my soul to *Sheol / Hades*, or let your Holy One see corruption', along with Acts 2: 2 7, in which the fulfilment of this verse in the person of Jesus was preached by St Peter.

By the thirteenth century Thomas Aquinas explained with as much clarity as possible what the harrowing involved.[9] He was clear that Christ in his person descended only to the *limbus* of the fathers, whom he immediately liberated. However, other parts of hell experienced him in effect, though not in person. For the souls in purgatory, the effect of the descent was to bring hope; but for the souls of the damned, the effect was to bring further condemnation of their disbelief and wickedness. So far, Aquinas's exposition chimed perfectly with the conventional conception of the harrowing of hell, in which Christ in triumph broke down the gates of hell and terrified those of its inhabitants who deserved to be terrified. But another note is also sounded. It is mentioned only in passing, but it appears in the important first article of Aquinas's *quaestio* on the *descensus*, which explains why the descent happened at all. It was fitting that Christ should descend into hell, Aquinas explains, because two of the consequences of the Fall for humankind had been the death of the body and the going down of the soul into hell. It was right, therefore, that the Christ who has borne our griefs and carried our sorrows should not only die in order to deliver us from death but also descend into hell in order to deliver us from its

---

[7] For the various versions of the *descensus* section of the Gospel of Nicodemus, see *The Apocryphal New Testament*, ed. J. K. Elliott (Oxford, 2005), 185–204; see ibid. 165 for the question of dating.

[8] Augustine, in his letter to Evodius (Ep. 63; PL 33: 709–18), expressly denied that the Petrine verses referred to the descent, and his interpretation was generally followed by medieval theologians, including Aquinas. See Quilliet, 'Descente de Jésus', col. 594.

[9] Thomas Aquinas, *Summa theologiae* III, qu. 52, 'De descensu Christi ad inferos' (Alba and Rome, 1962), 2124–30.

pains.[10] It is difficult to see how Christ's descent can be both the vicarious suffering of a penalty and a triumphal progress, and Aquinas does not attempt to reconcile the two: indeed, in the final article of this *quaestio* he explicitly denies that Christ's descent was for the purpose of offering satisfaction.[11] But this passing reference hints at another way of understanding the words 'He descended into Hell': not as part of the triumph of Easter, but as the continuation of the suffering of Good Friday.

By the middle of the fifteenth century, Aquinas's suggestion of vicarious suffering and his distinction between a death of the body and the descent of the soul had been developed into a fully-fledged idea of a descent in suffering. Nicholas of Cusa expounded it in a sermon preached in 1457.[12] According to Nicholas, the death of Christ's body on the cross was the 'first death'. The second death was Christ's descent into hell, not just to the *limbus* of the fathers but (and here Cusanus goes beyond Aquinas) to the place of the damned. In this place Christ experienced the punishments of hell in our stead and suffered, along with the damned, the *visio mortis*. It was at this point, when the jaws of death were closing about him, that God raised him up on Easter Sunday, fulfilling the prophecy of the Psalmist.

This was an extraordinary insight that challenged the traditional depictions, both in theology and art, of a harrowing of hell. It is not surprising if, as has been suggested, Nicholas of Cusa took care to express more orthodox sentiments on the subject shortly afterwards.[13]

---

[10] Ibid., art. 1, resp. 1 (2124).

[11] Ibid., art. 8 ad 2 (2130): 'Descensus autem Christi ad inferos non fuit satisfactorius. Operabatur tamen in virtute passionis, quae fuit satisfactoria.' Aquinas's concern was to demonstrate that faithful souls are still liable to the punishments of purgatory.

[12] Nicholas of Cusa, *Excitationum ex sermonibus*, book 10, 'Ex sermone, Qui per spiritum sanctum semetipsum obtulit' (preached 3 April 1457), in *Haec accurata recognitio trium voluminum operum clariss. P. Nicolae Cusae Card.*, ed. Jacques Lefèvre d'Étaples (Paris, 1514), vol. 2, fols 176ᵛ–177ʳ.

[13] Cusanus's words evidently created a stir. Shortly afterwards he was obliged to preach a sermon on the article 'Descendit ad inferna', where the emphasis was on Christ's perfect obedience to the Father (Ibid. fols 181ᵛ–182ʳ). In a sermon preached shortly after that, on 2 May 1457, concerning the duties of a shepherd of the flock, Cusanus again returned to the theme: a good shepherd would be damned in hell for the sake of his flock: 'Pastor non debet ad se respicere: dummodo qualitercunque in pascendo ea faciat quae deus praecipit pastori bono etiam si propterea conciperet se in inferno damnandum.' But lest his fellow pastors were unduly alarmed, he immediately added that a man who demonstrated such love would not be damned in hell, because 'a righteous man in hell would not suffer there the *poena* of the unrighteous'. (Nam siquis tantae charitatis esset: ille utique non esset damnatus in inferno. Iustus enim in inferno: non habet poenam iniustorum.): *Excitationum ex sermonibus*,

As developments in the next century were to prove, however, it was an idea whose time had come. In the first edition of his *Quincuplex Psalterium* (1509) Jacques Lefèvre d'Étaples followed Nicholas of Cusa's interpretation of Psalm 29 (30), speaking again in terms of Christ's suffering of hellish penalties as his 'second death'. Lefèvre confesses that, when he first came across Cusa's interpretation, he found it 'non modo extranea sed & stupenda & horrenda' and, like Cusa himself, he puts forward the view with some delicacy.[14] By the time of the second edition of the *Psalterium*, just four years later, he had evidently come under pressure from the ecclesiastical authorities to retract his earlier support for Cusanus's position: he still describes the idea as 'at first sight not only outlandish but also shocking and horrifying', but then he sets forth what he now feels to be the correct view of the descent as a glorious triumph. And with even greater care he distances his own views from those he is obliged to report: 'the foregoing treatment has contained no assertion, only discussion'.[15]

* * *

It is significant that the new approach to the descent had been espoused, however briefly, by a fifteenth-century mystic and a sixteenth-century biblical scholar. Nourished by both these traditions, the Reformation provided fertile ground for the growth of a variety of *descensus* theories. The sixteenth century saw it interpreted variously as literal or metaphorical, as corporeal or spiritual, as implying motion from one place to another or not, and of course as a descent in triumph or in suffering. 'Hell' itself was understood as Hades or as Gehenna, as the place of the dead or the place of punishment, or even (an interpretation which appealed particularly to the more humanistically-minded of the Reformers, on the basis of 1 Peter) a place where enlightened pagan philosophers were given a chance of hearing the Gospel.

The doctrinal historian's equivalent of an electrocardiogram would

book 10, 'Ex sermone "Ministrat nobis fratres" ', fol. 182[r]. It is at best an indirect correction, for no explicit reference is made here to Christ. However, one of the leading authorities on Nicholas's theology, Rudolf Haubst, believes that the 'ingenious idea' of Christ's vicarious suffering in hell is marginal to Cusanus's overall understanding of the descent. See the literature quoted in Herzog, *Descensus*, 172–73.

[14] Jacques Lefèvre d'Étaples, *Quincuplex Psalterium: Gallicum, Romanum, Hebraicum, Vetus, Conciliatum* (Paris, 1509), fols 50[v]–51[r], at Ps. (29) 30: 11.

[15] See Jacques Lefèvre d'Étaples, *Quincuplex Psalterium. Fac-similé de l'édition de 1513*, Travaux d'humanisme et renaissance 170 (Geneva, 1979), fol. 47[r].

show that concern with the *descensus* doctrine was fairly constant throughout the sixteenth and early seventeenth centuries, but that there were spikes of particularly intense activity on four occasions. The first of these occurred around 1550 and involved theologians in Germany and England in two separate controversies. In Hamburg, an intra-Lutheran debate was sparked by Johann Aepinus, who caused offence by his understanding of the descent in terms of suffering.[16] At the same time, he insisted in good Lutheran fashion that the descent was to be understood literally, involving the motion of Christ's body through space. The Hamburg controversy raged from 1549 to 1551, and it was to prove highly significant. Although Aepinus was eventually vindicated by the Marburg city council (largely because his opponent, Johann Gratz, refused to submit to the council's gagging order), Melanchthon himself weighed in to the debate with an opinion that would shape the Lutheran understanding of the descent for centuries.[17] Meanwhile, in England, the idea of the suffering descent, by now firmly associated with the name of Calvin, was being promoted by Hugh Latimer and Bishop John Hooper.[18] Possibly in an attempt to deflect attention from intra-Protestant debates on the subject, a disputation was arranged in Cambridge in autumn 1552 to disprove the Catholic doctrine of the *limbus patrum*, with Christopher Carlile acting for the defence and Sir John Cheke for the prosecution.[19] Genuine Catholic

[16] For the course of the Hamburg controversy, see Vogelsang, 'Höllenfahrtsstreitig-keiten', 107–19, an account which emphasizes the differences between Aepinus and Luther; D. G. Truemper, 'The *Descensus ad inferos* from Luther to the Formula of Concord' (S. T. D. dissertation, Concordia Seminary in Exile (Seminex) in cooperation with the Lutheran School of Theology at Chicago, 1974), 218–71, which challenges Vogelsang's evaluation of Aepinus on the basis of a previously undiscovered manuscript; and Herzog, *Descensus*, 176–81.

[17] The text of Melanchthon's (and Bugenhagen's) opinion is given in *Corpus Reformatorum: Philippi Melanthonis Opera Quae Supersunt Omnia*, eds K. G. Bretschneider and E. Bindseil, 28 vols (Halle and Brunswick, 1834–60), 7: 666–68. For an analysis of Melanchthon's contribution to the Hamburg debate, see Truemper, '*Descensus*', 206–08 and 238–39.

[18] In a sermon preached before Edward VI in 1549, Latimer (after summing up controversies over the descent in typically direct fashion as 'much ado'), suggested tentatively that '[Christ] suffered in hell such pains as the damned spirits did suffer there': *Sermons of Hugh Latimer*, ed. George E. Corrie, PS 27 (Cambridge, 1844), 234. Hooper expressed a similar view in his *Brief and Clear Confession* of c. 1550: *Later Writings of Bishop Hooper, Together with his Letters and Other Pieces*, ed. Charles Nevinson, PS 21 (Cambridge, 1852), 30.

[19] See Christopher Carlile, *A Discourse concerning two divine Positions. The first effectually concluding, that the soules of the faithfull fathers, deceased before Christ, went immediately to heaven. The second sufficientlye setting foorth unto us Christians what we are to conceive, touching the descension of our Saviour Christ into Hell: Publiquely disputed at a Commencement in Cambridge,*

voices were to be heard on this topic, but not until the early years of Elizabeth's reign, and then only from exile.[20]

The next peak of activity came in the early 1560s. In England, it was occasioned by revision of the articles of religion. The *Forty-two Articles* of 1553 had contained a minimal statement which failed to dot and cross any doctrinal 'i's or 't's:

> As Christ died, and was buried for us: so also it is to be believed that He went down into hell. For the body lay in the sepulchre until the resurrection: but his ghost departing from Him was with the ghosts that were in prison or in hell, and did preach to the same, as the place of St Peter doth testify.[21]

In the changed circumstances of 1563, this formula seemed to say both too much and too little. On one hand, the reference to a 'prison', with its suggestion of temporary detention, could imply the existence of a *limbus patrum* or even of purgatory.[22] On the other, the idea that Christ himself suffered the pangs of hell, an interpretation that was being popularized by the marginal comments of the Geneva Bible of 1560, was now noticeable by its absence.[23] The revision of the articles provided a perfect opportunity to bring greater clarity and precision to the Church's understanding of this doctrine, and this was the plea to Convocation of William Alley, Bishop of Exeter. Alley complained that his diocese was rent by 'great invective between preachers', with some denying a literal descent, others understanding it as a descent in suffering, and still others claiming that the doctrine was a late addition to the creed and deserved to be abandoned altogether.[24] Alley's request

---

anno domini 1552. *Purposely written at the first by way of a confutation, against a Booke of Richard Smith of Oxford* ([London], 1562). Further details of the disputation are given in John Strype, *The Life of the Learned Sir John Cheke* (Oxford, 1821), 89–90.

[20] While Catholic writers were generally cheered by disagreement on this doctrine within Protestant ranks, the idea of a suffering descent struck them as particularly offensive. This 'Calvinist' doctrine was attacked by Richard Smith in his *Refutatio luculenta crassae et exitiosae haeresis Joannis Calvini et Christophori Carlilus Angli; qua astruunt Christum non descendisse ad inferos alium, quam ad infernum infimum* ([London], 1562).

[21] Gibson, *Thirty-Nine Articles*, 159.

[22] The original form of the article added a clause which explained that that during his descent Christ freed no souls from imprisonment or torment. This would in effect have excluded the notion of a *limbus patrum*. It was, however, omitted from the article in its final form: Gibson, *Thirty-Nine Articles*, 159.

[23] The Geneva Bible's marginal notes relate Ps. 16: 10, Matt. 26: 37, 27: 46, Eph. 4: 8 and 1 Pet. 3: 19 to Christ's suffering in hell.

[24] See the summary of Alley's paper given in Wallace, 'Puritan and Anglican', 260.

was not heeded. Instead, the revisers decided that, on such a contentious matter, less was more, and struck out the second sentence of the 1553 article. To this day, the article 'Of the going down of Christ into Hell' remains the shortest of the *Thirty-nine Articles*.

In Germany, meanwhile, the infamously splenetic Lutherans erupted into controversy once more, this time in the south. It began in 1565 with an epistolary challenge delivered by Johann Matsperger (a champion of a literal descent by Christ in victory) to Johann Parsimonius.[25] News of Parsimonius's preaching of a metaphorical descent in suffering had evidently travelled the fifty miles or so from Stuttgart to Augsburg. The controversy is remarkable because, although Matsperger's view was eventually to prevail within Lutheranism, in this particular case it was Parsimonius who was vindicated and Matsperger who was deposed from his preaching office.[26] As with the Hamburg controversy, proponents of Christ's harrowing of hell proved to be (perhaps not inappropriately) the more belligerent of the two sides and fell foul of regulations designed to prevent inflammatory preaching. The same year, 1565, witnessed two other events in Germany which were more reliable indicators of the way the Lutheran wind was blowing on this subject. The first was the publication in Frankfurt of Nicholas Selneccer's influential exposition of the Apostles' Creed. This came down clearly on the side of a literal descent into hell, 'body and soul'.[27] The second was the confutation, by the Lutheran theologians of Mansfeld, of the Reformed Heidelberg Catechism, and picked out that Catechism's understanding of the descent as the suffering of Christ as their primary target. For them, the way in which the Heidelberg theologians had approached this article of faith was symptomatic of their fundamental theological weaknesses.[28]

The third peak of controversial activity concerning the doctrine of the *descensus Christi* occurred in the mid-1580s, and it consisted of a concerted effort by Catholic polemicists to exploit the lack of a united Protestant front on the issue, in the wake of the appearance of the

[25] For accounts of the south German controversy, see Vogelsang, 'Höllenfahrtsstreitigkeiten', 120–23; Truemper, '*Descensus*', 277–91.

[26] A point made forcefully in Truemper, '*Descensus*', 279–80.

[27] Selneccer, *Paedagogia christiana continens capita et locos doctrinae christianae, forma & serie catechetica vere, perspicue explicata* (Frankurt am Main, 1565), 570.

[28] For an account of the Mansfelders' response, see Kolb, 'Christ's Descent', 106–15. Kolb argues that it was this response (or at least the thinking behind it), and not the Hamburg controversy, which inspired the ninth article of the Formula of Concord.

Lutheran Book of Concord (1580). This was not a new tactic; we have already seen how the conservative Oxford theologian Richard Smith had tried to use the doctrine to drive a wedge between moderate and Calvinist Protestants in England. What was new was the concentration of theological firepower. In quick succession appeared substantial treatments by Henri de Vicq from Antwerp, Heinrich Ebingshausen from Cologne, and Hieronymus Montanus from Ingolstadt.[29] The contemporary appearance of Bellarmine's masterwork from the Ingolstadt presses might have been coincidental, but he took a similar line to the others in exposing Protestant divisions over the descent.[30]

The final flurry of debates on the *descensus* was a purely English phenomenon, and marked the last years of Elizabeth's reign and the first of James's. It has been suggested that it was occasioned by a 'conformist' backlash against extreme Calvinism, the fight being chosen over this issue partly because Lutheran Orthodoxy had provided the conformists with such a store of ready-made arguments.[31] The battle-lines drawn up were between a literal view of the descent with a belief in the harrowing of hell on the one side, and, on the other, a metaphorical view of the descent (often associated with a philological approach which explained Hades as merely a synonym for the grave) combined with a belief that Christ suffered the pangs of hell on the cross or in the garden of Gethsemane. The opening exchanges in 1592/3 involved Adam Hill arguing for the first position and Alexander Hume for the second.[32] They were succeeded by a protracted exchange, which lasted from 1597 to 1604, with Thomas Bilson, Bishop of Winchester, and Henry Jacob, replacing Hill and Hume respectively.[33] Meanwhile, in 1602, a John Higgins launched a literalist attack on the earlier writings of William Perkins.[34] In 1604, Bilson and Jacob gave way to two new

[29] Henri de Vicq (Vicus), *De descensv Iesv Christi ad inferos, ex symbolo apostolorvm et sacris scripturis liber* (Antwerp, 1586); Heinrich Ebingshausen, *De descensv Christi ad inferos dispvtatio theologica* (Cologne, 1586); Hieronymus Montanus, *Theses de descensv Christ ad inferos, et eivsdem ad caelos ascensu. In quibus refvtatvr impia et in Christvm blasphema doctrina Lutheranorum & Caluinianorum de hoc vtroque fidei articulo* (Ingolstadt, 1587).

[30] For a summary of Bellarmine's approach, see Quilliet, 'Descente de Jésus', cols 582–83.

[31] See Wallace, 'Puritan and Anglican', 269.

[32] Adam Hill, *Defence of the Article: Christ descended into Hell. With Arguments obiected agains the truth of the same doctrine: of one Alexander Humes* (London, 1592) and Alexander Hume, *A reioynder to Doctor Hill Concerning the Descense of Christ into Hell* (Edinburgh, 1593).

[33] For an account of the debate, see Wallace, 'Puritan and Anglican', 273–77.

[34] John Higgins, *An Answere to Master William Perkins, Concerning Christs Descension into Hell* (Oxford, 1602).

antagonists, Richard Parkes and Andrew Willet respectively, who exchanged treatises for three more years.[35] The 'Big Bertha' of this bombardment of books was rolled out in 1611, a four-volume defence of the metaphorical/suffering interpretation begun by Hugh Sanford and completed by Robert Parker.[36] By this time, however, the conformist counter-attack had run out of steam. On the other side, the idea of a suffering descent was also abandoned, and the idea that the 'hell' to which Christ descended was merely the grave, not the place of punishment, predominated.

This survey of the Reformation debates demonstrates that the questions which most commonly exercised the theologians were the related ones of understanding the descent literally or metaphorically and as a victory or a punishment. It was however a feature of the case for a suffering descent that – as with Cusanus and Lefèvre earlier – it did not generally attract the most steadfast of proponents. Two examples illustrate this point. Anton Zimmermann had been a student at Wittenberg University and could even have been present at Luther's second course of lectures on the Psalms (1519–21) in which Luther expressed the same views as Cusanus and the earlier Lefèvre on the descent.[37] By 1525 he was a Lutheran pastor, and preached at Weißenfels a sermon on John 6:44–47 in which he argued that, before his resurrection, Christ descended into hell and suffered there the punishment of the damned in our stead. His hearers, a congregation of about forty fellow pastors, objected that by this opinion he had diminished Christ's majesty. In response, Zimmermann sent the Weißenfelsers a defence filled with biblical references. Zimmermann published only two works: the first, in 1525, was the printed version of his defence. The second, in 1526, was, bizarrely, a refutation and recantation of his views published in the first book. His principled stand had lasted at best a matter of months.[38]

---

[35] See Wallace, 'Puritan and Anglican', 277–79.

[36] Hugh Sanford, *De descensu Domini Nostri Jesu Christi ad inferos, libri quatuor*, ed. Robert Parker (Amsterdam, 1611).

[37] For example, *WA* 5: 606, lines 10–20. Interestingly, in his marginal notes on the 1509 edition of the *Quincuplex Psalterium* (at *WA* 4: 487), which he used in preparing for his *Dictata super Psalterium* (1513–15), Luther seemed less than impressed by the orthodoxy of Lefèvre's suggestion. He commented that, although Cusanus and Lefèvre appear to be onto something ('[q]uanquam ista argumenta aliquid esse appareant'), their views conflict with Christ's promise to the good thief, 'Today you will be with me in Paradise' (Luke 23: 43). In confirmation, Luther cited John Cassian, *Collationes patrum* 1.14. See *Cassiani Opera: Collationes XXIIII*, ed. Michael Petschenig, CSEL 13 (Vienna, 2004), 23, lines 8–20.

[38] On Zimmermann, see Truemper, '*Descensus*', 153–59; Herzog, *Descensus*, 186–204.

A similar example is provided by the case of Jakob Thiele. Little is known about him except that he was a Lutheran pastor in Pomerania who in 1554 had preached the idea of a descent in suffering. Before the year was out, he had been summoned before the synod of Greifswald, had renounced his former views, and received absolution from his brother pastors.[39]

Lefèvre, Zimmermann and Thiele were not, therefore, very staunch defenders of the suffering motif in the face of pressure, and they collapsed at once. This might just be par for the course: most people in the sixteenth century did not go to stake for their beliefs. But I think the reason for these voltes-face is to be found not just in pusillanimity but in the nature of the insight itself. Not for nothing did Lefèvre find this way of looking at the *descensus* initially outlandish, shocking and horrible. The idea that Christ died in despair and went down to the hell of the damned, bereft of the beatific vision and filled with the vision of death, *is* a shocking idea. It is also not easy to maintain in terms of orthodox Christology, for it presupposes that Christ's divine conscious-ness, the Logos, was at least temporarily absent or suspended. The logical difficulties of when, where and how such a descent took place were not in themselves insuperable, but they further weighted the scales against such an interpretation. A suffering descent could find some support in the prophetic and therefore indirect witness of the Psalms, but the New Testament told uniformly against it: among Jesus's last words from the cross, he seemed to confirm in the cry 'It is finished!' (John 19: 30) that his sufferings were completed by his death, while the promise to the good thief rules out anything more than a fleeting visit to the infernal regions.[40] The most direct attestation of the descent in the New Testament depicts Christ more as a heavenly prison visitor than as a fellow inmate.[41] So it is not surprising that the defenders of this view were so easily persuaded to abandon it publicly, whatever they may have continued to believe privately. This makes all the more valuable the case of Martin Luther, who was not noted for renouncing his beliefs once he had made up his mind. His case is extraordinary because he held both these contradictory views of the descent, not successively (as Lefèvre, Zimmermann and Thiele did) but simultaneously. Luther's ambiguous position is the central problem of a

---

[39] Truemper, '*Descensus*', 273–76.
[40] Luke 23: 43.
[41] 1 Pet. 3–4.

generally problematic history of the doctrine in the sixteenth century, and I think one can best understand the dynamic of the wider debates by sorting out what is going on in the internal debate, as it were, within Luther's own mind.

The victory motif in Luther is the one with which, historically, most Lutherans have been familiar. The ninth article of the Formula of Concord, on the descent of Christ into hell, refers the reader to Luther's so-called 'Torgau' sermon (1532) for his definitive treatment of the topic, and this presents an entirely traditional view of the harrowing of hell.[42] 'Hold fast to your creed', he says, which proclaims 'I believe in Christ, the whole man, body and soul, who descended to Hell in body and soul and destroyed Hell.'[43] His insistence on a corporeal descent is striking, but Luther is not concerned with the difficulties that entails. Indeed, he explicitly dismisses those pedants who point out that the banner Christ was carrying would have burst into flames as he approached hell.[44] Luther insists that the only way of understanding the doctrine is not by biblical or theological expertise but by looking at the traditional depictions and singing the hymns (such as *Salve festa dies*) that everyone is familiar with. And then he says something that was once thought uncharacteristic of Reformation thinking, before we knew better: you will be saved, he assures his congregation, by gazing upon those pictures, in the same way that the Israelites were saved in the wilderness by looking upon the brazen serpent.[45]

So this is the sermon that made it into the Formula of Concord, and it is as forceful an affirmation of the harrowing of hell as could be imagined. As a result, it became axiomatic within Lutheran Orthodoxy that Luther taught the harrowing of hell, so much so that Lutherans came to reject as a matter of principle any spiritual or suffering interpretation as 'Calvinist'. But in doing this they were (in the most striking example of 'denominational disorientation' of all) actually condemning the way in which Luther himself far more characteristically spoke of the descent. From his earliest sustained theological writing in 1513/14

---

[42] For the texts of the article, see *The Book of Concord*, ed. Theodore G. Tappert (Philadelphia, PA, 1959), 492 (the Epitome), 610 (the Solid Declaration). The text of the 'Torgau' sermon for Easter 1533 may be found in *WA* 37: 62–72, while the text of the sermon for the afternoon of Easter Day (31 March) 1532, which is believed to be the more reliable text for a sermon that was later wrongly dated (see below), may be found at *WA* 36: 159–64.
[43] *WA* 36: 160, lines 22–24.
[44] Ibid., lines 6–9.
[45] Ibid., line 102.

(the first Psalms lectures) to the last (his lectures on Genesis in 1544), the suffering interpretation is paramount. When expounding Psalm 21 (22), he interpreted Christ's sense of abandonment by God, expressed in the cry of dereliction, as an experience of the pain of hell. 'To have the same consciousness as the damned – that is death, that is the descent into Hell'.[46] In his lectures on Genesis, Luther again affirmed that, in the Garden of Gethsemane, 'Christ our Lord and liberator was in very Hell for all our sakes. For truly he experienced death and Hell in his body.'[47]

This interpretation recurred throughout his writings. In 1527, a year in which he himself suffered particularly acutely from depression, Luther wrote in exposition of Ephesians 4:

> Christ has first descended, that is, he has become the least and most despised of all, so that he could not go deeper, and indeed no-one could fall lower than him, ... because he has made himself the lowest of all, beneath the Law, beneath the Devil, death, sin, and Hell, that is, I think, to the lowest and uttermost deep ...[48]

Luther's most sustained treatment of this theme came in the German version of his exposition of the Book of Jonah (1525–26). Jonah's sojourn in the belly of the whale for three days was a type of Christ's descent, but Luther sees Jonah more as a type of the believer who feels himself under the judgment of God, especially *in articulo mortis*. Jonah equates his experience with hell ('out of the belly of Sheol I cried'[49]), which Luther regards as a characteristic biblical trope, beloved not only of Jonah but also of the Psalmist. 'Hell' signifies the depths of despair and God-forsakenness in this life. But what does that mean for hell proper?

> But what Hell may be before the Last Judgement, I am not altogether sure. That it is some specific place (*eyn sonderlicher ort*), where the souls of the damned already suffer, as the painters paint and the

[46] Ibid. 5: 604.
[47] *Lectures on Genesis*, 1544 (*WA* 44: 524.6–7): 'Ita Christus Dominus et liberator noster pro nobis omnibus fuit in ipsissimo inferno. Vere enim sensit mortem et infernum in corpore suo.'
[48] *Eine gute Predigt von der Kraft der Himmelfahrt Christi*, 31 May 1527: *WA* 23: 702.11–703.1. For a description of the context of Luther's breakdown in 1527, see Heinrich Bornkamm, *Luther in Mid-Career, 1521–1530* (London, 1983), 554–61.
[49] Jonah 2: 2.

belly-preachers preach, is nonsense. For the devils are not in Hell but, as Peter says, are bound to Hell by ropes (II Peter 2: 4). ... Everyone carries his own Hell with him, wherever he goes, while he endures death's last agonies and God's wrath ...[50]

These sentiments, though with a different force, uncannily foreshadow Mephistopheles' famous lines in Marlowe's *Faustus*.

It will be evident that the purpose of this belief for Luther was not to establish a recondite point about Christ's *post mortem* whereabouts, but to comfort those who, like Luther himself, experienced anxiety over their final destination and especially feared that they did not measure up to God's demands – or rather that God had positively rejected them. The use of the *descensus* for this purpose had been present from his first consolatory writings. In his sermon of 1519 on the art of dying, for instance, he had already urged the saving function of pictures, physical and mental:

Look upon that heavenly image of Christ, who for your sake descended into Hell and was abandoned by God as one of those damned for all eternity, as he said from the cross, 'Eli, Eli, lama sabachthani – My God, my God, why hast thou forsaken me?' Look upon it, and in that image your [*sic!*] Hell is overcome and your uncertain hope is made certain.[51]

Given that this theme not only abounds in Luther's corpus but also serves such a crucial pastoral purpose, it is surprising that it was so completely overlaid by the approach taken by Lutheran Orthodoxy. It was only when the editors of the *Weimarer Ausgabe* began the project of tracking down and publishing all his writings in 1883 that the theme was once more unearthed. For scholars such as Althaus and Vogelsang in the first part of the twentieth century, this was a revelation.[52] For them it proved that the suffering motif was determinative for Luther, even when occasionally (as in the 'Torgau' sermon) he suggested other ways of looking at the descent. And it demonstrated the irony that, in

---

50 *Der Prophet Jona ausgelegt*, 1526 (*WA* 19: 225, lines 12–16, 28–29 = *LW* 19: 75).

51 *Ein Sermon von der Bereitung zum Sterben*, 1519 (*WA* 2: 690, lines 17–22 = *LW* 42: 105).

52 See esp. Erich Vogelsang, 'Luthers Torgauer Predigt von Jesu Christo vom Jahre 1532', *Luther Jahrbuch* 13 (1931), 114–30; idem, *Der angefochtene Christus bei Luther* (Berlin and Leipzig, 1932); idem, 'Höllenfahrtsstreitigkeiten', 90–132; Paul Althaus, 'Niedergefahren zur Hölle', *Zeitschrift für systematische Theologie* 19 (1942), 365–84.

persecuting 'Calvinist' interpretations, the theologians of Lutheran Orthodoxy were in reality persecuting Luther.

Although Vogelsang and Althaus undoubtedly had a case (their positions were not identical, as Althaus felt that Vogelsang had stressed the suffering motif in Luther too one-sidedly),[53] it went unheard or at least unacknowledged in much of worldwide Lutheranism, not least in North America. The editorial comments of the American edition of *Luther's Works* from the 1950s and 1960s, for instance, still reflect the viewpoint of Lutheran Orthodoxy.[54] It was not until 1974, in a Chicago doctoral dissertation that remains unpublished, that a determined attempt was made to re-evaluate Luther's *descensus* theology in the light of this research.[55]

The thesis by David G. Truemper attempts to reconcile the two conflicting themes of victory and suffering in Luther's *descensus* doctrine by appealing to his theology of the cross, in which victory and suffering are not two incompatible interpretations of the *descensus*, but two sides of the same coin. The sufferings of Christ, no matter how great, would have no effect whatever if it were not for the victory of Easter Sunday. On the other hand, the victory that God gave Christ and which he promises to believers is exclusively by way of the cross. Holy Saturday therefore has a dual nature, looking back to Good Friday and forward to Easter.[56] I think this is a very convincing interpretation, but the neatness of this theological solution requires Truemper to give equal weight to Luther's two interpretations of the *descensus*, when in fact the suffering motif is far more common in Luther than the theme of the harrowing of hell, and in fact the Torgau sermon is quite atypical of his output. Truemper takes the Torgau sermon as his starting-point (for understandable confessional reasons), and as such it overshadows his entire subsequent discussion of Luther's views. The result was that Truemper gives shorter shrift to the merits of Vogelsang's case than he should. I believe that, had Truemper situated the 'Torgau' sermon in its context, it would have been more obvious why Luther spoke in this way on this occasion.

---

[53] See Althaus, 'Niedergefahren', 379 n. 1.

[54] See, for example, *LW* 22: 325 n. 38, where a descent-as-suffering interpretation is glossed in the following words: 'Here Luther seems to equate the descent into hell with the death of Christ; ordinarily he distinguishes these two actions, as in the Torgau sermons of April 1533.'

[55] Truemper, '*Descensus*'.

[56] Ibid. 135.

The sermon was most probably given on Easter Day (31 March) 1532, at Wittenberg, not Torgau, and we know a good deal about Luther's personal and public circumstances at this time.[57] There was a new addition in the Luther household, a son by the name of Martin who was now four months old. One can only hope that young Martin spent most of his time sleeping, because his father was not in the best of health. The elder Martin took to his bed during Holy Week and was not well enough to preach the Good Friday sermon. He did manage to write or dictate a letter from his sickbed: 'I don't want to eat or drink. I am already dead. If only I were buried!'[58] On Holy Saturday, discussions began that would result in a truce between the Schmalkaldic League and the Emperor. Luther was for once a dove rather than a hawk in this initiative. His view was that the peace negotiations should not be jeopardized by a desire to get all one's demands accepted.[59] On Sunday he was recovered enough to enter the pulpit and began to preach, 'even though', he explained, 'I am sick and the Enthusiasts (*Schwermer*) are troubling me'.[60] This was a reference to an open letter on the Lord's Supper he had written earlier in the year against some Schwenckfelders who had settled in the Prussian territories of the Teutonic Knights, but which had caused great offence amongst the south German reformers.[61] And I think this is the key to understanding the line Luther takes in the 'Torgau' sermon. The so-called sacramentarians denied the real presence in the Eucharist on the grounds that it is impossible for Christ's natural body to be in more places than one. Since it is in heaven, seated at the right hand of God, it cannot also be in every consecrated host throughout the world. I believe that Luther's treatment of Holy Saturday was heavily coloured by this debate. He was keen to affirm that, by virtue of the *communicatio idiomatum*, the sharing of the properties of divine and human, it was perfectly possible for Christ's human body on Holy Saturday to be both lying in the tomb, and at the same

---

[57] I follow here, as does Truemper, Vogelsang's reconstruction. This demonstrates that the document known to the compilers of the Formula of Concord as Luther's 'Torgau' sermon of 1533 (in fact, the third and most extensive of three sermons) is a transcription of the sermon Luther gave on Easter Day (31 March) 1532 at Wittenberg. See Vogelsang, 'Torgauer Predigt', 114–30.

[58] See Martin Brecht, *Martin Luther: Shaping and Defining the Reformation, 1521–1532* (Minneapolis, MN, 1990), 430.

[59] Ibid. 421–27.

[60] *WA* 36: 159.8.

[61] Brecht, *Shaping and Defining*, 450.

time in heaven (for had he not promised the good thief '*Today* you will be with me in paradise'?), and at the same time throwing its weight around in hell, breaking down bronze gates, and doing other physical things that only a natural human body can do. In that context, with the south German notions of spiritual presence ringing in his ears, Luther could not afford to imply a spiritual (what we might call a 'metaphorical') descent by Christ into hell but was obliged to point to the clear words of the creed: 'Hold fast to what your creed tells you, that he descended into Hell'. This was exactly the same tactic he had employed earlier in the eucharistic debate: ignore all the clever sophistries and hold fast to the words, 'This is my body'.[62]

* * *

I suggested that if we could understand the internal tensions within Luther's own mind which led him to hold two apparently contradictory beliefs about Christ's descent into hell, this might provide us with a way of understanding the wider phenomenon of *descensus* controversy in the sixteenth century. I think it does. Despite Truemper's valiant attempt to assert the equal weight of both beliefs within the theology of the cross, it is clear from the sheer weight of evidence that, for Luther, the descent into hell that had the most value to a believer was the conviction that Christ himself had experienced abandonment by God, and that this was a guarantee to the believer that God was present even in absence: however far someone might fall from God, God in Christ has fallen further. The idea was not original to Luther, but had been learned from mystical writers such as Johann Tauler and the author of the *Theologia deutsch*, and it was a vital stage in his gaining of a new understanding of grace, righteousness and faith.[63] As Vogelsang maintained, this under-

---

[62] Robert Kolb also proposes that the 'Torgau' sermon was influenced by Christological considerations arising out of the sacramentarian controversies, though he relates this to Zwingli's death in 1531 rather than to the south German hostility to Luther's anti-Schwenkfeldian letter in 1532: Kolb, 'Christ's Descent', 116.

[63] Chapter 11 of the *Theologia deutsch* opens with the words 'Christ's soul had to visit hell before it came to heaven. This is also the pattern for man's soul.' See *The Theologia Germanica of Martin Luther*, ed. Bengt Hoffman (London, 1980), 72. The descent into hell was not an explicit concern of Tauler, whose focus was on the sufferings of Christ on the cross. However, his leading idea of following Christ through suffering; his conviction that, in the spiritual life, 'the greater the descent, the greater the ascent'; and perhaps also his notion that the *resignatio ad infernum* – cheerfully accepting eternal separation from God for God's sake – is the highest stage of the Christian life, all helped to point Luther towards what he called the *descensio spiritualis*. On the *resignatio*, see *Johannes Tauler: Sermons*, ed. Maria Schrady, Classics of Western Spirituality (New York, Mahwah, NJ, and Toronto, 1985), 96.

standing remained the primary way in which Luther thought about the descent. The alternative approach, that of the harrowing of hell, was also valued by him and forcefully preached; but there were relatively few occasions that it sprang to his mind as a primary association, as it were, except when he was in fierce controversy with the south German reformers over their denial of the ubiquity of Christ's body. Even then, the two understandings sat so awkwardly with one another that he was forced to develop clearly unsatisfactory explanations, such as his idea that there must have been two descents into hell, a suffering one before death and a triumphant one after.[64]

What we can conclude from this is, I think, that Luther exemplifies a tension that has always been present in Christian thought between two types of theology: affective or mystical theology on the one hand, and speculative or dogmatic theology on the other. The first is essentially personal, sometimes exaggerated, pastoral in intent and often geared to the specific religious needs of an individual. Luther's theology was almost all of this type: at times it worked spectacularly well, as the enormous popularity of his early consolatory writings testifies; at times it was misunderstood or misinterpreted. The second type of theology is essentially public, accessible, geared to the demands of unifying a believing community and defending it from false teaching. Its doctrines must be verifiable by reference to Scripture and other authorities.

The *descensus* controversies of the sixteenth century show ultimately that Protestantism was no more successful at resolving the tension between the two theologies than the medieval Church had been. Cusanus's idea of a descent of suffering was tolerable because it was expressed in the context of a sermon restricted to a limited audience. The same idea, expressed in the context of Lefèvre's commentary on the Psalms, a work of scholarship in the public domain, was not tolerable and Lefèvre himself (who could remember how shocking he had found the notion when he first read it) could see the objection. The same process operated after the Reformation in the case of the Lutherans

---

[64] See Luther's notorious expression in the macaronic transcript of his sermon for Holy Saturday 1538: 'This is the chief point: it was not for himself that Christ descended into hell a second time, but for us. That is to say, having been made lord over Devil, death, and sin, he now received the lordship' (Das ist die heubtmeinung, quod Christus non propter se, sed propter nos ist zum andern mal inn die helle, i.e. dominus factus supra Teufel, mortem, peccatum, hat eingenomen die herrschaft: *WA* 46: 308.15–17). The date is important, and refutes any suggestion that the 'Torgau' sermon represents Luther's 'mature' thoughts on the subject or that they superseded his earlier beliefs in a 'first' or spiritual descent.

Zimmermann and Thiele: the notion of Christ's descent in suffering was all very well for personal edification, but it could not be tolerated when broadcast in sermons and vernacular pamphlets. The Catholic controversialist Caspar Schatzgeyer evidently shared the view of the Lutheran authorities on this point, for he objected to Zimmermann that, for a doctrine to be publicly preached and then circulated in a pamphlet, it needs to be authorized by Scripture, tradition and reason.[65]

There was less of a tension for the Reformed tradition, because of its more critical attitude towards some standards of public theology such as creeds. That Calvin adopted an understanding of the descent as suffering was not scandalous in a climate in which Theodore Beza could delete the entire article 'descendit ad inferos' from his version of the creed. But when brought into contact with other traditions, the Calvinist position seemed bizarre. One thinks here not only of the knee-jerk reaction of Lutheran Orthodoxy, but also of more creedally minded Anglicans in the context of the *descensus* disputes in England in the 1590s and 1600s. Indeed, Wallace (in his study of these disputes) goes so far as to credit these *descensus* disputes with the birth of 'Anglicanism', as the more patristic-orientated and creedally minded members of the Church of England parted company with those who held fast to the Puritan *pietas crucis*. Wallace's more far-reaching claims about the nature and progress of Anglicanism have perhaps not stood up well to more recent advances in scholarship; but the bifurcation he notes between dogmatic and mystical strands in England is one that can be paralleled in other denominations at this time.[66]

The tension between mystical and dogmatic approaches to theology remains to this day. The popularity of von Balthasar's 'theology of Holy Saturday' is evidence that the idea of a suffering descent and a suffering Messiah has much more to offer to the Church of the late twentieth and early twenty-first centuries than the traditional idea of the harrowing of hell. But when an affective theology is judged by the alien categories of dogmatic theology, it will often look suspiciously like confessional confusion and denominational disorientation.

University of Hull

---

[65] Kaspar Schatzgeyer, *Verwerffung eines irrigenn artickels das die seel Christi nach abschaidt vom leib in absteigung zu den hellen hab darinn geliden hellische pein. Mit erklerung der warhayt warumb Christus zu der hellen gestigenn sey* (Landshut, 1526), Gii[v].

[66] Wallace, 'Puritans and Anglicans', 248–87.

REVELATION AND RECKONING:
ANGELS AND THE APOCALYPSE IN
REFORMATION ENGLAND, c. 1559–1625

by LAURA SANGHA

A NGELOLOGY – the science of angels – exercised a compelling hold on the medieval and early modern mind. The role that angels had in the belief and ritual associated with death was perhaps its most theologically resonant aspect – angels were intimately involved in the system of eschatology and the rites associated with dying, mourning and burial. Their responsibilities at the end of life included participation in the cosmic struggle enacted around the deathbed, where good and evil angels were thought to contend for the custody of the soul of the dying; and stewardship of the soul after death, when angels were believed to carry it to its final resting place, as Lazarus was carried to Abraham's bosom in Luke 16: 19–31. However, angels also assumed important responsibilities *after* death; they featured prominently in the narrative of the Last Judgement and the strategies adopted by Christians to conceptualize and prepare for the afterlife and the events of the Apocalypse.[1]

Although belief about angels was not an aspect of devotion that was to prove a major confessional battleground, through their roles in the afterlife angels were implicated in a corpus of beliefs that *were* fundamental to the Protestant world view: that is, the disconcerting concept of predestination. In his extensive study of early modern catechisms Ian Green has documented a tendency amongst the authors of these instructive texts to try to avoid the issue of predestination, or at least to treat it briefly with little controversy, suggesting that there was a reluctance on the part of the reformers to engage with this knotty question at a pastoral level.[2] This was perhaps understandable considering that

---

[1] For the importance of angels in Christian understandings of death, see David Keck, *Angels and Angelology in the Middle Ages* (Oxford, 1998), chs 9 and 44–6. Peter Marshall has recently explored the presence of angels around the early modern deathbed in 'Angels around the Deathbed: Variations on a Theme in the English Art of Dying', in Peter Marshall and Alexandra Walsham, eds, *Angels in the Early Modern World* (Cambridge, 2006), 83–103.

[2] Ian Green, *The Christian's ABC: Catechisms and Catechizing in England c. 1530–1740* (Oxford, 1996), ch. 8, esp. pp. 356–71. Alexandra Walsham has similarly identified an 'elas-

reformed perceptions of the afterlife left the laity bereft of strategies that previously provided them with the hope and means of achieving eventual salvation. But given that predestination lay at the heart of the reformed message, it was vital that some attempt was made to convey this fundamental concept to the people. Did angels have the qualifications to fill the emotional and spiritual void that the Reformation had created, providing comfort and hope and offering a 'softer' face to this daunting Protestant doctrine?

This question is formulated in the context of recent scholarship which has begun to examine the significance of celestial beings more closely, particularly as the enduring nature of belief about angels fits into a post-revisionist perspective. Post-revisionists recognize complex continuities in religious cultures, identifying a fusion of new and traditional elements and some accommodation to aspects of pre-Reformation religious life. Historians have argued that such accommodation catered to the intellectual and emotional capabilities of the laity and created points of intersection between old and new ideas, providing an explanation of how the reformers were able to obliterate inherited systems of custom and replace them with radical and disconcerting new concepts.[3]

This article will examine what the survival and mutation of belief about angels and the book of Revelation can tell us about continuity and change in people's expectations of what awaited them after death. Using evidence drawn mainly from contemporary vernacular commentaries on Revelation from the Elizabethan and Jacobean periods, I will seek to discover any disparity between the awesome and terrifying power exhibited by angels in Scripture and the way in which they were presented in this literature. In the process I will question the post-revisionist trend which tends to emphasize comfortable continuities across the pre- and post-Reformation eras. When discussing Revelation, it was not possible for reformers to side-step the fact that the chief function of heavenly beings in the Apocalypse was as instruments of God's divine justice and wrath, nor gloss over the harsh doctrine at its

---

ticity' of discourse that allowed ministers to gloss over the complexities of religious dogma at times of adversity: *Providence in Early Modern England* (Oxford, 1999), ch. 3.

[3] Important post-revisionist works include Tessa Watt, *Cheap Print and Popular Piety 1550–1640* (Cambridge, 1991); Judith Maltby, *Prayer Book and People in Elizabethan and Early Stuart England* (Cambridge, 1998); Walsham, *Providence*; Peter Lake and Michael Questier, *The Antichrist's Lewd Hat: Protestants, Papists and Players in Post-Reformation England* (London, 2002).

heart that only a portion of humanity was ultimately destined for heaven. But angels, I will argue, had the potential to make the hard doctrine of a novel faith more palatable to the laity.

Most of the detail relating to the angelic role in the events of the end was derived from Saint John's vision of God's judgement on the world in the book of Revelation. An angel is a central protagonist in the narrative, delivering the apocalyptic vision to John the Divine: 'the Lord God of the holy prophets sent his angel to shew unto his servants the things which must shortly be done' (Revelation 22: 6). Celestial beings are also integral to the scriptural action, as the book of the seven seals is opened and the earth destroyed. They separate the damned from the saved; they sound the trumpets that herald the annihilation of the earth; and they successfully take on the dragon in battle, casting him out of heaven. After this, seven angels dressed in pure and white linen visit seven plagues upon earth, culminating in its utter destruction. Finally, an angel casts a millstone into the sea, ensuring the downfall of Babylon, before John's celestial guide privileges him with a vision of the heavenly Jerusalem, its gates guarded by yet more heavenly beings.

The processes of reform in the sixteenth century were to have a profound effect on belief relating to the afterlife and the ways in which the Apocalypse was interpreted. The principle of justification by faith alone, the abolition of purgatory, and the eradication of prayers for the dead resulted in the dramatic restructuring of the soteriological landscape, and the traditional understanding of angels themselves encompassed certain indefensible elements that touched on issues at the heart of the reforming programme. Unsurprisingly, criticism focused on the angels' assumed role as mediators between human beings and the divine, and there were various Catholic devotional practices associated with them that to the reformers reeked of 'superstition'. The rejection of belief about angels was by no means unqualified, however; thanks to their sound scriptural credentials, perceptions of the nature and role of the celestial beings in the afterlife persisted, albeit in modified forms. Angels were less theologically suspicious in Protestant eyes than purgatory, transubstantiation, and veneration of the saints, and the inherently benevolent character of good angels meant that they were soon appropriated by reforming clergymen struggling to convert the laity to the true faith.

Perhaps the most noticeable characteristics of apocalyptic angels are the elements of continuity they represent. Descriptions of the last days continue to be replete with references to the angelic role in line with

their prominence in the book of Revelation. A sermon by John Bradford, published in 1562, related that 'with Angells of thy power, with a
mightie cry, shoute of an Archangell, blast of a trompe' the end of the
world is brought about, and Henry Bull's *Christian praiers*, published in
1568, also mentioned that angels perform the traditional celestial
responsibility of gathering together the souls of the saved.[4] The angelic
duty of standing witness during personal judgement was not forgotten
either, as Richard Day mentioned in 1578: 'my sinnes shal be opened in
ye sight of so many Angels, and not my misdeeds only, but thoughts
and words'.[5]

More specifically, reformed angels in commentaries on Revelation
and in sermons touching on the events of the Final Judgement betray
qualities that are entirely in keeping with pre-Reformation perceptions
of their roles. For example, in his *Praelections vpon the sacred and holy
Reuelation of S. Iohn*, William Fulke described how angels 'yelded
reuerence to God, with due submission', being 'continually most redely
prepared to the obedience of god'.[6] The notion of angels as fellow
worshippers of the Godhead alongside humankind was popular
amongst reformers, and the sentiment was enshrined in the Preface in
the Book of Common Prayer communion service.[7] Fulke also expanded
on the obedience of angels, introducing another theme that was particularly popular among Protestant authors, which was the notion that
angels provided a pious model for a godly life, 'an example of
aungelicall obedience, to the rule whereof we ought to frame our
obedience'.[8]

The sources also make reference to the most frequently mentioned
characteristic of angels, which was also an area of agreement amongst
the reformers – that they were provided by God because of the inherent
moral weakness of humanity, a potent symbol of his mercy. In *A plaine
explanation of the whole Revelation of Saint John*, Thomas Cartwright
acknowledged this when he maintained that certain chapters of Revela-

[4] John Bradford, *Godlie meditations upon the Lordes prayer* (London, 1562), L2v–r; Henry
Bull, *Christian praiers and holie medtations* (London, 1578), 216–22.
[5] Richard Day, *A booke of Christian prayers* (London, 1578), 136.
[6] William Fulke, *Praelections vpon the sacred and holy Reuelation of S. Iohn, written in latine
by William Fulke Doctor of Diuinitie, and translated into English by George Gyffard* (London, 1573),
fols 47r, 50v–r.
[7] Joseph Ketley, ed., *The Two Liturgies A. D. 1549 and A. D. 1552 with other Documents set
forth by Authority in the Reign of King Edward VI* (Cambridge, 1844), 87, 278; William Clay, ed.,
Liturgical Services of the Reign of Queen Elizabeth (Cambridge, 1847), 193.
[8] Fulke, *Praelections*, fol. 192r.

tion are 'put in for the comfort of God's children'.[9] Again, this is a theme that can be found throughout Protestant religious culture. In his *Institutes of the Christian Religion* Calvin established the pattern when he noted that the Scriptures especially insisted that angels are given to men 'in accommodation to the weakness of our capacity'. Thus when God employs angels it is because of man's inherent frailty – when men are 'filled with alarm and despair' celestial beings provide a remedy and act as a source of comfort and courage for the Christian believer.[10] This supports the idea that the angels were in fact eagerly embraced by the reformers as an antidote to the more disquieting aspects of the Protestant message. The very existence of angels was heartening to the laity, and their presence at the Final Judgement is evidence, if any were needed, of God's continued interest in and care of his people.

Of course this interpretation is somewhat at odds with the general tenor of Revelation, in which angels are more likely to function as the instruments of divine punishment than divine mercy. This is not a novel idea, however, as angels had never been unambiguously benevolent powers, a fact that set them apart from the saints. Scripture casts celestial beings as dispensers of divine justice, such as when God intervenes to prevent an angel destroying Jerusalem when he is displeased with David (2 Samuel 24: 16). This dual character is remarked upon in the literature on Revelation, Fulke noting that 'the selfe same Aungels whiche are the Ministers of Gods wrathe and seueritie vpon the wicked, do serue the godlye to their comforte, and consolation, and to the buyldinge vp of the Churche'.[11] Cartwright expresses a very similar opinion, declaring that at the Last Judgement 'the selfe same Angels that are Executioners of Gods iudgements vpon the wicked, are also Ministers of Gods mercie for the comfort of his Children'.[12]

It appears that the evidence provided by these texts does not really chime with Ian Green's hypothesis, as there is no indication that the reformers were shying away from the implications of their altered system of soteriology. The numerous commentaries rolling off the presses were testimony to the awareness and interest in the funda-

---

[9] Thomas Cartwright, *A plaine explanation of the whole Revelation of Saint John* (London, 1622), 42.

[10] John Calvin, *The Institutes of the Christian Religion: A New Translation by Henry Beveridge*, 2 vols (Grand Rapids, MI, 1957), I: 145, 149 (1.14.8, 11).

[11] Fulke, *Praelections*, fol. 110v.

[12] Cartwright, *A plaine explanation*, 103.

mental doctrines found in Revelation,[13] and there is no sense in this literature that the reformers were being forced to moderate their belief in predestination in order to give it a more popular appeal. At this juncture it is also worth noting that there were traditional apocalyptic elements that are conspicuously absent in post-Reformation England. For example, the removal of religious imagery from parish churches saw the disappearance of the ubiquitous Doom painting, previously dominating the nave in its position high on the chancel arch. This also deprived the congregation of a perennially popular angelic image that was part of the Doom, that of Saint Michael the Archangel presiding over the weighing of souls at the Judgement, the scales determining whether the person was to be granted salvation and entrance to heaven. Devoid of scriptural authority, this angelic duty is nowhere to be found in reformed religious literature, and without the imagery to sustain it, the traditional perception was quietly laid to rest.

The tendency to interpret 'Michael', the slayer of the dragon in Revelation, as a portrayal of Christ may be an associated development. This trend pervades the sources, with numerous authors identifying Michael as the prince of heaven. Cartwright noted 'the principall in this battell is first Michael, to wit, Christ'.[14] This is also the interpretation that Philip Stubbes put in the mouth of his dying young bride in the biography of her life which became one of the most popular chapbooks of the late seventeenth century: experiencing the temptations of the devil on her deathbed she cried 'get thee packing, or else I wil cal vpon my grand-captaine Christ Iesus, that valiant Michael, who beat thee in Heauen, and threw thee downe to hell'.[15]

These readings are in stark contrast to pre-Reformation belief which credited the Archangel Michael with being the chief of the celestial army and instrument of Satan's downfall at the Final Judgement. Indeed, depictions of Michael's defeat of the dragon were the stock visual image of late medieval angelic iconography, appearing on rood

---

[13] See for example Thomas Brightman, *The Reuelation of S.Iohn illustrated with an analysis & scholions* (Leiden, 1616); John Napier, *A plaine discouery of the whole Reuelation of Saint Iohn* (Edinburgh, 1593); William Perkins, *Lectures vpon the three first chapters of the Reuelation* (London, 1604); Samuel Smith, *The great assize, or, Day of iubilee* (London, 1622).

[14] Cartwright, *A plaine explanation*, 75.

[15] Phillip Stubbes, *A christal glasse for christian Women containing, a most excellent discourse, of the godly life and Christian death of Mistresse Katherine Stubs* (London, 1592), fol. C3r; Alexandra Walsham, 'Stubbes, Philip (b. c. 1555, d. in or after 1610)', *ODNB*, <http://www.oxforddnb.com/view/article/26737>, accessed 10 December 2007.

screens and in stained glass windows, and giving the English gold coin, the 'angel', its name. The identification of Michael with Christ is very much in keeping with reformed ideology, however, the subtle shift in understanding drawing attention to the absolutely fundamental Protestant tenet that Christ was the only mediator. Reformers were anxious to jettison any aspect of angelology that might lead their parishioners into error, and the cult of the Archangel Michael bore too close a resemblance to the cult of the saints for comfort. Subsequently, it is not surprising that Michael's role in Revelation was played down, redirecting attention to Christ instead, depersonalizing heavenly beings and making them less familial, and therefore less likely to attract the sin of idolatry.

These casualties of the reforming zeal again suggest that Protestants were not being forced to accommodate earlier religious traditions in order to make their new understanding of salvation more palatable to the laity. The survival of traditional understandings of the roles of angels at the Last Judgement indicates the large element of continuity that characterized the reformers' perceptions of what would happen to them after death. There were elements of change, however, as a process has been revealed whereby older belief was stripped of its non-scriptural features and dubious legacies were quietly suppressed. The result was a distinct understanding of angels that was entirely in line with the reformed world-view and which conformed wholesale to scriptural origins. However, recent historical scholarship on the Apocalypse suggests another potentially fruitful approach to the text.

The book of Revelation has attracted much attention from both contemporaries and historians, for, as Paul Christianson remarks in his study of apocalyptic visions, 'Revelation formed a veritable microcosm of holy writ and provided the Christian believer with a mirror in which he could discern his own true estate and the type of church to which he belonged.'[16] Accordingly, scholars such as Christianson, Bernard Capp, and Katherine Firth have ceased to consider the seventeenth century as awash with irrational eschatological expectations, perceiving rational and persuasive elements to the concepts and analysing them in light of this.[17] John Bale in *The image of bothe churches* is understood to have been

[16] Paul Christianson, *Reformers and Babylon: English Apocalyptic Visions from the Reformation to the Eve of the Civil War* (London, 1978), 15.
[17] See ibid.; Bernard Capp, *Astrology and the Popular Press: English Almanacs 1500–1800* (London, 1979), 164–78; idem, 'The Political Dimension of Apocalyptic Thought', in C. A.

the first of many who saw Revelation as the key to the past and present, providing an allegorical explanation of the upheavals of the Reformation and the rejection of Catholicism, a tradition that was later taken up and built upon by John Foxe in his *Actes and Monuments*.[18] Each viewed Christian history as a continuing struggle between the 'true' church, based on Jesus' teachings in the gospel, and the 'false' Church of Rome, subverted by the Antichrist and by the misinterpretation of Scripture. This reading of Revelation became the mainstream tradition, assuming a crucial part in the defence of the Church of England and solving the problem of lineage and authority by providing reformers with an answer to the question 'Where was your church before Luther?'

However, it is not only a polemical understanding of Revelation in its capacity as a prophecy of God's plan for the world that has received scholarly attention. In a recent article Patrick O'Banion lamented the tendency for the book to be considered mainly in association with its contribution to the roots of radical seventeenth-century English apocalypticism, a tendency which has led to a teleological approach where interpretation focuses on the development towards radicalism. O'Banion makes a plea for the pastoral significance of the book to be reinstated, arguing that Revelation was not only used as a tool for descrying the future or unlocking the meaning of the past, but also as a 'source of comfort for the present sufferings of readers'.[19] He identifies two groups of writings in early modern eschatological literature whose authors display distinct intentions and objectives when expounding Revelation: the first he categorizes as the 'playne and easye' group, whose professed aim is making the book accessible to the 'common sort' of believers; the second group are works similar to those of Bale and Foxe, intended for an educated audience and propagating sophisticated and speculative interpretations.

O'Banion's approach is a useful one, which is strengthened when angels are brought into the centre of the picture. His 'playne and easye' authors include Fulke and Cartwright, on whose works I have been focusing in the course of this essay. Such texts do not shy away from the

Patrides and Joseph Wittereich, eds, *The Apocalypse in English Renaissance Thought and Literature* (Manchester, 1984), 93–124; Katherine Firth, *The Apocalyptic Tradition in Reformation Britain 1530–1645* (Oxford, 1979).

[18] John Bale, *The image of bothe churches after reuelacion of saynt Iohan the euangelyst* (Antwerp, 1545); John Foxe, *Actes and Monuments of these latter and perilous days* (London, 1563).

[19] Patrick O'Banion, 'The Pastoral Use of the Book of Revelation in Late Tudor England', *JEH* 57 (2006), 711–37, at 702.

fact that angels will be the instruments of God's righteousness after death, but they frequently offer consolation through a variety of means. For example, Cartwright argued that 'God in his righteous judgement giues them [angels] power to hurt and deceiue', but this is tempered by the knowledge that they will be the means by which the 'ouerthrowe and ruine of Babell' will be achieved. Cartwright is keen to make a distinction between the different types of angels or messengers in Revelation, maintaining that this demonstrates that 'the gifts of God are diuerse in his ministers; as namely, some of exhortation, some of denouncing iudgements'.[20] The underlying message is simple: the day of judgement will be terrible for unrepentant sinners, but the elect can look forward to the end of suffering and eternal life among the angels, and this is a substantial consolation.

These texts set out to perpetuate the message that the Apocalypse is a reasonable working out of God's providential justice, and that ultimately it is more merciful than wrathful. The final episode of Revelation is crucial here, as this is the part of the book that foretells what existence will be like after the second coming of Christ. Angels figure large in discussions of this heavenly state. For Arthur Dent the chapter is designed to 'enlarge the ioyes of Gods people' through its description of the heavenly city with angels stationed at every gate, and other texts perpetuate the message: in 1613 the Bishop of Bangor, Lewis Bayly, in his *Practice of pietie directing a Christian how to walke*, talked of the bliss that will be felt when the soul will 'behold thousand thousandes of Cherubims, Seraphims, Angels, Thrones, Dominions, Principalities, Powers'.[21]

It is clear that within these sources angels *do* assume pastoral roles and they are discussed in terms that emphasize the rewards they offer to humankind. However, this does not mean that these authors are attempting to downplay the more severe aspects of the Protestant message on predestination. Rather they are crafting their message carefully to emphasize the fairness and justice of God's providential plan, detailing the impressive extent of his wrath yet also reminding the reader of the mercy and wisdom of a God who will never neglect his special care for his chosen people. The angels that feature in Revelation

---

[20] Cartwright, *Plaine Explanation*, 87–88.
[21] Arthur Dent, *The ruine of Rome: or an exposition vpon the whole Reuelation* (London, 1603), 297–98; Lewis Bayly, *Practice of pietie directing a Christian how to walke* (London, 1613), 147.

are used as instruments to convey this message: faithful servants and messengers of the Lord's will, they provide protection for humanity but also smite the wicked and put down the forces of evil.

These sources therefore indicate the utility of heavenly beings in the fight to embed reformed ideas in the hearts and minds of the populace. Reformers were evidently confident enough of the usefulness and potency of angelic beings to enlist them eagerly in this struggle, apocalyptic angels providing just one example of a wider trend in which angels were proving increasingly useful in providing support for the Protestant message and the reformed perception of the functioning of the universe. The ubiquity of references to angels in the Bible meant that they were an especially useful tool to the reformers – rather than being forced to compromise with earlier angelic belief, it would appear that the reformers eagerly embraced celestial beings as a salve to the potentially alarming implications of the rejection of purgatory and endorsement of double predestination.

For some time the Reformation was seen as a largely destructive process, which destroyed the sophisticated structures of traditional belief without offering much to replace these. However, this survey of differing interpretations of the role of angels within the book of Revelation would appear to support recent scholarship that has challenged this supposition. It has shown that in this context it was possible for angels to retain a significant pastoral role as the comforters and protectors of humankind whilst simultaneously acting as the dispensers of God's divine wrath, in the process presenting the laity with an unflinching interpretation of double predestination. The message was not solely one of fire and brimstone because, as has been shown, these sources also reflected genuine attempts to supply comfort and consolation for the harsher truths on offer, mollifying understandable fears about the ultimate fate of the dead with the bright hope of eventual salvation and the promise of better things to come.

University of Warwick

HEAVEN AND HEAVENLY PIETY IN COLONIAL AMERICAN ELEGIES

by ADRIAN CHASTAIN WEIMER

WHEN the Massachusetts schoolteacher Benjamin Tompson pictured his unmarried sister Elizabeth in heaven, he saw her in a palace-like 'nunnerye' where 'Chast virgins have faire entertainment free'. Elizabeth and the other virgins in heaven 'Enjoy their purest love in sacred mirth' as 'Great Jesus daily steps of his bright throne / And gives them hart embraces every one.'[1] Colonial Puritan elegies such as this one challenge our inherited scholarly categories, which contrast a spiritualized Christian heaven with a corporeal Muslim one and set 'a distant, majestic [Protestant] God' in opposition to the intimate afterlife of medieval Catholic mystics.[2] The most interesting part about Elizabeth Tompson's elegy, however, is that she narrates it herself. Benjamin imagined her speaking to him from the bosom of Christ, saying 'I Dare not tell what hear in heart i find', and then going on to describe her experience of the afterlife in the first person. Christ leads her to the top of a 'mount of pleasure' where, she says, 'i [have] all [the] flowers of paradice to Crop.' A Protestant saint embracing a physical Jesus, picking flowers to her heart's content, and telling her brother about it – these are all images which challenge our notions of early modern views of heaven and demonstrate the fruitfulness of elegies, or funeral poems, for opening up the imaginative worlds of early modern belief.

Historians have most often argued that when Protestants did away with purgatory, prayers for the dead and nearly all funerary ritual, they unwittingly isolated believers from their deceased friends and relatives. The Office of the Dead, a ubiquitous medieval liturgy offered on behalf of souls in purgatory, had been, Natalie Zemon Davis writes, a form of ritual communication that helped to establish the dead as an 'age group … to put alongside the children, the youth, the married, and the old'.

---

[1] Benjamin Tompson, 'The Amiable Virgin Memorized – Elizabeth Tompson' (1712), in Kenneth Murdock, ed., *Handkerchiefs from Paul* (New York, 1970), 9–10.

[2] Philip Almond, *Heaven and Hell in Enlightenment England* (New York, 1994), 105; Colleen McDannell and Bernhard Lang, *Heaven: A History* (London, 2001), 176–78.

When it was proscribed, Protestant believers were left 'more alone with their memories, more vulnerable to the prick of the past', and, in the words of Keith Thomas, 'each generation could be indifferent to the spiritual fate of its predecessor'.[3] In one sense, these scholars are right. No godly man or woman in Puritan New England would have believed they were actually interacting with a deceased friend or relative. At the same time, elegies reveal ambiguity in the firmness of the boundary between the living and the dead. Written by laypeople and ministers alike, circulated among mourners, and pinned to the coffin, these rough poems provide hints about the ways Protestants in early New England continued to negotiate the presence of departed saints in their own lives, revealing an imaginative openness to the ongoing role of the Church in heaven in the Church on earth.[4]

Porosity in the boundary between earth and heaven is not surprising when we remember the ways Puritan ministers conceptualized heaven itself. In catechisms and elegies, heaven is not infrequently referred to as 'the third heaven', drawing on the apostle Paul's account of a mystical experience in 2 Corinthians 12. Thomas Shepard's catechism describes the 'third heaven' both as a location and as an ongoing experience: it is 'a most glorious place above the starry heaven … to which the soules of just men goe when they depart this world', and it is also a place 'wherein … they are to have their conversation in the world'.[5] This conflation of the realm of the afterlife with Paul's ecstatic journey and a Christian's daily conversation (or habits) highlights the practical, experiential nature of Puritan views of heaven.

Popular treatments of colonial New England, influenced by the textbook-ubiquity of Jonathan Edwards's sermon 'Sinners in the Hands of an Angry God', assume hellfire to have been more prevalent than heavenly bliss in Puritan imaginations, yet Puritan literature on heaven

---

3 Natalie Zemon Davis, 'Ghosts, Kin, and Progeny: Some Features of Family Life in Early Modern France', *Daedalus* 106 (1977), 87–114, at 92, 96; Keith Thomas, *Religion and the Decline of Magic: Studies in Popular Beliefs in Sixteenth and Seventeenth Century England* (New York, 1970), 603. See also Andrea Brady, *English Funerary Elegy in the Seventeenth Century: Laws in Mourning* (New York, 2006), 53.

4 Ian Green, *Print and Protestantism in Early Modern England* (New York, 2000), 383; David D. Hall, 'Scribal Publication in Seventeenth-Century New England: An Introduction and Checklist', *Proceedings of the American Antiquarian Society* 115 (2006), 29–80, at 35–36; Gordon Geddes, *Welcome Joy: Death in Puritan New England* (Ann Arbor, MI, 1981), 130.

5 Thomas Shepard, *A Short Catechism familiarly teaching the knowledg* [sic] *of God, and of our selves…* (Cambridge, [MA], 1654), 11.

is surprisingly rich.[6] In one sense all of Puritan spirituality was about the pursuit of heaven: 'life was to get ready for afterlife, for salvation in its full sense.'[7] The Puritan afterlife was conceived as glorification, the final stage in the order of salvation (*ordo salutis*, the stages of Christian experience). It began on earth through communion with Christ in prayer and culminated when the believer was fully united with Christ after death.[8] One of the last things which Cambridge, Massachusetts, minister Jonathan Mitchel wrote in his journal was a reminder to himself: 'Heaven is here begun upon Earth: shall I be Thinking on, and Talking with, Christ, to all Eternity, and not Discourse with Him, one quarter of an Hour in a Day now?'[9]

While it has yet to be explored in any depth, we know there was a movement later in the seventeenth century towards devotional meditation on heaven. In this prayerful and discursive quest for 'heavenlymindedness', devotional manuals instructed believers how to 'call forth, by a meditative process emphasizing the sense and the imagination, some foretaste of heavenly joys'.[10] Tracts such as Richard Sibbes's *A Glance of Heaven* (1638), Joseph Hall's *The Invisible World* (1651), and, the most well-known of all, Richard Baxter's *The Saints Everlasting Rest* (1650), encouraged the faithful to imagine themselves partaking of the sights and sounds of heaven along with the departed saints.[11] In New England this movement seems to have dovetailed with the late seventeenth-century interest in devotional preparation for the Lord's Supper. Thomas Shepard explained the connection in his *Theses Sabbaticae* when he described the 'holy Rest of the Sabbath' as 'the twilight and dawning of Heaven'.[12] Though few would go so far in assigning their own role as

---

[6] Carl R. Trueman, 'Heaven and Hell in Puritan Theology', *Epworth Review* 22 (1995), 75–85. It is true, however, that even in their works on heaven, New England Puritans spent some time describing the pains of hell.

[7] Charles Hambrick-Stowe, *The Practice of Piety: Puritan Devotional Disciplines in Seventeenth Century New-England* (Chapel Hill, NC, 1982), 219.

[8] Ibid. 152; Sargent Bush, Jr, *The Writings of Thomas Hooker: Spiritual Adventure in Two Worlds* (Madison, WI, 1980), 299; Trueman, 'Heaven and Hell'.

[9] Cotton Mather, *Ecclesiastes, The Life of the Reverend & Excellent Jonathan Mitchel: a Pastor of the church*... (Boston, [MA], 1697), 105.

[10] Barbara Lewalski, *Protestant Poetics and the Seventeenth-century Religious Lyric* (Princeton, NJ, 1979), 162–64.

[11] Ibid. 166.

[12] Thomas Shepard, *Theses Sabbaticae: Or, The doctrine of the Sabbath* ... (London, 1650), 79; Hambrick-Stowe, *Practice of Piety*, 98. Though not devotional manuals, early New England treatises on the afterlife include Jonathan Mitchel's *A discourse of the glory to which God hath called believers by Jesus Christ* ... (London, 1677; Boston, [MA], 1721) and Increase Mather, *Meditations on the glory of the heavenly world* (Boston, [MA], 1711).

'assistant' as Cotton Mather did in his *Coelestinus: A Conversation in Heaven, Quickened and Assisted by Cotton Mather,* colonists did see explorations of the nature of heaven as a potent spiritual resource. It is in their elegies, above all, that we find laypeople and ministers expressing their imaginative conceptions of the afterlife and the ongoing influence of the Protestant saints.

In accord with the immediacy and experiential nature of heaven in Puritan literature, elegists vividly articulated a sense of permeability in the boundary between this life and the next.[13] This connectedness between heaven and earth took three primary forms. The first was an insistence that heaven had already been experienced on earth through prayer, and so devotion to Christ formed a strong continuity between earth and heaven. The second appears in imaginative communications from the saints in heaven, and the third is expressed in the conviction that the saints' piety continued to circulate in New England churches as their memories were kept alive. While literal encounters were proscribed, there was nonetheless a sense of close connectedness, even of being 'graffted … [t]o all in Heaven' through Christ.[14]

Elegists commonly reflected on the ways people had experienced heaven before arriving there. So John Cotton 'Convers'd in Heaven while he was on Earth', Nathanael Mather 'liv'd in Heaven whilst on Earth', and Mary Tompson was known during her life for the 'entercourse twixt heau'n & her'.[15] This dynamic of access to heaven through prayer and devotional exercises had the potential to expand to access to the saints in heaven themselves. Mourners for Mary Gerrish were told they could reach her through devotion to Christ: 'You want her Much: SEEK HER IN CHRIST / AND YOU WILL FIND HER THERE.' As a kind of foretaste of this communication they were also told of Gerrish's continuing desires for those on earth. She was now 'Joyn'd to the

---

[13] For a view that emphasizes the 'great gulf' and 'marked contrast' between earth and heaven in seventeenth-century thought, epitomized by the contrast between 'suffering' and 'felicity', see Almond, *Heaven and Hell*, 110.

[14] Edward Taylor, Meditation 1.29, in *The Poems of Edward Taylor*, ed. Donald E. Stanford (Chapel Hill, NC, 1989), 47.

[15] Benjamin Woodbridge, 'Upon the TOMB of the most Reverend Mr. John Cotton …', in Harrison T. Meserole, *American Poetry of the Seventeenth Century* (University Park, PA, 1985), 410; R. Hale, 'Epitaph for Nathanael Mather', in Cotton Mather, *Early piety, exemplified in the life and death of Mr. Nathanael Mather …* (London, 1689), 60; Benjamin Tompson, 'A short memorial & Revew of sum Vertues in that exemplary Christian Mary Tompson …' (1679), in Murdock, ed., *Handkerchiefs*, 5.

Church in Heav'n' even though she had never become a full church member on earth (i.e. one who gained access to the Lord's Supper by giving a relation of her experience of grace), and 'craves, by Friends here left ... to be Visited' and to see everyone 'at th' Heav'nly Table fed'.[16] In a later treatise, Cotton Mather would develop this idea further, urging his readers to ask and seek for 'Communion with the Departed Saints' as a part of pursuing sanctity and experiencing 'a Conversation in Heaven'. By imagining the enjoyments, manner of worship and earthly accomplishments of the departed saints, men and women could, in a sense, 'go up thither after them'. Mather insisted: '[i]t will be no faulty Necromancy for us thus to Converse with the Dead: and partake in the Joys of their Heaven with them.'[17]

As indicated by Mather's aversion to necromancy, on a literal level no orthodox Puritan would have initiated a conversation with the dead. John Fiske was expressing the orthodoxy of his community when, in an elegy on John Cotton, he asked him questions, but acknowledged 'thou no Answer give or shall'.[18] At the same time, ambiguity in the boundary between the living and the dead is revealed in the surprising number of elegies written in the first person, as imaginative messages from the afterlife.

These first-person elegies are sometimes prefixed with a poetic conceit of a mystical experience on the part of the writer that enables him to hear the voice of the deceased. So John Saffin began his elegy on John Hull, 'My lowly Muse now takes her flight on high / I am Envellop'd in an Extasie / As one Surrounded with some Dazleing Ray, / Mee thinks I heare his blessed Genious say ...'. And Cotton Mather, writing in the voice of Nathanael Collins's parents, described 'Thick Mists amain / About us gathering; a Murmur there / Of the blest Shade himself we then might here [hear]'.[19] The voice of Collins himself narrates the bulk of the poem, until 'He vanisht; They [his parents]

16 John Danforth, 'Profit and Loss: An Elegy Upon the Decease of Mrs. Mary Gerrish ...' (1710), in Meserole, *American Poetry*, 317–19.
17 Cotton Mather, *Coelestinus: A conversation in heaven, quickened and assisted by Cotton Mather* (London, 1723), 39–42, 54.
18 John Fiske, 'Upon the much-to-be lamented desease of the Reverend Mr John Cotton ...', in Meserole, *American Poetry*, 187.
19 John Saffin, 'An Elegie On the Deploreable Departure of the Honered and truly Religious Chieftain John Hull ...' (1683), in Meserole, *American Poetry*, 201–02; Cotton Mather, *An elegy on the much-to-be-deplored death of that never-to-be-forgotten person, the Reverend Nathanael Collins...* (Boston, [MA], 1684), 17.

retir'd; confused I [Mather] / Now quite alone …'.[20] Most often, however, these elegies begin abruptly in the voice of the deceased.

The imagery in the first-person elegies tends to be more vivid and concrete than that in other elegies, as the saints speak from their experience to console, exhort and inform the living about the realities of heaven. Lydia Minot's narrative takes over at the moment of death: 'When Breath expir'd my Life cam flowing in'. She describes the 'New Light, new Love, new Joy' she is given, as well as her 'New Robes' and her new musical 'Skill' to join in the heavenly 'new Song'.[21] In Benjamin Tompson's hands Edmund Davie depicts heaven as a Renaissance court, with angels instead of nobility, and each saint reigning on bejewelled streets with 'piles of Scepters, Diadems of Gold'.[22]

The voices from the afterlife urge the living not to weep, but to attend to their own souls. Abigaill Tompson, who died walking in the snow to church while her husband was away preaching in Virginia, tells her husband that she has been conducted 'Into a better Church' and pleads urgently, 'O, if thou euer louest me at all, / Whom thou didst by such loueing titles Call … Then do not thou my Death too much deplore.'[23] Edward Taylor has Samuel Hooker pleading with his wife: 'My Honey, mourn no more for mee … But stay thy Sorrow: bless my Babes. Obey.'[24]

Tension arises in these poems when the bliss of heaven is coloured by the saints' concern for their family on earth. Abigaill Tompson confesses: 'i do hope for the to Come err long / To sing thy part in this

[20] Cotton Mather, *Nathanael Collins*, 20.

[21] Anon., *Upon the death of the virtuous and religious Mrs. Lydia Minot …* (Cambridge, [MA], 1668). On pastoral imagery, see John Knott, 'Milton's Heaven', *Proceedings of the Modern Language Association* 85 (1970), 487–95, at 487–88. In spite of a lack of consensus among Protestant theologians on the ability of the soul to experience full bliss before reunion with the body at the resurrection, most colonists did not seem bothered by the problem. William M. Spellman, 'Between Death and Judgment: Conflicting Images of the Afterlife in Late Seventeenth-Century English Eulogies', *HThR* 87 (1994), 49–65, at 49–51; Brady, *English Funerary Elegy*, 41–42; Trueman, 'Heaven and Hell', 76–77.

[22] Tompson, 'Edmund Davie', in Meserole, *American Poetry*, 223; on Renaissance court imagery, see Knott, 'Milton's Heaven', 488–89. For more on angels in early modern culture, including their common role, also found in the elegies, of escorting saints to heaven, see Peter Marshall, 'Angels around the Deathbed: Variations on a Theme in the English Art of Dying', in Alexandra Walsham and Peter Marshall, eds, *Angels in the Early Modern World* (New York, 2006), 83–103, at 85, 94, 98.

[23] Wilson, 'Anagram made by mr John Willson of Boston upon the Death of Mrs. Abigaill Tompson …', in Murdock, ed., *Handkerchiefs*, 8–9.

[24] Taylor, 'An Elegy upon the Death of that Holy and Reverend Man of God, Mr. Samuel Hooker', in *Poems of Edward Taylor* (New Haven, CT, 1960), 483.

most glorious song.'[25] Elizabeth Stetson, who died delivering twins, urges her husband Samuel to 'season' her children 'With truths Divine' and teach them to 'avoid' the 'Doctrines of Devils'. She also feels concern for the sorrow of her friends on earth, an emotion which William Witherel, her elegist, couches in the conditional mood for the sake of meticulous orthodoxy: 'Could Griefs climb hither, I should grieved be, / To see my Friends, grieve and lament for me.'[26] The heavenly saints' concern for their friends and family on earth reveals strain in the lived theology of Puritan communities over whether grief could intrude on heaven, and the extent to which the dead remained emotionally connected to the living.

In keeping with the consolatory function of elegies, however, these messages from the afterlife affirm to the living that the person they have lost is indeed now in heaven, enjoying peace and bliss. This message could be especially important in situations where the person had not found peace on earth. William Tompson, who in the last decade of life was plagued with severe depression, told his children not to weep, for 'My pains are Cur[e]d, no greif doth me anoy'.[27]

The godly also felt connected to the inhabitants of heaven through the ongoing circulation of their virtue in the memory of the living. In a fascinating counterpoint to the prevalent jeremiad theme – that the death of New England's worthies spelled judgement and potential disaster for the colonies – elegies affirm repeatedly that those in the afterlife could continue to nourish the Church on earth as stories of their piety were told and retold. The activity here was partly simple imitation: friends and family could end up in heaven by following the example of the deceased's piety. But much of the language also implies a spiritual infusion of their sanctity.

We see this circulation of virtue most frequently in elegies on popular New England ministers. For example, John Cotton, in an elegy written by John Fiske, identifies himself as a source of grace and enrichment after death: 'And eeke remind that once I was, and blesse / that Hand that me you lent, yea and confesse / your portion greate that his

[25] Wilson, 'Anagram', in Murdock, ed., *Handkerchiefs*, 8–9.

[26] William Witherel, *Upon the immature death of that virtuous and truly religious young woman Elizabeth Stetson* . . . (Boston, [MA], 1682).

[27] Samuel Danforth, 'William Tompson, anagram I; lo, now i am past ill', and 'anagram 2: now i am slipt home', in Murdock, ed., *Handkerchiefs*, 19–20.

rich grace in Mee / enricheth you, abids, tho cea'st I bee'.[28] Benjamin Woodbridge, also writing on Cotton, affirmed, 'His death hath made him an Ubiquitary: / Where is his Sepulchre is hard to tell, / Who in a thousand Sepulchres doth dwell; / (Their Hearts, I mean, whom he hath left behind,) / In them his Sacred Relique's now Enshrin'd.'[29] In this interesting adaptation of the Catholic concept of a saint's reliquary, Cotton's exemplary piety continued to influence his earthly flock. In a similar way, Urian Oakes describing Thomas Shepard wrote, 'But live he shall in many a gratefull Breast / Where he hath rear'd himself a Monument … Could you but into th' Hearts of thousands peep, There would you read his Name engraven deep.'[30]

Cotton and Shepard's ministries extended beyond the grave: '[e]legy rendered the piety of the dead into a circulating commodity. Released by death and redistributed by the poet throughout the grieving community, the holiness of the deceased was thereby placed within reach of all who mourned the loss properly.'[31] In Puritan minister John Norton's succinct formulation, 'It is the priviledg of the blessed who lived in Heaven, whilst they lived on Earth; That they may live on Earth, whilst they live in Heaven.'[32] Norton explained this relationship by drawing upon the description of Abel in Hebrews 11, who 'being dead, yet speaketh'. 'And 'tis a part of the Portion of the Saints, that (together with the benefit of the living) they may enjoy both the life and death of those, who both lived and dyed in the Faith.' The godly on earth could continue to enjoy the spiritual resources of the saints in heaven.

The ongoing circulation of the piety of the saints in heaven also drew on the story of Elijah and Elisha from 2 Kings 2. In the Biblical narrative Elisha, wracked with grief at the translation of Elijah to heaven, suddenly, through Elijah's cloak, inherits a double portion of his mentor's prophetic spirit and power. In the elegies the spirit of the

[28] John Fiske, 'Ad Matronam pietissimam spectatissimamque Ipsius domini vixit Conthoralem dilectissimam Sobolemque eique Charissimum John Cotton', in Harold Jantz, ed., *First Century of New England Verse* (New York, 1962), 122.

[29] Woodbridge, 'Upon the TOMB of the most Reverend Mr. John Cotton …', in Meserole, *American Poetry,* 411.

[30] Urian Oakes, 'An Elegie upon that Reverend, Learned, Eminently Pious, and Singularly Accomplished Divine, my ever Honoured BROTHER Mr. Thomas Shepard …', in Meserole, *American Poetry*, 211.

[31] Jeffrey Hammond, *The American Puritan Elegy* (Cambridge, 2000), 157.

[32] John Norton, *Abel being Dead Yet Speaketh* (Boston, [MA], 1658), 3.

deceased could fall not on one protégé, but on many. An elegist for John Wilson prayed, 'Lord pour a double portion / Of his sweet, gracious, pious Spirit / On poor Survivers! let each one / Somewhat thereof at least inherit!'[33]

The ongoing availability of the piety of the dead for the community on earth in one sense offers a counterbalance to the theme of judgement in many jeremiad sermons, articulated in such phrases as 'Our sins have slain our Shepard!'[34] An elegy on Zechariah Symmes juxtaposes the two themes directly. In classic jeremiad tradition, the colonists, on the occasion of Symmes's death, 'may justly feare / we are forsaken of a loveing god' unless they 'morne and repent returne and mend our wayes / and for chastisements great Jehoveh praise'. Yet they may also 'pray that he would make elishas to inherit / a dubele porttion of elijahs sperit / and that he would be plesd to give to all / that standing pillow that will never fall'.[35] Symmes's death could thus be interpreted both as a judgement and as an opportunity for inheriting an infusion of piety.

Connecticut minister John James summarized the impulse to retain the influence of the deceased in economic terms: 'May Heaven, that takes our Treasures, make Retrievements!' The circulation of the piety of the saints in heaven still placed the burden on the living, however, to avail themselves of this resource. Though the 'goodness' of saints such as the magistrate John Haynes 'could ... circulate around' and form a channel of 'heavens influence', offsetting the community's bereavement, it is only a 'few' who 'do his Steps pursue' in such a way that they benefit from his piety.[36] The 'precious useful Memory' of the saints in heaven could cause 'everlasting Gains' only for 'wise Improvers', in a dynamic that may have added to, rather than simply balanced, the weighty moral imperatives of the jeremiads.[37]

[33] Nathaniel Morton, *New Englands Memoriall* (Cambridge, [MA], 1669), 187. See also John Danforth, *A funeral elegy humbly dedicated to the renowned memory of the Honorable, Thomas Danforth Esq. of Cambridge ...* (Boston, [MA], 1699); Benjamin Colman, 'A POEM on ELIJAHS Translation, Occasion'd by the DEATH of ... Samuel Willard', in Meserole, *American Poetry*, 343–46.

[34] Urian Oakes, 'Thomas Shepard', in Meserole, *American Poetry*, 219.

[35] Anon., 'Lines on the Death of Rev. Zechariah Symmes', *The New England Historical and Genealogical Register* 13 (1859), 207.

[36] John James, 'On the Decease of the Religious and Honourable Jno Haynes' (1713), in Meserole, *American Poetry*, 426.

[37] John Danforth, 'Two vast Enjoyments commemorated, and two great Bereavements lamented, in two excellent Persons, viz. the Reverend Mr. PETER THACHER ... And the

We do not, in early Puritan New England, find encounters with ghosts, miraculous interventions by saints, or literal conversations with the dead.[38] Even so, the Church in the afterlife continued to play an important role in the life of the community. As literary scholars have found, these elegies 'attempt to maintain a lineage between the living and the dead'.[39] While the deceased may not have been an 'age group' in the same way that they were for medieval Christians, Puritan elegies bear witness to an interaction, and even a kind of transfer of virtue, between the dead and the living.

We now know that the paradisal afterlife, as well as the burning underworld, occupied prime and colourful terrain in the imaginations of early New Englanders. It was not, however, uncomplicated territory. Much remains to be done to understand the anxieties, as well as the desires, of Puritan men and women as they relate to the life to come. There is some evidence that thinking about heaven too much had its own perils. As Giles Firmin, a former New Englander and relation of Massachusetts governor John Winthrop, expressed, there was a serious danger 'of screwing weak ones too high' so that their meditations on heaven would 'increase their sorrows'.[40] Conversing in heaven while living on earth was no easy ideal. In a culture where the most deep-rooted fear was of hypocrisy, or self-deluded security that might keep you from a true experience of grace, contemplating hell might seem safer than letting the mind visit heaven. Yet this reservation did not extend to friends and relatives who had made the journey already. Their residence and their piety were secure, at least in the world of the elegies. By imagining messages from their family and friends in heaven, and by appropriating their piety for the living, believers might vicariously participate in their assurance: the afterlife was a realm, above all, where salvation could not be counterfeit.

Harvard University

Reverend Mr. SAMUEL DANFORTH ...', in Meserole, *American Poetry*, 314.

38 David D. Hall, *Worlds of Wonder, Days of Judgment: Popular Religious Belief in Early New England* (Cambridge, MA, 1989), 295 n. 130.

39 Brady, *English Funerary Elegy*, 209–10; Hammond, *American Puritan Elegy*, 148.

40 Giles Firmin, *Meditations upon Mr. Baxter's review of his treatise of the duty of heavenly meditation ...* (London, 1672), 9. See also Richard Baxter, *The Duty of Heavenly Meditation: reviewed by Richard Baxter at the invitation of Mr. Giles Firmin's exceptions ...* (London, 1671), 4.

'BUT WHERE SHALL MY SOUL REPOSE?': NONCONFORMITY, SCIENCE AND THE GEOGRAPHY OF THE AFTERLIFE, c. 1660–1720

by ANDREW CAMBERS

L IFE, the afterlife, and life beyond the Earth are matters of scientific inquiry as well as religious belief. As we might expect, in the wake of the scientific revolution of the seventeenth century, the afterlife was subjected to new scrutiny. Such scrutiny, notably the demonology of Joseph Glanvill and Henry More, both fellows of the Royal Society, was undoubtedly scientific and serious, even if it has rarely been treated as such by scholars preferring to treat belief in witchcraft as a hangover from an earlier age.[1] Far from being opposed, or necessarily pulling in opposite directions, the conjunction of science and religion in this era breathed new life into old problems and opened up new questions for debate. One such area, with a long history as a philosophical conundrum, was the possibility of life beyond Earth. It is this question, its place within religious cultures, and its relation to traditional ideas about the afterlife, that is the subject of this essay.

The possibility of a plurality of worlds had a long history as a philosophical parlour game, from Epicurus in the ancient world to Nicholas of Cusa in medieval Europe. But the revolutionary discoveries of Copernicus gave new emphasis to the plurality of worlds as a *real* and not just a *theoretical* problem. And with the optical advances of Kepler and Galileo, man gained the potential not only to debate but also to observe extra-terrestrial life-forms. The debates about the plurality of worlds became real and urgent.[2] As David Cressy has shown, the seemingly playful English works about the possibility of life on the Moon, such as John Wilkins's *The Discovery of a World in the Moone* (London, 1638) and Francis Godwin's *The Man in the Moone* (London, 1638), in

---

[1] Joseph Glanvill, *Saducismus triumphatus* (London, 1681). For a powerful corrective, see Stuart Clark, *Thinking with Demons: The Idea of Witchcraft in Early Modern Europe* (Oxford, 1997), ch. 19.
[2] On the plurality of worlds, see especially Giordano Bruno, *De l'infinito universo e mondi* (London, 1584); Nicholas Hill, *Philosophia epicurea, democritiana, theophrastica* (Paris, 1601); Johannes Kepler, *Dissertatio cum nuncio sidereo* (Prague, 1610); Philip Melanchthon, *Initia doctrina physicae* (Wittenberg, 1550).

fact confronted serious philosophical and scientific problems and raised important theological questions: did other worlds compete with Earth for God's attention? Did God show them his love and his anger? Did their inhabitants share in Adam's sin and benefit from Christ's atonement, or did Christ die only for earthlings?[3]

These questions, which were debated throughout Europe and with reference to faraway planets, as well as Earth's nearest neighbours, were not airbrushed out of the mechanical universe – they persisted into the eighteenth century.[4] They surfaced in Descartes's physics and Pascal's terror about the 'infinite spaces' of the universe which harboured life ignorant of the wonders of Earth. And they were important in the scientific and theological debates about the sacred history of the Earth. Although at odds over their readings of Scripture, Thomas Burnet's *The theory of the earth* (London, 1681–89, in Latin; London, 1684–90, in English) and William Whiston's A *new theory of the earth* (London, 1696) both saw the world ending in a second deluge and final conflagration. Such theories prompted vital questions of what would happen thereafter and where it would take place. In what follows, I trace the story of an individual digesting these debates and thinking about the nature of the afterlife.

* * *

That individual is John Rastrick. Born in Lincolnshire in 1650 and educated at Trinity College, Cambridge, Rastrick was first the conforming Vicar of Kirton, near Boston, from 1673 until, troubled by his conscience and his bishop, he resigned his post in 1687. In 1688 he became the Dissenting minister at Spalding, Lincolnshire, where he stayed until 1697, when he accepted an invitation to move to Rotherham in Yorkshire. In 1701, Rastrick moved to the Presbyterian meeting at Spinner Lane, King's Lynn, where he stayed until his death in 1727. Throughout his career, within and without the Church of England, Rastrick was a divisive character with a talent for rubbing people up the wrong way and a gift for interpreting the misfortunes of others as the intervention of the providence of God. His personal life was just as complex: he married three times; his intimate spiritual rela-

---

[3] See David Cressy, 'Early Modern Space Travel and the English Man in the Moon', *AHR* 111 (2006), 961–82.

[4] For example, Emanuel Swedenborg, *De telluribus in mundo nostri* (London, 1758). Unlike Swedenborg, not everyone claimed to be able to communicate with extra-terrestrials.

tions with maidservants caused contention; he had twenty-three children; and he made a string of personal and professional enemies.

Rastrick was brought up on the classic devotional literature of early Stuart England yet developed an enduring love for the works of Richard Baxter (1615–91). His theology was complex and (on his account) frequently misunderstood by his opponents – who branded him a Baxterian and an Arminian – and sometimes by his former friends – who decried his 'Pelagianism Popery and Heresie'. Rastrick could hardly object to being called a Baxterian but – in a seemingly heated debate over the universal sufficiency of Christ's death – insisted that he was not an Arminian because he agreed with the judgement of the Synod of Dort (1618–19) and in any case he believed that God's grace was extended only to the elect.[5] A well-read individual, Rastrick had a highly developed understanding of the workings of the universe. His ideas about theology and natural history throw considerable light onto a series of debates surrounding the afterlife. They are contained in a lengthy appendix to a manuscript entitled 'Plain and Easy Principles of Christian Religion and Obedience; or The necessity of keeping Christ's Commandments'. Although the manuscript is now lost, we can get some idea of its contents from the description of it provided by the Baptist minister and historian William Richards.[6]

The manuscript was a commentary on John 15: 10 and apparently written as a response to the Salter's Hall dispute of 1719 – the meeting of London ministers which was designed to settle the question of whether the Dissenters should be required to subscribe to a creedal statement affirming the doctrine of the Trinity (to distance themselves from Arianism) but which in the end served only to shatter any doctrinal unity that Presbyterians, Independents and Baptists still shared. Rastrick's manuscript was also informed by a careful reading of the vitriolic printed exchanges between the Arian-leaning Samuel Clarke (1675–1729) and his follower John Jackson (1686–1763) and the orthodox Whig Daniel Waterland (1683–1740) over the doctrine of the

[5] This biographical sketch is drawn from San Marino, CA, Huntington Library, MS HM 6131, 'A narrative; or an historical account of the most materiall passages in the life of John Rastrick etc.' For further detail, see Andrew Cambers, ed., *The Life of John Rastrick, 1650–1727* (Cambridge, forthcoming). Rastrick made reference to the Canons of the Synod of Dort, ch. 2, art. 6 (*The Judgement of the Synode holden at Dort, Concerning the five Articles* (London, 1619), 19): 'But forasmuch as many beeing called by the Gospel doe not repent, nor beleeve in Christ, but perish in their infidelitie, this comes not to passe for want of, or by any insuffiency of the sacrifice of Christ offered upon the crosse, but by their owne proper fault.'

[6] See *ODNB*, s.v. 'Richards, William (1749–1818)'.

Trinity which had preceded and precipitated the Salter's Hall dispute. Rastrick apparently agreed with the Presbyterian minister James Peirce (1674–1726) in the debate – and so presumably denied that he was an Arian but argued that Christ was subordinate in the Trinity. Doubtless, Rastrick's position was also informed by what he described as the 'antinomian' faction among his congregation in King's Lynn.[7] The manuscript was lengthy and carefully presented. Rastrick pinned to it a letter to his son William urging him to publish it – 'I leave it to you to tell the world' – and to attach the letters he had received from Samuel Wright (1683–1746) and his own 'last Thoughts about the Trinity and Son of God'.[8] According to Richards, this appendix contains 'many striking and curious thoughts':

> Some of those thoughts relate to the *Theory of Comets*, which he supposed to be worlds in a state of conflagration and dissolution; and he thought it probable our Earth will hereafter become a comet and be seen as such in remote regions of the universe. This comet state of a heavenly body he considered as a state of judgment, and indicating the previous apostasy and irreclaimable impenitence or rebellion of its rational inhabitants, which caused the very world they inhabited to be so devoted to destruction. Each of those devoted worlds, he thought, had its *saviour* and offers of mercy sent to it long previous to that awful and fatal catastrophe. Christ he believed to be the saviour only of this world ...[9]

In thinking with comets, Rastrick was far from alone. Comets occupied a central role in the sacred physics of the late seventeenth century, whether in writings about the natural history of the Earth or in ideas about its future. As such, the astronomical discoveries of Halley and Newton should be interpreted within, rather than opposed to, an astrological framework, as Simon Schaffer has argued. The task of natural philosophy 'was to locate the restorative, transformative and prophetic effects of astronomical signs'.[10] Newton's vision of the solar system as a

---

[7] Rastrick did not elaborate on the theology of the 'antinomian' faction, but his use of the term was more likely polemical than descriptive.

[8] See William Richards, *The History of Lynn*, 2 vols (Lynn, 1812), 2: 1063–64. For Salter's Hall, see Michael. R. Watts, *The Dissenters*, 2 vols (Oxford, 1978–95), 1: 371–82. The publications of Clarke, Jackson, Waterland and Peirce are well charted in *ODNB*.

[9] Richards, *History of Lynn*, 2: 1060–61.

[10] Simon Schaffer, 'Newton's Comets and the Transformation of Astrology', in Patrick Curry, ed., *Astrology, Science and Society: Historical Essays* (Woodbridge, 1987), 219–43, at 219.

stable system of forces raised the importance of comets in explaining change. Comets passing close to the Earth were thus the key forces of change in Whiston's *New Theory of the Earth*, as Christian millennial hopes were transposed from eschatology onto nature.[11] In Whiston's account, the Earth was created when a comet was knocked off its path to orbit the Sun; the impact of a comet presaged the end of paradise, jolting the Earth from its axis and creating seasons, winds and tides; the Flood occurred as a result of the tail of a comet passing too close to the Earth; and it was to be the heat of a passing comet which would dry the oceans and bring fire (and the end) to the Earth. After the millennium and the final conflagration, the Earth would be hit by another comet, be pushed off its orbit and become a comet once more. As Philip Almond notes, with considerable understatement, 'cometology was the key to Whiston's theory of the earth'.[12]

The notes on Rastrick's missing treatise, in which he conceived of comets as former worlds burning through space in judgement for the sins of their inhabitants, can, of course, only take us so far. However, his other writings – a printed account of his Nonconformity; a remarkable manuscript autobiography; an extensive book of reading notes, draft dialogues and sermons; some intriguing poetry; a series of letters; and a will – shed further light on his own opinions and on how he received and adapted the substance of Whiston's work. They show, far from the centres of England's intellectual life, a learned if eccentric minister grappling with the challenges posed to his understanding of the after-life by the new science.[13]

Perhaps unsurprisingly, Rastrick's printed publications shed little light on his opinions about the afterlife. The same is true of the letters,

---

[11] Roy Porter, *The Making of Geology: Earth Science in Britain 1660–1815* (Cambridge, 1977), 87.

[12] Philip C. Almond, *Heaven and Hell in Enlightenment England* (Cambridge, 1994), 127.

[13] John Rastrick, *An account of the nonconformity of John Rastrick, M. A. Sometime Vicar of Kirkton, near Boston, in Lincolnshire* (London, 1705); Huntington Library, MS HM 6131; Washington, DC, Folger Shakespeare Library, MS V. a. 472, 'Note-book of a dissenting minister, ca. 1695–1707'. Rastrick's poems are reproduced in Richards, *History of Lynn*, 2: 1065–66; Sylvanus Urban, *The Gentleman's Magazine: and Historical Chronicle* 59 (1789), 1033–34, with commentary at 977; and John Evans, *Memoirs of the Life and Writings of the Rev. William Richards* (Chiswick, 1819), 163. For Rastrick's letters, see D. H. Atkinson, *Ralph Thoresby the Topographer: His Town and Times*, 2 vols (Leeds, 1885–87), 2: 418–19; *The Diary of Ralph Thoresby*, ed. J. Hunter, 2 vols (London, 1830), 2: 331–2; and London, Dr Williams's Library, MS 24.115, fols 44–46. For Rastrick's will, see Norwich, Norfolk Record Office, Will Register, Kirke, 82–84.

although they display his engagement with contemporary scientific debates, and also of his notebook, which focused instead upon issues like baptism and on the practical problems he faced in his ministry. His epitaph, at St Nicholas' Chapel, King's Lynn, goes little further, alluding to a man 'of remarkable study and pains; / And an adept in almost every part of learning/ But especially the mathematics.'[14] Rastrick's will talks conventionally, if suggestively, of his 'departure out of this world' and his 'hopes of a glorious resurrection to eternall Life thro' the merits of Jesus Christ'. More interestingly, it also informs us that Rastrick had the tools with which to observe the stars – he left his son William his books, manuscripts, mathematical instruments, double barometer and telescopes.[15]

More informative is Rastrick's manuscript autobiography which was written some time after 1713. This sets out Rastrick's life story, from his birth, upbringing and education, through to his career and ministry, family and enemies. The autobiography is punctuated by his ideas about the afterlife. As a teenager, his fears were heightened by books about heaven and hell. As an undergraduate at Cambridge in the 1660s, a melancholic Rastrick was tormented by the temptations of Satan and fears of an early death. He recalled how he became 'a great Observer of Signs', using books of astrology to mark up the Calendar in his Prayer Book with the 'criticall or unlucky days'. He was fixated by the descriptions of the punishments awaiting sinners in hell in the books he read and they fuelled his spiritual anxieties: 'Why,' he wrote, 'do I not make my whole life a continued act and trade of Prayer and Praise and the Worship of God? Can I make God and eternall happiness too sure? What if I should finally miss of Heaven? What then!?'[16] Such fears were perhaps conventional but Rastrick's blend of practical divinity and science, his equal admiration for Richard Baxter and René Descartes, caused consternation among his hearers when he moved from Cambridge out into the world, notably in July 1676, when he preached at Boston on Ephesians 2: 2 with the subject 'A Saint or a Devil', combining stories of spirits with ideas drawn from the works of Henry More, one of the most important proponents of the reality of witchcraft in Restoration England. Rastrick's learned appreciation of this debate

---

[14] Richards, *History of Lynn*, 2: 1062.
[15] Norwich, Norfolk Record Office, Will Register, Kirke, 83.
[16] Huntington Library, MS HM 6131, fols 14v, 16r, 29r.

appears to have done him little good, however, and he recalled that the sermon was 'received with laughter and Contempt'.[17]

To his credit, Rastrick continued his education after he left Cambridge, whether he pulled on his boots or pulled out his books. His autobiography describes a remarkable trip through the Peak District in 1697, which (by his own account) prompted him to read Burnet's *Theory of the Earth*, debate the presence of fish skeletons on high mountains, and think about the formation of the planet. Rastrick was struck with awe at the sight of Peak Cavern at Castleton (commonly known as the Devil's Arse) and with fear at Elden Hole (a pit near Castleton which was believed to be bottomless). The latter, he recalled: made him 'Shrink in my bed that night to think on it. The Lord save us from the Bottomless Pit.' In the study, Rastrick plunged himself further into astronomy and mathematics:

> I soon became wedded to the Copernican Hypothesis or the Pythagorick Scheme and System of the World unable to resist the Evidence I saw for it. The Thoughts I had of the Frame of the World and Order of the Creation the Multiplicity of habitable earths like this of ours (which I thought most highly probable) and especially of the vast Extent of the Universe were thoughts that at once surprised, enterteined, and amazed me! I often tryed in my mind to think or suppose that there were or should be nothing, no World, and I could not. I tryed to limit the Universe, or if I could suppose or believe that it has limits, and I could not: for let me travail never so far in my thoughts into the Universe and above the starry Firmament and I was constrained to think and believe that there must be something thick or thin i.e. Space empty or full beyond it; and this also into what Quarter soever my mind or Fancy darted it Self!

These ideas – of the multiplicity of worlds and the infinity of the universe – confirmed his belief in God: 'O then methought how wonderfully Great is God, and how incomprehensible the Divine Immensity!' He became convinced 'that the World is in God' rather than 'God is in the World!' and 'was assured that all our Conceptions of him as a Person … are false; and that God is rather a Nature … than a person'.[18]

---

[17] Ibid. fol. 52r.
[18] Ibid. fols 60r–61r, 74r–v.

Not only was his view of God unconventional, especially for a man who accused his opponents in King's Lynn of denying the Trinity, but his view of the afterlife followed suit. He was convinced that 'the Ethereall Interspaces' were 'inhabited with blessed Spirits, and conteined the Mansions of the Noblest Beings'. And that the dead – 'seperated Souls' – 'acquired new Senses by which the invisible world they go into and the things of it are known and discerned'. These ideas were deeply informed by reading the works of Henry More, Boyle and Hooke and by studying optics, 'so much as might help me in some measure to understand a Tellescope'.[19]

Rastrick's influences were undoubtedly diverse, but it seems clear that his ideas were shaped not only by the new work of Burnet and Whiston but also by the older work of Henry More. Rastrick had met More as a student and recalled discussing with him how the inhabitants of other planets might survive after the Sun had been extinguished. More's early work, in particular his poetry, drew on the discoveries of Galileo, Copernicus and Descartes, and highlighted his belief in the immortality of the soul. Two relatively early works had a pronounced impact upon Rastrick's ideas: *Democritus Platonissans* and *The Immortality of the Soul*. The latter work expounded More's belief in the reality of spirits. The treatise speculated about the impediments to the immortality of the soul, especially the idea of a final conflagration of the Earth and the subsequent predicament of the souls of men and demons. More argued that those souls which had gained their 'aetherial vehicles' would be out of the reach of the fire, while 'the unrecovered souls of wicked men and daemons' would burn. Life was not confined to Earth and he suggested that there were other planets where souls – 'aethereal creatures' – lived. He put the matter more simply in verse in *Democritus Platonissans*:

> ... long ago there Earths have been
> Peopled with men and beasts before this Earth,
> And after this shall be again
> And other beasts and other humane birth.
> Which once admit, no strength that reason bear'th
> Of this worlds Date and Adams efformation,
> Another Adam once received breath
> And still another in endlesse repedation,
> And this must perish once by finall conflagration.

19 Ibid. fols 74v–75r.

As evidence, More pointed to the 'flaming Comets wandering on high', and argued that 'Some Comets be but single Planets brent.'[20]

That More's works, alongside those of Burnet and Whiston, had continued influence is clear when we turn to Rastrick's own poetry. Two of Rastrick's poems survive, both undated. Addressed to his daughter Martha (1699–1756) and thus the product of his adult life, 'An evening hymn' is ambiguous. It reads:

> Now that *the Sun* hath veil'd his light,
>   And bid the world good night,
> To the soft bed my body I dispose –
>   But where shall my soul repose?
> Great God! even in thy arms; and can there be
>   Any so sweet security? –
> Then to thy Rest, my soul, and sing in praise
>   The mercy that prolongs thy days!

On one level this might be read, taking up More's ideas from *The Immortality of the Soul*, as a meditation on what happens to souls after the Sun has expired.[21]

Rastrick's longer poem, 'The dissolution', which in the absence of an easily accessible modern edition is printed in full below, offers the most fully elaborated picture of his imaginative vision of the final conflagration. It reads:

> Happy the man, to whom the Sacred Muse
> Her nightly visit pays;
> And, with her magic rod,
> Opens his mortal eyes:
> He Nature at one glance surveys,
> And past and future, near and distant, views.
>
> I'm mounted on Fancy, and long to be gone
> To some age or some world unknown:
> Swifter than Time, and impatient of stay,
> To the West, to the uttermost limit of day,
> To the end of the world, I'll hasten away;

[20] Ibid. fol. 74v; Henry More, *The immortality of the soul* (London, 1659), 529, 541; idem, *Democritus platonissans; or, an essay upon the infinity of worlds out of platonick principles* (Cambridge, 1646), stanzas 76, 77, 93.

[21] John Rastrick, 'An evening hymn', in Evans, *William Richards*, 163.

Where I may see it all expire,
And melt away in everlasting fire.

'Tis done! – I see a flaming Seraph fly,
And light his flambeau at the Sun:
Then, hastening down, to the curst globe
His blazing torch apply.
See the green forests crackling burn!
The oily pastures sweat
With intolerable heat!
The mines to hot volcanos turn!
Their horrid jaws, extended wide,
The sulphurous contagion spread.
Why do the aged mountains skip?
And little hills, like their own sheep,
Like lambs, which on their grizzly head
Once wanton play'd?
Expanded vapours, struggling to the birth,
Roar in the bowels of the earth.
And now the earth's foundations crack assunder,
Burst with subterraneous thunder:
Dusky flames, and livid flashes,
Rend the trembling Globe to ashes;
Fiery torrents, rolling down,
The naked valleys drown;
And, with their ruddy waves, supply
The channels of th'exhausted sea.
Seas, to thin vapours boil'd away,
Leave their crooked channels dry:
And not one drop returns again,
To cool the thirsty earth with rain.

And must all earth th'impartial ruin share?
Spare, ye revengeful Angels! spare,
Spare the Muses' blissful seat!
Let me for *Wickham's* peaceful walls intreat.
No! 'tis in vain! and *Bodley's* spicy nest
Of learning too must perish with the rest.
THE ORACLES OF GOD alone
An hasty Angel snatch'd away,

And bore them high, through parted flames,
To the Eternal Throne.

Behold fond soul, all thou didst once admire!
The objects of thy hope, and thy desire;
Houses, and lands, and large estate;
The little things that make men great;
The empty trifles are no more,
But vanish all in smoke, scarce lighter than before!

Was it for this the statesman rack'd his thought!
Was it for this the soldier fought!
While grumbling drums like thunder beat,
And clanging trumpets rais'd the martial heat!

I burn! my soul is all on flame!
The raging image fires my brain!
Cool it, ye Sacred Nine,
In Aganippe's flowing stream,
Lest I pursue the noble theme too long,
Let frequent rests stop the bold song!

Now Nature is unstrung!
The Spheres their musick lose!
The song of ages now
Ends in a solemn close!

The poem gets us as close as we can to Rastrick's ideas about the apocalypse and the afterlife, at least in the absence of his manuscript. Taking us 'To some age or some world unknown', Rastrick confirms in verse his belief in the reality of the plurality of worlds. At 'the end of the world', he sees the Earth 'melt away in everlasting fire'. Rastrick's characterization of the horrors of the final conflagration is clearly informed by Whiston's writings, but the work of Henry More is never far from the surface, and Rastrick's own idiosyncrasies are also present, notably his pondering the fate of the Bodleian Library shortly before the burning of souls in the final conflagration.[22]

For all their cosmic significance, debates about the history of early

---

[22] John Rastrick, 'The dissolution', as printed in Sylvanus Urban, *The Gentleman's Magazine: and Historical Chronicle* 59 (1789), 1033–34. An alternative version, lacking one verse, is reproduced in Richards, *History of Lynn*, 2: 1065–6.

modern religion are often strangely earthbound, more at home in the diocese and deanery than on the Moon or in the Milky Way. Although Rastrick's ideas, in particular those relating to life on other planets, were not mainstream, neither were they unthinking. They were informed by a conjunction of scientific debates, from Henry More through to William Whiston, and religious ideas, and he took some care in reconciling the ramifications of the new science with his own religious culture without stepping over the line into theological error. If Rastrick's ideas sound a little like early science fiction, or a Nonconformist's space odyssey, it is perhaps no coincidence. They certainly bring to mind Swift's flying island of Laputa, whose inhabitants he mocked in *Gulliver's Travels* for their dread of 'celestial bodies', their conviction that the next comet to pass close by the Earth would reduce it to ashes, and their fears that the Sun would in the end expire and bring an end to those planets which relied on its light. Swift sneered at Whig credulity and the outlandish ideas of the likes of Whiston about comets. But, as this short excursion into John Rastrick's views about the afterlife has shown, ideas about life on comets and the final conflagration were not so very far from the practical life of the ministry on Earth.[23]

Lancaster University

---

[23] Jonathan Swift, *Gulliver's Travels* (London, 1726), Part 3, ch. 2; for Laputa as a satire on Whiston, see Chris Wroth, 'Swift's "Flying Island": Buttons and Bomb-Vessels', *Review of English Studies* 42 (1991), 343–60.

THE CHINESE RITES CONTROVERSY: CONFUCIAN AND CHRISTIAN VIEWS ON THE AFTERLIFE

by PAUL RULE

T HE Chinese Rites Controversy is a question that is as much ecclesiastical or missiological as sinological, and the researcher, therefore, has to attempt to embrace two very complex and demanding fields.[1] It was, of course, an argument about cross-cultural understanding (and misunderstanding), and the peculiarities of Chinese religion and language; and an episode in the fraught historical relations between China and the West. But the controversy itself was ecclesiastical, among ecclesiastics, and it was the papacy and its offices which determined the outcome.

What embittered the argument, which lasted in the Catholic Church from the early seventeenth to the mid-eighteenth century (with a coda, the so-called 'terms controversy' among Protestant missionaries in the nineteenth century), were theological and institutional *partis pris*. The Chinese Rites Controversy became a proxy battle-ground over Augustinian pessimism, especially in its Jansenist form; over grace, between Jesuits and Dominicans; and (most fundamental of all) over the theology of religions, the question of salvation outside Christianity.

Moreover, and this brings me to the theme of this volume, the vast controversial literature in many languages, published and unpublished, which has occupied me for a long time is mostly concerned with questions of understandings of an afterlife. Are the dead still existing, still in contact with the living? How should they be approached or celebrated?

---

[1] The writer's current major research projects fortuitously straddle the two. The first is a multi-volume history of the Chinese Rites Controversy, which has been conducted under the auspices of the Ricci Institute for Chinese-Western Cultural History at the University of San Francisco, which has a unique collection of manuscripts, copies of archival material and rare books collected by Francis Rouleau, SJ, and augmented by the founding Director, Edward Malatesta, SJ. I am also editing for the Macau Ricci Institute an English translation of the most important document of the Chinese Rites Controversy, the *Acta Pekinensia*, a Latin account, running to nearly 1,500 pages, of the activities in China from 1705 to 1710 of the papal legate, Charles Maillard de Tournon. A preliminary account of the controversy is to be found in Paul A. Rule, *K'ung-tzu or Confucius? The Jesuit Interpretation of Confucianism* (Sydney, 1986), chs 2–3.

Are some more deserving of special respect and ritualizing than others? Can the dead help the living, and the living the dead? Are Chinese understandings of such issues compatible with Christian understandings (and I use the plural advisedly in both cases)? And, centrally, are rituals in their honour 'worship' and hence idolatrous?

These questions, ecclesiastical and theological, will then be the focus of my paper. Only indirectly will I address the substantive issue of the nature of the rituals in question. However, to understand the problems faced by early modern Christians in China, it is necessary to begin with some remarks about earlier attempts to preach monotheistic religions in the Chinese social and religious environment.

Monotheism in China

It could be argued that the key issues of the Chinese Rites Controversy, the appropriate Chinese names for the Christian God (in shorthand, 'terms') and the moral permissibility of Christians performing ancestor rituals and rituals in honour of Confucius ('rites'), can be found causing concern to all proponents of monotheism in China, and, indeed, all proponents of non-indigenous religions, as far back as records go. Even Buddhism, which eventually was accepted as a Chinese religion, had a long struggle to inculturate its otherworldliness and monastic tradition to Chinese humanism and familism.[2] Not the least controversial was the Buddhist doctrine of *anatta*, 'no soul', as received by a people whose major religious activities centred on the spirits of the dead. Chinese Buddhism became a soul-centred religion with elaborate rituals to ensure the successful entry of the souls of the dead into paradise. Its transformation demonstrated that no introduced religion could neglect rituals for the dead.

But there was a special problem for the monotheistic world religions: Judaism, Christianity and Islam. Exclusivism of belief and cult was never part of the indigenous tradition. There was an official orthodoxy, a state authoritarianism supported by a privileged Confucian scholar-official class, which prosecuted overt public expressions of heterodoxy, whether in the form of sectarian activities or moral and ritual deviancy:[3] but even those entrusted with its implementation, and

---

[2] See E. Zürcher, *The Buddhist Conquest of China*, 2 vols (Leiden, 1959).

[3] The best history of this remains J. J. M. de Groot, *Sectarianism and Religious Persecution in China: A Page in the History of Religions,* 2 vols (Leyden, 1901, repr. Taipei, 1963). While

certainly their women, often followed an eclectic personal religion. The fixation of early modern Christian missionaries in China on Confucianism led them, on the whole, to neglect not only the spiritual riches of the Chinese Buddhist and Daoist traditions – meditation and ascetic techniques, the rituals of everyday life and the seasons, and an elaborate eschatology – but also popular or folk religion. This was less true of missionaries in the provinces than those in Beijing: the writings of the former show an effective use of folk traditions of hungry ghosts, visions of the dead and moral retribution, in many ways reminiscent of medieval and early modern European folk religion.[4] Reluctantly, I must leave aside this fascinating and largely unexplored question.[5]

There was considerable adaptation in China of the God-language of Judaism and Islam and of the earliest Christians we know to have been in China, the Jing Jiao (Brilliant Religion) of the Tang.[6] We know nothing of the attitude of these Syrian Christians towards Chinese ancestor rituals or Confucius. Nor is there any evidence in the few surviving documents of accommodation to Chinese culture in terminology or ritual on the part of the thirteenth- and fourteenth-century western European Dominican and Franciscan friars who came to China during the Pax Mongolica. Perhaps in their case, as with that of the Syrian monks, their confinement to convents and monasteries largely insulated them from such problems. However, the Jews certainly, and probably at least some Muslims, practised ancestor rituals and expressed an admiration for Confucius, equating him with their own sages and patriarchs. Significantly, however, both Muslims and Jews excluded those holding official positions from mosque and synagogue respectively during their term of office. The grounds seem to have been

somewhat overstated, the documentation provides a devastating rebuttal of alleged Chinese tolerance.

[4] See Erik Zürcher, 'The Jesuit Mission in Fukien in Late Ming Times: Levels of Response', in E. B. Vermeer, ed., *Development and Decline of Fukien Province in the 17th and 18th Centuries* (Leiden, 1990), 417–57, and, in this volume, R. N. Swanson, 'Ghosts and Ghostbusters in the Middle Ages', 143–73.

[5] A major source for this is the record of the 'daily conversations' between Jesuit missionaries in Fuzhou and a large number of scholars, Christian and non-Christian, between 1630 and 1640, entitled *Kouduo richao*. An annotated English translation edited by Erik Zürcher has recently been published: *Kouduo richao. Li Jiubiao's Diary of Oral Admonitions. A Late Ming Christian Journal*, Monumenta Serica Monographs, 2 vols (Nettetal, 2007).

[6] On this form of Eastern Christianity, often misnamed 'Nestorian', introduced in the seventh century, see Roman Malek, ed., *The Chinese Face of Jesus Christ*, Volume 1 (Sankt Augustin, 2002), Part One.

twofold: obligatory participation in official sacrifices and the impossibility of observing dietary rules, both issues that arose in the later Chinese Rites Controversy.

Let me now attempt the impossible, a brief historical sketch of the enormously complex events that are generally labelled 'the Chinese Rites Controversy'.

The Internal Jesuit Debate on 'Terms'

The Jesuits were the first Christian missionaries effectively to evangelize China in the modern era. Beginning in 1582, they broke the prohibition on Europeans residing permanently in China proper. Almost by accident they adopted the felicitous term, *Tianzhu* ('Lord of Heaven') for the Christian God and this has resulted in the labelling of Chinese Catholic Christianity down to the present as the *Tianzhu Jiao*. *Tianzhu* implied an identification of their God with the ancient Chinese classical high god, *Tian* ('Heaven'), but without specifically claiming to do so. In their earliest works of apologetics such as Matteo Ricci's *Tianzhu Shiyi* ('The True meaning of the Lord of Heaven'), they further identified the attributes of the Christian God with those of *Tian* and the equivalent *Shangdi* ('Ruler on High').

These pioneer missionaries also appreciated the centrality of ritual in Confucianism as the key to ethics and good living. 'Master yourself and return to ritual and you will become fully human.'[7] Ricci and his companions were convinced from observing ancestor rituals, studying ritual texts and discussions with Chinese scholar-converts that such rituals were not idolatrous. The 'sacrifices' were offerings of food, flowers, and incense in memory of the dead, to incite their descendants to imitate their virtues. Some aspects of these rituals and of funerary rituals were perhaps superstitious but could be easily omitted as non-essential.

Matteo Ricci's view of the rituals in honour of Confucius was very straightforward. He wrote in his memoirs that 'the literati offer to [Confucius] a certain kind of sacrifice with incense and dead animals which they offer up, although they acknowledge no divinity in him and

---

[7] *The Analects of Confucius (Lun Yu)* 12: 1. 'Ritual' here is *li* in Chinese, a term with a semantic range far beyond liturgy or religious performance. It embraces all forms of correct social behaviour.

ask nothing of him. And so it cannot be called a true sacrifice'.[8] In other words, while it may be in a certain sense a 'religious' act, it is not an act of worship of the sort due to God alone. Later Jesuit polemicists complicated the issue unduly by denying there was anything religious in either ancestor rituals or Confucian rituals and declared them purely 'political'.[9] Ricci himself, educated in late Renaissance Christian humanism, saw such rituals as manifestations of a natural religion and, as such, precursors of revealed religion.

Ricci also believed that since the twelfth century there had been in the Ru Jiao, the teaching of the scholars,[10] a kind of secularization amounting at times to materialism and atheism. This even extended on the part of some to a denial of the immortality of the soul.[11] However, such an understanding of Neo-Confucianism, which has been contested recently,[12] would further strengthen the case for the permissibility of rituals in honour of Confucius. Atheists are not idolaters; militant materialists, rarely superstitious. But Ricci did not think that the Neo-Confucians denied the existence of spirit. Rather, they were monists.[13]

It was because he believed that the simple theism of the Chinese classics was more compatible with Christianity than the sophisticated metaphysics of Neo-Confucianism or Lixue, 'the Science of Principle', as the Chinese more appropriately label the philosophy of Zhu Xi (1130–1200), that Ricci advocated a return to 'original Confucianism'. But he was careful on the whole to avoid European labels for what he recognized as a very complex reality.

In the second generation of the Jesuit mission in China dissent arose from two chief sources. One was the influx of experienced missionaries after their expulsion from Japan who associated Confucianism with Buddhism and interpreted Chinese ideas and practices through Japanese glasses. The second came from Ricci's successor as head of the

[8] M. Ricci, *Storia dell'introduzione del Cristianesimo in Cina*, in *Fonti Ricciane*, ed. P. M. D'Elia, 3 vols (Roma, 1942), 1: 40 (paragraph N55).
[9] The term *politicus* in Latin embraced not just politics and government as in our usage, but the 'polite', correct behaviour.
[10] Despite the recent claim of Lionel Jensen in *Manufacturing Confucianism* (Durham, 1997), the Jesuits never used the term 'Confucianism', a nineteenth-century neologism.
[11] See D'Elia, ed., *Fonti Ricciane*, 1: 115–16 (paragraph N176).
[12] See R. C. Neville, *Boston Confucianism* (Albany, NY, 2000). Tu Wei-ming is perhaps the best known of the 'Boston Confucians', who argue for the religious nature of Confucianism, including Neo-Confucianism, and for its continuing relevance to modern society.
[13] D'Elia, ed., *Fonti Ricciane*, 1: 116 (paragraph N176).

mission, Niccolò Longobardo. But such dissent as there was never concerned rituals, always 'terms'. I can find no disagreement whatsoever over ancestor rites or Confucian rituals at any point during the first half-century of modern Chinese Christianity.

Longobardo's position has often been misrepresented as opposition to 'Chinese Rites',[14] but a close examination of the treatise in which his views are crystallized makes it clear that he was solely concerned with 'terms'. Further this sprang from his interpretation of Chinese tradition as being from the beginning materialistic, which should logically have ruled out idolatry and perhaps even superstition in Chinese rituals.

During the internal Jesuit dispute over terms in the 1620s Longobardo became an outspoken adherent of the party opposed to the use of *Tian* and *Shangdi* for the Christian God. He wrote a treatise on the subject around 1623 or 1624 entitled 'A brief reply on the controversies relating to *Tian*, *Tianshen*,[15] *Linghun*,[16] and other Chinese names and terms to determine which of them can and which of them cannot be used by Christians'.[17] When the Franciscan opponent of the Rites, Antonio Caballero de Santa Maria, came across the treatise in a Jesuit house in 1662, he seized on it as evidence of internal Jesuit dissent on 'Rites' before the advent of the Spanish friars in the 1630s. It become notorious through its publication in Spanish translation by the Dominican friar, Domingo Navarrete, in his *Tratados* (Madrid, 1676),[18] and even more through the French translation of 1701.[19]

It is curious that many eminent scholars have misread the 'Treatise'

[14] For example, in Joseph Needham, *Science and Civilisation in China*, 2: *History of Scientific Thought* (Cambridge, 1956), 500; and recently Benjamin Elman, *On their Own Terms* (Cambridge, MA, 2005), 161. This interpretation goes back as far as Antonio de Santa Maria, who in his letter to Propaganda Fide accompanying the treatise says 'there it will be seen whether or not the Chinese sacrifice to Confucius and their dead ancestors': Fortunato Margiotti, *Relationes et Epistolas Fratrum Minorum Hispanorum in Sinis qui a. 1697–1698 Missionum Ingressi Sunt*, eds Gaspar Han and Antolín Abad, Sinica Franciscana 9/2 (Madrid, 1995), 986.
[15] *Tianshen* ('heavenly spirit') was the term commonly used for angels.
[16] *Linghun* is one of many terms roughly corresponding to the Western notion of 'soul'.
[17] 'Reposta breve …', Rome, Historical Archives of the Congregation 'De Propaganda Fide' (now the Congregation for the Evangelization of Peoples), Scritture Referite nei Congressi, Indie Orientali e Cina, Vol. 1 (1623–1674), fols 145–68.
[18] *Tratados historicos, politicos, ethicos, y religiosos de la monarchia de China* (Madrid, 1676), especially 'Repuesta Breve', 246–89.
[19] *Traité sur quelques points de la religion des Chinois* (Paris, 1701); it was reprinted with critical annotations by Leibniz in his *Opera Omnia*, ed. L. Dutens (Geneva, 1768), 4: 89–144; and an English translation, 'A short answer concerning the controversy about Xang Ti, Tien Xim, and Ling Hoen …', is to be found in Navarrete, *An Account of the Empire of China*, (n. pl., n. d.; probably from Churchill's *Voyages*, 1704), Book V, 183–224.

PAUL RULE

or perhaps simply relied too heavily on second-hand authorities in categorizing it. And there is a marked imprecision of theological and anthropological language in their analysis. The great sinologist of the early twentieth century, Paul Demieville, says that Longobardo presents the Chinese as pantheistic and at the same time atheistic.[20] His successor at the College de France, Jacques Gernet, in *China and the Christian Impact*, correctly quotes Longobardo as claiming that 'their secret philosophy is pure materialism' but sees no problem with his further comment about it being a 'universal substance' which embraces non-material as well as material activities.[21] Neither see any problem with writing about 'the Chinese' (and both are prone to this kind of lumping together of very diverse systems of thought) being simultaneously materialists and idolaters.[22]

Longobardo's own confusions are partly responsible. He, like Ricci before him, simply could not deal with a non-dualistic system of thought. That most elusive of Chinese concepts, *qi*, at once physical energy and spiritual activity, was reduced by both to Aristotelean 'Prime Matter'. This was almost inevitable to anyone educated in the kind of Aristotelean scholasticism that culminated in the great Jesuit *Cursus Conimbricensis* (1593–1606). Since Zhu Xi insisted that *li* ('principle') and *qi* do not exist independently but combine to produce and explain all that is, they were read as form and matter respectively.

Longobardo has little to say about Chinese rituals. In one passage he seems bothered by the inconvenient fact that his Chinese materialists seem overly fond of rituals directed to spirits whose existence they deny.[23] He recognizes that there is something strange in the Chinese making offerings to their dead ancestors who are now nothing but 'Air'[24] (so he translates *qi*, probably by analogy with the Greek *ether*).[25]

---

[20] Paul Demiéville, 'The First Philosophical Contacts between China and Europe', *Diogenes* 58 (1967), 75–103, at 94.

[21] Jacques Gernet, *China and the Christian Impact* (Cambridge, 1985), 203.

[22] See the index to *China and the Christian Impact*, where under 'materialism' Gernet has 'see also idolatry' and under 'idolatry', 'see also materialism'.

[23] 'Short Answer', 206 (I will generally refer thus to the 1704 English edition which appears in the *Account of the Empire of China*, 183–224, under the title of 'A short answer concerning the controversies about *Xang Ti, Tien Xin*, and *Ling Hoen* ...'); cf. Navarrete, *Tratados*, 270.

[24] 'Short Answer', 210; cf. Navarrete, *Tratados*, 274.

[25] Leibniz's commentary on this is very shrewd. He seems to have found this talk of 'air' nonsensical and refuses to accept that this is the Chinese view. 'Tout le contraire', he wrote in the margin (*Opera*, ed. Dutens, 4: 125 n. 81). On an earlier mention of 'air' Leibniz pointed

286

Longobardo certainly did not regard such sacrifices to 'Air' as idolatry. In fact, he goes on to present the standard Confucian justification: 'When they shed the Wine, burnt Perfumes, slew Victims, and offer'd Pieces of Silk, all was to express the true respect of their Heart.'[26] But Navarrete in his notes to this section (and it must be remembered that these explanatory notes accompanied the text of Longobardo when first made public) concludes that all Chinese sacrifices are true sacrifices and hence idolatrous, and those to the dead are not of a different order to those to other Chinese spirits. 'Either', he says, 'they are all good, or all bad.'[27]

It is clear that Longobardo's 'Brief reply' to his confrères was solely concerned with the moral permissibility of using terms like *Tian* and *Shangdi* for the Christian God and that his dissertation on Chinese materialism was dedicated to demonstrating that as representations of this basic philosophy such terms could not be appropriate. But, to do so, besides tendentious translations and Europeanizing interpretations, he had also to reject Matteo Ricci's key distinction between ancient Confucianism and modern Confucianism. While this distinction is one which modern scholarship, Chinese and Western, accepts, Longobardo was on sound grounds in claiming that the late Ming Confucians did not see themselves as innovators but as continuing a 'Transmission of the Way' that went back to Mencius, Confucius and beyond them to the Sage Kings.

The Neo-Confucian naturalistic world-view was, perhaps, incompatible with traditional Christianity (a debate just beginning in Europe at the time), but its proponents could hardly be accused of *worshipping* Heaven and Earth, of idolatry. Yet this was just what Navarrete concluded. He wrote: 'From what has been said and shall be said it follows, that the Sect of the Learned has a religious Worship ... It is also a plain inference that the Learned are Idolaters.'[28] Leibniz, on the other hand, noted with impeccable logic in the margin of his copy of the French translation: 'It is then wrong to accuse them of invoking false gods.'[29] I

---

out that in European thought 'spirit' is analogously labelled 'air' (Greek *pneuma* / Latin *spiritus*). This led him to ask why the term *qi* should not be similarly metaphorical: ibid. 4: 116 n. 61.

26 'Short Answer', 210; cf. Navarrete, *Tratados*, 274.
27 Ibid.
28 'Short Answer', 207 n. 1.
29 Leibniz, *Opera*, ed. Dutens, 4: 120 n. 73: 'On les accuse donc à tort d'invoquer les faux Dieux.'

think the verdict on the implications must go to Leibniz. And there is no evidence that Longobardo saw it differently.

The issue of terms was finally solved by a general meeting of the Jesuits at Jiading in 1628, and the personal intervention of the Jesuit General in Rome upheld the majority position. *Tianzhu* was to be used as the normal name for God. It was legitimate to draw parallels between *Tianzhu* on the one hand and *Tian* or *Shangdi* on the other in works of apologetics, so long as all the connotations of the latter in Chinese discourse were not claimed as adequate or true.

The Spanish Friars Raise the Question of Rites

Soon, however, this hard-won consensus was again thrown into confusion by the arrival in China of Spanish friars, Dominican and Franciscan, from Manila.[30] Far too much has been made of the difference in missionary methods of Jesuits and friars.[31] The Jesuits accused the friars of marching through the streets displaying a crucifix, and the friars retorted that the Jesuits concealed the crucifixion even from their converts. The mendicant orders claimed the Jesuits were only interested in converting the high and mighty and lived a lavish lifestyle; the Jesuits pointed out that on many occasions the missions of the friars survived only through intervention at court or with local mandarins, and that Chinese customs required the public wearing of silk and observance of the customs of polite society. It is true that initially the friars followed a policy of direct and public evangelization derived from the missions of the New World and the Philippines, but experience quickly taught them that in China an indirect and literary apostolate was necessary. They too had to win over the all-powerful scholar-officials. They mostly worked in regions remote from the national and provincial capitals, but so did the majority of the Jesuits, very few of whom, even those at court, could be entitled 'missionary

[30] The best general history of the early missions of the Dominicans in China is Benno Biermann, *Die Anfänge der neueren Dominikermission im China* (Münster in Westfalen, 1927). On the Franciscans there is the continuing series of published letters and relations, Sinica Franciscana, 10 vols so far (various places, 1929 onwards). The best work on the Spanish Franciscans and the Chinese rites remains F. Margiotti, 'L'atteggiamento dei Francescani spagnoli nella questione dei riti cinesi', *Archivo Ibero-Americano* 38 (1978), 125–80.
[31] See J. S. Cummins, 'Two Missionary Methods in China: Mendicants and Jesuits', *Archivo Ibero-Americano* 38 (1978), 33–108, repr. in idem, *Jesuit and Friar in the Spanish Expansion to the East* (London, 1986), ch. 5.

288

and mandarin'.[32] And the notion of the Jesuits 'working from the top down' is a half-truth: they worked both ways from the beginning, but protection at the top was necessary for grassroots evangelization to flourish.

Nevertheless, from the very beginning of their mission the friars took up an oppositional position to the Jesuits on Chinese Rites. And on rituals themselves they were the first to ban them, and the first to bring the issue to Rome. Not only did they challenge the use of Chinese terms in Christian worship and teaching, they opposed their converts performing ancestor rituals and rituals in the Confucian hall (or 'temple' as they preferred to call it).

The alarm was raised by the Franciscan friar Antonio Caballero de Santa Maria and his Dominican companion Juan Bautista de Morales, who crossed from Manila to Fujian in June 1633. The story of their discovery of the terrible fact that the Jesuits were allowing their converts to 'worship' their ancestors is worth quoting at length in Diego Aduarte's account.[33] Fray Antonio was in Fu'an in Fujian studying Chinese:

> While this Father was engaged in studying a book printed in Chinese characters, he came across a letter pronounced *chi* or *zi*,[34] and not knowing its meaning, and not being able to understand it, he was obliged to ask for an explanation from a Christian who was teaching him: 'What does it really mean, Thaddeus (for that was what the said Christian was called)? He, not being able to make him understand any other way, said: 'Father, this letter means to sacrifice and is the same as what you have in the mass.'[35]

A few questions immediately come to mind. In what language was this

---

[32] A misconception spread by Arnold Rowbotham in his pioneering work *Missionary and Mandarin: The Jesuits at the Court of China* (Berkeley, CA, 1942). Very few of the 'Court Jesuits', or *Patres Pekinenses* as they called themselves, even those who actually worked for the emperor, were formally 'mandarins', i.e. holders of official positions. See my paper, 'Kangxi and the Jesuits: Missed Opportunity or Futile Hope?' (Dixième colloque international Ricci de sinologie, Paris, 6–8 septembre 2004), forthcoming in a volume edited by Michel Cartier.

[33] The whole passage from Aduarte, *Historia de la Provincia del Santo Rosario de la Orden de Predicadores en Philippinas, Japon, y China* (Manila, 1640), 1: 255ff, is given in Biermann, *Die Anfänge*, 44–45 n. 61.

[34] Presumably *ji*, the usual word for a ritual in which offerings of food, wine etc. are made.

[35] The Spanish reads: 'Padre, esta letra significa sacrificar, y explica lo mismo que vosostros haceis en la misa.'

conversation conducted? Antonio does not seem to have learned Chinese in Manila, unlike some Dominican friars who worked in the Chinese quarter there.[36] But it is even less likely that Thaddeus Wang spoke Spanish. So presumably poor Thaddeus, struggling to explain a term with many connotations deeply embedded in the complexities of Chinese society to a European with little Chinese in desperation, hit on the comparison with the Christian *misa*. It was after all a ritual action. It would surely be too much to interpret Thaddeus's remark as a theological statement: an act of worship such as Christians give to God.

But this is just what Antonio did. He asked Thaddeus whether Christians performed *ji* to their ancestors and was told they did. In great concern he wrote to Angelo Cocchi in Dingzhou, who interrogated his Christians who 'confessed':

> that all this Kingdom from the King down, young and old, have great reverence for and carry out a cult[37] of their ancestors and dead progenitors and offer them solemn sacrifices at their tombs or sumptuous temples[38] that they have built to this end in all the cities, towns and villages of the kingdom. Furthermore, they said that in all their houses they had tablets on which were written the names of the dead in this form: 'This is the seat or throne of the soul of such and such a deceased.' These tablets so inscribed were assembled on their corresponding altars, adorned with altar-cloths, candles, lamps and incense-sticks.

Cocchi continues:

> When I asked if the Christians in China participated in such sacrifices they replied, no;[39] but, that was not so, as we will see later, since they keep such tablets in their houses, make reverences to

---

[36] He had taught theology and worked with Japanese lepers in Manila with a view to trying to enter the now closed Japan.

[37] *Daban culto*, a highly prejudicial term given the implications of *cultus* in scholastic theology. Again what did they say in Chinese without begging the question of the meaning of expressions like *ji*?

[38] *Suntuosos templos*, again assuming they are 'temples' like Buddhist and Daoist temples. In South China there are often elaborate clan ancestral halls, unlike North China where the rituals are performed in domestic family shrines.

[39] There was probably a misunderstanding here over precisely which ancestor rituals were being discussed: domestic rituals or large public rituals in the clan *citang* which the Jesuits advised avoiding because of superstitious actions such as burning paper money on the part of non-Christian relatives.

them, keep incense-sticks burning before them; all in the kingdom observe this in common, Christians and non-Christians, in memory of the veneration that they owe to their progenitors and as a kind of polite behaviour,[40] owing from sons to fathers. When I grasped what was implied in this, my soul, going on what I had heard, determined that the whole of our Christian community that up until now we had made and retained in the whole kingdom, was nothing but a treaty of Christ with Belial and an Ark of the Covenant with Dagon.

The two friars in Fu'an, Caballero and Morales, having observed ancestor rituals of the Miu family, then proceeded in late 1635 to conduct a formal inquisition amongst the Christians as to the meaning of ancestor rituals and those in honour of Confucius. They had come from Manila armed with formal investigative powers from the Inquisition which suggests some degree at least of prejudgement. It is interesting too that they did not ask what Christians did or thought. They seem to have believed that there was some intrinsic unalterable meaning in a ritual enshrined in its name and independent of the intention. Their inquiry focused on whether 'the Chinese' (again that lumping of regions, classes and gender) were expecting favours of their ancestors. As the Franciscan historian Fortunato Margiotti notes, perhaps ironically, 'the results coincided perfectly with the opinions of the members of the tribunal, namely, that in the sacrifices they sought favours and help in their material and spiritual needs, hence the rituals involved superstition'.[41]

The great concern shown in this and the slightly later inquiry presided over by the Franciscan Provincial superior, Bermundez,[42] over whether the spirits of the dead were regarded as actually present and whether prayers of petition were offered to them must, I think, be placed in the context of contemporary theology. Heaven and hell seem to have been regarded as physical places in which the spirits of the dead were confined; hence to locate them in the tablets was, at the least, superstitious. I leave aside the question whether any Chinese really thought of the souls as residing in the tablets spatially 'like worms in a

[40] *Cortesia politica.*
[41] Margiotti, 'L'Atteggiamento', 134.
[42] Francesco de la Madre de Dios Bermudez de la Almeida, to give him his full name.

291

piece of wood or like little birds sitting on them', as one Jesuit wrote sarcastically.[43]

The anxiety over praying to, and seeking help from, the ancestors is again a product of contemporary ecclesiastical concerns. In Europe, and especially Spain, there was a vigorous campaign against alleged remnants of paganism and Jewish or Islamic notions.[44] This had been strengthened in the minds of the Spanish friars by their experience in Mexico of the tenacity of indigenous beliefs. Orthodoxy of 'cult' was a central concern of the Tridentine reformers.

But, it might be asked, did not the Dominicans at least share with the Jesuits a theology based on St Thomas Aquinas which should have resulted in a comparatively liberal attitude towards indigenous cultures?[45] The answer seems to be that by the early seventeenth century, partly as a result of the disputes over grace, the major Dominican theologians, while espousing strict Thomism, had adopted an 'Augustinianized Thomism' more closed to humanist perspectives and theological optimism.[46] As Pascal was to wickedly point out in his *Lettres provinciales*, it was hard to see any difference between the positions on grace of the French Dominicans and the Jansenists.

That the disputes were not just over rites but more general in scope is shown clearly in a letter of J. B. Morales to the Cardinals of Propaganda Fide. He accuses the Jesuits of 'erroneous doctrines and the worst sort of theology, as is seen in China and other places'. And he goes on to charge that 'the new church of China (following the teaching of the said Fathers) is not the Catholic Church but a schismatic one, full of a thousand errors and pagan superstitions',[47] a prime example of *odium theologicum.*

[43] Francisco Furtado, the Jesuit Vice-Provincial, in a reply to the friars written in 1640 but published only in 1700 as *Informatio Antiquissima de Praxi Missionariorum Sinensium Societatis...*, 2nd edn (Paris, 1700), 30–31.

[44] See William A. Christian, Jr, *Local Religion in Sixteenth-Century Spain* (Princeton, NJ, 1981); Jean Delumeau, *Catholicism between Luther and Voltaire: A New View of the Counter-Reformation* (London, 1977).

[45] See the treatments in Francis A. Sullivan, *Salvation Outside the Church?* (New York, 1992) of St Thomas's views (47–62) and of the liberal opinions of the Salamanca Dominicans Francisco de Vitoria, Melchior Cano and Domingo Soto (69–76); also James Muldoon, *Popes, Lawyers, and Infidels: The Church and the Non-Christian World 1250–1550* (Philadelphia, PA, 1979).

[46] See Emile Baudin, *Études historiques et critiques sur la philosophie de Pascal*, tome 2 (Neuchâtel, 1946), on the 'thomisme réaugustiné' of theologians like John of St Thomas, Domingo Bañez and Thomas de Lemos.

[47] Morales to Propaganda Fide, Manila, 15 October 1648; Rome, Historical Archives of

Not that theological differences alone explain the immediate and fierce challenge posed to the Jesuit practices by the newly arrived friars. There had long been hostility over the attempts of the Jesuits to exclude them first from Japan and then from China. Tensions between Spanish and Portuguese over the forcible union of the two kingdoms under the Spanish crown (1580–1640) had exacerbated relations between Manila and Macao. And the Dominican Province of San Gregorio, centred on the Philippines, had a proud tradition of ultra-asceticism and ultra-orthodoxy.

The attacks on Jesuit practices were not only on rites. There was a general attempt at 'Europeanizing' the Chinese Church, or, in a more benign interpretation, pulling China into the Tridentine mould of uniform law, liturgy and discipline. A long list of further complaints was made in the reports, first to the Archbishop of Manila then to Rome. The Jesuits had not enforced the positive law of the church on matters such as Sunday observance and fasting (they replied that it was impossible to observe the Sabbath in a ten-day market system, most of their converts could not afford meat, and in any case papal exemptions had been obtained much earlier). They allowed formal acts of respect to the emperor with formulas such as *wan wan sui* ('ten thousand times ten thousand years of life to the emperor'). They encouraged astrology (there was an ambiguity about this term in Europe as well as China, and the Jesuits' work in the Bureau of Astronomy in Beijing was incorporated in the imperial calendar with its listing of lucky and unlucky days). They allowed participation of Christian officials in rituals in the temple of the City God (which the Jesuits always denied). They did not preach that Confucius and the Sages of ancient China were in hell. They administered baptism to women omitting the application of saliva, salt and oil (a charge the Jesuits readily admitted, justifying it on grounds of Chinese notions of propriety). They allowed scholars and officials to attend rituals in honour of Confucius in the local Confucian temples (which the Jesuits counter-claimed were merely 'halls', places for lectures and study in which there were tablets – but not images – of Confucius and his major disciples). They allowed fruit, incense and candles to be placed before the coffins at funerals and on the graves at Chinese New Year and the Spring festival.

the Congregation 'de Propaganda Fide', Scritture Originali riferite nelle Congregazioni Generali: Informationum Libri, Lib. 193: India, China, Japonia, 1652 ad 1654, fols 112v, 113r.

All these questions were to reappear regularly in the literature as successive generations of polemicists took up the baton. In some ways the details were not important and most of those who raised them had no first-hand knowledge of China. They became symbols of anti-Jesuit and, it is tempting to say, anti-Chinese prejudices. In fact, one of the most striking features of the Chinese Rites Controversy is repetition of issues, arguments and positions. Little new evidence was produced, with one important exception, that of the Chinese themselves, which was ignored. The decisions seem to have been based not on evidence but on deeply held party positions.

The Appeal to Rome

One side effect of the disputes of the late 1630s in which the Jesuits rebuffed and attempted to refute the friars' charges was that the question was referred to Rome for the first time. Successive Roman tribunals handed down decisions either for or against the Jesuit arguments. These can only be mentioned briefly for lack of space.[48] In 1645 the Congregation of Propaganda Fide condemned the rites as described by Morales, who had gone to Rome to prosecute the case. In 1656 the Holy Office, with the approval of Pope Alexander VII, upheld the appeal by the Jesuit procurator Martino Martini and approved the Jesuit practices 'if things are as they are narrated'. In 1669 the Holy Office rejected a counter-appeal by the Dominicans and declared that both previous decisions stood. In 1674 the Dominican Domingo Navarrete attempted to reopen the question, but the consultors of the Holy Office refused to hear his *quaesita*; he went to Spain and published his *Tratados*.

A number of observations could be made here. Firstly, it was the Holy Office, the Sacred Congregation of the Roman and Universal Inquisition, which showed itself more favourable. I can only make some suggestions as to why this might be. Although this body was rightly regarded as being in the hands of the Dominicans, it was composed of theologians who appreciated the complexities of the question. They refused to make judgments on Chinese realities and in the apparently contradictory 1669 decree were saying, in effect, that it was not a theological issue but one of fact, and fact that should be deter-

---

[48] For a more detailed treatment of the Roman dimension of the question, see George Minamiki, SJ, *The Chinese Rites Controversy from its Beginning to Modern Times* (Chicago, IL, 1985).

mined in China rather than Rome. Propaganda Fide, on the other hand, was a new body (founded in 1622). It adopted a centralizing project. All foreign missions which had been the province of religious orders and were largely under either the Portuguese *Padroado* or the Spanish *Patronato* were to be brought under the direct control of the papacy and its agencies. It also favoured the secular clergy and the development in mission countries of an indigenous clergy not belonging to religious orders. On the spot control was to be vested in bishops who would initially be Vicars Apostolic, ordained bishops *in partibus infidelium* (given a title of an abandoned see, usually in the East, but with jurisdiction over a mission area).

This scheme, initiated by Propaganda Fide in 1658, put Rome in immediate confrontation with the Portuguese and Spanish, jealous of their privileges, but also with the French king Louis XIV, who had his own project of using missionary activities to promote French commercial and political ends. A further complication was that the main agents for Propaganda Fide and the bulk of the Vicars Apostolic were French, members of the new Missions Étrangères de Paris.

At the outset of this venture, in its instructions to the new Vicars Apostolic, Propaganda Fide produced one of the most enlightened documents of its time. The new bishops were urged to avoid conflict with the Portuguese; to 'accommodate themselves to the nature and customs of others'; not to act as if they had been sent to make visitations or give legal judgments; to avoid nationalism; to translate theological works into the local languages; and above all to establish seminaries everywhere for suitable local candidates for the priesthood.

In its key passage, the 'Instruction' states:

> Do not attempt or for any reason try to persuade these peoples to change their rites, customs or behaviour provided they are not openly contrary to religion and good morals. What could be more absurd than to drag France, Spain, Italy or some other part of Europe into China? Introduce not them but the faith which respects and does not insult the rituals and customs of any people, so long as they are not harmful, but on the contrary wishes them to be maintained and preserved.[49]

[49] My translation from the Latin text in Adrien Launay, *Documents historiques relatifs à la Société des missions étrangères* (Vannes, 1905), 33.

The new Vicars Apostolic and their successors were to do precisely the opposite, with the possible exception of the establishment of seminaries.

Charles Maigrot and the Reopening of the Controversy

To many missionaries, especially the Jesuits, the question was closed. During the minority of the young Kangxi Emperor,[50] the nascent Chinese Christianity became a victim of court factionalism and most of the missionaries were exiled to Canton, where they spent some years under house arrest. In December 1667 and January 1668 the nineteen Jesuits, three Dominicans and one Franciscan (Antonio de Santa Maria) held a conference on the main issues of church practice in China and reached agreement. Although this soon broke down, with Antonio and Domingo Navarrete repudiating the document they had signed, it seems to have been agreed to allow all parties to follow their own customs. Since Jesuits were in a large majority, this meant that in most of China ancestor rituals (with some minor caveats concerning such matters as the wording on the tablets) and the simple rites to Confucius were tolerated, even encouraged.

When he assumed personal power, the Emperor reinstated the Jesuit astronomers and became close to a number of the Beijing Jesuits. In 1692 he issued a decree tolerating Christianity as a religion that was not opposed to the basic values of China and therefore not to be persecuted as a seditious sect. But the very next year cause for such an adverse judgment was given by Charles Maigrot, Vicar Apostolic of Fujian and a member of the Société des Missions Étrangères.

Maigrot claimed that the ground for his decree of 26 March 1693 condemning Chinese rites and the use of terms *Tian* and *Shangdi* had been laid by several years of study of Chinese tradition, but his surviving treatises suggest a slight and mostly second-hand understanding of Confucianism. He was immensely proud of being a Doctor of the Sorbonne, and once again theological considerations seem to have predominated.

This raises the interesting question of the extent of the influence of Jansenism on the Chinese Rites Controversy. Malcolm Hay's arguments to that effect are exaggerated.[51] His chief villain, William Leslie, was a

---

[50] Kangxi was the reign title of the Emperor, whose personal name Xuanye was taboo.
[51] Malcolm Hay, *Failure in the Far East* (London, 1956).

minor figure, a somewhat venal archivist for Propaganda Fide.[52] However, after his expulsion from China, Maigrot fell out of favour in Rome for open lobbying on behalf of the Jansenists. Jansenist apologists such as Arnauld and Pascal used the alleged crimes of the Jesuits in China as key pieces of evidence supporting their charge of Jesuit 'laxity', and several of the Paris Society missionaries were proven Jansenist sympathizers.

The major effect of Maigrot's decree was to reopen the case in Rome and this time the Roman authorities did not hesitate to make judgments about what the Chinese did and believed while refusing to listen to their testimony, even that of Christians. Of course they could not read the vast bulk of Chinese documentation sent to Rome by the Jesuits,[53] but they also refused to accept the translations offered by the Jesuit procurators.

Perhaps the most important testimony was from the Emperor himself. In late 1700 the Jesuits of the court presented him with a statement in Manchu of their understanding of the nature of Chinese rituals, which he endorsed. The Peking Jesuits printed it in its original form together with the official Chinese translation, a Latin translation and additional testimony from Chinese scholars and officials.[54] To their astonishment – perhaps they had become too assimilated to the Chinese view of the Emperor as the supreme authority – this was attacked as intruding the testimony of a pagan and atheist into a theological controversy. For them it was a simple question of fact.

Proceedings in Rome had been going on since May 1697, in a special commission instigated by Propaganda Fide. While agents of both parties lobbied and produced memorials in Rome, the Sorbonne censured some Jesuit writings and a veritable war of printed words broke out, with literally hundreds of publications on both sides. A new pope, Clement XI, apparently more favourable to the Jesuits, switched

---

[52] His letters to the superiors of the Société des Missions Étrangères (in Launay, *Documents*, 1: 248–83) show him selling copies of secret correspondence to Paris.
[53] Much of this unpublished material is in the Jap. Sin. collection of the Jesuit Archives in Rome. Some of the more formal treatises have been published in Nicholas Standaert and Adrian Dudink, eds, *Chinese Christian Texts from the Roman Archives of the Society of Jesus*, 12 vols (Taipei, 2002).
[54] *Brevis Relatio eorum quae spectant ad declarationem Sinarum Imperatoris Kam Hi, circa coeli, Cumfucii et eorum cultum, datam anno 1700. Accedunt primatum doctissimorumque virorum et antiquissimae traditionis testimonia. Opera Patrum Soc. Jesu Pekini pro Evangelii propagatione laborantium*, xylograph [Beijing, 1701].

the issue to the Holy Office, but the commission of investigation had a majority of known opponents of the Jesuits, including the Augustinian Cardinal Noris, leader of the Neo-Augustinian school of theology. Clement decided in addition to send a papal legate to China, choosing a young Piedmontese aristocrat, Charles Maillard de Tournon, who departed in July 1702.

The decision of the papal commission, against the permissibility of the Rites, was given in the decree *Cum Deus Optimus* on 20 November 1704. Clement, however, withheld publication, apparently awaiting a report from his legate. In his last audience with the Jesuit procurator, Kaspar Castner, he assured the Jesuits that the decision was in their favour.[55] Did he believe he had averted something even worse, as the decree pointedly did not accuse the Jesuits of idolatry as their opponents wanted? Was it just another example of his notorious duplicity?[56] Or did he believe that de Tournon would report in a way that would negate the decision?

In many ways the de Tournon legation (1705–1710) was the crucial act in the whole drama. It has never been fully examined, and the forthcoming publication of the annotated translation of the *Acta Pekinensia*[57] may clear up much of the misinformation in existing sources.[58]

It is unclear what Maillard de Tournon's personal agenda, if any, might have been. His patron, Cardinal Cenci, seems to have regarded him as a friend of the Jesuits. On the other hand, his correspondence with the papal secretary of state, Fabrizio Paolucci, throughout his legation suggests the opposite. The key to his actions may lie in his personality and his health. In India, Manila and China he acted precipitately, was given to acute fits of anger and irritation, refused advice and was

55   Castner's 'Diarium' for 9 December 1704, 'Diarium Actorum circa Controversias de ritibus Sinicis'; Rome, Archivum Historicum Societatis Jesu, Fondo Gesuitico, 724, reg. 2, fol. 12v.

56   Lucien Ceyssens, in 'Autour de *l'Unigenitus*: Le pape Clément XI', *Bulletin de l'Institut historique belge de Rome* 53–54 (1983–84), 253–304, writes of 'le caractère mensonger de Clément XI' (279) and notes a contemporary judgement that 'chez Albani le oui et le non ne sont pas très distinct l'un de l'autre' (261).

57   The work of Kilian Stumpf, SJ, it is found as Jap. Sin. 138 in the Jesuit Roman Archives. An annotated English translation is currently being prepared by the Macau Ricci Institute. The mostly undocumented commentary that follows is based on this work and the huge volume of contemporary documentation too vast to be noted here. Partial listings are given in the *Bibliotheca Missionum* (Freiburg / Rome, 1916–1964), esp. vols 5 and 7, and Henri Cordier, *Bibliotheca Sinica* (Paris, 1904–1924), esp. cols 869–926, 3580–3600.

58   Such as Antonio Sisto Rosso, *Apostolic Delegations to China of the Eighteenth Century* (South Pasadena, CA, 1948).

highly partisan. He was extremely conscious of his status and authority, claiming (falsely) that a *legatus a latere* (a legate with authority to speak in the name of the pope, appointed for a specific task) had plenary powers which overrode canon law. He was frequently bed-ridden, had bouts of paralysis of the limbs, suffered severe stomach pains and was susceptible to the cold.

Much more seriously, given his mission, de Tournon seems to have disliked Chinese culture and even the Chinese themselves. He dismissed the views of the Emperor as those of an atheist and therefore worthless, and he seems to have fatally underestimated his intelligence and political shrewdness. He attempted to introduce European funeral customs and papal court procedures such as the levee, kneeling and hand kissing despite the advice of the experienced court Jesuits that all that happened would be observed and reported to the Emperor, who would regard it as a challenge to his authority. He was rude and dismissive in his encounters with Chinese Christians and the Manchu court functionaries who acted as intermediaries. And he refused to be bothered to consider Chinese law and custom.

De Tournon concealed his anti-Rites mission from the Emperor, who rightly suspected he was not telling the full truth. Originally he claimed he came simply to thank Kangxi for his kindness to Christianity. Then he requested a permanent diplomatic presence in Peking, despite the Jesuits' warning that this was contrary to the Chinese custom of short-term embassies. Furthermore, when on his return journey from Peking to Canton he issued in February 1707 a decree condemning the Chinese Rites, he appears surprised that Kangxi reacted fiercely. The Emperor ordered that he not be allowed to depart from Macao until the Jesuit imperial emissaries to the Pope returned. And he ordered to be expelled from China any missionary who did not promise to observe 'the regulations of Matteo Ricci'. Meanwhile de Tournon had been made a cardinal on the strength of his early optimistic reports, and when news of the contretemps arrived, the Pope felt that he had no alternative but to confirm his legate's decree.

De Tournon died in Macao in 1710 under house arrest before the Emperor's legates returned. In fact, two had died en route, one was too ill to return and the remaining one, Antonio Provana, was not allowed to leave. It was only when the reports from de Tournon's supporters were belied by an official poster circulated to all incoming ships in effect saying 'where are my envoys?' that the Pope and his curia realized that Provana must be allowed to return. He too died on the way, off the Cape of Good Hope.

A second papal legate, Carlo Mezzabarba, was dispatched in 1720, who eventually made a series of compromises in his 'Eight Permissions' only to find on his return that opinion in Rome had hardened further. The rites were condemned again in 1724 and definitively by Benedict XIV in 1742. From that time no missionary could go to China without taking an oath to observe the papal constitutions.

Conclusion: Tragedy or Farce?

It is often said that the Chinese Rites Controversy was a tragedy, and so it was, not only for the majority of the Catholic missionaries in China but especially for the Chinese Christians faced with a stark choice of being Christian or Chinese. But it was also farce. Parts of the *Acta Pekinensia* read almost like a script for a certain kind of black comedy film. There were, of course, other reasons than the Rites fiasco for this setback, not the least being the personal agendas of Kangxi's successors. But the hostility to Chinese culture and society, internal divisions and (one has to say) arrogance of many Catholic clerics exhibited in the Chinese Rites Controversy are still today obstacles to the spread of Christianity in China.

On an even deeper level, however, it was a tragic lost opportunity for a widening of Christian perspectives, a beginning of a true universalizing of Christian concepts and rituals. Conceptions of the afterlife and links to the present-day lives of descendants were central here. One can imagine a gradual absorption of notions of 'filial piety', of ritualized cross-generational links, into the understanding of theological concepts such as the Communion of Saints and praying for the dead. It is probably too late now, since the culture that embodied such notions has been largely destroyed by revolution and social and economic modernization. But if eschatology matters and has repercussions for all aspects of life, it may not be too late to learn from the sad story of the Chinese Rites Controversy.

La Trobe University, Melbourne / Ricci Institute for Chinese-Western Cultural History, University of San Francisco

STRATEGIES FOR THE AFTERLIFE IN EIGHTEENTH-CENTURY MALTA

by FRANS CIAPPARA

ACCORDING to Protestant eschatology, the dead are no longer with us. In the forceful words of Eamon Duffy they are 'gone beyond the reach of human contact, even of human prayer'.[1] But if this was the most devastating change in the mind of Protestants, Catholics affirmed Tridentine teaching on the cult of the dead by an 'obsessional multiplication' of suffrages or intercessory prayers, especially *post mortem* masses. This belief was still strong in eighteenth-century Catholic Europe. Italy,[2] Spain[3] and south-west Germany[4] all exhibited such religious 'frenzy'. Only France may be cited as an example to the contrary. Michel Vovelle has successfully proved that in Provence the will became simply a legal act distributing fortunes, with no reference to the pious clauses.[5] However, we cannot extend this thesis, as Philippe Ariès has mistakenly done, to the entire Catholic West.[6]

This paper argues that Malta was a bastion of these traditions. It seeks to explore how the Maltese tried to ensure that enough intercessory prayers would be offered for their souls not to stay too long in purgatory. Their preoccupation with death, the masses that they

---

[1] Eamon Duffy, *The Stripping of the Altars: Traditional Religion in England 1400–1580* (New Haven, CT, and London, 1992), 475. For this cultural transformation, see also Craig M. Koslofsky, *The Reformation of the Dead: Death and Ritual in Early Modern Germany, 1450–1700* (New York, 2000).

[2] R. Colapietra, *Gli Aquilani d'antico regime davanti alla morte 1535–1780* (Rome, 1986); Michael P. Carroll, *Veiled Threats: The Logic of Popular Catholicism in Italy* (Baltimore, MD, and London, 1996), chs. 4 and 5. For Modena, see Susan V. Nicassio, '"For the Benefit of my Soul": A Preliminary Study of the Persistence of Tradition in Eighteenth-Century Mass Obligations', *CathHR* 78 (1992), 75–96.

[3] Carlos M. N. Eire, *From Madrid to Purgatory: The Art and Craft of Dying in Sixteenth-Century Spain* (Cambridge, 1995).

[4] Marc R. Forster, *Catholic Revival in the Age of the Baroque: Religious Identity in Southwest Germany, 1550–1750* (Cambridge, 2001), 140–41.

[5] Michel Vovelle, *Piété baroque et déchristianisation en Provence au XVIIIe siècle* (Paris, 1978), 114–19.

[6] Philippe Ariès, *Western Attitudes towards Death: From the Middle Ages to the Present* (Baltimore, MD, 1974), 64.

bought, the indulgences they earned, the alms they distributed, the processions in which their bodies were carried to church, and the places where they were interred, are all important elements in the argument. An attempt will also be made to analyse whether the elite viewed these practices in different ways than the commoners. The data come from wills,[7] the petition registers at the ecclesiastical court and, especially, the 'pious dispositions' which people dictated to their parish priest on their deathbed.[8]

Fear of death in former centuries haunted the imagination of man.[9] Death was certain as well as unpredictable, and it would have been unwise not to be on the watch. Conversion at the last moment, when the devil rushed to the dying in the pangs of death like a hunting dog to a quail, was exceptionally rare.[10] One sermon *exemplum* identified winter, when the Sun is most distant from the Earth, with one's last days. God is the true sun, and he stays away from the sinner. The angels could put off the temptations 'but I don't think that the sinner merits so much'. 'Is there no mercy?', the preacher asked. 'No, not at this time. This is time for Justice.'[11]

The best way to die well is to live well,[12] like the pious Cornelius in Erasmus's colloquy 'The Funeral'.[13] Even so, to die in the state of God's grace does not necessarily mean that the soul goes straight to heaven. The catechism of the Council of Trent taught that sin produces two effects, a wound and a stain on the soul. When a wound has been healed some scars remain which demand attention; likewise with regard to the soul, after the guilt of sin (*culpa*) is remitted by the priest some of its effects remain, from which the soul requires to be cleansed.

---

[7] For wills and the religious attitudes of testators, see R. Po-chia Hsia, 'Civic Wills As Sources For The Study of Piety in Muenster, 1530–1618', *Sixteenth Century Journal* 14 (1983), 321–48.

[8] For a detailed study of these 'pious dispositions', see Frans Ciappara, 'Intercessory Funerary Rites in Malta 1750–1797', *Nuova Rivista Storica*, Anno 91 (2007), 145–71. For England, see Stephen Coppel, 'Willmaking on the Deathbed', *Local Population Studies* no. 40 (1988), 37–45.

[9] J. Huizinga, *The Waning of the Middle Ages* (Harmondsworth, 1955), 140–52.

[10] For an optimistic belief in this final hour, see Richard Wunderli and Gerald Broce, 'The Final Moment before Death in Early Modern England', *Sixteenth Century Journal* 20 (1989), 259–75.

[11] Valletta, National Library, Library 48, pp. 362–67 [hereafter: NL and Libr.]

[12] For this expression, see Robert Bellarmine, 'The Art of Dying Well', ch. 1, in *Spiritual Writings*, trans. and eds J. P. Donnelly and R. J. Teske (Mahwah, NJ, 1989), 239–40: 'The first rule for dying well, which is that one who desires to die well should live well'.

[13] Erasmus, 'Funus', in *Opera Omnia*, 10 vols (Lyons, 1703), 1: 10, cols 810–18.

These stains are removed by temporal punishment (*poena*), 'which disarms the vengeance of God'. Nevertheless, it is only saints who die in a state of full contrition; for all others a period in purgatory is necessary for their soul to be wholly acceptable to God.[14]

It was believed that these souls deserve our prayers because they are suffering pains that exceed all the torments of this life. Moreover, they are in the greatest necessity since they cannot possibly help themselves. Catholics ought to pray for them also out of love and gratitude. 'Wild animals like lions', a preacher told his listeners in 1745, 'are thankful to whoever is good to them. And dogs love their masters so that they die on their graves'.[15] Besides, it is in one's own interest to pray for the dead. 'They will show themselves grateful', Alphonsus Liguori told his readers in a classic of late eighteenth-century ascetic literature, 'by obtaining great graces for us, not only when they reach heaven, if they arrive sooner through our prayers, but also in purgatory.'[16]

The curfew bell reminded people every evening of this duty, and priests prayed God at mass to remember the dead and give them a 'place of refreshment, light and peace'. A popular devotion, started in 1766 by Don Francesco Wzzino, was to recite a prayer each day of the week for a particular soul; for example, Sunday was reserved for the most forsaken soul.[17] Furthermore, several testators who provided for intercessory prayers generally shared their benefits with others, especially their kin.[18]

Nonetheless, I want to emphasize that it was deemed unwise to rely fully on the generosity of one's fellow men. Did not the dead sometimes have to appear to their relatives to make them offer suffrages for them?[19] Most of the faithful, therefore, sought to curtail and offset the pains of purgatory by trying to control their affairs from beyond the

---

[14] *The Catechism of the Council of Trent*, trans. John A. McHugh and Charles J. Callan (Rockford, IL, 1982), 300–01.

[15] Valletta, NL, Libr. 48, p. 536.

[16] See his *Preparation for Death*, ed. Eugene Grimm (Brooklyn, NJ, 1926), 444. Note that the dead could be prayed *for* as well as *to*. On this point, see Carroll, *Veiled Threats*, 29–36.

[17] F. Wzzino, *Il Purgatorio aperto alla Pietà de' Viventi* (Malta, 1766).

[18] Valletta, Notarial Archives [hereafter: NA], Notary Tommaso Magri, 4 / 924, fol. 26r; 16 November 1728.

[19] For one such incident see Mdina, Archives of the Inquisition, Malta, Proceedings 102A, fols 390r–95v [hereafter: AIM and Proc.]. On this subject, see Theo Brown, *The Fate of the Dead: A Study in Folk Eschatology in the West Country after the Reformation* (Ipswich, 1979); Nancy Caciola, 'Wraiths, Revenants and Ritual in Medieval Culture', *P&P* no. 152 (August 1996), 3–45.

grave themselves.[20] Wearers of the scapular trusted that Our Lady would descend into purgatory on the first Sunday after their death to release them into heaven.[21] Similarly, people built up credit for the afterlife by means of indulgences. These promissory notes, which enjoyed such wide dissemination, were not only the most secure, but could also be the cheapest, ticket to heaven. Crusading indulgences like the *bolla crociata* cost money, as did those that assisted the building of churches. But ordinary people contented themselves with indulgences that required no money, such as visits to churches or repetition of prayers.[22] For example, in 1762 Bishop Rull granted forty days' remission to whoever recited a 'Hail Mary' before a statue of Our Lady of the Annunciation at Tarxien.[23]

But Catholics could bind others to pray for them. To this end they enrolled in one or more of the parish's confraternities to have a decent burial and earn the suffrages of the other brothers and sisters.[24] Brotherhoods were burial clubs and offered *post mortem* benefits, at least an obit for their deceased members. Ghaxaq's *confraternità di San Giuseppe* ruled that each member was to fast after the death of each brother; and a high mass was celebrated on the first Tuesday of every month for all living and dead members.[25]

Another way to secure the prayers of the living was to distribute alms. The most common item was cash, for instance dowries for poor girls,[26] but testators also left their kitchenware[27] and their clothes,[28] among other things. Giovanni Maria Agius of Mqabba (d. 1777) left all

[20] Jean-Loup Lemaître, 'La commémoration des défunts et les obituaires dans l'occident chrétien', *Revue d'Histoire de l'Église de France* 71 (1985), 131–45.

[21] Carroll, *Veiled Threats*, 125–29.

[22] R. N. Swanson, *Religion and Devotion in Europe, c. 1215–c. 1515* (Cambridge, 1995), 217–25. For the granting of indulgences in return for prayers for the faithful departed, see idem, 'Indulgences for Prayers for the Dead in the Diocese of Lincoln in the Early Fourteenth Century', *JEH* 52 (2001), 197–219. The standard work on indulgences is idem, ed., *Promissory Notes on the Treasury of Merits: Indulgences in Late Medieval Europe* (Leiden and Boston, MA, 2006).

[23] Floriana, Archbishop's Palace, Archiepiscopal Archives, Malta, Registrum Supplicationes 8, fols 49v–50r [hereafter: AAM and RS].

[24] Christopher C. Black, *Italian Confraternities in the Sixteenth Century* (Cambridge, 1989), 104–07.

[25] Floriana, AAM, RS 6, fols 523v–25r.

[26] Floriana, AAM, RS 7, fols 1237v–38r; Valletta, NA, Not. Bernardo Azzopardi, 18 January 1631; Floriana, AAM, Conti (Qrendi) 17A, no. 18, 49.

[27] Valletta, NA, Not. Tommaso Magri, 3 / 924, fols 59v–61v.

[28] Mdina, Parish Archives, Liber Defunctorum 3, pp. 570–71 [hereafter: PA and Lib. Def.].

his agricultural implements including a pickaxe and a mattock to his son,[29] while Margherita of Tarxien (d. 1790) rewarded her daughter with a chest of drawers.[30] These remembrances were also distributed in the form of landed property,[31] agricultural products,[32] livestock,[33] jewellery,[34] firearms,[35] spinning wheels and looms.[36]

In their desire to have as many suffrages as possible the Maltese of the eighteenth century fragmented their wealth into several small charitable gifts. Grazia Magro of Mqabba (d. 1788) divided her possessions among her two brothers, her niece and her sister-in-law to have her soul remembered in their devotions.[37] One wonders how many benefited from the pious legacy of Don Michel'Angelo Dalli of Tarxien, who in 1797 left the rent of a house to be distributed among the poor of the village.[38] And how many were the 'poor of Our Lord Jesus Christ' who received a loaf from the proceeds of a field bequeathed by Grazia Camilleri to the churchwardens of Qrendi in 1749?[39]

Charity was a meritorious act in itself, for which donors could demand nothing in return from the recipients. Teresa Gatt (d. 1784) donated a skirt to her two daughters for having stood by her in her dying days.[40] But these donations were essentially contractual, the donor obliging the beneficiaries to offer a counter-gift for the remission of his or her sins and the repose of his or her soul. For these bequests benefactors demanded the recipients to pray for them and often to fast on bread and water.[41] In 1751 Maria Sant of Mosta bequeathed a field to her children and ordered them to recite the rosary for five years on All Souls' Day.[42] Gratia Vella, a widow from Ghaxaq (d. 1798), requested her son to pay for the candles burning before the Stations of the Cross.[43]

[29] Mqabba, PA, Lib. Def. 4, p. 35.
[30] Tarxien, PA, Lib. Def. 5, 10 May 1790.
[31] Mdina, PA, Lib. Def. 3, p. 483.
[32] Valletta, NA, Not. Tommaso Magri, 2 / 924, fols 75r–v; 19 May 1725.
[33] B'Kara, PA, Lib. Def. 5, fol. 110v.
[34] Siggiewi, PA, Lib. Def. 4 (10 July 1769, Anna Pace).
[35] Valletta, NA, Not. Tommaso Magri, 6 / 924, fols 90r–92v.
[36] Mdina, PA, Lib. Def. 4, fols 9v–10r.
[37] Mqabba, PA, Lib. Def. 4, p. 79.
[38] Tarxien, PA, Lib. Def. 5, fol. 12v.
[39] Valletta, NA, Not. Gio. Francesco Farrugia, 21 / 816, fols 10r–11v.
[40] Lija, PA, Lib. Def. 4, p. 126.
[41] Valletta, NA, Not. Tommaso Magri, 2 / 924, fols 75r–v; 1725.
[42] Mdina, PA, Lib. Def. 3, pp. 482–83.
[43] Ghaxaq, PA, Lib. Def. (1747–1814), p. 128.

Even so, the suffrages of the whole parish were preferable to individual prayers. Margherita Ellul, her husband and children of Siggiewi had three 'Holy Fathers' and 'Hail Marys', the litany of Our Lady and the hymn to St Anne recited in suffrage of their souls after mass every Tuesday at the altar of the Agony.[44] And when in 1784 Giovanni Filippo Vella of St Saviour's founded the feast of St Theresa with a high mass and vespers, he ordered the hymn *Libera me Domine* ('Deliver me, O Lord') to be sung and the bells rung 'for his soul's release from purgatory'.[45]

In fact, of all the suffrages that benefited the dead there was nothing more meritorious for them than the mass. Such was the efficacy of this sacrifice of Christ himself, according to the Tridentine catechism, that its benefits extend to all the faithful whether living with us on earth or already numbered with those who are dead in the Lord, but whose sins have not yet been fully expiated.[46]

Except for the very poor who, like Giovanni Briffa of St Andrew's, were buried 'for love of God' at the parish priest's expense,[47] most Maltese paid for their funeral and 'bought' a few masses for their soul. An example in 1780 of such practice is seen in the case of Grazio Attard. When this beggar from the village of Nadur (Gozo) died he had somehow succeeded, to the great surprise of the assistant pastor, to save twenty *scudi* to ensure a proper burial service.[48] Usually, people 'purchased' a sung mass for their day of death and an additional sequence of masses for the second, third, seventh and thirtieth days after their death as well as on their anniversary,[49] a clear reference to the five wounds of Christ.[50] Generally, they dictated these modest 'pious dispositions' to the parish priest just before they died.

The rich, who were greatly concerned with the 'accounts of the hereafter' – Jacques Chiffoleau's favourite phrase – could afford a much larger number of masses and took pains to specify their performance in detail to a notary in a will.[51] In 1762 Crispino di Candia of Cospicua left

44 Floriana, AAM, RS 9, fols 1171r–v.
45 Lija, PA, Lib. Def. 4, p. 128.
46 *Catechism of the Council of Trent*, 259.
47 Luqa, PA, Lib. Def. 3, fol. 120r; 27 May 1772.
48 Mdina, AIM, Reverenda Fabbrica (Incartamenti, 1783–1797), 32, fol. 5r.
49 See, for instance, Lija, PA, Lib. Def. 4, p. 6.
50 For the votive mass of the Five Wounds, see Duffy, *Stripping of the Altars*, 243–44.
51 Jacques Chiffoleau, 'Sur l'usage obsessionnel de la Messe pour les morts à la fin du Moyen Âge', in *Faire croire: Modalités de la diffusion et de la réception des messages religieux du XIIe au XVe Siècle*, Collection de l'École française de Rome 51 (1981), 235–46.

a thousand *scudi* to endow with their interest three low masses daily.[52] But the rich did not only differ from the poor in the amount of masses they financed. They sought a long-term suffrage and preferred *post obit* services over a more extended period, possibly till the end of the world.[53] That is, they wished rather to perpetuate their memory, while the poor were concerned more to alleviate the pains of purgatory.[54]

We have several kinds of information about the obits. Liturgically they were a repetition of the rites accompanying the interment of the body, which explains why they were also referred to as 'funerals'.[55] They were generally celebrated on the anniversary of the testator's death,[56] but some testators requested the most important liturgical feasts associated with Christ or the Virgin, like Christmas and the Annunciation.[57] The saints already had access to God and therefore were all the more able to intercede with him for the poor souls. St Joseph, the protector of the dying, was especially loved,[58] but Catarina Dalli of Gudja in 1758 chose her own patron saint, St Catherine of Alexandria,[59] and Don Marcello Mallia of Ghaxaq (d. 1796) founded an obit on the feast of the martyr St Fedele.[60] The first Monday of each month was another day especially chosen for masses for the dead. This devotion could have owed its origin to the widespread pious belief that the flames of purgatory burned more strongly on Mondays following the day of the Lord.[61]

I have laboured this point enough, but people did not only try to

52 Floriana, AAM, RS 8, fol. 480r.

53 Frans Ciappara, '*Una Messa in Perpetuum*: Perpetual Mass Bequests in Traditional Malta, 1750–1797', *CathHR* 91 (2005), 278–99.

54 S. T. Strocchia, *Death and Ritual in Renaissance Florence* (London, 1992), 208.

55 Floriana, AAM, RS 6, fol. 530v.

56 Clive Burgess, 'A Service for the Dead: The Form and Function of the Anniversary in Late Medieval Bristol', *Transactions of the Bristol and Gloucestershire Archaeological Society* 105 (1987), 183–211; see also, in this volume, idem, ' "An Afterlife in Memory": Commemoration and its Effects in a Late Medieval Parish', 196–217.

57 Valletta, NA, Not. Gio. Francesco Farrugia, 9 / 816, fols 61r–v (22 February 1738); AAM, RS 6, fol. 516r.

58 Floriana, AAM, RS 10, fols 316r–v. On St Joseph as a model of a man who died well, see Michael W. Maher, *Devotion, the Society of Jesus, and the Idea of St. Joseph* (Philadelphia, PA, 2000).

59 Floriana, AAM, RS 7, fol. 1161v.

60 Ghaxaq, PA, Lib. Def. (1747–1814), fol. 39v.

61 For this belief, see Mario Rosa, 'The Italian Churches', in William J. Callahan and David Higgs, eds, *Church and Society in Catholic Europe of the Eighteenth Century* (Cambridge, 1979), 74, and Arturo Graf, 'Il riposo dei dannati', in idem, *Miti, leggende e superstizioni del medio evo* (Milan, 1984), 151–66. For St Patrick's purgatory in Ireland, see Jacques Le Goff, *The Birth of Purgatory* (Aldershot, 1984), 193–201.

control their destiny by an intricate arrangement of masses. They
ensured that their corpse was interred on the day of death or, at the
latest, by the end of the day following. The reason for this prompt
burial was primarily spiritual, since all funeral rites were imbued with
an intercessory value and the quicker they were accomplished the
better. To lack prayers at that moment was to endanger salvation and
therefore testators left money for the attendance of priests, members of
confraternities, acquaintances and friends at the funeral.[62] In Malta
reference to the poor accompanying funerals is rare, but in one instance
Baldassare Ferer (d. 1707) gave one *tarì* each to twenty paupers to escort
his body to the grave at the Carmelite church at Valletta, each one
holding a torch in their hand.[63]

The place where people were buried participated in the strategies for
the afterlife, too.[64] Parishioners would have preferred, therefore, to be
laid to rest where they would gain most intercessory prayers. Pasquale
Delceppo, who died at St Bartholomew's in 1793, ordered his corpse to
be carried to Senglea. He wanted to be with the other brothers in the
oratory of the Confraternity of the Holy Crucifix, of which he was a
member.[65] Monks had ranked as the chief intercessors in the Middle
Ages, and, plausibly, people hoped that being buried in some convent
they would secure the intercession of the order's founder. Furthermore,
they would also benefit from the prayers of the whole community, who
prayed corporately for the dead.[66] Between 1750 and 1797, 209 parishioners from Vittoriosa were interred with the Dominicans, while
eighty-six inhabitants of the nearby city of Cospicua chose the
Discalced Carmelites.[67] In contrast, villagers rarely opted to be buried
in friaries for the simple reason that these institutions were predomi-

[62] Ciappara, 'Intercessory Funerary Rites in Malta, 1750–1797', 157–60.
[63] Valletta, NLM, Archives 1723, fol. 121r.
[64] For the religious significance of burial choice, see the beautiful pages in Philippe
Ariès, *The Hour of Our Death*, trans. Helen Weaver (Harmondsworth, 1981), 29–92; and
Nicholas Rogers, 'Hic Iacet …: The Location of Monuments in Late Medieval Parish
Churches', in Clive Burgess and Eamon Duffy, eds, *The Parish in Late Medieval England*
(Donington, 2006), 261–81.
[65] Gargur, PA, Lib. Def. 2, fol. 143r.
[66] Adriaan H. Bredero, 'Le moyen age et le purgatoire', *Revue d'histoire ecclésiastique* 78
(1983), 429–52, at 448–49; Patrick J. Geary, *Living with the Dead in the Middle Ages* (Ithaca, NY,
and London, 1994), 95; M. McLaughlin, *Consorting with Saints: Prayer for the Dead in Early
Medieval France* (Ithaca, NY, and London, 1994), 230–33.
[67] Calculated from data in Cospicua, PA, Lib. Def. 4–8, and Vittoriosa, PA, Liber
Mortuorum 4–5.

nantly located in urban areas. Thus the widow from St Helen's who bequeathed her body for burial with the Capuchins at Floriana in 1790, must have been an exception.[68]

Primarily, however, people preferred to be interred in their resident parish, where they hoped to earn the prayers of their kin and acquaintances. Domenicuzza, a fifty-two year-old woman from Mqabba, died at her sister's at Zejtun in 1758, but she directed that her burial should be at her own parish.[69] This impulse for suffrages can also be exemplified by the arrangement made by the members of the Sodality of Consolation at St Andrew's to reclaim their members who died in hospital.[70] But even those Maltese who could not return to their parish or died abroad were still commemorated in their former parish.[71] For most of them a requiem mass was said; for others only the bell was rung, but this was enough to remind the parishioners to say a prayer for the soul of their former compatriots.[72]

According to canon law, all parishioners had an equal right to choose the church in which they wished to be buried but not all shared the right to be laid to rest in the most prestigious positions within the church.[73] Most were disposed of in burial pits with the rest[74] but a few had privileged places reserved for them. Between 1750 and 1797 twenty-three applications were made at the ecclesiastical court for a private grave.[75] By having a separate burial site, with an inscribed floor-slab[76] or, more rarely, a memorial surmounting it',[77] they ensured that their bones rested with those of their ancestors and that they would be remembered forever.[78]

Unlike Protestants,[79] Catholics cherished the idea that burial adja-

---

[68] B'Kara, PA, Lib. Def. 5, fols 85r, 116r.

[69] Mqabba, PA, Lib. Def. 3, p. 151.

[70] Floriana, AAM, RS 7, fols 1271r–v.

[71] This is how the parish priest of Ghaxaq described the death of one of his parishioners in Spain in 1795, 'Habimus notionem mortis in Hispania Gratio Schembri': Ghaxaq, Lib. Def. (1747–1814), fol. 37r.

[72] See, for instance, Cospicua, PA, Lib. Def. 7, fol. 4r.

[73] 'Canon Law of Burial', *New Catholic Encyclopedia* (New York, 1967), 2: 896.

[74] Floriana, AAM, RS 8, fols 35r–v.

[75] Calculated from data in Floriana, AAM, RS 6–12.

[76] Floriana, AAM, RS 8, fol. 8v.

[77] For the marble image in the collegiate church at Rabat (Gozo) of Baron Giovanni Antonio Azzopardi Castelletti as a young man in military dress, see Floriana, AAM, RS 7, fol. 1176r, and Floriana, AAM, RS 8, fol. 105v.

[78] David Cressy, *Birth, Marriage and Death: Ritual, Religion and the Life-Cycle in Tudor and Stuart England* (Oxford, 1999), 456–73.

[79]

cent to spiritually potent parts of the church acquired posthumous merit for them. Sanctity permeated the whole church but, as has well been said, 'there were gradations of the sacred'.[80] The prime location was near the high altar where the mass was celebrated.[81] A variant of this request was to be buried before the Blessed Sacrament.[82] The next most favoured location was to be interred near a favourite image, especially one of Our Lady.[83] Others found their place near the church door where the faithful entered and left the church – no doubt an ideal place to receive the benefit of their prayers. A frequent demand was to be laid to rest in the nave. This was the most conspicuous spot of the church, and whoever was interred there prompted the grateful prayers of the faithful.[84] Likewise, being placed near the fonts meant a constant sprinkling of holy water.[85]

To conclude, the evidence from eighteenth-century Malta suggests a society still deeply imbued with traditional concern for the state of souls after death and convinced that the living could affect this. Two centuries after the Reformation, and well into the Roman Catholic Church's response to this challenge, people still assumed that most who died in a state of grace would have to spend some time in purgatory. They therefore spent resources in bequests to bind others to pray, fast and especially to hear masses for them; and they made arrangements to be buried in places where they would catch the attention of those they left behind. While only elites had the money to 'buy' perpetual masses, the poor showed no less interest in intercession. Almost everyone did what they could – at least in providing for their burial service – to secure prayers to alleviate their coming trials.

University of Malta

Vanessa Harding, *The Dead and the Living in Paris and London, 1500–1670* (Cambridge, 2006). Among her articles, see 'Burial on the Margin: Distance and Discrimination in Early Modern London', in M. Cox, ed., *Grave Concerns: Death and Burial in England, 1700–1850* (York, 1988), 54–64; ' "And one more may be laid there": The Location of Burials in Early Modern London', *London Journal* 14 (1989), 112–29.

80 Will Coster, 'A Microcosm of Community: Burial, Space and Society in Chester, 1598 to 1633', in W. Coster and A. Spicer, eds, *Sacred Space in Early Modern Europe* (Cambridge, 2005), 124–43, at 124.

81 Floriana, AAM, RS 8, fols. 69r–v.

82 Floriana, AAM, RS 9, fol. 659v.

83 Our Lady of Sorrows – Floriana, AAM, RS 8, fol. 8v; Our Lady of the Rosary – ibid. fol. 111v; Our Lady of Carmel – ibid. fol. 556v.

84 Floriana, AAM, RS 7, fol. 856r.

APPARITIONS AND ANGLICANISM
IN 1750s WARWICKSHIRE

by SASHA HANDLEY

O
N Thursday, 1 May 1755, the small churchyard in Harbury, Warwickshire, was the scene of an extraordinary incident. An unnamed member of the local community claimed to have met and had a long conversation with an apparition, which emerged from amongst the tombstones. The precise details of this encounter no longer survive, but it clearly had a powerful impact upon the inhabitants of this sleepy rural village. The interest excited by the appearance persuaded Richard Jago, Vicar of Harbury, to put the episode to a useful didactic purpose. Just a few days later Jago based his Sunday sermon upon this event, which had quickly become the focus of intense curiosity.

The appropriation of the Harbury apparition tale by Richard Jago forms the central core of this essay. Jago's complex response provides a rich example of how educated clerics were successfully able to manipulate tales of ghosts and apparitions to manage and integrate the pressures of shifting theological and philosophical realms with the quotidian understandings of their parishioners, in order to build an effective defence of the Anglican faith and to encourage parish devotion. Jago's use of the apparition report therefore offers an interface through which the exigencies of lay spirituality and the demands of the theological and philosophical worlds were negotiated. To illustrate this complex dynamic, Jago is positioned at the centre of a network of influences, each of which shaped the way in which he thought and acted in relation to the apparition. The first and most significant influence was Jago's pastoral priorities in Harbury, and especially his need to secure lines of communication with some of his more recalcitrant parishioners. I will examine how Jago channelled the fascination created by the apparition to call for improved devotional habits, and to affirm his own spiritual and moral authority within his parish. The second closely related influence was Jago's position as an Anglican minister. Of interest here is how he reconciled the extraordinary occurrence in the churchyard with the broader interests and emphases of the Church of England in the 1750s. Finally, I will consider how Jago's own cultural interests and intellectual pursuits shaped his interpretation of the Harbury apparition and of the preternatural world more generally.

Jago's multi-layered response suggests that narratives of ghosts and apparitions occupied an important yet contested place within the culture of mid-eighteenth century Anglicanism. This is an important point to make since the relationship between the Church, society and seemingly miraculous signs, visions and wonders has been largely discussed in relation to narratives of disenchantment in an age of enlightened rationalism. Recent revisionist work has however documented the extent to which ghosts, witches and fairies still commanded considerable attention in post-Reformation spirituality.[1] This essay contributes to ongoing efforts to redraw the boundaries between the material and spiritual worlds. Yet more specifically it demonstrates how stories of ghosts and apparitions, when examined in specific social contexts, could play an important role in moulding positive relationships between the Church and its people.

On the Sunday following the report of the apparition, the parish church in Harbury was full to bursting. A flurry of speculation about the meaning of the apparition had drawn an unusually large crowd to the church in the hope of illumination. When Jago declared the purpose of his speech, he deliberately steered clear of wider intellectual debates that rendered problematic the very possibility that apparitions, or any kind of supernatural agent, could make contact with the living. Jago chose instead to interpret the event as a serious call to repentance, which was a legitimate subject of devotional contemplation according to the 'fundamental Principles of Reason and Revelation' to which he was committed as a clergyman.[2] Jago did not deny the possibility that God occasionally issued extraordinary signs, nor did he wish 'to dissuade Men from making the most serious Use of them when offered'.[3] He asserted that if the apparition in the churchyard was indeed a messenger from God, it represented the direst warning to the parishioners of Harbury to mend their irreverent ways and to worship

---

[1] Jonathan Barry, 'Public Infidelity and Private Belief? The Discourse of Spirits in Enlightenment Bristol, 1640–1714', in W. de Blécourt and O. Davies, eds, *Beyond the Witch Trials: Witchcraft and Magic in Enlightenment Europe* (Manchester, 2004), 117–43; Owen Davies, *Witchcraft, Magic and Culture, 1736–1951* (Manchester, 1999); Peter Marshall, *Mother Leakey and the Bishop: A Ghost Story* (Oxford, 2007).

[2] Richard Jago, *The Cause of Impenitence Consider'd: As well in the Case of extraordinary Warnings, as under the general Laws of Providence, and Grace* (Oxford, 1755), 4.

[3] Ibid.

God in a more consistent and heartfelt manner. According to this minister, those who believed that the apparition had a supernatural origin had been issued with 'an extraordinary Call in their own Minds to Seriousness, and Reformation'.[4]

Jago's sermon was carefully constructed to address a number of different groups within the parish, which, though small, encompassed a group of people who varied widely in their commitment to the set forms of Anglican worship. Firstly Jago addressed the newest members of his congregation. The vicar observed that many new faces had been drawn to the church on this particular Sunday in search of spiritual guidance about the celebrated vision. For their trouble they were chided for their previous absence, with Jago insisting that 'God requireth your public Worship of him, and your thankful Use of his Ordinances', which may indicate that a number of the local inhabitants were rather negligent in their formal religious observances.[5]

Aside from those who were reluctant to attend services, Jago also used this rare opportunity to rebuke the more familiar faces in the crowd. There were those, he declared, who were often '*slow* and *heartless*' when 'summon'd to attend the Duty of Public Prayer'.[6] These parishioners also demonstrated their devotional laxity by loitering around the doors of the church after service had already begun. Jago's pastoral zeal clearly extended beyond the assurance of mere external conformity to the set forms of the liturgy, and he advised those who attended services 'out of mere Form, or Custom' not to profane the 'holy Sanctuary' of the church by offering such empty gestures. Solemn prayers and catechisms were undoubtedly designed as aids to devotion, but the performance of such prosaic activities were viewed by Jago 'but as sounding Brass, and a tinkling Cymbal' unless they were offered 'in Spirit and Truth'.[7]

Nonetheless, although Jago acknowledged the convenience of this particular providential intervention in reinforcing the moral imperative of the Anglican faith, his sermon was by no means an endorsement of a faith based on such occurrences. Jago had no wish to deny that God *could* call upon providential signs and wonders if he chose to do so. But that he would *ordinarily* do so was declared 'a vain Thing for us to

[4] Ibid. 17–18.
[5] Ibid. 21.
[6] Ibid. 24.
[7] Ibid. 23–24.

imagine, and an unwise one to desire'.[8] Along with many of his peers Richard Jago believed that there existed more reliable and more *reasonable* tools with which to encourage parish piety. There was little doubt that spectacular revelations had a dramatic and immediate effect upon those who witnessed them, but such instances, he believed, did not always ensure long-term commitment to the ordinances of God. Jago thus affirmed the accepted hierarchy of authorities endorsed by the Church of England, which regarded Scripture, human reason and the writings of the early Church fathers as more authoritative than extra-biblical revelations.[9]

To illustrate this point Jago read from Luke 16: 31 and drew parallels between the parable of Dives and Lazarus and reactions to the Harbury apparition. In simple words he retold the story of Lazarus and of the rich man who was blinded to his spiritual duties by material luxuries and repented too late. From his fiery pit in hell, Dives begged Abraham to let him appear to his brothers as a spirit to warn them of their future torment. But his request met with a sharp rebuke. Abraham insisted that men had already been provided with sufficient proofs of God's work in Scripture – in a famous response he declared that 'if they hear not Moses and the *Prophets*, neither will they be persuaded tho' one rose from the *dead*'.[10]

The choice of parable was significant. It strongly suggests that the 'apparition' in the churchyard had been conceived of as a departed soul or as a restless ghost. The linguistic distinction between 'ghost' and 'apparition' had important philosophical implications, which I have explained elsewhere.[11] The story of Dives and Lazarus also allowed Jago to imitate the posture of Abraham by chiding his parishioners for their excessive attachment to material comforts. His interpretation of the apparition narrative therefore supported the Church's emphasis upon moral and holy living.

Nonetheless, the main use to which Jago put the event was to admonish his congregation for relying upon extraordinary interventions to strengthen their faith in Almighty God. According to the Vicar

[8] Ibid. 15.
[9] This point is discussed more fully by Ian Green, 'Anglicanism in Stuart and Hanoverian England', in S. Gilley and W. J. Sheils, eds, *A History of Religion in Britain* (Oxford, 1994), 168–87, at 170.
[10] Jago, *Causes of Impenitence*, 9.
[11] Sasha Handley, *Visions of an Unseen World: Ghost Beliefs and Ghost Stories in Eighteenth-Century England* (London, 2007), 9, 212–13.

of Harbury, the best way to ensure the safety of one's soul was to abide by the '*ordinary* Means of Instruction, and Grace, which God affords us, – and not to expect, or wait for *extraordinary*, and *supernatural* Providences'.[12] These *ordinary* methods were identified as public prayer, catechism and observance of the Sabbath, which together gave 'full and sufficient Provision' for salvation.[13] This was not an attempt to exorcize ghostly visitations entirely from religious life, but rather to deprioritize them and to move them down the scale of devotional tools available to Anglican ministers and their congregations.

Jago's interpretation of the Harbury apparition was heavily influenced by the specific pastoral context of Harbury, but his views were also mediated by the philosophical climate of the day. Jago's preferred path to salvation was well-established within the Church of England and his words were reminiscent of early Protestant reformers like Archbishop Sandys, who in 1585 optimistically declared that 'the gospel hath chased away walking spirits'.[14] Jago's thoughts on this controversial subject must, however, be situated within the much altered intellectual and theological climate of mid-eighteenth century England. This minister was reluctant to express his own personal views about the nature and reality of apparitions, but it is possible to reconstruct his viewpoint from his wider cultural interests and activities. When he was not ministering to his parishioners, Jago was often to be found in the company of poet William Shenstone. The two men were firm friends, both attending Solihull School and going on to Oxford University together in 1732. Here Jago attended as a servitor before gaining his MA in 1739. In 1746 he moved from the parish of Lapworth to take up the livings of Harbury and neighbouring Chesterton, which had been secured by his patron, Lord Willoughby de Broke. The two livings brought in a combined annual income of approximately £90, but Jago still struggled to meet the financial needs of a rapidly growing family. As a result, and under Shenstone's supervision, he spent much of his spare time writing poetry. Indeed, it was Shenstone who effectively acted as Jago's literary patron, and who introduced him to the influential publisher Robert Dodsley, who included a number of Jago's verses in his miscellaneous collections. Surviving correspondence between Jago and Dodsley makes clear that the former composed his poems not

12 Jago, *Causes of Impenitence*, 10.
13 Ibid. 13–14.
14 E. Sandys, *Sermons*, ed. J. Ayre, PS 41 (Cambridge, 1841), 60.

just for pleasure, but in hope of a modest profit to supplement his clerical income.[15]

A brief examination of Jago's literary work and milieu is relevant here for revealing the lively intellectual environment in which he circulated outside of his parish, and which framed the subject of apparitions in a different way. Although Jago had a few contacts in London, his main artistic influences were closer to home. He was a member of the so-called 'Warwickshire Coterie', a literary group centred on Lady Luxborough at Barrel's Hall, Ullenhall. It was here that Jago engaged with intellectual debates à la mode, and discussions may well have touched upon metaphysical topics, of which there are strong traces in the work of both Jago and Shenstone.

In contrast to Jago, Shenstone was a confirmed Deist who rejected the Trinity in favour of belief in a God who had created the universe but who no longer exerted any direct influence over natural phenomena. It was in keeping with these principles that Shenstone penned his highly sceptical prose piece *An Opinion of Ghosts* in 1764. Aside from his brand of natural religion, Shenstone's thoughts were clearly influenced by Enlightenment discourse and by the polite world of letters. Shenstone engaged with physiological research on mental delusions and on the defects of the human brain and eyes, which had circulated widely since the publication of Isaac Newton's *Optics* in 1704. What were once perceived to be apparitions or ghosts could now be revealed as chimeras of a defective imagination that were likely to occur when human passions were roused to an excessive pitch. Yet whether such visions were real or not, Shenstone conceded that they nonetheless retained 'some real use in God's moral government'.[16] Shenstone articulated the views of a growing number of poets and novelists in these years who believed that it was immaterial whether the image received by the brain was true or false since '[t]he effect, the conviction, and the resolution consequent, may be just the same in either of the cases'.[17]

Jago shared a similar appreciation for the aesthetic and moral value of ghost stories, although he clearly did not share Shenstone's confes-

[15] R. Dodsley, *The Correspondence of Robert Dodsley, 1733–1794*, ed. J. E. Tierney (Cambridge, 1988), 309–10, 389–91.

[16] W. Shenstone, 'An Opinion of Ghosts', in *The works, in verse and prose, of William Shenstone, Esq; in three volumes*, 5th edn (London, 1777), 2: 64.

[17] Ibid.

sional affiliation. Jago's poem *Peytoe's Ghost* (1759–63) illustrates the point well. When walking home one evening from Warwick, a clergyman (presumably Jago) met with the ghost of his recently deceased patron. The metaphysical status of the ghost was irrelevant; instead, de Broke was called upon to confirm the moral character of William Craven, who had recently been appointed as a Knight in the county of Warwickshire. The poem was also a celebration of the Warwickshire landscape and particularly of its ethereal qualities, which appealed to the vogue for the picturesque and later to followers of Romanticism.[18] In Jago's most famous poem *Edge-Hill* (1767) the sense of an enchanted landscape was similarly pronounced. The unseen haunts of sprites and spectres were described with awe and admiration. But they were decidedly allegorical, and in a famous phrase coined by Joseph Addison (1672–1719) they were categorized as 'pleasures of the imagination'.[19] According to this purveyor of politeness, ghosts and apparitions were legitimate objects of contemplation because they liberated the creative imagination from the narrow confines of the domestic world, and because they were so often infused with firm moral principles which were essential components of gentlemanly identity and civic humanism. Jago's view of apparitions was clearly influenced by Addison, with passages of *Edge-Hill* reminiscent of Addison's most famous publication, *The Spectator*, in which his artistic-supernatural manifesto was first set out. Jago was probably convinced that the moral utility of ghosts and apparitions was more significant than their sometimes flimsy empirical foundations, an opinion which was clearly articulated in his apparition sermon in Harbury.

The wider intellectual climate of the 1750s had very important consequences for the way in which apparitions and ghosts were envisaged, and this encompassed a very particular understanding of divine providence which was closely associated with poets and intellectual elites. The wonders and judgements of the divine were no longer to be discerned in dramatic outbreaks of plague or in monstrous births. A more indirect approach was instead favoured, one in which the wonders of God were reflected, rather than realized, in aspects of the natural world. Towering mountains, raging waters and wild forbidding woodland epitomized the boundless and impenetrable wonders of

---

[18] R. Jago, *Poems, Moral and Descriptive, By the Late Richard Jago A. M.* (London, 1784), 181–84.

[19] R. Jago, *Edge-hill, or, the rural prospect delineated and moralized* (London, 1767), title page.

creation.[20] In a similar vein the poetry of Thomas Gray and his fellow Graveyard Poets purposely conjured up images of the ephemeral condition of mankind through descriptions of churchyard topography.[21] The 'special status' of sacred verse in the eighteenth-century Church has been duly noted by Jeremy Gregory, and the work of prominent clerics Robert Lowth and Christopher Smart helped to fashion this genre as an acceptable outlet for spiritual expression.[22] Studying the intricate workings of the natural world was in itself considered to be an act of piety because it led the mind from the visible to the invisible and from secondary causes to the original Cause. The subtle shift in meaning witnessed in Jago's nature poetry allowed tales of ghosts and apparitions to be accepted either as real manifestations of divine power, or in Jago's terms as symbolic narratives. The meanings drawn from such reports were often the same despite this important philosophical distinction.

If Jago's literary pursuits led him to adopt this more sophisticated interpretation, then the parishioners of Harbury did not – something which Jago clearly understood. It seems highly significant that Jago subdued his own scepticism about the existence of real apparitions for the sake of the spiritual welfare of his parishioners. The compromise was justified by Jago when he claimed that 'what makes such things proper and sometimes necessary is owing to Circumstances peculiar to a Minister and his own Congregation, which can never affect others in exactly the same Manner'.[23] Jago's sermon was first and foremost a considered response to local circumstance; the work might then be termed a negotiated form of Anglicanism since it involved a genuine attempt to accommodate the beliefs of the Harbury people within a flexible devotional framework.

But how representative was Richard Jago's experience? Although his sermon was designed with his own congregation in mind, his publication of it in 1755 suggests that he believed the Harbury apparition would be of interest to a wider audience. Indeed, Jago's words may well

[20] R. J. Mayhew, *Landscape, Literature and English Religious Culture, 1660–1800* (Basingstoke, 2004), 70–126.

[21] T. Gray, *An elegy written in a country church yard* (London, 1751); Mayhew, *Landscape, Literature*, 44.

[22] J. Gregory, 'Anglicanism and the Arts: Religion, Culture and Politics in the Eighteenth Century', in J. Black and J. Gregory, eds, *Culture, Politics and Society in Britain, 1660–1800* (Manchester, 1991), 82–109, at 94.

[23] Jago, *Causes of Impenitence*, 3.

have resonated with the kind of people that James Ramble met in Northern England. In a travelogue which was also published in 1755, Ramble noted with wonder that this remote group of parishioners was entirely convinced 'that persons departed visited the upper regions again'. During Ramble's visit, reports broke out that a ghostly vision had been seen. As a result, the local churchyard became thronged with spectators who looked on whilst two local parsons recited prayers to try and exorcize the restless spirit. Ramble's contempt for this scene was thinly disguised and he particularly resented the fact that these two churchmen were 'hailed for their sanctity, and adored for their authority over the realms of darkness'.[24] In 1826 the Reverend Richard Polwhele similarly noted that 'some of the rusticated clergy used to favour the popular superstition by pretending to the power of laying ghosts. I could mention the name of several persons whose influence over their flocks was solely attributable to this circumstance'.[25] Despite the disapproval of Ramble and Polwhele it is clear that, in some regions, appearances of ghosts and attempts to exorcize them were an important component in the cultural adhesive that united incumbents with their parishioners. The active engagement of churchmen with both oral and written ghost stories represented a highly creative way of communicating with parishioners. Moreover, if we accept John Spurr's characterization of post-1714 Anglicanism as a pragmatic and less formal body of theological beliefs and devotional practices, ghost stories appear to blend seamlessly into this fluid cultural milieu rather than appearing anomalous.[26]

The spiritual overtones of these narratives also proved useful in negotiating the well-publicized doctrinal struggles of the 1750s and 1760s. These decades were dominated by intense theological debate about the continued value of revelation in religious life. The controversial clergyman Francis Blackburne brought these disagreements to a head in 1755 when his incendiary tract *No Proof in the Scriptures of an Intermediate State* was first published. Blackburne's mortalist philosophies were here given full rein; the human soul was rendered immortal only through Christ's sacrifice and the soul slept between death and the resurrection to eternal life.

---

[24] E. Kimber, *The Life and Adventures of James Ramble*, 2 vols (London, 1755), 1: 29.
[25] R. Polwhele, *Traditions and Recollections*, 2 vols (London, 1826), 2: 605.
[26] Green, 'Anglicanism', 168; J. Spurr, ' "Latitudinarianism" and the Restoration Church', *HistJ* 31 (1988), 61–82.

Blackburne's view was dangerously reminiscent of those of the radical religious sects of the English Civil War and he was denounced by his more orthodox and firmly Trinitarian colleagues within the Church, who set out to restore the precarious balance between a faith of the head and one of the heart. The Bishop of Gloucester, William Warburton, was among Blackburne's most prominent opponents, but Warburton's viewpoint was supported by many others both within and outside the Anglican fold. Baptist sympathizer Grantham Killingworth offered a vigorous defence of revealed religion in his 1761 tract *On the Immortality of the Soul*.[27] Lancashire curate Richard Dean firmly believed in the reality of ghosts, and he broadcast his providential ideas in an essay of 1767.[28] In 1778 Benjamin Caulfield's *Essay on the Immateriality and Immortality of the Soul* insisted that God worked by both general and particular laws of providence, which were experienced on a regular basis. If God was the divine watchmaker of the universe, it was only common sense to believe that 'the watch does sometimes want both to be wound up, and to be repaired'.[29]

Despite these words of support, however, clerical defences of miracles, visions and wonders were constrained by the discourses of enlightened empiricism and civic humanism, which encouraged contributions to public life that promoted ideals of human progress. Richard Jago justified his foray into print on the grounds that all profits would be given to the Free-School at Harbury. This was an admirable civic venture and a work which Jago described as 'providentially design'd' to improve the religion and humanity of the local community for years to come.[30] Augustus Toplady, Vicar of St Olave Jewry in London, similarly preached on the possibility of ghosts and apparitions to collect money for his parochial school. In a 1775 sermon Toplady insisted that there was nothing absurd in the philosophy of apparitions. 'I do not suppose' he continued 'that one story, in an hundred of this kind, is true. But I am speaking, as to the naked possibility of such phaenomena. And this I am satisfied of.'[31] Toplady maintained a 'stedfast and mature

---

[27] G. Killingworth, *On the Immortality of the Soul, the Resurrection of the Body, the Glorious Millennium, the most glorious kingdom of God, and the prophet Daniel's numbers* (London, 1761), 11.

[28] R. Dean, *On the future life of brutes, introduced with observations upon evil, its nature and origin* (London, 1767), 81, 91–99.

[29] B. Caulfield, *Essay on the immateriality and immortality of the soul* (London, 1778), 6.

[30] Jago, *Causes of Impenitence*, 1, 5.

[31] A. M. Toplady, 'The Existence and the Creed of Devils Considered: With a Word Concerning Apparitions', in idem, *Sermons and Essays* (London, 1793), 269–94, at 282.

belief, not only that there are unembodied spirits; but also that, upon some special occasions, unembodied spirits and disembodied spirits have been permitted, and may again, to render themselves visible and audible'.[32] For Toplady the idea of ghosts could hardly be considered unreasonable when 'God the Holy Ghost' was 'an unembodied spirit', who shared a kinship with 'disembodied spirits' and the 'glorified souls of the departed elect'.[33] Ghosts commanded a logical place in Toplady's Trinitarian theology, which allowed descriptions of the spirit world to form part of wider attacks upon Unitarian heresies as well as strengthening the faith of his parishioners. The priorities of lay spirituality could thus shape the contours of parish life, and in certain circumstances they could also influence wider philosophical debates about the links between the visible and invisible worlds.

Clearly not everybody chose to utilize ghost and apparition stories to preserve a balance between the marvellous and the mundane. Nonetheless, the preoccupations of theologians and philosophers ensured that ghost stories could be called upon as potentially valuable resources for apologists seeking to secure the faith from extremist attack. When ghost stories were verified by substantial evidence and supported by the philosophical scaffolding of civic humanism, a theological compromise was possible; it was a compromise which provided a veneer of respectability for the telling and retelling of ghost stories both in parish and in print.

By the mid-eighteenth century, reports of ghosts and apparitions remained an important, if occasional, tool of devotional encouragement for a select number of Anglican clergy. On the public stage these narratives still had a part to play in some of the key theological debates and confessional struggles of this period, especially at times of religious and political crisis. Nonetheless, a rapidly changing intellectual climate saw many such reports exposed to the ridicule of satirists. As a result they were rarely allowed to stand on their own merit, but were instead buttressed by the language of empiricism and civic humanism and by the conventions of moral philosophy.

At parish level, perceptions of ghosts and apparitions offer partial yet valuable insights into the nature and variety of lay spirituality. The spectral encounter in Harbury reveals much about varying degrees of

---

[32] Toplady, cited in R. M. Baine, *Daniel Defoe and the Supernatural* (Athens, GA, 1968), 94.
[33] Toplady, *Sermons*, 282.

commitment to formal Anglican worship. Richard Jago's decision to adopt the episode as part of his pastoral reform strategy shows that this particular clergyman was tuned into the preoccupations of his parishioners and committed to improving their spiritual welfare through a variety of imaginative methods. Jago's flexibility also suggests that we must find some kind of middle ground between Peter Virgin's pessimistic assessment of the eighteenth-century Church as an 'age of neglect' and Jonathan Clark's optimistic vision of harmonious relations in parish life.[34] Jago's approach suggests that the lived realities of parish life were much messier than these two historical models allow, and whilst Harbury was not without its tensions, Jago was at least actively engaged in trying to improve relations with his flock. Interpretations of the relative success or failure of the Church do of course depend upon the kind of source material consulted. The somewhat optimistic picture painted here may well be offset by further research into the trials and tribulations of this Warwickshire parish. Moreover, the very fact that several ministers utilized the popular cultural form of the ghost story as leverage to secure loyalty to the Church of England might in itself be interpreted as a sign of weakness. When placed in their immediate contexts, however, these efforts seem rather to demonstrate an innovative pastoral strategy through which ministers engaged their flocks and brought their hearts and minds towards God. The experiences of Richard Jago and his congregation were distant from one another in educational and cultural terms, but accommodation was possible and often actively sought. What is equally clear from the few glimpses of ghostly appearances discussed here is that the shape of devotional life was crafted by multiple forces, including wider intellectual trends, and not least by the laity themselves. This essay can touch upon just a few of the myriad debates engaged in by historians of eighteenth-century Anglicanism, and it certainly offers no comprehensive answers. I hope, however, that it might recommend a fresh and interesting set of sources to enrich debates about the nature of lay spirituality and the contours of parish life in the eighteenth-century Church.

University of Manchester

---

[34] J. C. D. Clark, *English Society 1660–1832: Religion, Ideology and Politics during the Ancien Regime* (Cambridge, 2000); P. Virgin, *The Church in an Age of Negligence: Ecclesiastical Structure and Problems of Church Reform 1700–1840* (Cambridge, 1989).

RESCUING THE PERISHING HEATHEN: THE BRITISH EMPIRE VERSUS THE EMPIRE OF SATAN IN ANGLICAN THEOLOGY, 1701–1721

by ROWAN STRONG

IN 1493–94, Pope Alexander VI divided the globe between Spain and Portugal with reference to their conquest of the territories of the New World. In the eighteenth century, Anglicans divided the globe into the territory of Christ and the lands and peoples under the dominion of Satan. The Bishop of Carlisle in 1719 was adamant that that indigenous heathen peoples were 'insensible of the great Concernments of their immortal Souls, and very much uncertain, at best, in their apprehensions of a future life; they are abandoned to their lusts and passions; and under the dominion of Satan'.[1] Consequently, affirmed Edward Waddington of Eton College in 1720, Satan was alarmed by the formation of a new Anglican mission society for work in British North American and West Indian colonies 'at the approaching Loss of so many Millions of Subjects'.[2] Through heathen ignorance of their spiritual captivity the Devil 'supported an Empire of almost equal extent with the Universe, and led the World captive at his pleasure', except where Christ had delivered humankind from devilish tyranny and dominion.[3]

This essay examines the views of the afterlife propounded by the annual preachers of the anniversary sermons of the Society for the Propagation of the Gospel in Foreign Parts (SPG) in the first twenty years following its foundation in 1701. Although some preachers attended to the future eternal fate and condition of the colonial heathen in these sermons, this aspect was not as prominent as their present perishing condition as subjects of the worldly empire of Satan

---

[1] Samuel Bradford, *A Sermon Preached before the Incorporated Society for the Propagation of the Gospel in Foreign parts at their Anniversary Meeting in the Parish-Church of St Mary le Bow, on Friday the 10th of February, 1719* (London, 1720), 22.

[2] Edward Waddington, Fellow of Eton College and royal chaplain, *A Sermon* (London, 1721), 33.

[3] John Waugh, Dean of Gloucester, *A Sermon* (London, 1723), 14–15.

for these preachers. Ultimately, it was this world, rather than the next, which mattered primarily for missionary motivation for these early Anglican mission supporters.

The Society was legally incorporated by Royal Charter to provide Anglican ministrations to the English overseas and to evangelize non-Christian peoples in crown territories. It was the brainchild of Thomas Bray who, when Rector of Sheldon, Warwickshire, responded in 1695 to the Bishop of London's request to be his commissary in Maryland. This North American engagement gave Bray a lifelong concern for the colonial church and had earlier resulted in his founding the Society for Promoting Christian Knowledge in 1698. The annual anniversary sermons of the SPG, which were delivered throughout the eighteenth century and into the nineteenth, constitute the first and most sustained construction of an Anglican missionary theology and theological engagement with the British Empire.

At this time Anglican views of the afterlife for the heathen of the British Empire were varied, reflecting domestic theological differences between Latitudinarians and High Churchmen. Some simply asserted the hellish destiny of the heathen; a few flirted with an intermediate state; and most remained uncertain as to the divine determination of heathen destinations. Judgement in the afterlife, however, was certain; and what could tip the balance in favour of a better outcome for the heathen was for the British Empire to be an effective agent of extending the Gospel and thereby taking the heathen from denizens of hell to becoming citizens of heaven. But, as preachers in the name of a new society, undertaking a missionary task that was not familiar to members of the Church of England, the SPG preachers' primary focus was on what could be done here and now for the perishing heathen, which entailed inculcating support for an agency which could be seen to make a difference. The concentration on this life, rather than the afterlife, among the SPG preachers was also in keeping with the metropolitan task of the Church of England in this period of changing the lives of the English to make them more moral, more devout and more active members of the Church of England. Arguably, this was in response to the reigns of two Stuart kings which had not resulted in the strong alliance between throne and altar that churchmen had dreamed of.

The new missionary focus on the heathen abroad came at a time of concern for moral reformation at home, through voluntary societies, and the Societies for the Reformation of Manners endorsed by the Church of England in 1699 but existing for a decade before that. These societies had both a devotional and a prosecuting dimension, endeavouring both to encourage and to compel the English into virtue. But it seems that the afterlife and the threat of eternal punishment did not play as large a role in the theology and propaganda of these societies and their preachers as did ascetical theology, personal sin, the love of God in this life, or the providential theology that retribution for immorality would follow in this life and in national chastisement by God.[4]

However, promotion of an eternal afterlife of heaven or hell was not entirely subsumed by a focus on temporal existence, as it was a commonplace that such belief was essential for the inculcation of social and moral virtue, especially among the lower orders. This was a recipe held by many of their social betters, even Deists such as Lord Shaftesbury.[5] Thomas Burnet, for example, the exotic cosmologist and disciple of the Cambridge Platonists, wrote in 1728 '[t]hat whatever you decide, in your own Breast of these Eternal Punishments, the people, too easily prone to Vice and easily terrified from Evil must have the commonly received Doctrine'.[6] While the orthodox resiled from such a socially pragmatic view of the afterlife, they certainly upheld the importance of eternal reward and punishment as central to religion, and as revealed truth; as did Bishop Fell of Oxford who in 1675 asserted: 'the great business of religion, is to oblige its votaries to present duty by awe and expectation of future retribution'.[7]

But this customary view of the afterlife had been brought into serious question in the later seventeenth century for the educated elite by the infamous work of the philosopher Thomas Hobbes. Hobbes's call for empirical evidence to substantiate every religious claim not only undermined folk or popular religion with its love of apparitions and revelations, but also challenged orthodox understandings of heaven and hell. One historian has posited that this intellectual threat to both levels of religion may have accounted for the storm of antagonism

---

[4] John Spurr, 'The Church, the Societies and the Moral Reformation of 1688', in John Walsh, Colin Haydon and Stephen Taylor, eds, *The Church of England c. 1689–c. 1833: From Toleration to Tractarianism* (Cambridge, 1983), 127–42, at 130, 140.

[5] Paul C. Davies, 'The Debate on Eternal Punishment in Late Seventeenth- and Eighteenth-Century English Literature', *Eighteenth-Century Studies* 4 (1971), 257–76, at 267.

[6] Quoted in Peter Harrison, *'Religion' and the Religions in the English Enlightenment* (Cambridge, 1990), 95.

[7] Quoted in John Spurr, *The Restoration Church of England, 1646–1689* (New Haven, CT, 1991), 259.

towards Hobbes.[8] Indeed, John Redwood has drawn attention to the serious questioning by the end of the seventeenth century of the whole orthodox worldview, including the afterlife, the miraculous and a spirit-centred universe, by Deists and others who emphasized reason and empiricism so that even the existence of the soul was under question. Theology was increasingly emphasizing reason, to the detriment of revelation, as a more secure ground for faith, as the Latitudinarians proposed, notwithstanding the doughty defence of the old cosmology of this life and the afterlife by some conservative champions.[9]

In that respect, Anglican Latitudinarians were also major contributors to the declining emphasis on the torments of hell as a deterrent to immorality, believing that such a view of the afterlife was contrary to the idea of a just and compassionate God. In 1690 a funeral sermon by John Tillotson, later Archbishop of Canterbury, became a source of controversy between himself and the leading Nonjuror, George Hickes. In his pamphlet Hickes accused Tillotson of diminishing the torments of hell, which had been divinely decreed by Christ. Hickes also upbraided Tillotson for preaching that there was a possibility of repentance in the afterlife, which was, for Hickes, a wanton disturbing of the divine cosmological order and heretical.[10] The Roman Catholic Alexander Pope was another who disagreed with the Latitudinarians' sanitizing the traditional horrors of hell and presenting a more palatable afterlife.

> The following license of the Foreign Reign
> Did all the Dregs of bold Socinus drain;
> Then Unbelieving Priests reform'd the Nation,
> And taught more Pleasant Methods of Salvation;
> Where Heav'ns Free Subjects might their Rights dispute,
> Lest God himself shou'd seem too Absolute.[11]

But while there was concern for moral reform at home in the moral societies, with their focus on the battle between sin and sanctity in the human soul and on the providential consequences in this life of English ungodliness, there was little contemporary English theological interest

---

[8] John Redwood, *Reason, Ridicule and Religion: The Age of Enlightenment in England, 1660–1750* (London, 1996), 74.

[9] Ibid. 153–54.

[10] Davies, 'The Debate on Eternal Punishment', 260–61.

[11] Ibid. 265.

in the eternal destiny of the heathen in these or other sources. At the same time as SPG preachers were asserting the hellish afterlife of the heathen under Satan's empire, a small controversy on the afterlife of the heathen was initiated in England by the erudite Nonjuror Henry Dodwell. Dodwell, in *An Epistolary Discourse* (1706), surprised and disgusted his more orthodox contemporaries by his speculation on the fate of those peoples that had never heard the Christian gospel. He propounded an intermediate state into which the heathen would enter after death. At the general resurrection on the Last Day Christians would be reborn to eternal bliss, and those who heard the gospel and rejected it to eternal torment. The heathen, then, would have the breath of God withdrawn from them and be annihilated. This fate, Dodwell argued, was the decree of a just God because the heathen, not having heard the Gospel, did not deserve hell and could not have heaven, and there was no third eternal state for them. While most of his contemporaries derided his argument, one who did answer it was the Platonist John Norris in 1709, who argued that it was incompatible with the love of God to destroy so many heathen and pagans. Platonists such as Norris, and the Cambridge Platonists of whom he was a late disciple, argued for there being a better fate deserved by virtuous pagans.[12]

But this was an erudite argument among a tiny theological minority. The SPG preachers, who had a larger audience, held the orthodox line that the heathen needed to hear and embrace the gospel if they were to be certain of a life of bliss rather than of torment. The most common ways used by SPG preachers to describe the situation of the heathen were to quote the Benedictus, which referred to those who 'sit in darkness and in the shadow of death' (Luke 1: 79), or to insist that they needed to be turned 'from darkness to light, and from the power of Satan unto God' (Acts 26: 18). Mostly the preachers were content to describe the state of these damned with words such as 'fear', 'trouble' or 'punishment'.

Bishop William Fleetwood went a little further in his sermon of 1711 to talk of 'The Wrath of God [which] is now Reveal'd against all Unrighteousness, and the Effect of it, is endless Punishment, in Pains most exquisite'.[13] Hell was the place of no escape or redemption, said John Waugh, Dean of Gloucester, at the beginning of his sermon in

---

[12] Philip C. Almond, *Heaven and Hell in Enlightenment England* (Cambridge, 1994), 62–63.
[13] William Fleetwood, Bishop of St Asaph, *A Sermon* (London, 1712), 9.

1722. On the basis of the verse about Christ preaching to the spirits in prison after his death (1 Peter 3: 19–20), he suggested that some early Fathers posited a middle state as distinct from purgatory. These writers, he said, opined that it was, unlike purgatory, not a place of painful purging but a state of incomplete blessedness where souls remained until the general resurrection. But he thought this theological construction unlikely as the verse spoke of spirits in prison, not in some semi-blissful paradise, and he rather preferred to interpret the text to mean those in this world dead in their sins, which included the heathen of the New World.[14]

But while the preachers were confident that the heathen lived under the dominion of Satan and that, consequently, the likelihood was that they would perish eternally, these early SPG spokesmen declared themselves uncertain that this was definitely their lot in the afterlife. For the earliest preachers of the Society, the eternal perishing of the heathen was probable, though not quite assured. However, a state of damnation was certain for Christians who rejected the evangelical command of Jesus Christ, a state for which the few preachers who described it in detail were content to use biblical imagery. In the very first sermon given at the foundation of the Society, Dean Richard Willis of Lincoln left his hearers in no doubt as to what was expected of them as Christians or the state of their afterlife if they did not fulfil such evident Christian obligations:

> Infidelity is constantly in Scripture reckoned as destructive of Salvation. Thus when Our Saviour sent His Disciples at first to Preach the Gospel, He Orders them, Go, preach the Gospel to every Creature, and then tells them, He that believeth and is baptized shall be saved, but he that believeth not shall be damned. To the same effect St. John tells us in the Revelations, That the fearful, and unbelieving shall have their portion in the lake that burns with fire and Brimstone, that is the second death. These places I believe are chiefly to be understood of those who have the Gospel Preached to them, but who through an evil heart of unbelief don't receive it. As for those who never heard of the Gospel, and so have not the guilt of rejecting it, I shall leave them to their own Master, before whom they must stand or fall. I have shewed before, That they have no Covenant-title or Promise either to the

14 Waugh, *Sermon*, 5–7.

Assistance of God's Holy Spirit, or the Pardon of their Sins, or Eternal Life, but still they are the Creatures of God, and he will find ways to deal with them as a Wise and a Merciful Creator.[15]

Two years later John Williams, the Bishop of Chichester, was following Willis's line that the eternal destiny of the heathen was uncertain; unlike Christians, whose assurance of heaven was definite, their fate remained with the mysterious judgement of God.

> As to the Case of the Heathens to whom Christ was never preached, they *stand and fall their own Master*, and according to that which *right* he [God] will give them. It is amongst the Secrets which belong to God ... As for our Parts, we can only judge by the Law, which is our Rule, and so cannot take upon us either to absolve them whom the Lord doth condemn, or to make that which is not certain to be certain ... But this is plain, that the Gospel is to be preached to all.[16]

These preachers, and others such as John Hough, Bishop of Lichfield and Coventry, maintained that while Christ's warning was clear that those without faith in him would perish, no one could be held accountable for a proposition they had never heard, and therefore the fate of the heathen was fundamentally unknown.[17] But certainty of salvation and the afterlife was unquestionably a desideratum for these orthodox Christians, and for that the heathen needed the Gospel. Both the perishing heathens of the colonies and the Christians at home had the same immortal souls and were designed for an 'eternal State of happiness'. If the English Christians did nothing to bring this about by transmitting to them the Gospel, then they would suffer a heavy charge 'at the great day of account'.[18] But if this duty was carried out, affirmed the Bishop of Carlisle, then such dutiful Christians 'who are now in another World, are receiving the Reward of so great a Service done to their Blessed Redeemer, as well as to their Brethren by Nature'.[19] Earlier, in 1704, his colleague had pointed to one such instance of a (not so) anonymous donor (Queen Anne) who had given £1000 to the Society, commenting that the donor 'would have no Share of her

[15] Richard Willis, Dean of Lincoln, *A Sermon* (London, 1702), 14.
[16] John Williams, Bishop of Chichester, *A Sermon* (London, 1706), 14.
[17] John Hough, Bishop of Lichfield and Coventry, *A Sermon* (London, 1705), 7–8.
[18] Philip Bise, Bishop of Hereford, *A Sermon* (London, 1718), 39–40.
[19] Bradford, *Sermon*, 30.

Reward on Earth that she might have it full, shaken together, and running over in Heaven'.[20]

Judgement was inescapable for Christian and heathen alike, though that judgement would be made more bearable and merciful by the fact that the judge, Jesus Christ, had shared our human nature. 'When the awful and tremendous Majesty of God is to be approach'd the Thought is terrible … Our Lord therefore has taken Humane [sic] Nature upon him, and exerts through it all the Benignity of the Deity, while the Dread is restrained'.[21] In 1712 the Bishop of Ely, John Moore, was content to be a bit more expansive on heaven and hell, again using biblical images. All would go to judgement after death to give an account of the actions of their lives. For this to happen the earth and sea would give up their dead and the parts of each individual's body would be rejoined in their old shape and to their same soul. Assembled before the judgement throne of Christ, these reconstituted human persons would then be separated into good and evil, the former to enter heaven and the latter to depart for eternity from Christ's presence. The good would be blessed with the fullness of joy; the damned would be consigned to everlasting fire which they would share with the Devil and his angels.[22]

Generally, however, the preachers were restrained in their depictions of the afterlife. The Dean of St Asaph, William Stanley, in 1707, was characteristic in his confessed ignorance about the detail of the blissful afterlife:

> As to the other life, tho we cannot particularly describe what the Glories of Heaven are, no more than what the Business of that State is, yet we are sure that it will be very happy to all that shall enjoy it. But to all those great benefactors, they may be sure to say as St. John said, who was one of the great and happy Instruments of Converting the World; It doth not yet appear what we shall be, but we shall see our Saviour as he is himself, and that must needs be the highest pitch of Felicity.[23]

Other than Bishop Moore, the only preacher who dwelt more graphically upon the afterlife was Bishop Hough, who was uncharacteristi-

[20] Gilbert Burnet, Bishop of Salisbury, *A Sermon* (London, 1705), 24.
[21] Hough, *Sermon*, 15.
[22] John Moore, Bishop of Ely, *A Sermon* (London, 1713), 38.
[23] William Stanley, Dean of St Asaph, *A Sermon* (London, 1709), 19–20.

cally detailed in his views. Both the life of the saved and of the damned, he maintained, had degrees of eternal existence, of life and happiness in the former state and death and misery in the latter one. It was not possible, he asserted, to define this too far or to specify the ingredients of their happiness, but 'its fundamental constituent was the enjoyment of' the presence of God. In such enjoyment some 'shall be nearer, and some more remote from Him'. That is, some of the blessed had larger spiritual capacities and consequently 'more compleat and fuller Idea's of God's Perfections than others; for even the Angels themselves have different Powers'. As heaven had spiritual distinctions and subordination, so also did hell: not all its denizens would be 'in the same degrees of Pain, whether sensible or intellectual'. There may even be some, the bishop piously hoped, who would suffer no extra misery than was attendant upon eternal exclusion from the face of God.[24] This conception of spiritual gradations in heaven and hell was not unusual in post-Restoration England, as it was common for contemporary theologians who upheld the traditional view of the afterlife to maintain such *post mortem* diversity based on the degree of sinfulness or sanctity at death.[25]

These SPG preachers believed there was an imperial remedy for the battle their society had recently undertaken for the salvation of the heathen. In order to rescue the souls of the eternally perishing heathen from the empire of Satan they endeavoured to enlist the emerging English Empire (British from 1707) in this spiritual Christian contest between God and Satan. For example, the Bishop of Carlisle in 1719 commented that the British 'are under very peculiar obligations' now that Providence had given them success in seeking out foreign countries 'that we might also be useful to them in concernments of much greater moment [than secular ones], namely, those which relate to the spiritual and eternal well-being' of the colonial heathen. Bishop Edward Chandler told his hearers that God had placed English colonists in places where they could observe the 'thick Darkness, the blind Ignorance and gross Idolatry, the entire neglect of God's worship these Natives live in and the Hazard their immortal Souls are in', and consequently it was the obligation of the English to bring Christianity to them. 'Are we not answerable for these Souls: May not their Blood be

---

24 Hough, *Sermon*, 10–11.
25 Almond, *Heaven and Hell in Enlightenment England*, 144.

required at our Hands?', he asked rhetorically.[26] Their Society and the Empire, the preachers repeatedly proclaimed, were the new divine instruments for the English to take up (belatedly, compared with their Spanish and French Catholic imperial rivals) this self-evident Christian task in the battlefield of their North American colonies. The colonies had brought before these SPG Anglicans at least the existence of heathen souls as distinct from Christian ones at home, or dubiously Christian ones in the form of their colonists. On a material level the English faced Spanish and French foes contesting their hold on overseas territories and the intervening ocean between colonies and metropole. But on a spiritual level the British Empire, through the SPG, was also contesting with the empire of the Devil for the souls of its heathen indigenous peoples, and for the equally non-Christian slaves in those territories. The Society's preachers, as part of their attempts to engage the interest of their countrymen and co-religionists in this imperial spiritual engagement, were consciously bringing the afterlife into play as a motivation for spurring the interest of their Anglican audience in this colonial engagement. Just as continued colonization of their souls by Satan would bring the heathen into hell, so also a passive acquiescence in that perilous state by the English at home or abroad would bring them into God's unfavourable judgement in their afterlife. The eternal destinies of both Christians and heathens were intertwined, they asserted in this early Anglican missionary theological construction.

In essence, the colonial heathen were viewed as the passive recipients and the Christians as the active partners in this battle of spiritual empires for the eternal life of the heathen. They were, affirmed Bishop Chandler of Coventry and Lichfield, 'the most miserable and helpless object', deserving, consequently, of the charity of the English.[27] The heathen, slaves or indigenes, were seen as spiritually and morally powerless. The identities of these two heathen groups, as proposed by these metropolitan Anglicans, meant they were regarded as incapable of securing heaven and avoiding hell unless Christians intervened. Hough, early in the series of sermons, is characteristic in proposing that it was the Christians who are commanded by Christ to go into all the world and preach the Gospel; Christians who had the power to 'open the Eyes of the deluded Gentiles, and to turn them from darkness to light and

26 Edward Chandler, Bishop of Coventry and Lichfield, *A Sermon* (London, 1719), 23–24; the title of the diocese was not at this stage fixed.
27 Ibid. 23.

from the power of Satan to God'.[28] The slaves 'know no better, and they are bad with a bad religion ... destitute of the means of Grace'.[29] The Indians were of a 'tractable, sweet, and gentle disposition, and indued with all those good Qualities which made them fit for it [the Christian Religion]'.[30] It was the slaves and the Indians whose condition paralleled that of the Gentiles of the New Testament - under the thrall of Satan; while the English Christians stood in the place of St Paul and the first Christian missionaries with the power to 'come over and help'.[31]

A number of these preachers were Latitudinarians, and presumably they agreed with the general theological position of their kind in diluting the terrors of hell in favour of more reasoned motives for mission. These included Bishops Hough, Lloyd, Burnet, Trimnell, Fleetwood and White, and Dean Willis.[32]

Consequently, the views of the afterlife held by these preachers were fairly mainstream in this regard. Most, presumably, would have agreed with the Bishop of Chichester in his assertion that an eternal reward of heaven or punishment in hell for disbelief in Christianity or an immoral life was a revealed truth of Christ's gospel.[33] How then do we account for this dimension of orthodox Anglicanism being so little to the fore in their sermons? The contemporary intellectual climate of increasing challenge to orthodox eschatology is one factor. For all their ultimate concern about the eternal destination of the heathen as a motive for this first Anglican mission, the SPG preachers, even those identified here as being the most detailed in their descriptions of the afterlife, devoted far more attention to expatiating upon the morally destructive consequences for the heathen of their rule by Satan in this world than attending to the details of the afterlife. Dean Waugh, who allowed the possibility of some *post mortem* middle state, dwelt far more upon the difficulties and obligations English Christians had here and now to 'preach to the Spirits in Prison, to bring degenerate Mankind out of Pagan Darkness, from the Power of Satan, and the Dominion of their own unruly lusts, into the glorious Light and Liberty of the

---

[28] Hough, *Sermon*, 8.

[29] Ibid. 23–24.

[30] Ibid. 27–28.

[31] Ibid. 8, 25; this was a reference to the SPG's motto, which was taken from Acts 16: 9.

[32] Rowan Strong, 'A Vision of an Anglican Imperialism: The Annual Sermons of the Society for the Propagation of the Gospel in Foreign Parts 1701–1714', *Journal of Religious History* 30 (2006), 175–98, at 181–83.

[33] John Williams, Bishop of Chichester, *A Sermon* (London, 1706), 12.

Gospel of Christ'.[34] Dean Willis, describing the lake of fire for unbelievers and disobedient Christians, occupied himself more in his inaugural sermon with the barbarity and idolatry of the heathen natives, for whom it was an act of charity pleasing to God to relieve, a duty which lay especially upon those who had grown rich from trade with these parts of the globe.[35] Even Hough's detailed exposition of heaven and hell was only a small part of a sermon devoted much more to the dangerous state of the heathen here and now. Heathenism in the present life was 'a state of Blindness and Thraldom, as a state of Death and Damnation' – and the obligation of the Christian was to relieve that servile life which led inevitably to hell. Hough used at length the writings of Bartolomé de Las Casas (1484–1566), the fiercely pro-Indian Roman Catholic Bishop of Chiapa in Guatemala, which also gave him the opportunity to dabble in the standard anti-popish polemic of Anglicans, in this case as an illustration of the defects of Roman Catholicism among the Indians of the New World.[36]

The reduction in the prominence of heaven and hell in these sermons may also have had much to do with the contemporary theological emphasis on benevolence and charity. But there was little benevolent pulling of theological punches about the threat posed by immorality in the work of the Society for the Reformation of Manners, which fervently pursued the punishment of sinners through the courts. Nor did any contemporary charitable theological impulse put any of these heathen in heaven or propose a universalist salvation accessible without a knowledge of Christ. They merely asserted uncertainty about divine judgement in the case of unwitting ignorance of the Saviour.

While the preachers either portrayed the heathen in hell unless liberated by the Gospel, or, more commonly, they remained reserved about the details of the final destiny of the heathen, they were more definite about the hellish doom that would befall English Christians who did not support this self-imposed rescue mission for the colonial heathen. However, the diminution of the afterlife as one of a suite of motives for rescuing the perishing heathen of the New World may have had more to do with the newly-founded position of their Society than with any declining belief in heaven or hell among the preachers. Conscious of the need to recruit supporters for a society founded only a

34 Waugh, *Sermon*, 25.
35 Willis, *Sermon*, 18–22.
36 Hough, *Sermon*, 8, 26–39.

few years before, with a totally unprecedented institutional task for the Church of England of missionary work among the colonists and indigenes of English/British colonies, the preachers understood their task as finding the most effective ways of inculcating support among their metropolitan and colonial audiences.[37] While one of these ways was the avoidance of hell and the hope of heaven, it seems that they preferred to concentrate on a range of this-worldly motives for mission, from inculcation of loyalty to spiritual repayment for material trading riches.[38] This suggests that the afterlife was less powerful than facets of this life as an inducement for mission at the beginning of the eighteenth century, either because it was intellectually and theologically under cogent challenge from non-orthodox thinkers in the period, or because it was insufficiently stimulating to the pockets of the better-off among the laity, on whom the Society depended for financial support. Whatever the reason, rescuing the heathen from perishing eternally in the afterlife, at least in these early decades of Anglican mission, was less urgent than liberating them from the destructive consequences of rule by their hellish overlord in this life and this world.

Murdoch University

---

[37] The annual sermon was printed each year and distributed throughout the SPG networks in England and overseas, using supportive domestic clergy, as well as colonial chaplains supported financially by the Society.

[38] Rowan Strong, *Anglicanism and the British Empire 1700–c. 1850* (Oxford, 2007), ch. 2.

'IN THEIR MADNESS THEY CHASE THE WIND': THE CATHOLIC CHURCH AND THE AFTERLIFE IN LATE CHOSŎN KOREA

by ANDREW J. FINCH

FOLLOWING its introduction to Korea in 1784, the Catholic Church grew and developed within a rich and varied religious milieu. An indigenous tradition of popular religion, characterized in part by shamanistic practices, existed alongside two imported traditions: Confucianism and Mahāyāna Buddhism.[1] The latter had enjoyed state patronage in the Koryŏ period (918/935–1392) but, with the establishment of the Chosŏn dynasty (1392–1911), it was supplanted by Chu-Hsi Neo-Confucianism (Chuja-hak). This became central to a policy of social reformation and was elevated to the position of state orthodoxy. Neo-Confucianism thereby became the dominant social, political and metaphysical system, and, during the course of the seventeenth and eighteenth centuries, its influence spread to all levels of Korean society.[2] Buddhism was increasingly discriminated against, while popular religion was disparaged as superstitious and potentially subversive.[3] Buddhist monks and nuns, together with shamans (mudang), were classed among the ch'ŏnmin, the 'base people', the very bottom of society whose members included butchers as well as slaves.[4] Nevertheless, all three traditions continued to exist in a form of antagonistic harmony, and the influence and attraction of popular religion and Buddhism remained strong at the lower levels of society and

[1] Interestingly Daoism, the third of the three 'pillars' of religion in China, did not develop as a distinct tradition in Korea, although it influenced both geomancy and magic: J. H. Grayson, *Korea: A Religious History*, 2nd edn (London, 2002), 51–52; Suk-jay Yim, R. L. Janelli and Dawnhee Yim Janelli, 'Korean Religion', in J. M. Kitagawa, ed., *The Religious Traditions of Asia* (London and New York, 1989), 333–46, at 333.

[2] M. Deuchler, *The Confucian Transformation of Korea: A Study of Society and Ideology* (Cambridge, MA, 1992), 27, 126–28, 286–87; Grayson, *Korea*, 83, 103–04, 112–13; B. Walraven, 'Popular Religion in a Confucianized Society', in JaHyun Kim Haboush and M. Deuchler, eds, *Culture and the State in Late Chosŏn Korea* (Cambridge, MA, 1999), 160–98, at 161.

[3] Grayson, *Korea*, 120–23, 137–38; Walraven, 'Religion', 160, 167.

[4] Deuchler, *Transformation*, 13, 302; S. J. Palmer, *Korea and Christianity: The Problem of Identification with Tradition* (Seoul, 1986), 44.

among women in general.[5] Indeed, the second half of the eighteenth century witnessed outbreaks of Buddhist millenarianism as individuals appeared claiming to be the future Buddha, Maitreya (Korean: Mirŭk).[6]

Each of the three traditions had more or less distinct beliefs concerning the afterlife, and the intention here is to outline these and then compare them with those held by Catholicism. This will, it is hoped, highlight elements which may have helped or, alternatively, hindered Catholicism's assimilation in the period between 1784 and about 1840. Much of the existing interest regarding the accommodation or otherwise of Catholicism within late Chosŏn Korea has focused on the reaction of the Confucian elite. Accommodation has been seen principally in terms of Catholicism's intellectual appeal, together with Western science and mathematics, to a group of reform-minded scholars, some of whom may also have been attracted by the message of asceticism prominent in the Jesuit texts they received from Beijing.[7] One line of inquiry to be pursued here will consider the significance of Catholicism's superficial – but nonetheless striking – resemblance to Pure Land Buddhism in its potential appeal to groups beyond this elite. The Confucian elite also provided Catholicism with its fiercest opponents, with the principal divide being opened up after 1790 when the papal prohibition concerning participation in the ancestral rites became known. This created an unbridgeable intellectual and social fissure between Catholicism and Confucian society in Korea. The principal interest in what follows will be to consider the extent to which contemporary Catholic eschatology may have created a further barrier to Catholicism's acceptance.

Confucianism ascribes particular importance to the respect to be accorded to one's elders and to one's ancestors, in the latter case through the performance of the ancestral rites.[8] Chu Hsi's synthesis of the Neo-Confucian schools added a metaphysical dimension to Confu-

---

[5] Grayson, *Korea*, 139; Walraven, 'Religion', 197.

[6] D. L. Baker, 'Tasan's World: Korea on the Eve of a Monotheistic Revolution' (typescript), 4. I am grateful to Dr Baker for providing me with a copy of this paper and for allowing me to cite from it.

[7] D. L. Baker, 'A Different Thread: Orthodoxy, Heterodoxy, and Catholicism in a Confucian World', in Kim Haboush and Deuchler, eds, *Culture*, 199–230, at 210–12; idem, 'A Confucian Confronts Catholicism: Truth Collides with Morality in Eighteenth Century Korea', *Korean Studies Forum* 6 (1979–80), 1–44, at 6.

[8] On ancestral rites, see, in this volume, Paul Rule, 'The Chinese Rites Controversy: Confucian and Christian Views on the Afterlife', 280–300.

cianism's ethical and social concerns.[9] This, however, did not allow for
a distinct and eternal soul distinguishing man from the physical world,
as in Christianity. Everything in the universe was considered 'natural':
that is subject to, and encompassed by, *i* (principle) which manifests
itself in *ki* (raw, unformed matter and energy). Man and the rest of the
universe therefore shared a common substance, and man was a balance
of universal *i* and the *ki*, which gave form and character to an individual. However, as all phenomena appear and disappear through the
natural condensation and dispersion of *ki*, so too would an individual's
ki eventually disperse after death.[10]

It was held that after death an individual's upper (intellectual) soul
(*hon*) would enter the afterlife, while the lower (animal) soul (*paek*)
would descend with the body into the grave.[11] Great emphasis was
placed on the proper forms of mourning and burial. Particular care was
taken over the auspicious siting of graves as the essential connections
between the worlds of the living and the dead, and considerable efforts
were made to slow the decay of the body. If the link between the living
and the dead could be preserved, and if the ancestors found peace in the
ground, then their descendants would find peace in the world. Such
concerns over proper burial and appropriate mourning were seen as
spontaneous expressions of the most natural of human emotions: filial
piety.[12] This was held to separate man from brute animals, and its ultimate manifestation was to be found in the performance of the ancestral
rites. These formal sacrifices, known in Korea as *chesa*, were made by
the males of a household in respect of up to four generations of ancestors, before their memorial tablets. Fr Dallet's introduction to Korean
culture, published in 1874, described such tablets as being

> generally of chestnut wood … [The] tablet is a small flat board on
> which they paint using white lead, and on each they inscribe the
> name of the deceased in Chinese characters. Around the edge they
> make holes through which the soul has to enter. The tablet, placed

9 Grayson, *Korea*, 102.
10 Walraven, 'Religion', 163–64.
11 J. Ching, 'East Asian Religions', in W. G. Oxtoby, ed., *World Religions: Eastern Traditions*
(Toronto, 1996), 346–467, at 396; Xinzhong Yao, *An Introduction to Confucianism* (Cambridge,
2000), 201.
12 C. Dallet, *Histoire de l'église de Corée, précédée d'une introduction sur l'histoire, les institutions,
la langue, les moeurs et coutumes coréennes: avec carte et planches*, 2 vols (Paris, 1874; repr. Seoul,
1975), 1: cxli; Deuchler, *Transformation*, 197.

in a square box, is kept by the wealthy in a special hall or chamber, and by the common people in a sort of niche in the corner of the house. Poor people make their tablets from paper.[13]

The significance of the offerings of food and wine made during *chesa* was open to interpretation. For some, the rites were a symbolic cere-mony which expressed the dignified respect and gratitude of children towards their parents. For others, the tablets became the site where the upper and lower souls would be reunited (hence the holes described by Dallet) and from which the deceased could in some way partake of the offerings. However, whether a symbolic or literal view was taken, the crucial matter was that the rites be conducted as sincere and respectful expressions of the filial piety which was the foundation of the social and moral order.[14]

The existence in some form or another of the spirits of the dead was, in any case, generally accepted, and some scholars subscribed to the view that the *ki* of exceptional individuals might persist long after their demise.[15] The potential threat to the living posed by restless spirits was accepted too, and measures taken to reduce it. Confucian sacrifices (*yŏje*) had been instituted in 1401 for the benefit of all abandoned spirits (*yŏgwi*), those hungry ghosts without – or neglected by – relatives who could not enjoy the benefits of the rites and whose collective resent-ments were held to cause epidemics. The restless spirits of those who had died violently were placated in more specific ways: 'chaste women' (*yŏllyŏ*) who had chosen death rather than dishonour, whether through slander or defilement, had gates and stelae erected in their honour; and soldiers who had died in battle were worshipped at special altars (*minch'ungdan*). These actions rewarded and promoted, in the former, the Confucian virtue of chastity and, in the latter, the civic virtue of loyalty; but both activities served additionally to appease and placate these potentially dangerous spirits.[16]

Acceptance of the existence of ancestral spirits and the potential

[13] Dallet, *Histoire*, 1: cxliii.

[14] Baker, 'Confucian', 11; idem, 'The Martyrdom of Paul Yun: Western Religion and Eastern Ritual in Eighteenth Century Korea', *Transactions of the Royal Asiatic Society, Korea Branch* 54 (1979), 33–58, at 44–47; Ki-bok Ch'oe, 'La rencontre du confucianisme et du catholicisme en Corée: Les conséquences de la "querelle des rites" ', trans. An Ŭng-yŏl, *Revue de Corée* 16 (1984), 21–41, at 33–34, 36–37.

[15] Walraven, 'Religion', 164, 166.

[16] Ibid. 175–76, 189–91.

dangers posed by restless spirits formed a continuum between scholarly
Confucian thought and popular beliefs concerning the afterlife. Korean
popular religion too considered that the spirits of the dead, invisibly
intermingled with the living as they were, required special care and
attention in order to reduce the risk of the deliberate or inadvertent
harm that they might cause. However, while Confucianism tended to
regard spirits as a generality, and its true focus was on the filialism
expressed through the *chesa* rites, popular religious practice dealt with
spirits on an individual level and was more concerned with practical
matters. Korean shamans, *mudang*, were employed as psychopomps
(specialists whose task is to guide spirits to the world of the dead) or to
prevent or remedy the harm caused by spirits with lingering grudges.[17]
Buddhism too had absorbed the concern that the dead might cause
harm to the living, and the blind exorcists (*p'ansu*, *sogyŏng* or *changmin*)
who specialized in healing diseases caused by angry or malevolent
spirits employed Buddho-Daoist rites.[18] Unlike Catholicism, or indeed
Buddhism, neither Confucianism nor popular religion held to any
belief in posthumous rewards or retributive punishments; and while
both maintained that the conduct of the living could affect the condition of the dead, this was viewed in terms of improving the physical
well-being of the departed, by providing them with access to the necessities of life, rather than in ensuring their speedy progress through a
place of temporary punishment such as purgatory.

Buddhism, in contrast to both Confucianism and Korean popular
religion, has – like Catholicism – a clear interest in the nature of an
afterlife and a sophisticated soteriology. Essential to Buddhist teaching
in this regard are the concept of transmigration determined by the law
of karma – the accumulation of good and bad actions during an individual's life – and the suffering (*duhkha*) inherent within existence itself.
Release from the cycle of transmigration and hence from continual and
repeated suffering comes through the realization that suffering is
caused by desire, that the cessation of desire will bring about the end of
suffering, and that the means to achieve this is to follow the Holy
Eightfold Path. This realization will enable an individual to achieve
nirvana: a transcendent, perfect state in which all the causes of
suffering, together with suffering itself, have been extinguished. Once

17 Ibid. 170–71, 182.
18 Ibid. 167.

nirvana has been achieved an individual will no longer be reborn.[19] Mahāyāna Buddhism, historically the dominant form in East Asia, developed these essentials to stress the centrality of devotion and faith and the importance of the *bodhisattva* (Korean: *posal*) – an individual well advanced on the path to enlightenment who has chosen to delay entry into this state in order to assist others. Mahāyāna cosmology envisages many such spiritually advanced beings, each presiding over a transcendental region, from which each will bestow merit on anyone who prays for aid.[20]

Buddhism's encounter with Chinese indigenous religion gave rise to the concept of an underworld in which condign but temporary punishment would be assigned and the nature of a subsequent rebirth determined. After death, the dead faced judgement by the Ten Kings of Hell to determine whether reincarnation should be in the world, following a relatively short expiation of their misdeeds, or – if particularly sinful – in hell, the terrors of which were graphically described in the *Kśitigarbha Sutra*. Each king presided over his own court, and the dead moved sequentially from one to another, spending seven days in each. Those not deserving of a rebirth in hell could hope for dispatch to a new existence after forty-nine days.[21]

Given the terrors associated with hell, many looked for ways to escape from or lessen its sufferings. Relatives could intercede for the deceased to enhance their chances of obtaining a favourable rebirth by having intercessory rites celebrated at set times, with that on the forty-ninth day after the death being of particular importance; Confucianists condemned such practices as unfilial and profligate.[22] The bodhisattva Kśitigarbha (Korean: Chijang), was also looked to as one who had promised to rescue individuals from hell.[23] Pure Land Buddhism, however, went further in offering salvation from hell and rebirth in the Pure Land of the Buddha Amitābha (Korean: Amit'a).

[19] P. Harvey, *An Introduction to Buddhism: Teachings, History and Practices* (Cambridge, 1990), 37–39, 47–48, 61–62.

[20] R. C. Amore and J. Ching, 'The Buddhist Tradition', in Oxtoby, ed., *Eastern Traditions*, 214–345, at 268–69.

[21] Younghee Lee, 'Hell and Other Karmic Consequences: A Buddhist Vernacular Song', in R. Buswell, ed., *Religions of Korea in Practice* (Princeton, NJ, 2007), 100–11, at 103; B. Walraven, 'Eighteenth-Century Buddhist Beliefs and Practice in *Yŏmbul pogwŏnmun*', in I. Sancho et al., eds, *Proceedings of the 30th Anniversary Conference of the Association for Korean Studies in Europe* (Dourdan, 2007), 81–84, at 83.

[22] Deuchler, *Transformation*, 197–98; Lee, 'Hell', 104.

[23] Amore and Ching, 'Tradition', 306; Harvey, *Buddhism*, 133.

This was linked to the belief that humanity had already entered the degenerate Latter Age of the Law in which most individuals would be unable to achieve enlightenment through their own efforts.[24] The *Larger Sutra on the Pure Land* contains Amitābha's promise, made while still a bodhisattva, that even after attaining buddhahood he would continue to assist those seeking enlightenment. He would accomplish this by establishing a Pure Land in the western part of the universe, rebirth in which would bring easy progress towards nirvana. Rebirth in this Western Paradise is ensured by the performance of meritorious deeds combined with faith and devotion towards Amitābha, who is assisted in his task by the intercessory figure of the bodhisattva Avalokiteśvara (Korean: Kwanŭm) – the very embodiment of compassion who has vowed not to become a Buddha until all beings are saved.[25]

Pure Land Buddhism enjoyed widespread popular appeal in Korea, and the eighteenth-century *Yŏmbul pogwŏnmun* (Exhortation to Practise the Invocation of the Buddha [Amitābha]), compiled in both Chinese and Korean, has at its heart the conviction that reliance on Amitābha is the best method in this degenerate age to ensure rebirth in the Pure Land. Amitābha's Pure Land is described in the Pure Land Sutras as a physical paradise of beauty and abundance, filled with both gods and men, in which there is nothing unpleasant or painful, and where it is possible to hear the Law (*dharma*) of the Buddha everywhere.[26] The Korean version of the *Yŏmbul pogwŏnmun* likewise presents the Pure Land as a place of freedom not only from birth and death, but also from illness, where instantaneous buddhahood is promised alongside the satisfaction of all material wants. The chief means to attain rebirth in the Pure Land is through the invocation of Amitābha's name (*yŏmbul*): anyone who at the moment of death invokes Amitābha ten times using the phrase 'Namu Amit'abul' ('Hail to Amitābha Buddha') will be reborn in the Pure Land, even if they have committed sins deserving of a rebirth in hell. However, *yŏmbul* is clearly linked with the pursuit of

---

[24] The advent of this age was dated to fifteen hundred years after the death of Gautama Buddha, and for Korean and Japanese Buddhists the 'period of the latter-day *Dharma*' (Japanese: *mappō*) had begun in 1052; the calculations made by the Chinese Pure Land patriarch, Tao-ch'o, however, dated its inception to 549: Harvey, *Buddhism*, 153, 162; L. Lancaster, 'Maitreya in Korea', in A. Sponberg and H. Hardacre, eds, *Maitreya, the Future Buddha* (Cambridge, 1988), 135–53, at 141.

[25] Amore and Ching, 'Tradition', 274–75; Harvey, *Buddhism*, 131.

[26] K. K. S. Ch'en, *Buddhism in China: A Historical Survey* (Princeton, NJ, 1964), 338–39.

virtuous behaviour, often in conformity with Confucian standards, such as filial piety and moderation.[27]

Catholicism too has well-developed doctrines concerning the afterlife, having subscribed for a significant part of its history to a tripartite division: heaven; hell; and the intermediate state of purgatory where the majority of souls will receive condign, but temporary, punishment. Individuals may take action to alleviate the sufferings of souls in purgatory through prayers and the foundation of memorial masses. Although Catholicism came to Korea initially through contacts with missionaries in Beijing, it remained essentially coloured by the concerns of contemporary European and, increasingly, French Catholicism.[28] Developments within the Counter-Reformation Church led to a renewed emphasis on the stark contrast between the rewards of heaven and the pains and torments of hell. Clerical thinking was characterized by contempt for the world and a desire to keep the laity on the path of moral rectitude through a pastoral message of fear. This world was simply a vale of tears; salvation lay elsewhere in another world with no connection to the present one. Contemporary preachers concentrated on death, judgement, hell, salvation and the dreadful consequences of sin (even the most venial of sins, if unconfessed, might land an individual in purgatory, which itself was often portrayed as an extremely unpleasant and terrifying, though temporary, mini-hell), and they left their audiences in no doubt about the intense and eternal physical suffering to be experienced in hell.[29]

This Tridentine Catholicism was rapidly assimilated by the Korean laity, and it found expression in the words of the Church's martyrs. Yu Chin-gil, during his interrogation in 1839, maintained that, in following the doctrine of the Europeans, an individual could escape the eternal torments of hell and enjoy the eternal rewards of heaven.[30] At an earlier date, Yi Sŏng-rye had compared the brevity of this life with the eternity of the future life, while Yi Kwang-nyŏl, writing shortly before his execution in July 1839, told his readers that 'life is but an

[27] Walraven, 'Beliefs', 82–83.

[28] Kyong-suk Min, *Catholic Socio-Religious Survey of Korea*, Part I: *Findings of Content Analysis, The Spiritual Ethos of Korean Catholicism*, 2 vols (Seoul, 1971), 1: 34–35. Initially dependent on the Diocese of Beijing, Korea became a Vicariate Apostolic of the Société des Missions Étrangères de Paris in 1831, and French missionaries began to enter the country from 1836.

[29] R. Gibson, *A Social History of French Catholicism, 1789–1914* (London, 1989), 15, 22–23, 26–28, 242, 245–48; Min, *Survey*, 1: 9–14, 18.

[30] Dallet, *Histoire*, 2: 169.

instant'. He went on to dwell upon the stark contrast between this world and the next, a contrast in which the transience and vanity of the mundane world were epitomized by the decay and dissolution of the body after death. Sin featured prominently, and for Yi his accumulated sins were like mountain ranges.[31] Although purgatory was absent from the accounts of the martyrs – who were purging their sins through earthly suffering – the existence of prayers for the dead shows that the laity were exposed to the doctrine.[32]

The complex religious milieu pertaining in late Chosŏn Korea ensured that Catholicism encountered a rich variety of established beliefs and practices concerning the afterlife. Confucianism was to a degree agnostic about such matters: what was important was the moral behaviour of the living towards the dead, wherever or whatever they might be.[33] The practical management of the dead was a particular concern of popular religion, while Buddhism – like Catholicism – preached a message of potential rewards and punishments and the possibility of salvation. All three accepted in their different ways the permeability of the divide between the worlds of the living and the dead in that the condition of the dead could influence, and be influenced by, the living. Korean Catholic apologists, sensitive as they were to the inherent prejudices of this milieu, sought to make common cause with Confucianism and to distance their religion from Buddhism. However, the outward similarities between Buddhism and Catholicism were striking, and were duly noted by Confucians in their own anti-Catholic polemics.[34] In their popular form, Buddhist beliefs concerning the afterlife comprised: the physical existence of the Pure Land and hell, in which rewards and punishments were meted out according to the tally of one's moral behaviour; a necessity for judgement and purgation; the intercession of the living on behalf of the dead; the intercession in this world by spiritually advanced beings; and an emphasis on faith, devotion and moral behaviour as a means of release from a condition of suffering. These found parallels within Catholicism, where, although heaven and hell stood as polar opposites with an

[31] Ibid. 2: 164, 235–38.
[32] Ibid. 2: 115.
[33] Baker, 'Confucian', 12; idem, 'Paul Yun', 46, 48, 53.
[34] Wŏn-sun Yi, 'The Sirhak Scholars' Perspectives of Sŏhak in the Late Chosŏn Society', trans. Yun-sŏng Kim, in Chai-shin Yu, ed., *The Founding of Catholic Tradition in Korea* (Mississauga, Ont., 1996), 45–102, at 54–55, 59, 61–65.

unbridgeable gulf between the two, purgatory played a role analogous to the Buddhist hell as a place of temporary and purgative suffering. Catholicism too stressed the efficacy of intercession by the living, or the intercessory figures of Jesus, Mary and the saints, in alleviating purgatorial suffering. The assignment of posthumous reward, punishment and purgation was determined by an individual's moral behaviour, and Catholicism preached a message of salvation through faith and morality set within the context of an imperfect and transient world. As Boudewijn Walraven suggests, such similarities – although grounded in distinct doctrinal premises – may have made Catholicism appear both familiar and acceptable to its largest group of converts: women, whose religious habits were associated with both Buddhism and popular religion, and whose religious needs were poorly catered for by Confucianism.[35]

Whatever the positive influence of such similarities, limits existed to any potential accommodation, especially as Catholicism was itself not shy about presenting a face that was unfamiliar and often unacceptable to East Asian societies. Catholicism clashed most famously and spectacularly with Confucianism over the ancestral rites. In Korea, this conflict arose during 1791 when Yun Chi-ch'ung and his cousin destroyed all the ancestral tablets in their possession following the death of Yun's mother. Their action, by which the cousins were held to have lowered themselves to the level of beasts and barbarians, ensured not only their trial and execution, but also the classification of Catholicism as a perverse teaching (*sahak*), which had moved beyond the private questioning of accepted ideas to the public rejection of orthodox ritual and precepts.[36] The ancestral rites controversy can be viewed as one manifestation of a conceptual divide between different worldviews, in this case Catholicism's insistence on the paramouncy of divinely-ordained truth as opposed to Confucianism's concern with the pre-eminence of socially determined morality.[37] Other manifestations of this divide were the doctrine of an afterlife characterized by a stark division between heaven and hell, and the special significance of martyrdom for the Catholic Church. Martyrdom formed a pervasive element in East

---

[35] Walraven, 'Beliefs', 82, 84; idem, 'Religion', 185–88, 197. It is possible that up to two-thirds of the laity were women: Masahiko Sawa, *Mikan Chōsen Kirisutokyōshi* [A History of Korean Christianity (Unfinished Work)] (Tokyo, 1991), 60.

[36] Baker, 'Different Thread', 220, 230; idem, 'Paul Yun', 49.

[37] Baker, 'Paul Yun', 48, 51, 53–55.

Asian Catholic missions, and in Korea, with persecutions occurring intermittently after 1785, a martyr cult had developed even before the arrival of French missionaries in 1836.[38] When dealing with Catholics, until the Great Persecution (1866–71), the authorities sought to encourage apostasies in preference to executions: by the acceptance of equivocal responses; by the use of threats and blandishments; and in the final resort by the application of torture.[39] This could be sustained and brutal.[40] For Catholics, though, while apostasy might briefly prolong their lives, it would ultimately cause the death of the soul.[41] A martyr's death, however, would guarantee the soul's salvation.[42] The belief in a better world to come, coupled with the fear of eternal punishment, led some Korean Catholics to endure intense and often prolonged physical suffering, and ultimately to accept death, in the expectation of the eternal rewards of heaven. Some even courted this fate with several examples of laity surrendering voluntarily to the authorities being recorded during the Kihae persecution in 1839.[43]

Martyrs by the manner of their deaths were guaranteed a place among the 'very special dead', the saints in heaven, and with it release from their sins and a continuing intercessory role on earth.[44] Korean Catholics often spoke of their desire for martyrdom, and government records of interrogations of Catholics commented on the willingness and determination with which they faced their deaths.[45] Catholics, it seemed, regarded death as a 'glory'; martyrdom was to be accepted 'like a lamb'.[46] This apparent disdain for life set Catholicism apart. Popular religion held no such precept, and, while Confucian teachings encouraged the imitation of the Sages, many of whom had suffered death by adhering to their moral convictions, Confucianism provided no developed eschatological or soteriological teaching encouraging a desire for

[38] *Annales de la Propagation de la Foi* 11 (Lyon, 1838–39), 353; Dallet, *Histoire*, 1: 55, 103, 136, 305, 321; 2: 64, 236.
[39] Dallet, *Histoire*, 2: 144, 146, 149, 163–64, 200.
[40] See for example, ibid. 2: 171, 193–94, 198.
[41] Ibid. 2: 194.
[42] Ibid. 2: 193, 226, 328.
[43] Ibid. 2: 139–40, 170, 198.
[44] P. R. L. Brown, *The Cult of the Saints: Its Rise and Function in Latin Christianity* (London, 1981), 62, 70, 72–73, 80; Dallet, *Histoire*, 2: 236.
[45] Sŭngjŏngwŏn [The Royal Secretariat [of the Chosŏn kingdom]], *Sŭngjŏngwŏn Ilgi* [Diary of the Royal Secretariat] (Seoul, 1975), 117: 945, 952; Mission de Seoul, *Documents relatifs aux martyrs de Corée de 1839 et 1846* (Hong Kong, 1924), 7–9, 49, 54–55.
[46] Mission de Seoul, *Documents*, 3; Sŭngjŏngwŏn, *Ilgi*, 117: 917; Dallet, *Histoire*, 2: 137.

martyrdom.[47] Similarly, while the compassionate giving of one's life to aid others may be viewed positively in Buddhism, and the Mahāyāna has a small tradition of 'religious suicides' undertaken as demonstrations of piety or to call attention to persecutions and the sufferings of others, there are again no such imperatives promoting martyrdom: rebirth in the Pure Land is achieved through moral behaviour and complete devotion to Amitābha.[48] Korean Catholics, however, through their belief in an eternal soul, subject to suffering in this world and judgement in the next, and their understanding of martyrdom as the pre-eminent path to salvation, came to demonstrate attitudes to death that were novel and shocking to contemporaries.[49] Faced in 1839 with Catholics who would willingly rather die than apostatize, Yi Chi-yŏn, president of the Royal Secretariat reacted with incomprehension: 'To love life and to avoid death is a sentiment common to humanity, but for them it is not so: the sword or fetters they regard as if they were going to a place of ease; demented men, demented women, in their madness they chase the wind.'[50]

Following its foundation in 1784, the Korean Catholic Church developed in a religious milieu in which its own teachings on the afterlife encountered a range of established beliefs more or less distinct from its own. Neo-Confucianism, the guiding ideology of the intellectual elite, provided the most marked contrast. Its essentially monistic view of the universe did not allow for the existence of a distinct and eternal soul, and its emphasis on the moral behaviour of the living left no room for a system of posthumous rewards and punishments. In fact, Confucianism was to a large degree agnostic about the nature of an afterlife, and the fate of the dead was firmly linked with, and largely subordinated to, the moral behaviour of the living. Similarly, although one of the principal concerns of Korean popular religion was to ensure the wellbeing of the dead, this was seen largely in terms of reducing the risk

[47] J. Ching, *Confucianism and Christianity: A Comparative Study* (Tokyo, 1977), 87.

[48] Harvey, *Buddhism*, 203. This tradition, however, appears most pronounced within Vietnamese Buddhism, and the example generally cited is that of the self-immolation of Buddhist monks protesting against the Diem regime in 1963: Amore and Ching, 'Tradition', 329–31; F. Fitzgerald, *Fire in the Lake: The Vietnamese and the Americans in Vietnam* (New York, 1972), 129–34.

[49] Baker, 'Paul Yun', 55; Min, *Survey*, 13.

[50] Mission de Seoul, *Documents*, 1–2; Sŭngjŏngwŏn, *Ilgi*, 117: 917. The Chinese, *mi ran sui feng*, translated as 'ils suivent le vent', conveys the sense of following a trend or a fancy. I am grateful to Kejun Yan, formerly of the London School of Economics, for explaining the meaning of this phrase.

that disgruntled spirits might pose to the living. The Confucian elite also provided the membership for the earliest group of Christian believers in Korea, and the inherent prejudices of their social and religious milieu led Catholic apologists, in their arguments for the intellectual and moral respectability of Catholicism, to seek common cause with Confucianism against Buddhism. However, much Catholic belief and practice concerning the afterlife bore a striking resemblance to elements within Pure Land Buddhism, in which devotion was emphasized as the means of escape from the purgatorial pains of hell and to achieve other-worldly salvation in the Pure Land. Such resemblances may have facilitated Catholicism's adoption by those groups, in particular women, whose religious concerns Confucianism either discounted or ignored, and who had traditionally found solace in popular religion and Buddhism. However, the soteriological pre-eminence of martyrdom engendered and encouraged by Catholic eschatology set potential limits to any accommodation. Martyrdom, like non-participation in the *chesa* rites, marked Catholicism out, not only from Confucianism, but also from Buddhism and popular religion; and, for its Confucian critics at least, the willingness of Catholics to die for their faith would have been further proof that Catholicism was irrational and that its adherents were indeed lower than savages and animals.[51]

Ambleside, Cumbria

---

[51] Mission de Seoul, *Documents*, 3; Sŭngjŏngwŏn, *Ilgi*, 117: 917.

THE 'RESTITUTION OF ALL THINGS' IN NINETEENTH-CENTURY EVANGELICAL PREMILLENNIALISM*

by MARTIN SPENCE

THIS paper explores the nineteenth-century doctrine of the 'restitution of all things', a concept of the afterlife which emphasized material continuity with the present and generated detailed speculation about the activities and events which would take place in the eternal realm. Such beliefs, it will be suggested, resonated with broader developments in nineteenth-century theology which tended to soften the boundary between this life and the life to come, and increasingly suggested that the Christian hope was for the coming of the kingdom of God on earth rather than for the soul to go to heaven after an individual's death. This belief has been almost completely neglected in previous historiographical discussions of nineteenth-century evangelical eschatology. To recognize its existence challenges many historiographical depictions of the 'world-denying' nature of Evangelicalism in general and the pessimistic temperament of pre-millennialism in particular.

The 'restitution of all things' was a shorthand term for a set of beliefs about the future destiny of individuals and the world which came to prominence among a group of evangelical Protestants in Britain in the middle decades of the nineteenth century. Those propounding this position argued that God's ultimate purpose was to establish his kingdom on a renovated earth populated by resurrected human beings. William Pym, the Rector of Willian, Hertfordshire, and author of a book devoted to explaining the doctrine, summarized it this way in 1843: 'By the restitution of all things ... we understand to mean, that almighty act whereby every thing, which has been cursed for the sin of man, shall be restored to at least its primitive state of perfection and blessing'.[1]

---

* The research upon which this article is based was funded by a grant from the Arts and Humanities Research Council.

[1] W. W. Pym, *The Restitution of All Things* (London, 1843), xi.

The doctrine was one strand of a broader eschatological position called premillennialism.[2] Premillennialists believed that there would be a period of righteousness on earth lasting one thousand years, an idea for which they claimed to find support in Revelation 20. They claimed that the physical return of Christ to earth was the only way in which this period of godly rule could be inaugurated and sustained. They objected to the postmillennial view, popular among the previous generation of Evangelicals, which held that missionary exertion would produce an earthly millennium before the return of Christ.

There were two varieties of premillennialism in the nineteenth century, historicism and futurism.[3] The difference between these positions related primarily to the interpretation of prophecy. Historicists believed that the prophetic scriptures were being fulfilled in the long course of western history. Futurists, by contrast, believed that apocalyptic passages in Scripture referred to events that would occur in a short span of time in the near future. It was historicist premillennialists who believed most strongly in the restitution of all things. This was not coincidental, since their commitment to the way in which God acted in space and time shaped the historicist premillennialist expectation that he would eventually establish his kingdom within the temporal-spatial realm. As the well-known historicist premillennialist Thomas Rawson Birks (1810–83) put it, during the millennium 'the separate elements, prepared for thousands of years, are all to be combined in one vast and glorious exhibition of the moral dominion of God'.[4] Historicist premillennialism gained many adherents in the middle decades of the nineteenth century, including the social reformer Lord Shaftesbury (1801–85), the publisher Robert Benton Seeley (1798–1886), and the former Church Missionary Society missionary Edward Bickersteth (1786–1850). The *British and Foreign Evangelical Review* reckoned in 1855

[2] The most comprehensive study of the premillennialist movement remains Ernest Sandeen, *The Roots of Fundamentalism: British and American Millenarianism, 1800–1930* (Chicago, IL, 1970). Several recent studies have supplemented this work, including Crawford Gribben and Timothy C. F. Stunt, eds, *Prisoners of Hope? Aspects of Evangelical Millennialism in Britain and Ireland, 1800–1880* (Carlisle, 2004); Crawford Gribben and Andrew Holmes, eds, *Protestant Millennialism, Evangelicalism and Irish Society, 1790–2005* (Basingstoke, 2006). The most detailed, although highly subjective, work on historicist premillennialism is Le Roy Edwin Froom, *The Prophetic Faith of Our Fathers*, 4 vols (Washington, DC, 1946).
[3] See D. W. Bebbington, *Evangelicalism in Modern Britain: A History from the 1730s to the 1980s* (London, 1989), 85–86.
[4] Thomas Rawson Birks, 'The Resurrection to Glory', in W. W. Pym, ed., *Good Things to Come* (London, 1847), 227–72, at 253.

that 'probably the majority' of evangelical clergy in the Church of England adhered to premillennialist views.[5]

Although belief in the restitution of all things emerged from a revived belief in the idea of an approaching earthly millennium, historicist premillennialists did not believe that a reinvigorated terrestrial existence was limited to this period of one thousand years. Rather, it was something that comprised their entire eschatological hope. Thomas Nolan (1809–82), the minister of St John's, Bedford Row, London, thus affirmed in 1855 the belief that the gamut of millennial promises could in fact be read as pertaining to the whole span of eternal life:

> This blessed period begins with the coming in glory of Christ at the commencement of the millennium ... It is not, however, necessary to suppose that it is to terminate at the close of that period, especially when so many passages speak of reigning for ever and ever.[6]

The restitution of all things was therefore proposed by these premillennialists as an alternative vision of life after death to that which they believed was held by many Evangelicals. They criticized the notion of a 'heavenly' future life which was ethereal and immaterial, claiming that such a hope owed more to the 'phantomizing system of the Buddhists, who believe that the future happiness of mankind will consist in moving about in the air'.[7] Historicist premillennialists argued that there was in fact no 'heaven' to which believers would go after death; no hope for the future life other than that Christ would return to establish his kingdom on earth. As the Irish historicist premillennialist journal *The Christian Herald* put it in 1830, 'when Christ return[s] to earth, then this earth will be all that we are used to fancy heaven would be'.[8]

The remainder of this paper examines three significant aspects of the belief in the restitution of all things as it occurred amongst some historicist premillennialists of this era. First, it will outline the way in

[5] The article, a review of Samuel Waldegrave's 1854 Bampton Lecture on 'New Testament Millenarianism, also noted that 'the Tractarians are at least favourably inclined to it': *British and Foreign Evangelical Review* 4 (1855), 697–710, at 698.
[6] Thomas Nolan, 'The Saviour's Throne', in Robert Bickersteth, ed., *The Gifts of the Kingdom* (London, 1855), 289–334, at 323–24.
[7] *Christian Ladies' Magazine*, April 1841, 7.
[8] *Christian Herald* 1 (1830), 159.

which their hope for the rescue of the whole earth led to a strong endorsement of the material world and the physical body. Secondly, it will offer further detail concerning their beliefs about the quality of life in the world to come, paying particular attention to the way in which they expected it to be a sphere of activity. Thirdly, it will discuss the ways in which the implications of this idea of 'restitution' moved some historicist premillennialists towards a modified soteriology. The sources for this discussion are journals, sermons and tracts produced by historicist premillennialist writers. In particular I draw upon the regular Lenten lectures given by Church of England clergymen at St George's, Bloomsbury, under the auspices of the Prophecy Investigation Society between 1843 and 1859.

The Physicality of Redemption

Premillennialism is often interpreted as a pessimistic or gloomy creed.[9] Such descriptions seem especially apposite when the premillennialist temperament of mid-nineteenth century Evangelicals is contrasted with the optimism of the previous generation's postmillennial hope. Whilst the dominant postmillennialism of late eighteenth-century Evangelicalism believed that human missionary effort would bring about a period of righteousness on earth before the return of Christ, the premillennialist had no such confidence in human ability to transform society. 'Until Christ comes again', wrote Baptist historicist pre-millennialist John Cox (1802–78) in 1862, '... man will go on chasing shadows, and creation will groan under its heavy burden'.[10] However, historicist premillennialists did not believe that the second coming of Christ marked the end of the world. The 'coming of the Lord' should not be 'regarded as the final dealing of God with mankind and the earth, as the end of all history and of time itself,' suggested the *Quarterly Journal of Prophecy*, a publication edited by the Scot Horatius Bonar (1808–89), for 'when the Lord comes he has much to do upon the earth'.[11] Thus, far from being 'world-denying', to use Clyde Binfield's

[9] Kenneth G. C. Newport, *Apocalypse and Millennium: Studies in Biblical Eisegesis* (Cambridge, 2000), 12–13.
[10] John Cox, *The Future – An Outline of Events Predicted in the Holy Scriptures* (London, 1862), 120.
[11] Anon., 'God's Purpose Concerning Man and the Earth', *Quarterly Journal of Prophecy* 6 (1854), 250–67, at 264.

ascription, many premillennialists desired to find a central place for the terrestrial globe in their expectations of the future life, a belief which anticipated, albeit in a different guise, later nineteenth-century 'social gospel' beliefs about the coming of the kingdom of God on earth.[12]

Because historicist premillennialists believed that Christ would come to repair the material globe, they believed that their future life was essentially continuous with the world with which they were familiar. 'If the illustration is not too remote', suggested the minister of St Mary's Episcopal Chapel, Reading, Charles Goodhart, 'we may liken all the thought and feeling and conduct of our present condition to so many pencils of rays, which, instead of being abruptly terminated at the close of our present existence, are to be refracted through the prism of coming judgement'.[13] Although there would certainly be a change in the nature of things, historicist premillennialists believed that eternal life would be a ripening or perfecting of what was already known. The *Churchman's Monthly Review*, an historicist premillennialist journal published by Robert Benton Seeley, thus stated in 1842 that the future for a Christian would be 'a perpetuity and perfection of *his present chief delights*'.[14] Far from decrying the current scene, then, the belief that heaven would actually look a lot like the current sphere of existence suggested a rather higher estimation of the world and temporal life than that often assumed to have existed among premillennialists. The hope of restitution, argued the Curate of St Mary Magdalene, Richmond, Surrey, Gerard Noel (1782–1851), 'consecrates all the variety and loveliness of the material objects around us, by their connexion with a Paradise yet to be restored to our full, and perhaps eternal enjoyment'.[15]

If the idea of restitution applied to the material creation, it equally applied to the human body. The *Churchman's Monthly Review* concluded in 1844 that because 'both body and soul ... were comprehended in the fall ... the body as well as the soul is capable of redemption by the

---

[12] Clyde Binfield, 'Jews in Evangelical Dissent', in M. Wilks, ed., *Prophecy and Eschatology*, SCH.S 10 (Oxford, 1994), 225–70, at 234.

[13] C. J. Goodhart, 'The Established Holiness of the Church at the Lord's Advent', in T. R. Birks, ed., *The Hope of the Apostolic Church* (London, 1845), 79–118, at 112.

[14] 'Life in the Sick Room: Essays by an Invalid' [review article], *Churchman's Monthly Review*, April 1844, 253–68, at 262 (italics mine). All articles in the *Churchman's Monthly Review* were anonymous.

[15] Gerard Noel, *A Brief Enquiry into the Prospects of the Christian Church* (London, 1828), 65.

blood of Jesus'.[16] The fleshly nature of the future life was thus believed to be of essence to the Christian hope. 'I can find in the Bible', concluded Norfolk Evangelical Benjamin Philpot in 1843, 'no other happiness provided for redeemed man than one which involves the corporeal condition in which he came from the hand of the Creator. We can have no sympathies with any other condition.'[17]

Historicist premillennialists realized that they were being somewhat iconoclastic in making this argument about the physicality of the future life. Much nineteenth-century popular religious sentiment imagined that the soul proceeded directly to heaven at the point of death, where it would enjoy everlasting bliss. The Scottish hymnwriter James Drummond Burns (1823–64) thus penned such typical lines as the following: 'So when the Christian's eyelid droops and closes / In nature's parting strife, / A friendly Angel stands where he reposes, / To wake him up to life.'[18] Such sentiment suggested that it was a small step from the deathbed to heavenly glory and thus had little place for a physical restoration. Historicist premillennialists vehemently rejected this popular eschatology. 'Paul does not console those who have lost friends in the modern way, by telling them that soon they would die, and that thus they would join the spirits of their departed friends in heaven', complained the *Christian Herald* in 1830.[19] In particular, historicist premillennialists feared that such presentations of the after-life suggested that death was a thing to be hoped for, the moment of release from the physical body and material earth, rather than a scar on God's created order. Thomas Rawson Birks thus complained that 'it is a serious defect in our popular theology that death has been made to occupy the place which the Bible every where assigns to the great contrast of death, the resurrection'.[20]

In its insistence upon the materiality of salvation, historicist premillennialism must be seen as an important stream within broader debates about eschatology in mid-nineteenth century Britain. Indeed, F. D. Maurice, the mid-century Christian thinker most commonly

[16] *Churchman's Monthly Review,* August 1843, 555–56. The statement was made as part of a review of John Cheyne's *Essays on Partial Derangement of the Mind, in Supposed Connexion with Religion* (Dublin, 1843).

[17] Benjamin Philpot, 'The Last Invitations of the Gospel', in William Cadman, ed., *The Parables Prophetically Explained* (London, 1853), 103–28, at 121.

[18] J. D. Burns, 'The Apostle Slept', quoted in Brian Castle, *Sing a New Song to the Lord* (York, 1998), 35.

[19] *Christian Herald* 1 (1830), 64.

[20] Thomas Rawson Birks, *The Victory of Divine Goodness* (London, 1867), 11.

associated with the drift of eschatology towards an emphasis on the coming of the kingdom on earth, had fulsome words of praise for historicist premillennialists. 'I think that the Millenarians [*sic*] are right', he wrote, 'when they bid us think more of Christ's victory over the earth and redemption of it to its true purposes, than of any new condition into which we may be brought when we go out of the earth.'[21] This perhaps somewhat surprising endorsement suggests that the currents helping to shape evangelical premillennialism's belief concerning the recuperation of the earth and the materiality of Christian salvation washed over a broad range of religious thinkers in this era, creating surprising affinities of outlook and eschatological hope.

Progress and Development in the Afterlife

What, then, would one do in this afterlife of reinvigorated material existence? Historicist premillennialists believed that the earth would be a place of development, activity and progress. First, they suggested that there would be reproduction and growth in population in the age to come. The prominent evangelical historicist premillennialist Edward Bickersteth argued that the earth would continue to be fertile in the age to come. 'Even now', he noted, 'two-thirds of our world is ocean, incapable of increase, half of the rest, and perhaps more, is almost desert, and of the remainder, the largest part is very imperfectly tilled. There is room even in the latter, for a vast increase, when the whole earth might become like the garden of the Lord.'[22] The *Quarterly Journal of Prophecy* in 1850 believed that the absence of water, as predicted in the vision of the new heaven and new earth recorded in Revelation 21: 1, would provide extra room for an expanded population, and pointed to Holland as an example of how draining the land might increase space for human habitation.[23]

Secondly, historicist premillennialists believed that the future realm would be one of great adventure and exploration. They presented a vivid picture of an unbounded universe waiting to be discovered. It would be the age of science, discovery and skill. Presbyterian Church of

---

21 John Frederic Maurice, *The Life of Frederick Denison Maurice*, 2 vols (London, 1884), 2: 244.

22 Edward Bickersteth, 'The Earth Yielding Her Increase', in Alexander Dallas, ed., *Lift Up Your Heads. Glimpses of Messiah's Glory* (London, 1848), 330–59, at 337–38.

23 Anon. 'The Earth: Its Curse and Regeneration', *Quarterly Journal of Prophecy* 2 (1850), 281–97, 444–69, at 457.

England minister John Cumming (1807–81) believed that in the world to come 'we shall grow in all kinds and in all degrees of knowledge. The telescope gives us now but a glimpse of the magnificence of that universe which we shall then see no more through a glass darkly.'[24] The millennial and eternal ages would thus constitute a field upon which the creative interests of humanity might be expressed indefinitely. Such hopes for expanded mental and physical powers led Birks to propose that humans would be able to fly in the world to come. 'To be tied down to one little spot alone is rather a humiliation than a natural condition', he contended in 1863.[25]

Thirdly, historicist premillennialists conceived of the world to come as a busy and active place. 'Ours shall be an eternity of *holy activity* as well as heartfelt praise', argued the Vicar of St Paul's, Wolverhampton, William Dalton (1805–80), at the St George's lecture series in 1843.[26] In his Lenten lecture of 1849 Mourant Brock asserted that '*a place of society*, as well as a place of meeting, is this City of God. The future state is not figured by solitude, and by eremites, but by a *city* and its *inhabitants;* every thing replete with life, and with society.'[27]

For historicist premillennialists the future was a place in which time and space continued to exist. People would reproduce, learn and discover new things. This element of their thought was part of a broader change of perceptions of the future life which occurred during the course of the nineteenth century. Although often still imagined as a remote geographical place, depictions of heaven increasingly looked like another version of earthly society. Gail Malmgreen pointed out that even Queen Victoria 'found special comfort in the decidedly un-orthodox doctrine that the dear departed had gone on not to a Heaven far removed from earthly cares but to one in which … the deity had taken Albert to continue *working* above at all those tasks in which he had excelled on earth'.[28] Such an idea, proposed to Victoria by Charles Kingsley, was very similar to the concept of an afterlife which consisted

---

[24] Cumming, *Millennial Rest*, 363.

[25] Thomas Rawson Birks, *The Ways of God* (London, 1863), 114.

[26] W. Dalton, 'The Delay of the Second Advent, its Causes and Practical Lessons', in Edward Bickersteth, ed., *The Second Coming* (London, 1854), 105–35, at 133.

[27] Mourant Brock, 'The City which hath Foundations Prepared for the Faithful and Suffering Pilgrim', in Robert Haldane Stewart, ed., *The Priest Upon His Throne* (London, 1849), 289–332, at 317.

[28] Gail Malmgreen, *Religion in the Lives of English Women, 1760–1930* (London, 1986), 106 (italics are the author's).

of the 'mighty stirring activity of busy holiness' proposed by historicist premillennialists. [29]

A Broadening Soteriology

Given the universality of the restoration and the hope of infinite improvement proposed in this vision of restitution, there was notable discomfort amongst some historicist premillennialists about limiting the scope of salvation to a small elect of believers. Gerard Noel was among those who appeared to move towards a universal idea of salvation within his discussion of the restitution of all things. Noel argued that the return of Christ should be understood as God coming amongst the fallen creation 'not to annihilate but to repair'. Rather than punish and destroy, thought Noel, 'he might educate, enlighten, protect, and reward – he might bring into exercise the latent sympathies of this misguided and the ignorant'.[30]

Noel's ideas on this matter may well have been shaped by his good friend, the Scottish lay theologian Thomas Erskine (1788–1870). In *The Unconditional Freeness of the Gospel* (1828), Erskine spoke of his 'fixed and longing expectation, of the sure and fast approaching accomplishment of those promises which announce the final triumph of the Messiah'.[31] He lamented that 'the expectation of the restitution of all things occupies a much less space in the common announcements of the gospel, or in the thoughts of Christians, than it ought to do'.[32] Moreover, he linked his expectation for restitution to the 'universality of the declaration and purpose of the gospel'. Restitution, he argued, would involve 'the destruction of evil, and the restoration of the ruined race'. Individuals could thus only have hope for personal salvation in the future, Erskine concluded, because God would act at that time to restore all humanity. At the time of restitution 'the individual drops are thus merged in the ocean, and self is lost in the "liberty, the universality, the impartiality of heaven"'.[33]

[29] C. J. Goodhart, 'The Powers of the World to Come', in Stewart, ed., *The Priest Upon His Throne*, 183–231, at 216.

[30] Noel, *A Brief Enquiry*, 14–15.

[31] T. Erskine, *The Unconditional Freeness of the Gospel in Three Essays*, 2nd edn (Edinburgh, 1828), 111. For a detailed discussion of the development of Erskine's theology, see D. Horrocks, *Laws of the Spiritual Order* (Carlisle, 2004).

[32] Erskine, *The Unconditional Freeness of the Gospel*, 111.

[33] Ibid. 112.

The most unequivocal statement by an historicist premillennialist concerning the 'wider hope' was made by Thomas Rawson Birks in his work *The Victory of Divine Goodness* (1867), a book which he claimed was the summation of the development of his eschatological thought over the past thirty years.[34] For Birks, restitution meant the triumph of good over evil, a belief that led him to conclude there was no place for a material hell in the future life. 'To assume the perpetual continuance of active malice and permitted blasphemies', he argued, 'is to ascribe to God a dominion shared for ever with the powers of evil. It makes hell the scene of Satan's triumphant malice, just as heaven is that of the Creator's triumphant love.'[35] Birks imagined a universe in which the reprobate were constrained and contained by the triumph of love. 'Will they not be saved, in a strange, mysterious sense, when the depth of their unchangeable shame and sorrow finds beneath it a still lower depth of Divine compassion, and the creature, and its most forlorn estate, is shut in by the vision of surpassing and infinite love?'[36]

Not all historicist premillennialists adopted such radical views about the scope of redemption, but the idea of restoration of the universe did lead several into a theological journey away from their Calvinist evangelical heritage and towards a soteriology more in keeping with the 'liberal' theology of thinkers such as F. D. Maurice. Indeed, the Dean of Wells, Edward H. Plumptre (1821–91), thought that the similarities between Birks' *Victory of Divine Goodness* and the views of Maurice were uncanny. 'In not a few passages it presents so close a verbal identity with the language of Mr. Maurice's *Theological Essays*, that in a writer of inferior calibre it would suggest the thought of a literary plagiarism', he observed.[37]

Conclusion

Historicist premillennialists were certain that 'heaven' should be understood not as an ethereal, immaterial realm, but rather as a regenerated terrestrial earth, inhabited by human beings in physical bodies who

[34] Birks, *The Victory of Divine Goodness*, vi. For a recent discussion of Birks and the emergence of modified views of hell during the mid-nineteenth century, see Ralph Brown, 'Victorian Anglicanism: The Radical Legacy of Edward Irving', *JEH* 58 (2007), 675–704, esp. 698–99.

[35] Birks, *The Victory of Divine Goodness*, 47.

[36] Ibid. 190–92.

[37] E. H. Plumptre, *The Spirits in Prison* (New York, 1894), 232.

would continue to learn, explore and reproduce. Any eschatological vision which implied that the soul alone could find rest was dismissed, an opinion which had implications for the evangelical view of death as an entry point into heaven. Historicist premillennialists believed that eternity was the fullness and culmination of all that existed. Humans would participate in a future life where 'time' continued to operate upon creatures having a spatial existence and where it might even be possible for the reprobate to find redemption. Such thought was the result of a theology which posited that God was more intimately concerned with temporal and earthly affairs than had sometimes been imagined in evangelical depictions of 'heaven' as discontinuous with 'earth', and of eternity as remote from the affairs of 'time'.[38] As Gerard Noel concluded, 'Jesus Christ is linked to our world by ties less fragile than those which human theology has framed. Surely He will COME AGAIN, and exhibit those ties in all their beauty and in all their strength.'[39]

Many of the themes associated with later nineteenth-century theology – a stress on the incarnation, an emphasis on Christ's solidarity with the earth, the hope that progress and education were possible in the afterlife – were announced by historicist premillennialists, demonstrating that the theological innovation commonly associated with 'liberal' figures in nineteenth-century religious thought was also evident among what were apparently the most 'conservative' sections of the church. Such complexity should cause us to continue the work of deconstructing the false ecclesiastical demarcations bequeathed to us by nineteenth-century commentators, and strive to recover the often surprising fluidity of theological speculation in Victorian Britain.

Corpus Christi College, Oxford

---

[38]   Boyd Hilton, *The Age of Atonement: The Influence of Evangelicalism on Social and Economic Thought, 1785–1865* (Oxford, 1988), 300.
[39]   Noel, *Brief Enquiry*, 27.

'ANGELS SEEN TODAY'.
THE THEOLOGY OF MODERN SPIRITUALISM AND ITS IMPACT ON CHURCH OF ENGLAND CLERGY,
1852–1939

by GEORGINA BYRNE

IN 1852 an American medium, Maria Hayden, crossed the Atlantic, landed in London and began offering séances in fashionable salons.[1] From this point on, and certainly well into the twentieth century, spiritualism proved attractive to many. What spiritualism offered was, primarily, an extravagant claim: that it was possible for the living to communicate with the departed. By various means, people from all classes, religious traditions and geographical locations 'tried' the spirits, seeking to make contact with famous characters from history or departed family members. Spiritualism offered, sometimes, spectacular signs and wonders: flying furniture, levitating mediums and ghostly presences, all of which attracted the attention of journalists.[2] Fashions for such signs came and went; the claim to communicate with the dead, however, remained at the heart of spiritualism.

Most histories of spiritualism concentrate their attention on the séance phenomena and the lives of the mediums; this paper offers instead an account of the *teachings* of spiritualism. I will argue that these teachings proved compelling for a number of Anglican clergy, some of whom quietly incorporated the ideas and images of spiritualism into their own accounts of the Christian faith, others of whom hoped more explicitly that spiritualism would alter the Church's teaching about the afterlife. Finally, I will suggest, albeit briefly, that the language and images of spiritualism permeated sermons from some of spiritualism's critics during the First World War.

It is important to acknowledge first of all that experimentation with spiritualism extended far beyond the boundaries of any sort of authorized movement. Although, by 1939, the Spiritualists National Union

---

[1] It is usually acknowledged that modern spiritualism began in the home of the Fox family, in Hydesville, New York State, in 1848. For a good account, see Joseph McCabe, *Spiritualism: A Popular History from 1847* (London, 1920).

[2] See, for example, *Cornhill Magazine* 2 (1860), 219–24.

claimed that there were 520 local spiritualist societies serving some 160,000 individuals, thousands more attended séances, visited spiritualist lectures and read about it in newspapers.[3] It was popular across the country and among people of all classes. Queen Victoria was known to have tried the spirits, and Gladstone, Thackeray and Dickens visited séances. In 1862 *The Times* complained that the country was beset by a passion for spiritualism:

> We have clear proofs of its existence, and some reason to fear that it is on the increase both in the highest and the lowest classes of society. While Mr Home and Mr Forester hold their fashionable seances at the West-end of London, gipsies and fortune-tellers are pandering to a like morbid craving for communion with the kingdom of darkness among peasants and servant girls.[4]

One early chronicler of spiritualism claimed that it was 'impossible' to visit any town or hamlet without discovering the 'way-marks' of spiritual power.[5] Even by 1919, at the Anglican Church Congress, one speaker complained that 'Spiritualism, like the spirits, is in the air. It is more than a craze. It is a passion. There is a wave of psychic feeling, I will not call it altogether power, which is passing through England today.'[6]

It is also important to acknowledge that modern spiritualism, with its claim to communicate with the departed, arrived in England at a time when a number of theological debates concerning the afterlife were taking place among Anglican theologians. These focused primarily on the nature and duration of eternity, the punishment of the wicked and the possibility of *post mortem* repentance and spiritual progress, and they are well documented.[7] That there was a significant theological shift during this period can be observed by comparing the responses to the work of F. D. Maurice in 1853 and Hastings Rashdall in 1915. Maurice lost his position at King's College London and was

---

[3] This claim was made to the committee set up by the Archbishop of Canterbury examining spiritualism. See 'Archbishop's Committee on Spiritualism. Report of the Committee to the Archbishop of Canterbury' (unpublished report, 1939), 6.

[4] *The Times*, 15 March 1862.

[5] Emma Hardinge Britten, *Nineteenth Century Miracles, or Spirits and their Work in every Country of the Earth* (Manchester, 1883), 165.

[6] The debate was held on 15 October 1919: *Authorized Report of the Church Congress held in Leicester* (London 1919), 113.

[7] See Geoffrey Rowell, *Hell and the Victorians* (1974; republ. Oxford, 2000).

accused of universalism for attacking, in his *Theological Essays*, the generally accepted belief that after judgement God punished the wicked for an endless amount of time. By 1915 the Bampton lecturer Hastings Rashdall could go so far as to describe Jesus's teaching as 'latent universalism'[8] without fear of similar reprisal.

Although, in the second half of the nineteenth century, the theological debates shifted in a universalist direction, the Church's *public* presentation of the afterlife remained largely unchanged during this same period. This was significant because although few members of the public engaged with theological debate, many experienced the Church's teaching as mediated by the services of the Prayer Book, by sermons and, increasingly, by hymnody. In the Prayer Book burial service a sense of sin and the certainty of judgement pervaded the text. There was no guarantee that the departed individual was one of the elect and no prayer that he might be made so, only a hope that he was among the saved. The tone of the service – and the final prayers in particular – suggested that the rite was concerned much more with the spiritual life of the living, rather than the state of the departed. Sermons similarly exhorted the living to be aware of impending judgement, occasionally speculating on the horrors of hell, but rarely on the bliss of heaven. One preacher claimed, for example, that if the Son of Man found 'open rebellion and indifference' in a person at judgement, then

> instead of loving recognition there will be a glance from the throne reproachful and terrible. From the fury of that glance there will be no hiding place; from the wrath of the Lamb no covering; it will then be too late to cry for mercy when it is the time of judgement.[9]

Importantly, the exhortation to repent and lead a godly life came from a belief – still widely held – that a person's eternal state was fixed for eternity at death, and that there was no possibility of *post mortem* repentance or forgiveness.[10]

Modern spiritualism, by its teachings, provided a contrasting vision of the afterlife to that of the Church of England. Spiritualists remained largely unconcerned to provide a theological system for the purpose of

[8] Hastings Rashdall, *The Idea of Atonement in Christian Theology* (London, 1920), 437.
[9] R. S. Beloe, *Be Ye Ready: A Sermon Preached in the Parish Church of Holton* (London, 1861), 15.
[10] The controversy over the Athanasian Creed in the 1870s, for example, gave rise to a number of sermons upholding this belief.

evangelizing.[11] However, the ideas and images of spiritualism permeated séances and lectures whenever the spirits apparently communicated or a spiritualist gave testimony. By piecing together the
communications of alleged spirits and the teachings of spiritualists it is
possible to discern a theology of spiritualism and a presentation of the
afterlife that remained largely consistent.

In the first place, death was of supreme importance because it
brought an individual to the point of entry into the afterlife. Rather
than being an abrupt moment of ending or beginning, it was a seamless
movement of 'transition', 'passing over' or 'passing on' into the next life;
a junction along a person's life rather than a terminus. Spiritualist
newspapers thus contained personal columns entitled 'Births, Marriages
and Transitions'.[12] When a person died there was no interruption
before their entry into the next life and, contrary to what spiritualists
characterized as the Church's teaching, neither was there a period of
'slumbering in the grave' before the spirit rose to a new life.[13] Accounts
were given by the departed spirits of how, on their deathbed, they had
been surrounded not only by living family members, but also the spirits
of departed loved ones, who offered encouragement as transition
approached.[14]

Once the departed spirit reached its destination it began to acclima-
tize to the new surroundings, in a place known variously as 'Summerland', 'the Spirit World' or 'Spirit Land'. Some spirits presented this
acclimatization as like waking after a good and refreshing sleep. Mabel
Corelli Green, a young woman who died in 1921, communicated to her
mother that on arrival in the next life she was taken to the 'Hill of Rest',
to a bower of roses where everything was peaceful. There she slept
before being woken by the presence of a bright shining spirit.[15]

Other spirits explained that they were initially confused by their
surroundings and did not realize that they had died because they awoke
in a place that appeared similar to the earth they had left. So one young
child spirit could say, 'I was not absolutely conscious that I had passed

---

[11] This may, in part, have been due to the fact that spiritualism did not become a single
definable movement. For an overview of the attempts to unite spiritualists as a movement,
see Geoffrey K. Nelson, *Spiritualism and Society* (London, 1969), 89–110.

[12] See, for example, *Two Worlds*, 18 January 1918.

[13] Robert Dale Owen, *Footfalls on the Boundary of Another World* (London, 1860), 352; also
Charles Tweedale, *Present Day Spirit Phenomena and the Churches* (Chicago, 1920), 5.

[14] See, for example, *Spiritualist*, 19 November 1869.

[15] Mabel Corelli Green, *Life in the Summerland* (London, 1922), 7–8.

the gates of death'.[16] And Sir Oliver Lodge's departed son Raymond could report that similarities with earthly life included the availability of whisky sodas and cigars.[17]

Gradually the newly arrived spirits were 'weaned' away from their earthly tastes and took in the new surroundings. Many of the communicating spirits described the sheer beauty of what they saw as they developed in their spiritual life. What they saw was 'earth made perfect'.[18] Thus communications were full of vivid descriptions of landscape, of streams, flowers, trees, colour and light. The following is typical:

> I lay on a couch of rest which was the most beautiful garden, and was, itself, formed by living flowers and fruits, and canopied over by a graceful vine. I stretched forth my hand to gather these fruits and flowers and as my touch came near them did I receive nourishment and strength, by the aromal [sic] essence that was at once infused into my spirit life in all its senses, of tasting, hearing and smelling as well as seeing.[19]

Departed friends were recognized in their spiritual bodies, but altered by their time in the Summerland, having had all traces of sadness, weakness and pain removed. Old people had 'straightened out'. The landscape was imbued with a sense of the spiritual, described in terms of light, colour, joy and beauty. It was a place for self-improvement, described as 'full of interest and occupation', where music, art and science were developed.[20]

In contrast to what the spiritualists characterized as 'traditional' Church teaching, where the soul, once judged, waited for the final resurrection, the spiritualist afterlife was a dynamic life. A spirit was not merely expected to wonder at its surroundings, but to grow in spiritual understanding. Most commonly this growth was described as an upward movement. The afterlife was stratified into 'spheres' or 'realms', and a spirit was considered to have made progress when it rose upward through these realms. The higher the realm, the more refined and

[16]   F. J. Theobald, *Heaven Opened, or, Messages for the Bereaved from our Little Ones in Glory* (London, 1870), 7.

[17]   Oliver Lodge, *Raymond* (London, 1916), 197–98.

[18]   George Vale Owen, *Life Beyond the Veil* (London, 1926), 17.

[19]   F. J. Theobald, *Homes and Work in the Future Life*, 3 vols (London, 1885–87), 2: 55–56.

[20]   Arthur Conan Doyle, *The New Revelation* (London, 1981; first publ. 1918), 41.

perfect in spiritual knowledge the spirit had become. There was little agreement among spiritualists as to how many spheres there were; but the importance of progressing through them was a consistent teaching.[21] What was clear from the accounts, however, was that the afterlife was generally divided into three sections. The communicating spirits tended to be located in the middle section and had little knowledge of life in the highest realms, or in the lowest, darkest realms, where lurked the obstinate ones who refused to grow in love and spiritual understanding.

Even from the darkest realms there was the possibility of spiritual growth and forgiveness. The doctrine of eternal punishment was 'almost always explicitly denied',[22] and many spirits communicated that hell did not exist.[23] Neither was there any divine judgement. Instead, when a person died their spirit simply entered a sphere that was appropriate to their earthly spiritual development. This bore little relation to a person's professed faith, but rather to their habits of life and thought on earth. The spirits therefore advised the living to pay attention to their spiritual health on earth, as this determined their sphere at death. The living were not discouraged from professing a faith, but were told that righteousness of life was of more importance. One spiritualist lecturer taught that: 'When you come to the spirit life you will find that you will not be asked, What have you believed? but, What have you done?'[24] After death a spirit was drawn to the sphere to which it was best suited and from that sphere was encouraged to grow in understanding.

The spirits who found themselves in the lower regions of the afterlife were those who had made little progress in life and who responded only slowly beyond death. Here spirits were encouraged to examine their misdeeds and remedy their defects. This took time and some found the process painful, but even murderers and suicides could work themselves upwards eventually, guided and assisted by spirits from the higher realms.[25]

---

[21] Adin Ballou thought that there were seven: Ballou, *An Exposition of Views Respecting the Principal Facts, Causes and Peculiarities Involved in Spirit Manifestations* (London, 1852), 55. The *Yorkshire Spiritual Telegraph*, August 1855, divided six spheres into a further six grades, making thirty-six. Another spirit thought twelve: *New Spiritualist*, 27 September 1922.

[22] R. H. Benson, *Spiritualism* (London, 1911), 9.

[23] *Spiritualist*, 31 December 1869.

[24] Report of lecture given to the Mechanics' Institute, Openshaw, by Mrs Green of Heywood; *Two Worlds*, 9 December 1887.

[25] Georgina Houghton, *Evenings at Home in Spiritual Séance* (London, 1881), 9; Ballou, *Spirit Manifestations*, 56. It ought to be added that some spiritualists argued that spirits could

Alongside the busyness there was, occasionally, worship of God. One spirit described a temple where beautiful worship took place and cherubs sang, another spoke of cathedral-like architecture and uplifting liturgy, but there was little beyond vague descriptions. Worship was more often described as being a function of the higher spirits, and not something in which communicating spirits participated. There did not appear to be much church attendance in the afterlife. God, when he was mentioned, was an all-pervading force, the Supreme Spirit or father of all spirits. He was believed to be loving and merciful, rather than judgemental, but the communicating spirits did not feel it necessary to mention him much.

Jesus seemed to be problematic for spiritualists. His teaching was revered, his presence in the afterlife was certainly noted, but the Christian belief in his divinity proved troublesome. For some spiritualists Jesus was the supreme medium, capable of conversing not only with the dead but also with the very centre of the Godhead. For others he was the highest and best of spirits. The problem with the Christian teaching about his divinity was that if all spirits were capable of progressing through spheres and reaching perfection then Jesus could not be unique. Some spiritualists tried to maintain that Christ was divine, but more often he was described in terms of a role model or teacher. The spirits testified that his simple teaching was revered in the afterlife, but that it bore little resemblance to what they characterized as the complicated doctrines of the Church.

Despite the ambivalence among the communicating spirits towards God, Jesus and worship, some clergy found spiritualism extraordinarily compelling – irrespective of their churchmanship. Anglo-Catholics such as William Geike Cobb, secretary to the English Church Union; Evangelicals such as Frederick Lees of the Missions to Seamen; and Hugh Haweis, the popular Vicar of Marylebone, were associated with it.[26] Percy Dearmer, Vicar of St Mary's, Primrose Hill and Canon of Westminster Abbey, put his name to a book communicated to his wife by a departed spirit through automatic writing. He said of the alleged communication, that it was 'written as from one who was urgent to

fall as well as rise. A base nature and refusal to conform to God's laws might halt or reverse progress: see, for example, Thomas Colley, *Sermons on Spiritualism at Stockton* (London, 1907), 16.

[26] A number of clergy were exposed as spiritualists by fellow clergyman and spiritualist Charles Tweedale: see his *Man's Survival after Death* (London, 1909), 409.

give a message to the world, who was the friend we had known and whose identity was familiar and unmistakable'.[27] A group formed in the 1930s called the Confraternity of Clergy and Spiritualists included on its headed notepaper the names of over thirty clergy members, who were diverse in their churchmanship, age and geographical location.[28] Greame Maurice Elliott, Vice-Chairman of the Confraternity, Rector of St Peter's, Cricklewood, and author of the book *Angels Seen Today* (1919), was the subject of a frank correspondence between the Bishop of Guildford and the Archbishop of Canterbury's chaplain in 1935 after speaking about spiritualism to clergy chapters in Surrey.[29] There were other clergy who, reluctant to make public their support for spiritualism by joining the Confraternity, nevertheless spoke at meetings or allowed spiritualists to speak in their churches.[30]

Some clergymen came to spiritualism, as other people did, during bereavement, examples being Charles Maurice Davies (1828–1910), best known as the author of works cataloguing the variety of religious life in London, Percy Dearmer (1867–1936) and George Vale Owen (1860–1931), Vicar of Orford in Lancashire.[31] Others investigated spiritualism as part of an interest in psychic science.[32]

Perhaps more surprisingly, some thought that spiritualism might rekindle the Christian faith, and in particular the belief in life after death. Thomas Colley, a convinced spiritualist who became Archdeacon of Natal, speaking in 1875, criticized the Church's grey and gloomy religion, preferring the possibility of birdsong, flowers and sunshine after death.[33] Davies thought that spiritualism offered people

[27] Percy and Nancy Dearmer, *The Fellowship of the Picture: An Automatic Script Taken Down by Nancy Dearmer* (London, 1920), 8.
[28] For an example, see 'The Confraternity of Clergy and Spiritualists' to the Archbishop of Canterbury, 9 December 1939: London, Lambeth Palace Library, Papers of Cosmo Gordon Lang, Vol. 70, fol. 205.
[29] John Victor Macmillan to Alan Don, 27 November 1935: Lang Papers, Vol. 133, fol. 297.
[30] The president of the London Spiritualist Alliance in 1900, following a lecture by Hugh Haweis of St James, Marylebone, commented that finding clergy who were spiritualists was not a novelty, although finding them proclaiming this in public was: *Light*, 5 May 1900.
[31] 'A Church of England clergyman' [Charles Maurice Davies], *The Great Secret and its Unfoldment in Occultism* (London, 1895); Owen, *Life beyond the Veil*; Nancy Dearmer, *The Life of Percy Dearmer* (London, 1940), esp. 275.
[32] There were many clergy members of the Society for Psychical Research, founded in 1882.
[33] *Spiritualist*, 19 February 1875.

imaginative ways of conceiving life beyond death not present in the Church of England. In an open letter to the Archbishop of Canterbury he complained that the Church was 'timid' when it came to speaking about life beyond death, whereas spiritualism offered a way of preaching it in fullness.[34] He began to interpret Scripture in the light of spiritualism, suggesting, for example, that St Paul, in 2 Corinthians 12, supported the teaching about spheres.[35]

Charles Tweedale, Vicar of Weston, Yorkshire, in the 1920s, thought that spiritualism offered something superior to the Church's teaching. Drawing on his ministry to the bereaved, he claimed that spiritualism promised 'the joy of the resurrection to those who either do not possess it, or see it so dimly that it affords no real consolation to the mind.'[36] George Vale Owen saw that spiritualism offered a rich and vivid landscape of the afterlife. In *Life beyond the Veil* (1922), his mother's spirit described this landscape as beautiful, with hills, rivers and forests. But for Owen there was more to spiritualism than vivid language. From his encounters with the spirits he came to believe that the Church's teaching about death, and particularly about hell and judgement, was wrong. He hoped, instead, that the assimilation of spiritualism into the Church would encourage a doctrine of *post mortem* forgiveness, purgation and progress.

Arthur Chambers, Vicar of Brockenhurst, Hampshire, in the 1890s, was initially sceptical of spiritualism but came to support its teachings. He remained uneasy about séances; but the teachings of spiritualism were, he thought, evident in the Bible and therefore acceptable. From Scripture he deduced levels of spiritual progress beyond death and possibilities for repentance. It was this teaching that he eventually commended to his readers, rather than the plausibility of séance phenomena.[37] Percy Dearmer wrote fourteen years after his first visits to mediums that he understood the afterlife as a place of forgiveness and spiritual progress and connected spiritualism with the Christian belief in the communion of saints.[38]

Spiritualism explicitly shaped the theology and teaching of some Anglican clergy. Yet the language and ideas also found a way into

---

34 *Light*, 26 March 1881.
35 Charles Maurice Davies, *London Sermons* (London, 1875), 173.
36 Tweedale, *Man's Survival after Death*, 11.
37 See esp. Arthur Chambers, *Problems of the Spiritual* (London, 1907).
38 Percy Dearmer, *The Communion of Saints* (London, 1906), 21–22.

mainstream Church of England sermons and writings; this was especially the case during the Great War.[39] It is impossible, within the
constraints of a short paper, to elaborate at length, and four examples
must be allowed to suffice for now. To a gathering of clergy in 1916 the
Bishop of London, Arthur Foley Winnington-Ingram readily used the
common spiritualist expressions, 'passing into' or 'passing over' to
describe the deaths of soldiers. 'Every single day', he said, 'thousands
pass into the other world.'[40] Elsewhere he told a congregation that souls,
like flowers, grew best in sunshine. Those who died grew 'in the sunny
land of paradise'.[41] He spoke of the dead as being in the 'spirit world'.[42]
He remained vehemently critical of spiritualism, regarding it as a waste
of time and a mistake. The Bishop of Kensington suggested in 1915
that the afterlife was a place of employment and usefulness, that each
person found their own 'sphere', and even that the dead assisted the
living in the winning of the war.[43] Canon Burnett Streeter of Hereford,
writing in 1917, judged that the expression 'progress' was crucial to a
Christian understanding of life after death.[44] Ernest Barnes, Bishop of
Birmingham, was keen to note that this 'progress' was not the same as
'purgatory'.[45]

None of this suggests that the Church of England adopted spiritualism lock, stock and barrel. It did no such thing. Rather, some of the
images and ideas of spiritualism, widely known across the country,
became useful at a time when the Church was already reframing its
own teachings about the afterlife. Thus the idea of 'progress' was
perhaps preferable to 'purgatory' in the early twentieth century, at a
time when Roman Catholicism was still viewed with suspicion. It was
also, pastorally, helpful for preachers to draw on images of sunshine
and to suggest that those who died young continued to grow spiritually
when they were speaking to those bereaved by war.

This paper has argued that the vision of the afterlife presented by
modern spiritualism influenced how a number of clergy thought about

[39] See, in this volume, Michael Snape, 'Civilians, Soldiers and Perceptions of the Afterlife in Britain during the First World War', 371–403.
[40] A. F. Winnington-Ingram, *The Church in Time of War* (London, 1916), 159.
[41] Idem, *The Spirit of Peace* (London, 1921), 159.
[42] Idem, *The Church in Time of War*, 299.
[43] John Primat Maud, *Our Comradeship with the Blessed Dead* (London, 1915), 72.
[44] B. H. Streeter, 'The Resurrection of the Dead', in idem et al., *Immortality: An Essay in Discovery, Co-ordinating Scientific, Psychical and Biblical Research* (London, 1917), 75–129, at 139.
[45] Ernest Barnes, *Spiritualism and the Christian Faith* (London, 1920), 3.

and preached about the Christian faith. The teachings of spiritualism, neglected by historians but encountered from 1852 onwards by large numbers of people from different classes and geographical locations, presented something quite different from the traditional teaching of the Church offered in the Prayer Book and in sermons. Spiritualism did not offer profundity, but it proved attractive to a small yet significant number of clergy. Even beyond this number, spiritualism's images and ideas provided a way of speaking about the afterlife that both reflected the theological shift towards universalism taking place in the late nineteenth-century Church, and at the same time presented an afterlife to the general public that was comprehensible, comprehensive and gently domestic. All of this serves to underline the extent to which Christianity was susceptible to the influence of an alternative, yet popular, belief.

Romsley, Worcestershire

CIVILIANS, SOLDIERS AND PERCEPTIONS OF THE AFTERLIFE IN BRITAIN DURING THE FIRST WORLD WAR

by MICHAEL SNAPE

OR most educated Britons the First World War is synonymous with death on a massive scale. Although reliable estimates remained elusive for many years (this deceptively straightforward process being complicated by issues such as determining the nationality of the fallen and when to stop counting deaths as war-related), the figures are sobering enough: according to research published in the 1980s, as many as 772,000 Britons died in military service during the First World War.[1] Despite the problems of the statistician, the fact of mass mortality was acutely and painfully obvious to contemporaries, so much so that, in an important essay published in 1981, David Cannadine characterized inter-war Britain as a society that was 'obsessed with death'.[2] Since 1918, the identification of death with the experience of the First World War has lodged itself deep in the national psyche, spawning the myth of 'the lost generation' and dominating the perceptions of posterity. As Dan Todman recently observed:

> The terrible cost of the war underpins many of our other received beliefs about it: the incompetence of the generals whose actions resulted in so many lost lives; the purposelessness of any war with such a butcher's bill; and the miraculous veneration of any veteran who managed to survive the carnage.[3]

However, this perception of an all-engulfing tide of death requires further analysis and considerable qualification. Such is the strength of the mythology itself that it seems almost callous to point out that a third of British males of military age never served in the armed forces and that, despite vast numbers of wounded,[4] nearly ninety per cent of

[1] D. Todman, *The Great War: Myth and Memory* (London, 2005), 44.
[2] D. Cannadine, 'War and Death, Grief and Mourning in Modern Britain', in J. Whaley, ed., *Mirrors of Mortality: Studies in the Social History of Death* (London, 1981), 187–242, at 189, 230.
[3] Todman, *Great War*, 44.
[4] As many as 2,270,000, although many soldiers were wounded more than once; A. Rawson, ed., *The British Army Handbook 1914–1918* (Stroud, 2006), 349.

the men who served in the British army (which sustained the over-whelming majority of British casualties) actually *survived* the war.[5] Furthermore, far from being a society in which the loss of an immediate family member was universal, this was true of an average of one in six British families. However, these bereavements were not evenly borne across the country or between social classes. Scotland (and most notably the Highlands) was particularly badly affected, along with some smaller English towns (such as Barnsley and Accrington) which raised their own 'Pals' battalions for Lord Kitchener's volunteer army.[6] Nor can the common assumption that the war was 'a betrayal of the ruled by the rulers' be sustained from the social incidence of mortality: the aristocracy suffered more than any other social class; the church press testified to the enormous extent of clerical bereavement; and the impact upon the upper and middle classes as a whole can be inferred from the fact that a disproportionate number of Britain's war dead were officers.[7] Finally, nowhere is the mendacity of this 'morbid revelling in mass fatality'[8] (as Todman describes it) more obvious than in its sheer Anglocentricity; far from being uniquely afflicted by the First World War, in both relative and absolute terms Britain suffered much less than either France, Germany or Austria-Hungary. Furthermore, it was a reflection of the savagery of the war on the forgotten Eastern Front that, whereas sixteen out of every thousand Britons perished, Serbia lost as many as fifty-seven per thousand of its population.[9]

The subject of British religion and the mass mortality of 1914–18 is not virgin territory for historians; nevertheless, it has been locked into this popular and misleading paradigm. For example, in his landmark study *The Church of England and the First World War* (1978), Alan Wilkinson stressed the scale of Britain's losses by citing the casualties suffered by the British army on 1 July 1916, which he insisted were 'the heaviest losses ever suffered in a single day by any army in the first

[5] M. Middlebrook, *Your Country Needs You* (Barnsley, 2000), 134; Todman, *Great War*, 44–45; J. M. Winter, *The Experience of World War I* (London, 2006), 207.

[6] Todman, *Great War*, 46; J. L. MacLeod, ' "Greater Love Hath No Man Than This": Scotland's Conflicting Religious Responses to Death in the Great War', *ScHR* 81 (2002), 70–96, at 70.

[7] B. Bond, *The Unquiet Western Front: Britain's Role in Literature and History* (Cambridge, 2002), 65; Todman, *Great War*, 46; S. Lee, *Rural Society and the Anglican Clergy, 1815–1914* (Woodbridge, 2006), 190–91; War Office, *Statistics of the Military Effort of the British Empire During the Great War* (London, 1922; repr. London, 1992), 29, 237.

[8] Todman, *Great War*, 67.

[9] Ibid. 45.

war'.[10] This is not true; the French army alone went through a much more sanguinary experience on at least one, and probably two, occasions in 1914 and 1917.[11] Moreover, Wilkinson delivered a largely negative verdict as to the Church's ability to meet the needs of the bereaved. While it could offer the consolation of the familiar, most notably in the Prayer Book's 'Order for the Burial of the Dead', it was largely unable to accommodate popular religious sentiment and aspiration: '[T]he Church of England was nervous of folk religion: its Evangelicalism was too puritan, biblicist and pietistic, its liberalism too detached and academic, its catholicism too self-conscious, dogmatic and nostalgic.'[12] Other historians have happily concurred with this verdict. In his highly influential essay on 'War and Death, Grief and Mourning in Modern Britain', David Cannadine pronounced that 'the established Church – concerned, like all Christianity, with explaining the significance of death in this world and life in the next – seemed unable to cope when confronted with so much mortality and grief'. Moreover, and on the basis of very little new evidence, he broadened this criticism by extending it to 'traditional religion' in general which, he averred, 'seemed inadequate in the face of so much death and bereavement'.[13]

In this seminal essay, Cannadine identified two subjects as worthy of note in relation to religion, death and the afterlife in the First World War, namely the rise of the cult of remembrance and the surging popularity of spiritualism; these, he maintained, had two things in common: 'they were in large part generated by the bereaved for their own comfort'.[14] Historical research has tended to pursue this agenda ever since, with little thought being spared by historians of spiritualism in particular for the abiding influence of institutional religion, much of which is simply subsumed in an expansive and rather misleading definition of spiritualism itself. However, this preoccupation with the issues of spiritualism and remembrance masks a more complex reality. Even before the war, the relationship between spiritualism and more orthodox Christianity was far more ambivalent and varied than is often

[10] A. Wilkinson, *The Church of England and the First World War* (London, 1978), 169.
[11] H. Strachan, *The First World War*, Volume I: *To Arms* (Oxford, 2001), 230; A. Clayton, *Paths of Glory: the French Army 1914–18* (London, 2005), 140.
[12] Wilkinson, *Church of England*, 196.
[13] Cannadine, 'War and Death', 218–19.
[14] Ibid. 219.

imagined.[15] Furthermore, during the war, and again largely as a result of developments spanning several decades, the principal British Churches showed that they were able to adjust, both devotionally and theologically, to the needs of the time and to provide comfort and meaning for the bereaved. If insufficient attention has been paid to the evidence of wartime eschatology, sermons, worship and pastoralia, our existing understanding of contemporary British society, death and the afterlife is also marred by its largely civilian focus. Although they were the subjects of an enormous weight of concern and speculation, the perspectives and experience of the men who served in the British army during the First World War have been tacitly ignored, except to provide colourful vignettes for advocates and historians of spiritualism.[16] However, at no time in its history has the British army been so large (5.7 million men served in its ranks during the First World War)[17] and never had it been so educated as in 1914–18, a distinction that was largely a function of its unprecedented social diversity. This paper aims to shed some new light on the artificially circumscribed subject of British society and the afterlife in the First World War by quarrying a new seam of evidence relating to contemporary perceptions of the hereafter in the British army. In doing so, it will eschew sensational stories of ghosts and phantasms (so beloved of civilians at home and of cultural historians ever since) in order to focus attention on prevailing discourses on the afterlife that reveal much about the convergence of academic and popular eschatology, the emergence of new or distinctive liturgical and sacramental practices, and the underlying links between religious belief and military morale.

Before proceeding, however, it is necessary to give a broad outline of the impact of the First World War on the relevant theology and practices of Britain's main Churches. By the turn of the twentieth century, the cumulative effect of theological, intellectual and moral developments over the previous half-century meant that hell (along with many other old orthodoxies) was in rapid retreat across a broad front. While Bishop of Birmingham, Charles Gore observed that:

15 See, in this volume, Georgina Byrne, ' "Angels Seen Today": The Theology of Modern Spiritualism and its Impact on Church of England Clergy, 1852–1939', 360–70.
16 See, for example, A. Conan Doyle, *The History of Spiritualism*, 2 vols (London, 1926), 1: 224–45.
17 P. Simkins, 'The Four Armies 1914–1918', in D. Chandler and I. Beckett, eds, *The Oxford Illustrated History of the British Army* (Oxford, 1994), 235–57, at 241.

Some thirty years ago there was a sort of Protestant religion, with a doctrine of the Trinity, Heaven and Hell, of Atonement and Judgment, of Resurrection and Eternal Life, which for good or evil could be more or less assumed. Such a standard has gone. I seriously doubt whether nearly half the men of the country could seriously say that they believed that Christ is God or that he actually rose from the dead on the third day ... their religious opinions are in complete chaos.[18]

The mass bereavement that occurred under the impact of war merely put the seal on the fate of hell. In 1917, C. W. Emmet, a New Testament scholar and the Vicar of West Hendred in Berkshire, claimed that 'It is probably safe to say that except in a few restricted circles a living belief in hell has practically vanished to-day in the Church of England'.[19] The state of opinion in the Free Churches was more varied. However, in 1907 the Congregationalist R. J. Campbell, then the standard-bearer of English liberal theology, denounced a raft of 'dogmatic beliefs' including hell as 'not only misleading but unethical'.[20] This liberalization of thought, it must be emphasized, was by no means confined to English Christianity. By the turn of the twentieth century, mainstream Scottish Presbyterianism had freed itself from a narrowly Calvinistic interpretation of the Westminster Confession, and, for the ministers of the Church of Scotland and the United Free Church, 'theological precision' had duly 'given way to a licensed (if still cautious) breadth of interpretation and a less rigorous degree of uniformity'.[21] By 1914, it appeared that 'the modern Scottish sermon' was distinguished by its 'practical teaching' centred 'round the Person of Christ'; those 'doctrines which may be subsidiary or doubtful [were], for the most part, quietly ignored'.[22] However, the old eschatology was by no means entirely vanquished. To conservative Evangelicals (a tendency that was represented across the principal Protestant Churches and which

---

[18] H. G. Wood, 'The Middle Classes', in W. K. Lowther Clarke, ed., *Facing the Facts: Or, an Englishman's Religion* (London, 1911), 55–87, at 70–71.

[19] C. W. Emmet, 'The Bible and Hell', in B. H. Streeter, ed., *Immortality: An Essay in Discovery, Co-ordinating Scientific, Psychical and Biblical Research* (London, 1917), 167–217, at 208.

[20] R. J. Campbell, *The New Theology* (London, 1907), 8–9.

[21] G. Parsons, 'Victorian Britain's Other Establishment: The Transformation of Scottish Presbyterianism', in idem, ed., *Religion in Victorian Britain. Volume 1: Traditions* (Manchester, 1988), 117–45, at 127–29.

[22] D. Macmillan, 'Scotland', in Lowther Clarke, ed., *Facing the Facts*, 223–50, at 228–30.

subsumed most Baptists) the threat of hell was as real and compelling as ever, an outlook that was also shared by the smaller and more conservative Presbyterian Churches in Scotland.[23] Furthermore, while the nineteenth century had seen the development of a milder, more ameliorative concept of purgatory in English Catholicism,[24] the place of hell remained secure in Roman Catholic eschatology. Indeed, by the end of the nineteenth century, popular Roman Catholic depictions of hell were considered so severe as to have spawned a new variety of anti-Catholic rhetoric among freethinkers and more liberal Protestants.[25]

As hell was being pushed to the margins, in the Church of England at least there was a growing conviction of the existence of an 'intermediate' purificatory state between death and the last judgement. Advocated by the Tractarians since the 1830s, this concept complemented the Broad Church rebellion against hell and was increasingly in tune with the religious and moral outlook of late Victorian Britain. Significantly, by the turn of the century even some evangelical theologians were prepared to entertain the possibility of an intermediate state. Although personally unconvinced, Edward Litton cautioned his readers not to apply 'the name of heresy ... to opinions which, even if erroneous, do not affect the fundamentals of the faith, or to interpretations of Scripture which vary from those to which we have been accustomed'.[26] As Litton reasoned:

> The Romish doctrine of purgatory must not be confounded with the belief of spiritual progress in the intermediate state, against which latter no objection from reason or Scripture can be urged. If the soul survives its separation from the body, and if it exists, not in a state of unconscious slumber ... but with its moral and intellectual faculties in activity, the inference seems to be that between death and the final judgment there must be progress, either in the one direction or the other.[27]

---

[23] H. McLeod, *Class and Religion in the Late Victorian City* (London, 1974), 69–70, 226; C. Brown, *Religion and Society in Scotland since 1707* (Edinburgh, 1997), 30–31; MacLeod, '"Greater Love"', 93–94.

[24] G. Rowell, *Hell and the Victorians* (Oxford, 1974), 163–69.

[25] Ibid. 172–73; J. A. Hill, ed., *Letters from Sir Oliver Lodge* (London, 1932), 82–83.

[26] E. A. Litton, *Introduction to Dogmatic Theology on the Basis of the Thirty-Nine Articles* (London, 1912), 542.

[27] Ibid. 308, 540–42.

Once again, the impact of the First World War served to accelerate existing trends. In 1916, Charles Gore, now Bishop of Oxford, published his summary of *The Religion of the Church as Presented in the Church of England*. Speedily compiled, Gore admitted that it could 'supply little in the way of proofs or justifications', its contents being the fruits of 'the meditation and study of a lifetime'.[28] This was especially true of his chapter on 'The Last Things and the Communion of Saints', where he rejected the traditional hell of 'unending conscious torment for the lost', argued instead for the dissolution of 'irretrievably lost spirits',[29] and maintained that:

> [W]e are led to believe in an intermediate state of (in some sense) disembodied souls, in a condition of waiting or expectancy, following on the 'particular judgement' – that is, the disclosure of a man's real state which appears to be associated with each one's death. About this intermediate state we are told exceedingly little, but we are led to suppose that there is such a state both for good and bad ... We almost all instinctively tend to believe in some sort of purgatory, a state of cleansing and gradual emancipation and enlightenment for the imperfect ... In that we may – nay, I feel, we must – believe; but it is rather a conclusion of our reasoning than a part of what is revealed.[30]

However, while this belief in an intermediate state had some currency by the early 1900s, public prayers for the dead were not common in the Victorian or Edwardian Church of England. Although Anglo-Catholics had always argued that such prayers were consistent with the Prayer Book's 'Order for the Burial of the Dead' and were a natural corollary of the intermediate state and of the communion of saints,[31] it was a sign of the vestigial strength of Protestant orthodoxy that public prayers for the dead were rare in the Church of England prior to the First World War. For example, in 1903 only 217 churches marked All Souls' Day with special services, a figure that accounted for only one in ten of those churches that could be deemed Anglo-Catholic.[32] However, the coming

---

[28] C. Gore, *The Religion of the Church as Presented in the Church of England* (London, 1916), v.

[29] Ibid. 91–92.

[30] Ibid. 93–95.

[31] Rowell, *Hell and the Victorians*, 99–100.

[32] N. Yates, *Anglican Ritualism in Victorian Britain 1830–1910* (Oxford, 1999), 278–79.

of war saw a rapid transformation of the situation. In a sermon preached on All Souls' Day 1914, Archbishop Davidson noted with cautious approval the rapid diffusion of prayers for the dead since the outbreak of war.[33] Naturally, the Bishop of Oxford staunchly defended prayers for the dead in *The Religion of the Church*. While invoking the communion of saints and appealing for the proper observance of All Souls' Day, Gore proclaimed that:

> We must recover without apology or concealment the practice of prayer for the dead. It is [a] matter of revelation that the departed are alive and waiting their final perfection. They need something and we need something. And therefore we may pray for them. That is a practice inevitably resulting from the revealed belief about the efficacy of prayer for others in all their real needs.[34]

Significantly, by this time a vocal element of Nonconformist opinion fully concurred with these sentiments. While minister of London's City Temple, R. J. Campbell made his opinion quite clear as to the merits of praying for the dead: 'It has antiquity on its side', he wrote, 'and, though greatly abused in pre-Reformation days, satisfies such a natural instinct, and is such a solace to the bereaved, that it is a pity Protestants everywhere should not be encouraged to return to it forthwith.'[35] Bernard Snell, another Congregationalist minister, was no less insistent in his endorsement of the practice.[36]

However, these developments were strongly resisted in other quarters. In the Church of England, matters came to a head in the summer of 1917 when forms of prayer were issued under the authority of the two archbishops to mark the third anniversary of Britain's declaration of war. Reflecting the prevailing mood, for the first time these included explicit prayers for the dead, a fact that prompted the evangelical Bishop of Liverpool, F. J. Chavasse, to lodge a strongly worded complaint with the Archbishop of Canterbury.[37] Another dissenting voice was that of E. A. Knox, the evangelical Bishop of Manchester. Although public prayers for the dead were already so common in his

[33] G. K. A. Bell, *Randall Davidson: Archbishop of Canterbury*, 2 vols (Oxford, 1935), 2: 830–31 n. 2.
[34] Gore, *Religion of the Church*, 96–97.
[35] R. J. Campbell, *The War and the Soul* (London, 1916), 14.
[36] B. J. Snell, 'If Only They Had Remained!', in F. Hastings, ed., *Our Boys Beyond the Shadow* (London, 1917), 35–44, at 43–44.
[37] Bell, *Randall Davidson*, 2: 828–30.

diocese that some of his clergy had inferred his tacit approval of them, Knox now bestirred himself to state that he could grant 'no permission' for the use of the prayers in question; this prohibition was then made public, prompting a flurry of debate in his diocese as well as a revolt among his cathedral clergy.[38] However, little seems to have been achieved by the rather isolated stand of Chavasse and Knox. At the end of the war, the forms of prayer issued under authority for Sunday 17 November 1918 were fulsome in their intercessions for the now victorious dead.[39] A few months later, the archbishops' committee charged with considering 'The Worship of the Church' in the wake of the 1916 National Mission of Repentance and Hope came down strongly in favour of including prayers for the dead in a revised Prayer Book.[40] Significantly, controversy over the intermediate state and prayers for the dead even rocked Presbyterian Scotland in 1917, after Norman Maclean (of the Church of Scotland) and J. R. P. Sclater (of the United Free Church)[41] expressed their approval of both in a volume of essays entitled *God and the Soldier*.[42] Unsurprisingly, such a radical break with Reformed orthodoxy was greeted with dismay by more conservative Presbyterians. The Free Presbyterian condemnation of *God and the Soldier* was unequivocal: it was 'a dark symptom of the Romeward drift in the Protestant church' and imperilled 'the future of religion in Scotland'.[43] Furthermore, in one of the island presbyteries of the Church of Scotland an overture was considered that would have had Maclean 'summoned to the Bar of the General Assembly to be accused of Popish practices'.[44]

1917 was a turbulent year in another related respect, for in November 1916, and as the Battle of the Somme fizzled to an end, Sir Oliver Lodge published *Raymond: or Life and Death*. This book, which is probably the most powerful claim for spirit communication ever to have been published in Britain, had a deep resonance with a nation in

---

[38] 'What Lancashire Thinks', *The Guardian*, 2 August 1917, 582, and 9 August 1917, 609.

[39] *Forms of Thanksgiving to Almighty God to be used on Sunday, the 17th November, 1918: Being the Sunday after the Cessation of Hostilities between the Allied Powers and the German Empire. Issued under the Authority of the Archbishops of Canterbury and York* (London, 1918), 2.

[40] Wilkinson, *Church of England*, 82–84, 178.

[41] S. J. Brown, ' "A Solemn Purification By Fire": Responses to the Great War in the Scottish Presbyterian Churches, 1914–19', *JEH* 45 (1994), 82–104, at 94.

[42] N. Maclean and J. R. P. Sclater, *God and the Soldier* (London, 1917), 206–08.

[43] MacLeod, ' "Greater Love" ', 94.

[44] Ibid. 87.

trauma and was a publishing phenomenon. As Herbert Thurston wrote for *The Month* in February 1917:

> The appearance at the present time of such a book as *Raymond* was bound to create something of a sensation. Published at the beginning of last November, a sixth edition of this half-guinea volume had already been called for before the middle of the following month. On every hand one heard it discussed . . .[45]

Ever since spiritualism had taken root in mid-Victorian Britain, most clergymen had taken a dim view of its pseudo-scientific claims and forbidden practices. However, while it was often seen as fraudulent or even diabolical, a handful of Anglican clergymen had been enthusiastic exponents of it, partly because its claims stood as a refutation of the greater threat of materialistic science. Furthermore, from 1882 the investigations of the Cambridge-based Society for Psychical Research (SPR) had given the claims of spiritualism some intellectual credibility and provided respectable scope for clerical interest. Indeed, such were developments in the SPR during the Edwardian period that Sir Oliver Lodge had boldly announced to the British Association for the Advancement of Science in September 1913:

> The evidence ... goes to prove that discarnate intelligence, under certain conditions, may interact with us on the material side, thus indirectly coming within our scientific ken; and that gradually we may hope to attain some understanding of the nature of a larger, perhaps ethereal, existence, and of the conditions regulating intercourse across the chasm. A body of responsible investigators has even now landed on the treacherous but promising shores of a new continent.[46]

The war years inevitably saw a growing demand for the services of mediums at all levels of British society and unleashed a flood of spiritualist publications, many of which – such as J. S. M. Ward's *Gone West* and Wellesley Tudor Pole's *Private Dowding* – were of dubious provenance and quality. *Raymond* was very different. Written in a sober and reasoned style, there was no mystery as to its subject's identity

---

[45] H. Thurston, 'Communicating with the Dead', *The Month*, February 1917, 134–44, at 134.

[46] 'Extracts from Sir Oliver Lodge's Presidential Address', *Journal of the Society for Psychical Research*, November 1913, 132–44, at 144.

(Raymond Lodge had been a subaltern in the 2nd South Lancashire Regiment who had been killed in September 1915), and its author possessed the threefold attraction of being an eminent man of science, a grieving father and a professing Christian. Ironically, *Raymond* even contained an explicit caution against absorption in spiritualism, and its conception of a purposeful and progressive eternity, though not unique in spiritualist writing, bore a strong if superficial resemblance to more orthodox and dynamic conceptions of the intermediate state. Reactions from the Churches were mixed and seldom dispassionate. In an address at St Martin-in-the-Fields in February 1917, Lord Halifax, then President of the English Church Union, even accused Lodge of necromancy and of consorting with familiar spirits;[47] in turn, Halifax was attacked by the Master of the Temple, Ernest Barnes, a modernist churchman who had as little time for inflated Anglo-Catholic rhetoric as he had for spiritualism:

> The difference between my own view of spiritualism and that of Lord Halifax can be summed up in a sentence by using an oft-employed metaphor. I do not think that there is any evidence to prove that telephonic communication with the other side has been established; his lordship thinks that a devil is speaking into the receiver at the other end.[48]

As the public debates surrounding the eternal prospects of the fallen, prayers for the dead, and the claims and practice of spiritualism serve to illustrate, there was intense interest (not to say fevered speculation) among civilians as to the fate and circumstances of the war dead. This evidence highlights the commonly neglected fact that Britain's first industrialized war was seen and experienced in religious, or spiritual, as well as in material terms. Naturally, the Churches took the lead in defining its religious parameters. As Stuart Mews has wryly observed, the war saw the 'identification of Germany with devilry', it being 'remarkable how quickly the devil and hell – topics which had been quietly and gradually discarded by the majority of leading preachers ... suddenly reappeared and took on a new significance'.[49] However, such views were widely shared in British popular culture; while the early war

---

[47] 'Life After Death', *The Guardian*, 15 February 1917, 133.
[48] 'Evil Spirits', *The Guardian*, 22 February 1917, 155.
[49] S. P. Mews, 'Religion and English Society in the First World War' (unpublished Ph. D. thesis, Cambridge University, 1973), 74.

myths of the Angels of Mons, the White Comrade, and even 'the drums of Ypres' gained great currency, a strong apprehension of the cosmic and even apocalyptic significance of the struggle persisted until the end of the war. In 1916, for example, a 'Patriotic Photoplay' was released entitled *It is For England*. The central character of the film was an army chaplain – the fearless Christian St. George – who was reincarnated as England's patron saint in order to thwart a diabolical plot hatched by naturalized Germans. In 1917, a collection of essays by Protestant clergymen appeared entitled *Our Boys Beyond the Shadow* in which R. C. Gillie remarked how 'some persons declare that young men are being called out of this life because they are needed in a great battle between right and wrong in the spiritual world'.[50] Finally, in the *Occult Review* of April 1918, one pundit was at hand to explain how its readers could give 'Psychic Help for Soldiers and Sailors' and who spoke of how 'a certain veteran Colonel, the chief of a Highland clan' could dream himself onto the battlefield – 'And whenever he has such a dream, some of the men of the regiment have said with sincere conviction – "The old Colonel is with us, we shall come through all right." '[51]

The eminent cultural historian Jay Winter has seen in all of this, and in wartime publications such as *Raymond* and *Private Dowding*, strong evidence of a 'spiritualist embrace' that linked the home and the fighting fronts.[52] However, many contemporaries would have taken issue with Winter's expansive definition of 'spiritualist' as it was very much a contested term. Leading spiritualists preferred the term 'spiritism', or even 'psychic science', while a broad definition of 'spiritualism' could include miscellaneous phenomena such as apparitions, hypnotism, telepathy, clairvoyance, pre-cognition and prophecy. This terminological slipperiness caused some problems, for, as M. A. Bayfield, an Anglican clergyman and a leading figure in the SPR, pointed out at the Church Congress held at Southend in 1920: 'Everyone is a spiritualist who is not a materialist, and Christianity itself is essentially a spiritualistic religion.'[53] What most people actually understood spiritualism to be was quite simply 'communication with the spirits of the dead'

[50] R. C. Gillie, 'Is Purgatory Necessary?', in Hastings, ed., *Our Boys Beyond the Shadow*, 175–86, at 178.
[51] J. W. Brodie-Innes, 'Psychic Help for Soldiers and Sailors', *Occult Review*, April 1918, 211–21, at 216–17.
[52] J. M. Winter, 'Spiritualism and the First World War', in R. W. Davis and R. J. Helmstadter, eds, *Religion and Irreligion in Victorian Society* (London, 1992), 185–200, at 193.
[53] 'Spiritualism', *Report of the Church Congress* (London, 1920), 146–75, at 154, 161–62.

through mediums, a point made emphatically by Sir William Barrett, a founding member of the SPR, in his wartime book *On the Threshold of the Unseen*.[54] Taking this definition of spiritualism, there was a clear disjuncture between the prevalence of spiritualism at home and its remarkable absence in the army.

Of course, there were soldiers serving in the British army who had either dabbled in spiritualism or who had spiritualist tendencies. Under the influence of a younger sister, Sir Douglas Haig had attended seances in the pre-war years, on one occasion being told by a medium of the interest shown in his career by 'a small man named Napoleon [who] had become changed for the better in the spirit world'.[55] As late as June 1916, Haig's sister had this reformed Napoleon very much in mind, assuring her brother that he had now been charged by God to attend him as a military advisor.[56] While Haig's religion had veered in a more orthodox direction by this stage of the war, Sir John French, his prede-cessor as commander-in-chief of the British Expeditionary Force (BEF), was highly susceptible to spiritualist ideas. Early in 1915, and after only a few months of war, French wrote how his room at his headquarters was '*thick* with the spirits of my dead friends'. He even confessed that 'I sometimes people my room with these glorious friends (all boys compared to me!), who have gone over. That "Silent Army". Alas, alas! The room is getting [too] small to hold even my intimate friends.'[57]

Nevertheless, army life was stony ground for spiritualism as most contemporaries understood it; adequate conditions for a seance could seldom be obtained or sustained in camps, billets and dugouts. Further-more, in one of those rare examples where they were attainable over time, namely in an officers' prison camp at Yozgad in Anatolia, the seances held between February 1917 and October 1918 were entirely fraudulent. However, they did result in the repatriation of the two 'mediums' involved on the ground of insanity.[58] In the execution of their novel plan to escape, Lieutenants E. H. Jones of the Indian army and C. W. Hill of the Royal Flying Corps succeeded in convincing

[54] Ibid. 162; W. F. Barrett, *On The Threshold of the Unseen* (London, 1917), 8–9.

[55] D. Cooper, *Haig* (London, 1935), 114.

[56] G. DeGroot, ' "We are safe whatever happens" – Douglas Haig, the Reverend George Duncan, and the Conduct of War, 1916–1918', in N. MacDougal, ed., *Scotland and War* (Edinburgh, 1991), 193–211, at 193.

[57] R. Holmes, *The Little Field Marshal: A Life of Sir John French* (London, 2005), 276–77.

[58] E. H. Jones, *The Road to En-Dor* (London, 1920).

some of their captors and some of their fellow prisoners of the reality of spirit communication. As Jones ruefully remarked:

> [I]n the atmosphere of the séance, men whose judgment one respects and whose mental powers one admires lose hold of the criteria of sane conclusions and construct for themselves a fantastic world on their hypothesis. The messages we received from 'the world beyond' and from 'other minds in this sphere' were in every case, and from beginning to end, of our own invention. Yet the effect both on our friends and on the Turks was to lead them, as earnest investigators, to the same conclusions as Sir Oliver Lodge has reached, and the arrival of his book *Raymond* in the camp in 1918 only served to confirm them in their views.[59]

What compounded the difficulties for spiritualism in the army was the fact that mediums tended to be women; as Alex Owen has shown in her studies of women and late nineteenth-century spiritualism, mediumship was strongly associated with the vaunted feminine virtue of passivity.[60] In addition to the conspicuous lack of female mediums, or generally females of any kind, army culture was at odds with spiritualism in other respects. Plebeian spiritualism in the north of England was radical in its political orientation and inclined towards pacifism; after the introduction of conscription in 1916, eligible males from this background often became conscientious objectors. Furthermore, while Christian spiritualist churches had existed since the 1860s,[61] the army had no spiritualist chaplains and there is no evidence to suggest that any were ever sought from the War Office. Consequently, and in marked contrast to the situation on the home front, even in the later years of the war spiritualism hardly registered as an issue for army chaplains and church workers. Significantly, only one per cent of the three hundred memoranda received by the compilers of *The Army and Religion* report of 1919 made any reference to the existence of 'spiritualistic ideas' at all.[62] In fact, here the Churches had the opposite problem, as the young, male and overwhelmingly working-class soldiers of the British army were judged to be usually indifferent to spiritual matters. As David Cairns testified, their social environment, economic background and

---

[59] Ibid. x.
[60] A. Owen, *The Darkened Room* (London, 1989), 8, 10.
[61] G. K. Nelson, *Spiritualism and Society* (London, 1969), 143–47.
[62] D. S. Cairns, *The Army and Religion* (London, 1919), vi, 19–20.

defective education meant that 'The greatly prevailing drift of the evidence is that the men as a whole take a material view of life.'[63] Largely sheltered from the storm generated by *Raymond*, even at its height army chaplains could take an objective and dispassionate view of the threat from this quarter. In June 1917, William Duncan Geare, an evangelical Anglican, concluded from the popularity of *Raymond* that better standards of religious teaching were required from the Church of England; similarly, for the more Anglo-Catholic F. W. Worsley of the Chaplains' School of Instruction at Saint-Omer, the antidote seemed to lie in the growing revival of prayers for the dead.[64]

What must be stressed, however, is that this dearth of interest in spiritualism did not betoken a lack of interest in the afterlife among British soldiers of 1914–18. Based on their work with the YMCA, Maclean and Sclater found that:

> There is little need for any man to go to our soldiers in order to convince them of Immortality, for they are convinced already that 'death's true name is Onward'. Votes have sometimes been taken in [YMCA] huts where the men congregate, as to whether they believe that their dead friends have gone out like the flame of a candle; and the usual majority against such a thought was in the proportion of nine to one.[65]

Similarly, in a volume of essays published in 1917 entitled *Our Mess*, which claimed to be a collection of 'Mess Table Talks in France', a chaplain confirmed the depth of interest in the afterlife among front-line troops in particular:

> The interest is keener and more intelligent the nearer one gets to the front. [At base] men are saturated with the minor incidents of military life, drills … food and drink, tent talk, promotions, decorations, and the rivalries to which these give rise; but when men realise that [the next] twelve hours may see them ushered into eternity, they want to know what the words mean.[66]

63 Ibid. 74.
64 W. D. Geare, *Letters of an Army Chaplain* (London, 1918), 84–85; F. W. Worsley, 'Beliefs Emphasised by the War', in F. B. MacNutt, ed., *The Church in the Furnace: Essays by Seventeen Temporary Church of England Chaplains on Active Service in France and Flanders* (London, 1917), 71–96, at 93–95.
65 Maclean and Sclater, *God and the Soldier*, 181.
66 D. MacFadyen, *Our Mess: Mess Table Talks in France* (London, 1917), 114–15.

Nevertheless, and as in civilian life, this firm belief in the survival of the soul masked a great deal of uncertainty regarding its details. As Maclean and Sclater noted, the general outlook was positive but nebulous: 'They believe that the dead are alive, and that they will meet them again some summer morning.'[67] While belief in eternal punishment had waned in late Victorian and Edwardian Britain, the war brought home not only the extent of its decline but also the confusion it had left in its wake. A YMCA worker who spent his period of wartime service 'among skilled mechanics' at a major base of the BEF observed that hell was largely dismissed by this more educated constituency. However, they had no firm idea as to what they could expect after death, only that 'men will get [a] fair judgment and chances for improvement in another world'.[68] Another witness for *The Army and Religion Report*, this time an infantry officer and former minister, confirmed that this confidence was also typical of the average infantryman, although here again it was more a product of hope than sound reasoning: 'Surely if Christianity is right, God will give the well-meaning multitude a second chance, and in the end smuggle them in.'[69]

Despite the use of hell as a literary motif by the more celebrated war poets, perhaps most powerfully by Wilfred Owen in 'Strange Meeting' (1918), the prevailing disdain for hell as a concept (not to mention a striking familiarity with Corinthians 15) was reflected in a contemporary soldiers' ditty that was put to a Salvation Army tune and widely sung in billets and estaminets:

> The bells of Hell go ting-a-ling-a-ling
> For you but not for me:
> And the little devils how they sing-a-ling-a-ling
> For you but not for me,
> O Death where is thy sting-a-ling-a-ling,
> O Grave, thy victor-ee?
> The bells of Hell go ting-a-ling-a-ling,
> For you but not for me.[70]

This lack of clarity and consensus about the afterlife prevailed as much

[67] Maclean and Sclater, *God and the Soldier*, 182.
[68] Cairns, *Army and Religion*, 18.
[69] Ibid. 19.
[70] J. Brophy and E. Partridge, eds, *The Long Trail: Soldiers' Songs and Slang 1914–18* (London, 1969), 46, 48.

among junior officers as it did among the other ranks. The celebrated Anglican layman Donald Hankey, who died as a subaltern on the Somme in October 1916, was alleged to have led his platoon over the top, and to his death, with the words, 'Men, if you are wounded it is Blighty; if you are killed it is the resurrection.'[71] However, this fore-shortened eschatology was by no means the sum of Hankey's personal theology of the afterlife. In earlier reflections on the question of eternal torment, he had concluded that sometimes 'utterly corrupt' souls would be destroyed 'in the unquenchable fire' but most would be puri-fied therein: 'Surely', he reasoned, 'it is more biblical (not to mention common sense) to suppose that fire is an instrument of purification and destruction rather than of torture.'[72] On the other hand, while concur-ring with the existence of an intermediate state, Alec De Candole, a lieutenant in the Wiltshire Regiment, saw its function in universalist terms when he wrote in 1918:

> There is ... further progress in the life after death; and progress means struggle, and perhaps pain. Perhaps this progress will be endless, since the goal is infinite; but the idea that all eternity depends on this little space of earthly life is too disproportionate to be believed, and too terrible to be borne ... All we who have come from GOD shall return to GOD: for if GOD be GOD, Whose power is equal to His Will, no evil will, human or demonic, shall in the end withstand Him ...[73]

Despite overwhelming belief in an afterlife, there were some symp-toms of doubt, especially among junior officers, whose superior educa-tion and notoriously limited life expectancy were conducive to habits of reflection on this question. James Hannay, a canon of St Patrick's cathedral, Dublin, who served as an army chaplain, was struck by the agitation of a young subaltern who was about to depart from Le Havre for the front. Noting his strongly Anglo-Catholic background, Hannay concluded that in this case religious education had proved worthless in the face of the ultimate test:

> [T]hat boy had some teaching, quite definite as far as it went. He knew his Creed. He knew, or at one time had known, his Catechism.

---

[71] Maclean and Sclater, *God and the Soldier*, 202.
[72] D. Hankey, *A Student in Arms* (London, 1918), 103–04.
[73] A. De Candole, *The Faith of a Subaltern: Essays on Religion and Life* (Cambridge, 1919), 72–73.

He had been prepared for Confirmation. He actually carried about with him a little book of Eucharistic meditations, glowing with teaching so definite and so 'churchy' that many people would have cursed it. Yet after all that, he wanted to know whether he would live on in any fashion after the German bullet which he expected went through his head. I have no doubt that definite Church teaching is an excellent thing ... but no amount of definiteness will create the sense of reality.[74]

However, in another case, lingering doubts as to immortality were dispelled in an instant after a mute appeal to God in the midst of a heavy bombardment. As the officer in question told Maclean and Sclater:

Shells still burst all around, with smoke and an incredible roar everywhere ... the earth blasted and thrown high into the air – that was what girt me around. But these things were no longer real. As a dreamer awakes from a ghastly nightmare ... the danger and horror of the trench became unreal. *I* was the reality. *I* could not be destroyed. *I* was filled with great comfort ... *I* was raised above destruction ... It made a great difference to me.[75]

While there were disagreements as to the nature of an intermediate state beyond death and even some isolated doubts as to immortality itself, conceptions of the afterlife tended to be fairly mundane. Writing in October 1917, William St. Leger, a lieutenant in the 2nd Coldstream Guards, averred that: 'everyone comes into this world for two purposes', namely:

(1) To do a certain work.
(2) To fit himself for a better existence.
When he has done these two things I believe he is taken away by God to enjoy his rest.

Hence, St. Leger maintained that his fallen comrades were 'happy together – supremely happy' and that they were 'waiting for me to join them'; when he did, he believed, they would give him 'a great welcome .... I will understand everything, and be happy and content.'[76]

74 J. O. Hannay, 'Man To Man', in MacNutt, ed., *Church in the Furnace*, 335–46, at 340.
75 Maclean and Sclater, *God and the Soldier*, 109.
76 London, Imperial War Museum, Department of Documents, P239 W. B. St Leger

However, these rather prosaic perceptions were almost sublime in comparison with the views that were widely entertained by the other ranks. Private Frank Richards of the 2nd Royal Welch Fusiliers recalled one discussion in which he and his comrades debated 'whether the spirits of the soldiers that were killed early in the War could wander through space and could look down upon us', one of them being of the opinion that they were 'looking down on us and dancing a two-step and clicking their heels together in holy glee to think that they have scrounged out of this blasted misery'.[77] As one Anglican chaplain lamented in a wartime article for the *Church Times*:

> The ideas of many of the men as to the actual state of those who have 'gone west' are vague and even grotesque. This is largely due to the fact that when left to think the matter out for themselves their thoughts run along the line of life as they know it here. It is not surprising, therefore, that they are attracted by a poem that describes the soldiers' valhalla as a place of 'never-ending Wood-bines and never-closed canteen', or the ideas set forth in a book like 'Raymond'.[78]

While they might despair over its aesthetics, army chaplains did much to foster the prevailing mood of optimism regarding the afterlife. Militarily speaking, the old theology of hell was not only passé but positively demoralizing; as E. C. Crosse acknowledged, 'Gloomy subjects like the terrors of death made the worst possible subject for a sermon … any attempt at profiteering of this nature was universally resented.'[79] However, for compelling personal and theological reasons, most were disinclined to believe that God would deal harshly with their former comrades. For many chaplains the conduct of their fellow soldiers (in whom they often discerned a host of latent virtues) made hell unthinkable. As Oswin Creighton wrote from Gallipoli in June 1915, 'I don't think that the war makes people more religious at once. But it makes them a great deal more serious and unselfish … The men

(every effort has been made to trace the copyright holder, and the author and the Imperial War Museum would be very grateful for any information which may enable them to do so).

[77] F. Richards, *Old Soldiers Never Die* (London, 1983), 97.

[78] 'A Padre', 'The Religion of the Man at the Front', *Church Times*, 13 July 1917, 33.

[79] London, Imperial War Museum, Department of Documents, 80/22/1, E. C. Crosse (every effort has been made to trace the copyright holder, and the author and the Imperial War Museum would be very grateful for any information which may enable them to do so).

who are killed I feel absolutely sure must have many sins forgiven.'[80]
This vision was shared by G. A. Studdert Kennedy, who in 1918 urged
that the war had served to push the parameters of salvation far beyond
the confines of the Churches:

> There are many men who die fine deaths who have no faith, or at
> least no conscious faith, in God or Christ as Son of God. How
> about them? Well, God is greater than the Churches ... The river
> of eternal life breaks through a thousand channels and finds the
> soul of man.[81]

Studdert Kennedy's strident rejection of traditional eschatology was a
theme that ran through much of his celebrated wartime verse. For
example, in his poem 'Eternal Hope', he expressed his revulsion at the
thought of eternal punishment:

> Can the Father in His Justice burn in Everlasting flame
> Souls that, sunk in foulest squalor, never knew the Father's Name?
>
> Can the Love of man be greater than Eternal Love divine?
> Can the heart of God be harder than this hardened heart of mine?
>
> Can the pangs of Hell be endless, void of object, void of gain,
> Save to pay for years of sorrow with Eternity of Pain?
>
> Cursèd be the foul contortion, that hath turned His Love to Hate,
> That hath cried at death's dim portal, 'Enter here, and 'tis too late,'
>
> Cruel pride and vain presumption claim to grasp where angels grope,
> 'Tis not God but mean man blindness dims the deathless star of
> Hope.[82]

The popular eschatology of military and civilian society was thus
broadly similar: a rejection of the traditional hell prevailed alongside a
widespread belief in an intermediate state, however vaguely or diver-
gently this may have been understood. However, one area in which
army chaplains seem to have been in advance of civilian practice was in
praying for the dead. This was widely adopted, even by evangelical
Anglicans, from the early months of the war. Since 1901, Anglican

---

80   L. Creighton, ed., *Letters of Oswin Creighton, C. F. 1883–1918* (London, 1920), 130.
81   G. A. Studdert Kennedy, *The Hardest Part* (London, 1918), 172–73.
82   G. A. Studdert Kennedy, *Rough Rhymes of a Padre* (London, 1918), 45–46; see also, in
the same volume, 'Well?', 'To-day Thou shalt be with Me' and 'Judgment'.

chaplains had been appointed for the regular army by Bishop John Taylor Smith, a former Church Missionary Society (CMS) missionary and a staunch Evangelical. However, few of his younger protégés were prepared to eschew a practice that the Chaplain-General was known to oppose.[83] As Harry Blackburne, a regular chaplain who was attached to the 3rd Field Ambulance, wrote at Christmas 1914: 'Hearing of more deaths in the trenches, I went up the line, and did the sad work of burying; the men always asking me to "say a prayer for him and his relations at home," and yet there are still some at home who quibble about prayers for the dead!'[84] Likewise, and despite being of Taylor Smith's generation, Bishop Llewellyn Henry Gwynne, another Evangelical, CMS missionary and the Suffragan Bishop of Khartoum, commenced praying for the dead soon after he arrived in France in August 1914.[85] As Deputy Chaplain-General on the Western Front from the summer of 1915, his support for the practice was so well known that one chaplain could not help remarking on its irony: 'The C. M. S. Bishop of Khartoum prints prayers for the dead for the use of all chaplains, and yet the Low Church Party still think it is a matter in dispute.'[86]

While evangelical Anglicans were drawn to this practice from an early stage, even Presbyterian chaplains seem to have experimented with prayers for the dead. However, this required a little circumspection. John White, who served as a chaplain to the 5th Scottish Rifles (or Cameronians) and who made much of the militant Presbyterian lineage of his regiment, was a case in point. White's reflection on the fallen which concluded his published account of his service in France was highly suggestive of a personal departure from Reformed orthodoxy:

> They have entered on a higher curriculum; but they still remain the same living, thinking, loving sons and brothers that we knew and loved here. Do they minister to those for whom they have died, and who live through the weary days in loneliness and grief …? What says our heart? We think of them and retain our fellowship with them in prayer, and they with us; we cannot think other-

---

[83] M. Snape, *The Royal Army Chaplains' Department, 1796–1953: Clergy Under Fire* (Woodbridge, 2008), 178.

[84] H. W. Blackburne, *This Also Happened on the Western Front* (London, 1932), 32.

[85] Birmingham, University of Birmingham, CMS Archives, XACC /18/F/1/51, Diaries of L. H. Gwynne, 2 December 1914.

[86] R. Keable, *Standing By: War-Time Reflections in France and Flanders* (London, 1919), 42.

MICHAEL SNAPE

wise if we believe that they are not dead but live men who still love and serve.[87]

More directly, in one of the essays featured in *Our Mess*, a Presbyterian chaplain admitted that: 'I value highly ... the increasing desire to pray for our living dead, and I have even encouraged it'.[88]

Burial services were, of course, the main context in which prayers for the dead were offered. In this setting, the inadequacies of the Prayer Book's 'Order for the Burial of the Dead' were abundantly clear to many Anglican chaplains and a tendency to improvise was endemic.[89] For example, E. V. Tanner of the 2nd Worcestershire Regiment composed his own 'Shortened Form of Burial Service' which he thought 'followed in a general way that laid down in the Anglican Book of Common Prayer'.[90] In 1917, Eric Milner-White, in civilian life the chaplain of King's College, Cambridge, and now a senior army chaplain, complained that the Prayer Book's burial office had 'failed badly in the days of death', forcing chaplains to contrive their own services; significantly, he had only come across one chaplain who had refused to 'pray directly for the dead'. The cumulative result of these experiments had, he maintained, been very positive, producing a departure from the Prayer Book service that was 'no less beautiful but far more human, with not less but more true and ancient divinity in it; and thereby deeper suitability, honesty and comfort'.[91] Given their experiences, in the wake of the National Mission three senior Anglican army chaplains were among the most strident advocates of reform on the archbishops' committee charged with considering 'The Worship of the Church'. While addressing sundry other weaknesses in the Prayer Book, they concluded their joint statement to the committee with the assertion that:

> [A]bundant use under strange and pathetic circumstances has revealed the defects of the Burial Service, and we are sure that

[87] J. White, *With the Cameronians (Scottish Rifles) in France: Leaves from a Chaplain's Diary* (Glasgow, 1917), 110.

[88] MacFadyen, *Our Mess*, 123.

[89] L. MacDonald, *1914–1918: Voices and Images of the Great War* (London, 1991), 179.

[90] London, Imperial War Museum, Department of Documents, P310, E. V. Tanner (every effort has been made to trace the copyright holder, and the author and the Imperial War Museum would be very grateful for any information which may enable them to do so); Amport, Andover, Amport House, Royal Army Chaplains' Department Archive, E. V. Tanner, 'An Army Chaplain's Work in War-Time'.

[91] E. Milner-White, 'Worship and Services', in MacNutt, ed., *Church in the Furnace*, 175–210, at 179–81.

those who have been at the Front will never wish to go back to its use unmodified ... a direct and simple commendation of the soul of the departed to God, and a prayer for the bereaved should be added.[92]

In addition to prayers for the dead, army chaplains also played a major role in helping to popularize the notion that those who gave their lives for their country would inherit eternal life, a 'doctrine of justification by works with a vengeance' as one critic sourly remarked in the *Expository Times*.[93] However, this common belief, which proved so obnoxious to conservative Protestants, cannot be dismissed simply as a knee-jerk product of an over-heated 'war theology'.[94] Firstly, it was implicitly based on the theology of an intermediate state; of those who died for their country, most *would* eventually reach heaven. Secondly, its roots also lay in the dauntless optimism of pre-war liberal theology. In his controversial summary of *The New Theology*, R. J. Campbell had made a passionate argument to the effect that salvation was being earned, usually quite unconsciously, by all who sought the betterment of humanity:

> Wherever you see a man trying to do something for the common good, you see the uprising of the spirit of Christ ... In church or out of church, with or without a formal creed, this is the true way in which the redemption of the world is proceeding. Every man who is trying to live so as to make his life a blessing to the world is being saved himself, saved by becoming a saviour. Ordinary observation ought to tell us that untold thousands of our fellow-beings, even among those who never dream of going to church, are being saved in this way ... The Christ – the true Christ, who was, and is, Jesus, but who is the deeper self of every human being – is saving individuals by filling them with the unselfish desire to save the race.[95]

If these sentiments applied, as Campbell claimed they did, even to

---

[92] *The National Mission of Repentance and Hope: Reports of the Archbishops' Committees of Inquiry. The Worship of the Church, being the Report of the Archbishops' Second Committee of Inquiry* (London, 1919), 39.

[93] H. Cernyw Williams, 'The Fate of those who have Fallen in the War', *Expository Times*, April 1919, 329.

[94] Mews, 'Religion and English Society', 80.

[95] Campbell, *New Theology*, 210.

Robert Blatchford, the fiercely anti-clerical editor of the *Clarion*,[96] it was clear from August 1914 that they were still more applicable to those millions of British soldiers engaged in saving Europe from what Lloyd George described as 'the thraldom of a military caste' which had plunged the world into 'a welter of bloodshed and death'.[97] While, for a combination of moral, theological and patriotic reasons, the intrinsic merit of their sacrifice was taken for granted by most British churchmen, as recruiting fever swept the nation in the autumn of 1914, it was also propounded by Lloyd George himself. Speaking at the City Temple that November, the Liberal (and Baptist) Chancellor of the Exchequer pronounced martial courage to be a redeeming Christian virtue and even offered some favourable reflections on Islam:

> It is appointed that men should die once, and after that the judgment. Brave men die, but they need not fear the judgment. I think we are too ready to scoff at creeds which promise the glories of their paradise to those who die for the cause or for the country they are devoted to. It is but a crude expression of a truth which is the foundation of every great faith, that sacrifice is the surest road to redemption.[98]

The concept of salvation through dying for one's country was, therefore, widely canvassed long before it became an unofficial tenet of the Army Chaplains' Department. Following Haig's appointment as commander-in-chief of the BEF in December 1915, chaplains played a burgeoning role in promoting morale among Haig's citizen soldiers on the Western Front. At a conference with his army commanders in January 1916, Haig, whose religious convictions proved a major source of personal support over the next three years, instructed them to take their chaplains firmly in hand. As the commander-in-chief put it, 'We must have large minded, sympathetic men as Parsons, who realise the <u>Great Cause</u> for which we are fighting, and can imbue their hearers with enthusiasm ... Any clergyman who is not fit for this work must be sent home.'[99] While this remodelling of the chaplains' role saw them

---

[96]   *ODNB*, s. v. 'Robert Peel Glanville Blatchford'.

[97]   F. L. Stevenson, ed., *Through Terror to Triumph: Speeches and Pronouncements of the Right Hon. David Lloyd George, M. P., since the Beginning of the War* (London, 1915), 13.

[98]   Ibid. 57–58.

[99]   D. Haig, *Haig's Autograph Great War Diary* (microfilm; Brighton, 1987), 15 January 1916.

acquire greater freedom of movement and unfettered access to front-line trenches, its theological corollaries were soon made clear as well. In March 1916, Lieutenant-General Sir Hubert Gough, a protégé of Haig's who was soon to take command of the Fifth Army, was invited by Bishop Gwynne to address a conference of Anglican chaplains. In his address, Gough made it clear that in their sermons salvation should be linked to sacrifice for the national cause:

> [I]n my opinion a great deal too much importance is laid in sermons on the individual's welfare and good, as it is in England in every walk of life. Not enough is made of our public duty, of one's duty to the whole Nation, or to the whole Army. We are entreated from the Pulpit to be 'good' in order that we may save our individual souls ... If you wish to rouse enthusiasm, harp not so frequently on the saving of my soul; but talk to me of how I can help to save the soul of England and the Empire. If I can do something for that, my own soul will be safe enough.[100]

Significantly, senior officers in the BEF came to expect a certain line of preaching from their chaplains. After cancelling all church parades for that particular Sunday, in September 1916 the commander of the 21st Division, Major-General D. G. M. Campbell, toured its constituent units in order to deliver his own religious address to the men. As one chaplain remembered:

> He told them ... that a man was much better for being a good Christian and saying his prayers [and] he further laid down that a man guilty of cowardice was lost for ever – his conception of eternal damnation being apparently the sentence of death by court martial. Then he quoted the Bishop of London to the effect that however deeply a man had sinned if he was killed on the battlefield and had faith he was sure of salvation.[101]

A few months later, the senior Anglican chaplain of the 8th Division was removed as being theologically unsatisfactory. As E. H. L. Beddington, one of its staff officers, remembered:

[100] H. Gough, *Address Delivered by a well-known Corps Commander to the Chaplains of his Corps in France* (London, 1916), 6.
[101] London, Imperial War Museum, Department of Documents, 67/180/1, J. B. Marshall (every effort has been made to trace the copyright holder, and the author and the Imperial War Museum would be very grateful for any information which may enable them to do so).

I went in to GHQ to see ... the [Assistant] Chaplain General [of the Fourth Army] ... He asked me the reason for my request and I said that our Chaplain would stress all the time that unless you were really good your chances of going to Heaven were poor, whilst the doctrine needed for men of an infantry division, whose expectation of life was bound to be short, should in my view approximate to that of the Mohammedan religion, i.e., he that dies in battle goes to Heaven. [He] nodded assent, but asked what I thought should happen to our Chaplain. I suggested duty at a Base Hospital.[102]

As a result of these developments, *The Army and Religion* report, which was compiled during the latter part of the war and published in 1919, sniffed that 'The idea of salvation by death in battle for one's country has been widely prevalent, and is one of those points in which the religion of the trenches has rather a Moslem than a Christian colour.'[103] While E. C. Crosse was emphatic that he did not preach 'the very doubtful theology of Mohammed, that the soldier who dies in battle for a just cause is thereby assured of eternal salvation',[104] many chaplains would have contested this depiction of their theology. E. S. Woods was unapologetic that certain smug, pre-war conceptions had been discarded, claiming that 'The official exponents of Christianity have too commonly allowed, or even encouraged, the notion that a Christian's chief function is to save his own soul; and religion, for many, has tended to become a refined form of selfishness.'[105] Another chaplain explained that:

We do not hold out to the British Tommy or Jock any expectation of a Valhalla where heroes feast eternally, or of a Mahommedan [*sic*] Paradise where he will have all the joys he has denied himself here; but we can say to him that so far as his act in serving his country has any quality in it of love for the highest, of sacrifice, of brotherhood, of solidarity, it is a real preparation for sharing the life of eternal blessedness; for that life is a life lived out on those principles.[106]

---

[102] London, King's College, Liddell Hart Centre for Military Archives, GB99 KCLMA Beddington.

[103] Cairns, *Army and Religion*, 19.

[104] IWM, 80/22/1, E. C. Crosse.

[105] E. S. Woods, 'The Great Adventure', in MacNutt, ed., *Church in the Furnace*, 429–54, at 434.

[106] Macfadyen, *Our Mess*, 125–26.

While very few wartime sermons by serving chaplains have survived,[107] this claim is borne out by the sermon notes of E. V. Tanner for a thanksgiving service held in September 1917, as the 2nd Worcestershire Regiment was recuperating after fighting in the Ypres salient. Here, the implication was not that their dead had been granted immediate access to heavenly glory but that they had been given gainful employment in an intermediate state:

> For them we need not mourn … A nobler activity is theirs today [and] greater opportunities for the development of character and a sphere of wider usefulness, as we Christians firmly believe … No, for our fallen comrades we need not grieve. God has other work for them to do.[108]

Similarly, while the sermon notes of Bishop Gwynne reflect a powerful sense of the activity and significance of 'the blessed Dead', he never presumed that they were actually in heaven. In a sermon preached at a memorial service for an officer of the Coldstream Guards in the winter of 1916–17, Gwynne declared that:

> They being dead yet speaketh [*sic*] … We are Trustees of the blessed Dead … There behind the line in Flanders [and] France are the forests of crosses which mark their resting places – They speak more eloquently than words – begging us never to lay down our arms … And so we think of Geoffrey Campbell … on active service in that other world.[109]

Inevitably, however, there were those who misconstrued this message or who were unhappy with its theological implications, especially its reliance on works and the promise of heaven that the intermediate state apparently implied. Firstly, there was a dissentient minority in the Chaplains' Department itself. One chaplain, for example, preferred the sharp demarcations of traditional eschatology and objected to the idea 'that the future life is a kind of heaven and hell amalgamation society'.[110] This theology also jarred with Guy Rogers, whom Bishop Gore had described as 'one of the most thoughtful and

[107] M. Brown, *The Imperial War Museum Book of the First World War* (London, 1991), 248.
[108] IWM, P310, E. V. Tanner.
[109] Birmingham, University of Birmingham, CMS Archives, XACC /18/F/4/4–9, Sermon books of L. H. Gwynne.
[110] Macfadyen, *Our Mess*, 117.

ablest of the young Evangelicals'.[111] While a chaplain with the Guards Division on the Somme, Rogers wrote in November 1916:

> It is absurd that, under the stress of the moment, we should commit ourselves to saying that death in obedience to duty strikes such a balance that it atones for a life which may have been one long dereliction of duty. The brave man, I say, would look at us and say, 'Do you think so much of bravery that you think more of it than of the Gospel you are supposed to preach …?' The real conclusion he would draw would be that our own faith in the unique value of Christ's redemptive work was on the wane.[112]

Although Anglo-Catholic in his views, F. W. Worsley was also scathing about 'the claim that a man who dies in battle is for that reason necessarily saved'. As Worsley remarked, 'Many of us have met a similar belief in popular theology before the war. We have stood at the bed upon which lay the body of a hardened and oft-convicted criminal to hear some relative say "Ah, poor dear, he's in heaven now." '[113]

While one Anglican chaplain remarked that it was those soldiers 'who had given little thought in the past to religious matters' who were most easily persuaded that death 'in the cause of righteousness … justifies a man in the sight of God',[114] a small but vocal element of conservative Evangelicals among the rank and file took strong exception to this kind of preaching from their chaplains. However, and because they ranked as officers, military etiquette seems to have ensured that chaplains were not directly challenged on this score. While a denominationally mixed group of fourteen evangelical soldiers protested 'To the Churches at Home' about this theology, which they argued 'belittles our Saviour's great Sacrifice',[115] most seem to have vented their spleen at services and meetings held by the safely civilian YMCA. Maclean and Sclater's *God and the Soldier* spoke of an awkward confrontation after a voluntary service in which a preacher had voiced some current perspectives on the subject of death and the afterlife. However, this sermon outraged one of his hearers, who consequently took him to task:

---

111 Birmingham, University of Birmingham, CMS Archives, XACC /18/Z/1, Army book of L. H. Gwynne.

112 G. Rogers, *A Rebel at Heart* (London, 1956), 125.

113 Worsley, 'Beliefs Emphasised by the War', in MacNutt, ed., *Church in the Furnace*, 93.

114 'A Padre', 'The Religion of the Man at the Front', 33.

115 Mews, 'Religion and English Society', 206–07.

A kilted, grim-faced Scot waited and asked this question: 'Do you really believe that every soldier who dies in battle goes to heaven?' ... The spirit of all the Puritans glowed in his deep-set eyes. He made it clear that he had no use for such a gospel. He was a Christian and not a Mohammedan. His body was cheap – a shilling a day; his life was cheap – mere fodder for guns; his self-respect required that his soul should not be cheap. And a heaven gained through a splinter of shell would be but a cheap heaven indeed![116]

Though not subjected to a similar tirade, J. D. Robertson, a Baptist minister from Burnley, was presented with a difficult dilemma during a 'Question Time' in a YMCA hut in 1918:

A soldier with a very serious countenance rose, and fixing his eyes on me, said: 'We were going into action recently, and assembled to hear an address from the Padre. In substance he said that we should be over the top in a short time, and it might be that all would not come back, but he added: "Fear not death, my lads; whoever dies for his country is sure of Heaven." Now I want to ask you if such an assurance was in harmony with the teaching of Jesus Christ?' He added one word more: 'It was the general opinion of the men who heard it that he was speaking what he thought was comforting rather than what was true.'[117]

Reluctant to contradict the chaplain in question directly, Robertson cautiously replied that 'the best preparation for death is to repent, and make peace with conscience and with God'.[118]

At the other end of the ecclesiastical spectrum, Roman Catholic eschatology also stood firm. While sacramental practice was adjusted to fit the needs of the time, there was no retreat from essentials. Much to the concern of one Catholic officer, even on active service Catholic soldiers could still be regaled with harrowing descriptions of hell. As C. P. Blacker noted of a sermon in July 1916:

Father Leahy then began to describe what would happen to those who cast aside the chance of salvation. Hell would be their fate. Hell, he said, was a fiery place peopled by hideous beings, half-

---

[116] Maclean and Sclater, *God and the Soldier*, 202–03.
[117] J. D. Robertson, 'Question Time in the Hut', *The Red Triangle*, November 1918, 103–04, at 104.
[118] Ibid.

animal, half-human, whose sole occupation was to devise and perform unthinkable tortures of which the worst feature was that they were never-ending.[119]

Similarly, *The Catholic Soldiers' and Sailors' Prayer-Book* of 1917 stated in a section entitled 'HOW TO GET TO HEAVEN':

> There is only one way of getting to Heaven and that is by dying in a state of grace, and remember that, as a general rule, we die in the state in which we are living ... If therefore you have the misfortune to be in the state of mortal sin, ask God's pardon at once for your sins by a fervent act of contrition ... and make up your mind to go to Confession at the first opportunity and to live in a state of grace in future.[120]

The vital task of making the sacraments available to the sometimes widely dispersed Roman Catholics of the British army was by no means an easy one. Nevertheless, it was made considerably easier by a frequent and even lax recourse to general absolutions on the part of many Roman Catholic chaplains. William Doyle, a Jesuit priest attached to the largely Roman Catholic 16th (Irish) Division, explained the rationale for these expedients in a letter to his father in 1917:

> We reap a good harvest with confessions every day, at any time the men care to come, but there are many who for one reason or another cannot get away, hence before going into the trenches, which nearly always means death for some poor fellows, we give them a General Absolution. I do not think there can be a more touching or soul-inspiring sight than to see a whole regiment go down upon their knees ... I love to picture the foul garment of sin falling from every man there at the words of Absolution, and to watch the look of peace and happiness on the men's faces as they lift their rifles and fall into rank, ready for anything.[121]

However, Doyle was unusual among Roman Catholic chaplains in ministering to a large concentration of his co-religionists. More typical was the situation of J. B. Marshall, who served the scattered Roman

---

[119] J. Blacker, ed., *Have You Forgotten Yet? The First World War Memoirs of C. P. Blacker* (Barnsley, 2000), 114.

[120] P. Casgrain, *The Catholic Soldiers' and Sailors' Prayer-Book* (London, 1917), 10.

[121] A. O'Rahilly, ed., *Father William Doyle S. J.: A Spiritual Study* (London, 1932), 494–95.

Catholics of the 62nd Infantry Brigade. On 12 June 1916, and following a visit to the 1st Lincolnshire Regiment in their front-line trenches, Marshall let slip:

> I met a couple of men and got them to make an act of contrition together while I gave them absolution. I could not hope to hear everybody's confession ... my plan was to get two or three together and give them absolution ... All seemed glad to see me. I chatted with them, heard a few confessions and scattered absolutions in the free and easy way we do out here. How my rector will have to look after me when at last I arrive on the English mission![122]

Nevertheless, even Marshall was taken aback by the methods employed by a more senior Roman Catholic colleague:

> He told me that when action was on he told men to make an act of contrition at any time, and they could know that he was absolving them, because he kept pronouncing a general absolution over the whole battlefield. This struck me as going a bit far even for the theology of the front.[123]

Although generally considered to be better instructed, Roman Catholic soldiers were by no means impervious to the notion of salvation by death in battle. Just after Major-General Campbell emphasized this message to the men of the 21st Division in September 1916, J. B. Marshall was surprised to discover 'a poor wounded Catholic who had long postponed his confession [who] told me that he had taken courage from this dictum to go into battle without approaching the sacraments!'[124] While Marshall deplored Campbell's usurpation of the Sabbath and dismissed his message as 'a shocking medley of bad theology',[125] Roman Catholic soldiers also seem to have envisaged the afterlife in much the same prosaic terms as their Protestant counterparts. In July 1917, William Doyle wrote:

> Before the last big battle I gave the men a few talks about Heaven, where I hope many of them are now ... I reminded them of the saying of the Blessed Curé d'Ars: 'When we get to Heaven and see all the happiness which is to be ours for ever, we shall wonder why

---

[122] IWM, 67/180/1, J. B. Marshall.
[123] Brown, *Imperial War Museum Book of the First World War*, 249.
[124] IWM, 67/180/1, J. B. Marshall.
[125] Ibid.

we wanted to remain even one day on earth' ... I said, the man who falls in the charge is not the loser but immensely the gainer, is *not* the unlucky one but the fortunate and blessed. You should have seen how the poor chaps drank in every word, for rough and ignorant as they are, they are full of Faith: though I fear their conception of an ideal Heaven, for some at least, would be a place of unlimited drinks and no closing time ...[126]

To summarize: what this paper has argued is that historians have too readily subscribed to the idea that such was the scale of mortality in Britain during the First World War that orthodox religion simply could not cope with the national trauma; indeed, it had so little to offer in terms of consolation for the bereaved that the rampant growth of spiritualism, particularly after the publication of *Raymond* in November 1916, registered not only the nation's grief but its sense of despair with the Churches as a whole. This is a view which Sir Arthur Conan Doyle, the most zealous and incautious propagandist for spiritualism, would have cheered to the echo. However, it clearly ignores some fundamental points. Firstly, the experience of immediate family bereavement was not as universal as the prevailing mythology of the First World War implies. Secondly, and not least because of theological developments in the later nineteenth century, orthodox religion was a broader, more flexible and more dynamic force than its detractors have allowed. During the First World War, and with relatively few exceptions, the Churches accommodated change with remarkable pragmatism and dexterity. The growing currency of an intermediate state, the rapid rise of public prayers for the dead, and, in Roman Catholicism, the adjustment of key sacramental practices reflected the extent of this change. Thirdly, the relationship between spiritualism and mainstream Christianity was much more complex than the prevailing analysis admits, not least because they were commonly locked together at a personal level as the example of Sir Oliver Lodge serves to illustrate. Fourthly and finally, neglected evidence from the British army shows a clear disjuncture with the situation on the home front. Here, and among the least religiously susceptible members of British society – namely young, working-class males – even at the end of the war spiritualism had remarkably little appeal or currency. Instead, current views of the afterlife reflected the progressive teaching of the Churches at home, the

---

[126] O'Rahilly, ed., *Father William Doyle*, 509–10.

concept of an intermediate state providing not only reassurance for the individual soldier but also an important means of buttressing collective morale by promising ultimate happiness in the hereafter. Although its orthodoxy was disputed by an evangelical minority, its underlying pragmatism was comparable to that demonstrated by Roman Catholic chaplains in their widespread – and again, sometimes questionable – use of general absolutions. Whatever his travails on earth, ultimate happiness was not to be denied the British soldier of 1914–18, however prosaically he may have envisaged it.

University of Birmingham

LIFE BEYOND THE GRAVE:
NEW CHURCHES IN YORK AND THE AFTERLIFE,
c. 1982–2007

by DAVID GOODHEW

OST studies of Christianity in recent British history are pessimistic about church life in Britain, varying only in the depth of their pessimism.[1] Alongside the assumption that Christianity in Britain is in inexorable decline is the assumption that traditional Christian notions about the afterlife – and indeed stress on the afterlife at all – are fast disappearing.[2] Even studies of charismatic Christianity, the most recent major Christian movement, see it as stagnant or in decline.[3] However, a study of the city of York shows such pessimism to be overstated. Whilst mainline denominations are mostly in slow or rapid decline, a large number of 'new churches' have arisen. This paper shows how these churches perceive the afterlife. It uncovers a rich seam of contemporary theology from below. Though largely unknown to those outside its congregations, this strand of belief is already of considerable significance and is likely to become more so in the twenty-first century. This paper offers contemporary religious history, showing that dramatic shifts within Christian history are not solely the preserve of previous centuries, but have taken place in recent decades.

Nomenclature can be confusing when studying recent church history, with references to house churches (which rarely, if ever, meet in houses), restorationist churches, neo-pentecostal churches, charismatic churches and so on. This paper refers to 'new churches', by which it simply means congregations which have been founded during the last

---

[1] G. Davie, *Religion in Britain since 1945* (Oxford, 1994); C. Brown, *The Death of Christian Britain* (London, 2001); S. Bruce, *God is Dead: Secularisation in the West* (Oxford, 2002).

[2] See, for instance, A. Hastings, *A History of English Christianity 1920–85* (London, 1987), 649–59. Hastings offers a discussion of late twentieth-century Christianity in which the afterlife is largely passed over.

[3] S. Hunt, M. Hamilton and T. Walter, eds, *Charismatic Christianity: Sociological Perspectives* (Basingstoke, 1997); M. Percy, 'A Place at High Table? Assessing the Future of Charismatic Christianity', in G. Davie, ed., *Predicting Religion: Christian, Secular and Alternative Futures* (Aldershot, 2003), 95–108.

twenty-five years.[4] Amongst them it has included four church plants which came from older congregations but which are in essence new.

York is a good place to study this development.[5] It is a substantial community with a broad social mix, neither wholly affluent nor wholly poor. Moreover, through the work of Robin Gill, its patterns of church attendance are better researched than those of any other city in Britain. Gill's work shows that mainline churches in York broadly followed national trends in recent decades. Despite pockets of growth, most mainline Churches are in long-term decline.[6] Even the Roman Catholics, who had kept growing long after Anglican and Free Churches had begun to shrink, have declined markedly in recent years, although immigration may yet bolster their numbers.[7]

However, there has been growth as well as decline in York's churches. In 1989 David Bebbington made the prediction that 'the charismatic movement' would soon become 'the prevailing form of Protestantism in twenty-first-century Britain'.[8] This paper illustrates the partial truth of that prediction. In the last quarter century twenty-one new congregations have been founded in the city, many of them influenced by the charismatic movement.

The tables below survey twenty-one new churches founded in York since the early 1980s, illustrating their variety and vitality, and summarize the contrasting decline in attendance among mainline denominations.

The bulk of such churches can be described as 'evangelical-charismatic' in theology, worship style and organization, although three of the new congregations are Orthodox. In size they constitute a 'new Nonconformity', probably eclipsing the old Nonconformity represented

---

[4] New churches tend to fly beneath the radar of contemporary academic discourse, but background to their growth can be found in Hunt, Hamilton and Walter, eds, *Charismatic Christianity*; W. Kay, *Pentecostals in Britain* (Carlisle, 2000); L. J. Thompson, 'New Churches in Britain and Ireland' (unpublished Ph. D. thesis, Queen's University, Belfast, 2000).

[5] A selection of the churches discussed here have been analysed by R. Warner, 'York's Evangelicals and Charismatics: An Emergent Free Market in Voluntarist Religious Activities', in S. Kim and P. Kollontai, eds, *Community Identity: Dynamics of Religion in Context* (London 2007), 183–202.

[6] R. Gill, *The Empty Church Revisited* (Aldershot, 2003), 199.

[7] M. Hornsby-Smith, 'English Catholics at the New Millennium', in idem, ed., *Catholics in England, 1950–2000: Historical and Sociological Perspectives* (London 1999), 291–306, at 300.

[8] D. W. Bebbington, *Evangelicalism in Modern Britain: A History from the 1730s to the 1980s* (London, 1989), 247.

Table One: New Churches in York, 2007[9]

	Adult Attendance (Sunday)	Under-18s Att. (Sunday)	Year Founded
The Ark	45	8	2003
Calvary Chapel	140	52	1997
Chinese Church	30	2	2003
Clifton Moor LEP	40	20	1990
Crossroads CF	40	20	2003
Elim	125	35	2004
G2 (Anglican)	80	20	2005
Gateway CF	120	30	1981
Global	120	80	2005
King's Church	40	15	1987
Korean Church	25	5	2004
Orthodox (Antiochian)	18	–	2004
Orthodox (Coptic)	20	–	c. 2000
Orthodox (Greek)	20	–	1980s
Orthodox (Syrian)	10	–	1995
The Rock	150 (est.)	30 (est.)	mid-1980s
York City Church (NFI)	110	20	1999
YCC	200	50	1993
YEC	120	25	1982
Vine Apostolic	26	5	1999
Vineyard	10	3	2005

Table Two: Adult Attendance at Mainline Churches in York, 1948–2001[10]

	1948	1989	2001
Anglican	3,384	2,989	2,248
Free Church	3,763	2,335	2,013[11]
Roman Catholic	3,073	3,160	2,540

[9] Statistics are based on my own observations and information supplied by the leaders I have interviewed. LEP, 'Local Ecumenical Project; CF, 'Christian Fellowship; NFI, 'New Frontiers International'; YCC, 'York Community Church'; YEC, 'York Evangelical Church'.

[10] Gill, *Myth*, 199.

[11] The 'Free Church' category includes a handful of the new congregations, without which Free Church decline would be more pronounced.

by Methodist, Baptist and United Reformed congregations, among others. Their particular strength amongst children and young adults suggests that they may well catch up with the Anglican Church during the next two decades.

However, the label 'evangelical-charismatic' is a broad term and it is important to recognise the wide variations between new churches. Such congregations stress the authority of the Bible but do so in different ways. Some have come out of existing denominations (Anglican, Elim Pentecostal, Assemblies of God) and their background colours their approach. Some are part of newer charismatic networks (Calvary Chapel, a highly conservative California-based church; New Frontiers International; Abundant Life; and Ministries Without Borders [also known as Covenant Ministries]) – most of which sprang from the British charismatic movement of the 1970s. York Evangelical Church is independent with Baptist and Brethren roots but adheres to the Westminster Confession. York Community Church is independent but has Brethren roots and an ex-Baptist pastor. Gateway Christian Fellowship began as a breakaway from a charismatic Anglican church in the early 1980s, but now it has connections with New Frontiers International. Some have a strong ethnic base – for example, the Korean and Chinese churches.

The result is a movement which is organizationally diffuse, has a theological 'family likeness' (marked by a high view of the Bible, a stress on the substitutionary understanding of the atonement, and a 'modern' worship style), but which retains significant theological variation. Some happily see themselves as 'charismatic' (City Church, Gateway), some explicitly do not (York Evangelical Church). For Colin Runciman of York Evangelical Church, biblical exposition is 'the central part of the service'; King's Church see themselves as 'people who are inwardly free and outwardly mobile to use their gifts, talents and abilities to take the message of hope, the Gospel of Good News, to a needy and dying world.' The Rock Church stressed the role of music, sometimes quiet, but 'most of the time WE WANT IT LOUD!'[12]

Orthodox congregations are a different world again. Some, such as the Greek congregation, have strong ethnic roots. The Antiochian congregation is ethnically diverse and uses English in worship. The

---

[12] Interview with Colin Runciman (York Evangelical Church), 23 May 2007; cf. the websites at <http://www.kcy.org.uk>; <http://www.rockchurch.org.uk>.

Syrian Orthodox Church centres on a monastery based in a terraced house – a curious mix of ancient tradition and 'house church' practice.

Apart from the Orthodox congregations, the new churches have readily adopted modern culture and eschew traditional church culture. They worship mostly in secular buildings, using a musical style closer to that of the wider culture. Ministers do not wear distinctive dress, and hymnbooks and service books are replaced by words projected onto screens. How, then, do these new churches approach the question of the afterlife? Is it something to be eschewed along with cassocks and hassocks, or is it recast?

The most striking aspect of new church views of the afterlife is that, whilst they may be in haste to avoid anything 'old fashioned' in liturgy, they are decidedly 'old fashioned' in their conceptualization of life beyond the grave. All of the leaders interviewed for this study stressed their belief in an afterlife and happily utilized traditional terminology about heaven and hell. Heaven and – for the most part – hell were seen as realities that all need to face. One leader spoke of how his church is 'very strong' on the importance of these subjects. The Gospel was seen as good news, although it included some unavoidable bad news. Hell was not stressed, but it was seen as a fact that decisions taken now affect a person's future in the afterlife.[13] Whilst most leaders were prepared to see biblical pictures of hell as poetical imagery rather than as accurate blueprints, they saw hell as a literal place and as eternal. Even the standpoint of annihilationism, in which death is indeed the end for those not reconciled to God in this life, was regarded with unease by a number of leaders – a contrast with much English Evangelicalism, which has drawn closer to this position through the writings of John Stott and others.[14] One leader went so far as to see such a view 'as heresy ... a denial of a fundamental of the Christian faith ... We don't know what hell is ... but since the soul is immortal, we would have a problem in saying that there is nothing afterwards.'[15] Asked if he held a traditional view of hell, the

---

[13] Interviews with Steve Hurd (York City Church), 6 June 2007; Graham Hutchinson (Elim York), 11 June 2007; Jim McNaughton (York Community Church), 27 June 2007; Steve Redman (The Ark), 4 May 2007; Dave Shore (Global), 18 June 2007; David Stephens (Crossroads Christian Fellowship), 19 June 2007; John Wilson (Gateway Christian Fellowship), 7 June 2007.

[14] Interviews with Hutchinson; Hurd; David Lavery (Kings Church), 16 May 2007; Mike Salmon (Calvary Chapel York), 17 May 2007; Redman; Shore; Stephens; Wilson. For Stott's views, see Timothy Dudley-Smith, *John Stott: A Global Ministry* (Leicester, 2001), 351–55.

[15] Interview with Stephens.

leader of Gateway Christian Fellowship, John Wilson, replied: 'I wish I didn't, but I've yet to be convinced of a biblically viable alternative.'[16] A leader in an American church plant, Calvary Chapel, felt that the afterlife was given 'a much higher priority than anywhere I'd experienced previously' with systematic teaching about judgement, the second coming and a pretribulation rapture (the belief in a secret 'rapture' of the Church which would precede the coming of Christ).[17] One leader commented on how he had left his career in the police specifically to build an 'eternal reward'. This did not imply disparagement of 'worldly work', but it did indicate a high view of the pastor's role as one who pointed people towards eternity.[18] Whilst the new churches are keen to adapt to modern culture in terms of styles of worship and publicity, they display no embarrassment about using traditional language regarding the afterlife. Certain aspects of Christian Britain may be dying, but those strands which show most vigour are also those which place a marked stress on traditional conceptions of life beyond the grave.

Whilst there was widespread consensus about heaven and hell, there was greater variety when it came to the millennium. Some held to the Augustinian view that the millennium was a symbolic reference to the time between the resurrection and second coming of Christ (amillennialism), others leaned towards the more literalistic view popularized in the nineteenth century by J. N. Darby, in which the personal advent of Christ precedes the millennium (one form of premillennialism). York Evangelical Church, coming from a strongly Calvinistic viewpoint, was firmly amillennialist. The pastor of Gateway, one of the leading charismatic congregations, said he would 'teach the main views' but was 'agnostic', with a leaning towards amillennialism. By contrast, York's Calvary Chapel is committed to premillennialism, although one leader felt there was latitude for disagreement about this amongst the leadership team.[19] One of the leaders of the newest and largest of the new churches stated his reliance on the teachings of David Pawson, a highly conservative, somewhat idiosyncratic Baptist who stresses a literal millennium, rapture and return of Christ as judge.[20]

---

16 Interview with Wilson.
17 Interview with Salmon.
18 Interview with Lavery.
19 Interview with Salmon.
20 Interview with Shore; cf. David Pawson, *Unlocking the Bible Omnibus: A Unique Overview of the Whole Bible* (London, 2003).

York's Elim Pentecostal Church came from a denomination which had been committed to premillennialism, but which had removed this from its basis of faith. The current pastor commented 'I'm fairly vague on it', favouring an 'undogmatic, broad view'. Others stressed their agnosticism about millennial matters and commented that there was 'a spectrum' of belief amongst the church's leaders.[21]

Nevertheless, sensitivity to context played a significant part in the way in which traditional truths were declared. Even the highly conservative Calvary Chapel stressed that their concern for the afterlife was balanced by a strong 'this-worldly' emphasis in their teaching, with a focus on working effectively in the kingdom of God now. One conservative Anglican who pastored the Chinese Church, when asked how he spoke of heaven, hell and the millennium, replied: 'Heaven, yes, but not the others!'[22] One member of an Anglican team leading the 'G2' church plant commented: 'Meetings are topically driven and, as yet, we haven't covered these themes [the afterlife]. Our evangelistic message is more about "following Jesus today" than "will you go to heaven when you die?"'[23] Although the content of new church thinking on the afterlife has consistently been traditional, there is some reticence, particularly among Anglican new churches, in the stress placed on teaching about the afterlife.

Dave Shore, leader of one of the most recent and fastest growing new churches, Global, said of heaven and hell, 'I'm not that big on it', and stressed that church was a means for dealing with life now, rather than in the future. However he also felt that people need to understand the eternal dimension of life to be effective here and now.[24] York City Church utilizes material from its parent body, New Frontiers International, a network of charismatic churches based in Brighton. What was striking about such material was how 'this-worldly' it was, stressing discipleship at home, work and in church. As a charismatic church, York City Church stressed the supernatural, but saw it as something to be expected very much before death, rather than after.[25]

Within the new churches, some denominational trends are visible

21 Interviews with Hutchinson, Hurd, Stephens.
22 Interviews with Salmon; Derek Wooldridge (Chinese Church, York), 27 June 2007.
23 Interview with Christian Salvaratnam (G2), 27 June 2007.
24 Interview with Shore.
25 On the growth of a this-worldly approach to Christianity in a different context, see, in this volume, Paul Gifford, 'African Christianity and the Eclipse of the Afterlife', 413–29.

with regard to views of the afterlife. Those with an Anglican connection appear less strong in their emphasis on the afterlife than those with a more independent background. The large church plant from Calvary Chapel was notable for retaining its parent church's emphasis on the afterlife and its particular teachings about the afterlife which stressed judgement, the second coming and a pretribulation rapture.

At one remove from such discussion are those new churches from the Orthodox tradition. Here teaching was coherent and in accordance with the Orthodox stress on the reality of the resurrection and of heaven. However, whilst such stress put them in the more conservative camp, this was coupled with elements of universalism. Orthodox priests in York stressed the strong possibility that anyone could turn to God and experience the afterlife. There was a willingness to take funerals of non-Orthodox, and whilst there was a readiness to entertain the possibility that someone might permanently turn from God, one priest commented that 'we don't know' what their fate is.[26]

Looking at York's churches there is a sense that we are seeing seeing 'old wine in new wineskins'. Here are churches which have been highly innovative in their use of modern culture and in their willingness to work outside normal denominational limits, yet which are highly conservative in their views on the afterlife. Admittedly, such views are somewhat muted by the concern of these churches to relate well to the surrounding culture; hence the stress has been as much on the Gospel as good news for now, as for eternity. Nonetheless, beneath this, the traditional beliefs about heaven and hell have been present and influential. There is certainly no sense in which such doctrines are seen as an embarrassment or outmoded. In a number of cases, such doctrines are highly prominent in teaching programmes. The new churches have retained a theology with which, as far as the four Last Things are concerned, many in the nineteenth century would have been comfortable, but they have also adjusted to a world where life expectancy is considerably longer than that which the Victorians knew. Questions about the afterlife are seen as ultimately vital but not immediately pressing.

York has been something of an ecclesiastical 'hot spot'. New churches have been noticeably more vigorous there than in less pros-

---

[26] Interview with Bishop Stephen Armitage (Syrian Orthodox Church), 11 May 2007. Similar views were expressed in an interview with Elwyn Richards (Antiochian Orthodox Church), 25 May 2007.

perous, less ethnically mixed or less socially mobile areas of northern England such as Hull or Middlesbrough. However, the new churches of York are not an isolated phenomenon. A number of York's new churches have been instrumental in planting congregations in nearby towns,[27] and there is considerable evidence of new church vitality across the UK.[28] They represent, arguably, the most significant development in the Christian Church over the past fifty years. At their heart is a reaffirmation of traditional teaching about the afterlife. They fly in the face of the significant number of scholars who regard Christianity as in severe decline and those who regard the charismatic movement as past its peak. To those academics, such as Callum Brown and Steve Bruce, who proclaim the death of Christian Britain or even the death of God himself,[29] they raise the question of whether for British Christianity there may be life beyond the grave.

Fulford, York

[27] Calvary Chapel has planted in Bridlington and Harrogate; New Frontiers International (the parent body for York City Church) have planted in Hull and Teesside (Interviews with Salmon, Hurd).

[28] A. Greeley, *Religion in Europe at the End of the Second Millennium: A Sociological Profile* (New Brunswick, NJ, 2003), xi, 73–74; Kay, *Pentecostals in Britain*; Thompson, 'New Churches in Britain and Ireland', 221. Studies of Swansea, Hull and Kendal suggest limited new church growth, but it should be noted that such towns are relatively 'poor soil' compared to larger, more cosmopolitan centres: see P. Chambers, *Religion, Secularisation and Social Change in Wales: Congregational Studies in a Post-Christian Society* (Cardiff, 2005); P. Forster, ed., *Contemporary Mainstream Religion: Studies from Humberside and Lincolnshire* (Aldershot, 1995); P. Heelas and L. Woodhead, *The Spiritual Revolution: Why Religion is Giving Way to Spirituality* (Oxford, 2005).

[29] Brown, *Death of Christian Britain*; Bruce, *God is Dead*.

AFRICAN CHRISTIANITY AND THE
ECLIPSE OF THE AFTERLIFE

by PAUL GIFFORD

W HEN asked to address the issue of the afterlife in African Christianity, my immediate reaction was to doubt whether there is much stress on the afterlife in contemporary African Christianity. This brought the response: 'Well, deal with that; a Christianity from which the afterlife has been displaced.' What follows is an attempt to do just that.

Three preliminary remarks are in order. The first could be called methodological. What I am drawing on below is my experience of attending African churches. I am speaking from what I have seen and heard. This is important, because if you asked any African Christian whether he or she believed in an afterlife, the answer would probably be 'Yes, of course.' If you took a questionnaire into a congregation, all would tick the box indicating a strong belief in an afterlife. Nevertheless, I am convinced from attending African churches over the years that the idea seldom really arises. My particular approach explains, too, my reservations about studies like Mbiti's *New Testament Eschatology in an African Background*.[1] If you begin from the position that crucial to the New Testament (or Christianity) is the notion of an afterlife, you will approach African Christianity to find what Africans have made of it. If you do not bring that assumption to the study, you are open to the possibility that they have not really made much of it at all, and that African Christianity is not primarily about that.

Secondly, there may in fact be a similar development in the West. In a novel of David Lodge, there is a remark about the collapse of the traditional Christian cosmology: 'At some point in the nineteen-sixties, hell disappeared.'[2] Lodge has remarked in another novel: 'The very idea of an afterlife for individual human beings has been regarded with scepticism and embarrassment – or silently ignored – by nearly every major twentieth-century theologian. Bultmann, Barth, Bonhoeffer,

---

[1] John S. Mbiti, *New Testament Eschatology in an African Background: A Study of the Encounter between New Testament Theology and African Traditional Concepts* (Oxford, 1971).
[2] David Lodge, *How Far Can You Go?* (Harmondsworth, 1980), 113.

Tillich, for example, even the Jesuit Karl Rahner, all dismissed traditional notions of personal survival after death.'[3] If it is true that the afterlife is in eclipse in Western Christianity too, I doubt that it is for the same reasons as in African Christianity.

Thirdly, the figure often cited from the *World Christian Encyclopedia* is that 28,000 Africans a day become Christian. There is no doubt that Christianity is exploding in sub-Saharan Africa.[4] Edward Gibbon gave belief in an afterlife as one of his five reasons for the triumph of Christianity in the Roman World.[5] Christianity's triumph in modern sub-Saharan Africa may be similar, but a belief in the afterlife is certainly not one of the reasons. Just the opposite: I will argue that it is precisely because a form of Christianity has developed that focuses so strongly on this life that African Christianity is flourishing.

In what follows, I will divide my remarks into two unequal sections. The first will deal briefly with traditional African notions of immortality, and the second will sketch Africa's contemporary Christianity. Africa is an enormous and diverse continent, and one could cite examples of every phenomenon imaginable. For my purposes I will subsume all the varieties into two admittedly rough and ready categories which I will call mainline and 'Pentecostal'. The divisions are crude, but adequate for my purposes and necessary because though both are characterized by this-worldliness, the dynamics are different in the two cases.

Traditional ideas relating to an afterlife

In his classic work on the religion of the Nuer of the Sudan, Evans-Pritchard noted 'their almost total lack of eschatology. Theirs is a this-worldly religion, a religion of abundant life and the fullness of days, and they neither pretend to know, nor, I think, do they care, what happens to them after death.'[6] Though one cannot generalize over the entire continent, that verdict does not seem out of place for many African peoples.[7] From the diverse practices, however, several scholars

---

[3] David Lodge, *Paradise News* (London, 1991), 352–53.

[4] David Barrett, George Kurian and Todd Johnson, *World Christian Encyclopedia*, 2nd edn (New York, 2001).

[5] Edward Gibbon, *The Decline and Fall of the Roman Empire*, abridged version (London, 1980), 260–327.

[6] E. E. Evans-Pritchard, *Nuer Religion* (Oxford, 1956), 154.

[7] 'To Africans this is the only world, and it is neither inferior to any other, nor "illusory"': Okot p'Bitek, *African Religions in Western Scholarship* (Nairobi, 1971), 110.

have suggested a sketch like the following.[8] The African idea of the soul is that of personality. At death, the soul leaves the body. The idea of the rebirth of the departed soul is widespread, but whether the word reincarnation is helpful here is debated: there is no idea of the cycles of rebirth from which one might escape only by reaching Nirvana, nor any idea of the reward or punishment of being reborn into a higher or lower estate. The departed is thought to be reborn in a child, and rituals may be undertaken to establish which ancestor it is. The same ancestor may be reborn in more than one person. It is perhaps not so much that the ancestral spirit is reborn, but the child comes under his (infrequently her) protecting influence and receives some of his vitality. The ancestral name is renewed in the family, and becomes a revitalized clan influence.

It is through the notion of the ancestors that we get the clearest picture of an afterlife. The ancestors are an integral part of the clan and play a very large part in African life. In some areas such as West Africa where there is a stronger pantheon of gods, the ancestors may be less prominent, but even here it is not clear whether gods have developed out of distant ancestors. Ancestors are thought to survive death and live in a spiritual world. There are different and not easily harmonized notions here. The departed soul may be invoked at the graveside, but is also thought to have travelled to the land of the dead, and in addition may be reincarnated on earth. Pictures of this future world are varied. Yet the departed are not far away, and are thought to watch over their families. Everything that concerns the family, including its health and fertility, are of interest to the ancestors, since they are the elders and will seek rebirth into the same family. The family land is their property, and they must be consulted in any decisions about that land. Often, there is an element of real fear in regard to ancestors. All sorts of evils are attributed to the ancestors – drought and famine, earthquakes and thunder, insomnia, epilepsy, other sicknesses and even death. Most usually, they are thought to be annoyed at neglect by their descendants. In causing sickness or misfortune, they are not evil, but just making

---

[8] For the remarks that follow I have consulted several standard books on African religion: Evans-Pritchard, *Nuer Religion*; E. G. Parrinder, *African Traditional Religion*, 3rd edn (London, 1974); E. Bolaji Idowu, *African Traditional Religion: A Definition* (London, 1973); Benjamin C. Ray, *African Religions: Symbol, Ritual and Community*, 2nd edn (Upper Saddle River, NJ, 2000); Michael Bourdillon, *The Shona Peoples*, 3rd revised edn (Gweru, 1987); Dominique Zahan, *The Religion, Spirituality and Thought of Traditional Africa* (Chicago, IL, 1979); Laurenti Magesa, *African Religion: The Moral Traditions of Abundant Life* (Nairobi, 1998).

their views known to their descendants in the only way they can. The ancestors are approached for benefits, often with some trepidation. They were invoked before battles. They are approached for oracles, and mediums pass on their messages. In dreams they still speak to descendants. Sacrifices must be made to them.

As is obvious from that short summary, there is hardly one fixed system of belief concerning the afterlife, and certainly no orthodoxy. It is equally clear that the focus is on this world. Ancestors matter because of their significance here. African religion was traditionally about this-worldly realities – flocks, crops, fertility, wives, children and animals. Ancestors were thought to be concerned with promoting and protecting these, and rituals were undertaken to bring this about. It is this religious world-view that I am suggesting has persisted into contemporary African Christianity. I therefore tend to disagree with the opinion of Richard Gray who claimed that Christianity brought a 'cosmological revolution' to African religion, and that the idea of an afterlife was a major attraction in conversion.[9] If that was the case in the past, I detect little trace of it today. In what follows I will outline the this-worldly nature of both of the broad classes of contemporary African Christianity.

Mainline Christianity

What I here call the mainline (or historic or mission) denominations – such as Anglican, Catholic, Presbyterian, Methodist and Lutheran – have a long and important history in Africa, and their contribution to health and education is well known. This continues, even intensifies. According to one estimate, sixty-four per cent of all Kenya's educational institutions are church-based.[10] Now, crowning the acknowledged contribution in primary and secondary education, Christian universities are opening. In Kenya there are seven public universities, but they are now outnumbered by private ones, nearly all Christian. In Uganda, there are now four public universities and eighteen recognized private universities. Of these eighteen, eleven are Christian institutions.

Involvement in health is diversifying too.[11] It is sometimes claimed

---

[9] Richard Gray, 'Christianity and Religious Change in Africa', *African Affairs* 77 (1978), 89–100, at 96–98.

[10] *National Mirror*, July 2006, 10 (this is a Kenyan Catholic monthly).

[11] The *Kenya Catholic Directory 2006* (Nairobi, 2006) gives some idea of the Catholic

that seventy per cent of all the HIV/AIDS care on the continent is provided by churches – in large parts of rural Africa, the figure would be a hundred per cent. The Catholic Church alone had over seven hundred AIDS projects in Kenya in 2006.

The last decades have seen a significant novelty. In a country like Kenya (with perhaps five thousand registered Non-Governmental Organizations), alongside Oxfam, Care, Médecins Sans Frontières and other secular agencies, increasing numbers of Christian funding bodies are found: World Vision International; Catholic Relief Services; the Lutheran World Federation (all in the very top league, alongside Oxfam); and other significant players like Christian Aid, CAFOD and Tearfund (from Britain); DanChurchAid; Norwegian Church Aid; Diakonia (Sweden); Cordaid (Holland); Trocaire (Ireland); Church World Service; Christian Reformed World Relief Committee and Samaritan's Purse (USA); Misereor and Bread for the World (Germany); Caritas Switzerland; Jesuit Refugee Services and the Adventist Development and Relief Agency. Smaller organizations include Malteser International (the aid arm of the Knights of Malta); DKA (DreiKönigs-Aktion of Austria); Ipsia (the development arm of the Italian Catholic Workers' Union); and KAAD (the Catholic Academic Exchange Service, the scholarship fund of the German Catholic bishops). Then there are the countless small-scale development schemes that are essentially personal initiatives, such as the Youth Sponsorship Programme started by a Lutheran missionary which has two hundred and fifty (mainly German) donors sponsoring two hundred Kenyans through school, or the Rafiki Trust for educating poor Kenyans established by the Methodists of London's suburb of Wimbledon. The list is literally endless.

But such institutional networks do not give half the picture. Individual Western missionaries are able to access funds from personal contacts in their home countries. In Nairobi I met one European missionary who, with funds provided by 'family and friends at home', had been able to build a block of flats in a middle-class suburb; on the security of those flats he had been able to raise a bank loan of a million US dollars to build twenty-two luxury apartments in an exclusive suburb. With the rent from those apartments, he has been able to embark on a whole range of development activities among the Maasai.

---

involvement, listing 178 dispensaries, 100 health centres, 54 hospitals, and so on – even 11 schools of nursing.

That is not an extreme case. One American Maryknoll priest, a doctor before becoming a priest and with extensive personal contacts in North American medical circles, has built St Mary's Hospital, Nairobi, from resources raised through his own networks, and he is now building two more. The Undugu Society of Kenya, involved in rehabilitating street children, was the personal project of a Dutch White Father, Arnold Grol. Nyumbani, a renowned home for and outreach to AIDS orphans, was the project of Fr Angelo D'Agostino, an American Jesuit who had such international clout that the Vatican issued a stamp commemorating his work (that stamp alone bringing him $620,000). Another American Maryknoll priest has built up the Eastern Deanery AIDS Relief Program in Nairobi, with a budget of $3.5 million.[12] All missionaries seem able to tap into funds from contacts back home (as one Irish missionary put it: 'There is no Irishman without relatives in the US') or in their native parish or diocese. Caritas Italiana, the aid organization of the Italian Catholic bishops, told me that the reason they are relatively uninvolved in Kenya is that Kenya has so many Italian missionaries (especially Consolata and Comboni priests and sisters) who can tap into personal channels that official assistance from Italy's Catholic Church is better directed elsewhere.

There is no limit to the range of their activities, everything from the rehabilitation of the justice system, to strengthening food production, micro-finance, nutrition outreach programmes, health and water sanitation, HIV and AIDS education, conflict resolution and agricultural productivity. Virtually none of these big agencies funds strictly spiritual or evangelistic or 'pastoral' activities, because they obtain most, even all, of their funds from governments or world bodies like USAID, the European Union or the United Nations, who are reluctant to give to corrupt governments and seek other service providers.[13] When asked what is the difference between themselves and Oxfam, most admit that,

---

[12] Only 30% of the funding for the Catholic AIDS programmes mentioned above came from local contributions: Kenya Catholic Secretariat, *Inventory of the Catholic Church's Response to HIV and AIDS in Kenya* (Nairobi, 2006), 14.

[13] Catholic Relief Services' $55 million for Ethiopia in 2005 came almost exclusively from USAID. The Lutheran World Federation in 2005 received over 50% of its Sudan/Kenya funds from UNHCR and the US Department of State. In 2004–05 DanChurchAid received only 35% of its 340 million Danish kroner from private donations. Caritas Switzerland in 2000 spent 60 million Swiss francs abroad, only 25% from (mainly church) donations. Christian Aid, by contrast, stresses that only 30% of its £60 million comes from governments. CAFOD, too, in 2004–05 received less than 20% of its £47 million from governments.

on the operational level, there is really none. Very few of them seem interested in even asking whether there is any specifically Christian way of, or contribution to, development.

In recent decades Africa has been marginalized, receiving little direct foreign investment and avoided by multinationals outsourcing to countries with cheaper labour. Even if investment, especially Chinese, is now increasing substantially, this is overwhelmingly in extractive industries like mining and petroleum. In such circumstances, Christian aid flows and what they involve have become increasingly significant for, even constitutive of, parts of mainline Christianity. This is the sense in which one can talk of secularization in Africa. It is not that Africans are noticeably becoming secularized, but much mainline Christianity effectively is. The identification of aid and Christianity obviously worries some; thus the Papal Nuncio to Kenya feels the need to stress: 'The role of the church is not just giving food and health services but also sharing its faith since it works for the eternal salvation of mankind.'[14] The link with development aid also determines the functioning of significant sectors of Christianity. In Kenya, eight remote Catholic dioceses in undeveloped regions are invariably headed by European bishops who can bring the resources, not least of their particular religious congregation, not only for evangelization but even more obviously for the extensive development work that characterizes all these dioceses. Nor do the local clergy, normally remarkably sensitive about missionary preferment, complain; it would be a waste of time appointing a Kenyan, given the requirements of those areas. In 2005 a Kenyan was appointed to the remote diocese of Isiolo, where the previous (Italian) bishop had been murdered, but, as the national Catholic monthly frankly admitted, he was as good as a European because, as a member of the Consolata Fathers, he could tap into the Italian resources of the Consolata missionary congregation.[15]

This increasing identification of mainline Christianity with western resources in Africa's current state of economic marginalization, is something rather new and demands more attention than it normally receives. There are political effects; all this Christian activity allows governments to avoid responsibility, and for this reason many of these

---

[14] At Nairobi's Strathmore University at a thanksgiving Mass for Opus Dei's founder, June 2007: *National Mirror*, July 2007, 24. Pope Benedict XVI in his first encyclical, *Deus Caritas Est* (25 December 2005), was insistent on the same point: sections 30–33.

[15] *National Mirror*, May 2006, 14.

bodies are moving from service provision to advocacy. Here, however, I want to mention the effects on Christianity itself. An enormous amount of Christian involvement is not obviously about relating to the divine; it is most obviously about access to Western resources and the whole range of things this brings: education; employment; modernization and global opportunities. Bishops are now not so much successors of the apostles as conduits of foreign aid (a point caught succinctly by this remark about an Tanzanian Anglican priest just promoted: 'He will be a fine bishop; he spent years in London, and has contacts everywhere'). This Christianity brings development as much as redemption. It is associated less with miracle, mystery and magic than with science and technology. It operates with a vocabulary less of grace, sacraments and conversion than of micro-finance, capacity building and women's empowerment. It instils virtues of accountability, transparency and good governance as much as faith, hope and charity. It operates as much from human rights reports and millennium development goals as from biblical texts and creeds. Its level of engagement is as much the natural and the human as the supernatural or the divine. Its sacramentals are as much software, spread sheets and four-wheel drives, as bread, wine and oil. Its register is as much social science as theology. Qualifications for leadership of a faith community are now not so much ordination or consecration as acceptability to donors.

Much more could be said. My point here is not that no African has ever found profound spiritual resources within Lutheranism or Methodism, nor that baroque and Italianate forms of Catholic devotion do not abound on the continent; the point is that as Africa becomes increasingly marginalized, these aid flows and what they involve become increasingly significant for, even constitutive of, parts of mainline Christianity.

A new twist has furthered this process, the growth of short-term missionaries (STMs). Definitions of 'short-term' differ – the label can mean anything from a few weeks up to one year. This is particularly obvious in the Protestant context (because of its more hierarchical and clericalized nature, Catholicism has much less scope for this). Short-term Protestant missionaries from North America to other countries have increased from 540 in 1965 to 120,000 in 1989, 450,000 in 1998, 600,000 in 2000 and one million in 2004.[16] Some US mega-

---

[16] Internal Serving In Mission (formerly Sudan Interior Mission) document, dated 2 July 2003.

churches now demand that everyone in the church have some experience of mission within, say, a five-year period. The increase is evident and undeniable. I flew to Kenya in June 2007 from London on British Airways; on that single flight there were six different groups of STMs going to East Africa: twenty-two Presbyterians from Nashville; twelve Baptists from Orlando building their ninth church in East Africa; twenty-three Methodists from Pennsylvania; and numbers I could not verify from the Fellowship of Christian Optometrists, the Lott Carey Mission and New Horizon Student Mission. There may have been other groups as well; these were evident from their T-shirts.

All the major Protestant mission agencies in Africa are changing to cater for this STM explosion, even if in some cases rather reluctantly. The reluctance arises from the awareness that STMs need careful organizing if they are not to do more harm than good. Some organizations realise that, as currently operating, they lack the resources and structures to screen, prepare and then (on arrival) orient the STMs. Even those aware of the limitations, though, are aware that often the short-term experience provides the seed for a long-term commitment and (just as important) lifelong financial support. These STMs are involved in many more activities than church planting, and they work for all sorts of local churches. Indeed, many of these mission bodies have to spend considerable effort finding sufficient churches to host their increasing numbers of STMs.

Most STMs are linked to official Churches or church agencies. For example, a team of 103 Canadian Anglicans comprising clergy, nurses, doctors, dentists and engineers visited the Kenyan diocese of Bungoma for two weeks in 2007. Each spent $3,500 dollars on the trip, and they brought goods valued at $150,000 covering everything from pairs of spectacles to computers.[17] Yet possibly the most interesting aspect of this phenomenon is the increasing independent sector that bypasses any recognised structures. Today, especially through the internet, contacts can be established without any intermediary agency. Neighbourhood churches in North America (this is still mainly a North American phenomenon) can initiate contacts with African churches, and entrepreneurial African pastors often actively seek out North American contacts. I know of Kenyan churches advertising on Californian radio stations inviting such links. These contacts can be with individuals,

[17]   *Nation*, 4 July 2007, 32.

families or whole churches, and they can lead to anything from one-off visits by individuals or couples to groups which return every year.

The effects of large numbers of well-meaning and (at least relatively) wealthy North Americans in Africa are considerable and serve to heighten this phenomenon. Most STMs are immediately struck by the poverty and want to help. Very often, they offer school fees, scholarships and other assistance. This is precisely the pitfall that the mission agencies seek to avoid.[18] Mission agencies admit the huge problem of dependency within African Christianity and seem genuinely concerned to address it; in orientation for their own STMs they put great stress on the harm that indiscriminate financial support can wreak. Yet many a church, school or orphanage is kept afloat through such Western contacts, and many an African makes a living from the 'Christianity Industry'. The rise in STMs makes increasing dependency almost unavoidable and furthers the identification of Christianity with Western aid, with all that that entails.

Pentecostal Christianity

With mainline Christianity taking the shape just outlined, another form of Christianity is becoming equally salient. Kenya requires that churches (not new parishes of existing denominations, but new entities) be registered before operating. In September 2007 the Attorney General announced that the country had 8,520 registered churches, with 6,740 applications pending, and that 60 new applications were filed every month.[19] The procedure for vetting new bodies was overwhelmed, and systems had totally broken down. Ghana has a similar requirement. During the 2005 calendar year, 443 new religious groups were registered – out of a total of 1,931 societies and companies altogether.[20] I will call these burgeoning churches Pentecostal, or perhaps better 'Pentecostal-like', because that enables me to avoid the debate over the

[18] The late John Wimber's Vineyard movement, with over sixty churches in its Association of Vineyard Churches East Africa in 2006, have drawn up 'Guidelines for Visiting Ministries' addressing this issue directly and at length. The tone is caught in this extract: 'It is our concern that the generosity of visitors be encouraged but that, instead of creating unhealthy, ongoing dependency, it strategically acts as a boost or launching-pad for ongoing fruitfulness that becomes self-sustaining.'

[19] *Standard*, 4 September 2007, 6.

[20] Statistics from Registrar General's Department of the Government of Ghana, for which I am indebted to Dr Michael Perry Kweku Okyerefo.

degree to which they resemble the classical Pentecostal denominations of North America.

They represent enormous variety, varying from urban mega-churches to groups of a few dozen. Some have numerous staff; others are effectively one-person enterprises. Some command few resources; others have built institutions such as universities. Yet I would argue that amid the variety they have two things in common, the emphasis on spiritual forces and the emphasis on success or prosperity. The emphasis on spiritual forces comes naturally from the traditional religious imagi-nation in which nothing is purely matter; spirit infuses everything. Although natural causality is not entirely disregarded, causality is to be discerned primarily in the spiritual realm. There is no matter or event that might not be influenced by the gods, ancestors, spirits or witches. The task of the religious professional is essentially to identify spiritual forces afflicting sufferers. This enchanted world-view largely persists in this Pentecostal-like form of Christianity; I would maintain that is the greatest reason for its appeal – particularly since the mainline churches just mentioned, engaged overwhelmingly in development, do not cater for this world-view. One does not go to a mainline missionary or Christian NGO or a mission church office for curses to be broken, witches to be identified or spirits to be exorcized.

The second feature of these churches, the stress on victory, achieve-ment, success, prosperity, is often seen in their names (for example, 'Victory Bible Church', 'Jesus Breakthrough Assembly' or 'Triumphant Christian Centre'). The titles and themes of their ubiquitous conven-tions, crusades and conferences repeat this emphasis ('Living a Life of Abundance', 'Taking your Territories' or 'Stepping into Greatness'). And for all these churches, size and numbers and expansion are tangible signs of success, hence the words 'global', 'world' or 'international' in the titles of so many. In talking to these Christians, or studying their sermons, testimonies and literature, the winning motif is characteristic.

A perfect example is the Nigerian multinational Living Faith Church Worldwide, better known as Winners' Chapel, founded in Lagos by David Oyedepo in 1983. It now has over four hundred branches in Nigeria and is present in forty African countries. Here, too, size is important, and Winners' boasts in Lagos the biggest church audi-torium in the world, seating 50,400; in Nairobi they are constructing the biggest church in East and Central Africa, seating about 20,000. In each country, the leading pastors tend to be Nigerians, all fiercely loyal to Oyedepo. Oyedepo labelled 2006 'Your Year of Laughter', and this was his pledge to all his followers, read out by pastors at services, with the congregation shouting 'Amen' after every assertion: 'In 2006, Everything that shall make your laughter complete and total shall be added unto you. The desires of everyone's heart shall be delivered. Every trial shall be turned to testimonies. Every struggle shall be turned to miracles. Every form of barrenness shall be turned to fruitfulness. Every frustration shall be turned to celebration. Every humiliation shall be turned into honour. Every shame shall be turned to glory. And every curse shall be turned into blessings.'

Oyedepo's 'prophetic focus' for 2007 was 'From Glory to Glory' (2 Corinthians 3: 18). In leaflets handed out to attenders, the preacher declared:

> God is saying in 2007 I am bringing you out of every shame and reproach into realms of glory you had never thought possible in your life-time. That for your shame you shall have double. That it shall be a year of supernatural restoration of his glory in all areas of our lives. Yea, it shall happen suddenly like most supernatural acts of God in scripture. It shall come like a dream of the night ... God is saying to all of us in the Winners' family that the year 2007 is a year of going forward. That we shall be moving from whatever level we are now to the next. That it shall be your year of restoration of colour. That it shall be your year of restoration of beauty. That it shall be your year of restoration of dignity. That it shall be your year of restoration of glory ... You are emerging more than a conqueror in all areas of your life this year. The news of your triumphs shall hit the headlines in the course of the year 2007.

Although the success promised at Winners' embraces all areas of life, it is material success that is paramount – perhaps to be expected from the account which Oyedepo gives of his calling by God. His experience is obviously modelled on the call to Moses, but whereas Moses in Midian was commanded: 'Go and set my people free', Oyedepo in the United States was simply told: 'Get down home quick and make my people rich.'[21] At Winners', the testimonies are almost all to material success, often scholarships, jobs, cars, promotion and salaries paid in dollars. And Winners' is characterized by a rhetorical insistence that the breakthrough will occur 'now', 'during this service', 'this week', 'this month'

---

[21] David Oyedepo, *Breaking Financial Hardship* (Lagos, 1995), 51.

or 'this year'. Every month promises some new advance, every year brings its particular blessing.

I think at least six distinct avenues to this success are discernible. First, success comes through motivation: a church can inculcate drive and determination, almost 'success through a positive mental attitude'. The theology is essentially that of Deuteronomy 30: 19 ('Choose today ...'), and it is your own fault if you are not successful and rich: 'Anything you want to become you can become; the only thing stopping you is you.'[22] Secondly, success is achieved through entrepreneurship. At Winners' at least once every service you will have to turn to your neighbour and ask: 'Have you started your own business yet?' This is often linked to having a new idea ('one idea that will make you rich'). Thirdly, success comes through practical life skills – like hard work, budgeting, saving, investing, organizing time and avoiding drink. Fourthly, faith, usually 'seed faith' from the biblical metaphor of 'sowing and reaping' (as in the 'faith movements' associated with the North American televangelists Kenneth Hagin, Oral Roberts and Kenneth Copeland), and giving tithes and offerings to the church become instruments of one's advancement. Fifthly, and increasingly, success and prosperity come through the 'anointing' of the 'man of God'; pastors increasingly claim the ability to make their followers prosper, and they often make themselves indispensable. Thus David Adeoye of Nairobi Winners' Chapel argues: 'God is saying believe Him and you will be established, but your prosperity, success and breaking forth on the right and the left is tied to a prophet ... Any trace of disregard for their role in your life is a showcase of unprofitability for you.'[23] Sixthly, and related to the last point, the pastor can drive out the spirits that impede the progress that is one's due as a Christian. These six ways in which Christianity is understood to entail success and wealth are obviously not incompatible, and many churches (like Winners') combine them all, seamlessly mixed together. It requires effort to separate out the different strands. Other churches are more associated with one way, less with others.

Let me make my point as clearly as I can. I am not just saying that in

---

[22] Winners' Chapel, second service, Nairobi, 20 August 2006. Cf. Mombasa's Wilfred Lai: 'You are not poor because you were born in a poor family ... It has nothing to do with your parents. It has everything to do with you. You are the way you are because of the way you believe': *God's Army*, January 2006, 9 (a Kenyan evangelical monthly).

[23] *Miracle Magazine*, March 2006, 19.

many cases the worldly success motif is added to foundational Christian doctrines and ideas. I am suggesting that it may presuppose them, but often it substitutes for them. I do not claim to have studied Winners' exhaustively, but over the years I have attended about forty services in various countries, watched a further forty or so on television, and read a good part of their literature. I have never encountered anything but the celebration of success and prosperity. In Accra in 2002, I attended Winners' on Easter Sunday, which in most churches would be a chance to say something about the Resurrection, for most Christians the key event of the whole Christian story. There was no reference to it at all, except the statement that through our tithes and offerings we could roll away the stone entombing us. On Easter Sunday 2007 I attended Winners' in Nairobi; there was one sentence that God's power had raised Jesus from the grave, but the theme was a totally predictable 'Turning your Obstacles into Miracles' with no reference to Easter. Even Winners' characteristic foot-washing ritual is not a re-enactment of Jesus' action at the Last Supper but a ritualizing of Joshua 14: 9: 'Whatsoever your feet tread upon shall be given unto you for a posses-sion.' Thus this ritual, performed by the man of God, becomes one more assurance of owning property. Even the central ritual of Christianity, the eucharist, is interpreted to fit this message of abundance, success and prosperity – Oyedepo can link it with Zechariah 9: 11–12: 'by the blood of thy covenant … I declare that I will render double unto thee'.[24] At a communion service in September 2006, Winners' Nairobi pastor explained the eucharist as 'a mystery to swallow every misfortune in your life … Let it eradicate all sickness and affliction.' The congregation were reminded that 'mediocrity is a sickness', and they were assured that 'if your business is sick, it can be healed'. Immediately after receiving communion, all received communion a second time, as an immunization: 'Jesus was never sick once. By this second communion you will never be sick again … Go and sack all your doctors. Tell your doctors, "I will not come to your clinic again." You will not contribute to buy their houses and cars; you will buy your own houses and cars.'

Winners' is only one of Africa's new trans-national denominations, but it is not unrepresentative. Its message is merely a heightened, more relentless and uncompromising expression of a theology that is wide-spread in Africa's new churches.

---

[24] David O. Oyedepo, *The Miracle Meal* (Lagos, 2002), 30–31.

One unavoidable consideration inevitably arises regarding this Christianity of this-worldly success. Many wonder how this success theology can appeal in circumstances where so many obviously do not, indeed cannot, prosper. At Winners' in Nairobi on New Year's Day 2007 the congregation were urged to buy Winners' bumper stickers for their cars, and other stickers for house windows. Those wanting to own a car this year, or a house, were to buy the stickers and to prophesy over them every day. Moreover, 'If you want to own ten cars, buy ten stickers, and prophesy over them every day.' It seems obvious that most attending Nairobi's Winners' Chapel, situated on the edge of Kibera, Africa's biggest slum, would not own one car, much less ten, by the end of the year. There is a genuine tension here. The previous night, at the 2007 New Year's Eve service, this tension was addressed. There seemed to be a genuine lowering of expectations. All should rejoice at the end of 2006, because at least they were alive to celebrate: 'One thing I know: Jesus has been faithful to you. Go to Langata cemetery if you are doubtful. Forget about the job (or) contract you didn't get; the money you wanted but didn't get. He makes all things beautiful in his time.' The pastor then told the story of a woman he knew who missed her plane, only to learn later that that particular plane was the one that crashed into the Pentagon on '9/11' – so what we might be tempted to see as a setback might not be when viewed from a longer perspective. 'Whether things are working or not, give thanks'. However, that message ('Whether things are working or not'; 'Forget about the money you wanted but didn't get') is definitely not the one normally heard at Winners'. When the pastor introduced the issue of delay ('in his time'), this merely heightened the tension, because through the rest of the year Winners' claimed to effect biblical promises *now*, with progress testable every month. The tension remains unresolved, and it is probably a large part of the reason for members' frequent migration between these churches.

The issue of 'seed faith' raises starkly the issue of the economics of this new Christianity. I have already drawn attention to the economics of mainline Christianity, the resources brought into Africa through the service provision of the mainline churches. Though in a very different way, the economics of these new churches is just as significant. The pastors of these newer churches are religious entrepreneurs, examples of an entire new class of religious professional, the church founder-owner-leader. The church is the source of livelihood. Nearly all the newer churches teach the necessity of giving to a greater or lesser extent. Nearly all are characterized by an emphasis on seed-planting. The doctrine of tithes and offerings has been essential to the rise of this entire sector.

I have just argued that both forms of contemporary African Christianity are overwhelmingly this-worldly, the mainline because of its association with aid and development, the Pentecostal-like because its focus is on success and achievement in this world. As confirmation of its this-worldly orientation, I might add the disappearance of millennialism. In contemporary African Christianity there is almost no mention of the end times. Sometimes someone will refer to 'these last days', but more often this is meant in a restorationist sense (these are the days when signs and wonders, or charismatic gifts more generally, are restored to the Church), rather than alluding to the end of the world that we know. Millennialism, used here to refer to the ideas associated with the books of Revelation and Daniel – dualism, the corruption of the present order and an imminent divine intervention to establish a totally new dispensation – seems to have disappeared. Harvey Cox is rather misleading when he puts millennialism at the very centre of Pentecostalism, which he effectively defines as a 'millennial sensibility'.[25] Africa has had its millennialists, such as John Chilembwe and Elliot Kamwana in Central Africa and William Wadé Harris and Garrick Braide in West Africa.[26] It has also been exposed to the pre-millennial dispensationalism of John Nelson Darby which has been so important in American fundamentalism and which reached its apogee, in a somewhat modified form, in Hal Lindsey's popular *The Late Great Planet Earth*, which in the 1980s was America's best-selling 'non-fiction' book (as it was classified).[27] Today the ubiquitous Christian media channels in Africa present programmes from Hal Lindsey and Jack van Impe, but the surprising thing is just how little their emphasis is taken up.[28] The popular Christianity outlined here is

[25] Harvey Cox, *Fire from Heaven: The Rise of Pentecostal Spirituality and the Reshaping of Religion in the Twenty-First Century* (London, 1996), 281–87.
[26] Chilembwe (c. 1871–1915) preached militant resistance to colonial rule in Nyasaland (now Malawi); Kamwana (c. 1870–1956) preached the millennialism of the Watchtower, predicting the return of Jesus in 1914; Harris (c. 1865–1929), a Liberian, preached divine judgement along the West African Coast; Braide (c. 1882–1918), a Nigerian visionary, preached the withdrawal of the British from Nigeria during World War I, contributing to a revolt.
[27] Hal Lindsey with C. C. Carlson, *The Late Great Planet Earth* (New York, 1970).
[28] It may be that even in the USA Pentecostalism is now jettisoning this pre-millennialism: see Margaret Poloma, 'The Millenarianism of the Pentecostal Movement', in

personal, not cosmic. It is not concerned with a renewed order or any 'New Jerusalem', but with a job, a husband, a child, a car, an education or a visa to the West. It is about succeeding in this realm, through faith, through giving and through deliverance from Satanic blockages. On the face of it, it might be thought that there are millennial images that could resonate powerfully with Africa's truly apocalyptic plight – most obviously the scourges of war, famine and disease (Revelation 6: 1–8) or (at least in the optimistic interlude of 1989–93) the imminent dethroning of evil powers and the dawning of a new order. But these images have not been widely developed. The books of Daniel and Revelation have posed no threat to Deuteronomy, Kings and Malachi.[29]

One still hears misleading characterizations of popular Christianity in the developing world, like that of the *Economist* on what it calls South America's 'sects': 'Mostly they offer political quietism, promising a reward in the next world for the miseries of this one.'[30] I am not sure about Latin America, but for Africa this view needs to be challenged. The message of African's flourishing new Christianity is one of fullness in this life, through development, or through faith, or through faith and deliverance, or through faith and a pastor's anointing, or through faith and entrepreneurship. Missionaries have been criticized for teaching Africans to endure hardship in this life in exchange for happiness hereafter. If the criticism was once valid, the missionary legacy has vanished with scarcely a trace, for it is this-worldly blessings that feature so prominently in African Christianity now.

School of Oriental and African Studies

Stephen Hunt, ed., *Christian Millenarianism: From the Early Church to Waco* (London, 2001), 166–86, at 169.

[29] Often one sees a this-worldly emphasis in the interpretation of biblical texts. For example, I have heard 'Enter into your rest' (Heb. 3: 11) interpreted as promising rest here and now: 'the promised land' as on this earth; expecting 'what eye hath not seen' (1 Cor. 2: 9) in this life, and so on. I have dealt with this interpretation of Scripture in Paul Gifford, 'The Bible in Africa: A Novel Usage in Africa's New Churches', *Bulletin of the School of Oriental and African Studies* 71 (2008), 203–18.

[30] *Economist*, 10 February 1996, 70.